**W9-CNZ-652**

# THE ASSOCIATED PRESS STYLEBOOK
# AND LIBEL MANUAL

## THE QUICK, EASY STYLEBOOK
## THAT SATISFIES A WRITER'S NEED TO KNOW

**THE AP STYLEBOOK AND LIBEL MANUAL** is more than the traditional stylebook. Writers and editors—especially those facing deadlines—told the AP they needed a reference at their fingertips that would help them spell place names and brand names; identify the correct form for government agencies, military titles, ship names, and corporation names; and verify correct punctuation, capitalization, and abbreviations. They wanted everything in one easy-to-use source—and they needed that source to be widely accepted throughout the world.

**THE AP STYLEBOOK AND LIBEL MANUAL** satisfies all those requirements and also provides a libel section for people writing for newspapers, newsletters, or anything that goes to the public in print. It's the most complete, helpful stylebook for writers now available in paperback. No professional or student should be without it.

# THE ASSOCIATED PRESS

# STYLEBOOK

## AND LIBEL MANUAL

### With Appendixes on
### PHOTO CAPTIONS
### FILING THE WIRE

*REVISED EDITION*

**Editor**
CHRISTOPHER W. FRENCH

A LAUREL BOOK
Published by
Dell Publishing
a division of
Bantam Doubleday Dell Publishing Group, Inc.
666 Fifth Avenue
New York, New York 10103

ISBN: 0-440-20601-4

Reprinted by arrangement with The Associated Press

Printed in the United States of America

Published simultaneously in Canada

August 1990

10  9  8  7  6  5  4  3  2  1

RAD

# CONTENTS

# FOREWORD

Work on this Stylebook began in mid-1975. The orders were: Make clear and simple rules, permit few exceptions to the rules, and rely heavily on the chosen dictionary as the arbiter of conflicts.

As work progressed, we became convinced that while style would remain the chief purpose, there were many factual references we should include to make things a bit easier for busy editors.

So we have a Stylebook, but also a reference work.

As for the "style" itself, we thought at the outset that it wouldn't be possible to please everyone. Of course, we were right.

Journalists approach these style questions with varying degrees of passion. Some don't really think it's important. Some agree that basically there should be uniformity for reading ease if nothing else. Still others are prepared to duel over a wayward lowercase.

We encountered all three types and, in their special ways, all were helpful.

It is customary at this place to thank those whose aid and counsel produced the volume that follows.

That list is long. It ranges from the staff of The Associated Press to editors and writers on member newspapers, to other individuals and groups with special interests in some subjects. In particular we sought and received member views on a variety of difficult questions so that this book could reflect what members wanted.

We are particularly grateful to those newspaper editors who agreed to review the final draft and give us their comments as well as those of their staffs. The completed book incorporates many of their suggestions.

We have tried to make the Stylebook current and trust it will be a lasting work. But language changes, and we will review entries annually, making necessary changes by wire notes during the review period.

Each new printing of the Stylebook will incorporate the changes that have been announced on the wires.

LOUIS D. BOCCARDI
President and
General Manager

# **STYLEBOOK**

# STYLEBOOK KEY

This updated and revised version of The Associated Press Stylebook has been organized like a dictionary. Need the acronym for a government agency? Look under the agency's name. Should you capitalize a word? Check the word itself or the **capitalization** entry. What's the format for baseball boxes? See **baseball.**

Following is a key to the entries:

**airport** Capitalize as part of a proper name: *La Guardia Airport, Newark International Airport.*

> Entry words, in alphabetical order, are in **boldface**. They represent the accepted word forms unless otherwise indicated.

The first name of an individual and the word *international* may be deleted from a formal airport name while the remainder is capitalized: *John F. Kennedy International Airport, Kennedy International Airport* or *Kennedy Airport.* Use whichever is appropriate in the context.

> Text explains usage.

Do not make up names, however. There is no *Boston Airport,* for example. The *Boston airport* (lowercase *airport*) would be acceptable if for some reason the proper name, *Logan International Airport,* were not used.

> Examples of correct and incorrect usage are in *italics.*

**airtight**

> Many entries simply give the correct spelling, hyphenation and/or capitalization.

**airways** The system of routes that the federal government has established for airplane traffic.

See the **airline, airlines** entry for its use in carriers' names.

> Abbrev. indicates the correct abbreviation of a word.

**Alabama** Abbrev.: *Ala.* See **state names.**

> Related topics are in **boldface**.

Other abbreviations used in the Stylebook:
**n.:** noun form     **adj.:** adjectives
**v.:** verb form     **adv.:** adverbs

**a, an** Use the article *a* before consonant sounds: *a historic event, a one-year term* (sounds as if it begins with a *w*), *a united stand* (sounds like *you*).

Use the article *an* before vowel sounds: *an energy crisis, an honorable man* (the *h* is silent), *an NBA record* (sounds like it begins with the letter *e*), *an 1890s celebration.*

**a-** The rules of **prefixes** apply, but in general, no hyphen. Some examples:

achromatic        atonal

**A&P** Acceptable in all references for *Great Atlantic & Pacific Tea Co. Inc.* Headquarters is in Montvale, N.J.

**abbreviations and acronyms** In this book the notation *abbrev.* is used to identify the abbreviated form that may be used for a word in some contexts.

A few universally recognized abbreviations are re-

quired in some circumstances. Some others are acceptable depending on the context. But in general, avoid alphabet soup. Do not use abbreviations or acronyms which the reader would not quickly recognize.

Guidance on how to use a particular abbreviation or acronym is provided in entries alphabetized according to the sequence of letters in the word or phrase.

Some general principles:

BEFORE A NAME: Abbreviate the following titles when used before a full name outside direct quotations: *Dr., Gov., Lt. Gov., Mr., Mrs., Rep., the Rev., Sen.* and certain military designations listed in the **military titles** entry. Spell out all except *Dr., Mr., Mrs.* and *Ms.* when they are used before a name in direct quotations.

For guidelines on how to use titles, see **courtesy titles; legislative titles; mil-**

**itary titles; religious titles;** and the entries for the most commonly used titles.

AFTER A NAME: Abbreviate *junior* or *senior* after an individual's name. Abbreviate *company, corporation, incorporated* and *limited* when used after the name of a corporate entity. See entries under these words and **company names.**

In some cases, an academic degree may be abbreviated after an individual's name. See **academic degrees.**

WITH   DATES   OR NUMERALS: Use the abbreviations *A.D., B.C., a.m., p.m., No.* and abbreviate certain months when used with the day of the month.

Right: *In 450 B.C.; at 9:30 a.m.; in room No. 6; on Sept. 16.*

Wrong: *Early this a.m. he asked for the No. of your room.* The abbreviations are correct only with figures.

Right: *Early this morning he asked for the number of your room.*

See **months** and individual entries for these other terms.

IN   NUMBERED   ADDRESSES: Abbreviate *avenue, boulevard* and *street* in numbered addresses: *He lives on Pennsylvania Avenue. He lives at 1600 Pennsylvania Ave.*

See **addresses.**

STATES AND NATIONS: The names of certain states, the *United States* and the *Union of Soviet Socialist Republics* (but not of other nations) are abbreviated with periods in some circumstances.

See **state names; datelines;** and individual entries.

ACCEPTABLE BUT NOT REQUIRED: Some organizations and government agencies are widely recognized by their initials: *CIA, FBI, GOP.*

If the entry for such an organization notes that an abbreviation is acceptable in all references or on second reference, that does not mean that its use should be automatic. Let the context determine, for example, whether to use *Federal Bureau of Investigation* or *FBI.*

See **second reference.**

AVOID   AWKWARD CONSTRUCTIONS: Do not follow an organization's full name with an abbreviation or acronym in parentheses or set off by dashes. If an abbreviation or acronym would not be clear on second reference without this arrangement, do not use it.

Names not commonly before the public should not be reduced to acronyms solely to save a few words.

SPECIAL CASES: Many abbreviations are desirable in tabulations and certain types of technical writing. See individual entries.

CAPS, PERIODS: Use capital letters and periods according to the listings in this book. For words not in this book, use the first-listed abbreviation in Webster's New World Dictionary.

If an abbreviation not listed in this book or in the dictionary achieves widespread acceptance, use capital letters. Omit periods unless the result would spell an unrelated word.

**ABC** Acceptable in all references for *American Broadcasting Cos.* (the plural is part of the corporate name).

Divisions are ABC News, ABC Radio and ABC-TV.

**ABCs**

**able-bodied**

**ABM, ABMs** Acceptable in all references for *anti-ballistic missile(s),* but the term should be defined in the story. Avoid the redundant phrase *ABM missiles.*

**A-bomb** Use *atomic bomb* unless a direct quotation is involved.

See **Hiroshima.**

**aboveboard**

**absent-minded**

**absent without leave** *AWOL* is acceptable on second reference.

**academic degrees** If mention of degrees is necessary to establish someone's credentials, the preferred form is to avoid an abbreviation and use instead a phrase such as: *John Jones, who has a doctorate in psychology.*

Use an apostrophe in *bachelor's degree, a master's,* etc.

Use such abbreviations as *B.A., M.A., LL.D.* and *Ph.D.* only when the need to identify many individuals by degree on first reference would make the preferred form cumbersome. Use these abbreviations only after a full name—never after just a last name.

When used after a name, an academic abbreviation is set off by commas: *Daniel Moynihan, Ph.D., spoke.*

Do not precede a name with a courtesy title for an academic degree and follow it with the abbreviation for the degree in the same reference:

Wrong: *Dr. Sam Jones, Ph.D.*

Right: *Dr. Sam Jones, a chemist.*

When in doubt about the proper abbreviation for a degree, follow the first listing in Webster's New World Dictionary.

See **doctor.**

**academic departments**
Use lowercase except for words that are proper nouns or adjectives: *the department of history, the history department, the department of English, the English department.*

**academic titles** Capitalize and spell out formal titles such as *professor, chancellor, chairman,* etc., when they precede a name. Lowercase elsewhere.

Lowercase modifiers such

as *history* in *history Professor Oscar Handlin* or *department* in *department Chairman Jerome Wiesner.*

See **doctor** and **titles.**

**academy** See **military academies.**

**Academy Awards** Presented annually by the Academy of Motion Picture Arts and Sciences. Also known as the *Oscars.*

Lowercase *the academy* and *the awards* whenever they stand alone.

**accept, except** *Accept* means to receive.

*Except* means to exclude.

**accommodate**

**accused** A person is *accused of,* not *with,* a crime.

To avoid any suggestion that an individual is being judged before a trial, do not use a phrase such as *accused slayer John Jones,* use *John Jones, accused of the slaying.*

For guidelines on related words, see **allege; arrest;** and **indict.**

**Ace** A trademark for a brand of elastic bandage.

### acknowledgment

**acre** Equal to 43,560 square feet or 4,840 square yards. The metric equivalent is .4 (two-fifths) of a hectare or 4,047 square meters.

To convert to hectares, multiply by .4 (5 acres × .4 = 2 hectares).

See **hectare.**

**acronyms** See the **abbreviations and acronyms** entry.

**act** Capitalize when part of the name for pending or implemented legislation: *the Taft-Hartley Act.*

**acting** Always lowercase, but capitalize any formal title that may follow before a name: *acting Mayor Peter Barry.*

See **titles.**

**act numbers** Use Arabic figures and capitalize *act: Act 1; Act 2, Scene 2.* But: *the first act, the second act.*

**actor** (man)
**actress** (woman)

**Actors Equity Association** Headquarters is in New York.

**A.D.** Acceptable in all references for *anno Domini:* in the year of the Lord.

Because the full phrase would read *in the year of the Lord 96,* the abbreviation *A.D.* goes before the figure for the year: *A.D. 96.*

Do not write: *The fourth century A.D. The fourth century* is sufficient. If *A.D.* is not specified with a year, the year is presumed to be A.D.

See **B.C.**

**-added** Follow this form in sports stories: *The $50,000-added sweepstakes.*

**addresses** Use the abbreviations *Ave., Blvd.* and *St.* only with a numbered address: *1600 Pennsylvania Ave.* Spell them out and capitalize when part of a formal street name without a number: *Pennsylvania Avenue.* Lowercase and spell out when used alone or with more than one street name: *Massachusetts and Pennsylvania avenues.*

All similar words (*alley, drive, road, terrace,* etc.) always are spelled out. Capitalize them when part of a formal name without a number; lowercase when used alone or with two or more names.

Always use figures for an

address number: *9 Morning-side Circle.*

Spell out and capitalize *First* through *Ninth* when used as street names; use figures with two letters for *10th* and above: *7 Fifth Ave., 100 21st St.*

Abbreviate compass points used to indicate directional ends of a street or quadrants of a city in a numbered address: *222 E. 42nd St., 562 W. 43rd St., 600 K St. N.W.* Do not abbreviate if the number is omitted: *East 42nd Street, West 43rd Street, K Street Northwest.*

See **highway designations.**

**adjectives** The abbreviation *adj.* is used in this book to identify the spelling of the adjectival forms of words that frequently are misspelled.

The **comma** entry in the **Punctuation** chapter provides guidance on punctuating a series of adjectives.

The **hyphen** entry in the **Punctuation** chapter provides guidance on handling compound modifiers used before a noun.

**ad-lib** (n., v., adj.)

**administration** Lowercase: *the administration, the president's administration, the governor's administration, the Reagan administration.*

See the **government, junta, regime** entry for distinctions that apply in using these terms and *administration.*

**administrative law judge** This is the federal title for the position formerly known as *hearing examiner.* Capitalize it when used as a formal title before a name.

To avoid the long title, seek a construction that sets the title off by commas: *The administrative law judge, John Williams, disagreed.*

**administrator** Never abbreviate. Capitalize when used as a formal title before a name.

See **titles.**

**admiral** See **military titles.**

**admissible**

**admit, admitted** These words may in some contexts

give the erroneous connotation of wrongdoing.

A person who announces that he is homosexual, for example, may be acknowledging it to the world, not admitting it. *Said* is usually sufficient.

**ad nauseam**

**adopt, approve, enact, pass** Amendments, ordinances, resolutions and rules are *adopted* or *approved*.

Bills are *passed*.

Laws are *enacted*.

**Adrenalin** A trademark for the synthetic or chemically extracted forms of epinephrine, a substance produced by the adrenal glands.

The non-proprietary terms are *epinephrine hydrochloride* or *adrenalin.*

**Adventist** See **Seventh-day Adventist Church.**

**adverbs** The abbreviation *adv.* is used in this book to identify the spelling of adverbial forms of words frequently misspelled.

See the **hyphen** entry in the **Punctuation** chapter for guidelines on when an adverb should be followed by a hyphen in constructing a compound modifier.

**adverse, averse** *Adverse* means unfavorable: *He predicted adverse weather.*

*Averse* means reluctant, opposed: *She is averse to change.*

**adviser** Not *advisor.*

**advisory**

**Aer Lingus** The headquarters of the airline is in Dublin, Ireland.

**Aeroflot** The headquarters of this airline is in Moscow.

**Aeromexico** This airline formerly was known as Aeronaves de Mexico.

Headquarters is in Mexico City.

**aesthetic**

**affect, effect** *Affect,* as a verb, means to influence: *The game will affect the standings.*

*Affect,* as a noun, is best avoided. It occasionally is used in psychology to describe an emotion, but there is no need for it in everyday language.

*Effect,* as a verb, means to

cause: *He will effect many changes in the company.*

*Effect,* as a noun, means result: *The effect was overwhelming. He miscalculated the effect of his actions. It was a law of little effect.*

**Afghan** (adj.) *Afghani* is the *Afghan* unit of currency.

**AFL-CIO** Acceptable in all references for the *American Federation of Labor and Congress of Industrial Organizations.*

**A-frame**

**African** Of or pertaining to Africa, or any of its peoples or languages. Do not use the word as a synonym for *black* or *Negro.*

In some countries of Africa, *colored* is used to describe those of mixed white and black ancestry. In other societies *colored* is considered a derogatory word.

Because of the ambiguity, avoid the term in favor of a phrase such as *mixed racial ancestry.* If the word cannot be avoided, place it in quotation marks and provide its meaning.

See **colored.**

**after-** No hyphen after this prefix when it is used to form a noun:

aftereffect          afterthought.

Follow *after* with a hyphen when it is used to form compound modifiers:

after-dinner         after-theater
  drink                  snack

**afterward** Not *afterwards.*

**Agency for International Development** *AID* is acceptable on second reference.

**agenda** A list. It takes singular verbs and pronouns: *The agenda has run its course.* The plural is *agendas.*

**agent** Lowercase unless it is a formal title used before a name.

In the FBI, the formal title is *special agent.* Use *Special Agent William Smith* if appropriate in special context. Otherwise, make it *agent William Smith* or *FBI agent William Smith.*

See **titles.**

**ages** Always use figures. When the context does not require *years* or *years old,* the figure is presumed to be *years.*

Ages expressed as adjectives before a noun or as substitutes for a noun use hyphens.

Examples: A *5-year-old boy,* but *the boy is 5 years old. The boy, 7, has a sister, 10. The woman, 26, has a daughter 2 months old. The law is 8 years old. The race is for 3-year-olds. The woman is in her 30s* (no apostrophe).

See also **boy; girl; infant;** and **youth.**

See **comma** in **Punctuation** chapter.

**ages of history** See the **historical periods and events** entry.

**agnostic, atheist** An *agnostic* is a person who believes it is impossible to know whether there is a God.

An *atheist* is a person who believes there is no God.

**aid, aide** *Aid* is assistance.

An *aide* is a person who serves as an assistant.

**aide-de-camp, aides-de-camp** A military officer who serves as assistant and confidential secretary to a superior.

**AIDS** Acronym for *acquired immune deficiency syndrome. AIDS* is acceptable on first reference, but full name should be included high in the story.

*AIDS* is an affliction in which a virus attacks the body's immune system, leaving victims susceptible to a wide variety of infections and cancers.

*AIDS* is most often transmitted through sexual contact, mostly between homosexual males. Other means of transmission include transfusions of blood or blood products, and the sharing of contaminated hypodermic needles or syringes by drug abusers. *AIDS* can also be passed from mother to child at or before birth.

A note about *AIDS* statistics: When a city reports a change in numbers of cases, be wary of extrapolating or implying a trend. Statistical variation and other factors can affect monthly case totals, giving an illusion of major trends. So make sure health officials, especially epidemiologists, give their interpretation of what changes in the numbers really mean.

A note about *AIDS* tests: A positive test indicates the

presence of *AIDS* antibodies. That means the person tested has been exposed to the *AIDS* virus. It does not mean the person has *AIDS*.

At least 60 percent of people with a positive antibody test carry the *AIDS* virus. Of those, some may continue to carry the virus but not get sick. They are carriers. They can transmit the disease to others.

**ain't** A dialectical or substandard contraction. Use it only in quoted matter or special contexts.

**air base** Two words. Follow the practice of the U.S. Air Force, which uses *air force base* as part of the proper name for its bases in the United States and *air base* for its installations abroad: *Lackland Air Force Base, Texas,* but *Clark Air Base, Philippines.*

On second reference: the *Air Force base, the air base,* or *the base.*

Do not abbreviate, even in datelines:

*LACKLAND AIR FORCE BASE, Texas (AP)— . . .*

*CLARK AIR BASE, Philippines (AP)— . . .*

**Air Canada** Headquarters is in Montreal.

**air-condition, air-conditioned** (v. and adj.) The nouns are: *air conditioner, air conditioning.*

**aircraft names** Use a hyphen when changing from letters to figures; no hyphen when adding a letter after figures.

Some examples for aircraft often in the news: *F-19, B-1, BAC-111, C-5A, DC-10, FH-227, F-4 Phantom 2, F-86 Sabre, L-1011, MiG-29, Tu-144, 727-100C, 747, 747B, VC-10.*

This hyphenation principle is the one used most frequently by manufacturers and users. Apply it in all cases for consistency. For other elements of a name, use the form adopted by the manufacturer or user. If in doubt, consult Jane's All the World's Aircraft.

NO QUOTES: Do not use quotation marks for aircraft with names: *Air Force One, the Spirit of St. Louis, Concorde.*

PLURALS: *DC-10s, 747s.* But: *747B's.* (As noted in **plurals,** the apostrophe is used in forming the plural of a single letter.)

SEQUENCE: Use Arabic figures to establish the sequence of aircraft, spacecraft and missiles: *Apollo 10.* Do not use hyphens.

**aircraft terms** Use *engine,* not *motor,* for the units that propel aircraft: a *twin-engine* plane (not *twin engined*).

Use *jet plane* or *jetliner* to describe only those aircraft driven solely by jet engines. Use *turboprop* to describe an aircraft on which the jet engine is geared to a propeller. Turboprops sometimes are called *propjets.*

Jet planes in commercial use include the *BAC-111; Boeing 707, 727, 737, 747; the Convair 880; the DC-8, DC-9, and DC-10; the L-1011;* and *the VC-10.*

See the **engine and motor** entry.

**air force** Capitalize when referring to U.S. forces: *the U.S. Air Force, the Air Force, Air Force regulations.* Do not use the abbreviation *USAF.*

Use lowercase for the forces of other nations: *the Israeli air force.*

This approach has been adopted for consistency, because many foreign nations do not use *air force* as the proper name.

See the **military academies** and **military titles** entries.

**air force base** See **air base.**

**Air Force One** The Air Force applies this name to any aircraft the president of the United States may be using.

In ordinary usage, however, *Air Force One* is the name of the airplane normally reserved for the president's use.

**Air France** Headquarters is in Paris.

**Air-India** The hyphen is part of the formal name.

Headquarters is in Bombay, India.

**Air Jamaica** Headquarters is in Kingston, Jamaica.

**airline, airlines** Capitalize *airlines, air lines* and *airways* when used as part of a proper airline name.

Major airlines are listed in this book separately by name.

Companies that use *airlines* include Alitalia, American, Continental, Eastern, Hawaiian, Northwest, Trans World, United and Western.

Companies that use *air lines* include Delta, Japan, and Ozark.

Companies that use *airways* include Braniff, British, Pan American World and Qantas.

Companies that use none of these include Aer Lingus, Aeromexico, Air Canada, Air France, Air-India, Air Jamaica, Iberia, KLM, USAir and Western Alaska.

On second reference, use just the proper name *(Delta),* an abbreviation if applicable *(Pan Am, TWA),* or *the airline.* Use *airlines* when referring to more than one line.

Do not use *air line, air lines* or *airways* in generic references to an airline.

**airmail**

**airman** See **military titles**

**Air National Guard**

**airport** Capitalize as part of a proper name: *La Guardia Airport, Newark International Airport.*

The first name of an individual and the word *international* may be deleted from a formal airport name while the remainder is capitalized: *John F. Kennedy International Airport, Kennedy International Airport,* or *Kennedy Airport.* Use whichever is appropriate in the context.

Do not make up names, however. There is no *Boston Airport,* for example. The *Boston airport* (lowercase *airport)* would be acceptable if for some reason the proper name, *Logan International Airport,* were not used.

**airtight**

**airways** The system of routes that the federal government has established for airplane traffic.

See the **airline, airlines** entry for its use in carriers' names.

**Alabama** Abbrev.: *Ala.* See **state names**.

**a la carte**

**a la king, a la mode**

**Alaska** Do not abbreviate. Largest land area of the 50 states—586,432 square miles.
See **state names**.

**Alaska-Hawaii Standard Time** The time zone used in Hawaii and most of Alaska.

There is an *Alaska Daylight Time,* but there is no daylight time in Hawaii.

*Bering time* applies in some far western sections of Alaska. *Yukon time* is used in a small section south of the Yukon border. *Pacific time* applies in most of the area that borders British Columbia, including the city of Juneau.

See **time zones.**

**Alberta** A province of western Canada. Do not abbreviate.

See **datelines.**

**albino, albinos**

**Alcoa** The acronym *Alcoa* is acceptable on second reference for *Aluminum Company of America.* The company has dropped the all-capitalized acronym *ALCOA* and made *Alcoa* the acceptable acronym for the company name.

*Alcoa* also is a city in Tennessee.

**alcoholic** Use *recovered,* not *reformed,* in referring to those afflicted with the disease of alcoholism.

**alderman** Do not abbreviate. See **legislative titles.**

**alert** See **weather terms.**

**Al Fatah** A Palestinian guerrilla organization. Drop the article *Al* if preceded by an English article: *the Fatah statement, a Fatah leader.*

**align**

**Alitalia Airlines** Headquarters is in Rome.

**all-** Use a hyphen:
all-around          all-out
(not all-round)     all-star
all-clear

See **all right** and the **all time, all-time** entries.

**allege** The word must be used with great care.

Some guidelines:

—Avoid any suggestion that the writer is making an allegation.

—Specify the source of an allegation. In a criminal case, it should be an arrest record, an indictment or the statement of a public official connected with the case.

—Use *alleged bribe* or similar phrase when necessary to make it clear that an unproved action is not being treated as fact. Be sure that the source of the charge is specified elsewhere in the story.

—Avoid redundant uses of *alleged*. It is proper to say: *The district attorney alleged that she took a bribe.* Or: *The district attorney accused her of taking a bribe.* But not: *The district attorney accused her of allegedly taking a bribe.*

—Do not use *alleged* to describe an event that is known to have occurred when the dispute is over who participated in it. Do not say: *He attended the alleged meeting* when what you mean is: *He allegedly attended the meeting.*

—Do not use *alleged* as a routine qualifier. Instead, use a word such as *apparent, ostensible* or *reputed*.

For guidelines on related words, see **accuse; arrest;** and **indict.**

**Allegheny Mountains** Or simply: *the Alleghenies.*

**alley** Do not abbreviate. See **addresses.**

**allies, allied** Capitalize *allies* or *allied* only when referring to the combination of the United States and its allies during World War I or World War II: *The Allies defeated Germany. He was in the Allied invasion of France.*

**allot, allotted, allotting**

**all right** (adv.) Never *alright*. Hyphenate only if used colloquially as a compound modifier: *He is an all-right guy.*

**all time, all-time** An *all-time high*, but *the greatest runner of all time.*

Avoid the redundant phrase *all-time record*.

**allude, refer** To *allude* to something is to speak of it without specifically mentioning it.

To *refer* is to mention it directly.

**allusion, illusion** *Allusion* means an indirect reference: *The allusion was to his opponent's war record.*

*Illusion* means an unreal or false impression: *The scenic director created the illusion of choppy seas.*

**alma mater**

**almost never** Do not use the phrase. Instead use *seldom* or *hardly ever*.

**also-ran** (n.)

**altar, alter** An *altar* is a tablelike platform used in a church service.

To *alter* is to change.

**Aluminum Company of America** *Alcoa* is acceptable on second reference.

Headquarters is in Pittsburgh.

**alumnus, alumni, alumna, alumnae** Use *alumnus (alumni* in the plural) when referring to a man who has attended a school.

Use *alumna (alumnae* in the plural) for similar references to a woman.

Use *alumni* when referring to a group of men and women.

**Alzheimer's disease** This is a progressive, irreversible neurological disorder with an estimated 2.5 million American victims. Most are older than 65, but Alzheimer's can strike in the 40s or 50s. Alzheimer's causes some 150,000 deaths a year.

Symptoms include gradual memory loss, impairment of judgment, disorientation, personality change, difficulty in learning and loss of language skills.

No cause or cure is known.

**AM** Acceptable in all references for the *amplitude modulation* system of radio transmission.

**a.m., p.m.** Lowercase, with periods. Avoid the redundant *10 a.m. this morning.*

**Amalgamated Clothing and Textile Workers** The shortened forms *Amalgamated Clothing Workers* and *Clothing Workers union* are acceptable in all references.

Headquarters is in New York.

**Amalgamated Transit Union** Use this full name on first reference.

Headquarters is in Washington.

**ambassador** Use for both men and women. Capitalize as a formal title before a name.

See **titles.**

**amendments to the Constitution** Use *First Amendment, 10th Amendment,* etc.

Colloquial references to the Fifth Amendment's protection against self-incrimination are best avoided, but where appropriate: *He took the Fifth seven times.*

**American** Do not limit the description to citizens or residents of the United States. It also may be applied to any resident or citizen of nations in North or South America.

**American Airlines** Headquarters is in Fort Worth, Texas.

**American Automobile Association** AAA is acceptable on second reference. Also: *the automobile association, the association.*

Headquarters is in Falls Church, Va.

**American Baptist Association** See **Baptist Churches.**

**American Baptist Churches in the U.S.A.** See **Baptist Churches.**

**American Bar Association** *ABA* is acceptable on second reference. Also: *the bar association, the association.*

Headquarters is in Chicago.

**American Broadcasting Cos.** See **ABC.**

**American Civil Liberties Union** *ACLU* is acceptable on second reference.

Headquarters is in New York.

**American Federation of Government Employees** Use this full name on first reference to prevent confusion with other unions that represent government workers.

Headquarters is in Washington.

**American Federation of Labor and Congress of Industrial Organizations** *AFL-CIO* is acceptable in all references.

Headquarters is in Washington.

**American Federation of Musicians** Use this full name on first reference.

The shortened form *Musi-*

*cians union* is acceptable on second reference.

Headquarters is in New York.

**American Federation of State, County and Municipal Employees** Use this full name on first reference to prevent confusion with other unions that represent government workers.

Headquarters is in Washington.

**American Federation of Teachers** Use this full name on first reference to prevent confusion with other unions that represent teachers.

Headquarters is in Washington.

**American Federation of Television and Radio Artists** *AFTRA* is acceptable on second reference.

Headquarters is in New York.

**American Hospital Association** *AHA* is acceptable on second reference. Also: *the hospital association, the association.*

Headquarters is in Chicago.

**Americanisms** Words and phrases that have become part of the English language as spoken in the United States are listed in Webster's New World Dictionary with a star.

Most Americanisms are acceptable in news stories, but let the context be the guide.

See **word selection.**

**American Legion** Capitalize also *the Legion* in second reference. Members are *Legionnaires,* just as members of the Lions Club are *Lions.*

*Legion* and *Legionnaires* are capitalized because they are not being used in their common-noun sense. A *legion* (lowercase) is a large group of soldiers or, by derivation, a large number of items: *His friends are legion.* A *legionnaire* (lowercase) is a member of such a legion.

See the **fraternal organizations and service clubs** entry.

**American Medical Association** *AMA* is acceptable on second reference. Also: *the medical association, the association.*

Headquarters is in Chicago.

**American Motors Corp.** *AMC* is acceptable on second reference.

Headquarters is in Southfield, Mich.

**American Newspaper Publishers Association** *ANPA* is acceptable on second reference. Also: *The newspaper publishers association, the publishers association, the association.*

Headquarters is in Washington.

**American Petroleum Institute** *API* is acceptable on second reference.

Headquarters is in Washington.

**American Postal Workers Union** This union represents clerks and similar employees who work inside post offices.

Use the full name on first reference to prevent confusion with the National Association of Letter Carriers. The shortened form *Postal Workers union* is acceptable on second reference.

Headquarters is in Washington.

**American Press Institute** *API* is acceptable on second reference.

Headquarters is in Reston, Va.

**American Society for the Prevention of Cruelty to Animals** This organization is limited to the five boroughs of New York City. *ASPCA* is acceptable on second reference.

See **Society for the Prevention of Cruelty to Animals.**

**American Society of Composers, Authors and Publishers** *ASCAP* is acceptable on second reference.

Headquarters is in New York.

**American Stock Exchange** In second reference: *the American Exchange, the Amex,* or *the exchange.*

**American Telephone & Telegraph Co.** *AT&T* is acceptable on second reference.

Headquarters is in New York.

**American Veterans of World War II, Korea and Vietnam** *AM-VETS* is acceptable in all references.

Headquarters is in Washington.

**Amex** See **American Stock Exchange.**

**amid** Not *amidst.*

**amidships**

**ammunition** See **weapons.**

**amnesty** See the entry that reads **pardon, parole, probation.**

**amok** Not *amuck.*

**among, between** The maxim that *between* introduces two items and *among* introduces more than two covers most questions about how to use these words: *The funds were divided among Ford, Carter and McCarthy.*

However, *between* is the correct word when expressing the relationships of three or more items considered one pair at a time: *Negotiations on a debate format are under way between the network and the Ford, Carter and McCarthy committees.*

As with all prepositions, any pronouns that follow these words must be in the ob-jective case: *among us, between him and her, between you and me.*

**ampersand (&)** See entry in **Punctuation** chapter.

**amplitude modulation** *AM* is acceptable in all references.

**Amtrak** This acronym, drawn from the words *American travel by track,* may be used in all references to the *National Railroad Passenger Corp.* Do not use *AMTRAK.*

The corporation was estab-lished by Congress in 1970 to take over intercity passenger operations from railroads that wanted to drop passenger ser-vice. Amtrak contracts with railroads for the use of their tracks and of certain other op-erating equipment and crews.

Amtrak is subsidized in part by federal funds appro-priated yearly by Congress and administered through the Department of Transporta-tion.

*Amtrak* should not be con-fused with *Conrail* (see sepa-rate entry). However, the leg-islation that established Con-rail provided for Amtrak to gradually take over ownership of certain trackage in the Boston-Washington corridor and from Philadelphia to Harrisburg.

Amtrak headquarters is in Washington.

**AMVETS** Acceptable in all references for *American Veterans of World War II, Korea and Vietnam.*

### anemia, anemic

### Anglican Communion

This is the name for the worldwide association of the 22 separate national Anglican churches.

Each national church is independent. A special position of honor is accorded to the archbishop of Canterbury, as the pre-eminent officer in the original Anglican body, the Church of England.

The test of membership in the Anglican Communion traditionally has been whether a church has been in communion with the See of Canterbury. No legislative or juridical ties exist, however.

BELIEFS: Anglicans believe in the Trinity, the humanity and divinity of Christ, the virginity of Mary, salvation through Christ, and everlasting heaven and hell.

Baptism and the Lord's Supper are recognized as sacraments, although belief in the degree to which Christ is present in the Eucharist may vary.

Together with Scripture, the Book of Common Prayer serves as the principal guide to belief and practice.

A principal difference between Roman Catholics and Anglicans is still the dispute that led to the formation of the Church of England—refusal to acknowledge that the pope, as bishop of Rome, has ruling authority over other bishops.

The communion also contends that its clergy have a direct link to Christ's apostles that is traceable through an unbroken series of ceremonies in which authority was passed down by a laying on of hands. The Roman Catholic Church, which claims the same type of historic succession for its clergy, has held that 16th-century Anglican practice broke the continuity of apostolic succession among its clergy.

Among individual Anglican (or *Episcopal* in the United States) parishes, practices fall into one of three categories—high, broad or low. A high parish stresses the sacraments and extensive ritual in worship. A low parish favors simpler services and emphasizes the preaching of the Gospel. A broad parish embraces portions of high and low worship practices, while tending to be activist on social questions and flexible in matters of church government.

The term *Anglo-Catholic* occasionally is used to describe high Anglican practices. See **catholic, catholicism.**

ANGLICAN CHURCHES: Members of the Anglican Communion, in addition to the Church of England, include the Scottish Episcopal Church, the Anglican Church of Canada, and in the United States, the Protestant Episcopal Church.

See **Episcopal Church.**

**Anglo-** Always capitalized. No hyphen when the word that follows is in lowercase:

Anglomania      Anglophobe
Anglophile

Use a hyphen when the word that follows is capitalized:

Anglo-American      Anglo-Indian

Anglo-Catholic      Anglo-Saxon

Never use *Anglo* standing alone as a synonym for people who are of English descent or whose primary language is English. This can be as offensive to them as other derogatory ethnic terms are to those who are not of English heritage.

**angry** *At* someone or *with* someone.

**animals** Do not apply a personal pronoun to an animal unless its sex has been established or the animal has a name: *The dog was scared; it barked. Rover was scared; he barked. The cat, which was scared, ran to its basket. Susie the cat, who was scared, ran to her basket. The bull tosses his horns.*

Capitalize the name of a specific animal, and use Roman numerals to show sequence: *Bowser, Whirlaway II.*

For breed names, follow the spelling and capitalization in Webster's New World Dictionary. For breeds not listed in the dictionary, capitalize words derived from proper nouns; use lowercase elsewhere: *basset hound, Boston terrier.*

**anno Domini** See **A.D.**

**annual** An event cannot be described as *annual* until it has been held in at least two successive years.

Do not use the term *first annual.* Instead, note that sponsors plan to hold an event annually.

**annual meeting** Lowercase in all uses.

**anoint**

**another** *Another* is not a synonym for *additional;* it refers to an element that somehow duplicates a previously stated quantity.

Right: *Ten women passed, another 10 failed.*

Wrong: *Ten women passed, another six failed.*

Right: *Ten women passed, six others failed.*

**Antarctic, Antarctica, Antarctic Ocean**

**ante-** The rules in **prefixes** apply, but in general, no hyphen. Some examples:

antebellum        antedate

**anthems** See **composition titles.** Lowercase the term *national anthem.*

**anti-** Hyphenate all except the following words, which have specific meanings of their own:

| | |
|---|---|
| antibiotic | antipasto |
| antibody | antiperspirant |
| anticlimax | antiphon |
| antidote | antiphony |
| antifreeze | antiseptic |
| antigen | antiserum |
| antihistamine | antithesis |
| antiknock | antitoxin |
| antimatter | antitrust |
| antimony | antitussive |
| antiparticle* | |

*And similar terms in physics such as *antiproton.*

This approach has been adopted in the interests of readability and easily remembered consistency.

Hyphenated words, many of them exceptions to Webster's New World, include:

| | |
|---|---|
| anti-aircraft | anti-labor |
| anti-bias | anti-slavery |
| anti-inflation | anti-social |
| anti-intellec- tual | anti-war |

See **Antichrist, anti-Christ.**

**Antichrist, anti-Christ**
*Antichrist* is the proper name for the individual the Bible says will challenge Christ.

The adjective *anti-Christ* would be applied to someone or something opposed to Christ.

**anticipate, expect** *Anticipate* means to expect and prepare for something; *expect* does not include the notion of preparation:

*They expect a record crowd. They have anticipated it by adding more seats to the auditorium.*

**Antiochian Orthodox Christian Archdiocese of North America** Formed in 1975 by the merger of the Antiochian Orthodox Christian Archdiocese of New York and All North America and the Archdiocese of Toledo, Ohio, and Dependencies in North America. It is under the jurisdiction of the patriarch of Antioch.

See **Eastern Orthodox churches.**

**anybody, any body, anyone, any one** One word for an indefinite reference: *Anyone can do that.*

Two words when the emphasis is on singling out one element of a group: *Any one of them may speak up.*

**AP** Use in logotypes. Acceptable on second reference for *The Associated Press.*

Do not capitalize *the* when it precedes *AP*.

**apostolic delegate, papal nuncio** An *apostolic delegate* is a Roman Catholic diplomat chosen by the pope to be his envoy to the church in a nation that does not have formal diplomatic relations with the Vatican.

A *papal nuncio* is the pope's envoy to a nation with which the Vatican has diplomatic relations.

**apostrophe (')** See entry in **Punctuation** chapter.

**Appalachia** In the broadest sense, the word applies to the entire region along the Appalachian Mountains, which extend from Maine into northern Alabama.

In a sense that often suggests economic depression and poverty, the reference is to sections of eastern Tennessee, eastern Kentucky, southeastern Ohio and the western portion of West Virginia.

The Appalachian Regional Commission, established by federal law in 1965, has a mandate to foster development in 397 counties in 13 states—all of West Virginia and contiguous parts of Alabama, Georgia, Kentucky, Maryland, Mississippi, New York, North Carolina, Ohio, Pennsylvania, South Carolina, Tennessee and Virginia.

When the word *Appalachia* is used, specify the extent of the area in question.

**Appalachian Mountains** Or simply: *the Appalachians.*

**appeals court** See **U.S. Court of Appeals.**

**apposition** A decision on whether to put commas around a word, phrase or clause used in apposition depends on whether it is essential to the meaning of the sentence (no commas) or not essential (use commas).

See the **essential phrases, non-essential phrases** entry for examples.

**approve** See the entry that reads **adopt, approve, enact, pass.**

**April** See **months.**

**April Fool's Day**

**Aqua-Lung** A trademark for an underwater breathing apparatus.

See **scuba.**

**Arabian American Oil Co.** *Aramco* is acceptable on second reference.

Headquarters is in Dhahran, Saudi Arabia.

**Arabic names** In general, use an English spelling that approximates the way a name sounds in Arabic.

If an individual has a preferred spelling in English, use that. If usage has established a particular spelling, use that.

Problems in transliteration of Arabic names often are traceable to pronunciations that vary from region to region. The g, for example, is pronounced like the *g* of *go* in North Africa, but like the *j* of *joy* in the Arab Peninsula. Thus it is *Gamal* in Egypt and *Jamal* in nations on the peninsula. Follow local practice in deciding which letter to use.

Arabs commonly are known by two names *(Fuad Butros)*, or by three *(Ahmed Zaki Yamani)*. Follow the individual's preference on first reference. On second reference, use only the final name in the sequence.

The articles *al-* or *el-* should not be used. They stand for an Arabic article similar to *the* and have an English meaning of *sir, lord* or *Mr.* The Arabic word for *son (ibn* or *bin* depending on personal preference and the nation) is sometimes part of a name *(Rashid bin Humaid)*. On second reference, use only the final word in the name: *Humaid.*

The word *abu*, meaning *father of*, occasionally is used as a last name *(Abdul Mohsen Abu Maizer)*. Capitalize and repeat it on second reference: *Abu Maizer.*

The titles *king, emir, sheik* and *imam* are used, but *prince* usually replaces *emir*. Some Arabs are known only by the title and a given name on first reference *(King Hussein)*. Others are known by a complete name *(Sheik Sabah Salem Sabah)*. Follow the common usage on first reference.

On second reference, drop the title, using only the given name if it stood alone *(Hussein)* or the final name in the sequence if more than one was used on first reference *(Sabah)*. Make an exception to this procedure for second reference if an individual commonly is known by some other one of the names used on first reference.

The *al*, when found in front of many newspaper names, means *the.* It should be capitalized, as in *The New York Times, El Pais, Die Welt.*

**Arabic numerals** The numerical figures *1, 2, 3, 4, 5, 6, 7, 8, 9, 10.*

In general, use Arabic forms unless denoting the sequence of wars or establishing a personal sequence for people or animals. See **Roman numerals.**

Separate entries list more details and examples. For a full list, see the **numerals** entry.

**arbitrate, mediate** Both terms are used in reports about labor negotiations, but they should not be interchanged.

One who *arbitrates* hears evidence from all people concerned, then hands down a decision.

One who *mediates* listens to arguments of both parties and tries by the exercise of reason or persuasion to bring them to an agreement.

**arch-** No hyphen after this prefix unless it precedes a capitalized word:

archbishop  arch-Republi-
archenemy  can
  archrival

**archbishop** See **Episcopal Church; Roman Catholic Church;** and **religious titles.**

**archbishop of Canterbury** In general, lowercase *archbishop* unless it is used before the name of the individual who holds the office.

Capitalize *Archbishop of Canterbury* standing alone only when it is used in a story that also refers to members of Britain's nobility. See the **nobility** entry for the relevant guidelines.

**archdiocese** Capitalize as part of a proper name: *the Archdiocese of Chicago, the Chicago Archdiocese.* Lowercase when it stands alone.

See the entry for the particular denomination in question.

**arctic, Arctic Circle, arctic fox, Arctic Ocean**

**are** A unit of surface measure in the metric system, equal to 100 square meters.

An *are* is equal to approximately 1,076.4 square feet or 119.6 square yards.

See **hectare** and **metric system.**

**area codes** See **telephone numbers.**

**Arizona** Abbrev.: *Ariz.* See **state names.**

**Arkansas** Abbrev.: *Ark.* See **state names.**

**Armenian Church of America** The term encompasses two independent dioceses that cooperate in some activities: the Eastern Diocese of the Armenian Church of America, for areas outside California, and the Western Diocese of the Armenian Church of America, which serves California.

See **Eastern Orthodox Churches.**

**Armistice Day** It is now *Veterans Day*.

**army** Capitalize when referring to U.S. forces: *the U.S. Army, the Army, Army regulations*. Do not use the abbreviation *USA*.

Use lowercase for the forces of other nations: *the French army*.

This approach has been adopted for consistency, because many foreign nations do not use *army* as the proper name.

See **military academies** and **military titles**.

**arrest** To avoid any suggestion that someone is being judged before a trial, do not use a phrase such as *arrested for killing*. Instead, use *arrested on a charge of killing*.

For guidelines on related words, see **accuse; allege;** and **indict**.

**arrive** It requires the preposition *at*. Do not omit, as airline dispatchers often do in: *He will arrive LaGuardia*.

**artifact**

**artillery** See **weapons**.

**art works** See **composition titles**.

**as** See **like, as**.

**ashcan, ashtray**

**Ash Wednesday** The first day of Lent, 46 days before Easter.

See **Easter** and **Lent**.

**Asian, Asiatic** Use *Asian* or *Asians* when referring to people.

Some Asians regard *Asiatic* as offensive when applied to people.

**Asian flu**

**Asian subcontinent** In popular usage the term applies to Bangladesh, Bhutan, India, Nepal, Sikkim and the island nation of Sri Lanka (formerly Ceylon) at the southeastern tip of India.

For definitions of the terms that apply to other parts of Asia, see **Far East; Middle East;** and **Southeast Asia**.

**as if** The preferred form, but *as though* is acceptable.

**assassin, killer, murderer** An *assassin* is a politically motivated killer.

A *killer* is anyone who kills with a motive of any kind.

A *murderer* is one who is convicted of murder in a court of law.

See **execute** and the **homicide, murder, manslaughter** entry.

**assassination, date of** A prominent person is shot one day and dies the next. Which day was he assassinated? The day he was attacked.

**assault, battery** Popularly, *assault* almost always implies physical contact and sudden, intense violence.

Legally, however, *assault* means simply to threaten violence, as in pointing a pistol at an individual without firing it. *Assault and battery* is the legal term when the victim was touched by the assaulter or something the assaulter put in motion.

**assembly** Capitalize when part of the proper name for the lower house of a legislature: *the California Assembly.* Retain capitalization if the state name is dropped but the reference is specific:

*SACRAMENTO, Calif. (AP)—The state Assembly . . .*

If a legislature is known as a general assembly: *the Missouri General Assembly, the General Assembly, the assembly. Legislature* also may be used as the proper name, however. See **legislature.**

Lowercase all plural uses: *the California and New York assemblies.*

**assemblyman, assemblywoman** Do not abbreviate. See **legislative titles.**

**assistant** Do not abbreviate. Capitalize only when part of a formal title before a name: *Assistant Secretary of State George Ball.* Whenever practical, however, an appositional construction should be used: *George Ball, assistant secretary of state.*

See **titles.**

**associate** Never abbreviate. Apply the same capitalization norms listed under **assistant.**

**Associated Press, The** The newsgathering cooperative dating from 1848.

Use *The Associated Press* on first reference (the capitalized article is part of the formal name).

On second reference, *AP* or *the AP* (no capital on *the*) may be used.

The address is 50 Rockefeller Plaza, New York, N.Y. 10020. The telephone number is (212) 621-1500.

The following are service names used most frequently by the AP.

CustomStocks
DataFeature
DataSpeed
DataStream
DataStream 500 Stocks
DigitalStocks
DigitalStocks II
LaserGraphics
LaserPhoto
LaserPhoto II
Newsfeatures
NewsPhoto
Newspower 1200
Network News
PhotoColor
SelectStocks
SportsStats

**Association** Do not abbreviate. Capitalize as part of a proper name: *American Medical Association.*

**astronaut** It is not a formal title. Do not capitalize when used before a name: *astronaut John Glenn.*

**Atchison, Topeka & Santa Fe Railway** A subsidiary of Santa Fe Industries.

Headquarters is in Chicago.

**atheist** See the **agnostic, atheist** entry.

**athlete's foot, athlete's heart**

**Atlanta** The city in Georgia stands alone in datelines.

**Atlantic Ocean**

**Atlantic Richfield Co.** *Arco* is acceptable on second reference.

Headquarters is in Los Angeles.

**Atlantic Standard Time, Atlantic Daylight Time** Used in the Maritime Provinces of Canada and in Puerto Rico.

See **time zones.**

**at large** Usually two words for an individual representing more than a single district: *congressman at large, councilman at large.*

But it is *ambassador-at-large* for an ambassador assigned to no particular country.

**Atomic Age** It began Dec. 2, 1942, at the University of Chicago with the creation of the first self-sustaining nuclear chain reaction.

**Atomic Energy Commission** It no longer exists. See **Nuclear Regulatory Commission**.

**attache** It is not a formal title. Always lowercase.

**attorney, lawyer** In common usage the words are interchangeable.

Technically, however, an *attorney* is someone (usually, but not necessarily, a lawyer) empowered to act for another. Such an individual occasionally is called an *attorney in fact*.

A *lawyer* is a person admitted to practice in a court system. Such an individual occasionally is called an *attorney at law*.

Do not abbreviate. Do not capitalize unless it is an office-holder's title: *defense attorney Perry Mason, attorney Perry Mason, District Attorney Hamilton Burger*.

See **lawyer**.

**attorney general, attorneys general** Never abbreviate. Capitalize only when used as a title before a name: *Attorney General Griffin B. Bell*.

See **titles**.

**augur** A transitive verb. Do not follow it with the preposition *for: The tea leaves augur a time of success.*

**August** See **months**.

**author** A noun used for both men and women. Do not use it as a verb.

**automaker, automakers**

**automatic** See **pistol** and **weapons** entries.

**automobiles** Capitalize brand names: *Buick, Ford, Mustang, MG, Impala.* Lowercase generic terms: *a Volkswagen van, a Mack truck.*

**Auto-Train Corp.** A private company that hauls passengers and their cars, leasing rails and equipment owned by other companies.

Headquarters is in Washington.

**autoworker, autoworkers** One word when used generically.

But *Auto Worker* when referring specifically to the membership and the activities of the United Automobile, Aerospace and Agricultural Implement Workers of America.

**autumn** See **seasons**.

**avenue** Abbreviate only with a numbered address. See **addresses**.

**average, mean, median, norm** *Average* refers to the result obtained by dividing a sum by the number of quantities added together: *The average of 7, 9, 17 is 33 divided by 3, or 11.*

*Mean* commonly designates a figure intermediate between two extremes: *The mean temperature of the day with a high of 56 and a low of 34 is 45.*

*Median* is the middle number of points in a series arranged in order of size: *The median grade in the group of 50, 55, 85, 88, 92 is 85. The average is 74.*

*Norm* implies a standard of average performance for a given group: *The child was below the norm for his age in reading comprehension.*

**average of** The phrase takes a plural verb in a construction such as: *An average of 100 new jobs are created daily.*

**averse** See **adverse, averse**.

**Avianca** The headquarters of this airline is in Bogota, Colombia.

**aviator** Use for both men and women.

**awards and decorations** Capitalize them: *Bronze Star, Medal of Honor,* etc.

See **Nobel Prize** and **Pulitzer Prize**.

**awe-struck**

**awhile, a while** *He plans to stay awhile.*

*He plans to stay for a while.*

**AWOL** Acceptable on second reference for *absent without leave*.

**ax** Not *axe*.

The verb forms: *ax, axed, axing.*

**Axis** The alliance of Germany, Italy and Japan during World War II.

# B

**Baby Bells** A collective description of the regional telephone companies formed out of the breakup of the Bell System of AT&T. Avoid except in quotes.

**baby-sit, baby-sitting, baby-sat, baby sitter**

**baccalaureate**

**bachelor of arts, bachelor of science** *A bachelor's degree* or *bachelor's* is acceptable in any reference.

See **academic degrees** for guidelines on when the abbreviations *B.A.* or *B.S.* are acceptable.

**back up** (v.) **backup** (n. and adj.)

**backward** Not backwards.

**back yard** (n.) **back-yard** (adj.)

**bad, badly** *Bad* should not be used as an adverb. It does not lose its status as an adjective, however, in a sentence such as *I feel bad.* Such a statement is the idiomatic equivalent of *I am in bad health.* An alternative, *I feel badly,* could be interpreted as meaning that your sense of touch was bad.

See the **good, well** entry.

**Bahamas** In datelines, give the name of the city or town followed by *Bahamas:*
*NASSAU, Bahamas (AP)—*
In stories, use *Bahamas, the Bahamas* or *the Bahama Islands* as the construction of a sentence dictates.

Identify a specific island in the text if relevant.

**bail** *Bail* is money or property that will be forfeited to the court if an accused individual fails to appear for trial. It may be posted as follows:
—The accused may deposit with the court the full amount

or its equivalent in collateral such as a deed to property.

—A friend or relative may make such a deposit with the court.

—The accused may pay a professional bail bondsman a percentage of the total figure. The bondsman, in turn, guarantees the court that it will receive from him the full amount in the event the individual fails to appear for trial.

It is correct in all cases to say that an accused *posted bail* or *posted a bail bond* (the money held by the court is a form of bond). When a distinction is desired, say that the individual *posted his own bail,* that *bail was posted by a friend or relative,* or that *bail was obtained through a bondsman.*

**Bakelite** A trademark for a type of plastic resin.

**baker's dozen** It means 13.

**Bakery and Confectionery Workers' International Union of America** The shortened form *Bakery Workers union* is acceptable in all references.

Headquarters is in Washington.

**balance of payments, balance of trade** The *balance of payments* is the difference between the amount of money that leaves a nation and the amount that enters it during a period of time.

The *balance of payments* is determined by computing the amount of money a nation and its citizens send abroad for all purposes—including goods and services purchased, travel, loans, foreign aid, etc. —and subtracting from it the amount that foreign nations send into the nation for similar purposes.

The *balance of trade* is the difference between the monetary value of the goods a nation imports and the goods it exports.

An example illustrating the difference between the two:

The United States and its citizens might send $10 billion abroad—$5 billion for goods, $3 billion for loans and foreign aid, $1 billion for services and $1 billion for tourism and other purposes.

Other nations might send $9 billion into the United States—$6 billion for U.S. goods, $2 billion for services and $1 billion for tourism and other purposes.

The United States would

have a *balance-of-payments* deficit of $1 billion but a *balance-of-trade* surplus of $1 billion.

**ball carrier**

**ballclub, ballpark, ballplayer, ballroom**

**ball point pen**

**baloney** Foolish or exaggerated talk.

The sausage or luncheon meat is *bologna.*

**Baltimore** The city in Maryland stands alone in datelines.

**Band-Aid** A trademark for a type of adhesive bandage.

**Bank of America** Acceptable in all references for *Bank of America National Trust & Savings Association.*

The parent company is BankAmerica Corp. of San Francisco.

**bankruptcy** The legal sense of the word applies only if a court has told an individual or organization to liquidate assets and distribute the proceeds to creditors.

The action may be involuntary, as the result of a suit by creditors, or it may be a voluntary effort to deal with bills that cannot be paid.

Often a company with financial problems announces that it is seeking to reorganize under federal bankruptcy laws. In such a case, it is incorrect to describe the company as *bankrupt.*

A story that announces such a filing should specify the chapter of the Federal Bankruptcy Act under which the reorganization is sought and describe the basic provisions.

Under Chapter 11, the most frequently used, a company obtains a federal court order that frees it from the threat of creditors' lawsuits until it can develop a plan to put its finances in order. While the reorganization proceeds, the activities of management must be approved by the court. The ultimate reorganization plan must be accepted by a majority of the creditors. It may involve various options, including a full or partial payment of debts.

Chapter 10, which is used occasionally, takes away management from the existing officers and turns it over to an independent trustee. Under a Chapter 10 reorganization, stockholders could lose their entire investment. By contrast, under a Chapter 11 reorganization, it is possible for stockholders to retain something even if creditors are not paid in full.

Some other chapters apply to specific types of companies or situations.

If a reorganization plan fails, a company may be forced into bankruptcy.

**baptism** See **sacraments.**

**baptist, Baptist** A person who baptizes is a *baptist* (lowercase).

A *Baptist* (uppercase) is a person who is a member of the Protestant denomination described in the next entry.

**Baptist churches** It is incorrect to apply the term *church* to any Baptist unit except the local church.

The ultimate governing power rests with members of the local congregation. Majority rule prevails.

This emphasis on the authority of the individual churches helps account for the existence of more than 20 Baptist bodies in the United States.

The largest, the Southern Baptist Convention, has more than 12 million members, most of them in the South, although it has churches in 50 states.

The largest Northern body is American Baptist Churches in the U.S.A., with about 1.5 million members.

Blacks predominate in three other large Baptist bodies, the National Baptist Convention of America, the National Baptist Convention U.S.A. Inc., and the Progressive National Baptist Convention Inc.

The roster of Baptist bodies in the United States also includes the Baptist General Conference, the Conservative Baptist Association of America, the General Association of Regular Baptist Churches, the General Association of General Baptists, and the North American Baptist General Conference.

The Baptist World Alliance, a voluntary association of Baptist bodies throughout the world, fosters communication among its members, provides a forum for discussion of doctrine and practice, and organizes the Baptist

World Congress meetings generally held every five years. Headquarters is in Washington.

BELIEFS: Baptists are free to interpret Scripture as their consciences dictate.

In general, however, Baptists believe that no one can be validly baptized without first giving a personal confession of faith in Christ as his savior. They also believe that the baptism should be by immersion.

In addition to belief in original sin and the need for redemption, Baptists generally believe in the Trinity, the humanity and divinity of Christ, salvation through Christ, and everlasting heaven and hell.

CLERGY: All members of the Baptist clergy may be referred to as *ministers. Pastor* applies if a minister leads a congregation.

On first reference, use *the Rev.* before the name of a man or woman. On second reference, use only the last name of a man; use *Miss, Mrs., Ms.* or no title before the last name of a woman depending on her preference.

See **religious titles.**

See **religious movements** for definitions of some descriptive terms that often apply to Baptists but are not limited to them.

**barbecue** Not *barbeque* or *Bar-B-Q.*

**barbiturate**

**barmaid**

**bar mitzvah** The Jewish religious ritual and family celebration that marks a boy's 13th birthday. Judaism regards the age of 13 as the benchmark of religious maturity. *Bar mitzvah* translates as "one who is responsible for the Commandments."

Conservative congregations have instituted the *bas mitzvah* or *bat mitzvah,* a similar ceremony for girls.

**baron, baroness** See **nobility.**

**barrel** A standard barrel in U.S. measure contains 31.5 gallons.

A standard barrel in British and Canadian measure contains 36 imperial gallons.

In international dealings with crude oil, a standard barrel contains 42 U.S. gallons or 35 imperial gallons.

See the **oil** entry for guidelines on computing the volume and weight of petroleum products.

**barrel, barreled, barreling**

**barrel-chested, barrelhouse** Also: *double-barreled shotgun.*

**barrister** See **lawyer.**

**barroom**

**battalion** Capitalize when used with a figure to form a name: *the 3rd Battalion, the 10th Battalion.*

**battlefield** Also: *battlefront, battleground, battleship.* But *battle station.*

**Bavarian cream**

**bay** Capitalize as an integral part of a proper name: *Hudson Bay, San Francisco Bay.*
Capitalize also *San Francisco Bay area* or *the Bay area* as the popular name for the nine-county region that has San Francisco as its focal point.

**bazaar** A fair. *Bizarre* means unusual.

**B.C.** Acceptable in all references to a calendar year in the period *before Christ.*
Because the full phrase would be *in the year 43 before Christ,* the abbreviation *B.C.* is placed after the figure for the year: *43 B.C.*
See **A.D.**

**because, since** Use *because* to denote a specific cause-effect relationship: *He went because he was told.*
*Since* is acceptable in a causal sense when the first event in a sequence led logically to the second but was not its direct cause: *He went to the game, since he had been given the tickets.*

**before Christ** See **B.C.**

**Beijing** The city in China (formerly Peking) stands alone in datelines.

**Belize** The former British Honduras.

**bellwether**

**benefit, benefited, benefiting**

**Benelux** Belgium, the Netherlands and Luxembourg.

If *Benelux* is used, explain that it is an inclusive word for these three nations.

**Ben-Gurion International Airport** Located at Lod, Israel, about 10 miles south of Tel Aviv.

See **airport**.

**Benzedrine** A trademark for a type of pep pill or stimulant.

**Bering Standard Time, Bering Daylight Time** Used in the far western section of Alaska, including Nome.

See **time zones.**

**Berlin** Stands alone in datelines.

When a distinction must be made between sections of the city, do so in the body of the story. Use *East Berlin, the eastern sector* or *the Communist sector* for the area controlled by East Germany. Use *West Berlin* or *the western sector* for the non-Communist part of the city.

**Berlin Wall** On second reference, *the wall.*

**Bermuda collar, Bermuda grass, Bermuda shorts**

**beside, besides** *Beside* means at the side of.

*Besides* means in addition to.

**besiege**

**best seller** (n.)

**betting odds** Use figures and a hyphen: *The odds were 5-4; he won despite 3-2 odds against him.*

The word *to* seldom is necessary, but when it appears it should be hyphenated in all constructions: *3-to-2 odds, odds of 3-to-2, the odds were 3-to-2.*

**bettor** A person who bets.

**between** See the **among, between** entry.

**bi-** The rules in **prefixes** apply, but in general, no hyphen. Some examples:

| | |
|---|---|
| bifocal | bimonthly |
| bilateral | bipartisan |
| bilingual | |

**biannual, biennial** *Biannual* means twice a year and

is a synonym for the word semiannual.

*Biennial* means every two years.

**Bible** Capitalize, without quotation marks, when referring to the Scriptures in the Old Testament or the New Testament. Capitalize also related terms such as the *Gospels, Gospel of St. Mark, the Scriptures, the Holy Scriptures.*

Lowercase *biblical* in all uses.

Lowercase *bible* as a nonreligious term: *My dictionary is my bible.*

Do not abbreviate individual books of the Bible.

The books of the Old Testament, in order, are: Genesis, Exodus, Leviticus, Numbers, Deuteronomy, Joshua, Judges, Ruth, 1 Samuel, 2 Samuel, 1 Kings, 2 Kings, 1 Chronicles, 2 Chronicles, Ezra, Nehemiah, Esther, Job, Psalms, Proverbs, Ecclesiastes, Song of Solomon, Isaiah, Jeremiah, Lamentations, Ezekiel, Daniel, Hosea, Joel, Amos, Obadiah, Jonah, Micah, Nahum, Habakkuk, Zephaniah, Haggai, Zechariah, Malachi.

The books of the New Testament, in order, are: Matthew, Mark, Luke, John, Acts, Romans, 1 Corinthians, 2 Corinthians, Galatians, Ephesians, Philippians, Colossians, 1 Thessalonians, 2 Thessalonians, 1 Timothy, 2 Timothy, Titus, Philemon, Hebrews, Epistles of James, 1 Peter, 2 Peter, 1 John, 2 John, 3 John, Jude, Revelation.

Citations listing the number of chapter and verse(s) use this form: *Matthew 3:16, Luke 21:1–13, 1 Peter 2:1.*

**Bible Belt** Those sections of the United States, especially in the South and Middle West, where fundamentalist religious beliefs prevail. Use with care, because in certain contexts it can give offense. See **religious movements.**

**bicycle**

**big-bang theory** The theory that the universe began with the explosion of a superdense primeval atom and has been expanding ever since.

The **oscillating theory,** another hypothesis, maintains that expansion eventually will stop, followed by contraction to a superdense atom, followed by another big bang.

The **steady-state theory,** an alternate hypothesis, maintains that the universe always has existed and that matter constantly is being created to replace matter that constantly is being destroyed.

**big brother** One's older brother is a *big brother. Big Brother* (capitalized) means under the watchful eye of big government, from George Orwell's "1984."

Capitalize *Big Brother* also in reference to members of Big Brothers Inc., an organization that encourages adult men to spend time with boys who need guidance. Headquarters is in New York.

**Big Three automakers** General Motors, Ford, Chrysler.

*Big Four:* The Big Three plus American Motors.

**bigwig**

**billion** A thousand million.

For forms, see the **millions, billions** entry.

**Bill of Rights** The first 10 amendments to the Constitution.

**bimonthly** Means every other month. *Semimonthly* means twice a month.

**birthday** Capitalize as part of the name for a holiday: *Washington's Birthday.* Lowercase in other uses.

**bishop** See **religious titles** and the entry for the denomination in question.

**biweekly** Means every other week. *Semiweekly* means twice a week.

**bizarre** Unusual. A fair is a *bazaar.*

**black** Acceptable in all references for *Negro.*

Do not use *colored* as a synonym. See the **colored** entry.

**Black Muslims** See **Muslim(s).**

**blackout, brownout** A *blackout* is a total power failure over a large area or the concealing of lights that might be visible to enemy raiders.

The term *rotating blackout* is used by electric companies to describe a situation in which electric power to some sections temporarily is cut off on a rotating basis to assure that voltage will meet minimum standards in other sections.

A *brownout* is a small, temporary voltage reduction, usually from 2 to 8 percent, implemented to conserve electric power.

**blast off** (v.) **blastoff** (n. and adj.)

**Blessed Sacrament, Blessed Virgin**

**blizzard** See **weather terms.**

**bloc, block** A *bloc* is a coalition of people, groups or nations with the same purpose or goal.
*Block* has more than a dozen definitions, but a political alliance is not one of them.

**blond, blonde** Use *blond* as a noun for males and as an adjective for all applications: She has *blond* hair.
Use *blonde* as a noun for females.

**bloodhound**

**Bloody Mary** A drink made of vodka and tomato juice. The name is derived

from the nickname for Mary I of England.

**blue blood** (n.) **blue-blooded** (adj.)

**blue chip stock** Stock in a company known for its long-established record of making money and paying dividends.

**B'nai B'rith** See the **fraternal organizations and service clubs** entry.

**board** Capitalize only when an integral part of a proper name. See **capitalization.**

**board of aldermen** See **city council.**

**board of directors, board of trustees** Always lowercase. See the **organizations and institutions** entry.

**board of supervisors** See **city council.**

**boats, ships** A *boat* is a watercraft of any size but generally is used to indicate a small craft. A *ship* is a large, seagoing vessel.
The word *boat* is used,

however, in some words that apply to large craft: *ferryboat, PT boat, gunboat.*

Use Arabic or Roman numerals in the names of boats and ships: *the Queen Elizabeth 2* or *QE2; Titan I, Titan II.*

The reference for military ships is Jane's Fighting Ships; for non-military ships, Lloyd's Register of Shipping.

**Boeing Co.** Formerly Boeing Aircraft Co.

Headquarters is in Seattle.

**boldface** Use boldface type for the slug lines, bylines and underlines for bylines atop a story, and for separate subhead lines if needed within a story.

Do not use boldface for individual words within a paragraph.

**bologna** The sausage. *Baloney* is foolish or exaggerated talk.

**bona fide**

**bonbon**

**bonds** See **loan terminology** in Business guidelines and style section.

**boo-boo**

**book titles** See **composition titles.**

**borscht** Exception to Webster's New World.

**Bosporus, the** Not the Bosporus Strait.

**Boston** The city in Massachusetts stands alone in datelines.

**Boston brown bread, Boston cream pie, Boston terrier**

**boulevard** Abbreviated only with a numbered address. See **addresses.**

**boundary**

**bowlegged**

**box office** (n.) **box-office** (adj.)

**boy** Applicable until 18th birthday is reached. Use man or young man afterward.

**boycott, embargo** A *boycott* is an organized refusal to buy a particular product or service, or to deal with a particular merchant or group of merchants.

An *embargo* is a legal restriction against trade. It usually prohibits goods from entering or leaving a country.

### boyfriend, girlfriend

**Boy Scouts** The full name of the national organization is *Boy Scouts of America.* Headquarters is in Irving, Texas.

*Cub Scouting* is for boys 8 through 10. Members are *Cub Scouts* or *Cubs.*

*Boy Scouting* is for boys 11 through 17. Members are *Boy Scouts* or *Scouts.*

*Exploring* is a separate program open to boys and girls from high school age through 20. Members are *Explorers,* not *Explorer Scouts.* Members of units that stress nautical programs are *Sea Explorers.*

See **Girl Scouts.**

**bra** Acceptable in all references for *brassiere.*

**brackets** They cannot be transmitted over news wires. Use parentheses or recast the material.

See **parentheses.**

**Brahman, Brahmin** *Brahman* applies to the priestly Hindu caste and a breed of cattle.

*Brahmin* applies to aristocracy in general: *Boston Brahmin.*

**brand names** When they are used, capitalize them.

Brand names normally should be used only if they are essential to a story.

Sometimes, however, the use of a brand name may not be essential but is acceptable because it lends an air of reality to a story: *He fished a Camel from his shirt pocket* may be preferable to the less specific *cigarette.*

When a company sponsors an event such as a tennis tournament, use the company's name for the event in first reference and the generic term in subsequent references: *The Buick Women's Open; the $200,000 women's tennis tournament; the tournament.*

Also use a separate paragraph to provide the name of a sponsor when the brand name is not part of the formal title.

Brand name is a non-legal term for *service mark* or *trademark.* See entries under those words.

**brand-new** (adj.)

**Braniff Airways** Headquarters is in Dallas.

**break in** (v.) **break-in** (n. and adj.)

**break up** (v.) **breakup** (n. and adj.)

**Bricklayers, Masons and Plasterers' International Union of America** The shortened form *Bricklayers union* is acceptable in all references.
Headquarters is in Washington.

**bride, bridegroom, bridesmaid** *Bride* is appropriate in wedding stories, but use *wife* or *spouse* in other circumstances.

**brigadier** See **military titles.**

**Bright's disease** After Richard Bright, the London physician who first diagnosed this form of kidney disease.

**Brill's disease** After Nathan E. Brill, a U.S. physician. A form of epidemic typhus fever in which the disease recurs years after the original infection.

**Britain** Acceptable in all references for *Great Britain,* which consists of England, Scotland and Wales.
See **United Kingdom.**

**British, Briton(s)** The people of Great Britain: the English, the Scottish, the Welsh.

**British Airways** The successor to British European Airways and British Overseas Airways Corp.
Headquarters is in Hounslow, England.

**British Broadcasting Corp.** BBC is acceptable in all references within contexts such as a television column. Otherwise, do not use *BBC* until second reference.

**British Columbia** The Canadian province bounded on the west by the Pacific Ocean. Do not abbreviate.
See **datelines.**

**British Commonwealth** See **Commonwealth, the.**

**British Petroleum Co. Ltd.** *BP* is acceptable on second reference.

Headquarters is in London.

**British thermal unit** The amount of heat required to increase the temperature of a pound of water one degree Fahrenheit. *Btu* (the same for singular and plural) is acceptable on second reference.

**British ton** See **ton.**

**British Virgin Islands** Use with a community name in datelines on stories from these islands. Do not abbreviate.

Specify an individual island in the text if relevant.

See **datelines.**

**broadcast** The past tense also is *broadcast,* not *broadcasted.*

**Broadway, off-Broadway, off-off-Broadway** When applied to stage productions, these terms refer to distinctions made by union contracts, not to location of a theater.

Actors Equity Association and unions representing craft workers have one set of pay scales for *Broadway* productions (generally those in New York City theaters of 300 or more seats) and a lower scale for smaller theaters, classified as *off-Broadway* houses.

The term *off-off-Broadway* refers to workshop productions that may use Equity members for a limited time at substandard pay. Other unions maintain a hands-off policy, agreeing with the Equity attitude that actors should have an opportunity to whet their talents in offbeat roles without losing their Equity memberships.

**broccoli**

**Bromo Seltzer** A trademark for a brand of bicarbonate of soda.

**Bronze Age** The age characterized by the development of bronze tools and weapons, from 3500 to 1000 B.C. Regarded as coming between the Stone Age and the Iron Age.

**brother** See **Roman Catholic Church.**

**Brotherhood of Railway, Airline and Steamship Clerks, Freight Handlers,** Express and Station

Employees The shortened form *Railway Employees union* is acceptable in all references.

Headquarters is in Rosemont, Ill.

**brothers** Abbreviate as *Bros.* in formal company names: *Warner Bros.*

For possessives: *Warner Bros.' profits.*

**brownout** See the **blackout, brownout** entry.

**brunet, brunette** Use *brunet* as a noun for males, and as the adjective for both sexes.

Use *brunette* as a noun for females.

**brussels sprouts**

**Btu** The same in singular and plural. See **British thermal unit.**

**Budapest** The capital of Hungary. In datelines, follow it with *Hungary.*

**Buddha, Buddhism** A major religion founded in India about 500 B.C. by Buddha. Buddha, which means enlightened one, was the name given to Gautama Siddhartha by his followers.

Buddhism has about 250 million followers, mostly in India, Tibet, China, Japan, Korea and Southeast Asia. About 250,000 practice Buddhism in North America.

BELIEFS: Buddhists believe that correct thinking and self-denial will enable the soul to reach nirvana, a state of release into ultimate enlightenment and peace. Until nirvana is reached, believers cannot be freed from the cycle of death and rebirth. Karma controls existence after rebirth. It says that all actions of an individual, no matter how small, have an effect on an individual's new life after rebirth.

The way to achieve nirvana is set out in three sets of rules or guidelines:

—Four Noble Truths: The existence of suffering, the cause of suffering is ignorance, suffering may end, there is a path to the end of suffering.

—Eightfold Path: Correct resolution, correct speech, correct action, correct living, right effort, right thinking and peace of mind through meditation.

—Six Paramitas: Almsgiving, observance of the truths and paths, patience, endeavor, meditation and wisdom.

ORGANIZATION: The sangha is the general term for the Buddhist organization and loosely means the ideal Buddhist community. It is made up of monks, nuns and the laity. Monks play the primary role in preserving and spreading the religion.

SECTS: There are four major groups within Buddhism.

—Hinayana or Theravada: Followers stress monastic discipline and attainment of nirvana by the individual through meditation. It is dominant among Buddhists in Burma, Cambodia, Laos, Thailand and Sri Lanka.

—Mahayana: Followers lay stress on idealism, disinterested love, and the relief of suffering. The ideal life is that of virtue and wisdom. The sect is found mostly in Japan, Korea and eastern China.

—Mantrayana: Major centers for this group are in the Himalayas, Mongolia and Japan. It basically follows the doctrines of the Mahayana but also has a structure of spiritual leaders and disciples, believes in various evil spirits and deities, uses magic, and has secret rituals.

—Zen: Followers seek enlightenment through introspection and intuition. The doctrines are again similar to Mahayana and like Mantrayana there is a loose structure of leaders and disciples. This group is found mostly in Japan.

**Bufferin** A trademark for buffered aspirin.

**bug, tap** A concealed listening device designed to pick up sounds in a room, an automobile, etc. is a *bug*.

A *tap* is a device attached to a telephone circuit to pick up conversations on the line.

**building** Never abbreviate. Capitalize the proper names of buildings, including the word *building* if it is an integral part of the proper name: *the Empire State Building.*

**build up** (v.) **buildup** (n. and adj.)

**bullet** See **weapons.**

**bullfight, bullfighter, bullfighting**

**bullpen** One word, for the place where baseball pitchers warm up, and for a pen that holds cattle.

**bull's eye**

**bureau** Capitalize when part of the formal name for an organization or agency: *the Bureau of Labor Statistics, the Newspaper Advertising Bureau.*

Lowercase when used alone or to designate a corporate subdivision: *the Washington bureau of The Associated Press.*

**burglary, larceny, robbery, theft** Legal definitions of *burglary* vary, but in general a *burglary* involves entering a building (not necessarily by breaking in) and remaining unlawfully with the intention of committing a crime.

*Larceny* is the legal term for the wrongful taking of property. Its non-legal equivalents are *stealing* or *theft.*

*Robbery* in the legal sense involves the use of violence or threat in committing larceny. In a wider sense it means to plunder or rifle, and may thus be used even if a person was not present: *His house was robbed while he was away.*

*Theft* describes a larceny that did not involve threat, violence or plundering.

USAGE NOTE: You *rob* a person, bank, house, etc., but you *steal* the money or the jewels.

**bus, buses** Transportation vehicles. The verb forms: *bus, bused, busing.*
See **buss.**

**bushel** A unit of dry measure equal to four pecks or 32 dry quarts. The metric equivalent is approximately 35.2 liters.

To convert to liters, multiply by 35.2 (5 bushels $\times$ 35.2 = 176 liters).
See **liter.**

**business editor** Capitalize when used as a formal title before a name. See **titles.**

**business names** See **company names.**

**buss, busses** Kisses. The verb forms: *buss, bussed, bussing.*
See **bus.**

**by-** The rules in prefixes apply, but in general, no hyphen. Some examples:

byline          byproduct
bypass          bystreet

*By-election* is an exception. See the next entry.

**by-election** A special election held between regularly scheduled elections. The term most often is associated with special elections to the British House of Commons.

**Byelorussian Soviet Socialist Republic** See **Russia, Soviet Union.**

**bylaw**

**bylines** Use only if the reporter was in the dateline community to gather the information reported.

Nicknames should not be used unless they specifically are requested by the writer.

# C

**cabinet** Capitalize references to a specific body of advisers heading executive departments for a president, king, governor, etc.: *The president-elect said he has not made his Cabinet selections.*

The capital letter distinguishes the word from the common noun meaning cupboard, which is lowercase.

See **department** for a listing of all the U.S. Cabinet departments.

**Cabinet titles** Capitalize the full title when used before a name; lowercase in other uses: *Secretary of State Cyrus R. Vance,* but *Juanita M. Kreps, secretary of commerce.* See **titles**.

**cactus, cactuses**

**cadet** See **military academies**.

**Caesarean section**

**caliber** The form: *.38-caliber pistol.* See **weapons**.

**California** Abbrev.: *Calif.* See **state names**.

**call letters** Use all caps. Use hyphens to separate the type of station from the basic call letters: *WBZ-AM, WBZ-FM, WBZ-TV.*

Until the summer of 1976, the format for citizens band operators was three letters and four figures: *KTE9136.* Licenses issued since then use four letters and four figures: *KTEM1234.*

Shortwave stations, which operate with greater power than citizens band stations and on different frequencies, typically mix letters and figures: *K2LRX.*

See **channel; citizens band; radio station;** and **television station**.

**call up** (v.) **call-up** (n. and adj.)

**Cambodia** Use this name rather than *Democratic Kampuchea* in datelines. When *Kampuchea* is used in the body of the story, it should be identified as the formal name of Cambodia.

**Cameroon** Not *Camerouns or Cameroun.* See **geographic names.**

**Camp Fire** The full name of the national organization is *Camp Fire, Inc.* It was founded in 1910 as Camp Fire Girls. The name was changed in 1979 to reflect the inclusion of boys. Headquarters is in Kansas City, Mo.

Both girls and boys are included in all levels of the organization. Boys and girls 6 through 8 are *Camp Fire Blue Birds.* Children 9 through 11 are *Camp Fire Adventure* members, or *Adventurers.* Children 12 and 13 are *Camp Fire Discovery* members. Youths 14 through 17 are *Camp Fire Horizon* members.

**campaign manager** Do not treat as a formal title. Always lowercase.
See **titles.**

**Canada** Montreal, Ottawa, Quebec and Toronto stand alone in datelines. For all other datelines, use the city name and the name of the province or territory spelled out.

The 10 provinces of Canada are Alberta, British Columbia, Manitoba, New Brunswick, Newfoundland (includes Labrador), Nova Scotia, Ontario, Prince Edward Island, Quebec and Saskatchewan.

The two territories are the Yukon and the Northwest Territories.

The provinces have substantial autonomy from the federal government.

The territories are administered by the federal government, although residents of the territories do elect their own legislators and representatives to Parliament.

See **datelines.**

**Canada goose** Not *Canadian goose.*

**Canadian Broadcasting Corp.** *CBC* is acceptable in all references within contexts such as a television column. Otherwise, do not use *CBC* until second reference.

**canal** Capitalize as integral part of a proper name: *the Suez Canal.*

**Canal Zone** Do not abbreviate. No longer used except when referring to the Panama Canal area during the time it was controlled by the United States, 1904–1979.

**cancel, canceled, canceling, cancellation**

**cannon, canon** A *cannon* is a weapon. See the **weapons** entry.
A *canon* is a law or rule, particularly of a church.

**cannot**

**cant** The distinctive stock words and phrases used by a particular sect or class.
See **dialect.**

**can't hardly** A double negative is implied. Better is: *can hardly.*

**cantor** See **Jewish congregations.**

**Canuck** It means a French Canadian, and often is considered a derogatory racial label. Avoid the word except in formal names (*the Vancouver Canucks,* a professional hockey team) or in quoted matter.
See the **nationalities and races** entry.

**canvas, canvass** *Canvas* is heavy cloth.
*Canvass* is a noun and a verb denoting a survey.

**cape** Capitalize as part of a proper name: *Cape Cod, Cape Hatteras.* Lowercase when standing alone.
Although local practice may call for capitalizing *the Cape* when the rest of the name is clearly understood, always use the full name on first reference in wire copy. On second reference in wire copy, either repeat the full name or use *the cape* in lowercase.

**Cape Canaveral, Fla.** Formerly Cape Kennedy. See **John F. Kennedy Space Center.**

**capital** The city where a seat of government is located. Do not capitalize.
When used in a financial sense, *capital* describes money, equipment or property used in a business by a person or corporation.

**capitalization** In general, avoid unnecessary capitals. Use a capital letter only if you can justify it by one of the principles listed here.

Many words and phrases, including special cases, are listed separately in this book. Entries that are capitalized without further comment should be capitalized in all uses.

If there is no relevant listing in this book for a particular word or phrase, consult Webster's New World Dictionary. Use lowercase if the dictionary lists it as an acceptable form for the sense in which the word is being used.

As used in this book, *capitalize* means to use uppercase for the first letter of a word. If additional capital letters are needed, they are called for by an example or a phrase such as *use all caps.*

Some basic principles:

PROPER NOUNS: Capitalize nouns that constitute the unique identification for a specific person, place, or thing: *John, Mary, America, Boston, England.*

Some words, such as the examples just given, are always proper nouns. Some common nouns receive proper noun status when they are used as the name of a particular entity: *General Electric, Gulf Oil.*

PROPER NAMES: Capitalize common nouns such as *party, river, street* and *west* when they are an integral part of the full name for a person, place or thing: *Democratic Party, Mississippi River, Fleet Street, West Virginia.*

Lowercase these common nouns when they stand alone in subsequent references: *the party, the river, the street.*

Lowercase the common noun elements of names in all plural uses: *the Democratic and Republican parties, Main and State streets, lakes Erie and Ontario.*

Among entries that provide additional guidelines are:

| | |
|---|---|
| animals | historical pe- |
| brand names | riods and |
| buildings | events |
| committee | holidays and |
| congress | holy days |
| datelines | legislature |
| days of the | months |
| week | monuments |
| directions and | nationalities |
| regions | and races |
| family names | nicknames |
| food | |

foreign governmental bodies
foreign legislative bodies
geographic names
governmental bodies
heavenly bodies
organizations and institutions
plants
planets
police department
religious references
seasons
trademarks
unions

noun elements of a name when they stand alone.

DERIVATIVES: Capitalize words that are derived from a proper noun and still depend on it for their meaning: *American, Christian, Christianity, English, French, Marxism, Shakespearean.*

Lowercase words that are derived from a proper noun but no longer depend on it for their meaning: *french fries, herculean, manhattan cocktail, malapropism, pasteurize, quixotic, venetian blind.*

POPULAR NAMES: Some places and events lack officially designated proper names but have popular names that are the effective equivalent: *the Combat Zone* (a section of downtown Boston), *the Main Line* (a group of Philadelphia suburbs), *the South Side* (of Chicago), *the Badlands* (of North Dakota), *the Street* (the financial community in the Wall Street area of New York).

The principle applies also to shortened versions of the proper names of one-of-a-kind events: *the Series* (for the World Series), *the Derby* (for the Kentucky Derby). This practice should not, however, be interpreted as a license to ignore the general practice of lowercasing the common

SENTENCES: Capitalize the first word in a statement that stands as a sentence. See **sentences** and **parentheses.**

In poetry, capital letters are used for the first words of some phrases that would not be capitalized in prose. See **poetry.**

COMPOSITIONS: Capitalize the principal words in the names of books, movies, plays, poems, operas, songs, radio and television programs, works of art, etc. See **composition titles; magazine names;** and **newspaper names.**

TITLES: Capitalize formal titles when used immediately before a name. Lowercase formal titles when used alone or in constructions that set them off from a name by commas.

Use lowercase at all times for terms that are job descriptions rather than formal titles.

See **academic titles; courtesy titles; legislative titles; military titles; nobility titles; religious titles;** and **titles.**

ABBREVIATIONS: Capital letters apply in some cases. See the **abbreviations and acronyms** entry.

**capitol** Capitalize *U.S. Capitol* and *the Capitol* when referring to the building in Washington: *The meeting was held on Capitol Hill in the west wing of the Capitol.*

Follow the same practice when referring to state capitols: *The Virginia Capitol is in Richmond. Thomas Jefferson designed the Capitol of Virginia.*

**captain** See **military titles** for military and police usage.

Lowercase and spell out in such uses as *team captain Carl Yastrzemski.*

**carat, caret, karat** The weight of precious stones, especially diamonds, is expressed in *carats*. A carat is equal to 200 milligrams or about 3 grains.

A *caret* is a writer's and a proofreader's mark.

The proportion of pure gold used with an alloy is expressed in *karats*.

**carbine** See **weapons.**

**cardinal** See **Roman Catholic Church.**

**cardinal numbers** See **numerals.**

**CARE** Acceptable in all references for *Cooperative for American Relief Everywhere Inc.*

Headquarters is in New York.

**carefree**

**caretaker**

**Caribbean** See **Western Hemisphere.**

**carmaker, carmakers**

**car pool**

**carry-over** (n. and adj.)

**cash on delivery** *c.o.d.* is preferred in all references.

**caster, castor** *Caster* is a roller.
*Castor* is the spelling for the oil and the bean from which it is derived.

**catalog, cataloged, cataloger, cataloging, catalogist**

**Caterpillar** A trademark for a brand of crawler tractor.
Use lowercase for the wormlike larva of various insects.

**catholic, catholicism** Use *Roman Catholic Church, Roman Catholic* or *Roman Catholicism* in the first references to those who believe that the pope, as bishop of Rome, has the ultimate authority in administering an earthly organization founded by Jesus Christ.
Most subsequent references may be condensed to *Catholic Church, Catholic* or *Catholicism. Roman Catholic* should continue to be used, however, if the context requires a distinction between Roman Catholics and members of other denominations who often describe themselves as Catholic. They include some high church Episcopalians (who often call themselves *Anglo-Catholics*), members of Eastern Orthodox churches, and members of some national Catholic churches that have broken with Rome. Among churches in this last category are the Polish National Catholic Church and the Lithuanian National Catholic Church.
Lowercase *catholic* where used in its generic sense of general or universal, meanings derived from a similar word in Greek.
Those who use *Catholic* in a religious sense are indicating their belief that they are members of a universal church that Jesus Christ left on Earth.

**cat** See **animals.**

**cattle** See **animals.**

**Caucasian**

**cave in** (v.) **cave-in** (n. and adj.)

**CB** See **citizens band radio.**

**CBS** Acceptable in all references for *CBS Inc.,* the former Columbia Broadcasting System.

Divisions include *CBS News, CBS Radio* and *CBS-TV.*

**cease-fire, cease-fires** (n. and adj.) The verb form is *cease fire.*

**celebrant, celebrator** Reserve *celebrant* for someone who conducts a religious rite: *He was the celebrant of the Mass.*

Use *celebrator* for someone having a good time: *The celebrators kept the party going until 3 a.m.*

**cellophane** Formerly a trademark, now a generic term.

**Celsius** Use this term rather than *centigrade* for the temperature scale that is part of the metric system.

The Celsius scale is named for Anders Celsius, a Swedish astronomer who designed it. In it, zero represents the freezing point of water, and 100 degrees is the boiling point at sea level.

To convert to Fahrenheit, multiply a Celsius temperature by 9, divide by 5 and add 32 (25 × 9 = 225, divided by 5 = 45, plus 32 = 77 degrees Fahrenheit.).

When giving a Celsius temperature, use these forms: *40 degrees Celsius* or *40 C* (note the space and no period after the capital *C*) if degrees and Celsius are clear from the context.

See **Fahrenheit** and **metric system** entries.

**cement** *Cement* is the powder mixed with water and sand or gravel to make *concrete.* The proper term is *concrete* (not *cement*) *pavement, blocks, driveways,* etc.

**censer, censor, censure** A *censer* is a container in which incense is burned.

To *censor* is to prohibit or restrict the use of something.

To *censure* is to condemn.

**centerfold**

**Centers for Disease Control** The centers, located in Atlanta, are the U.S. Public Health Service's national agencies for control of infectious and other preventable diseases. They work with state health departments to provide specialized services that the states are unable to maintain on an everyday basis.

The normal form for first reference is the *national Centers for Disease Control*. *CDC* is acceptable on second reference.

**centi-** A prefix denoting one-hundredth of a unit. Move a decimal point two places to the left in converting to the basic unit: *155.6 centimeters equals 1.556 meters.*

**centigrade** See **Celsius.**

**centimeter** One-hundredth of a meter.

There are 10 millimeters in a centimeter.

A centimeter is approximately the width of a large paper clip.

To convert to inches, multiply by .4 (5 centimeters × .4 = 2 inches).

See **meter; metric system;** and **inch.**

**Central America** See **Western Hemisphere.**

**Central Conference of American Rabbis** See **Jewish Congregations.**

**Central Intelligence Agency** *CIA* is acceptable in all references.

The formal title for the individual who heads the agency is *director of central intelligence.* On first reference: *Director George Bush of the CIA, Director of Central Intelligence George Bush,* or *CIA Director George Bush.*

**Central Standard Time (CST), Central Daylight Time (CDT)** See **time zones.**

**cents** Spell out the word cents and lowercase, using numerals for amounts less than a dollar: *5 cents, 12 cents.* Use the $ sign and decimal system for larger amounts: *$1.01, $2.50.*

Numerals alone, with or without a decimal point as appropriate, may be used in tabular matter.

**century** Lowercase, spelling out numbers less than 10: *the first century, the 20th century.*

For proper names, follow the organization's practice:

*20th Century Fox, Twentieth Century Fund, Twentieth Century Limited.*

**Ceylon** It is now *Sri Lanka,* which should be used in datelines and other references to the nation.

The people may be referred to as *Ceylonese* (n. or adj.) or *Sri Lankans.* The language is *Sinhalese.*

**cha-cha**

**Chagas' disease** After Charles Chagas, a Brazilian physician who identified the chronic wasting disease caused by a parasite that is carried by insects.

**chairman, chairwoman** Capitalize as a formal title before a name: *company Chairman Henry Ford, committee Chairwoman Margaret Chase Smith.*

Do not capitalize as a casual, temporary position: *meeting chairman Robert Jones.*

Do not use *chairperson* unless it is an organization's formal title for an office.

See **titles.**

**chamber of deputies** See **foreign legislative bodies.**

**chancellor** The translation to English for the first minister in the governments of West Germany and Austria. Capitalize when used before a name.

See the **premier, prime minister** entry and **titles.**

**changeable**

**changeover**

**change up** (v.) **change-up** (n. and adj.)

**channel** Capitalize when used with a figure; lowercase elsewhere: *He turned to Channel 3. No channel will broadcast the game.*

Also: *the English Channel,* but *the channel* on second reference.

**chapters** Capitalize *chapter* when used with a numeral in reference to a section of a book or legal code. Always use Arabic figures: *Chapter 1, Chapter 20.*

Lowercase when standing alone.

**character, reputation**
*Character* refers to moral qualities.

*Reputation* refers to the way a person is regarded by others.

**charismatic groups** See **religious movements.**

**Charleston, Charlestown, Charles Town**
*Charleston* is the name of the capital of West Virginia and a port city in South Carolina.

*Charlestown* is a section of Boston.

*Charles Town* is the name of a small city in West Virginia.

**chauffeur**

**chauvinism, chauvinist**
The words mean unreasoning devotion to one's race, sex, country, etc., with contempt for other races, sexes, countries, etc.

The terms come from Nicolas Chauvin, a soldier of Napoleon I, who was famous for his devotion to the lost cause.

**check up** (v.) **checkup** (n.)

**Chemical Mace** A trademark, usually shortened to *Mace,* for a brand of tear gas that is packaged in an aerosol canister and temporarily stuns its victims.

**chess** In stories, the names and pieces are spelled out, lowercase: *king, queen, bishop, pawn, knight, rook, kingside, queenside, white, black.*

Examples: *White was unable to defend his kingside bishop. The black pieces were cramped. Black brought pressure on the queenside knight file. White took black's kingside bishop's pawn.*

The news services use the descriptive notation in providing tabular summaries. Capital letters represent the pieces and files: *B* for bishop, *K* for king, *N* for knight, *Q* for queen, *R* for rook, *P* for pawn. Each file is given the name of the piece originally posted on it, and the ranks are numbered from 1 to 8 away from the player. Each rank thus has a dual designation, depending on which player makes the move.

The initial of the moving piece comes first, followed by the designation of the square moved to. Thus, moving a pawn to the fourth rank of the queen's bishop's file would be noted: *P-QB4*.

The castle, a move involving two pieces, is noted by lowercase *o*'s separated by a hyphen. The kingside castle: *o-o;* the queenside castle: *o-o-o.*

To note a capture, a lowercase *x* is substituted for the hyphen. Thus, if a pawn takes another pawn it would be noted: *PxP.*

The initials *ch* are used to indicate a check.

The word *mate* is used for a checkmate.

Indication of queenside *Q* or kingside *K* are omitted when no ambiguity would result.

The form, taken from the first modern international tournament in London in 1851:

| White<br>Anderson | Black<br>Kieseritzki |
|---|---|
| 1. P-K4 | P-K4 |
| 2. P-KB4 | PxP |
| 3. B-B4 | P-QN4 |
| 4. BxNP | Q-R5ch |
| 5. K-B1 | N-KB3 |
| 6. N-KB3 | Q-R3 |
| 7. P-Q3 | N-R4 |
| 8. N-R4 | P-QB3 |
| 9. N-B5 | Q-N4 |
| 10. P-KN4 | N-B3 |
| 11. R-N1 | PxB |
| 12. P-KR4 | Q-N3 |
| 13. P-R5 | Q-N4 |
| 14. Q-B3 | N-N1 |
| 15. BxP | Q-B3 |
| 16. N-B3 | B-B4 |
| 17. N-Q5 | QxP |
| 18. B-Q6 | BxR |
| 19. P-K5 | QxRch |
| 20. K-K2 | N-QR3 |
| 21. N-Pch | K-Q1 |
| 22. Q-B6ch | NxQ |
| 23. B-K7 | mate |

**Chevy** Not *Chevie* or *Chevvy.* This nickname for the *Chevrolet* should be used only in automobile features or in quoted matter.

**Chicago** The city in Illinois stands alone in datelines.

**chief** Capitalize as a formal title before a name: *He spoke to Police Chief Michael Codd. He spoke to Chief Michael Codd of the New York police.*

Lowercase when it is not a formal title: *union chief Walter Reuther.*

See **titles.**

**chief justice** Capitalize only as a formal title before a name: *Chief Justice William Rehnquist.* The officeholder is the chief justice of the United States, not of the Supreme Court.

See **judge.**

**Chile** The nation.

**chili, chilies** The peppers.

**chilly** Moderately cold.

**China** When used alone, it refers to the mainland nation. Use it in datelines and other routine references.

Use *People's Republic of China, Communist China, mainland China* or *Red China* only in direct quotations or when needed to distinguish the mainland and its government from Taiwan.

For datelines on stories from the island of Taiwan, use the name of a community and *Taiwan.* In the body of a story, use *Nationalist China* or *Taiwan* for references to the government based on the island. Use the formal name of the government, *the Republic of China,* when required for legal precision.

**Chinaman** A patronizing term. Confine it to quoted matter.

**Chinese names** For most Chinese place names and personal names, use the official Chinese spelling system known as Pinyin: *Vice Premier Deng Xiaoping* or *Zhejiang Province.*

Note that the Chinese usually give the family name first *(Deng)* followed by the given name *(Xiaoping).* Second reference should be the family name only: *Deng.*

The Pinyin spelling system eliminates the hyphen and/or apostrophe previously used in many given names.

If the new Pinyin spelling of a proper noun is so radically different from the traditional American spelling that a reader might be confused, provide the Pinyin spelling followed by the traditional spelling in parentheses. For example, the city of *Fuzhou (Foochow).* Or use a descriptive sentence: *Fuzhou is the capital of Fujian Province, on China's eastern coast.*

Use the traditional American spellings for these place names: *Canton, China, Inner Mongolia, Shanghai, Tibet.*

And use the traditional American spellings for well-known deceased people such as *Chou En-lai, Mao Tse-tung, Sun Yat-sen.*

Follow local spellings in stories dealing with Hong Kong and Taiwan.

Some Chinese have westernized their names, putting their given names or the initials for them first: *P. Y. Chen, Jack Wang.* In general, follow an individual's preferred spelling.

Normally, Chinese women do not take their husbands' surnames. Use the courtesy titles *Mrs., Miss,* or *Ms.* only when specifically requested. Never use *Madame* or *Mme.* unless in quoted material.

## Christian Church (Disciples of Christ)
The parentheses and the words they enclose are part of the formal name.

The body owes its origins to an early 19th century frontier movement to unify Christians.

The Disciples, led by Alexander Campbell in western Pennsylvania, and the Christians, led by Barton W. Stone in Kentucky, merged in 1832.

The local church is the basic organizational unit.

National policies are developed by the General Assembly, made up of representatives chosen by local churches and regional organizations. The regional units certify the standing of ministers and provide help and counsel to ministers and congregations.

The church lists more than 1 million members.

BELIEFS: The church allows for varied opinions and stresses freedom of interpretation, based on the historic conviction that there is no creed but Christ and no saving doctrines except those of the New Testament.

CLERGY: All members of the clergy may be referred to as *ministers. Pastor* applies if a minister leads a congregation.

On first reference, use *the Rev.* before the name of a man or woman. On second reference, use only the last name of a man; use *Miss, Mrs., Ms.* or no title before the last name of a woman depending on her preference.

See **religious titles.**

## Christian Science Church
See **Church of Christ, Scientist.**

## Christmas, Christmas Day
Dec. 25. The federal legal holiday is observed on Friday if Dec. 25 falls on a Saturday, on Monday if it falls on a Sunday.

Never abbreviate *Christmas* to *Xmas* or any other form.

**church** Capitalize as part of the formal name of a building, a congregation or a denomination; lowercase in other uses: *St. Mary's Church, the Roman Catholic Church, the Catholic and Episcopal churches, a Roman Catholic church, a church.*

Lowercase in phrases where the church is used in an institutional sense: *He believes in the separation of church and state. The pope said the church opposes abortion.*

See **religious titles** and the entry for the denomination in question.

**Churches of Christ** Approximately 18,000 independent congregations with a total U.S. membership of more than 2 million cooperate under this name. They sponsor numerous educational activities, primarily radio and television programs.

Each local church is autonomous and operates under a governing board of elders. The minister is an evangelist, addressed by members as *Brother.* The ministers do not use clergy titles. Do not precede their names by a title.

The churches do not regard themselves as a denomination.

Rather, they stress a non-denominational effort to preach what they consider basic Bible teachings. The churches also teach that baptism is an essential part of the salvation process.

See **religious movements.**

**churchgoer**

**Church of Christ, Scientist** This denomination was founded in 1879 by Mary Baker Eddy, who attributed her recovery from an illness to insights she gained from reading Scripture.

The Mother Church in Boston is the international headquarters. Its board of directors guides all of the approximately 3,200 branch churches throughout the world.

A branch church, governed by its own democratically chosen board, is named First Church of Christ, Scientist, or Second Church, etc., according to the order of its establishment in a community.

The terms *Christian Science Church* or *Churches of Christ, Scientist,* are acceptable in all references to the denomination.

BELIEFS: Christian Science describes God as the source of all real being, so that nothing except what he has created can ultimately be real. Death, disease and sin are regarded as having no real existence because they are not created by God. Scripture is cited as evidence that a true understanding of God heals sickness as well as sin.

The principal beliefs are contained in "Science and Health With Key to the Scriptures," the denominational textbook written by Mrs. Eddy.

The word *Christian* is used because New Testament writings are an integral element of the denomination's teachings. The word *science* denotes the concept that reality can be understood and proved in Christian experience.

A distinction is made between Christ, regarded as the divine nature or godliness of Jesus, and Jesus, regarded as the human Wayshower and Exemplar of man's sonship with God.

CLERGY: The church is composed entirely of lay members and does not have clergy in the usual sense. Either men or women may hold the three principal offices—*reader, practitioner* or *lecturer.*

*Readers* are elected from congregations to conduct worship services. *Practitioners* devote full time to the public healing ministry of the church. *Lecturers,* appointed by the directors of the Mother Church, give public lectures on Christian Science.

The preferred form for these titles is to use a construction that sets them off from a name with commas. Capitalize them only when used as a formal title immediately before a name. Do not continue use of the title in subsequent references.

The terms *pastor* and *minister* are not applicable. Do not use *the Rev.* in any reference. See **religious titles.**

**Church of England** See **Anglican Communion.**

**Church of Jesus Christ of Latter-day Saints** Note the capitalization and punctuation of *Latter-day. Mormon Church* is acceptable in all references, but always include the proper name in a story dealing primarily with church activities.

The church is based on revelations that Joseph Smith said were brought to him in the 1820s by heavenly messengers.

After Smith's death in 1844, his followers split into factions, the largest of them the Church of Jesus Christ of Latter-day Saints. Led west by Brigham Young, they founded Salt Lake City, Utah, in 1847.

Today, the church headquarters there directs more than 6,500 congregations with more than 3 million members worldwide.

Church hierarchy is composed of men known as general authorities. Among them, the policy-making body is the First Presidency, made up of a president and two or more counselors. It has final authority in all spiritual and worldly matters.

The Council of the Twelve Apostles, primarily an advisory body, helps the First Presidency direct church activities. When the church president dies, the First Presidency is dissolved and the Council of the Twelve Apostles selects a new president, traditionally the man who is the senior apostle in the council. He then chooses his counselors.

Other general authorities include the church patriarch, a spiritual adviser; a three-member Presiding Bishopric, which administers temporal affairs; and the First Quorum of Seventy, in charge of missionary work. Women may not become general authorities.

The church's basic geographical units are called stakes. They are governed by a stake presidency, made up of a president and two counselors, and a stake high council. Individual congregations within a stake are called wards. Missions, which oversee members where there are no stakes, are headed by a president and may include one or more congregations known as branches.

BELIEFS: Mormons believe that Jesus Christ established one church on earth, that it was taken away upon his death and not restored until the revelations to Smith. They believe that Jesus came to America after his Resurrection, visiting its people, who had immigrated to the continent in ancient times.

Among the revelations were directions to gold plates that Smith said he found on

Hill Cumorah, near Palmyra, N.Y. He taught that the plates, left by a prophet who lived some time after Jesus, contained the records of the people Jesus had visited in America and the true word of God.

The "Book of Mormon," written by Smith, contains what members believe are his translation of the hieroglyphics on the plates. The plates were later returned to Moroni, the heavenly messenger who led Smith to them. Smith also wrote the "Book of Doctrine and Covenants" and the "Pearl of Great Price." These three books and the Bible are the key church documents, although revelation is considered to continue today through members of the First Presidency.

CLERGY: All faithful male members over the age of 11 are members of the priesthood and may attain positions of leadership in the all-lay clergy. Younger members go through a series of ranks from deacon to teacher to priest before becoming elders sometime after their 18th birthdays. They may later become seventies or high priests. A high priest may become a bishop or one of two bishop's counselors, who lead local congregations.

The only formal titles are *president* (for the head of the First Presidency), *bishop* (for members of the Presiding Bishopric and for local bishops) and *elder* (for other general authorities and church missionaries). Capitalize these formal titles before a name on first reference; use only the last name on second reference.

The terms *minister* or *the Rev.* are not used.

See **religious titles.**

SPLINTER GROUPS: The term *Mormon* is not properly applied to the other Latter Day Saints churches that resulted from the split after Smith's death.

The largest is the Reorganized Church of Jesus Christ of Latter Day Saints (note the lack of a hyphen and the capitalized *Day*), with headquarters in Independence, Mo. It was founded by Smith's son Joseph III and claims to be the continuation of the original church. It has about 1,000 churches and 150,000 members.

**CIA** Acceptable in all references for *Central Intelligence Agency.*

**cigarette**

**Cincinnati** The city in Ohio stands alone in datelines.

**CIO** See **AFL-CIO.**

**Citibank** The former First National City Bank. The parent holding company is Citicorp of New York.

**cities and towns** Capitalize them in all uses. See **datelines** for guidelines on when they should be followed by a state or a country name.

Capitalize official titles, including separate political entities such as *East St. Louis, Ill.,* or *West Palm Beach, Fla.*

The preferred form for the section of a city is lowercase: *the west end, northern Los Angeles.* But capitalize widely recognized names for the sections of a city: *South Side* (Chicago), *Lower East Side* (New York).

Spell out the names of cities unless in direct quotes: *A trip to Los Angeles,* but: *"We're going to L.A."*

See **city.**

**citizen, resident, subject, national, native** A *citizen* is a person who has acquired the full civil rights of a nation either by birth or naturalization. Cities and states in the United States do not confer citizenship. To avoid confusion, use *resident,* not *citizen,* in referring to inhabitants of states and cities.

*Subject* is the term used when the government is headed by a monarch or other sovereign.

*National* is applied to a person residing away from the nation of which he is a citizen, or to a person under the protection of a specified nation.

*Native* is the term denoting that an individual was born in a given location.

**citizens band** Without an apostrophe after the *s,* an exception to Webster's New World based on widespread practice.

*CB* is acceptable on second reference.

The term describes a group of radio frequencies set aside by the Federal Communications Commission for local use at low power by individuals or businesses.

Until summer 1976, the format for call letters was

three letters and four figures: *KTE9136.* Licenses issued since then use four letters and four figures: *KTEM1234.*

**city** Capitalize *city* as part of a proper name: *Kansas City, New York City, Oklahoma City, Jefferson City.*

Lowercase elsewhere: *a Texas city; the city government; the city Board of Education;* and all *city of* phrases: *the city of Boston.*

Capitalize when part of a formal title before a name: *City Manager Francis McGrath.* Lowercase when not part of the formal title: *city Health Commissioner Frank Smith.*

See **city council** and **governmental bodies.**

**city commission** See the next entry.

**city council** Capitalize when part of a proper name: *the Boston City Council.*

Retain capitalization if the reference is to a specific council but the context does not require the city name:

*BOSTON (AP)—The City Council . . .*

Lowercase in other uses: *the council, the Boston and New York city councils, a city council.*

Use the proper name if the body is not known as a city council: *the Miami City Commission, the City Commission, the commission; the Louisville Board of Aldermen, the Board of Aldermen, the board.*

Use *city council* in a generic sense for plural references: *the Boston, Louisville and Miami city councils.*

**city editor** Capitalize as a formal title before a name. See **titles.**

**city hall** Capitalize with the name of a city, or without the name of a city if the reference is specific: *Boston City Hall, City Hall.*

Lowercase plural uses: *the Boston and New York city halls.*

Lowercase generic uses, including: *You can't fight city hall.*

**citywide**

**Civil Aeronautics Board** *CAB* is acceptable on second reference.

**civil cases, criminal cases** A *civil case* is one in which an individual, business or agency of government seeks damages or relief from another individual, business or agency of government. Civil actions generally involve a charge that a contract has been breached or that someone has been wronged or injured.

A *criminal case* is one that the state or the federal government brings against an individual charged with committing a crime.

**Civil War**

**claptrap**

**clean up** (v.) **cleanup** (n. and adj.)

**clear-cut** (adj.)

**clerical titles** See **religious titles.**

**Cleveland** The city in Ohio stands alone in datelines.

**clientele**

**cloak-and-dagger**

**Clorox** A trademark for a brand of bleach.

**closed shop** A *closed shop* is an agreement between a union and an employer that requires workers to be members of a union before they may be employed.

A *union shop* requires workers to join a union within a specified period after they are employed.

An *agency shop* requires that the workers who do not want to join the union pay the union a fee instead of union dues.

A *guild shop,* a term often used when the union is The Newspaper Guild, is the same as a *union shop.*

See the **right-to-work** entry for an explanation of how some states prohibit contracts that require workers to join unions.

**close-up** (n. and adj.)

**cloture** Not *closure,* for the parliamentary procedure for closing debate.

Whenever practical, use a phrase such as closing debate or ending debate instead of the technical term.

**co-** Retain the hyphen when forming nouns, adjectives and verbs that indicate occupation or status:

co-author      co-respondent
co-chairman    (in a
co-defendant   divorce
co-host        suit)
co-owner       co-signer
co-partner     co-star
co-pilot       co-worker

(Several are exceptions to Webster's New World in the interests of consistency.)

Use no hyphen in other combinations:

coed           cooperate
coeducation    cooperative
coequal        coordinate
coexist        coordination
coexistence

*Cooperate, coordinate* and related words are exceptions to the rule that a hyphen is used if a prefix ends in a vowel and the word that follows begins with the same vowel.

**Co.** See **company**.

**coast** Lowercase when referring to the physical shoreline: *Atlantic coast, Pacific coast, east coast.*

Capitalize when referring to regions of the United States lying along such shorelines: *the Atlantic Coast states, a Gulf Coast city, the West Coast, the East Coast.*

Do not capitalize when referring to smaller regions: *the Virginia coast.*

Capitalize *the Coast* when standing alone only if the reference is to the West Coast.

**coastal waters** See **weather terms**.

**coast guard** Capitalize when referring to the U.S. force: *the U.S. Coast Guard, the Coast Guard, Coast Guard policy, the Guard.* Do not use the abbreviation *USCG*.

Use lowercase for similar forces of other nations.

This approach has been adopted for consistency, because many foreign nations do not use *coast guard* as the proper name.

See **military academies**.

**Coast Guardsman** Note spelling. Capitalize as a proper noun when referring to an individual in a U.S. Coast Guard unit: *He is a Coast Guardsman.*

Lowercase *guardsman* when it stands alone.

See **military titles**.

**coastline**

**coattails**

**Coca-Cola, Coke** Trademarks for a brand of cola drink.

**cocaine** The slang term *coke* should appear only in quoted matter.
*Crack* is a refined cocaine in crystalline rock form.

**c.o.d.** Acceptable in all references for *cash on delivery* or *collect on delivery*. (The use of lowercase is an exception to the first listing in Webster's New World.)

**Cold War** Capitalize when referring specifically to the rivalry between the United States and the Soviet Union.

**collective nouns** Nouns that denote a unit take singular verbs and pronouns: *class, committee, crowd, family, group, herd, jury, orchestra, team.*
Some usage examples: *The committee is meeting to set its agenda. The jury reached its verdict. A herd of cattle was sold.*

PLURAL IN FORM: Some words that are plural in form become collective nouns and take singular verbs when the group or quantity is regarded as a unit.
Right: *A thousand bushels is a good yield.* (A unit.)
Right: *A thousand bushels were created.* (Individual items.)
Right: *The data is sound.* (A unit.)
Right: *The data have been carefully collected.* (Individual items.)

**collectors' item**

**college** Capitalize when part of a proper name: *Dartmouth College.*
Consult special sections of the Webster's New World for lists of junior colleges, colleges and universities in the United States and Canadian colleges and universities.
See the **organizations and institutions** entry.

**College of Cardinals** See **Roman Catholic Church.**

**collide, collision** Two objects must be in motion before they can *collide.* An automobile cannot *collide* with a utility pole, for example.

**colloquialisms** The word describes the informal use of a language. It is not local or regional in nature, as dialect is.

Webster's New World Dictionary identifies many words as colloquial with the label *Colloq.* The label itself, the dictionary says, "does not indicate substandard or illiterate usage."

Many colloquial words and phrases characteristic of informal writing and conversation are acceptable in some contexts but out of place in others. Examples include *bum, giveaway* and *phone.*

Other colloquial words normally should be avoided because they are substandard. Webster's New World notes, for example, that *ain't* is colloquial and not automatically illiterate or substandard usage. But it also notes that *ain't* is "a dialectical or substandard contraction." Thus it should not be used in news stories unless needed to illustrate substandard speech in writing.

See the **dialect** and **word selection** entries.

**colon** See the entry in the **Punctuation** chapter.

**colonel** See **military titles.**

**colonial** Capitalize *Colonial* as a proper adjective in all references to the *Colonies.* (See the next entry.)

**colonies** Capitalize only for the British dependencies that declared their independence in 1776, now known as the United States.

**Colorado** Abbrev.: *Colo.* See **state names.**

**colorblind**

**colored** In some societies, including the United States, the word is considered derogatory and should not be used.

In some countries of Africa, it is used to denote individuals of mixed racial ancestry. Whenever the word is used, place it in quotation marks and provide an explanation of its meaning.

**Columbia Broadcasting System** It no longer exists. See **CBS.**

**Columbus Day** Oct. 12. The federal legal holiday is the second Monday in October.

**combat, combated, combating**

**comedian** Use for both men and women.

**comma** See entry in **Punctuation** chapter.

**commander** See **military titles.**

**commander in chief** Capitalize only if used as a formal title before a name.
See **titles.**

**commissioner** Do not abbreviate. Capitalize when used as a formal title.
See **titles.**

**commitment**

**committee** Do not abbreviate. Capitalize when part of a formal name: *the House Appropriations Committee.*

Do not capitalize committee in shortened versions of long committee names: *the Special Senate Select Committee to Investigate Improper Labor-Management Practices,*

for example, became *the rackets committee.*
See **subcommittee.**

**commodity** When used in a financial sense, the word describes the products of mining and agriculture before they have undergone extensive processing.

**Common Market** *European Economic Community* is preferred for this part of the *European Community.*

There are 12 members: Belgium, France, West Germany, Italy, Luxembourg, Netherlands (the original six), Denmark, Greece, Ireland, Portugal, Spain, and United Kingdom.

See **European Community** and **European Economic Community.**

**commonwealth** A group of people united by their common interests.
See **state.**

**Commonwealth, the** Formerly the British Commonwealth. The members of this free association of sovereign states recognize the British sovereign as head of the Commonwealth. Some also recognize the sovereign as head of their state; others do not.

The members are: Australia, Bahamas, Bangladesh, Barbados, Botswana, Canada, Cyprus, Fiji, Gambia, Ghana, Grenada, Guyana, India, Jamaica, Kenya, Lesotho, Malawi, Malaysia, Malta, Mauritius, New Zealand, Nigeria, Papua New Guinea, St. Lucia, Seychelles, Sierra Leone, Singapore, Sri Lanka, Swaziland, Tanzania, Tonga, Trinidad and Tobago, Uganda, United Kingdom, Western Samoa and Zambia. Nauru, a special member, participates in activities but not in meetings of government heads.

**Communicable Disease Center** The former name of the *Centers for Disease Control.* See entry under that name.

**Communications Satellite Corp.** *Comsat* is acceptable on second reference.

Headquarters is in Washington.

**Communications Workers of America** The shortened form *Communications Workers union* is acceptable in all references.

Headquarters is in Washington.

**communism, communist** Lowercase *communism.* Capitalize *Communist* only when referring to the activities of the Communist Party or to individuals who are members of it: *The Communists won the election. She ran on the Communist ticket.*

See the **political parties and philosophies** entry.

**commutation** See the **pardon, parole, probations** entry.

**company, companies** Use *Co.* or *Cos.* when a business uses either word at the end of its proper name: *Ford Motor Co., American Broadcasting Cos.* But: *Aluminum Company of America.*

If *company* or *companies* appears alone in second reference, spell the word out.

The forms for possessives: *Ford Motor Co.'s profits, American Broadcasting Cos.' profits.*

THEATRICAL: Spell out *company* in names of theatrical organizations: *the Martha Graham Dance Company.*

**company** (military)
Capitalize only when part of a name: *Company B.* Do not abbreviate.

**company names** Consult the company or Standard & Poor's Register of Corporations if in doubt about a formal name. Do not, however, use a comma before *Inc.* or *Ltd.*

See the **organizations and institutions** entry.

**compared to, compared with** Use *compared to* when the intent is to assert, without the need for elaboration, that two or more items are similar: *She compared her work for women's rights to Susan B. Anthony's campaign for women's suffrage.*

Use *compared with* when juxtaposing two or more items to illustrate similarities and/or differences: *His time was 2:11:10, compared with 2:14 for his closest competitor.*

**compatible**

**complacent, complaisant** *Complacent* means self-satisfied.

*Complaisant* means eager to please.

**complement, compliment** *Complement* is a noun and a verb denoting completeness or the process of supplementing something: *The ship has a complement of 200 sailors and 20 officers. The hat complements her dress.*

*Compliment* is a noun or a verb that denotes praise or the expression of courtesy: *The captain complimented the sailors. She was flattered by the compliments on her outfit.*

**complementary, complimentary** *The husband and wife have complementary careers.*

*She received complimentary tickets to the show.*

**compose, comprise, constitute** *Compose* means to create or put together. It commonly is used in both the active and passive voices: *He composed a song. The United States is composed of 50 states. The zoo is composed of many animals.*

*Comprise* means to contain, to include all or embrace. It is best used only in the active voice, followed by a direct object: *The United States comprises 50 states. The jury comprises five men and seven women. The zoo comprises many animals.*

*Constitute,* in the sense of form or make up, may be the best word if neither *compose* nor *comprise* seems to fit: *Fifty states constitute the United States. Five men and seven women constitute the jury. A collection of animals can constitute a zoo.*

Use *include* when what follows is only part of the total: *The price includes breakfast. The zoo includes lions and tigers.*

**composition titles** Apply the guidelines listed here to book titles, movie titles, opera titles, play titles, poem titles, song titles, television program titles, and the titles of lectures, speeches and works of art.

The guidelines, followed by a block of examples:

—Capitalize the principal words, including prepositions and conjunctions of four or more letters.

—Capitalize an article— *the, a, an*—or words of fewer than four letters if it is the first or last word in a title.

—Put quotation marks around the names of all such works except the Bible and books that are primarily cata-

logs of reference material. In addition to catalogs, this category includes almanacs, directories, dictionaries, encyclopedias, gazetteers, handbooks and similar publications.

—Translate a foreign title into English unless a work is known to the American public by its foreign name.

EXAMPLES: *"The Star-Spangled Banner," "The Rise and Fall of the Third Reich," "Gone With the Wind," "Of Mice and Men," "For Whom the Bell Tolls," "Time After Time,"* the NBC-TV *"Today"* program, the *"CBS Evening News," "The Mary Tyler Moore Show."* See **television program titles** for further guidelines and examples.

*Reference works: Jane's All the World's Aircraft; Encyclopaedia Britannica; Webster's New World Dictionary of the American Language, Second Edition.*

Foreign works: *Rousseau's "War,"* not *Rousseau's "La Guerre."* But: *Leonardo da Vinci's "Mona Lisa,"* Mozart's *"The Marriage of Figaro"* and *"The Magic Flute."* But: *"Die Walkuere"* and *"Gotterdammerung" from Wagner's "The Ring of the Nibelungen."*

**compound adjectives** See the **hyphen** entry in the **Punctuation** chapter.

**comptroller, controller** *Comptroller* generally is the accurate word for government financial officers.

The U.S. comptroller of the currency is an appointed official in the Treasury Department who is responsible for the chartering, supervising and liquidation of banks organized under the federal government's National Bank Act.

*Controller* generally is the proper word for financial officers of businesses and for other positions such as *aircraft controller.*

Capitalize *comptroller* and *controller* when used as the formal titles for financial officers. Use lowercase for *aircraft controller* and similar occupational applications of the word.

See **titles.**

**conclave** A private or secret meeting. In the Roman Catholic Church it describes the private meeting of cardinals to elect a pope.

**concrete** See **cement.**

**Confederate States of America** The formal name of the states that seceded during the Civil War. The shortened form *the Confederacy* is acceptable in all references.

**confess, confessed** In some contexts the words may be erroneous.

See **admit.**

**confirmation** See **sacraments.**

**Congo** In datelines, give the name of the city followed by *Congo:*

BRAZZAVILLE, Congo (AP)—

In stories, *the Congo* or *Congo* as the construction of a sentence dictates.

**Congo River** Not *the Zaire River.* But when appropriate, stories may mention that *Zaire,* the nation on one of its banks, calls the river *the Zaire.*

**Congregationalist churches** The word *Congregational* still is used by some individual congregations. The principal national body that used the term dropped it in

1961 when the Evangelical and Reformed Church merged with the Congregational Christian Churches to form the United Church of Christ. It has some 1.8 million members.

The word *church* is correctly applied only to an individual local church. Each such church is responsible for the doctrine, ministry and ritual of its congregation.

The local churches also appoint delegates to associations. Their functions include recognizing local churches, promoting cooperation among the churches, and the licensing, ordination, installation and dismissal of ministers.

Conferences, generally organized along state lines, recognize associations and specialize in missionary and educational work.

A general synod, made up of delegates elected by associations and conferences, is designed primarily to discuss questions of concern to all the churches and to handle communications with other denominations.

A small body of churches that did not enter the United Church of Christ is known as the National Association of Congregational Churches. Churches in the association have more than 100,000 members.

BELIEFS: Jesus is regarded as man's savior, but no subscription to a set creed is required for membership. Emphasis is placed on the value of having people band together for common worship and to help each other lead religious lives.

CLERGY: Members of the clergy are known as *ministers.* *Pastor* applies if a minister leads a congregation.

On first reference, use *the Rev.* before the name of a man or woman. On second reference, use only the last name of a man; *Miss, Mrs., Ms.* or no title before the last name of a woman depending on her preference.

See **religious titles.**

**congress** Capitalize *U.S. Congress* and *Congress* when referring to the U.S. Senate and House of Representatives. Although *Congress* sometimes is used as a substitute for the House, it properly is reserved for reference to both the Senate and House.

Capitalize *Congress* also if

referring to a foreign body that uses the term, or its equivalent in a foreign language, as part of its formal name: *the Argentine Congress, the Congress.*

See **foreign legislative bodies.**

Lowercase when used as a synonym for *convention* or in second reference to an organization that uses the word as part of its formal name: *the Congress of Racial Equality, the congress.*

**congressional** Lowercase unless part of a proper name: *congressional salaries, the Congressional Quarterly, the Congressional Record.*

**Congressional Directory** Use this as the reference source for questions about the federal government that are not covered by this stylebook.

**congressional districts** Use figures and capitalize district when joined with a figure: *the 1st Congressional District, the 1st District.*

Lowercase *district* whenever it stands alone.

**Congressional Record** A daily publication of the proceedings of Congress in-

cluding a complete stenographic report of all remarks and debates.

**congressman, congresswoman** Use only in reference to members of the U.S. House of Representatives.

See **legislative titles.**

**Congress of Racial Equality** *CORE* is acceptable on second reference.

Headquarters is in New York.

**Connecticut** Abbrev.: *Conn.* See **state names.**

**connote, denote** *Connote* means to suggest or imply something beyond the explicit meaning: *To some people, the word marriage connotes too much restriction.*

*Denote* means to be explicit about the meaning: *The word demolish denotes destruction.*

**Conrail** This acronym is acceptable in all references to *Consolidated Rail Corp.* (The corporation originally used *ConRail,* but later changed to *Conrail.*)

A private, for-profit corporation, Conrail was set up by Congress in 1976 to reorganize and consolidate six bankrupt Northeast railroads—the Penn Central, the Erie Lackawanna, Reading, Central of New Jersey, Lehigh Valley, and Lehigh & Hudson River.

The legislation provided for a $2 billion federal loan to the corporation and set a phased schedule of repayments. A total of 25 million shares of common stock were created, but the shares were not made available for public trading. Instead, the shares were issued in the names of voting trustees chosen to represent the individuals designated as the ultimate recipients after the settlement of litigation over the value of the property that Conrail took over.

Do not confuse *Conrail* with *Amtrak* (see separate entry). However, the legislation that set up Conrail also provided for Amtrak to gradually acquire from Conrail some of the property that had been owned by the bankrupt railroads.

Headquarters is in Philadelphia.

**consensus**

**conservative** See the **political parties and philosophies** entry.

**Conservative Judaism** See **Jewish congregations.**

**constable** Capitalize when used as a formal title before a name.
See **titles.**

**constitute** See the **compose, comprise, constitute** entry.

**constitution** Capitalize references to the U.S. Constitution, with or without the *U.S.* modifier: *The president said he supports the Constitution.*

When referring to constitutions of other nations or of states, capitalize only with the name of a nation or a state: *the French Constitution, the Massachusetts Constitution, the nation's constitution, the state constitution, the constitution.*

Lowercase in other uses: *the organization's constitution.*

Lowercase *constitutional* in all uses.

**consul, consul general, consuls general** Capitalize when used as a formal title before a noun.
See **titles.**

**consulate** A *consulate* is the residence of a consul in a foreign city. It handles the commercial affairs and personal needs of citizens of the appointing country.

Capitalize with the name of a nation; lowercase without it: *the French Consulate, the U.S. Consulate, the consulate.*

See **embassy** for the distinction between a consulate and an embassy.

**consumer price index** A measurement of changes in the retail prices of a constant marketbasket of goods and services. It is computed by comparing the cost of the marketbasket at a fixed time with its cost at subsequent or prior intervals.

Capitalize when referring to the U.S. index, issued monthly by the Bureau of Labor Statistics, an agency of the Labor Department.

The *U.S. Consumer Price Index* should not be referred to as a *cost-of-living index,* because it does not include the impact of income taxes and Social Security taxes on the cost of living, nor does it reflect changes in buying patterns that result from inflation. It is, however, the basis for computing cost-of-living

raises in many union contracts.

The preferred form for second reference is *the index.* Confine *CPI* to quoted material.

**Consumer Product Safety Commission**

**Contac** A trademark for a brand of decongestant.

**contagious**

**contemptible**

**continent** The seven continents, in order of their land size: Asia, Africa, North America, South America, Europe, Antarctica and Australia.

Capitalize *the Continent* and *Continental* only when used as synonyms for Europe or European. Lowercase in other uses such as: *the continent of Europe, the European continent, the African and Asian continents.*

Capitalize *Dark Continent* when used as a synonym for *Africa.*

**Continental Airlines** Use this spelling of *airlines,* which Continental has adopted for its public identity.

Only its incorporation papers still read *air lines.*

Headquarters is in Los Angeles.

**Continental Divide** The ridge along the Rocky Mountains that separates rivers flowing east from those that flow west.

**continental shelf, continental slope** Lowercase. The *shelf* is the part of a continent that is submerged in relatively shallow sea at gradually increasing depths, generally up to about 600 feet below sea level.

The *continental slope* begins at the point where the descent to the ocean bottom becomes very steep.

**continual, continuous** *Continual* means a steady repetition, over and over again: *The merger has been the source of continual litigation.*

*Continuous* means uninterrupted, steady, unbroken: *All she saw ahead of her was a continuous stretch of desert.*

**contractions** Contractions reflect informal speech and writing. Webster's New World Dictionary includes many entries for contractions: *aren't* for *are not,* for example.

Avoid excessive use of contractions. Contractions listed in the dictionary are acceptable, however, in informal contexts where they reflect the way a phrase commonly appears in speech or writing.

See **Americanisms; colloquialisms; quotations in the news;** and **word selection.**

**Contra, Contras** Uppercase when used to describe Nicaraguan rebel groups.

**contrasted to, contrasted with** Use *contrasted to* when the intent is to assert, without the need for elaboration, that two items have opposite characteristics: *He contrasted the appearance of the house today to its ramshackle look last year.*

Use *contrasted with* when juxtaposing two or more items to illustrate similarities and/or differences: *He contrasted the Republican platform with the Democratic platform.*

**control, controlled, controlling**

**controller** See the **comp-troller, controller** entry.

**controversial** An over-used word; avoid it. See **non-controversial.**

**convention** Capitalize as part of the name for a specific national or state political convention: *the Democratic National Convention, the Republican State Convention.*

Lowercase in other uses: *the national convention, the state convention, the convention, the annual convention of the American Medical Association.*

**convict** (v.) Follow with preposition *of,* not *for: He was convicted of murder.*

**convince, persuade** You may be *convinced that* something or *of* something. You must be *persuaded to do* something.

Right: *The robbers persuaded him to open the vault.*

Wrong: *The robbers convinced him to open the vault.*

Right: *The robbers convinced him that it was the right thing to do.*

Wrong: *The robbers persuaded him that it was the right thing to do.*

**cookie, cookies**

**cooperate, cooperative** But *co-op* as a short term of *cooperative,* to distinguish it from *coop,* a cage for animals.

**Cooperative for American Relief Everywhere** See **CARE**

**coordinate, coordination**

**cop** Often a derogatory term for *police officer.* Confine it to quoted matter.

**copter** Acceptable shortening of *helicopter.* But use it only as a noun or adjective. It is not a verb.

**copy editor** Seldom a formal title. See **titles.**

**copyright** (n., v. and adj.) *The disclosure was made in a copyright story.*

Use *copyrighted* only as the past tense of the verb: *He copyrighted the article.*

**co-respondent** In a divorce suit.

**Corn Belt** The region in the north central Midwest where much corn and corn-fed livestock are raised. It extends from western Ohio to eastern Nebraska and northeastern Kansas.

**Corp.** See **corporation**.

**corporal** See **military titles.**

**corporate names** See **company names.**

**corporation** An entity that is treated as a person in the eyes of the law. It is able to own property, incur debts, sue and be sued.

Abbreviate *corporation* as *Corp.* when a company or government agency uses the word at the end of its name: *Gulf Oil Corp., the Federal Deposit Insurance Corp.*

Spell out *corporation* when it occurs elsewhere in a name: *the Corporation for Public Broadcasting.*

Spell out and lowercase *corporation* whenever it stands alone.

The form for possessives: *Gulf Oil Corp.'s profits.*

**corps** Capitalize when used with a word or a figure to form a proper name: *the Marine Corps, the Signal Corps, the 9th Corps.*

Capitalize when standing alone only if it is a shortened reference to *U.S. Marine Corps.*

The possessive form is *corps'* for both singular and plural: *one corps' location, two corps' assignments.*

**corral, corralled, corralling**

**correctional facility, correctional institution** See the **prison, jail** entry.

**Corsica** Use instead of *France* in datelines on stories from communities on this island.

**Cortes** The Spanish parliament. See **foreign legislative bodies.**

**cosmonaut** The applicable occupational term for Soviet astronauts. Always use lowercase.

See **titles.**

**cost of living** The amount of money needed to pay taxes and to buy the goods and services deemed necessary to make up a given standard of living, taking into account changes that may occur in tastes and buying patterns.

The term often is treated incorrectly as a synonym for the *U.S. Consumer Price Index,* which does not take taxes into account and measures only price changes, keeping the quantities constant over time.

Hyphenate when used as a compound modifier: *The cost of living went up, but he did not receive a cost-of-living raise.*

See the **consumer price index** and **inflation** entries.

**Cotton Belt** The region in the South and Southwestern sections of the United States where much cotton is grown.

**council, councilor, councilman, councilwoman** A deliberative body and those who are members of it.

See the **counsel** entry and **legislative titles.**

**Council of Economic Advisers** A group of advisers who help the U.S. president prepare his annual economic report to Congress and recommend economic measures to him throughout the year.

**counsel, counseled, counseling, counselor, counselor at law** To *counsel* is to advise. A *counselor* is one who advises.

A *counselor at law* (no hyphens for consistency with *attorney at law)* is a lawyer. See **lawyer.**

**count, countess** See **nobility.**

**counter-** The rules in **prefixes** apply, but in general, no hyphen. Some examples:

counteract     counterpro-
countercharge    posal
counterfoil      counterspy

**countryside**

**county** Capitalize when an integral part of a proper name: *Dade County, Nassau County, Suffolk County.*

Capitalize the full names of county governmental units: *the Dade County Commission, the Orange County Department of Social Services, the Suffolk County Legislature.*

Retain capitalization for the name of a county body if the proper noun is not needed in the context; lowercase the word *county* if it is used to distinguish an agency from state or federal counterparts: *the Board of Supervisors, the county Board of Supervisors; the Department of Social Services, the county Department of Social Services.* Lowercase *the board, the department,* etc. whenever they stand alone.

Capitalize *county* if it is an integral part of a specific body's name even without the proper noun: *the County Commission, the County Legislature.* Lowercase *the commission, the legislature,* etc. when not preceded by the word *county.*

Capitalize as part of a formal title before a name: *County Manager John Smith.* Lowercase when it is not part of the formal title: *county Health Commissioner Frank Jones.*

Avoid *county of* phrases where possible, but when necessary, always lowercase: *the county of Westchester.*

Lowercase plural combinations: *Westchester and Rockland counties.*

Apply the same rules to similar terms such as *parish.*

See **governmental bodies.**

**county court** In some states, it is not a court but the administrative body of a county. In most cases, the *court* is presided over by a *county judge,* who is not a judge in the traditional sense but the chief administrative officer of the county.

The terms should be explained if they are not clear in the context.

Capitalize all references to a specific *county court,* and capitalize *county judge* when used as a formal title before a name. Do not use *judge* alone before a name except in direct quotations.

Examples:

*SEVIERVILLE, Tenn. (AP)—A reluctant County Court approved a school budget today that calls for a 10 percent tax increase for property owners.*

*The county had been given an ultimatum by the state: Approve the budget or shut down the schools.*

*The chief administrative officer, County Judge Ray Reagan, said . . .*

**coup d'etat** The word *coup* usually is sufficient.

**couple** When used in the sense of two people, the word takes plural verbs and pronouns: *The couple were married Saturday and left Sunday*

*on their honeymoon. They will
return in two weeks.*

In the sense of a single unit,
use a singular verb: *Each couple was asked to give $10.*

**couple of** The *of* is necessary. Never use *a couple tomatoes* or a similar phrase.

The phrase takes a plural
verb in constructions such as:
*A couple of tomatoes were
stolen.*

**course numbers** Use
Arabic numerals and capitalize the subject when used with
a numeral: *History 6, Philosophy 209.*

**court decisions** Use figures and a hyphen: *The Supreme Court ruled 5-4, a 5-4
decision.* The word *to* is not
needed, but use hyphens if it
appears in quoted matter:
*"The court ruled 5-to-4; the 5-
to-4 decision."*

**court districts** See **court
names.**

**courtesy titles** In general, do not use the courtesy
titles *Miss, Mr., Mrs.* or *Ms.*
on first and last names of the
person: *Betty Ford, Jimmy
Carter.*

Do not use *Mr.* in any ref-

erence unless it is combined
with *Mrs.: Mr. and Mrs. John
Smith, Mr. and Mrs. Smith.*

On sports wires, do not use
courtesy titles in any reference unless needed to distinguish among people of the
same last name.

On news wires, use cour-
tesy titles for women on second reference, following the
woman's preference. If the
woman says she does not
want a courtesy title, refer to
her on second reference by
last name only. Some guidelines:

MARRIED WOMEN: The
preferred form on first reference is to identify a woman by
her own first name and her
husband's last name: *Susan
Smith.* Use *Mrs.* on the first
reference only if a woman requests that her husband's first
name be used or her own first
name cannot be determined:
*Mrs. John Smith.*

On second reference, use
*Mrs.* unless a woman initially
identified by her own first
name prefers *Ms.: Carla Hills,
Mrs. Hills, Ms. Hills;* or no title: *Carla Hills, Hills.*

If a married woman is
known by her maiden name,
precede it by *Miss* on second
reference unless she prefers

*Ms.: Jane Fonda, Miss Fonda, Ms. Fonda;* or no title, *Jane Fonda, Fonda.*

UNMARRIED WOMEN: For women who have never been married, use *Miss, Ms.* or no title on second reference according to the woman's preference.

For divorced women and widows, the normal practice is to use *Mrs.* or no title, if she prefers, on second reference. But, if a woman returns to the use of her maiden name, use *Miss., Ms.* or no title if she prefers it.

MARITAL STATUS: If a woman prefers *Ms.* or no title, do not include her marital status in a story unless it is clearly pertinent.

See **nobility** and **religious titles.**

**courthouse** Capitalize with the name of a jurisdiction: *the Cook County Courthouse, the U.S. Courthouse.* Lowercase in other uses: *the county courthouse, the courthouse, the federal courthouse.*

*Court House* (two words) is used in the proper names of some communities: *Appomattox Court House, Va.*

**court-martial, court-martialed, courts-martial**

**court names** Capitalize the full proper names of courts at all levels.

Retain capitalization if *U.S.* or a state name is dropped: *the U.S. Supreme Court, the Supreme Court, the state Superior Court, the Superior Court, Superior Court.*

For courts identified by a numeral: *2nd District Court, 8th U.S. Circuit Court of Appeals.*

For additional details on federal courts, see **judicial branch** and separate listings under **U.S.** and the court name.

See **judge** for guidelines on titles before the names of judges.

**Court of St. James's** Note the *'s.* The formal name for the royal court of the British sovereign. Derived from St. James's Palace, the former scene of royal receptions.

**courtroom**

**cover up** (v.) **cover-up** (n. and adj.) *He tried to cover up the scandal. He was prosecuted for the cover-up.*

**crack up** (v.) **crackup** (n. and adj.)

**crawfish** Not *crayfish*. An exception to Webster's New World based on the dominant spelling in Louisiana, where it is a popular delicacy.

**criminal cases** See the **civil cases, criminal cases** entry.

**Crisco** A trademark for a brand of vegetable shortening.

**crisis, crises**

**crisscross**

**criterion, criteria**

**cross-examine, cross-examination**

**cross-eye** (n.) **cross-eyed** (adj.)

**cross fire**

**crossover** (n. and adj.)

**cross section** (n.) **cross-section** (v.)

**Cub Scouts** See **Boy Scouts.**

**cuckoo clock**

**cup** Equal to eight fluid ounces. The approximate metric equivalents are 240 milliliters or .24 of a liter.

To convert to liters, multiply by .24 (14 cups × .24 = 3.36 liters, or 3,360 milliliters).

See **liter.**

**cupful, cupfuls** Not *cupsful.*

**curate** See **religious titles.**

**cure-all**

**Curia** See **Roman Catholic Church.**

**currency depreciation, currency devaluation** A nation's money *depreciates* when its value falls in relation to the currency of other nations or in relation to its own prior value.

A nation's money is *devalued* when its government deliberately reduces its value in relation to the currency of other nations.

When a nation devalues its currency, the goods it imports tend to become more expensive. Its exports tend to become less expensive in other nations and thus more competitive.

**curtain raiser**

**customs** Capitalize *U.S. Customs Service,* or simply *the Customs Service.*
Lowercase elsewhere: *a customs official, a customs ruling, he went through customs.*

**cut back** (v.) **cutback** (n. and adj.) *He cut back spending. The cutback will require frugality.*

**cut off** (v.) **cutoff** (n. and adj.) *He cut off his son's allowance. The cutoff date for applications is Monday.*

**cyclone** See **weather terms.**

**Cyclone** A trademark for a brand of chain-link fence.

**cynic, skeptic** A *skeptic* is a doubter.
A *cynic* is a disbeliever.

**czar** Not *tsar.* It was a formal title only for the ruler of Russia and some other Slavic nations.
Lowercase in all other uses.

# D

**Dacron** A trademark for a brand of polyester fiber.

**dalai lama** The traditional high priest of Lamaism, a form of Buddhism practiced in Tibet and Mongolia. *Dalai lama* is a title rather than a name, but it is all that is used when referring to the man. Capitalize *Dalai Lama* in references to the holder of the title, in keeping with the principles outlined in the **nobility** entry.

**Dallas** The city in Texas stands alone in datelines.

**Dalles, The** A city in Oregon.

**dam** Capitalize when part of a proper name: *Hoover Dam.*

**damage, damages** *Damage* is destruction: *Authorities said damage from the storm would total more than $1 billion.*

*Damages* are awarded by a court as compensation for injury, loss, etc.: *The woman received $25,000 in damages.*

**dame** See **nobility.**

**damn it** Use instead of *dammit,* but like other profanity it should be avoided unless there is a compelling reason.
See the **obscenities, profanities, vulgarities** entry.

**dangling modifiers** Avoid modifiers that do not refer clearly and logically to some word in the sentence.
Dangling: *Taking our seats, the game started.* (Taking does not refer to the subject, *game,* nor to any other word in the sentence.)
Correct: *Taking our seats, we watched the opening of the game.* (Taking refers to *we,* the subject of the sentence.)

**Danish pastry**

**Dardanelles, the** Not *the Dardanelles Strait*.

**Dark Ages** The period beginning with the sack of Rome in A.D. 476 and ending about the end of the 10th century. The term is derived from the idea that this period in Europe was characterized by intellectual stagnation, widespread ignorance and poverty.

**Dark Continent** Africa.

**dark horse**

**dash** See entry in the **Punctuation** chapter.

**data** A plural noun, it normally takes plural verbs and pronouns.
See the **collective nouns** entry, however, for an example of when *data* may take singular verbs and pronouns.

**date line** Two words for the imaginary line that separates one day from another.
See the **international date line** entry.

**datelines** Datelines on stories should contain a city name, entirely in capital letters, followed in most cases by the name of the state, county or territory where the city is located.

DOMESTIC DATELINES: A list of domestic cities that stand alone in datelines follows. The norms that influenced the selection were the population of the city, the population of its metropolitan region, the frequency of the city's appearance in the news, the uniqueness of its name, and experience that has shown the name to be almost synonymous with the state or nation where it is located.

No state with the following:

ATLANTA
BALTIMORE
BOSTON
CHICAGO
CINCINNATI
CLEVELAND
DALLAS
DENVER
DETROIT
HONOLULU
HOUSTON
INDIANAPOLIS
LOS ANGELES
MIAMI
MILWAUKEE
MINNEAPOLIS
NEW ORLEANS
NEW YORK

OKLAHOMA CITY
PHILADELPHIA
PITTSBURGH
ST. LOUIS
SALT LAKE CITY
SAN DIEGO
SAN FRANCISCO
SEATTLE
WASHINGTON

Also *HOLLYWOOD* when used instead of *LOS ANGELES* on stories about films and the film industry.

Stories from all other U.S. cities should have both the city and state name in the dateline, including *KANSAS CITY, Mo.,* and *KANSAS CITY, Kan.*

Spell out *Alaska, Hawaii, Idaho, Iowa, Maine, Ohio, Texas* and *Utah.* Abbreviate others as listed in this book under the full name of each state.

Use *Hawaii* on all cities outside Honolulu. Specify the island in the text if needed.

Follow the same practice for communities on islands within the boundaries of other states: *EDGARTOWN, Mass.,* for example, not *EDGARTOWN, Martha's Vineyard.*

REGIONAL CIRCUITS: On state wires, additional cities in a state or region may stand alone if requested by the newspapers served.

When this is done, provide a list to all offices in the region, to all newspapers affected and to New York headquarters.

U.S. POSSESSIONS: Apply the guidelines listed below in the ISLAND NATIONS AND TERRITORIES section and the OVERSEAS TERRITORIES section.

FOREIGN CITIES: These foreign locations stand alone in datelines:

BEIJING
EAST BERLIN
GENEVA
GIBRALTAR
GUATEMALA CITY
HAVANA
HONG KONG
JERUSALEM
KUWAIT
LONDON
LUXEMBOURG
MACAO
MEXICO CITY
MONACO
MONTREAL
MOSCOW
OTTAWA
PARIS
QUEBEC
ROME

SAN MARINO
SINGAPORE
TOKYO
VATICAN CITY
WEST BERLIN

In addition, use *UNITED NATIONS* alone, without an *N.Y.* designation in stories from *U.N.* headquarters.

CANADIAN DATELINES: Datelines on stories from Canadian cities other than Montreal, Ottawa, Quebec and Toronto should contain the name of the city in capital letters followed by the name of the province. Do not abbreviate any province or territory name.

SOVIET DATELINES: Datelines on stories from Soviet cities other than Moscow should contain the name of the city in capital letters followed by *U.S.S.R.*

OTHER FOREIGN NATIONS: Stories from other foreign cities that do not stand alone in datelines should contain the name of the country or territory (see the next section) spelled out.

SPELLING AND CHOICE OF NAMES: In most cases, the name of the nation in a dateline is the conventionally accepted short form of its official name: *Argentina,* for example, rather than *Republic of Argentina.* (If in doubt, look for an entry in this book. If none is found, follow Webster's New World Dictionary.)

Note these special cases:
—Instead of *United Kingdom,* use *England, Northern Ireland, Scotland* or *Wales.*

—For divided nations, use the commonly accepted names based on geographic distinctions: *East Germany, West Germany, North Korea, South Korea.*

—Use an article only with *El Salvador.* For all others, use just a country name: *Gambia, Netherlands, Philippines,* etc.

—Use *U.S.S.R.* throughout the *Union of Soviet Socialist Republics.* Identify specific republics, such as *Byelorussian Soviet Socialist Republic* or the *Ukrainian Soviet Socialist Republic,* in the text if necessary.

See **geographic names** for guidelines on spelling the names of foreign cities and nations not listed here or in separate entries.

ISLAND NATIONS AND TERRITORIES: When reporting from nations and territories that are made up primarily of islands but commonly are linked under one name, use the city name and the general name in the dateline. Identify an individual island, if needed, in the text:

Examples:

| | |
|---|---|
| British Virgin Islands | Netherlands Antilles |
| Indonesia | Philippines |

OVERSEAS TERRITORIES: Some overseas territories, colonies and other areas that are not independent nations commonly have accepted separate identities based on their geographic character or special status under treaties. In these cases, use the commonly accepted territory name after a city name in a dateline.

Examples:

| | |
|---|---|
| Bermuda | Martinique |
| Corsica | Puerto Rico |
| Faeroe Islands | Sardinia |
| Greenland | Sicily |
| Grenada | Sikkim |
| Guadeloupe | Tibet |
| Guam | |

WITHIN STORIES: In citing other cities within the body of a story:

—No further information is necessary if a city is in the same state as the datelined city in U.S. stories or if it is in the same nation as stories from abroad. Make an exception if confusion would result.

—Follow the city name with further identification in most cases where it is not in the same state or nation as the datelined city. The additional identification may be omitted, however, if no confusion would result—there is no need, for example, to refer to *Boston, Mass.,* in a story datelined *NEW YORK.*

—Provide a state or nation identification for the city if the story is undated. However, cities that stand alone in datelines may be used alone in undated stories if no confusion would result.

**dateline selection** A dateline should tell the reader that the AP obtained the basic information for the story in the datelined city.

Do not, for example, use a Washington dateline on a story written primarily from information that a newspaper reported under a Washington dateline. Use the home city of the newspaper instead.

This rule does not preclude the use of a story with a dateline different from the home city of a newspaper if it is from the general area served by the newspaper.

Use a foreign dateline only if the basic information in a story was obtained by a full- or part-time correspondent physically present in the date-lined community.

If a radio broadcast monitored in another city was the source of information, use the dateline of the city where the monitoring took place and mention the fact in the story.

When a story has been assembled from sources in widely separated areas, use no dateline.

When a datelined story contains supplementary information obtained in another city, make that point clear in the context. Do not put parentheses around such material, however, unless the correspondent in the datelined community was cut off from incoming communications. Note the following examples:

—Material from another area was available in the date-lined city:

*LONDON    (AP)—Prime Minister Wilson submitted his resignation today.*

*In Washington, a State Department spokesman said the change in government leadership would have no effect on negotiations involving the Common Market.*

—Material from another area was not available to the correspondent in the date-lined city because communications from the outside world were cut off:

*PHNOM PENH, Cambodia (AP)—Khmer Rouge troops pushed into Phnom Penh today, barely hours after the United States ran down the Stars and Stripes and abandoned Cambodia to the Communists.*

*(In Washington, the State Department said Americans evacuated in a mass airlift had arrived safely aboard aircraft carriers and at bases in Thailand.)*

**dates** Always use Arabic figures, without *st, nd, rd* or *th.* See **months** for examples and **Punctuation** chapter.

**daughter-in-law, daughters-in-law**

**Daughters    of    the American    Revolution**

*DAR* is acceptable on second reference.

Headquarters is in Washington.

**daylight-saving time** Not *savings*. Note the hyphen.

When linking the term with the name of a time zone, use only the word *daylight: Eastern Daylight Time, Pacific Daylight Time,* etc.

Lowercase *daylight-saving time* in all uses and *daylight time* whenever it stands alone.

A federal law, administered by the Transportation Department, specifies that daylight time applies from 2 a.m. on the first Sunday of April until 2 a.m. on the last Sunday of October in areas that do not specifically exempt themselves.

See **time zones.**

**daylong**

**days of the week** Capitalize them. Do not abbreviate, except when needed in a tabular format: *Sun, Mon, Tue, Wed, Thu, Fri, Sat* (three letters, without periods, to facilitate tabular composition).

See **time element.**

**daytime**

**day to day, day-to-day** Hyphenate when used as a compound modifier: *They have extended the contract on a day-to-day basis.*

**D-day** June 6, 1944, the day the Allies invaded Europe in World War II.

**DDT** Preferred in all references for the insecticide *dichloro - diphenyl - trichloro - ethane.*

**de-** See **foreign particles.**

**deacon** See the entry for the individual's denomination.

**dead center**

**dead end** (n.) **dead-end** (adj.) *She reached a dead end. He has a dead-end job.*

**Dead Sea Scrolls**

**deaf-mute** This term may be used, but the preferred form is to say that an individual cannot hear or speak. A *mute* person may be deaf or may be able to hear.

Do not use *deaf and dumb.*

**dean** Capitalize when used as a formal title before a name: *Dean John Jones, Deans John Jones and Susan Smith.*

Lowercase in other uses: *John Jones, dean of the college; the dean.*

**dean's list** Lowercase in all uses: *He is on the dean's list. She is a dean's list student.*

**deathbed** (n. and adj.)

**decades** Use Arabic figures to indicate decades of history. Use an apostrophe to indicate numerals that are left out; show plural by adding the letter *s: the 1890s, the '90s, the Gay '90s, the 1920s, the mid-1930s.*

See the **historical periods and events** entry.

**December** See **months.**

**deci-** A prefix denoting one-tenth of a unit. Move a decimal point one place to the left in converting to the basic unit: 15.5 decigrams = 1.55 grams.

**decimal units** Use a period and numerals to indicate decimal amounts. Decimalization should not exceed two places in textual material unless there are special circumstances.

See **fractions.**

**Declaration of Independence** Lowercase *the declaration* whenever it stands alone.

**decorations** See the **awards and decorations** entry.

**Deepfreeze** A trademark for a brand of home freezer.

If something is being postponed indefinitely, use two words: *The project is in the deep freeze.*

**deep-sea** (adj.)

**Deep South** Capitalize both words when referring to the region that consists of Alabama, Georgia, Louisiana, Mississippi and South Carolina.

**deep water** (n.) **deep-water** (adj.) *The creature swam in deep water. The ship needs a deep-water port.*

**defendant**

**defense** Do not use it as a verb.

**defense attorney** Always lowercase, never abbreviate.
See **attorney** and **titles**.

**defense spending** *Military spending* usually is the more precise term.

**definitely** Overused as a vague intensifier. Avoid it.

**degree-day** See **weather terms**.

**degrees** See **academic degrees**.

**deity** Lowercase. See **gods** and **religious references**.

**dek-** (before a vowel), **deka-** (before a consonant) A prefix denoting 10 units of a measure. Move a decimal point one place to the right to convert to the basic unit: 15.6 dekameters = 156 meters.

**Delaware** Abbrev.: *Del.* It has a land area of 2,057 square miles. Only Rhode Island is smaller in area, 1,049 square miles.
See **state names**.

**delegate** The formal title for members of the lower houses of some legislatures. Do not abbreviate. Capitalize only before their names. See **legislative titles**.
Always lowercase in other uses: *convention delegate Richard Henry Lee.*

**Delta Air Lines** Headquarters is in Atlanta.

**demagogue, demagoguery** Not *demagog.*

**democrat, democratic, Democratic Party** See the **political parties and philosophies** entry.

**Democratic Governors' Conference** Note the apostrophe.

**Democratic National Committee** On the second reference: *the national committee, the committee.*
Similarly: *Democratic State Committee, Democratic County Committee, Democratic City Committee, the state committee, the city committee, the committee.*

**demolish, destroy** Both mean to do away with something completely. Something cannot be partially *demolished* or *destroyed*. It is redundant to say *totally demolished* or *totally destroyed*.

**denote** See the **connote, denote** entry.

**Denver** The city in Colorado stands alone in datelines.

**depart** Follow it with a preposition: *He will depart from LaGuardia. She will depart at 11:30 a.m.*

Do not drop the preposition as some airline dispatchers do.

**Department of Agriculture; Department of Commerce; Department of Defense; Department of Education; Department of Energy** (*DOE* acceptable on second reference); **Department of Health and Human Services** (formerly the Department of Health, Education and Welfare); **Department of Housing and Urban Development** (*HUD* acceptable on second reference); **Department of the Interior; Department of Justice; Department of Labor; De-partment of State; Department of Transportation** (*DOT* acceptable on second reference); **Department of the Treasury.** Avoid acronyms when possible. A phrase such as *the department* is preferable on second reference because it is more readable and avoids alphabet soup.

The *of* may be dropped and the title flopped while capitalization is retained: *the State Department.*

Lowercase *department* in plural uses, but capitalize the proper name element: *the departments of Labor and Justice.*

A shorthand reference to the proper name element also is capitalized: *Kissinger said, "State and Justice must resolve their differences."* But: *Henry Kissinger, the secretary of state.*

Lowercase *the department* whenever it stands alone.

Do not abbreviate *department* in any usage.

See **academic departments.**

**dependent** (n. and adj.) Not *dependant*.

**depreciation** The reduction in the value of capital

goods due to wear and tear or obsolescence.

*Estimated depreciation* may be deducted from income each year as one of the costs of doing business.

**depression** Capitalize *Depression* and *the Great Depression* when referring to the worldwide economic hard times generally regarded as having begun with the stock market collapse of Oct. 28–29, 1929.

Lowercase in other uses: *the depression of the 1970s.*

**depths** See **dimensions.**

**deputy** Capitalize as a formal title before a name. See **titles.**

**derogatory terms** Do not use derogatory terms such as *krauts* (for Germans) or *niggers* (for Negroes) except in direct quotes, and then only when their use is an integral, essential part of the story.

See the **obscenities, profanities, vulgarities** entry and **word selection.**

**-designate** Hyphenate: *chairman-designate.* Capitalize only the first word if used

as a formal title before a name.

See **titles.**

**destroy** See the **demolish, destroy** entry.

**detective** Do not abbreviate. Capitalize before a name only if it is a formal rank: *police Detective Frank Serpico, private detective Richard Diamond.*

See **titles.**

**detente**

**detention center** See the **prison, jail** entry.

**Detroit** The city in Michigan stands alone in datelines.

**devil** But capitalize *Satan.*

**Dexedrine** A trademark for a brand of appetite suppressant. It also may be called *dextroamphetamine sulfate.*

**dialect** The form of language peculiar to a region or a group, usually in matters of pronunciation or syntax. Dialect should be avoided, even in quoted matter, unless it is clearly pertinent to a story.

There are some words and phrases in everyone's vocabulary that are typical of a particular region or group. Quoting dialect, unless used carefully, implies substandard or illiterate usage.

When there is a compelling reason to use dialect, words or phrases are spelled phonetically, and apostrophes show missing letters and sounds: *"Din't ya yoosta live at Toidy-Toid Street and Sekun' Amya? Across from da moom pitchers?"*

See **Americanisms; colloquialisms; quotes in the news;** and **word selection.**

**dialogue** (n.)

**diarrhea**

**Dictaphone** A trademark for a brand of dictation recorder.

**dictionaries** For spelling, style and usage questions not covered in this stylebook, consult Webster's New World Dictionary of the American Language, Second College Edition, published by Simon & Schuster of New York.

Use the first spelling listed in Webster's New World unless a specific exception is listed in this book. (The principal exception is the require-

ment that a hyphen be used in most words that begin with *anti-* or *non-.)*

If Webster's New World provides different spellings in separate entries *(tee shirt* and *T-shirt,* for example), use the spelling that is followed by a full definition *(T-shirt).*

If Webster's New World provides definitions under two different spellings for the same sense of a word, either use is acceptable. For example, *although* or *though.*

If there is no listing in either this book or Webster's New World, the backup dictionary, with more listings, is Webster's Third New International Dictionary, published by G. & C. Merriam Co. of Springfield, Mass.

Webster's New World is also the first reference for geographic names not covered in this stylebook. See **geographic names.**

**die-hard** (n. and adj.)

**Diet** The Japanese parliament. See **foreign legislative bodies.**

**dietitian** Not *dietician.*

**different** Takes the preposition *from,* not *than.*

**differ from, differ with**
To *differ from* means to be unlike.

To *differ with* means to disagree.

**dilemma** It means more than a problem. It implies a choice between two unattractive alternatives.

**dimensions** Use figures and spell out *inches, feet, yards,* etc., to indicate depth, height, length and width. Hyphenate adjectival forms before nouns.

EXAMPLES: *He is 5 feet 6 inches tall, the 5-foot-6-inch man, the 5-foot man, the basketball team signed a 7-footer.*

*The car is 17 feet long, 6 feet wide and 5 feet high. The rug is 9 feet by 12 feet, the 9-by-12 rug.*

*The storm left 5 inches of snow.*

Use an apostrophe to indicate feet and quote marks to indicate inches *(5'6")* only in very technical contexts.

**Diners Club** No apostrophe, in keeping with the practice the company has adopted for its public identity. Only its incorporation papers still read *Diners' Club.*

Headquarters is in New York.

**diocese** Capitalize as part of a proper name: *the Diocese of Rochester, the Rochester Diocese, the diocese.*

See **Episcopal Church** and **Roman Catholic Church.**

**directions and regions** In general, lowercase *north, south, northeast, northern,* etc. when they indicate compass direction; capitalize these words when they designate regions.

Some examples:

COMPASS DIRECTIONS: *He drove west. The cold front is moving east.*

REGIONS: *A storm system that developed in the Midwest is spreading eastward. It will bring showers to the East Coast by morning and to the entire Northeast by late in the day. High temperatures will prevail throughout the Western states.*

*The North was victorious. The South will rise again. Settlers from the East went West in search of new lives. The customs of the East are different from those of the West. The*

*Northeast depends on the Midwest for its food supply.*

*She has a Southern accent. He is a Northerner. Nations of the Orient are opening doors to Western businessmen. The candidate developed a Southern strategy. She is a Northern liberal.*

*The storm developed in the South Pacific. Leaders of Western Europe met leaders of Eastern Europe to talk about supplies of oil from Southeast Asia.*

**WITH NAMES OF NATIONS:** Lowercase unless they are part of a proper name or are used to designate a politically divided nation: *northern France, eastern Canada, the western United States.*

But: *Northern Ireland, East Germany, South Korea.*

**WITH STATES AND CITIES:** The preferred form is to lowercase compass points only when they describe a section of a state or city: *western Texas, southern Atlanta.*

But capitalize compass points:

—When part of a proper name: *North Dakota, West Virginia.*

—When used in denoting widely known sections: *Southern California, the South Side of Chicago, the Lower East Side of New York.* If in doubt, use lowercase.

**IN FORMING PROPER NAMES:** When combining with another common noun to form the name for a region or location: *the North Woods, the South Pole, the Far East, the Middle East, the West Coast* (the entire region, not the coastline itself—see **coast**), *the Eastern Shore* (see separate entry), *the Western Hemisphere.*

**director** The formal title for the individuals who head the Federal Bureau of Investigation and the Central Intelligence Agency. Capitalize when used immediately before their names or those of others for whom director is a formal title: *FBI Director J. Edgar Hoover.*

Most uses of *director,* however, involve an occupational description not capitalized in any use: *company director Joseph Warren.*

See **titles.**

**dis-** the rules in prefixes apply, but in general, no hyphen. Some examples:

dismember        disservice
dissemble        dissuade

**disc jockey** *DJ* is acceptable on second reference in a column or other special context. Use announcer in other contexts.

**discreet, discrete** *Discreet* means prudent, circumspect: *"I'm afraid I was not very discreet,"* she wrote.

*Discrete* means detached, separate: *There are four discrete sounds from a quadraphonic system.*

**diseases** Do not capitalize *arthritis, emphysema, leukemia, migraine, pneumonia,* etc.

When a disease is known by the name of a person identified with it, capitalize only the individual's name: *Bright's disease, Parkinson's disease,* etc.

**disinterested, uninterested** *Disinterested* means impartial, which is usually the better word to convey the thought.

*Uninterested* means that someone lacks interest.

**dispel, dispelled, dispelling**

**disposable personal income** The income that a person retains after deductions for income taxes, Social Security taxes, property taxes and for other payments such as fines and penalties to various levels of government.

**Disposall** A trademark for a type of mechanical garbage disposer.

**dissociate** Not *disassociate.*

**distances** Use figures for 10 and above, spell out one through nine: *He walked four miles.*

**Distant Early Warning Line** *DEW line* is acceptable on second reference for this series of radar stations near the 70th parallel in North America.

**district** Always spell it out. Use a figure and capitalize *district* when forming a proper name: *the 2nd District.*

**district attorney** Do not abbreviate. Capitalize when used as a formal title before a name: *District Attorney Hamilton Burger.*

Use *DA* (no periods) only in quoted matter.

See **titles.**

**district court** See **court names** and **U.S. District Court.**

**District of Columbia** Abbreviate as *D.C.* when the context requires that it be used in conjunction with *Washington.* Spell out when used alone.

*The district,* rather than *D.C.,* should be used in subsequent references.

**ditto marks** They can be made with quotation marks, but their use in newspapers, even in tabular material, is confusing. Don't use them.

**dive, dived, diving** Not *dove* for the past tense.

**divided nations** Use *East Germany, South Korea,* etc. See **datelines** and entries under the names of these nations.

**division** See the **organizations and institutions** entry; **military units;** and **political divisions.**

**divorcee** The fact that a woman has been divorced should be mentioned only if a similar story about a man would mention his marital status.

When the woman's marital status is relevant, it seldom belongs in the lead. Avoid stories that begin: *A 35-year-old divorcee* . . .

The preferred form is to say in the body of the story that a woman is divorced.

**Dixie cup** A trademark for a paper drinking cup.

**doctor** Use *Dr.* in first reference as a formal title before the name of an individual who holds a doctor of medicine degree: *Dr. Jonas Salk.*

The form *Dr.,* or *Drs.* in a plural construction, applies to all first-reference uses before a name, including direct quotations.

If appropriate in the context, *Dr.* also may be used on first reference before the names of individuals who hold other types of doctoral degrees. However, because the public frequently identifies *Dr.* only with physicians, care should be taken to assure that the individual's specialty is stated in first or second reference. The only exception would be a story in which the context left no doubt that the person was a dentist, psychologist, chemist, historian, etc.

In some instances it also is necessary to specify that an individual identified as *Dr.* is a physician. One frequent case is a story reporting on joint research by physicians, biologists, etc.

Do not use *Dr.* before the names of individuals who hold only honorary doctorates.

Do not continue to use *Dr.* in subsequent references.

See **academic degrees; courtesy titles;** and **religious titles.**

**dogs** See **animals.**

**dollars** Always lowercase. Use figures and the *$* sign in all except casual references or amounts without a figure: *The book cost $4. Dad, please give me a dollar. Dollars are flowing overseas.*

For specified amounts, the word takes a singular verb: *He said $500,000 is what they want.*

For amounts of more than $1 million, use the *$* and numerals up to two decimal places. Do not link the

numerals and the word by a hyphen: *He is worth $4.35 million. He is worth exactly $4,351,242. He proposed a $300 billion budget.*

The form for amounts less than $1 million: *$4, $25, $500, $1,000, $650,000.*

See **cents.**

**domino, dominoes**

**door to door, door-to-door** Hyphenate when used as a compound modifier: *He is a door-to-door salesman.*

But: *He went from door to door.*

**double-faced**

**doughnut** Not *donut.*

**Dow Jones & Co.** The company publishes The Wall Street Journal and Barron's National Business and Financial Weekly. It also operates the Dow Jones News Service.

For stock market watchers, it provides the Dow Jones industrial average, the Dow Jones transportation average, the Dow Jones utility average, and the Dow Jones composite average.

Headquarters is in New York.

**down-** The rules in **prefixes** apply, but in general, no hyphen. Some examples:

downgrade     downtown

**-down** Follow Webster's New World. Some examples, all nouns and/or adjectives:

breakdown    rundown
countdown    sit-down

All are two words when used as verbs.

**Down East** Use only in reference to Maine.

**downstate** Lowercase unless part of a proper name: *downstate Illinois.* But: *the Downstate Medical Center.*

**Down Under** Australia, New Zealand and environs.

**Dr.** See **doctor.**

**draft beer** Not *draught beer.*

**drama** See **composition titles.**

**Dramamine** A trademark for a brand of motion sickness remedy.

**Drambuie** A trademark for a brand of Scottish liqueur.

**dressing room**

**Dripolator** A trademark for a brand of drip coffeemaker.

**drive** See **addresses.**

**drive-in** (n.)

**drop out** (v.) **dropout** (n.)

**drought**

**drowned, was drowned** If a person suffocates in water or other fluid, the proper statement is that the individual *drowned.* To say that someone *was drowned* implies that another person caused the death by holding the victim's head under the water.

**Dr Pepper** A trademark (no period after Dr) for a brand of soft drink.

Headquarters is in Dallas.

**drugs** Because the word drugs has come to be used as a synonym for narcotics in recent years, *medicine* is frequently the better word to specify that an individual is taking medication.

**drunk, drunken** *Drunk* is the spelling of the adjective used after a form of the verb *to be: He was drunk.*

*Drunken* is the spelling of the adjective used before nouns: *a drunken driver, drunken driving.*

**drunkenness**

**duel** A contest between two people. Three people cannot duel.

**duffel** Not *duffle.*

**duke, duchess** See **nobility.**

**Dumpster** Trademark for a large metal trash bin.

Use trash bin or trash container instead.

**Dunkirk** Use this spelling rather than *Dunkerque,* in keeping with widespread practice.

**du Pont, E.I.** Note the spelling of the name of the U.S. industrialist born in France. Use *du Pont* on second reference.

The company named after him is *E.I. du Pont de Nemours & Co.* of Wilmington, Del. Capitalize the shortened form *Du Pont* in keeping with company practice. The shortened form is acceptable in all references.

See **foreign particles.**

**dust storm** See **weather terms.**

**Dutch oven, Dutch treat, Dutch uncle**

**dyed-in-the-wool** (adj.)

**dyeing, dying** *Dyeing* refers to changing colors.

*Dying* refers to death.

# E

**each** Takes a singular verb.

**each other, one another** Two people look at *each other*.

More than two look at *one another*.

Either phrase may be used when the number is indefinite: *We help each other. We help one another.*

**earl, countess** See **nobility.**

**earmark**

**earth** Generally lowercase; capitalize when used as the proper name of the planet. *She is down to earth. How does the pattern apply to Mars, Jupiter, Earth, the sun and the moon? The astronauts returned to Earth. He hopes to move heaven and earth.*

See **planets.**

**earthquakes** Hundreds of earthquakes occur each year. Most are so small they cannot be felt.

First reports on major earthquakes often come from the National Earthquake Information Service operated by the U.S. Geological Survey in Golden, Colo., or the Uppsala Seismological Institute in Uppsala, Sweden.

There are two important scales in measuring earthquakes, the Richter scale and the Mercalli scale.

The difference between them is what they measure. The Richter scale, the more common, provides information on the magnitude—the inherent strength—of a quake. The Mercalli scale describes the intensity of a quake—the degree to which it is felt in a given area.

Dr. Charles F. Richter, whose work in the 1930s led to the scale that bears his name, illustrates the difference by comparing a quake to a radio signal: The magnitude of the signal is the same no matter where you are. Its intensity varies depending on your distance from the transmitter.

RICHTER SCALE: The Richter scale is a gauge of the energy released by an earthquake, as measured by the ground motion recorded on a seismograph.

Every increase of one number, say from magnitude 5.5 to magnitude 6.5, means that the ground motion is 10 times greater. Some experts say the actual amount of energy released may be 30 times greater.

Theoretically, there is no upper limit to the scale, although it often erroneously is reported to be 10. Readings of 8.9, the highest on record, were computed from seismographic records of a quake off the coast of Ecuador in 1906 and from a quake off the coast of Japan in 1933.

A quake of magnitude 2 is the smallest normally felt by humans.

The relationship between a Richter reading and the potential for damage in populated areas is as follows:

—A quake of magnitude 3.5 can cause slight damage.

—Magnitude 4: The quake can cause moderate damage.

—Magnitude 5: The quake can cause considerable damage.

—Magnitude 6: The quake can cause severe damage.

—Magnitude 7: A major earthquake, capable of widespread, heavy damage.

—Magnitude 8: A "great" earthquake, capable of tremendous damage.

In 1977, a group of scientists suggested a new way to compute Richter readings. Officials of the National Earthquake Information Service and similar bodies said they would study the proposal. The method of providing Richter readings would not change, they said, at least until agreement on a new format could be reached through an international conference or similar forum.

MERCALLI SCALE: The Mercalli scale gauges the intensity of an earthquake as felt in a specific location.

The scale runs from 1 to 12: a 1 reading is "not felt except by very few, favorably situated." A 12 reading is "damage total, lines of sight disturbed, objects thrown into the air."

NOTABLE QUAKES: Earthquakes noted for both their magnitude and the amount of damage they caused include:

—Shensi province of China, January 1556: Killed 830,000 people, the largest number of fatalities on record from an earthquake.

—Tokyo and Yokohama, Japan, September 1923: Highest Richter reading later computed as 8.3. The quake and subsequent fires destroyed most of both cities, killing more than 100,000 people. Until the China quake of 1976, this was the highest fatality toll in the 20th century.

—San Francisco, April 1906: Highest Richter reading later computed as 8.3. The quake and subsequent fire were blamed for an estimated 700 deaths.

—Alaska, March 1964: Highest Richter reading 8.5. Killed 114 people.

—Guatemala, February 1976: Highest Richter reading later computed as 7.5. Authorities reported more than 234,000 deaths.

—Hopeh province of northern China, July 28, 1976: Highest Richter reading 8.3. A government document later said 655,237 people were killed and 779,000 injured. The fatality total was second only to the toll in the Shensi quake of 1556.

OTHER TERMS: The word *temblor* (not *tremblor*) is a synonym for *earthquake.*

The word *epicenter* refers to the point on the earth's surface above the underground center, or focus, of an earthquake.

**east, eastern** See the **directions and regions** entry.

**Easter** In the computation used by the Latin Rite of the Roman Catholic Church and by Protestant churches, it falls on the first Sunday after the first full moon that occurs on or after March 21. If the full moon falls on a Sunday, Easter is the next Sunday.

Easter may fall, therefore, between March 22 and April 25 inclusive.

**Eastern Airlines** Use this spelling of *airlines,* which Eastern has adopted for its public identity. Only its incorporation papers still read *air lines.*

Headquarters is in Miami.

**Eastern Hemisphere**
The half of the earth made up primarily of Africa, Asia, Australia and Europe.

**Eastern Orthodox churches** The term applies to a group of churches that have roots in the earliest days of Christianity and do not recognize papal authority over their activities.

Churches in this tradition were part of the undivided Christendom that existed until the Great Schism of 1054. At that time, many of the churches in the western half of the old Roman Empire accorded the bishop of Rome supremacy over other bishops. The result was a split between eastern and western churches.

The autonomous churches that constitute Eastern Orthodoxy are organized along mostly national lines. They recognize the patriarch of Constantinople (modern-day Istanbul) as their leader. He convenes councils, but his authority is otherwise that of a "first among equals."

Eastern Orthodox churches today count about 200 million members. They include the Greek Orthodox Church and the Russian Orthodox Church.

In the United States, organizational lines are based on the national backgrounds of various ethnic groups. The largest is the Greek Orthodox Archdiocese of North and South America, with about 2 million members. Next is the Orthodox Church in America, with about 1 million members, including people of Bulgarian, Romanian, Russian and Syrian descent.

BELIEFS: The term *orthodox* (literally "right believing") derives from the adherence of these churches to the teachings of only the seven ecumenical councils held before the Great Schism. The schism was caused, in part, by a Rome-approved change in wording that the Council of Nicaea had used in defining the doctrine of the Holy Spirit.

Aside from the question of papal supremacy, beliefs are generally the same as those described in the **Roman Catholic Church** entry.

Liturgies reflect cultural heritages. The principal worship service is called the Divine Liturgy.

The churches have their

own disciplines on matters such as married clergy—a married man may be ordained, but a priest may not marry after ordination.

CLERGY: Some of these churches call the archbishop who leads them a *metropolitan,* others use the term *patriarch.* He normally heads the principal archdiocese within a nation. Working with him are other archbishops, bishops, priests and deacons.

Archbishops and bishops frequently follow a monastic tradition in which they are known only by a first name. When no last name is used, repeat the title before the sole name in subsequent references.

Some forms: *Metropolitan Ireney, archbishop of New York and metropolitan of America and Canada.* On second reference: *Metropolitan Ireney. Archbishop* may be replaced by *the Most Rev.* on first reference. *Bishop* may be replaced by *the Rt. Rev.* on first reference.

Use *the Rev.* before the name of a priest on first reference; *Deacon* before the name of a deacon on first reference. Use only last names, customarily available for priests and deacons, in subsequent references.

See **religious titles.**

## Eastern Rite churches

The term applies to a group of Roman Catholic churches that are organized along ethnic lines traceable to the churches established during the earliest days of Christianity.

These churches accept the authority of the pope, but they have considerable autonomy in ritual and questions of discipline such as married clergy—a married man may be ordained, but marriage is not permitted after ordination.

Worldwide membership totals more than 10 million.

Among the churches of the Eastern Rite are the Antiochean-Maronite, Armenian Catholic, Byzantine-Byelorussian, Byzantine-Russian, Byzantine-Ruthenian, Byzantine-Ukrainian and Chaldean Catholic.

See **Roman Catholic Church.**

## Eastern Shore

A region on the east side of Chesapeake Bay, including parts of Maryland and Virginia.

*Eastern Shore* is not a synonym for *East Coast.*

**Eastern Standard Time (EST), Eastern Daylight Time (EDT)** See **time zones.**

**East Germany** Use both words, not *Germany* alone, after cities and towns in the German Democratic Republic.
See **Berlin** and **West Germany.**

**easygoing**

**ecology** The study of the relationship between organisms and their surroundings. It is not synonymous with *environment.*
Right: *The laboratory is studying the ecology of man and the desert.*
Wrong: *Even so simple an undertaking as maintaining a lawn affects ecology.* (Use *environment* instead.)

**editor** Capitalize *editor* before a name only when it is an official corporate or organizational title. Do not capitalize as a job description.
See **titles.**

**editorial, news** In references to a newspaper, reserve *news* for the news department, its employees and news articles. Reserve *editorial* for the department that prepares the editorial page, its employees and articles that appear on the editorial page.

**editor in chief** No hyphens. Capitalize when used as a formal title before a name: *Editor in Chief Horace Greeley.*
See **titles.**

**effect** See the **affect, effect** entry.

**Eglin Air Force Base, Fla.** Not *Elgin.*

**either** Use it to mean one or the other, not both.
Right: *She said to use either door.*
Wrong: *There were lions on either side of the door.*
Right: *There were lions on each side of the door. There were lions on both sides of the door.*

**either . . . or, neither . . . nor** The nouns that follow these words do not constitute a compound subject; they are alternate subjects and require a verb that agrees with the nearer subject:

*Neither they nor he is going.
Neither he nor they are going.*

**El Al Israel Airlines** An *El Al airliners* is acceptable in any reference.

Headquarters is in Tel Aviv.

**elder** For its use in religious contexts, see the entry for an individual's denomination.

**elderly** Use this word carefully and sparingly.

It is appropriate in generic phrases that do not refer to specific individuals: *concern for the elderly, a home for the elderly,* etc.

If the intent is to show that an individual's physical or mental capabilities have deteriorated as a direct result of age, cite a graphic example and give attribution for it.

Apply the same principle to terms such as *senior citizen.*

**-elect** Always hyphenate and lowercase: *President-elect Reagan.*

**Election Day** The first Tuesday after the first Monday in November.

**election returns** Use figures, with commas every three digits starting at the right and counting left. Use the word *to* (not a hyphen) in separating different totals listed together: *Jimmy Carter defeated Gerald Ford 40,827,292 to 39,146,157 in 1976* (this is the actual final figure).

Use the word *votes* if there is any possibility that the figures could be confused with a ratio: *Nixon defeated McGovern 16 votes to 3 votes in Dixville Notch.*

Do not attempt to create adjectival forms such as *the 40,827,292-39,146,157 vote.*

See **vote tabulations.**

**Electoral College** But *electoral vote(s).*

**electrocardiogram** *EKG* is acceptable on second reference.

**ellipsis** See entry in **Punctuation** chapter.

**El Salvador** The use of the article in the name of the nation helps to distinguish it from its capital, *San Salvador.*

Use *Salvadoran(s)* in references to citizens of the nation.

**embargo** See the **boycott, embargo** entry.

**embargo times** See **release times.**

**embarrass, embarrassing, embarrassed, embarrassment**

**embassy** An *embassy* is the official residence of an ambassador in a foreign country and the office that handles the political relations of one nation with another.

A *consulate,* the residence of a consul in a foreign city, handles the commercial affairs and personal needs of citizens of the appointing country.

Capitalize with the name of a nation; lowercase without it: *the French Embassy, the U.S. Embassy, the embassy.*

**emcee, emceed, emceeing** A colloquial verb and noun best avoided. A phrase such as *He was the master of ceremonies* is preferred.

**emeritus** This word often is added to formal titles to denote that individuals who have retired retain their rank or title.

When used, place *emeritus* after the formal title, in keeping with the general practice of academic institutions: *Professor Emeritus Samuel Eliot Morison, Dean Emeritus Cortney C. Brown, Publisher Emeritus Barnard L. Colby.*

Or: *Samuel Eliot Morison, professor emeritus of history; Cortney C. Brown, dean emeritus of the faculty of business; Barnard L. Colby, publisher emeritus.*

**emigrate, immigrate** One who leaves a country *emigrates* from it.

One who comes into a country *immigrates.*

The same principle holds for *emigrant* and *immigrant.*

**Emmy, Emmys** The annual awards by the National Academy of Television Arts and Sciences.

**Empirin** A trademark for a brand of aspirin compound.

**employee** Not *employe.*

**empty-handed**

**enact** See the **adopt, approve, enact, pass** entry.

**encyclopedia** But follow the spelling of formal names: *Encyclopaedia Britannica*.

**Energy Research and Development Administration** It no longer exists. Its functions were transferred in 1977 to the Department of Energy.

**enforce** But *reinforce*.

**engine, motor** An *engine* develops its own power, usually through internal combustion or the pressure of air, steam or water passing over vanes attached to a wheel: *an airplane engine, an automobile engine, a jet engine, a missile engine, a steam engine, a turbine engine*.

A *motor* receives power from an outside source: *an electric motor, a hydraulic motor*.

**England** London stands alone in datelines. Use *England* after the names of other English communities in datelines.

See **datelines** and **United Kingdom**.

**English muffin, English sparrow, English setter**

**Enovid** A trademark for a brand of birth control pill. It also may be called *norethynodrel with mestranol*.

**enquire, enquiry** The preferred words are *inquire, inquiry*.

**enroll, enrolled, enrolling**

**en route** Always two words.

**ensign** See **military titles**.

**ensure, insure** Use *ensure* to mean guarantee: *Steps were taken to ensure accuracy*.
Use *insure* for references to insurance: *The policy insures his life*.

**entitled** Use it to mean a right to do or have something. Do not use it to mean titled.
Right: *She was entitled to the promotion*.
Right: *The book was titled "Gone With the Wind."*

**enumerations** See examples in the **dash** and **periods** entries in the **Punctuation** chapter.

**envelop** Other verb forms: *enveloping, enveloped.* But: *envelope* (n.)

**environment** See **ecology.**

**Environmental Protection Agency** *EPA* is acceptable on second reference.

**envoy** Not a formal title. Lowercase. See **titles.**

**epicenter** The point on the earth's surface above the underground center, or focus, of an earthquake.
See **earthquakes.**

**epidemiology**

**Episcopal, Episcopalian** *Episcopal* is the adjective form; use *Episcopalian* only as a noun referring to a member of the Episcopal Church: *She is an Episcopalian.* But: *She is an Episcopal priest.*

Capitalize *Episcopal* when referring to the Episcopal Church. Use lowercase when the reference is simply to a body governed by bishops.

**Episcopal Church** Acceptable in all references for the *Episcopal Church in the United States of America,* the U.S. national church that is a member of the Anglican Communion.

The church is governed nationally by two bodies—the permanent Executive Council and the General Convention, which meets every three years.

After the council, the principal organizational units are, in descending order of size, provinces, dioceses or missionary districts, local parishes and local missions.

The National Council is composed of bishops, priests, laymen and laywomen. One bishop is designated the leader and holds the formal title of presiding bishop. The council is responsible for furthering the missionary, educational and social work of the church.

The General Convention has final authority in matters of policy and doctrine. All acts must pass both of its houses—the House of Bishops and the House of Deputies. The latter is composed of an equal number of clergy and lay delegates from each diocese.

A province is composed of several dioceses. Each has a provincial synod made up of a house of bishops and a house of deputies. The synod's primary duty is to coordinate the work of the church in its area.

Within a diocese, a bishop is the principal official. He is helped by the Diocesan Convention, which consists of all the clergy in the diocese and lay representatives from each parish. The convention adopts a budget, elects a bishop in the case of a vacancy, and elects delegates to the General Convention and the Provincial Synod.

The parish or local church is governed by a vestry, composed of the pastor and lay members elected by the congregation.

BELIEFS: See **Anglican Communion.**

CLERGY: The clergy consists of bishops, priests, deacons and brothers. A priest who heads a parish is described as a *rector* rather than a pastor. The term *minister* seldom is used.

For first reference to bishops, use *Bishop* before the individual's name: *Bishop John M. Allin.* An acceptable alternative in referring to U.S. Bishops is *the Rt. Rev.* The designation *the Most Rev.* is used before the names of the archbishops of Canterbury and York.

For first reference to men, use *the Rev.* before the name of a priest, *Deacon* before the name of a deacon, *Brother* before the name of a brother. On second reference, use only the last name.

For first reference to women, use *the Rev.* before the name of a priest, *Deacon* before the name of a deacon. On second reference, use *Miss, Mrs. or Ms.* or no title before the woman's last name, depending on her preference.

See **Anglican Communion** and **religious titles.**

**epoch** See the **historical periods and events** entry.

**equal** An adjective without comparative forms.

When people speak of a *more equal* distribution of wealth, what is meant is *more equitable.*

**equal, equaled, equaling**

**Equal Employment Opportunity Commission** *EEOC* is acceptable on second reference.

**equally as** Do not use the words together; one is sufficient.

Omit the *equally* shown here in parentheses: *She was (equally) as pretty as Marilyn.*

Omit the *as* shown here in parentheses: *She and Marilyn were equally (as) pretty.*

**Equal Rights Amendment** *ERA* is acceptable on second reference.

Ratification required approval by three-fourths (38) of the 50 states by June 30, 1982. Ratification failed when only 35 states had approved the amendment by the deadline. The original deadline was March 22, 1979, but was extended by Congress.

The text:

Section 1. Equality of rights under the law shall not be denied or abridged by the United States or by any state on account of sex.

Section 2. The Congress shall have the power to enforce, by appropriate legislation, the provisions of this article.

Section 3. This amendment shall take effect two years after the date of ratification.

**equal time, fairness doctrine** *Equal time* applies to the Federal Communications Commission regulation that requires a radio or television station to provide a candidate for political office with air time equal to any time that an opponent receives beyond the coverage of news events.

If a station broadcasts material that takes a stand on an issue, the FCC's *fairness doctrine* may require it to give advocates of a different position an opportunity to respond.

**equator** Always lowercase.

**equitable** See **equal**

**ERA** Acceptable in all references to baseball's *earned run average.*

Acceptable on second reference for *Equal Rights Amendment.*

**eras** See the **historical periods and events** entry.

**escalator** Formerly a trademark, now a generic term.

**escalator clause** A clause in a contract providing for increases or decreases in wages, prices, etc., based on fluctuations in the cost of living, production, expenses, etc.

**escapee** The preferred words are *escaped convict* or *fugitive*.

**Eskimo, Eskimos** Do not use *Inuit* unless in direct quotes.

**espresso** The coffee is *espresso*, not *expresso*.

**essential clauses, non-essential clauses** These terms are used in this book instead of *restrictive clause* and *non-restrictive clause* to convey the distinction between the two in a more easily remembered manner.

Both types of clauses provide additional information about a word or phrase in the sentence.

The difference between them is that the *essential clause* cannot be eliminated without changing the meaning of the sentence—it so *restricts* the meaning of the word or phrase that its absence would lead to a substantially different interpretation of what the author meant.

The *non-essential clause,* however, can be eliminated without altering the basic meaning of the sentence—it does not *restrict* the meaning so significantly that its absence would radically alter the author's thought.

PUNCTUATION: An essential clause must not be set off from the rest of a sentence by commas. A non-essential clause must be set off by commas.

The presence or absence of commas provides the reader with critical information about the writer's intended meaning. Note the following examples:

—*Reporters who do not read the stylebook should not criticize their editors.* (The writer is saying that only one class of reporters, those who do not read the stylebook, should not criticize their editors. If the *who . . . stylebook* phrase were deleted, the meaning of the sentence would be changed substantially.)

—*Reporters, who do not read the stylebook, should not criticize their editors.* (The writer is saying that all reporters should not criticize their editors. If the *who . . . stylebook* phrase were deleted, this meaning would not be changed.)

USE OF WHO, THAT, WHICH: When an essential or non-essential clause refers to a human being or animal with a name, it should be introduced by *who* or *whom*. (See the **who, whom** entry.) Do not use commas if the clause is essential to the meaning; use them if it is not.

*That* is the preferred pronoun to introduce clauses that refer to an inanimate object or an animal without a name. *Which* is the only acceptable pronoun to introduce a non-essential clause that refers to an inanimate object or an animal without a name.

The pronoun *which* occasionally may be substituted for *that* in the introduction of an essential clause that refers to an inanimate object or an animal without a name. In general, this use of *which* should appear only when *that* is used as a conjunction to introduce another clause in the same sentence: *He said Monday that the part of the army which suffered severe casualties needs reinforcement.*

See **that (conjunction)** for guidelines on the use of *that* as a conjunction.

## essential phrases, non-essential phrases

These terms are used in this book instead of *restrictive phrase* and *non-restrictive phrase* to convey the distinction between the two in a more easily remembered manner.

The underlying concept is the one that also applies to clauses:

An *essential phrase* is a word or group of words critical to the reader's understanding of what the author had in mind.

A *non-essential phrase* provides more information about something. Although the information may be helpful to the reader's comprehension, the reader would not be misled if the information were not there.

PUNCTUATION: Do not set an essential phrase off from the rest of a sentence by commas:

*We saw the award-winning movie "One Flew Over the Cuckoo's Nest."* (No comma, because many movies have won awards, and without the name of the movie the reader would not know which movie was meant.)

*They ate dinner with their daughter Julie.* (Because they have more than one daughter, the inclusion of Julie's name is critical if the reader is to know which daughter is meant.)

*We saw the 1976 winner in the Academy Award competition for best movie, "One Flew Over the Cuckoo's Nest."* (Only one movie won the award. The name is informative, but even without the name no other movie could be meant.)

*They ate dinner with their daughter Julie and her husband, David.* (Julie has only one husband. If the phrase read *and her husband David,* it would suggest that she had more than one husband.)

*The company chairman, Henry Ford II, spoke.* (In the context, only one person could be meant.)

*Indian corn, or maize, was harvested. (Maize* provides the reader with the name of the corn, but its absence would not change the meaning of the sentence.)

DESCRIPTIVE WORDS: Do not confuse punctuation rules for non-essential clauses with the correct punctuation when a non-essential word is used as a descriptive adjective. The distinguishing clue often is the lack of an article or pronoun:

Right: *Julie and her husband David went shopping. Julie and her husband, David, went shopping.*

Right: *Company Chairman Henry Ford II made the announcement. The company chairman, Henry Ford II, made the announcement.*

**Eurasian** Of European and Asian descent.

**European Community** The European Community is the umbrella organization of the European Economic Community, which is also called the Common Market; the European Iron and Steel Community, and some other bodies.

The community consists of 12 member nations. They are France, West Germany, Italy, Luxembourg, Belgium, Netherlands (the original six), Denmark, Greece, Ireland, Portugal, Spain, and United Kingdom.

The community's executive body is known as the European Commission and is based in Brussels. The commission is subordinate to the countries themselves, which speak through a Council of

Ministers, which has its own secretariat based in Brussels.

The Council of Ministers can meet by category—for example, the finance ministers of the member states can meet as a Finance Council, the foreign ministers as the Foreign Ministers' Council, etc. A summit of the heads of government of the member states is known as a European Council.

Every six months, the chairmanship of the Council of Ministers, and therefore of the community as a whole, rotates to another nation.

*EC* is acceptable on second reference if the full name has appeared earlier in the story.

**European Economic Community** *EEC* is acceptable on second reference.

*Common Market* may be used later in a story.

See **Common Market** or **European Community** for listing of members.

**evangelical** See **religious movements.**

**Evangelical Friends Alliance** See **Quakers.**

**evangelism** See **religious movements.**

**evangelist** Capitalize only in reference to the men credited with writing the Gospels: *The four Evangelists were Matthew, Mark, Luke and John.*

In lowercase, it means a preacher who makes a profession of seeking conversions.

**eve** Capitalize when used after the name of a holiday: *New Year's Eve, Christmas Eve.* But: *the eve of Christmas.*

**even-steven** Not *even-stephen.*

**every day** (adv.) **everyday** (adj.) *He goes to work every day. She wears everyday shoes.*

**every one, everyone** Two words when it means each individual item: *Every one of the clues was worthless.*

One word when used as a pronoun meaning all persons: *Everyone wants his life to be happy.* (Note that *everyone* takes singular verbs and pronouns.)

**ex-** Use no hyphen for words that use *ex-* in the sense of *out of:*

excommuni-   expropriate
cate

Hyphenate when using *ex-* in the sense of *former:*

ex-convict          ex-president

Do not capitalize *ex-* when attached to a formal title before a name: *ex-President Nixon.* The prefix modifies the entire term: *ex-New York Gov. Nelson Rockefeller;* not *New York ex-Gov.*

Usually *former* is better.

### exaggerate

**Excedrin** A trademark for a brand of aspirin compound.

**except** See the **accept, except** entry.

**exclamation point** See entry in **Punctuation** chapter.

**execute** To *execute* a person is to kill him in compliance with a military order or judicial decision.

See the **assassin, killer, murderer** entry and the **homicide, murder, manslaughter** entry.

**executive branch** Always lowercase.

**executive director** Capitalize before a name only if it is a formal corporate or organizational title.

See **titles.**

**Executive Mansion** Capitalize only in references to the White House.

**Executive Protective Service** It is now the *Secret Service Uniformed Division.*

See **Secret Service.**

**executor** Use for both men and women.

Not a formal title. Always lowercase.

See **titles.**

**exorcise, exorcism** Not *exorcize.*

**expel, expelled, expelling**

**Explorers** See **Boy Scouts.**

**Export-Import Bank of the United States** *Export-Import Bank* is acceptable in all references; *Ex-Im Bank* is acceptable on second reference.

Headquarters is in Washington.

**extol, extolled, extolling**

**extra-** Do not use a hyphen when *extra-* means outside of unless the prefix is followed by a word beginning with *a* or a capitalized word:

extralegal        extraterrestrial
extramarital      extraterritorial

But:

extra-alimen-     extra-Britannic
  tary

Follow *extra-* with a hyphen when it is part of a compound modifier describing a condition beyond the usual size, extent or degree:

extra-base hit    extra-mild
extra-dry drink     taste
extra-large
  book

**extrasensory perception** *ESP* is acceptable on second reference.

**extreme unction** See **sacraments.**

**Exxon Corp.** Formerly Standard Oil Co. (New Jersey).

Headquarters is in New York.

**eye, eyed, eyeing**

**eyestrain**

**eye to eye, eye-to-eye** Hyphenate when used as a compound modifier: *an eye-to-eye confrontation.*

**eyewitness**

# F

**facade**

**face to face** When a story says two people meet for discussions, talks or debate, it is unnecessary to say they met *face to face*.

**fact-finding** (adj.)

**Faeroe Islands** Use in datelines after a community name in stories from this group of Danish islands in the northern Atlantic Ocean between Iceland and the Shetland Islands.

**Fahrenheit** The temperature scale commonly used in the United States.

The scale is named for Gabriel Daniel Fahrenheit, a German physicist who designed it. In it, the freezing point of water is 32 degrees and the boiling point is 212 degrees.

To convert to Celsius, subtract 32 from Fahrenheit figure, multiply by 5 and divide by 9 (77-32 = 45, × 5 = 225, divided by 9 = 25 degrees Celsius).

In cases that require mention of the scale, use these forms: *86 degrees Fahrenheit* or *86 F* (note the space and no period after the *F*) if degrees and Fahrenheit are clear from the context.

See **Celsius** and **Kelvin.**

For guidelines on when Celsius temperatures should be used, see **metric system** entry.

## TEMPERATURE CONVERSIONS

Following is a temperature conversion table. Celsius temperatures have been rounded to the nearest whole number.

| F | C | F | C | F | C |
|---|---|---|---|---|---|
| 26 | -32 | 19 | -7 | 64 | 18 |
| -24 | -31 | 21 | -6 | 66 | 19 |
| -22 | -30 | 23 | -5 | 68 | 20 |
| -20 | -29 | 25 | -4 | 70 | 21 |
| -18 | -28 | 27 | -3 | 72 | 22 |
| -17 | -27 | 28 | -2 | 73 | 23 |
| -15 | -26 | 30 | -1 | 75 | 24 |
| -13 | -25 | 32 | 0 | 77 | 25 |

| F | C | F | C | F | C |
|---|---|---|---|---|---|
| -11 | -24 | 34 | 1 | 79 | 26 |
| -9 | -23 | 36 | 2 | 81 | 27 |
| -8 | -22 | 37 | 3 | 82 | 28 |
| -6 | -21 | 39 | 4 | 84 | 29 |
| -4 | -20 | 41 | 5 | 86 | 30 |
| -2 | -19 | 43 | 6 | 88 | 31 |
| 0 | -18 | 45 | 7 | 90 | 32 |
| 1 | -17 | 46 | 8 | 91 | 33 |
| 3 | -16 | 48 | 9 | 93 | 34 |
| 5 | -15 | 50 | 10 | 95 | 35 |
| 7 | -14 | 52 | 11 | 97 | 36 |
| 9 | -13 | 54 | 12 | 99 | 37 |
| 10 | -12 | 55 | 13 | 100 | 38 |
| 12 | -11 | 57 | 14 | 102 | 39 |
| 14 | -10 | 59 | 15 | 104 | 40 |
| 16 | -9 | 61 | 16 | 106 | 41 |
| 18 | -8 | 63 | 17 | 108 | 42 |

**fairness doctrine** See the **equal time, fairness doctrine** entry

**fall** See **seasons.**

**fallout** (n.)

**false titles** Often derived from occupational titles or other labels.
Always lowercase. See **titles.**

**family names** Capitalize words denoting family relationships only when they precede the name of a person or when they stand unmodified

as a substitute for a person's name: *I wrote to Grandfather Smith. I wrote Mother a letter. I wrote my mother a letter.*

**Fannie Mae** See **Federal National Mortgage Association.**

**Fannie May** A trademark for a brand of candy.

**Far East** The easternmost portions of the continent of Asia: China, Japan, North and South Korea, Taiwan, Hong Kong and the eastern portions of the Soviet Union.
Confine *Far East* to this restricted sense. Use the *Far East and Southeast Asia* when referring to a wider portion of southern Asia.
See the **Asian subcontinent** and **Southeast Asia** entries.

**far-flung** (adj.)

**far-off** (adj.)

**far-ranging** (adj.)

**farsighted** When used in a medical sense, it means that a person can see objects at a distance but has difficulty seeing materials at close range.

**farther, further** *Farther* refers to physical distance: *He walked farther into the woods.*

*Further* refers to an extension of time or degree: *She will look further into the mystery.*

**Far West** For the U.S. region, generally west of the Rocky Mountains.

**fascism, fascist** See the **political parties and philosophies** entry.

**father** Use *the Rev.* in first reference before the names of Episcopal, Orthodox and Roman Catholic priests. Use *Father* before a name only in direct quotations.

See **religious titles.**

**father-in-law, fathers-in-law**

**Father's Day** The third Sunday in June.

**Father Time**

**faze, phase** *Faze* means to embarrass or disturb: *The snub did not faze her.*

*Phase* denotes an aspect or stage: *They will phase in a new system.*

**FBI** Acceptable in all references for *Federal Bureau of Investigation.*

**feather bedding, featherbedding** *Feather bedding* is a mattress stuffed with feathers.

*Featherbedding* is the practice of requiring an employer to hire more workers than needed to handle a job.

**features** They are not exempt from normal style rules. See **special contexts** for guidelines on some limited exceptions.

**February** See **months.**

**federal** Use a capital letter for the architectural style and for corporate or governmental bodies that use the word as part of their formal names: *Federal Express, the Federal Trade Commission.* (See separate entries for governmental agencies.)

Lowercase when used as an adjective to distinguish something from state, county, city, town or private entities: *federal assistance, federal court, the federal government, a federal judge.*

Also: *federal District Court* (but *U.S. District Court* is pre-

# Federal Housing Administration 135

ferred) and *federal Judge John Sirica* (but *U.S. District Judge John Sirica* is preferred).

**Federal Aviation Administration** *FAA* is acceptable on second reference.

**Federal Bureau of Investigation** *FBI* is acceptable in all references. To avoid alphabet soup, however, use *the bureau* in some references.

**Federal Communications Commission** *FCC* is acceptable on second reference.

**federal court** Always lowercase.

The preferred form for first reference is to use the proper name of the court. See entries under **U.S.** and the court name.

Do not create non-existent entities such as *Manhattan Federal Court.* Instead, use *a federal court in Manhattan.*

See **judicial branch.**

**Federal Crop Insurance Corp.** Do not abbreviate.

**Federal Deposit Insurance Corp.** *FDIC* is acceptable on second reference.

**Federal Emergency Management Agency** *FEMA* is acceptable on second reference, but *the agency* is preferred.

**Federal Energy Regulatory Commission** This agency replaced the Federal Power Commission in 1977. It regulates interstate natural gas and electricity transactions.

*FERC* is acceptable on second reference, but *the agency* or *the commission* is preferred.

**Federal Farm Credit Board** Do not abbreviate.

**Federal Highway Administration** Reserve the *FHA* abbreviation for the *Federal Housing Administration.*

**Federal Home Loan Bank Board** Do not abbreviate.

**Federal Housing Administration** *FHA* is acceptable on second reference.

**federal legal holidays**
See the **holidays and holy days** entry.

**Federal Mediation and Conciliation Service** Do not abbreviate. Use *the service* on second reference.

**Federal National Mortgage Association** *Fannie Mae* is acceptable on second reference, but it should be identified as the nickname for the agency if the story is not being written primarily for business-oriented readers.

The association's bonds are known as *Fannie Maes.*

**Federal Power Commission** It no longer exists. See **Federal Energy Regulatory Commission.**

**Federal Register** This publication, issued every workday, is the legal medium for recording and communicating the rules and regulations established by the executive branch of the federal government.

Individuals or corporations cannot be held legally responsible for compliance with a regulation unless it has been published in the Register.

In addition, executive agencies are required to publish in advance some types of proposed regulations.

**Federal Reserve System, Federal Reserve Board** On second reference, use the *Federal Reserve, the Reserve, the Fed, the system* or *the board.*

Also: *the Federal Reserve Bank of New York (Boston,* etc.), *the bank.*

**Federal Trade Commission** *FTC* is acceptable on second reference.

**felony, misdemeanor**
A *felony* is a serious crime. A *misdemeanor* is a minor offense against the law.

A fuller definition of what constitutes a felony or misdemeanor depends on the governmental jurisdiction involved.

At the federal level, a *misdemeanor* is a crime that carries a potential penalty of no more than a year in jail. A *felony* is a crime that carries a potential penalty of more than a year in prison. Often, however, a statute gives a judge options such as imposing a fine or probation in addition to or instead of a jail or prison sentence.

A *felon* is a person who has been convicted of a *felony,* regardless of whether the individual actually spends time in confinement or is given probation or a fine instead.

See the **prison, jail** entry.

**Ferris wheel**

**ferryboat**

**fertility rate** As calculated by the federal government, it is the number of live births per 1,000 females age 15 through 44 years.

**fewer, less** In general, use *fewer* for individual items, *less* for bulk or quantity.

Wrong: *The trend is toward more machines and less people.* (People in this sense refers to individuals.)

Wrong: *She was fewer than 60 years old.* (Years in this sense refers to a period of time, not individual years.)

Right: *Fewer than 10 applicants called.* (Individuals.)

Right: *I had less than $50 in my pocket.* (An amount.) But: *I had fewer than 50 $1 bills in my pocket.* (Individual items.)

**fiance** (man) **fiancee** (woman)

**Fiberglas** Note the single *s.* A trademark for fiberglass or glass fiber.

**figuratively, literally** *Figuratively* means in an analogous sense, but not in the exact sense. *He bled them white.*

*Literally* means in an exact sense; do not use it figuratively.

Wrong: *He literally bled them white.* (Unless the blood was drained from their bodies.)

**figure** The symbol for a number: *the figure 5.*
See **numerals.**

**filibuster** *To filibuster* is to make long speeches to obstruct the passage of legislation.

A legislator who used such methods also is a *filibuster,* not a *filibusterer.*

**Filipinos** The people of the Philippines.

**film ratings** See **movie ratings.**

**financial editor** Capitalize only as a formal title before a name.
See **titles.**

**fiord** Not *fjord*.

**firearms** See **weapons**.

**fire department** See the **governmental bodies** entry for the basic rules on capitalization.

See **titles** and **military titles** for guidelines on titles.

**firefighter, fireman** The preferred term to describe a person who fights fire is *firefighter*.

One meaning of *fireman* is a person who tends fires in a furnace. *Fireman* is an also acceptable synonym for *firefighter*.

**firm** A business partnership is correctly referred to as a *firm. He joined a law firm.*

Do not use *firm* in references to an incorporated business entity. Use *the company* or *the corporation* instead.

**first degree, first-degree** Hyphenate when used as a compound modifier: *It was murder in the first degree. He was convicted of first-degree murder.*

**first family** Always lowercase.

**first lady** Not a formal title. Do not capitalize, even when used before the name of a chief of state's wife.

See **titles.**

**first quarter, first-quarter** Hyphenate when used as a compound modifier: *He scored in the first quarter. The team took the lead on his first-quarter goal.*

**fiscal, monetary** *Fiscal* applies to budgetary matters.

*Monetary* applies to money supply.

**fiscal year** The 12-month period that a corporation or governmental body uses for bookkeeping purposes.

The federal government's fiscal year starts three months ahead of the calendar year—fiscal 1987, for example, runs from Oct. 1, 1986, to Sept. 30, 1987.

**fitful** It means restless, not a condition of being fit.

**flack, flak** *Flack* is slang for press agent.

*Flak* is a type of anti-aircraft fire, hence, figuratively, a barrage of criticism.

**flagpole, flagship**

**flail, flay** *To flail* is to swing the arms widely.

*To flay* is, literally, to strip off the skin by whipping. Figuratively, *to flay* means to tongue-lash a person.

**flair, flare** *Flair* is conspicuous talent.

*Flare* is a verb meaning to blaze with sudden, bright light or to burst out in anger. It is also a noun meaning a flame.

**flak** See the **flack, flak** entry.

**flare up** (v.) **flare-up** (n.) See the **flair, flare** entry.

**flash flood** See **weather terms.**

**flaunt, flout** *To flaunt* is to make an ostentatious or defiant display: *She flaunted her beauty.*

*To flout* is to show contempt for: *He flouts the law.*

**flautist** The preferred word is *flutist.*

**fleet** Use figures and capitalize *fleet* when forming a proper name: *the 6th Fleet.*

Lowercase *fleet* whenever it stands alone.

**flier, flyer** *Flier* is the preferred term for an aviator or a handbill.

*Flyer* is the proper name of some trains and buses: *The Western Flyer.*

**flimflam, flimflammed**

**flip-flop**

**floods, flood stage** See **weather terms.**

**floodwaters**

**floor leader** Treat it as a job description, lowercased, rather than a formal title: *Republican floor leader John Smith.*

Do not use when a formal title such as *majority leader, minority leader* or *whip* would be the accurate description.

See the **legislative titles** and **titles** entries.

**Florida** Abbrev.: *Fla.* See **state names.**

**Florida Keys** A chain of small islands extending southwest from the southern tip of mainland Florida.

Cities, or the islands themselves, are followed by *Fla.* in datelines:

*KEY WEST, Fla. (AP)—*

**flounder, founder** A *flounder* is a fish; *to flounder* is to move clumsily or jerkily, to flop about: *The fish floundered on land.*

*To founder* is to bog down, become disabled or sink: *The ship floundered in the heavy seas for hours, then foundered.*

**flout** See the **flaunt, flout** entry.

**flowers** See **plants.**

**fluid ounce** Equal to 1.8 cubic inches, two tablespoons or six teaspoons. The metric equivalent is approximately 30 milliliters.

To convert to milliliters, multiply by 30 (3 ounces × 30 = 90 milliliters).

See **liter.**

**fluorescent**

**flush** To become red in the face. See **livid.**

**flutist** The preferred term, rather than *flautist.*

**flyer** See the **flier, flyer** entry.

**FM** Acceptable in all references for the *frequency modulation* system of radio transmission.

**f.o.b.** Acceptable on first reference for *free on board.* The concept should be explained, however, in contexts not addressed to business-oriented audiences: The seller agrees to put an item on a truck, ship, etc. at no charge, but the transportation costs must be paid by the buyer.

**-fold** No hyphen:
twofold        fourfold

**folk singer, folk song**

**following** The word usually is a noun, verb or adjective: *He has a large following. He is following his conscience. The following statement was made.*

Although Webster's New World records its use as a preposition, the preferred word is *after: He spoke after dinner.* Not: *He spoke following dinner.*

**follow up** (v.) **follow-up** (n. and adj.)

**food** Most food names are lowercase: *apples, cheese, peanut butter.*

Capitalize brand names and trademarks: *Roquefort cheese, Tabasco sauce.*

Most proper nouns or adjectives are capitalized when they occur in a food name: *Boston brown bread, Russian dressing, Swiss cheese, Waldorf salad.*

Lowercase is used, however, when the food does not depend on the proper noun or adjective for its meaning: *french fries, graham crackers, manhattan cocktail.*

If a question arises, check the separate entries in this book. If there is no entry, follow Webster's New World. Use lowercase if the dictionary lists it as an acceptable form for the sense in which the word is used.

The same principles apply to foreign names for foods: *mousse de saumon* (salmon mousse), *pomme de terre* (literally, "apple of the earth"— for potato), *salade Russe* (Russian salad).

**Food and Agriculture Organization** Not *Agricultural. FAO* is acceptable on second reference to this U.N. agency.

**Food and Drug Administration** *FDA* is acceptable on second reference.

**foot** The basic unit of length in the measuring system that has been used in the United States. Its origin was a calculation that this was the length of the average human foot.

The metric equivalent is exactly 30.48 centimeters, which may be rounded to 30 centimeters for most comparisons.

For most conversions to centimeters, it is adequate to multiply by 30 (5 feet × 30 = 150 centimeters). For more exact figures, multiply by 30.48 (5 feet × 30.48 = 152.4 centimeters).

To convert to meters, multiply by .3 (5 feet × .3 = 1.5 meters).

See **centimeter, meter;** and **dimensions.**

**foot-and-mouth disease**

**forbear, forebear** *To forbear* is to avoid or shun.

A *forebear* is an ancestor.

**forbid, forbade, forbidding**

**forcible rape** A redundancy that usually should be avoided. It may be used, however, in stories dealing with both rape and statutory rape, which does not necessarily involve the use of force.

**Ford Motor Co.** Use *Ford*, not *FMC*, on second reference.

Headquarters is in Dearborn, Mich.

**fore-**The rules in prefixes apply, but in general, no hyphen. Some examples:

forebrain    foregoing
forefather   foretooth

There are three nautical exceptions, based on long-standing practice:

fore-topgallant  fore-topsail
fore-topmast

**forecast** Use *forecast* also for the past tense, not *forecasted*.

See **weather terms**.

**forego, forgo** *To forego* means to go before, as in *foregone conclusion*.

*To forgo* means to abstain from.

**foreign governmental bodies** Capitalize the names of the specific foreign governmental agencies and departments, either with the name of the nation or without it if clear in the context: *the French Foreign Ministry, the Foreign Ministry.*

Lowercase *the ministry* or a similar term when standing alone.

**foreign legislative bodies** In general, capitalize the proper name of a specific legislative body abroad, whether using the name of a foreign language or an English equivalent.

The most frequent names in use are *congress, national assembly* and *parliament.*

GENERIC USES: Lowercase *parliament* or a similar term only when used generically to describe a body for which the foreign name is being given: *the Diet, Japan's parliament.* But capitalize *parliament* or similar term when used independently of the foreign name:

*TOKYO (AP)—Demonstrators gathered outside the Parliament today.*

*Parliament* is the appropriate generic descriptive for the Diet, the Cortes in Spain, the Knesset in Israel and the Supreme Soviet in the Soviet Union.

PLURALS: Lowercase *parliament* and similar terms in plural constructions: *the parliaments of England and France, the English and French parliaments.*

INDIVIDUAL HOUSES: The principle applies also to individual houses of the nation's legislature, just as *Senate* and *House* are capitalized in the United States:

*ROME (AP)—New leaders have taken control in the Chamber of Deputies.*

PARLIAMENTS: Nations in which *parliament* is the name include: Australia, Canada, Denmark, Finland, France, India, Ireland, Italy, New Zealand, Norway, Poland and the United Kingdom.

NATIONAL ASSEMBLIES: Nations in which *national assembly* is the name include: Bulgaria, Czechoslovakia, Egypt, Hungary, Nepal, Pakistan, Portugal, Tunisia, Uganda, Zaire and Zambia.

Lowercase *assembly* when used as a shortened reference to *national assembly.*

In many countries, *national assembly* is the name of a unicameral legislative body. In some, such as France, it is the name for the lower house of a legislative body known by some other name such as *parliament.*

**foreign money** Generally, amounts of foreign money mentioned in news stories should be converted to dollars. If it is necessary to mention the foreign amount, provide the dollar equivalent in parentheses.

The basic monetary units of nations are listed in Webster's New World Dictionary among the M's under "Monetary Units of All Nations." Do not use the exchange rates listed in the dictionary. Instead, use, as appropriate, the official exchange rates, which change from day to day on the world's markets.

**foreign names** For foreign place names, use the primary spelling in Webster's New World Dictionary. If it has no entry, follow the National Geographic Atlas of the World.

For personal names, follow

the individual's preference for an English spelling if it can be determined. Otherwise:

—Use the nearest phonetic equivalent in English if one exists: *Alexander Solzhenitsyn,* for example, rather than *Aleksandr,* the spelling that would result from a transliteration of the Russian letters into the English alphabet.

If a name has no close phonetic equivalent in English, express it with an English spelling that approximates the sound in the original language: *Anwar Sadat.*

For additional guidelines, see **Arabic names; Chinese names; Russian names;** and **Spanish and Portuguese names.**

When a question arises, the news services will announce a common policy.

**foreign particles** Lowercase particles such as *de, la,* and *von* when part of a given name: *Charles de Gaulle, Baron Manfred von Richthofen.*

Capitalize the particles only when the last name starts a sentence: *De Gaulle spoke to von Richthofen.*

**foreign words** Some foreign words and abbreviations have been accepted universally into the English language: *bon voyage; versus, vs.; et cetera, etc.* They may be used without explanation if they are clear in the context.

Many foreign words and their abbreviations are not understood universally, although they may be used in special applications such as medical or legal terminology. Such words are marked in Webster's New World by a double dagger. If such a word or phrase is needed in a story, place it in quotation marks and provide an explanation: *"ad astra per aspera,"* a Latin phrase meaning "to the stars through difficulty."

**foreman, forewoman** Seldom a formal title.

**formal titles** See **titles.**

**former** Always lowercase. But retain capitalization for a formal title used immediately before a name: *former President Nixon.*

**Formica** A trademark for a brand of laminated plastic.

**Formosa** See **Taiwan.**

**Formosa Strait** Not *the straits of Taiwan.*

**formula, formulas** Use figures in writing formulas, as illustrated in the entries on metric units.

**forsake, forsook, forsaken**

**fort** Do not abbreviate, for cities or for military installations.
In datelines for cities:
*FORT LAUDERDALE, Fla. (AP)—*
*In datelines for military installations:*
*FORT BRAGG, N.C. (AP)—*

**fortnight** The expression *two weeks* is preferred.

**fortuneteller, fortunetelling**

**forty, forty-niner** *'49er is acceptable.*

**forward** Not *forwards.*

**foul, fowl** *Foul* means offensive, out of line.
A *fowl* is a bird, especially the larger domestic birds used as food: chickens, ducks, turkeys.

**founder** See the **flounder, founder** entry.

**four-flush** (stud poker)

**Four-H Club** *4-H Club* is preferred. Members are *4-H'ers.*

**four-star general**

**Fourth Estate** Capitalize when used as a collective name for journalism and journalists.
The description is attributed to Edmund Burke, who is reported to have called the reporters' gallery in Parliament a "Fourth Estate."
The three estates of early English society were the Lords Spiritual (the clergy), the Lords Temporal (the nobility) and the Commons (the bourgeoisie).

**Fourth of July, July Fourth** Also *Independence Day.* The federal legal holiday is observed on Friday if July 4 falls on a Saturday, on Monday if it falls on a Sunday.

**fractions** Spell out amounts less than one in stories, using hyphens between the words: *two-thirds, four-fifths, seven-sixteenths,* etc.

Use figures for precise amounts larger than one, converting to decimals whenever practical.

Fractions are preferred, however, in stories about stocks. See **stock market prices.**

When using fractional characters, remember that most newspaper type fonts can set only 1/8, 1/4, 3/8, 1/2, 5/8, 3/4 and 7/8 as one unit; use 11/2, 25/8, etc., with no space between the figure and the fraction. Other fractions require a hyphen and individual figures, with a space between the whole number and the fraction: *1 3-16, 2 1-3, 5 9-10.*

In tabular material, use figures exclusively, converting to decimals if the amounts involve extensive use of fractions that cannot be expressed as a single character.

See **percentages.**

**fragment, fragmentary**
*Fragment* describes a piece or pieces broken from the whole: *She sang a fragment of the song.*

*Fragmentary* describes dis-connected and incomplete parts: *Early returns were fragmentary.*

**frame up** (v.) **frame-up** (n.)

**frankfurters** They were first called hot dogs in 1906 when a cartoonist, T.A. "Tad" Dorgan, showed a dachshund inside an elongated bun.

**fraternal organizations and service clubs** Capitalize the proper names: *American Legion, Lions Club, Independent Order of Odd Fellows, Rotary Club.*

Capitalize also words describing membership: *He is a Legionnaire, a Lion, an Odd Fellow, an Optimist and a Rotarian.* See **AMERICAN Legion** for the rationale on *Legionnaire.*

Capitalize the formal titles of officeholders when used before a name.

See **titles.**

**free-for-all** (n. and adj.)

**free-lance** (n. and adj.)
The noun: *free-lancer.*

**free on board** See **f.o.b.**

**freewheeling**

**Free World** An imprecise description. Use only in quoted matter.

**freeze-dry, freeze-dried, freeze-drying**

**freezing drizzle, freezing rain** See **weather terms.**

**French Canadian, French Canadians** Without a hyphen. An exception to the normal practice in describing a dual ethnic heritage.

**French Foreign Legion** Retain capitalization if shortened to the Foreign Legion.

Lowercase *the legion* and *legionnaires.* Unlike the situation with the American Legion, the French Foreign Legion is a group of active soldiers.

**french fries** See **capitalization** and **food.**

**frequency modulation** *FM* is acceptable in all references.

**Friday** See **days of the week.**

**Friends General Conference, Friends United Meeting** See **Quakers.**

**Frigidaire** A trademark for a brand of refrigerator.

**Frisbee** A trademark for a plastic disk thrown as a toy. Use *Frisbee disk* for the trademarked version and *flying disk* for other generic versions.

**front line** (n.) **front-line** (adj.)

**front page** (n.) **front-page** (adj.)

**front-runner**

**frost** See **weather terms.**

**fruits** See **food.**

**fulfill, fulfilled, fulfilling**

**full-** Hyphenate when used to form compound modifiers:

full-dress    full-page
full-fledged   full-scale
full-length

See the listings that follow and Webster's New World

Dictionary for the spelling of other combinations.

**full house** (poker)

**full time, full-time** Hyphenate when used as a compound modifier: *He works full time. She has a full-time job.*

**fulsome** It means disgustingly excessive. Do not use to mean lavish, profuse.

**fundamentalist** See **religious movements.**

**fund raising, fund-raising, fund-raiser** *Fund raising is difficult. They planned a fund-raising campaign. A fund-raiser was hired.*

**funnel cloud** See **weather terms.**

**furlough**

**further** See the **farther, further** entry.

**fuselage**

**fusillade**

**F.W. Woolworth Co.** *Woolworth's* is acceptable in all references.

Headquarters is in New York.

# G

**G** *The general audience* rating. See **movie ratings**.

**gage, gauge** A *gage* is a security or a pledge.

A *gauge* is a measuring device.

*Gauge* is also a term used to designate the size of shotguns. See **weapons**.

**gaiety**

**gale** See **weather terms**.

**gallon** Equal to 128 fluid ounces. The metric equivalent is approximately 3.8 liters.

To convert to liters, multiply by 3.8 (3 gallons × 3.8 = 11.4 liters).

See **imperial gallon; liter;** and **metric system**.

**Gallup Poll** Prepared by The American Institute of Public Opinion, Princeton, N.J.

**game plan**

**gamut, gantlet, gauntlet** A *gamut* is a scale or notes of any complete range or extent.

A *gantlet* is a flogging ordeal, literally or figuratively.

A *gauntlet* is a glove. *To throw down the gauntlet* means to issue a challenge. *To take up the gauntlet* means to accept a challenge.

**gamy, gamier, gamiest**

**garnish, garnishee** *Garnish* means to adorn or decorate.

As a verb, *garnishee* (*garnisheed, garnisheeing*) means to attach a debtor's property or wages to satisfy a debt. As a noun, it identifies the individual whose property was attached.

**gauge** See the **gage, gauge** entry.

**gay** Do not use as a noun meaning a homosexual unless it appears in the formal name of an organization or in quoted matter.

In a story about homosexuals, *gay* may be used as an adjective meaning homosexual.

**general, general of the air force, general of the army** See **military titles.**

**General Accounting Office** The *General Accounting Office* is a nonpartisan congressional agency that audits federal programs.

*GAO* is acceptable on second reference.

**general assembly** See legislature for its treatment as the name of a state's legislative body.

Capitalize when it is the formal name for the ruling or consultative body of an organization: *the General Assembly of the World Council of Churches.*

**General Assembly (U.N.)** *General Assembly* may be used on the first reference in a story under a United Nations dateline.

Use *U.N. General Assembly* in other first references, *the General Assembly* or *the assembly* in subsequent references.

**general court** Part of the official proper name for the legislatures in Massachusetts and New Hampshire. Capitalize specific references with or without the state name: *the Massachusetts General Court, the General Court.*

In keeping with the accepted practice, however, *Legislature* may be used instead and treated as a proper name. See **legislature.**

Lowercase *legislature* in a generic use such as: *The General Court is the legislature in Massachusetts.*

**General Electric Co.** *GE* is acceptable on second reference.

Headquarters is in Fairfield, Conn.

**general manager** Capitalize only as a formal title before a name.

See **titles.**

**General Motors Corp.** *GM* is acceptable on second reference.

Headquarters is in Detroit.

**General Services Administration** *GSA* is acceptable on second reference.

**genie** Not *jinni,* the spelling under which Webster's New World gives the definition.

**gentile** Generally, any person not a Jew; often, specifically a Christian. But to Mormons it is anyone not a Mormon.

**gentleman** Do not use as a synonym for *man.* See **lady.**

**geographic names** The basic guidelines:

DOMESTIC: The authority for spelling place names in the 50 states and territories is the U.S. Postal Service Directory of Post Offices, with two exceptions:

—Do not use the postal abbreviations for state names. For acceptable abbreviations, see entries in this book under each state's name. See **state names** for rules on when the abbreviations may be used.

—Abbreviate *Saint* as *St.* (But abbreviate *Sault Sainte Marie* as *Sault Ste. Marie.*)

FOREIGN: The first source for the spelling of all foreign place names is Webster's New World Dictionary as follows:

—Use the first-listed spelling if an entry gives more than one.

—If the dictionary provides different spellings in separate entries, use the spelling that is followed by a full description of the location. There are four exceptions:

1. Use *West Germany, East Germany,* etc., for divided nations. See the **datelines** entry.

2. Use *Cameroon,* not *Cameroons* or *Cameroun.*

3. Use *Maldives,* not *Maldive Islands.*

4. Use *Sri Lanka,* not *Ceylon.*

The latter three exceptions have been made to conform with the practices of the United Nations and the U.S. Board of Geographic Names. (See the NEW NAMES paragraph below.)

If the dictionary does not have an entry, use the first-listed spelling in the National Geographic Atlas of the World.

NEW NAMES: Follow the styles adopted by the United

Nations and the U.S. Board of Geographic Names on new cities, new independent nations and nations that change their names. If the two do not agree, the news services will announce a common policy.

DATELINES: See the **datelines** entry.

CAPITALIZATION: Capitalize common nouns when they form an integral part of a proper name, but lowercase them when they stand alone: *Pennsylvania Avenue, the avenue; the Philippine Islands, the islands; the Mississippi River, the river.*

Lowercase common nouns that are not a part of a specific name: *the Pacific islands, the Swiss mountains, Chekiang province.*

For additional guidelines, see **addresses; capitalization;** the **directions and regions** entry; and **island.**

**Georgia** Abbrev.: *Ga.* See **state names.**

**German measles** Also known as *rubella.*

**Germany** Use *East Germany* in datelines after the names of communities in the German Democratic Republic.

Use *West Germany* after the names of communities in the Federal Republic of Germany.

*Berlin* stands alone in datelines. See the **Berlin** entry.

**getaway** (n.)

**get-together** (n.)

**ghetto, ghettos** Do not use indiscriminately as a synonym for the sections of cities inhabited by minorities or the poor. *Ghetto* has a connotation that government decree has forced people to live in a certain area.

In most cases, *section, district, slum, area* or *quarter* is the more accurate word. Sometimes a place name alone has connotations that make it best: *Harlem, Watts.*

**GI, GIs** *Soldier* is preferred unless the story contains the term in quoted matter or involves a subject such as the *GI Bill of Rights.*

**gibe, jibe** *To gibe* means to taunt or sneer: *They gibed him about his mistakes.*

*Jibe* means to shift direction or, colloquially, to agree:

*They jibed their ship across the wind. Their stories didn't jibe.*

**Gibraltar, Strait of** Not *Straits*. The entrance to the Mediterranean from the Atlantic Ocean. The British colony on the peninsula that juts into the strait stands alone in datelines as *GIBRALTAR*.

**giga-** A prefix denoting 1 billion units of a measure. Move a decimal point nine places to the right, adding zeros if necessary, to convert to the basic unit: 5.5 gigatons = 5,500,000,000 tons.

**girl** Applicable until 18th birthday is reached. Use *woman* or *young woman* afterward.

**girlfriend, boyfriend**

**Girl Scouts** The full name of the national organization is *Girl Scouts of the United States of America.* Headquarters is in New York.
   Girls 6 through 8 are *Brownie Girl Scouts* or *Brownies*. Girls 9 through 11 are *Junior Girl Scouts* or *Juniors*. Girls 12 through 14 are *Cadette Girl Scouts* or *Cadettes*. Girls 15 through 17 are *Senior Girl Scouts* or *Seniors*.

See **Boy Scouts.**

**glamour** One of the few *our* endings still used in American writing. But the adjective is *glamorous*.

**globe-trotter, globe-trotting** But the proper name of the basketball team is the *Harlem Globetrotters*.

**GMT** For *Greenwich Mean Time*. See **time zones.**

**gobbledygook**

**go-between** (n.)

**godchild, goddaughter** Also: *godfather, godliness, godmother, godsend, godson, godspeed.* Always lowercase.

**gods and goddesses** Capitalize *God* in references to the deity of all monotheistic religions. Capitalize all noun references to the deity: *God the Father, Holy Ghost, Holy Spirit,* etc. Lowercase personal pronouns: *he, him, thee, thou.*
   Lowercase *gods* and *goddesses* in references to the deities of polytheistic religions.
   Lowercase *god, gods* and *goddesses* in references to false gods: *He made money his god.*

See **religious references.**

**go-go**

**good, well** *Good* is an adjective that means something is as it should be or is better than average.

When used as an adjective, *well* means suitable, proper, healthy. When used as an adverb, *well* means in a satisfactory manner or skillfully.

*Good* should not be used as an adverb. It does not lose its status as an adjective in a sentence such as *I feel good.* Such a statement is the idiomatic equivalent of *I am in good health.* An alternative, *I feel well,* could be interpreted as meaning that your sense of touch was good.

See the **bad, badly** entry and **well.**

**goodbye** Not *goodby.*

**Good Conduct Medal**

**Good Friday** The Friday before Easter.

**good will** (n.) **goodwill** (adj.)

**GOP** See **Grand Old Party.**

**Gospel(s), gospel** Capitalize when referring to any or all of the first four books of the New Testament: *the Gospel of St. John, the Gospels.*

Lowercase in other references: *She is a famous gospel singer.*

**gourmand, gourmet** A *gourmand* is a person who likes good food and tends to eat to excess; a glutton.

A *gourmet* is a person who likes fine food and is an excellent judge of food and drink.

**government** Always lowercase, never abbreviate: *the federal government, the state government, the U.S. Government.*

**government, junta, regime** A *government* is an established system of political administration: *the U.S. government.*

A *junta* is a group or council that often rules after a coup: *A military junta controls the nation.* A junta becomes a government after it establishes a system of political administration.

The word *regime* is a synonym for *political system: a democratic regime, an authoritarian regime.* Do not use *re-*

*gime* to mean government or junta. For example, use *the Franco government* in referring to the government of Spain under Francisco Franco, not *Franco regime.* But: *The Franco government was an authoritarian regime.*

An *administration* consists of officials who make up the executive branch of a government: *the Reagan administration.*

**governmental bodies**
Follow these guidelines:

FULL NAME: Capitalize the full proper names of governmental agencies, departments, and offices: *The U.S. Department of State, the Georgia Department of Human Resources, the Boston City Council, the Chicago Fire Department.*

WITHOUT JURISDICTION: Retain capitalization in referring to a specific body if the dateline or context makes the name of the nation, state, county, city, etc., unnecessary: *The Department of State* (in a story from Washington), *the Department of Human Resources* or *the state Department of Human Resources* (in a story from Geor-

gia), *the City Council* (in a story from Boston), *the Fire Department* or *the city Fire Department* (in a story from Chicago).

Lowercase further condensations of the name: *the department, the council, etc.*

For additional guidance see **assembly; city council; committee; congress; legislature; house of representatives; senate; Supreme Court of the United States;** and **supreme courts of the states.**

FLIP-FLOPPED NAMES: Retain capital letters for the name of a governmental body if its formal name is flopped to delete the word *of: the State Department, the Human Resources Department.*

GENERIC EQUIVALENTS: If a generic term has become the equivalent of a proper name in popular use, treat it as a proper name: *Walpole State Prison,* for example, even though the proper name is the *Massachusetts Correctional Institute-Walpole.*

For additional examples, see **legislature; police department;** and the **prison, jail** entry.

PLURALS, NON-SPE-CIFIC REFERENCES: All words that are capitalized when part of a proper name should be lowercased when they are used in the plural or do not refer to a specific, existing body. Some examples:

*All states except Nebraska have a state senate. The town does not have a fire department. The bill requires city councils to provide matching funds. The president will address the lower houses of the New York and New Jersey legislatures.*

FOREIGN BODIES: The same principles apply. See **foreign governmental bodies** and **foreign legislative bodies.**

**governor** Capitalize and abbreviate as *Gov.* or *Govs.* when used as a formal title before one or more names in regular text. Capitalize and spell out when used as a formal title before one or more names in direct quotations.

Lowercase and spell out in all other uses.

See the next entry and **titles.**

**governor general, governors general** The formal title for the British sovereign's representatives in Canada and elsewhere.

Do not abbreviate in any use.

**grade, grader** Hyphenate both the noun forms (*first-grader, second-grader, 10th-grader,* etc.) and the adjectival forms (*a fourth-grade pupil, a 12th-grade pupil.*)

**graduate** (v.) *Graduate* is correctly used in the active voice: *She graduated from the university.*

It is correct, but unnecessary, to use the passive voice: *He was graduated from the university.*

Do not, however, drop *from: John Adams graduated from Harvard.* Not: *John Adams graduated Harvard.*

**graham, graham crackers** The crackers are made from a finely ground whole-wheat flour named for Sylvester Graham, a U.S. dietary reformer.

**grain** The smallest unit in the system of weights that has been used in the United States. It originally was defined as the weight of one grain of wheat.

It takes 437.5 grains to make an ounce. There are 7,000 grains to a pound.

See **ounce (weight)** and **pound**.

**gram** The basic unit of weight in the metric system. It is the weight of one cubic centimeter of water at 4 degrees Celsius.

A gram is roughly equivalent to the weight of a paper clip, or approximately one-twenty-eighth of an ounce.

To convert to ounces, multiply by 035 (86 grams × .035 = 3 ounces).

See **metric system**.

**grammar**

**granddad, granddaughter** Also: *grandfather, grandmother, grandson*.

**grand jury** Always lowercase: *a Los Angeles County grand jury, the grand jury*.

This style has been adopted because, unlike the case with *city council* and similar governmental units, a jurisdiction frequently has more than one grand jury session.

**Grand Old Party** *GOP* is acceptable as a second-reference synonym for *Republican Party* without first spelling out *Grand Old Party*.

**grant-in-aid, grants-in-aid**

**gray** Not grey. But: *greyhound*.

**great-** Hyphenate *great-grandfather, great-great-grandmother*, etc.

Use *great grandfather* only if the intended meaning is that the grandfather was a great man.

**Great Atlantic & Pacific Tea Co. Inc.** A&P is acceptable in all references.

Headquarters is in Montvale, N.J.

**Great Britain** It consists of England, Scotland and Wales, but not Northern Ireland.

*Britain* is acceptable in all references.

See **United Kingdom**.

**Great Depression** See **Depression**.

**greater** Capitalize when used to define a community and its surrounding region: *Greater Boston*.

**Great Lakes** The five, from the largest to the smallest: Lake Superior, Lake Huron, Lake Michigan, Lake Erie, Lake Ontario.

**Great Plains** Capitalize *Great Plains* or *the Plains* when referring to the U.S. prairie lands that extend from North Dakota to Texas and from the Missouri River to the Rocky Mountains.

Use *northern Plains, southwestern Plains,* etc., when referring to a portion of the region.

**Greek Orthodox Archdiocese of North and South America** See **Eastern Orthodox churches.**

**Greek Orthodox Church** See **Eastern Orthodox churches.**

**Green Revolution** The substantial increase in agricultural yields that resulted from the development of new varieties of grains.

**Greenwich Mean Time (GMT)** See **time zones** and **meridians.**

**gringo** See the **nationalities and races** entry.

**grisly, grizzly** *Grisly* is horrifying, repugnant.
*Grizzly* means grayish or is a short form for *grizzly bear.*

**grits** Ground hominy. The word normally takes plural verbs and pronouns: *Grits are to country ham what Yorkshire pudding is to roast beef.*

**gross national product** The total value at retail prices of all the goods and services produced by a nation's economy in a given time period.

As calculated quarterly by the Department of Commerce, the gross national product of the United States is considered the broadest available measure of the nation's economic activity.

Lowercase in all uses.

**Groundhog Day** Feb. 2.

**groundskeeper**

**groundswell**

**group** Takes singular verbs and pronouns: *The group is reviewing its position.*

**grown-up** (n. and adj.)

**Grumman Corp.** Headquarters is in Bethpage, N.Y.

**G-string**

**Guadalupe** (Mexico)

**Guadeloupe** (West Indies)

**Guam** Use in datelines after the name of a community. See **datelines.**

**guarantee** Preferred to *guaranty,* except in proper names.

**guard** Usually a job description, not a formal title. See **titles.**

**guardsman** See **National Guard** and **Coast Guardsman.**

**Guatemala City** Stands alone in datelines.

**gubernatorial**

**guerrilla** Unorthodox soldiers and their tactics.

**guest** Do not use as a verb except in quoted matter. (An exception to a use recorded by Webster's New World.)

**Guild, The** See **Newspaper Guild, The.**

**Gulf & Western Industries Inc.** Headquarters is in New York.

**Gulf Coast** Capitalize when referring to the region of the United States lying along the Gulf of Mexico. See **coast.**

**Gulf Oil Corp.** Headquarters is in Pittsburgh.

**Gulf Stream** But the racetrack is *Gulfstream Park.*

**gunbattle, gunboat, gunfight, gunfire, gunpoint, gunpowder**

**gung-ho** A colloquialism to be used sparingly.

**guns** See **weapons.**

**guru**

**gypsy, gypsies** Capitalize references to the wandering Caucasoid people found throughout the world.
Lowercase when used generically to mean one who is constantly on the move: *I plan to become a gypsy. She hailed a gypsy cab.*

**gypsy moth**

**habeas corpus** A writ ordering a person in custody to be brought before a court. It places the burden of proof on those detaining the person to justify the detention.

When *habeas corpus* is used in a story, define it.

**Hades** But lowercase *hell*.

**Hague, The** In datelines: *THE HAGUE, Netherlands (AP)*—

In text: *The Hague.*

**half** It is not necessary to use the preposition *of: half the time* is correct, but *half of the time* is not wrong.

**half-** Follow Webster's New World Dictionary. Hyphenate if not listed there.

Some frequently used words without a hyphen:

halfback          halftone
halfhearted       halftrack

Also: *halftime,* an exception to the dictionary in keeping with widespread practice in sports copy.

Some frequently used combinations that are two words without a hyphen:

half brother      half size
half dollar       half sole (n.)
half note         half tide

Some frequently used combinations that include a hyphen:

half-baked        half-life
half-blood        half-moon
half-cocked       half-sole (v.)
half-hour         half-truth

**half-mast, half-staff** On ships and at naval stations ashore, flags are flown at *half-mast.*

Elsewhere ashore, flags are flown at *half-staff.*

**hallelujah**

**Halley's comet** After Edmund Halley, an English astronomer who predicted the comet's appearance once every 75 years, last seen in 1985–86.

**Halloween**

**halo, halos**

**handmade**

**hand-picked**

**hands off, hands-off** Hyphenate when used as a compound modifier: *He kept his hands off the matter. He follows a hands-off policy.*

**hand to hand, hand-to-hand, hand to mouth, hand-to-mouth** Hyphenate when used as compound modifiers: *The cup was passed from hand to hand. They live a hand-to-mouth existence.*

**handicapped, disabled, impaired** In general do not describe an individual as *disabled* or *handicapped* unless it is clearly pertinent to a story. If such a description must be used, make it clear what the handicap is and how much the person's physical or mental performance is affected.

Some terms include:

*disabled* A general term used for a condition that interferes with an individual's

ability to do something independently.

*handicap* It should be avoided in describing a disability.

*blind* Describes a person with complete loss of sight. For others use terms such as *partially blind.*

*deaf* Describes a person with total hearing loss. For others use *partial hearing loss* or *partially deaf.*

*mute* Describes a person who physically cannot speak. Others with speaking difficulties are *speech impaired.*

*wheelchair-bound* Do not use this or variations. A person may use a wheelchair occasionally or may have to use it for mobility. If it is needed, say why.

**hang, hanged, hung** One *hangs* a picture, a criminal or oneself.

For past tense or the passive, use *hanged* when referring to executions or suicides, *hung* for other actions.

**hangar, hanger** A *hangar* is a building.

A *hanger* is used for clothes.

**hangover**

**hanky-panky**

**Hanukkah** The Jewish Feast of Lights, an eight-day commemoration of the rededication of the Temple by the Macabees after their victory over the Syrians.

Usually occurs in December but sometimes falls in late November.

**harass, harassment**

**harebrained**

**harelip**

**Harris Survey** Prepared by Louis Harris & Associates of New York.

**Havana** The city in Cuba stands alone in datelines.

**Hawaii** Do not abbreviate. Residents are *Hawaiians,* technically natives of Polynesian descent.

The state comprises 132 islands about 2,400 miles southwest of San Francisco. Collectively, they are the *Hawaiian Islands.*

Eight islands—Hawaii, Kahoolawe, Kauai, Lanai, Maui, Molokai, Niihau and Oahu—account for all but three square miles of the 6,450 in the state.

The largest island in land area is Hawaii. Honolulu and Pearl Harbor are on Oahu, where more than 80 percent of the state's residents live.

*Honolulu* stands alone in datelines. Use *Hawaii* after all other cities in datelines, specifying the island in the text, if needed.

See **datelines** and **state names.**

**Hawaiian Airlines** Headquarters is in Honolulu.

**H-bomb** Use *hydrogen bomb* unless a direct quotation is involved.

**he, him, his, thee, thou** Personal pronouns referring to the deity are lowercase.

See **deity.**

**headlong**

**head-on** (adj., adv.)

**headquarters** May take a singular or a plural verb.

Do not use *headquarter* as a verb.

**hearing examiner** See **administrative law judge.**

**hearsay**

**heaven**

**heavenly bodies** Capitalize the proper names of planets, stars, constellations, etc.: *Mars, Arcturus, the Big Dipper, Aries.* See **earth.**

For comets, capitalize only the proper noun element of the name: *Halley's comet.*

Lowercase *sun* and *moon,* but if their Greek names are used capitalize them: *Helios* and *Luna.*

Lowercase nouns and adjectives derived from the proper names of planets and other heavenly bodies: *jovian, lunar, martian, solar, venusian.*

**hect-** (before a vowel), **hecto-** (before a consonant) A prefix denoting 100 units of a measure. Move a decimal point two places to the right, adding zeros if necessary, to convert to the basic unit: 5.5 hectometers = 550 meters.

**hectare** A unit of surface measure in the metric system equal to 100 ares or 10,000 square meters.

A hectare is equal to 2.47 acres, 107,639.1 square feet or 11,959.9 square yards.

To convert to acres, multiply by 2.47 (5 hectares × 2.47 = 12.35 acres).

See **are** and **metric system.**

**heights** See **dimensions.**

**heliport**

**hell** But capitalize *Hades.*

**helter-skelter**

**hemisphere** Capitalize *Northern Hemisphere, Western Hemisphere,* etc.

Lowercase *hemisphere* in other uses: *the Eastern and Western hemispheres, the hemisphere.*

**hemorrhage**

**hemorrhoid**

**her** Do not use this pronoun in reference to nations or ships, except in quoted matter.

Use *it* instead.

**here** The word is frequently redundant, particularly in the lead of a datelined story. Use only if there is some specific need to stress that the event being reported took place in the community.

If the location must be stressed in the body of the story, repeat the name of the datelined community, both for the reader's convenience and to avoid problems if the story is topped with a different dateline.

**Her Majesty** Capitalize when it appears in quotations or is appropriate before a name as the long form of a formal title.

For other purposes, use the woman's name or *the queen*.

See **nobility**.

**heroin** The narcotic, originally a trademark.

**hertz** This term, the same in singular or plural, has been adopted as the international unit of frequency equal to one cycle per second.

In contexts where it would not be understood by most readers, it should be followed by a parenthetical explanation: *15,400 hertz (cycles per second)*.

Do not abbreviate.

**hideaway**

**hi-fi**

**highway designations** Use these forms, as appropriate in the context, for highways identified by number: *U.S. Highway 1, U.S. Route 1, U.S. 1, state Route 34, Route 34, Interstate Highway 495, Interstate 495.* On second reference only for *Interstate: I-495.*

When a letter is appended to a number, capitalize it but do not use a hyphen: *Route 1A.*

See **addresses.**

**highway patrol** Capitalize if used in the formal name of a police agency: *the Kansas Highway Patrol, the Highway Patrol.* Lowercase *highway patrolman* in all uses.

See **state police.**

**hike** People take *hikes* through the woods, but they *increase* prices.

**Hindu, Hinduism** The dominant religion of India. It has about 470 million followers, making it the world's third largest religion after Christianity and Islam. There are more than 300,000 followers in North America.

BELIEFS: The basic teaching is that the soul never dies, but is reborn each time the body dies. The soul may be reborn in either human or animal form. The following rule is that of karma and states that no matter how small the action or thought of an individual it will affect how the soul will be reborn in the next incarnation. The cycle of death and rebirth continues until a soul reaches spiritual perfection. At that point the soul is united in total enlightenment and peace with the supreme being and the cycle is ended.

There are a number of gods and goddesses, all of whom are different focuses of the one supreme being. The primary gods are Brahma, the creator, Vishnu, called the preserver, and Siva, the destroyer. Vishnu has had important human incarnations as Krishna and Rama. The primary goddess is Devi, who is also known as Durga, Kali, Sarasvati, Lakshimi and other names. She represents in her forms either motherhood and good fortune or destruction.

There are thousands of other deities and saints who also may receive prayers and offerings.

Hindus also believe that animals have souls and many are worshiped as gods.

WRITINGS: Hindus have no single book of teachings such as the Bible or the Koran. The primary written sources of doctrine are the Vedas, Puranas, the Ramayana, the Mahabharata, the Bhagavad-Gita and the Manu Smriti.

The Vedas deal with ritual, theology and philosophy. The Manu Smriti is the basic source of Hindu religious and social law and contains the basis for the Indian caste system. The other writings contain philosophical stories and discourses supporting the religion's doctrines.

ORGANIZATION: There are thousands of sects and organization runs from virtually none to very strict depending on the group. Basically, doctrines are passed along and practices are taught by leaders with varying degrees of holiness but there is no formal clergy.

**Hiroshima** On Aug. 6, 1945, this Japanese city and military base were the targets of the first atomic bomb dropped as a weapon. The explosion had the force of 20,000 tons (20 kilotons) of TNT. It destroyed more than four square miles and killed or injured 160,000 people.

**his, her** Do not presume maleness in constructing a sentence, but use the pronoun *his* when an indefinite antecedent may be male or female: *A reporter attempts to protect his sources.* (Not *his or her* sources, but note the use of the word *reporter* rather than *newsman.*)

Frequently, however, the best choice is a slight revision of the sentence: *Reporters attempt to protect their sources.*

**His Majesty** Capitalize when it appears in quotations or is appropriate before a name as the long form of a formal title.

For other purposes, use the man's name or *the king.*

See **nobility.**

**Hispaniola** The island shared by the Dominican Republic and Haiti.

See **Western Hemisphere.**

**historic, historical** A *historic* event is an important occurrence, one that stands out in history.

Any occurrence in the past is a *historical* event.

**historical periods and events** Capitalize the names of widely recognized epochs in anthropology, archaeology, geology and history: *the Bronze Age, the Dark Ages, the Middle Ages, the Pliocene Epoch.*

Capitalize also widely recognized popular names for periods and events: *the Atomic Age, the Boston Tea Party, the Civil War, the Exodus* (of the Israelites from Egypt), *the Great Depression, Prohibition.*

Lowercase *century: the 18th century.*

Capitalize only proper nouns or adjectives in general descriptions of a period: *ancient Greece, classical Rome, the Victorian era, the fall of Rome.*

For additional guidance, see separate entries in this book for many epochs, events and historical periods. If this book has no entry, follow the capitalization in Webster's

New World Dictionary, using lowercase if the dictionary lists it as an acceptable form for the sense in which the word is used.

**history** Avoid the redundant *past history.*

**hit and run** (v.) **hit-and-run** (n. and adj.) *The coach told him to hit and run. He scored on a hit-and-run. She was struck by a hit-and-run driver.*

**hitchhike, hitchhiker**

**hocus-pocus**

**hodgepodge**

**Hodgkin's disease** After Thomas Hodgkin, the English physician who first described the disease of the lymph nodes.

**ho-hum**

**hold-up** (v.) **holdup** (n. and adj.)

**holidays and holy days** Capitalize them: *New Year's Eve, New Year's Day, Groundhog Day, Easter, Hanukkah,* etc.

The legal holidays in federal law are New Year's, Washington's Birthday, Memorial Day, Independence Day, Labor Day, Columbus Day, Veterans Day, Thanksgiving and Christmas. See individual entries for the official dates and when they are observed if they fall on a weekend.

The designation of a day as a federal legal holiday means that federal employees receive the day off or are paid overtime if they must work. Other requirements that may apply to holidays generally are left to the states. Many follow the federal lead in designating holidays, but they are not required to do so.

**Hollywood** Stands alone in datelines when used instead of *Los Angeles* on stories about films and the film industry.

**Holocaine** A trademark for a type of local anesthetic.

**Holy Communion** See **sacraments.**

**Holy Father** The preferred form is to use *the pope* or *the pontiff,* or to give the individual's name.

Use *Holy Father* in direct

quotations or special contexts where a particular literary effect is desired.

**Holy Orders** See **sacraments.**

**Holy See** The headquarters of the Roman Catholic Church in Vatican City.

**Holy Spirit** Now preferred over *Holy Ghost* in most usage.

**Holy Week** The week before Easter.

**homemade**

**hometown** See **comma** in **Punctuation** chapter for guidelines on how to list a hometown after an individual's name.

**homicide, murder, manslaughter** *Homicide* is a legal term for slaying or killing.

*Murder* is malicious, premeditated homicide. Some states arbitrarily define certain homicides as murder if the killing occurs in the course of armed robbery, rape, etc.

*Manslaughter* is homicide without malice or premeditation.

A person should not be described as a *murderer* until convicted of the charge.

Unless authorities say premeditation was obvious, do not say that a victim *was murdered* until someone has been convicted in court. Instead, say that a victim *was killed* or *slain.*

See **execute** and the **assassin, killer, murderer** entries.

**Hong Kong** Stands alone in datelines.

**honky** A term of abuse directed toward whites by blacks. Use it only in quoted matter.

See the **nationalities and races** entry.

**Honolulu** The city in Hawaii stands alone in datelines. It is on the island of Oahu.

See **Hawaii.**

**honorary degrees** All references to honorary degrees should specify that the degree was honorary.

Do not use *Dr.* before the name of an individual whose only doctorate is honorary.

**honorary titles** See **nobility.**

**hoof-and-mouth disease** Use *foot-and-mouth disease.*

**hooky** Not *hookey.*

**hopefully** It means in a hopeful manner. Do not use it to mean it is hoped, let us or we hope.
Right: *It is hoped that we will complete our work in June.*
Right: *We hope that we will complete our work in June.*
Wrong as a way to express the thought in the previous two sentences: *Hopefully, we will complete our work in June.*

**horsepower**

**horse races** Capitalize their formal names: *Kentucky Derby, Preakness, Belmont Stakes,* etc.

**horses' names** Capitalize. See **animals.**

**host** Do not use it as a verb. (Exception to a usage recorded in Webster's New World.)

**hotel** Capitalize as part of the proper name for a specific hotel: *the Waldorf-Astoria Hotel.*
Lowercase when standing alone or used in an indefinite reference to one hotel in a chain: *The city has a Sheraton hotel.*

**Hotel and Restaurant Employees and Bartenders International Union.** The shortened forms *Hotel and Restaurant Employees union* and *Bartenders union* acceptable in all references.
Headquarters is in Cincinnati.

**hot line** The circuit linking the United States and the Soviet Union.
Lowercase.

**household, housing unit** In the sense used by the Census Bureau, a *household* is made up of all occupants of a *housing unit.*
A *housing unit,* as defined by the bureau, is a group of rooms or single room occupied by people who do not live and eat with any other person in the structure. It must have either direct access from the outside or through a common hall, or have a

kitchen or cooking equipment for the exclusive use of the occupants.

**House of Commons, House of Lords** The two houses of the British Parliament.

On second reference: *Commons* or *the Commons, Lords* or *the Lords.*

**house of delegates** See the next entry.

**house of representatives** Capitalize when referring to a specific governmental body: *the U.S. House of Representatives, the Massachusetts House of Representatives.*

Capitalize shortened references that delete the words *of Representatives: the U.S. House, the Massachusetts House.*

Retain capitalization if *U.S.* or the name of a state is dropped but the reference is to a specific body.

*BOSTON (AP)—The House has adjourned for the year.*

Lowercase plural uses: *the Massachusetts and Rhode Island houses.*

Apply the same principle to similar legislative bodies such

as *the Virginia House of Delegates.*

See the **organizations and institutions** entry for guidelines on how to handle the term when it is used by a non-governmental body.

**housing unit** See the **household, housing unit** entry.

**Houston** The city in Texas stands alone in datelines.

**Hovercraft** A trademark for a vehicle that travels on a cushion of air.

**howitzer** See **weapons.**

**Hughes Airwest** Headquarters is in San Mateo, Calif.

**human, human being** *Human* is preferred, but either is acceptable.

**hurly-burly**

**hurricane** Capitalize hurricane when it is part of the name that weather forecasters assign to a storm: *Hurricane Hazel.*

But use *it* and *its*—not *she,*

*her or hers*—in pronoun references.

And do not use the presence of a woman's name as an excuse to attribute sexist images of women's behavior to a storm. Avoid, for example, such sentences as: *The fickle Hazel teased the Louisiana coast.*
See **weather terms.**

**husband, widower** Use *husband,* not *widower,* in referring to the spouse of a woman who dies.

**hush-hush**

**Hyannis Port, Mass.**

**hydro-** The rules in **prefixes** apply, but in general, no hyphen. Some examples:

hydroelectric     hydrophobia

**hyper-** The rules in **prefixes** apply, but in general, no hyphen. Some examples:

hyperactive     hypercritical

**hyphen** See entry in **Punctuation** chapter.

**Iberia Air Lines of Spain** An *Iberia airliner* is acceptable in any reference.

Headquarters is in Madrid.

**IBM** Acceptable as first reference for *International Business Machines.* Headquarters is in Armonk, N.Y.

**ICBM, ICBMs** Acceptable on first reference for *intercontinental ballistic missile(s),* but the term should be defined in the body of a story.

Avoid the redundant *ICBM missiles.*

**ice age** Lowercase, because it denotes not a single period but any of a series of cold periods marked by glaciation alternating with periods of relative warmth.

Capitalize the proper nouns in the names of individual ice ages, such as the *Wisconsin ice age.*

Together, the ice ages, which began about 600,000 years ago, make up glacial epochs. During the first, called the *Pleistocene,* glaciers covered much of North America and northwestern Europe.

The present epoch, the *Helocene* or *Recent,* began about 12,000 years ago, with continental glaciers restricted to Antarctica and Greenland.

**Icelandair** Headquarters is in Reykjavik, Iceland.

**ice storm** See **weather terms.**

**Idaho** Do not abbreviate. See **state names.**

**illegal** Use *illegal* only to mean a violation of the law. Be especially careful in labor-management disputes, where one side often calls an action by the other side *illegal.* Usually it is a charge that a contract or rule, not a law, has been violated.

**Illinois** Abbrev.: *Ill.* See **state names.**

**illusion** See the **allusion, illusion** entry.

**imam** Lowercase when describing the leader of prayer in a Moslem mosque. Capitalize before a name when used as the formal title for a Moslem leader or ruler.
See **religious titles.**

**immigrate** See the **emigrate, immigrate** entry.

**impassable, impassible, impassive** *Impassable* means that passage is impossible: *The bridge was impassable.*
*Impassible* and *impassive* describe lack of sensitivity to pain or suffering. Webster's New World notes, however, that *impassible* suggests an inability to be affected, while *impassive* implies only that no reaction was noticeable: *She was impassive throughout the ordeal.*

**impel, impelled, impelling**

**imperial gallon** The standard British gallon, equal to 277.42 cubic inches or about 1.2 U.S. gallons.
The metric equivalent is approximately 4.5 liters.
See **liter.**

**imperial quart** One-fourth of an imperial gallon.

**implausible**

**imply, infer** Writers or speakers *imply* in the words they use.
A listener or reader *infers* something from the words.

**impostor** Not *imposter*

**impromptu** It means without preparation or advance thought.

**in, into** *In* indicates location: *He was in the room.*
*Into* indicates motion: *She walked into the room.*

**"in"** When employed to indicate that something is in vogue, use quotation marks only if followed by a noun: *It was the "in" thing to do. Raccoon coats are in again.*

**in-** No hyphen when it means *not:*

inaccurate          insufferable

Often solid in other cases:
inbound             infighting
indoor              inpatient (n.,
infield             adj.)
A few combinations take a hyphen, however:
in-depth            in-house
in-group            in-law
Follow Webster's New World when in doubt.

**-in** Precede with a hyphen:
break-in            walk-in
cave-in             write-in

### inasmuch as

**Inauguration Day** Capitalize only when referring to the total collection of events that include inauguration of a U.S. president; lowercase in other uses: *Inauguration Day is Jan. 20. The inauguration day for the change has not been set.*

**Inc.** See **incorporated.**

**inch** Equal to one-twelfth of a foot.
The metric equivalent is exactly 2.54 centimeters.
To convert to centimeters, multiply by 2.54 (6 inches × 2.54 = 15.24 centimeters).

See **centimeter; foot;** and **dimensions.**

**inches per second** A rating used for the speed of tape recorders.
The abbreviation *ips* (no periods) is acceptable on first reference in specialized contexts such as a records column; otherwise do not use *ips* until second reference.

**include** Use *include* to introduce a series when the items that follow are only part of the total: *The price includes breakfast. The zoo includes lions and tigers.*
Use *comprise* when the full list of individual elements is given: *The zoo comprises 100 types of animals, including lions and tigers.*
See the **compose, comprise, constitute** entry.

**income** See **profit terminology** in Business Guidelines chapter.

**incorporated** Abbreviate and capitalize as Inc. when used as part of a corporate name. It usually is not needed, but when it is used, do not set off with commas: *J.C. Penney Co. Inc. announced . . .*

See **company names.**

**incorporator** Do not capitalize when used before a name.
See **titles.**

**incredible, incredulous**
*Incredible* means unbelievable.
*Incredulous* means skeptical.

**incur, incurred, incurring**

**Independence Day** *July Fourth* or *Fourth of July* also are acceptable.
The federal legal holiday is observed on Friday if July 4 falls on a Saturday, on Monday if it falls on a Sunday.

**index, indexes**

**Index of Leading Economic Indicators** A composite of 12 economic measurements that was developed to help forecast likely shifts in the U.S. economy as a whole.
It is compiled by the Commerce Department.

**Indiana** Abbrev.: *Ind.* See **state names.**

**Indianapolis** The city in Indiana stands alone in datelines.

**Indian Ocean** See **oceans.**

**Indians** In news stories about American Indians, such words as *wampum, warpath, powwow, tepee, brave, squaw,* etc., can be disparaging and offensive. Avoid them.
Also avoid the use of *Native American* except in quotations. American Indians migrated to the continent over a land bridge from Asia.

**indict** Use *indict* only in connection with the legal process of bringing charges against an individual or corporation.
To avoid any suggestion that someone is being judged before a trial, do not use phrases such as *indicted for killing* or *indicted for bribery.* Instead, use *indicted on a charge of killing* or *indicted on a bribery charge.*
For guidelines on related words, see the entries under **accuse; allege;** and **arrest.**

**indiscreet, indiscrete**
*Indiscreet* means lacking pru-

dence. Its noun form is *indiscretion.*

*Indiscrete* means not separated into distinct parts. Its noun form is *indiscreteness.*

## indiscriminate, indiscriminately

## indispensable

**indo-** Usually hyphenated and capitalized:

Indo-Aryan     Indo-Hittite
Indo-German   Indo-Iranian
But: *Indochina.*

**Indochina** Formerly French Indochina, now divided into Cambodia, Laos and Vietnam.

**Indochinese peninsula** Located here are the nations of Burma, Cambodia, Laos, Thailand and Vietnam.

**Indonesia** Use after the name of a community in datelines on stories from this nation.

Specify an individual island, if needed, in the text.

**indoor** (adj.) **indoors** (adv.) *He plays indoor tennis. He went indoors.*

**infant** Applicable to children through 12 months old.

**infantile paralysis** The preferred term is *polio.*

**inflation** A sustained increase in prices. The result is a decrease in the purchasing power of money.

There are two basic types of inflation:

—*Cost-push inflation* occurs when rising costs are the chief reason for the increased prices.

—*Demand-pull inflation* occurs when the amount of money available exceeds the amount of goods and services available for sale.

**infra-** The rules in prefixes apply, but in general, no hyphen. Some examples:

infrared            infrastructure

**initials** Use periods and no space when an individual uses initials instead of a first name: *H.L. Mencken.*

This format has been adopted to assure that in typesetting the initials are set on the same line.

Do not give a name with a single initial *(J. Jones)* unless it is the individual's preference or a first name cannot be learned.

See **middle initials.**

**injuries** They are *suffered* or *sustained,* not *received.*

**in-law**

**Inner Light** See **Quakers.**

**innocent** Use *innocent,* rather than *not guilty,* in describing a defendant's plea or a jury's verdict, to guard against the word *not* being dropped inadvertently.

**innocuous**

**innuendo**

**inoculate**

**inquire, inquiry** Not *enquire, enquiry.*

**insignia** Same form for singular and plural.

**insofar as**

**in spite of** *Despite* means the same thing and is shorter.

**intelligence quotient** *IQ* is acceptable in all references.

**inter-** The rules in **prefixes** apply, but in general, no hyphen. Some examples:

inter-American interstate interracial

**intercontinental ballistic missile** See **ICBM, ICBMs.**

**Internal Revenue Service** *IRS* is acceptable on second reference.

Capitalize also *Internal Revenue,* but lowercase *the revenue service.*

**International Association of Machinists and Aerospace Workers** The shortened form *Machinists union* is acceptable in all references.

Headquarters is in Washington.

**International Bank for Reconstruction and Development** *World Bank* is acceptable in all references.

Headquarters is in Washington.

**International Brotherhood of Electrical Workers** Use the full name on first reference to avoid confusion with the United Electrical,

Radio and Machine Workers of America.

*IBEW* is acceptable on second reference.

Headquarters is in Washington.

**International Brotherhood of Painters and Allied Trades of the United States and Canada** The shortened form *Painters union* is acceptable in all references.

Headquarters is in Washington.

**International Brotherhood of Teamsters, Chauffeurs, Warehousemen and Helpers of America** The shortened form *Teamsters union* is acceptable in all references.

Capitalize *Teamsters* and *the Teamsters* in references to the union or its members.

Lowercase *teamster* when no specific reference to the union is intended.

Headquarters is in Washington.

**International Court of Justice** The principal judicial organ of the United Nations, established at The Hague in 1945.

The court is not open to individuals. It has jurisdiction over all matters specifically provided for either in the U.N. charter or in treaties and conventions in force. It also has jurisdiction over cases referred to it by U.N. members and by non-members such as Switzerland that subscribe to the court statute.

The court serves as the successor to the Permanent Court of International Justice of the League of Nations, which also was known as the World Court.

On second reference use *international court* or *world court* in lowercase. Do not abbreviate.

**International Criminal Police Organization** *Interpol* is acceptable in all references.

Headquarters is in Paris.

**international date line** The imaginary line drawn north and south through the Pacific Ocean, largely along the 180th meridian.

By international agreement, when it is 12:01 a.m. Sunday just west of the line, it is 12:01 a.m. Saturday just east of it.

See **time zones.**

**International Labor Organization** *ILO* is acceptable on second reference.

Headquarters is in Geneva.

**International Ladies' Garment Workers Union** The shortened forms *Ladies' Garment Workers* and *Ladies' Garment Workers union* are acceptable in all references.

*ILGWU* is acceptable on second reference if the full name has been used.

Lowercase *garment workers* when no specific reference to the union is intended.

Headquarters is in New York.

**International Longshoremen's and Warehousemen's Union** *ILWU* is acceptable on second reference.

Headquarters is in San Francisco.

**International Longshoremen's Association** *ILA* is acceptable on second reference.

Headquarters is in New York.

**International Monetary Fund** *IMF* is acceptable on second reference.

Headquarters is in Washington.

**International Telecommunications Satellite Organization** *Intelsat* is acceptable on first reference, but the body of the story should identify it as the shortened form of the full name.

(The original name was International Telecommunications Satellite Consortium.)

Headquarters is in Washington.

**International Telephone and Telegraph Corp.** Note the *and,* not an ampersand. *ITT* is acceptable on second reference.

Headquarters is in New York.

**International Union, United Automobile, Aerospace and Agricultural Implement Workers of America** This is the full, formal name for the union known more commonly as the *United Auto Workers*.

See the entry that begins **United Automobile.**

**Interpol** Acceptable in all references for *International Criminal Police Organization.*

**Interstate Commerce Commission** *ICC* is acceptable on second reference.

**intra-** The rules in **prefixes** apply, but in general, no hyphen. Some examples:

intramural    intrastate

**IOU, IOUs**

**Iowa** Do not abbreviate. See **state names.**

**ips** See **inches per second.**

**IQ** Acceptable in all references for **intelligence quotient.**

**Iran** The nation formerly called Persia. It is not an Arab country.

The people are *Iranians,* not *Persians* or *Irani.*

For the language, use *Persian,* the word widely accepted outside Iran. Inside Iran, the language is called *Farsi.*

**Iraq** The Arab nation coinciding roughly with ancient Mesopotamia.

Its people are *Iraqis.* The dialect of Arabic is *Iraqi.*

**Ireland** Acceptable in most references to the independent nation known formally as the Irish Republic.

Use *Irish Republic* when a distinction must be made between this nation and *Northern Ireland,* a part of the United Kingdom.

**Irish coffee** Brewed coffee containing Irish whiskey, topped with cream or whipped cream.

**Irish International Airlines** The preferred name is *Aer Lingus.*

Headquarters is in Dublin, Ireland.

**Irish Republican Army** A group that fights to wrest Northern Ireland from British rule and unite it with the Irish Republic.

*IRA* is acceptable on second reference.

**Iron Curtain** Use it only in quoted matter.

**irregardless** A double negative. *Regardless* is correct.

**Islam** Followers are called Moslems. Their holy book is the Koran, which according to Islamic belief was revealed by Allah (God) to the prophet Mohammed in the 7th century in Mecca and Medina. Their place of worship is a mosque. Their weekly holy day, equivalent to the Christian sabbath, is Friday.

MEMBERSHIP: It is the religion of about 850 million people in the world.

Although Arabic is the language of the Koran and Moslem prayers, not all Arabs are Moslems and not all Moslems are Arabs. Most of the world's Moslems live in a wide belt that stretches halfway around the world: across West Africa and North Africa, through the Arab countries of the Middle East and on to Turkey, Iran, Afghanistan, Pakistan and other Asian countries, parts of the Soviet Union and western China, to Indonesia and the southern Philippines.

BELIEFS: Islam is the youngest of the world's three major monotheistic religions. Like the other two—Judaism and Christianity—its followers believe in a single deity instead of several.

The Koran includes many of the stories—or variations of them—also found in the Jewish and Christian bibles. Moslems regard Abraham, Moses and Jesus as early prophets of their faith.

Islam sets five duties for its adherents:

—Acceptance of the one God and of Mohammed as his prophet.

—Five daily prayers, which are said facing Mecca.

—The giving of alms.

—Fasting from dawn to dusk during the Moslem month of Ramadan, which follows Islam's lunar calendar and therefore starts on a different day each year in the Western calendar.

—If able, make a pilgrimage (called a *Hajj* in Arabic) to Mecca.

HOLY PLACES: The holiest city in Islam is Mecca, in modern-day Saudi Arabia. Mecca is the site of the Kaaba, the cube-shaped black rock which is Islam's holiest shrine.

The second-holiest city is Medina. The Mosque of Mohammed, which contains Mohammed's grave, is the second-holiest shrine.

The third-holiest city is Jerusalem, which Islamic tradition holds was the place where Mohammed stopped before his nocturnal journey to heaven. The third-holiest shrine is Jerusalem's al-Aqsa Mosque, which is the sanctuary for the nearby Dome of the Rock.

SECTS: There are a number of sects in Islam. The following lists the largest and other major sects:

—*Sunni* The biggest single sect in Islam, comprising about 85 percent of all Moslems. Nations with Sunni majorities include Egypt, Saudi Arabia and most other Arab nations, as well as non-Arab Turkey and Afghanistan. Most Palestinian Moslems and most West African Moslems are Sunnis.

The Saudis sometimes are referred to as Wahhabi Moslems. This is a sub-group within the Sunni branch of Islam.

—*Shiite* The second-largest sect, after the Sunni. Iran, home of Ayatollah Ruhollah Khomeini's militant Islamic fundamentalism, is the only nation with an overwhelming Shiite majority. Iraq, Lebanon and Bahrain have large Shiite communities, in proportion to their overall populations.

(The schism between Sunni and Shiite stems from the very early days of Islam and arguments over Mohammed's successors as caliph, the spiritual and temporal leader of Moslems. The Shiites wanted the caliphate to descend through Ali, Mohammed's son-in-law. Ali eventually became the fourth caliph, but he was murdered; Ali's son al-Hussein was massacred with his fighters at Karbala, in what is now Iraq. Shiites considered the later caliphs to be usurpers. The Sunnis no longer have a caliph.)

OTHERS INCLUDE:

—*Druse* A mystical but pragmatic sect whose members are found in Lebanon, Syria, Israel and Jordan. An offshoot of Shiite Islam, the Druse use the Koran but also follow other teachings considered heretical by mainstream Islam. They call their faith "a way of Islam."

—*Ismaili* Another offshoot of the Shiites. The Aga Khan is their hereditary leader. Ismailis live mostly in Pakistan, India and East Africa.

—*Alawite* Also a Shiite offshoot. A minority found in Syria and northern Lebanon.

**CLERGY:** Titles vary from sect to sect and from country to country, but these are the most common:

*Grand Mufti*—The highest authority in Koranic law and interpretation, a title used mostly by Sunnis.

*Sheik*—Used by most clergymen in the same manner that *the Rev.* is used as a Christian clerical title, especially common among Sunnis. (Not all sheiks are clergymen. *Sheik* can also be a secular title of respect or nobility.)

*Ayatollah*—Used by Shiites, especially in Iran, to denote senior clergymen, such as *Ayatollah Ruhollah Khomeini.*

*Hojatoleslam*—A rank below ayatollah.

*Mullah*—Lower level clergy.

*Imam*—Used by some sects as a title for the prayer leader at a mosque. Among the Shiites, it usually has a more exalted connotation.

The adjective is *Islamic.*
See **Moslem.**

**island** Capitalize *island* or *islands* as part of a proper name: *Prince Edward Island, the Hawaiian Islands.*

Lowercase *island* and *islands* when they stand alone or when the reference is to the islands in a given area: *the Pacific islands.*

Lowercase all *island of* constructions: *the island of Nantucket.*

**U.S. DATELINES:** For communities on islands within the boundaries of the United States, use the community name and the state name:

*EDGARTOWN, Mass. (AP)* —

*Honolulu* stands alone, however.

**DATELINES ABROAD:** If an island has an identity of its own *(Bermuda, Prince Edward Island, Puerto Rico, Sardinia, Taiwan,* etc.) use the community name and the island name:

*HAMILTON, Bermuda (AP)*—

*Havana, Hong Kong, Macao* and *Singapore* stand alone, however.

If the island is part of a chain, use the community name and the name of the chain:

*MANILA, Philippines (AP)* —

Identify the name of the island in the text if relevant: *Manila is on the island of Luzon.*

For additional guidelines, see **datelines**.

**it** Use this pronoun, rather than *she,* in references to nations and ships.

**it's, its** *It's* is a contraction for *it is* or *it has: It's up to you. It's been a long time.*

*Its* is the possessive form of the neuter pronoun: *The company lost its assets.*

**IUD** Acceptable on second reference for *intrauterine device.*

**Ivy League** Brown University, Columbia University, Cornell University, Dartmouth College, Harvard University, Princeton University, the University of Pennsylvania and Yale University.

# J

**jail** Not interchangeable with *prison*. See the **prison, jail** entry.

**Jamaica rum** Not *Jamaican rum*.

**Jane's All the World's Aircraft, Jane's Fighting Ships** The reference sources for questions about aircraft and military ships not covered in this book.

The reference for non-military ships is Lloyd's Register of Shipping.

**January** See **months**.

**Japan Air Lines** *JAL* is acceptable on second reference.

Headquarters is in Tokyo.

**Japan Current** A warm current flowing from the Philippine Sea east of Taiwan and northeast past Japan.

**jargon** The special vocabulary and idioms of a particular class or occupational group.

In general, avoid jargon. When it is appropriate in a special context, include an explanation of any words likely to be unfamiliar to most readers.

See **dialect** and **word selection**.

**Jaycees** The proper name for the former Junior Chamber of Commerce. The United States Jaycees, the parent domestic organization, is affiliated with the worldwide body, the Jaycees International.

U.S. headquarters is in Tulsa, Okla.

See the **fraternal organizations and service clubs** entry.

**J.C. Penney Co. Inc.** Headquarters is in Dallas.

**jeep, Jeep** Lowercase the military vehicle.

Capitalize if referring to the

rugged, four-wheel drive civilian vehicle so trademarked.

## Jehovah's Witnesses

The denomination was founded in Pittsburgh in 1872 by Charles Taze Russell, a former Congregationalist layman.

Witnesses do most of their work through three legal corporations: the Watch Tower and Tract Society of Pennsylvania, the Watchtower Bible and Tract Society of New York Inc., and, in England, the International Bible Students Association. The principal officers of the corporations elect a director, who becomes the international head of the Jehovah's Witnesses.

U.S. membership is listed at more than 500,000.

BELIEFS: Witnesses believe that they adhere to the oldest religion on earth, the worship of Almighty God revealed in the Bible as Jehovah.

They regard civil authority as necessary and obey it "as long as its laws do not contradict God's law." Witnesses refuse to bear arms, salute the flag or participate in secular government.

They refuse blood transfusions as being against the Bible, citing the section of Leviticus that reads, "Whatsoever man . . . eats any manner of blood, I will cut him off from among his people."

CLERGY: Witnesses consider themselves a society of ministers. A public ceremony of water immersion sets an individual apart as a minister of Jehovah.

There are no formal titles, but there are four levels of ministry: *publishers* (part-time workers expected to devote 60 hours a month to distributing literature), *general pioneers* and *special pioneers* (terms for part-time workers who devote more than 60 hours a month to activities) and *pioneers* (full-time workers).

**Jell-O** A trademark for a brand of gelatin dessert.

**Jerusalem** Stands alone in datelines.

**Jesus** The central figure of Christianity, he also may be called *Jesus Christ*.

Personal pronouns referring to him are lowercase.

**jet, jetliner, jet plane** See **aircraft terms**.

**Jew** Use for men and women. Do not use *Jewess*.

## Jewish congregations

A Jewish congregation is autonomous. No synods, assemblies or hierarchies control the activities of an individual synagogue.

In the United States, there are three major expressions of Judaism:

1. Orthodox Judaism. Most of its congregations are represented nationally by the Union of Orthodox Jewish Congregations of America. Most of its rabbis are members of the Rabbinical Council of America.

2. Reform Judaism. Its national representatives are the Union of American Hebrew Congregations and the Central Conference of American Rabbis.

3. Conservative Judaism. Its national representatives are the United Synagogue of America and the Rabbinical Assembly.

These six groups make up the New York-based Synagogue Council of America. It is the vehicle for consultation among the three expressions and coordinates joint activities.

The council estimates that its members represent about 3 million synagogue-affiliated American Jews, divided about equally among the three major groups. The council also estimates that 1 million American Jews, most of them Orthodox, are members of congregations not represented by council members.

BELIEFS: Jews generally believe that a divine kingdom will be established on earth, opening a messianic era that will be marked by peace and bliss. They also believe that they have a mandate from God to work toward this kingdom.

The key to beliefs is the Torah, or Law of Moses, which consists of the Pentateuch, the first five books of the Bible. Jewish Scripture also includes the other books of the Old Testament. Additional elements of Jewish belief are contained in the Talmud, a detailed interpretation of the written and oral law of the faith.

Orthodox Jews expect the coming of the Messiah, who is to be a descendant of King David. They are strict adherents of the biblical dietary laws, ritual forms and traditional holy days.

Reform Jews believe in the coming of a messianic age, but not a personal Messiah. They regard dietary laws and ritual forms as concessions to the customs of ancient times that may be adapted to modern needs.

Conservative Jews take a middle position, generally adhering to traditional customs of diet and ritual but stressing that faith is not static and should adapt to the needs of contemporary culture.

CLERGY: The only formal titles in use are *rabbi,* for the spiritual leader of a congregation, and *cantor,* for the individual who leads the congregation in song. Capitalize these titles before an individual's full name on first reference. On second reference use only the last name of a man; use *Miss, Mrs., Ms.* or no title before the last name of a woman depending on her preference.

See **religious titles** and **Zionism.**

**Jewish holy days** See separate listings for **Hanukkah, Passover, Purim, Rosh Hashana, Shavuot, Sukkot** and **Yom Kippur.**

The High Holy Days are Rosh Hashana and Yom Kippur.

**jibe** See the **gibe, jibe** entry.

**job descriptions** Always lowercase. See **titles.**

**John F. Kennedy Space Center** Located in Cape Canaveral, Fla., it is the National Aeronautics and Space Administration's principal launch site for manned spacecraft.

*Kennedy Space Center* is acceptable in all references.

For datelines on launch stories:

*CAPE CANAVERAL, Fla. (AP)—*

See **Lyndon B. Johnson Space Center.**

**Johns Hopkins University** No apostrophes.

**Joint Chiefs of Staff** Also: *the Joint Chiefs.* But lowercase *the chiefs* or *the chiefs of staff.*

**Jr.** See the **junior, senior** entry.

**judge** Capitalize before a name when it is the formal title for an individual who presides in a court of law. Do not continue to use the title in second reference.

Do not use *court* as part of the title unless confusion would result without it:

—No *court* in the title: *U.S. District Judge John Sirica, District Judge John Sirica, federal Judge John Sirica, Judge John Sirica, U.S. Circuit Judge Homer Thornberry, appellate Judge John Blair.*

—*Court* needed in the title: *Juvenile Court Judge John Jones, Criminal Court Judge John Jones, Superior Court Judge Robert Harrison, state Supreme Court Judge William Cushing.*

When the formal title *chief judge* is relevant, put the court name after the judge's name: *Chief Judge John Sirica of the U.S. District Court in Washington, D.C.; Chief Judge Clement F. Haynsworth Jr. of the 4th U.S. Circuit Court of Appeals.*

Do not pile up long court names before the name of a judge. Make it *Judge John Smith of Allegheny County Common Pleas Court.* Not: *Allegheny County Common Please Court Judge John Smith.*

Lowercase *judge* as an occupational designation in phrases such as *beauty contest judge Bert Parks.*

See **administrative law judge; court names; judicial branch;** and **justice.**

**judge advocate** The plural: *judge advocates.* Also: *judge advocate general, judge advocates general.*

Capitalize as a formal title before a name.

See **titles.**

**judgment** Not *judgement.*

**judicial branch** Always lowercase.

The federal court system that exists today as the outgrowth of Article 3 of the Constitution is composed of the Supreme Court of the United States, the U.S. Court of Appeals, U.S. District Courts, the U.S. Court of Claims, the U.S. Court of Customs and Patent Appeals, and the U.S. Customs Court. There are also four district judges for U.S. territories.

The U.S. Tax Court and the U.S. Court of Military Appeals are not part of the judicial branch as such.

For more detail on all federal courts, see separate entries under the names listed here.

**Judicial Conference of the United States** This rule-making body for the courts of the judicial branch meets twice a year. Its 25 members are the chief justice, the chief judges of the 11 circuit courts, one district judge from each of the circuits, and the chief judges of the U.S. Court of Claims and the U.S. Court of Customs and Patent Appeals.

Day-to-day functions are handled by the Administrative Office of U.S. Courts.

**jukebox**

**July** See **months.**

**jumbo jet** Any very large jet plane, including the Boeing 747, the DC-10, the L-1011 and the C-5A.

**June** See **months.**

**junior, senior** Abbreviate as *Jr.* and *Sr.* only with full names of persons or animals. Do not precede by a comma: *Joseph P. Kennedy Jr.*

The notation *II* or *2nd* may be used if it is the individual's preference. Note, however, that *II* and *2nd* are not necessarily the equivalent of *junior* —they often are used by a grandson or nephew.

If necessary to distinguish between father and son in second reference, use the *elder Smith* or the *younger Smith.*

See **names.**

**Junior Chamber of Commerce** It no longer exists. See **Jaycees.**

**junta** See the **government, junta, regime** entry.

**jury** The word takes singular verbs and pronouns: *The jury has been sequestered until it reaches a verdict.*

Do not use awkward phrases such as *seven-man, five-woman jury.* Make it: *a jury of seven men and five women.*

Do not capitalize: *a U.S. District Court jury, a federal jury, a Massachusetts Superior Court jury, a Los Angeles County grand jury.*

*See* **grand jury.**

**justice** Capitalize before a name when it is the formal title. It is the formal title for members of the U.S. Supreme Court and for jurists on some state courts. In such cases, do not use *judge* in first or subsequent references.

See **judge**; **Supreme Court of the United States**; and **titles**.

**justice of the peace** Capitalize as a formal title before a name. Do not abbreviate.
See **titles**.

**juvenile delinquent** Juveniles may be declared delinquents in many states for antisocial behavior or for breaking the law. In some states, laws prohibit publishing or broadcasting the names of juvenile delinquents.

Follow the local practice unless there is a compelling reason to the contrary. Consult with the General Desk if you believe such an exception is warranted.

# K

**Kansas** Abbrev.: *Kan.* See **state names.**

**Kansas City** Use *KANSAS CITY, Kan.,* or *KANSAS CITY, Mo.,* in datelines to avoid confusion between the two.

**karat** See the **carat, caret, karat** entry.

**Kelvin scale** A scale of temperature based on, but different from, the Celsius scale. It is used primarily in science to record very high and very low temperatures. The Kelvin scale starts at zero and indicates the total absence of heat (absolute zero).

Zero on the Kelvin scale is equal to minus 273.15 degrees Celsius and minus 460 degrees Fahrenheit.

The freezing point of water is 273.16 degrees Kelvin. The boiling point of water is 373.16 degrees Kelvin.

To convert from Celsius to Kelvin, add 273.15 to the Celsius temperature.

See **Celsius** and **Fahrenheit.**

**Kennedy Space Center** See **John F. Kennedy Space Center.**

**Kentucky** Abbrev.: *Ky.* Legally a commonwealth, not a state.

See **state** and **state names.**

**kerosene** Formerly a trademark, now a generic term.

**ketchup** Not *catchup* or *catsup.*

**keynote address** Also: *keynote speech.*

**Keystone Kops**

**KGB** Acceptable on first reference, but the story should contain a phrase identifying it as the Soviet secret police and intelligence agency.

The initials stand for the Russian words meaning *Committee for State Security.*

**kibbutz** An Israeli collective settlement.

The plural is *kibbutzim.*

**kidnap, kidnapped, kidnapping, kidnapper**

**kids** Use *children* unless you are talking about goats, or the use of *kids* as an informal synonym for *children* is appropriate in the context.

**killer** See the **assassin, killer, murderer** entry.

**kilo-** A prefix denoting 1,000 units of a measure. Move a decimal point three places to the right, adding zeros if necessary, to convert to the basic unit: 10.5 kilograms = 10,500 grams.

**kilocycles** The new term is *kilohertz.*

**kilogram** The metric term for 1,000 grams.

A kilogram is equal to approximately 2.2 pounds or 35 ounces.

To convert to pounds, mul-tiply by 2.2 (9 kilograms × 2.2 = 19.8 pounds).

See **gram; metric system;** and **pound.**

**kilohertz** Equals 1,000 hertz (1,000 cycles per second), replacing *kilocycles* as the correct term in applications such as broadcast frequencies.

The official abbreviation *kHz* is acceptable on second reference if clear in the context.

**kilometer** The metric term for 1,000 meters.

A kilometer is equal to approximately 3,281 feet, or five-eighths (0.62) of a mile.

To convert to miles, multiply by 0.62 (5 kilometers × 0.62 = 3.1 miles).

See **meter; metric system;** and **miles.**

**kiloton, kilotonnage** A unit used to measure the power of nuclear explosions. One kiloton has the explosive force of 1,000 tons of TNT.

The atomic bomb dropped Aug. 6, 1945, on Hiroshima, Japan, in the first use of the bomb as a weapon had an explosive force of 20 kilotons.

A *megaton* has the force of a million tons of TNT. A

*gigaton* has the force of a billion tons of TNT.

**kilowatt-hour**　　The amount of electrical energy consumed when 1,000 watts are used for one hour.

The abbreviation *kwh* is acceptable on second reference.

**kindergarten**

**king** Capitalize only when used before the name of royalty: *King George VI.* Continue in subsequent references that use the king's given name: *King George,* not *George.*

Lowercase *king* when it stands alone.

Capitalize in plural uses before names: *Kings George and Edward.*

Lowercase in phrases such as *chess king Bobby Fischer.*

See **nobility** and **titles.**

**Kitty Litter** A brand of absorbent material used in cat litter boxes.

**Klan in America** See **Ku Klux Klan.**

**Kleenex** A trademark for a brand of facial tissue.

**KLM Royal Dutch Airlines** A *KLM airliner* is acceptable in any reference.

Headquarters is in Amsterdam, Netherlands.

**K mart** No hyphen, lowercase *m.* Headquarters is in Troy, Mich.

**Knesset** The Israeli parliament. See **foreign legislative bodies.**

**knickknack**

**knight** See **nobility.**

**Knights of Columbus** *K. of C.* or *the Knights* may be used on second reference.

See the **fraternal organizations and service clubs** entry.

**knot** A knot is one nautical mile (6,076.10 feet) per hour. It is redundant to say *knots per hour.*

A knot is computed as the length of one minute of a meridian. To convert knots into approximate statute miles per hour, multiply knots by 1.15.

Always use figures: *Winds were at 7 to 9 knots; a 10-knot wind.*

See **nautical mile.**

**know-how**

**Kodak** A trademark for cameras and other photographic products made by Eastman Kodak Co. of Rochester, N.Y.

**Koran** The sacred book of Moslems, who believe that it contains the words of Allah dictated to the prophet Mohammed through the angel Gabriel.

**Korean War** But lowercase *Korean conflict.*

**kosher** Always lowercase.

**kowtow**

**Kriss Kringle** Not *Kris.*

**kudos** It means credit or praise for an achievement.
The word takes plural verbs: *Kudos go to John Jones.*

**Ku Klux Klan** There are 42 separate organizations known as the *Klan in America.*
Some of them do not use the full name *Ku Klux Klan,* but each may be called that, and the *KKK* initials may be used for any of them on second reference.
The two largest Klan organizations are the National Knights of the Ku Klux Klan, based at Stone Mountain, Ga., and the United Klans of America, based at Tuscaloosa, Ala.
An Imperial Board, composed of leaders from the various groups, meets occasionally to coordinate activities.
Capitalize formal titles before a name: *Imperial Wizard James R. Venable, Grand Dragon Dale Reusch.* Members are *Klansmen.*

**Kuomintang** The Chinese Nationalist political party. Do not follow with the word *party. Tang* means party.

**Kuril islands** Use in datelines after a community name in stories from these islands. Name an individual island, if needed, in the text.
Explain in the text that the islands are claimed by Japan but have been occupied by the Soviet Union since 1945.

**Kuwait** Stands alone in datelines.

# L

**Ia** See **foreign particles**.

**Labor Day** The first Monday in September.

**Laborers' International Union of North America** The shortened form *Laborers' union* is acceptable in all references.

Headquarters is in Washington.

**Labor Party** Not *labour*, even if British.

**Labrador** The mainland portion of the Canadian province of Newfoundland.

Use *Newfoundland* in datelines after the name of a community. Specify in the text that it is in Labrador.

**Ladies' Home Journal**

**lady** Do not use as a synonym for *woman*. *Lady* may be used when it is a courtesy title or when a specific reference to fine manners is appropriate without patronizing overtones.

See **nobility**.

**Laetrile** A trademark for a substance derived from the chemical amygdalin, found naturally in the pits of apricots and peaches and in bitter almonds. It is believed by some to be an effective cancer treatment. The U.S. Food and Drug Administration has said that the substance has not been proved safe and effective as an anti-cancer agent and has banned it in interstate transportation. Marketed in some areas under the names *Bee-Seventeen* or *Aprikern*.

**lager** (beer)

**lake** Capitalize as part of a proper name: *Lake Erie, Canandaigua Lake, the Finger Lakes.*

Lowercase in plural uses: *lakes Erie and Ontario; Canandaigua and Seneca lakes.*

**lamebrain**

**lame duck** (n.) **lame-duck** (adj.)

**Land-Rover** With a hyphen. A trademark for a brand of all-terrain vehicle.

**languages** Capitalize the proper names of languages and dialects: *Aramaic, Cajun, English, Gullah, Persian, Serbo-Croatian, Yiddish.*

**lanolin** Formerly a trademark, now a generic term.

**larceny** See the **burglary, larceny, robbery, theft** entry.

**last** Avoid the use of last as a synonym for latest if it might imply finality. *The last time it rained, I forgot my umbrella,* is acceptable. But: *The last announcement was made at noon today* may leave the reader wondering whether the announcement was the final announcement, or whether others are to follow.

The word *last* is not necessary to convey the notion of most recent when the name of a month or day is used:
Preferred: *It happened Wednesday. It happened in April.* Correct, but redundant: *It happened last Wednesday.*
But: *It happened last week. It happened last month.*

**Lastex** A trademark for a type of elastic yarn.

**Last Supper**

**late** Do not use it to describe someone's actions while alive.
Wrong: *Only the late senator opposed this bill.* (He was not dead at that time.)

**latex** A resin-based substance used in making elastic materials and paints.

**Latin America** See **Western Hemisphere.**

**Latin Rite** See **Roman Catholic Church.**

**latitude and longitude** *Latitude,* the distance north or south of the equator, is designated by parallels. Longitude, the distance east or west of Greenwich, England, is designated by meridians.
Use these forms to express degrees of latitude and longitude: *New York City lies at 40 degrees 45 minutes north latitude and 74 degrees 0 minutes*

*west longitude; New York City lies south of the 41st parallel north and along the 74th meridian west.*

**Latter Day Saints, Latter-day Saints** See **Church of Jesus Christ of Latter-day Saints.**

**Laundromat** A trademark for a coin-operated laundry.

**Law Enforcement Assistance Administration** *LEAA* is acceptable on second reference.

**laws** Capitalize legislative acts but not bills: *the Taft-Hartley Act, the Kennedy bill.*

**lawsuit**

**lawyer** A generic term for all members of the bar.

An *attorney* is someone legally appointed or empowered to act for another, usually, but not always, a lawyer. An *attorney at law* is a lawyer.

A *barrister* is an English lawyer who is specially trained and appears exclusively as a trial lawyer in higher courts. He is retained by a solicitor, not directly by the client. There is no equivalent term in the United States.

*Counselor,* when used in a legal sense, means a person who conducts a case in court, usually, but not always, a lawyer. A *counselor at law* is a lawyer. *Counsel* frequently is used collectively for a group of counselors.

A *solicitor* in England is a lawyer who performs legal services for the public. A solicitor appears in lower courts but does not have the right to appear in higher courts, which are reserved to barristers.

A *solicitor* in the United States is a lawyer employed by a governmental body. *Solicitor* is generally a job description, but in some agencies it is a formal title.

*Solicitor general* is the formal title for a chief law officer (where there is no attorney general) or for the chief assistant to the law officer (when there is an attorney general). Capitalize when used before a name.

Do not use *lawyer* as a formal title.

See the **attorney, lawyer** entry and **titles.**

**lay, lie** The action word is *lay.* It takes a direct object.

*Laid* is the form for its past tense and its past participle. Its present participle is *laying*.

*Lie* indicates a state of reclining along a horizontal plane. It does not take a direct object. Its past tense is *lay*. Its past participle is *lain*. Its present participle is *lying*.

When *lie* means to make an untrue statement, the verb forms are *lie, lied, lying*.

Some examples:

PRESENT OR FUTURE TENSES:

Right: *I will lay the book on the table. The prosecutor tried to lay the blame on him.*

Wrong: *He lays on the beach all day. I will lay down.*

Right: *He lies on the beach all day. I will lie down.*

IN THE PAST TENSE:

Right: *I laid the book on the table. The prosecutor has laid the blame on him.*

Right: *He lay on the beach all day. He has lain on the beach all day. I lay down. I have lain down.*

WITH THE PRESENT PARTICIPLE:

Right: *I am laying the book on the table. The prosecutor is laying the blame on him.*

Right: *He is lying on the beach. I am lying down.*

**Leaning Tower of Pisa**

**leatherneck** Lowercase this nickname for a member of the U.S. Marine Corps. It is derived from the leather lining that was formerly part of the collar on the Marine uniform.

**lectern, podium, pulpit, rostrum** A speaker stands *behind a lectern, on a podium* or *rostrum,* or *in the pulpit*.

**lecturer** A formal title in the Christian Science Church. An occupational description in other uses.

**lectures** Capitalize and use quotation marks for their formal titles, as described in **composition titles.**

**left hand** (n.) **left-handed** (adj.) **left-hander** (n.)

**leftist, ultra-leftist** In general, avoid these terms in favor of a more precise description of an individual's political philosophy.

As popularly used today, particularly abroad, *leftist*

often applies to someone who is merely liberal or believes in a form of democratic socialism.

*Ultra-leftist* suggests an individual who subscribes to a communist view or one holding that liberal or socialist change cannot come within the present form of government.

See **radical** and the **rightist, ultra-rightist** entry.

**left wing** (n.) But: *left-wing* (adj.), *left-winger* (n.).

**legal holiday** See the **holidays and holy days** entry.

**legerdemain**

**legion, legionnaire** See **American Legion** and **French Foreign legion.**

**Legionnaires' disease** The disease takes its name from an outbreak at the Pennsylvania American Legion convention held at the Bellevue-Stratford Hotel in Philadelphia in July 1976. Thirty-four people died—29 Legionnaires or family members and five other people who had been near the hotel. The disease was diagnosed for the first time after 221 people contracted the illness in Philadelphia.

The bacterium believed to be responsible is found in soil and grows in water, such as air conditioning ducts, storage tanks and rivers.

The Centers for Disease Control in Atlanta estimates that 25,000 people a year in the United States get the disease, whose pneumonia-like symptoms begin two–three days after exposure.

**legislative titles**

FIRST REFERENCE FORM: Use *Rep., Reps., Sen.* and *Sens.* as formal titles before one or more names in regular text. Spell out and capitalize these titles before one or more names in a direct quotation. Spell out and lowercase *representative* and *senator* in other uses.

Spell out other legislative titles in all uses. Capitalize formal titles such as *assemblyman, assemblywoman, city councilor, delegate,* etc., when they are used before a name. Lowercase in other uses.

Add *U.S.* or *state* before a title only if necessary to avoid confusion: *U.S. Sen. Herman*

*Talmadge spoke with state Sen. Hugh Carter.*

**FIRST REFERENCE PRACTICE:** The use of a title such as *Rep.* or *Sen.* in first reference is normal in most stories. It is not mandatory, however, provided an individual's title is given later in the story.

Deletion of the title on first reference is frequently appropriate, for example, when an individual has become well known: *Barry Goldwater endorsed President Ford today. The Arizona senator said he believes the president deserves another term.*

**SECOND REFERENCE:** Do not use legislative titles before a name on second reference unless they are part of a direct quotation.

**CONGRESSMAN, CONGRESSWOMAN:** *Rep.* and *U.S. Rep.* are the preferred first-reference forms when a formal title is used before the name of a U.S. House member. The words *congressman* or *congresswoman,* in lowercase, may be used in subsequent references that do not use an individual's name, just

as *senator* is used in references to members of the Senate.

*Congressman* and *congresswoman* should appear as capitalized formal titles before a name only in direct quotation.

**ORGANIZATIONAL TITLES:** Capitalize titles for formal, organizational offices within a legislative body when they are used before a name: *Speaker Thomas P. O'Neill, Majority Leader Robert C. Byrd, Minority Leader John J. Rhodes, Democratic Whip James C. Wright, Chairman John J. Sparkman of the Senate Foreign Relations Committee, President Pro Tem John C. Stennis.*

See **party affiliation** and **titles.**

**legislature** Capitalize when preceded by the name of a state: *the Kansas Legislature.*

Retain capitalization when the state name is dropped but the reference is specifically to that state's legislature:

*TOPEKA, Kan. (AP)— Both houses of the Legislature adjourned today.*

Capitalize *legislature* in subsequent specific references and in such constructions as:

*the 100th Legislature, the state Legislature.*

Although the word *legislature* is not part of the formal, proper name for the lawmaking bodies in many states, it commonly is used that way and should be treated as such in any story that does not use the formal name.

If a given context or local practice calls for the use of a formal name such as *Missouri General Assembly,* retain the capital letters if the name of the state can be dropped, but lowercase the word *assembly* if it stands alone. Lowercase *legislature* if a story uses it in a subsequent reference to a body identified as a general assembly.

Lowercase *legislature* when used generically: *No legislature has approved the amendment.*

Use *legislature* in lowercase for all plural references: *The Arkansas and Colorado legislatures are considering the amendment.*

In 49 states the separate bodies are a *senate* and a *house* or *assembly.* The *Nebraska Legislature* is a unicameral body.

See **assembly; governmental bodies; general assembly; house of representatives;** and **senate.**

**Lent** The period from Ash Wednesday through Holy Saturday, the day before Easter. The 40-day Lenten period for penance, suggested by Christ's 40 days in the desert, does not include the six Sundays between Ash Wednesday and Easter.

See **Easter** for the method of computing when Easter occurs.

**lesbian, lesbianism** Lowercase in references to homosexual women, except in names of organizations.

**less** See the **fewer, less** entry.

**-less** No hyphen before this suffix:
childless        waterless
tailless

**let up** (v.) **letup** (n. and adj.)

**Levi's** A trademark for a brand of jeans.

**liaison**

**liberal, liberalism** See the **political parties and philosophies** entry.

**lie** See the **lay, lie** entry.

**lie in state** Only people who are entitled to a state funeral may formally lie in state. In the United States, this occurs in the rotunda in the Capitol.

Those entitled to a state funeral are a president, a former president, a president-elect or any other person designated by the president.

Members of Congress may lie in state, and a number have done so. The decision is either house's to make, although the formal process normally begins with a request from the president.

Those entitled to an official funeral, but not to lie in state, are the vice president, the chief justice, Cabinet members and other government officials when designated by the president.

**lieutenant** See **military titles.**

**lieutenant governor** Capitalize and abbreviate as *Lt. Gov.* or *Lt. Govs.* when used as a formal title before one or more names in regular text. Capitalize and spell out when used as a formal title before one or more names in direct quotations.

Lowercase and spell out in all other uses.

See **titles.**

**Life Saver, Life Savers** Trademarks for a brand of roll candy.

**life-size**

**lifestyle** This form, an exception to Webster's New World, has been adopted in keeping with the spelling used by many newspapers.

**lifetime**

**lift off** (v.) **liftoff** (n. and adj.)

**light, lighted, lighting** Do not use *lit* as the past tense form.

**lightning** The electrical discharge.

**light-year** The distance that light travels in one year at the rate of 186,282 miles per second. It works out to about 5.88 trillion miles (5,878,612,800,000 miles).

**likable** Not *likeable*.

**like, as** Use like as a preposition to compare nouns and pronouns. It requires an object: *Jim blocks like a pro.*

The conjunction *as* is the correct word to introduce clauses: *Jim blocks the linebacker as he should.*

**like-** Follow with a hyphen when used as a prefix meaning similar to:

like-minded    like-natured

No hyphen in words that have meanings of their own:

likelihood    likewise
likeness

**-like** Do not precede this suffix by a hyphen unless the letter *l* would be tripled:

bill-like    lifelike
businesslike    shell-like

**limousine**

**linage, lineage** *Linage* is the number of lines.

*Lineage* is ancestry or descent.

**Lincoln's Birthday** Capitalize *birthday* in references to the holiday.

Lincoln was born Feb. 12. His birthday is not a federal legal holiday.

**line numbers** Use figures and lowercase the word line in naming individual lines of a text: *line 1, line 9.* But: *the first line, the 10th line.*

**linoleum** Formerly a trademark, now a generic term.

**Linotype** A trademark for a brand of typesetting machine that casts an entire line of type in one bar or slug.

**lion's share** The term comes from an Aesop fable in which the lion took all the spoils of a joint hunt.

Use it to mean the whole of something, or the best and biggest portion.

Do not use it to mean majority.

**liter** The basic unit of volume in the metric system. It is defined as the volume occupied by one kilogram of distilled water at 4 degrees Celsius. It works out to a total of 1,000 cubic centimeters (one cubic decimeter).

It takes 1,000 milliliters to make a liter.

A liter is equal to approximately 34 fluid ounces or 1.06 liquid quarts. A liter equals .91 of a dry quart. The metric system makes no distinction between dry volume and liquid volume.

To convert to liquid quarts, multiply by 1.06 (4 liters × 1.06 = 4.24 liquid quarts).

To convert to dry quarts, multiply by .91 (4 liters × .91 = 3.64 dry quarts).

To convert to liquid gallons, multiply by .26 (8 liters × .26 = 2.08 gallons).

See **gallon; kilogram; metric system; quart (dry);** and **quart (fluid).**

**literally** See the **figuratively, literally** entry.

**literature** See **composition titles.**

**livable** Not *liveable.*

**livid** It is not a synonym for *fiery, bright, crimson, red* or *flaming.* If a person turns *livid* with rage, his face becomes ashen or pale. It can mean *blue, bluish gray, gray, dull white, dull purple* or *grayish black.*

**Lloyds Bank International Ltd.** A prominent bank with headquarters in London.

**Lloyd's of London** A prominent group of insurance companies with headquarters in London.

**Lloyd's Register of Shipping** The reference source for questions about non-military ships not covered in this book.

It is published by Lloyd's Register of Shipping Trust Corp. Ltd. in London.

**local** Avoid the irrelevant use of the word.

Irrelevant: *The injured were taken to a local hospital.*

Better: *The injured were taken to a hospital.*

**local of a union** Always use a figure and capitalize *local* when giving the name of a union subdivision: *Local 222 of The Newspaper Guild.*

Lowercase *local* standing alone or in plural uses: *The local will vote Tuesday. He spoke to locals 2, 4 and 10.*

**Lockheed Aircraft Corp.** Headquarters is in Burbank, Calif.

**lodges** See the **fraternal organizations and service clubs** entry.

**London** The city in England stands alone in datelines.

**long distance, long-distance** Always a hyphen in reference to telephone calls: *We keep in touch by long-distance. He called long-distance. She took the long-distance call.*

In other uses, hyphenate only when used as a compound modifier: *She traveled a long distance. She made a long-distance trip.*

**longitude** See the **latitude and longitude** entry.

**longshoreman** Capitalize *longshoreman* only if the intended meaning is that the individual is a member of the International Longshoremen's and Warehousemen's Union or the International Longshoremen's Association.

**long term, long-term** Hyphenate when used as a compound modifier: *We will win in the long term. He has a long-term assignment.*

**long time, longtime** *They have known each other a long time. They are longtime partners.*

**long ton** Also known as a *British ton.* Equal to 2,240 pounds. See **ton.**

**Lord's Supper** See **sacraments.**

**Los Angeles** The city in California stands alone in datelines.

Confine *LA* to quoted matter.

**LOT Polish Airlines** Headquarters is in Warsaw, Poland.

**Louisiana** Abbrev.: *La.* See **state names.**

**Low Countries** Belgium, Luxembourg and Netherlands.

**lowercase** One word (n., v., adj.) when referring to the absence of capital letters. An exception to Webster's New World, in keeping with printers' practice.

**LSD** Acceptable in all references for *lysergic acid diethylamide.*

**Lt. Gov.** See **lieutenant governor.**

**Lucite** A trademark for an acrylic plastic.

**Lufthansa German Airlines** A *Lufthansa airliner* is acceptable in any reference.

Headquarters is in Cologne, West Germany.

**Lutheran churches** The basic unit of government in Lutheran practice is the congregation. It normally is administered by a council, headed either by the senior pastor or a lay person elected from the membership of the council. The council customarily consists of a congregation's clergy and elected lay persons.

National church bodies are made up of congregations and governed by conventions. Congregations are grouped into territorial districts or synods whose functions vary. The term *synod* also is used in the names of some national bodies.

The Lutheran Church in America is the largest of three major Lutheran bodies in the United States. Of the three, it takes the least rigid or literalistic stand on doctrine and Bi-

ble interpretation. Formed in 1962 from a merger of four bodies with Danish, Finnish, German and Swedish backgrounds, it has almost 3 million members.

The Lutheran Church-Missouri Synod, with about 2.7 million members, is regarded as the most conservative of the three bodies. A split has developed within the synod over the question of Bible interpretation and synod leadership. Its background is predominantly German.

The American Lutheran Church, with some 2.4 million members, generally is regarded as middle-of-the-road in doctrinal emphasis. It was formed in 1960 through a merger of four bodies with Danish, German and Norwegian backgrounds.

All three bodies are members of the New York-based Lutheran Council in the U.S.A., which coordinates various joint activities.

BELIEFS: Lutheran teachings go back to Martin Luther, a 16th-century Roman Catholic priest whose objections to elements of Roman Catholic practice began the movement known as the Protestant Reformation.

Lutherans believe in the Trinity and emphasize both the divinity and humanity of Christ. There are two sacraments, baptism and the Lord's Supper.

In recent years, the question of Bible interpretation has divided Lutherans into "moderate" and "conservative" camps. Conservatives argue for a literal interpretation of passages others consider symbolic. Moderates argue that some truths in the Bible are expressed in allegories.

CLERGY: Members of the clergy are known as *ministers*. *Pastor* applies if a minister leads a congregation.

On first reference, use *the Rev.* before the name of a man or woman. On second reference, use only the last name of a man; use *Miss, Mrs., Ms.* or no title before the last name of a woman, depending on her preference.

In the American Lutheran Church, the president and district presidents are often referred to as bishops. Use *Bishop* before such an individual's name on first reference.

See **religious titles.**

OTHER OFFICIALS: Lay members of a church council frequently are designated *elders, deacons* or *trustees.* The preferred form for identifying them is a construction that requires commas to set their names off from these titles. Capitalize *elder, deacon* or *trustee* when used before a name on first reference. On second reference, use only the last name of a man; use *Miss, Mrs., Ms.* or no title before the last name of a woman, depending on her preference.

**Luxembourg** Stands alone in datelines.

**-ly** Do not use a hyphen between adverbs ending in *-ly* and adjectives they modify: *an easily remembered rule, a badly damaged island, a fully informed woman.*

See the *compound modifiers* section of the **hyphen** entry in **Punctuation** chapter.

**Lyndon B. Johnson Space Center** Formerly the Manned Spacecraft Center. Located in Houston, it is the National Aeronautics and Space Administration's principal control and training center for manned spaceflight.

*Johnson Space Center* is acceptable in all references.

In datelines:

*SPACE CENTER, Houston (AP)—*

See **John F. Kennedy Space Center.**

# M

**Macao** Stands alone in datelines.

**Mace** A trademark, shortened from *Chemical Mace,* for a brand of tear gas that is packaged in an aerosol canister and temporarily stuns its victims.

**machine gun** (n.) But: *machine-gun* (v. and adj.), *machine-gunner.*
See **weapons.**

**Mach number** Named for Ernst Mach, an Austrian physicist, the figure represents the ratio of the speed of an object to the speed of sound in the surrounding medium, such as air, through which the object is moving.

A rule of thumb for speed of sound is approximately 750 miles per hour at sea level and approximately 660 miles per hour at 30,000 feet above sea level.

A body traveling at *Mach 1* would be traveling at the speed of sound. *Mach 2* would equal twice the speed of sound.

**Mafia, Mafiosi** The secret society of criminals and its members. Do not use as a synonym for *organized crime* or *the underworld.*

**magazine names** Capitalize the name but do not place it in quotes. Lowercase *magazine* unless it is part of the publication's formal title: *Harper's Magazine, Newsweek magazine, Time magazine.*
Check the masthead if in doubt.

**magistrate** Capitalize when used as a formal title before a name. See **titles.**

**Magna Carta** Not Magna Charta. An exception to Webster's. The charter the English barons forced King John of England to grant at Runnymede in June 1215. It guaranteed certain civil and political liberties.

**Mailgram** A trademark for a telegram sent to a post office near the recipient's address and delivered to the address by letter carrier.

**mailman** Letter carrier is preferable because many women hold this job.

**Maine** Do not abbreviate. See **state names.**

**mainland China** See **China.**

**major** See **military titles.**

**Majorca** Use instead of Spain in datelines on stories from communities on this island.

**majority, plurality** *Majority* means more than half of an amount.
*Plurality* means more than the next highest number.

COMPUTING MAJORITY: To describe how large a majority is, take the figure that is more than half and subtract everything else from it: If 100,000 votes were cast in an election and one candi-

date received 60,000 while opponents received 40,000, the winner would have a *majority* of 20,000 votes.

COMPUTING PLURALITY: To describe how large a plurality is, take the highest number and subtract from it the next highest number: If, in the election example above, the second-place finisher had 25,000 votes, the winner's *plurality* would be 35,000 votes.

Suppose, however, that no candidate in this example had a majority. If the first-place finisher had 40,000 votes and the second-place finisher had 30,000, for example, the leader's *plurality* would be 10,000 votes.

USAGE: When *majority* and *plurality* are used alone, they take singular verbs and pronouns: *The majority has made its decision.*

If a plural word follows an *of* construction, the decision on whether to use a singular or plural verb depends on the sense of the sentence: *A majority of two votes is not adequate to control the committee. The majority of the houses on the block were destroyed.*

**majority leader** Capitalize when used as a formal title before a name: *Majority Leader Robert C. Byrd.* Lowercase elsewhere.

See **legislative titles** and **titles.**

**make up** (v.) **makeup** (n., adj.)

**malarkey** Not *malarky.*

**Maldives** Use this official name with a community name in a dateline. The body of the story should note that the nation frequently is called the *Maldive Islands.*

**man, mankind** Either may be used when both men and women are involved and no other term is convenient. In these cases, do not use duplicate phrases such as *a man or a woman* or *mankind and womankind.*

Frequently the best choice is a substitute such as *humanity, a person* or *an individual.*

See **women.**

**manageable**

**manager** Capitalize when used as a formal title before a name: *Manager Casey Sten-gel, General Manager Dick O'Connell.*

Do not capitalize in job descriptions such as *equipment manager John Smith.*

See **titles.**

**managing editor** Capitalize when used as a formal title before a name.

See **titles.**

**Manitoba** A province of central Canada. Do not abbreviate.

See **datelines.**

**manslaughter** See the **homicide, murder, manslaughter** entry.

**mantel, mantle** A *mantel* is a shelf. A *mantle* is a cloak.

**Maoism (Maoist)** The communist philosophy and policies of Mao Tse-tung. See the **political parties and philosophies** entry.

**March** See **months.**

**Mardi Gras** Literally "fat Tuesday," the term describes a day of merrymaking on the Tuesday before Ash Wednesday.

In New Orleans and many Roman Catholic countries,

the Tuesday celebration is preceded by a week or more of parades and parties.

**marijuana** Not *marihuana*.

**Marines** Capitalize when referring to U.S. forces: *the U.S. Marines, the Marines, the Marine Corps, Marine regulations*. Do not use the abbreviation *USMC*.

Capitalize *Marine* when referring to an individual in a Marine Corps unit: *He is a Marine*.

**Maritime Provinces** The Canadian provinces of Nova Scotia, New Brunswick and Prince Edward Island.

**marketbasket, marketplace**

**marquess, marchioness, marquis, marquise** See **nobility**.

**marshal, marshaled, marshaling, Marshall** *Marshal* is the spelling for both the verb and the noun: *Marilyn will marshal her forces. Erwin Rommel was a field marshal.*

*Marshall* is used in proper names: *George C. Marshall,* *John Marshall, the Marshall Islands.*

**Marshall Islands** Named for John Marshall, a British explorer.

In datelines, give the name of a city and *Marshall Islands*. List the name of an individual island in the text.

**Marxism (Marxist)** The system of thought developed by Karl Marx and Friedrich Engels. See the **political parties and philosophies entry.**

**Maryland** Abbrev.: *Md.* See **state names.**

**Mason-Dixon Line** The boundary line between Pennsylvania and Maryland, generally regarded as separating the North from the South.

**Masonite** A trademark for a brand of hardboard.

**Mass** It is *celebrated, said* or *sung*. Always capitalize when referring to the ceremony, but lowercase any preceding adjectives: *high Mass, low Mass, requiem Mass.*

In Eastern Orthodox churches the correct term is *Divine Liturgy.*

See **Roman Catholic Church.**

**Massachusetts** Abbrev.: *Mass.* Legally a commonwealth, not a state.

See **state** and **state names.**

**master of arts, master of science** A *master's degree* or a *master's* is acceptable in any reference.

See **academic degrees** for guidelines on when the abbreviations *M.A.* and *M.S.* are acceptable.

**matrimony** See **sacraments.**

**maturity** In a financial sense, the date on which a bond, debenture or note must be repaid.

See **loan terminology** in Business Guidelines.

**May** See **months.**

**May Day, mayday** *May Day* is May 1, often observed as a festive or political holiday.

*Mayday* is the international distress signal, from the French *m'aidez,* meaning "help me."

**mayors' conference** See **U.S. Conference of Mayors.**

**MC** For *master of ceremonies,* but only in quoted matter. See **emcee.**

**McDonnell Douglas Corp.** Headquarters is in St. Louis.

**M.D.** A word such as *physician* or *surgeon* is preferred.

See **doctor** and **academic titles.**

**meager**

**mean** See the **average, mean, median, norm** entry.

**Medal of Freedom** It is now the *Presidential Medal of Freedom.* See entry under that name.

**Medal of Honor** The nation's highest military honor, given by Congress for risk of life in combat beyond the call on duty.

There is no *Congressional Medal of Honor.*

**media** In the sense of mass communication, such as magazines, newspapers, the news services, radio and television, the word is plural: *The news media are resisting attempts to limit their freedom.*

**median** See the **average, mean, median, norm** entry.

**mediate** See the **arbitrate, mediate** entry.

**Medicaid** A federal-state program that helps pay for health care for the needy, aged, blind and disabled, and for low-income families with children.

A state determines eligibility and which health services are covered. The federal government reimburses a percentage of the state's expenditures.

**Medicare** The federal health care insurance program for people aged 65 and over, and for the disabled. Eligibility is based mainly on eligibility for Social Security.

Medicare helps pay charges for hospitalization, for stays in skilled nursing facilities, for physician's charges and for some associated health costs. There are limitations on the length of stay and type of care.

In Canada, *Medicare* refers to the nation's national health insurance program.

**medicine** See the **drugs, medicine** entry.

**medieval**

**mega-** A prefix denoting 1 million units of a measure. Move a decimal point six places to the right, adding zeros if necessary, to convert to the basic unit: 5.5 megatons = 5,500,000 tons.

**melee**

**Melkite Church** See **Eastern Rite churches.**

**memento, mementos**

**memo, memos**

**memorandum, memorandums**

**Memorial Day** Formerly May 30. The federal legal holiday is the last Monday in May.

**menage a trois**

**menswear** Not *men's wear.*

**Mercalli scale** See **earthquakes.**

**Mercurochrome** A trademark for a brand of antiseptic for wounds.

**meridians** Use numerals and lowercase to identify the imaginary locater lines that ring the globe from north to south through the poles. They are measured in units of 0 to 180 degrees east and west of the *prime meridian,* which runs through Greenwich, England.

Examples: *33rd meridian* (if location east or west of Greenwich is obvious), *1st meridian west, 100th meridian.*

See the **latitude and longitude** entry.

**merry-go-round**

**messiah** Capitalize in religious uses. Lowercase when used generically to mean a liberator.

**meter** The basic unit of length in the metric system. It is defined as being equal to 1,650,763.73 wavelengths of the orange-red radiation of an isotope of krypton.

It is equal to approximately 39.37 inches, which may be rounded off to 39.5 inches in most comparisons.

It takes 100 centimeters to make a meter.

It takes 1,000 meters to make a kilometer.

To convert to inches, multiply by 39.37 (5 meters × 39.37 = 196.85 inches).

To convert to yards, multiply by 1.1 (5 meters × 1.1 = 5.5 yards).

See **inch; metric system;** and **yards.**

**Methodist churches** The term *Methodist* originated as a nickname applied to a group of 18th-century Oxford University students known for their methodical application to Scripture study and prayer.

The principal Methodist body in the United States is the United Methodist Church, which also has some member conferences outside the United States. It was formed in 1968 by the merger of the Methodist Church and the Evangelical United Brethren church. It has about 10 million members.

The government of the United Methodist Church follows a stratified pattern from the General Conference through several intermediate conferences down to the local congregation.

The General Conference, which meets every four years, has final authority in all matters. Its members, half lay and half clergy, are elected by the annual conferences.

Jurisdictional conferences covering major sections of the nation are composed of ministers and lay delegates. Their principal function is to elect bishops.

Annual conferences, generally organized along state lines, elect delegates to higher conferences and make official appointments within their areas.

A Methodist bishop presides over a "church area," which may embrace one or more annual conferences. Bishops have extensive administrative powers, including the authority to place, transfer and remove local church pastors, usually in consultation with district superintendents.

Districts in each conference are responsible for promotion of mission work, support of colleges, hospitals and publications, and examination of candidates for the ministry.

Members of a congregation form a charge conference. It elects officers to a board that assists the pastor.

Methodism in the United States also includes three major black denominations: the African Methodist Episcopal Church, the African Methodist Episcopal Zion Church and the Christian Methodist Episcopal Church.

BELIEFS: Methodist teachings emphasize that the Holy Scriptures contain all the knowledge necessary for salvation. Tradition is not acknowledged as a valid source of revelation, although the writings of John Wesley, a leader of the Oxford University group, are regarded as sound interpretations of the Scriptures.

Methodists believe in the Trinity and the humanity and divinity of Christ. There are two sacraments, baptism and the Lord's Supper.

CLERGY: Ordained individuals are known as *bishops* and *ministers. Pastor* applies if a minister leads a congregation.

For first references to bishops use the word: *Bishop W. Kenneth Goodson of Richmond, Va.* The designations *the Most Rev.* or *the Rt. Rev.* do not apply.

For first reference to ministers, use *the Rev.* before the name of a man or woman. On second reference, use only the last name of a man; use *Miss, Mrs., Ms.* or no title before the last name of a woman depending on her preference.

See **religious titles.**

**metric system** In general, metric terms should be included in a story when they are relevant.

There are no hard-and-fast rules on when they are relevant, but the following two guidelines have been developed to cover questions likely to arise as metric measurements gain increased acceptance in the United States:

—Use metric terms when they are the primary form in which the source of a story has provided statistics. Follow the metric units with equivalents in the terms more widely known in the United States. Normally, the equivalent should be in parentheses after the metric figure. A general statement such as: *A kilometer equals about five-eighths of a mile,* would be acceptable, however, to avoid repeated use of parenthetical

equivalents in a story that uses kilometers many times.

—Provide metric equivalents for traditional forms if a metric unit has become widely known. As speedometers with kilometer markings become more prevalent, for example, a story about speed limits might list miles per hour and provide kilometers per hour in parentheses.

CONVERSION FORMULAS: A conversion table for frequently used metric terms follows.

In addition, separate entries for **gram, meter, liter, Celsius** and other frequently used metric units define them and give examples of how to convert them to equivalents in the terminology that has been used in the United States.

Similarly, entries for **pound, inch, quart, Fahrenheit,** etc., contain examples of how to convert these terms to metric forms.

To avoid the need for long strings of figures, prefixes are added to the metric units to denote fractional elements or large multiples. The prefixes are: *pico-* (one-trillionth), *nano-* (one-billionth), *micro-* (one-millionth), *milli-* (one-thousandth), *centi-* (one-hundredth), *deci-* (one-tenth), *deka-* (10 units), *hecto-* (100 units), *giga-* (1 billion units), *tera-* (1 trillion units). Entries for each prefix show how to convert a unit preceded by the prefix to the basic unit.

ABBREVIATIONS: The abbreviation *mm* for millimeter is acceptable in references to film widths *(8 mm film)* and weapons *(1 105mm cannon).*

Do not otherwise use metric abbreviations in news copy.

The principal abbreviations, for reference in the event they are used by a source, are: *g* (gram), *kg* (kilogram), *t* (metric ton), *m* (meter), *cm* (centimeter), *km* (kilometer), *mm* (millimeter), *L* (liter, capital *L* to avoid confusion with the figure *1),* and *mL* (milliliter).

**metric ton** Equal to approximately 2,204.62 pounds. See **ton.**

**Metro-Goldwyn-Mayer Inc.** *MGM* is acceptable in all references.

Headquarters is in Culver City, Calif.

**Mexico City** The city in Mexico stands alone in datelines.

**Miami** The city in Florida stands alone in datelines.

**Michigan** Abbrev.: *Mich.* See **state names.**

**micro-** A prefix denoting one-millionth of a unit.

Move a decimal point six places to the left in converting to the basic unit: 2,999,888.5 microseconds = 2.9998885 seconds.

**mid-** No hyphen unless a capitalized word follows:

| | |
|---|---|
| mid-America | midsemester |
| mid-Atlantic | midterm |

But use a hyphen when *mid-* precedes a figure: *mid-30s.*

**Middle Ages** A.D. 476 to approximately A.D. 1450.

**Middle Atlantic States** As defined by the U.S. Census Bureau, they are New Jersey, New York and Pennsylvania.

Less formal references often consider Delaware part of the group.

See **Northeast region.**

# METRIC CONVERSION CHART

## INTO METRIC

| If You Know | Multiply By | To get |
|---|---|---|
| **LENGTH** | | |
| inches | 2.54 | centimeters |
| feet | 30 | centimeters |
| yards | 0.91 | meters |
| miles | 1.6 | kilometers |
| **AREA** | | |
| sq. inches | 6.5 | sq. centimeters |
| sq. feet | 0.09 | sq. meters |
| sq. yards | 0.8 | sq. meters |
| sq. miles | 2.6 | sq. kilometers |
| acres | 0.4 | hectares |
| **MASS (Weight)** | | |
| ounces | 28 | grams |
| pounds | 0.45 | kilograms |
| short ton | 0.9 | metric ton |
| **VOLUME** | | |
| teaspoons | 5 | milliliters |
| tablespoons | 15 | milliliters |
| fluid ounces | 30 | milliliters |
| cups | 0.24 | liters |
| pints | 0.47 | liters |
| quarts | 0.95 | liters |
| gallons | 3.8 | liters |
| cubic feet | 0.03 | cubic meters |
| cubic yards | 0.76 | cubic meters |
| **TEMPERATURE** | | |
| Fahrenheit | Subtract 32 then multiply by 5/9ths | Celsius |

## OUT OF METRIC

| If You Know | Multiply By | To get |
|---|---|---|
| **LENGTH** | | |
| millimeters | 0.04 | inches |
| centimeters | 0.4 | inches |
| meters | 3.3 | feet |
| kilometers | 0.62 | miles |
| **AREA** | | |
| sq. centimeters | 0.16 | sq. inches |
| sq. meters | 1.2 | sq. yards |
| sq. kilometers | 0.4 | sq. miles |
| hectares | 2.47 | acres |
| **MASS (Weight)** | | |
| grams | 0.035 | ounces |
| kilograms | 2.2 | pounds |
| metric tons | 1.1 | short tons |
| **VOLUME** | | |
| milliliters | 0.03 | fluid ounces |
| liters | 2.1 | pints |
| liters | 1.06 | quarts |
| liters | 0.26 | gallons |
| cubic meters | 35 | cubic feet |
| cubic meters | 1.3 | cubic yards |
| **TEMPERATURE** | | |
| Celsius | Multiply by 9/5ths, then add 32 | Fahrenheit |

**middle class, middle-class** *He is a member of the middle class. She has middle-class values.*

**Middle East** The term applies to southwest Asia west of Pakistan (Afghanistan, Iran, Iraq, Israel, Kuwait, Jordan, Lebanon, Oman, Qatar, Saudi Arabia, South Yemen, Syria, Turkey, United Arab Emirates and Yemen), northeastern Africa (Egypt and Sudan), and the island of Cyprus.

Popular usage once distinguished between the *Near East* (the westerly nations in the listing) and the *Middle East* (the easterly nations), but the two terms now overlap, with current practice favoring *Middle East* for both areas.

Use *Middle East* unless *Near East* is used by a source in a story.

*Mideast* is also acceptable, but *Middle East* is preferred.

**middle initials** In general, use them. They are an integral part of a person's name.

Particular care should be taken to include middle initials in stories where they help identify a specific individual.

Examples include casualty lists and stories naming the accused in a crime.

A middle initial may be dropped if a person does not use one or is publicly known without it: *Mickey Mantle* (not *Mickey C.*), *the Rev. Billy Graham* (not *Billy F.*).

See **names.**

**middleman**

**Middle West** Definitions vary, but the term generally applies to the 12 states that the U.S. Census Bureau includes in the North Central region. See **North Central region.**

The shortened form *Midwest* is acceptable in all references.

The forms for adjectives are *Middle Western, Midwestern.*

See the **directions and regions** entry.

**midnight** Do not put a *12* in front of it. It is part of the day that is ending, not the one that is beginning.

**midshipman** See **military academies.**

**MiG** The *i* in this designation for a type of Soviet fighter is lowercase because it is the Russian word for *and*. The initials are from the last names of the designers, Arten Mikovan and Mikhail Gurevich.

The forms: *MiG-19, MiG-21s.*

See **aircraft names.**

**mile** Also called a statute mile, it equals 5,280 feet.

The metric equivalent is approximately 1.6 kilometers.

To convert to kilometers, multiply by 1.6 (5 miles × 1.6 = 8 kilometers).

See **foot; kilometer; knot;** and **nautical mile.**

Use figures for amounts under 10 in dimensions, formulas and speeds: *The farm measures 5 miles by 4 miles. The car slowed to 7 mph. The new model gets 4 miles more per gallon.*

Spell out below 10 in distances: *He drove four miles.*

**miles per gallon** The abbreviation *mpg* (no periods) is acceptable on second reference.

**miles per hour** The abbreviation *mph* (no periods) is acceptable in all references.

**military academies** Capitalize *U.S. Air Force Academy, U.S. Coast Guard Academy, U.S. Military Academy, U.S. Naval Academy.* Retain capitalization if the *U.S.* is dropped: *the Air Force Academy,* etc.

Lowercase *academy* whenever it stands alone.

*Cadet* is the proper title on first reference for men and women enrolled at the Army, Air Force and Coast Guard academies. *Midshipman* is the proper title for men and women enrolled at the Naval Academy.

Use the appropriate title on first reference. On second reference to a man, use his last name; on second reference to a woman, use *Miss, Mrs., Ms.* or no title before her last name depending on her preference.

**military titles** Capitalize a military rank when used as a formal title before an individual's name.

See the lists that follow to determine whether the title should be spelled out or abbreviated in regular text. Spell out any title used before a name in a direct quotation.

On first reference, use the appropriate title before the full name of a member of the military.

In subsequent references, do not continue using the title before a name. Use only the last name of a man. Use *Miss, Mrs., Ms.* or no title before the last name of a woman depending on her preference.

Spell out and lowercase a title when it is substituted for a name: *Gen. John J. Pershing arrived today. An aide said the general would review the troops.*

In some cases, it may be necessary to explain the significance of a title: *Army Sgt. Maj. John Jones described the attack. Jones, who holds the Army's highest rank for enlisted men, said it was unprovoked.*

In addition to the ranks listed here, each service has ratings such as *machinist, radarman, torpedoman,* etc., that are job descriptions. Do not use any of these designations as a title on first reference. If one is used before a name in a subsequent reference, do not capitalize or abbreviate it.

ABBREVIATIONS: The abbreviations, with the highest ranks listed first:

## MILITARY TITLES

| Rank | Usage before a name |
|------|---------------------|

### ARMY

#### Commissioned Officers

| | |
|------|---------------------|
| general | Gen. |
| lieutenant general | Lt. Gen. |
| major general | Maj. Gen. |
| brigadier general | Brig. Gen. |
| colonel | Col. |
| lieutenant colonel | Lt. Col. |
| major | Maj. |
| captain | Capt. |
| first lieutenant | 1st Lt. |
| second lieutenant | 2nd Lt. |

#### Warrant Officers

| | |
|------|---------------------|
| chief warrant officer | Chief Warrant Officer |
| warrant officer | Warrant Officer |

#### Enlisted Personnel

| | |
|------|---------------------|
| sergeant major of the Army | Army Sgt. Maj. |
| command sergeant major | Command Sgt. Maj. |
| staff sergeant major | Staff Sgt. Maj. |
| first sergeant | 1st Sgt. |
| master sergeant | Master Sgt. |
| platoon sergeant | Platoon Sgt. |
| sergeant first class | Sgt. 1st Class |
| specialist seven | Spec. 7 |
| staff sergeant | Staff Sgt. |
| specialist six | Spec. 6 |

| | |
|---|---|
| sergeant | Sgt. |
| specialist five | Spec. 5 |
| corporal | Cpl. |
| specialist four | Spec. 4 |
| private first class | Pfc. |
| private 2 | Pvt. 2 |
| private 1 | Pvt. 1 |

## NAVY, COAST GUARD

### Commissioned Officers

| | |
|---|---|
| admiral | Adm. |
| vice admiral | Vice Adm. |
| rear admiral | Rear Adm. |
| commodore | Commodore |
| captain | Capt. |
| commander | Cmdr. |
| lieutenant commander | Lt. Cmdr. |
| lieutenant | Lt. |
| lieutenant junior grade | Lt. j.g. |
| ensign | Ensign |

### Warrant Officers

| | |
|---|---|
| chief warrant officer | Chief Warrant Officer |
| warrant officer | Warrant Officer |

### Enlisted Personnel

| | |
|---|---|
| master chief petty officer | Master Chief Petty Officer |
| senior chief petty officer | Senior Chief Petty Officer |
| chief petty officer | Chief Petty Officer |
| petty officer first class | Petty Officer 1st Class |
| petty officer second class | Petty Officer 2nd Class |
| petty officer third class | Petty Officer 3rd Class |
| seaman | Seaman |
| seaman apprentice | Seaman Apprentice |
| seaman recruit | Seaman Recruit |

## MARINE CORPS

Ranks and abbreviations for commissioned officers are the same as those in the Army. Warrant officer ratings follow the same system used in the Navy. There are no specialist ratings.

### Others

| | |
|---|---|
| sergeant major | Sgt. Maj. |
| master gunnery sergeant | Master Gunnery Sgt. |
| master sergeant | Master Sgt. |
| first sergeant | 1st Sgt. |
| gunnery sergeant | Gunnery Sgt. |
| staff sergeant | Staff Sgt. |
| sergeant | Sgt. |
| corporal | Cpl. |
| lance corporal | Lance Cpl. |
| private first class | Pfc. |
| private | Pvt. |

## AIR FORCE

Ranks and abbreviations for commissioned officers are the same as those in the Army.

## Enlisted Designations

| | |
|---|---|
| chief master sergeant of the Air Force | Chief Master Sgt. of the Air Force |
| senior master sergeant | Senior Master Sgt. |
| master sergeant | Master Sgt. |
| technical sergeant | Tech. Sgt. |
| staff sergeant | Staff Sgt. |
| sergeant | Sgt. |
| senior airman | Senior Airman |
| airman first class | Airman 1st Class |
| airman | Airman |
| airman basic | Airman |

PLURALS: Add *s* to the principal element in the title: *Majs. John Jones and Robert Smith; Maj. Gens. John Jones and Robert Smith; Specs. 4 John Jones and Robert Smith.*

RETIRED OFFICERS: A military rank may be used in first reference before the name of an officer who has retired if it is relevant to a story. Do not, however, use the military abbreviation *Ret.*

Instead, use *retired* just as *former* would be used before the title of a civilian: *They invited retired Army Gen. John Smith.*

FIREFIGHTERS, PO-LICE OFFICERS: Use the abbreviations listed here when a military-style title is used before the name of a firefighter or police officer outside a direct quotation. Add *police* or *fire* before the title if needed for clarity: *police Sgt. William Smith, fire Capt. David Jones.*

Spell out titles such as *detective* that are not used in the armed forces.

**military units** Use Arabic figures and capitalize the key words when linked with the figures: *1st Infantry Division* (or *the 1st Division*), *5th Battalion, 395th Field Artillery, 7th Fleet.*

But: *the division, the battalion, the artillery, the fleet.*

**milli-** A prefix denoting one-thousandth of a unit. Move a decimal three places to the left in converting to the basic unit: 1,567.5 millimeters = 1.5675 meters.

**milligram** One-thousandth of a gram.

Equal to approximately twenty-eight-thousandths of an ounce.

To convert to ounces, multiply by 0.000035 (140 milligrams × 0.000035 = 0.0049 ounces).

See **metric system.**

**milliliter** One-thousandth of a liter.

Equal to approximately one-fifth of a teaspoon.

Thirty milliliters equal one fluid ounce.

To convert to teaspoons, multiply by .2 (5 milliliters × .2 = 1 teaspoon).

See **liter** and **metric system.**

**millimeter** One-thousandth of a meter.

It takes 10 millimeters to make a centimeter.

A millimeter is roughly equal to the thickness of a paper clip.

To convert to inches, multiply by .04 (5 millimeters × .04 = .2 of an inch).

May be abbreviated as *mm* (no space) when used with a numeral in first or subsequent references to film or weapons: *35mm film, 105mm artillery piece.*

See **meter; metric system;** and **inch.**

**millions, billions** Use figures with *million* or *billion* in all except casual uses: *I'd like to make a billion dollars.* But: *The nation has 1 million citizens. I need $7 billion.*

Do not go beyond two decimals: *7.51 million persons, $2.56 billion, 7,542,500 persons, $2,565,750,000.* Decimals are preferred where practical: *1.5 million.* Not: *1½ million.*

Do not mix *millions* and *billions* in the same figure: *2.6 billion.* Not: *2 billion 600 million.*

Do not drop the word *million* or *billion* in the first figure of a range: *He is worth from $2 million to $4 million.* Not: *$2 to $4 million,* unless you really mean $2.

Note that a hyphen is not used to join the figures and the word *million* or *billion,* even in this type of phrase: *The president submitted a $300 billion budget.*

**milquetoast** Not *milk toast* when referring to a shrinking, apologetic person. Derived from Caspar Milquetoast, a character in a comic strip by H.T. Webster.

**Milwaukee** The city in Wisconsin stands alone in datelines.

**mimeograph** Formerly a trademark, now a generic term.

**mini-** The rules in prefixes apply, but in general, no hyphen. Some examples:

minibus          miniskirt
miniseries

**minister** It is not a formal title. Do not use it before the name of a member of the clergy.

See **religious titles** and the entry for an individual's denomination.

**ministry** See **foreign governmental bodies.**

**Minneapolis** The city in Minnesota stands alone in datelines.

**Minnesota** Abbrev.: *Minn.* See **state names.**

**Minnesota Mining & Manufacturing** Its products are known under the names *3M* and *Scotch*. The company is popularly known as *3M*.

Headquarters is in St. Paul, Minn.

**minority leader** Treat the same as *majority leader*. See that entry and **legislative titles.**

**minuscule** Not *miniscule*.

**minus sign** Use a hyphen, not a dash, but use the word *minus* if there is any danger of confusion.

Use a word, not a minus sign, to indicate temperatures below zero: *minus 10* or *5 below zero.*

**MIRV, MIRVs** Acceptable on first reference for *multiple independently targetable reentry vehicle(s)*.

Explain in the text that an *MIRV* is an intercontinental ballistic missile with several warheads, each of which can be directed to a different target.

**misdemeanor** See the **felony, misdemeanor** entry.

**mishap** A minor misfortune. People are not killed in *mishaps*.

**Miss** See **courtesy titles.**

**missile names** Use Arabic figures and capitalize the proper name but not the word *missile: Pershing 2 missile*.

See **ABM; ICBM; MIRV;** and **SAM.**

**Mississippi**  Abbrev.: *Miss.* See **state names.**

**Missouri**  Abbrev.: *Mo.* See **state names.**

**mix up** (v.)  **mix-up** (n. and adj.)

**Mobil Corp.**  Headquarters is in New York.
Mobil Oil Corp. is a subsidiary.

**mock-up** (n.)

**model numbers**  See **serial numbers.**

**Mohammed**  The preferred spelling for the name of the founder of the Islamic religion.

**Monaco**  After the Vatican, the world's smallest state.
The *Monaco* section stands alone in datelines. The other two sections, *La Condamine* and *Monte Carlo*, are followed by *Monaco:*
*MONTE CARLO, Monaco (AP)—*

**Monday**  See **days of the week.**

**Monday morning quarterback**  One who second guesses.

**M-1, M-14**  See **weapons.**

**monetary**  See the **fiscal, monetary** entry.

**monetary units**  See **cents; dollars;** and **pounds.**

**moneymaker**

**monsignor**  See **Roman Catholic Church.**

**Montana**  Abbrev.: *Mont.* See **state names.**

**Montessori method**  After Maria Montessori. A system of training young children, it emphasizes training of the senses and guidance to encourage self-education.

**monthlong**

**months**  Capitalize the names of months in all uses. When a month is used with a specific date, abbreviate only *Jan., Feb., Aug., Sept., Oct., Nov.* and *Dec.* Spell out when using alone, or with a year alone.
When a phrase lists only a month and a year, do not sep-

arate the year with commas. When a phrase refers to a month, day and year, set off the year with commas.

EXAMPLES: *January 1972 was a cold month. Jan. 2 was the coldest day of the month. His birthday is May 8. Feb. 14, 1987, was the target date.*

In tabular material, use these three-letter forms without a period: *Jan, Feb, Mar, Apr, May, Jun, Jul, Aug, Sep, Oct, Nov, Dec.*

See **dates** and **years.**

**Montreal** The city in Canada stands alone in datelines.

**monuments** Capitalize the popular names of monuments and similar public attractions: *Lincoln Memorial, Statue of Liberty, Washington Monument, Leaning Tower of Pisa,* etc.

**moon** Lowercase. See **heavenly bodies.**

**mop up** (v.) **mop-up** (n. and adj.)

**Moral Majority** Not *the* Moral Majority.

**more than** See **over.**

**Mormon Church** Acceptable in all references for *Church of Jesus Christ of Latter-day Saints,* but always include the full name in a story dealing primarily with church activities.

See the entry under the formal name.

**Moscow** The city in the Soviet Union stands alone in datelines.

**Moslem(s)** The preferred term to describe adherents of Islam.

**mosquito, mosquitoes**

**mother-in-law, mothers-in-law**

**Mother Nature**

**Mother's Day** The second Sunday in May.

**motor** See the **engine, motor** entry.

**mount** Spell out in all uses, including the names of communities and of mountains: *Mount Clemens, Mich.; Mount Everest.*

**mountains** Capitalize as part of a proper name: *Appalachian Mountains, Ozark Mountains, Rocky Mountains.*

Or simply: *the Appalachians, the Ozarks, the Rockies.*

**Mountain Standard Time (MST), Mountain Daylight Time (MDT)** See **time zones.**

**Mountain States** As defined by the U.S. Census Bureau, the eight are Arizona, Colorado, Idaho, Montana, Nevada, New Mexico, Utah and Wyoming.

**movie ratings** The ratings used by the Motion Picture Association of America Inc. are:

*G* For *general audiences.* All ages admitted.

*PG* For *parental guidance.* All ages admitted.

*PG-13 Parental guidance* advised. Some material may not be suitable for 13-year-olds and under.

*R* For *restricted.* Persons under 17 must be accompanied by a parent or adult guardian.

*X* No one under 17 admitted. (The age limit may be different in some areas.)

When the ratings are used in news stories or reviews, use these forms as appropriate: *the movie has an X rating, an X-rated movie, the movie is X-rated.*

**movie titles** See **composition titles.**

**mph** Acceptable in all references for *miles per hour* or *miles an hour.*

**Mr., Mrs.** The plural of *Mr.* is *Messrs.;* the plural of *Mrs.* is *Mmes.*

These abbreviated spellings apply in all uses, including direct quotations.

See **courtesy titles** for guidelines on when to use *Mr.* and *Mrs.*

**Ms.** This is the spelling and punctuation for all uses of the courtesy title, including direct quotations.

There is no plural. If several women who prefer *Ms.* must be listed in a series, repeat *Ms.* before each name.

See **courtesy titles** for guidelines on when to use *Ms.*

**Muhammad** The preferred spelling is *Mohammed.*

**multi-** The rules in prefixes apply, but in general, no hyphen. Some examples:

| | |
|---|---|
| multicolored | multimillion |
| multilateral | multimillionaire |

**Multigraph** A trademark for a brand of dictating machine.

**Multilith** A trademark for a brand of duplicating machine.

**murder** See the **homicide, murder, manslaughter** entry.

**murderer** See the **assassin, killer, murderer** entry.

**Murphy's law** The law is: *If something can go wrong, it will.*

**music** The basic guidelines for capitalizing and using quotations marks on the titles on musical works are listed in **composition titles.**

Capitalize, but do not use quotation marks on descriptive titles for orchestral works: *Bach's Suite No. 1 for Orchestra; Beethoven's Serenade for Flute, Violin and Viola.* If the instrumentation is not part of the title but is added for explanatory purposes, the names of the instruments are lowercased: *Mozart's Sinfonia Concertante in E flat major* (the common title) *for violin and viola.* If in doubt, lowercase the names of the instruments.

Use quotation marks for non-musical terms in a title: *Beethoven's "Eroica" Symphony.* If the work has a special full title, all of it is quoted: *"Symphonie Fantastique," "Rhapsody in Blue."*

In subsequent references, lowercase *symphony, concerto,* etc.

**musket** See **weapons**

**Muslim(s)** The preferred term to describe adherents of Islam is *Moslem.*

A *Black Muslim* is a member of a predominantly black Islamic sect in the United States. However, the term is considered derogatory by members of the sect, who call themselves *Muslims.*

See **Moslem.**

**Mutual Broadcasting System Inc.** *Mutual Radio* is acceptable in all references.

Use *Mutual,* not *MBS,* in subsequent references.

**Muzak** A trademark for a type of recorded background music.

# N

**n.** See **nouns**.

**naive**

**names** In general, people are entitled to be known however they want to be known, as long as their identities are clear.

When an individual elects to change the name by which he has been known, such as Cassius Clay's transition to Muhammad Ali, provide both names in stories until the new name is known by the public. After that, use only the new name unless there is a specific reason for including the earlier identification.

See the **junior, senior** entry and the entries under **middle initials; nicknames;** and **sex changes**.

**nano-** A prefix denoting one-billionth of a unit. Move a decimal point nine places to the left in converting to the basic unit: 2,999,888,777.5

nanoseconds = 2.9998887775 seconds.

**naphtha** See the **oil** entry.

**narrow-minded**

**national** See the **citizen, resident, subject, national, native** entry.

**National Aeronautics and Space Administration** *NASA* is acceptable on first reference.

If *NASA* is used in first reference to avoid a cumbersome lead, mention the full name later.

**National Airlines** This company name went out of use in mid-1980 after the airline was acquired by Pan American World Airways. See entry under that name.

**national anthem** Lowercase. But: *"The Star-Spangled Banner."*

**National Association for the Advancement of Colored People** *NAACP* is acceptable on first reference to avoid a cumbersome lead, but provide the full name in the body of the story.

Headquarters is in Baltimore.

**National Association of Letter Carriers** the shortened form *Letter Carriers union* is acceptable in all references.

Headquarters is in Washington.

**National Baptist Convention of America** See **Baptist churches.**

**National Baptist Convention U.S.A. Inc.** See **Baptist churches.**

**National Broadcasting Co.** See **NBC.**

**national chairman** Capitalize when used before the name of the individual who heads a political party: *Democratic National Chairman Kenneth M. Curtis.*

**National Conference of Catholic Bishops** See **Roman Catholic Church.**

**National Council of the Churches of Christ in the U.S.A.** This interdenominational, cooperative body includes most major Protestant and Eastern Orthodox denominations in the United States.

The shortened form *National Council of Churches* is acceptable in all references.

Headquarters is in New York.

See **World Council of Churches.**

**National Education Association** *NEA* is acceptable on second reference.

Headquarters is in Washington.

**National Governors' Association** Note the apostrophe. Represents the governors of the 50 states and five territories.

Its office is in Washington.

**national guard** Capitalize when referring to U.S. or state-level forces: *the National Guard, the Guard, the Iowa National Guard, Iowa's National Guard, National Guard troops.*

Use lowercase for the forces of other nations.

**National Guardsman**
Note spelling. Capitalize as a proper noun when referring to an individual in a federal or state National Guard unit: *He is a National Guardsman.*

Lowercase *guardsman* when it stands alone.

See **military titles.**

**National Hurricane Center** See **weather terms.**

**National Institutes of Health** This agency within the Department of Health and Human Services is the principal biomedical research arm of the federal government.

It consists of the National Library of Medicine, 11 separate institutes and various divisions that provide centralized support services for the individual institutes.

The 11 institutes are: National Cancer Institute; National Eye Institute; National Heart, Lung, and Blood Institute; National Institute of Allergy and Infectious Diseases; National Institute of Arthritis, Metabolism, and Digestive Diseases; National Institute of Child Health and Human Development; National Institute of Dental Research; National Institute of Environmental Health Sciences; National Institute of General Medical Sciences; National Institute of Neurological and Communicative Disorders and Stroke; National Institute on Aging.

**nationalist** Lowercase when referring to a partisan of a country. Capitalize only when referring to alignment with a political party for which this is the proper name.

See the **political parties and philosophies** entry.

**Nationalist China** See **China.**

**nationalities and races** Capitalize the proper names of nationalities, peoples, races, tribes, etc.: *Arab, Arabic, African, Afro-American, American, Caucasian, Cherokee, Chinese* (both singular and plural), *Eskimo* (plural *Eskimos*), *French Canadian, Gypsy (Gypsies), Japanese* (singular and plural), *Jew, Jewish, Latin, Negro (Negroes), Nordic, Oriental, Sioux, Swede,* etc.

Lowercase *black* (noun or adjective), *white, red, mulatto,* etc. See **colored.**

See **race** for guidelines on when racial identification is pertinent in a story.

Lowercase derogatory terms such as *honky* and *nigger.* Use them only in direct quotes when essential to the story.

**National Labor Relations Board** *NLRB* is acceptable on second reference.

**National League of Cities** Its members are the governments of cities with 30,000 or more residents, and some state and municipal leagues.

It is separate from the U.S. Conference of Mayors, whose membership is limited to mayors of cities with 30,000 or more residents. The organizations often engage in joint projects, however.

The office is in Washington.

**National Organization for Women** Not *of.* *NOW* is acceptable on second reference.

Headquarters is in Washington.

**National Rifle Association** *NRA* is acceptable on second reference.

Headquarters is in Washington.

**National Weather Service** No longer the U.S. Weather Bureau. *The weather service* (lowercase) may be used in any reference.

See **weather terms.**

**nationwide**

**native** See the **citizen, resident, subject, national, native** entry.

**NATO** Acceptable in all references for the *North Atlantic Treaty Organization,* but use it sparingly. A phrase such as *the alliance* is less burdensome to the reader.

**Naugahyde** A trademark for a brand of simulated leather.

**nautical mile** It equals one minute of arc of a great circle or 6,076.11549 feet or 1,852 meters. To convert to approximate statute miles (5,280 feet), multiply the number of nautical miles by 1.15.

See **knot.**

**naval, navel** *Naval* pertains to a navy.

A *navel* is a bellybutton.

A *navel orange* is a seedless orange, so named because it has a small depression, like a navel, at its apex.

**naval station** Capitalize only as part of a proper name: *Norfolk Naval Station*.

**navy** Capitalize when referring to U.S. forces: *the U.S. Navy, the Navy, Navy policy.* Do not use the abbreviation *USN*.

Lowercase when referring to the naval forces of other nations: *the British navy*.

This approach has been adopted for consistency, because many foreign nations do not use *navy* as the proper name.

See **military academies** and **military titles.**

**Nazi, Nazism** Derived from the German for the National Socialist German Workers' Party, the fascist political party founded in 1919 and abolished in 1945. Under Adolf Hitler, it seized control of Germany in 1933.

See the **political parties and philosophies** entry.

**NBC** Acceptable in all references for the *National Broadcasting Co.,* a subsidiary of General Electric Co.

Divisions are NBC News, NBC Radio and NBC-TV.

**NCR Corp.** Formerly National Cash Register Co.

Headquarters is in Dayton, Ohio.

**Near East** There is no longer a substantial distinction between this term and *Middle East.*

See the **Middle East** entry.

**nearsighted** When used in a medical sense, it means an individual can see well at close range but has difficulty seeing objects at a distance.

**Nebraska** Abbrev.: *Neb.* See **state names.**

**negligee**

**neither . . . nor** See the **either . . . or, neither . . . nor** entry.

**Netherlands** In datelines, give the name of the community followed by *Netherlands:* AMSTERDAM, *Netherlands (AP)—*

In stories: *the Netherlands* or *Netherlands* as the construction of a sentence dictates.

**Netherlands Antilles** In datelines, give the name of the community followed by

*Netherlands Antilles.* Do not abbreviate.

Identify an individual island, if needed, in the text.

**net income, net profit** See **profit terminology** in the Business Guidelines section.

**neutron weapon** A small warhead designed to be mounted on a Lance missile or fired from an 8-inch gun. It produces twice the deadly radiation of older, tactical nuclear warheads but less than one-tenth as much explosive power, heat and fallout. This means the warhead can kill people while causing little damage to buildings and other structures.

It is not a *bomb*. It is a *weapon* or a *warhead*.

*If neutron bomb* is used in a direct quote, explain in a subsequent paragraph that the warhead would be fired on a missile or from artillery and not dropped, like a bomb, from a plane.

The weapon officially is known as an *enhanced radiation weapon*.

**Nevada** Abbrev.: *Nev.* See **state names.**

**New Brunswick** One of the three Maritime Provinces of Canada. Do not abbreviate. See **datelines.**

**New England** Connecticut, Maine, Massachusetts, New Hampshire, Rhode Island and Vermont.

**Newfoundland** This Canadian province comprises the island of Newfoundland and the mainland section known as Labrador. Do not abbreviate.

In datelines, use Newfoundland after the names of all cities and towns. Specify in the text whether the community is on the island or in Labrador.

See **datelines.**

**New Hampshire** Abbrev.: *N.H.* See **state names.**

**New Jersey** Abbrev.: *N.J.* See **state names.**

**New Mexico** Abbrev.: *N.M.* See **state names.**

**New Orleans** The city in Louisiana stands alone in datelines.

**New South** The era that began in the South in the

1960s with a thriving economy and the election of state officials who advocated the abolition of racial segregation.

*Old South* applies to the South before the Civil War.

**Newspaper Guild, The** Formerly the American Newspaper Guild, it is a union for newspaper and news service employees, generally those in the news and business departments.

On second reference: *the Guild.*

Headquarters is in Washington.

**newspaper names** Capitalize *the* in a newspaper's name if that is the way the publication prefers to be known.

Lowercase *the* before newspaper names if a story mentions several papers, some of which use *the* as part of the name and some of which do not.

Where location is needed but is not part of the official name, use parentheses: *The Huntsville (Ala.) Times.*

Consult the International Year Book published by Editor & Publisher to determine whether a two-name combination is hyphenated.

**newsstand**

**New Testament** See **Bible.**

**New World** The Western Hemisphere.

**New Year's, New Year's Day, New Year's Eve** But: *What will the new year bring?*

The federal legal holiday is observed on Friday if Jan. 1 falls on a Saturday, on Monday if it falls on a Sunday.

**New York** Abbrev.: *N.Y.* Use *New York state* when a distinction must be made between state and city. See **state names.**

**New York City** Use *NEW YORK* in datelines, not the name of an individual community or borough such as *Flushing* or *Queens.*

Identify the borough in the body of the story if pertinent.

**New York Stock Exchange** *NYSE* is acceptable on second reference as an adjective. Use *the stock exchange* or *the exchange* for other second references.

Capitalize the nickname *Big Board* when used.

**nicknames** A nickname should be used in place of person's given name in news stores only when it is the way the individual prefers to be known: *Jimmy Carter.*

When a nickname is inserted into the identification of an individual, use quotation marks: *Sen. Henry M. "Scoop" Jackson.* Also: *Jackson is known as "Scoop."*

In sports stories and sports columns, commonly used nicknames may be substituted for a first name without the use of quotation marks: *Woody Hayes, Bear Bryant, Catfish Hunter, Bubba Smith,* etc. But in sports stories where the given name is used, and in all news stories: *Paul "Bear" Bryant.*

Capitalize without quotation marks such terms as *Sunshine State, the Old Dominion, Motown, the Magic City, Old Hickory, Old Glory, Galloping Ghost.*

See **names.**

**nightclub**

**nighttime**

**nitpicking**

**nitty-gritty**

**No.** Use as the abbreviation for *number* in conjunction with a figure to indicate position or rank: *No. 1 man, No. 3 choice.*

Do not use in street addresses, with this exception: *No. 10 Downing St.,* the residence of Britain's prime minister.

Do not use in the names of schools: *Public School 19.*

**Nobel Prize, Nobel Prizes** The five established under terms of the will of Alfred Nobel are: Nobel Peace Prize, Nobel Prize in chemistry, Nobel Prize in literature, Nobel Prize in physics, Nobel Prize in physiology or medicine. (Note the capitalization styles.)

The Nobel Memorial Prize in Economic Science is not a Nobel Prize in the same sense. The Central Bank of Sweden established it in 1968 as a memorial to Alfred Nobel. References to this prize should include the word *Memorial* to help make this distinction. Explain the status of the prize in the story when appropriate.

Nobel Prize award ceremonies are held on Dec. 10, the anniversary of Alfred Nobel's death in 1896. The award ceremony for peace is in Oslo and the other ceremonies are in Stockholm.

Capitalize *prize* in references that do not mention the category: *He is a Nobel Prize winner. She is a Nobel Prize-winning scientist.*

Lowercase *prize* when not linked with the word Nobel: *The peace prize was awarded Monday.*

**nobility** References to members of the nobility in nations that have a system of rank present special problems because nobles frequently are known by their titles rather than their given or family names. Their titles, in effect, become their names.

The guidelines here relate to Britain's nobility. Adapt them as appropriate to members of nobility in other nations.

Orders of rank among British nobility begin with the royal family. The term *royalty* is reserved for the families of living and deceased sovereigns.

Next, in descending order, are dukes, marquesses, (also called marquises), earls, viscounts and barons. Many hold inherited titles; others have been raised to the nobility by the sovereign for their lifetimes. Occasionally the sovereign raises an individual to the nobility and makes the title inheritable by the person's heirs, but the practice is increasingly rare.

Sovereigns also confer honorary titles, which do not make an individual a member of the nobility. The principal designations, in descending order, are baronet and knight.

In general, the guidelines in **courtesy titles** and **titles** apply. However, honorary titles and titles of nobility are capitalized when they serve as an alternative name.

Some guidelines and examples:

ROYALTY: Capitalize *king, queen, prince* and *princess* when they are used directly before one or more names; lowercase when they stand alone:

*Queen Elizabeth II, Queen Elizabeth II of the United Kingdom of Great Britain and Northern Ireland, the queen. Kings George and Edward. Queen Mother Elizabeth, the queen mother.*

Also capitalize a longer form of the sovereign's title when its use is appropriate in a story or it is being quoted: *Her Majesty Queen Elizabeth.*

Use *Prince* or *Princess* before the names of a sovereign's children: *Princess Anne, the princess.*

The male heir to the throne normally is designated *Prince of Wales,* and the title becomes, in common usage, an alternative name. Capitalize when used: *The queen invested her eldest son as Prince of Wales. Prince Charles is now the Prince of Wales. The prince is a bachelor. Charles, Prince of Wales, was married today. His wife is known as the Princess of Wales, not Princess Diana.*

DUKE: The full title—*Duke of Wellington,* for example—is an alternative name, capitalized in all uses. Lowercase *duke* when it stands alone.

The designation *Arthur, Duke of Wellington,* is appropriate in some cases, but never *Duke Arthur* or *Lord Arthur.*

The wife of a *duke* is *a duchess: the Duchess of Wellington, the duchess,* but never *Duchess Diana* or *Lady Diana.*

A duke normally also has a lesser title. It is commonly used for his eldest son if he has one. Use the courtesy titles *Lord* or *Lady* before the first names of a duke's children.

Some examples:

*Lady Jane Wellesley, only daughter of the eighth Duke of Wellington, has been linked romantically with Prince Charles, heir to the British throne. One of Lady Jane's four brothers is Arthur Charles, the Marquess Douro. The Wellingtons, whose family name is Wellesley, are not of royal blood. However, they rank among the nation's most famous aristocrats thanks to the first duke, the victor at Waterloo.*

MARQUESS, MARQUIS, EARL, VISCOUNT, BARON: The full titles serve as alternative names and should be capitalized. Frequently, however, the holder of such a title is identified as a lord: *The Marquess of Bath,* for example, more commonly known as *Lord Bath.*

Use *Lady* before the name of a woman married to a man who holds one of these titles. The wife of a marquess is a marchioness, the wife of a marquis is a marquise, the wife of an earl is a countess (earl is the British equivalent of count), the wife of a viscount is a viscountess, the wife of a baron is a baroness.

Use *Lord* or *Lady* before the first names of children of a marquess.

Use *Lady* before the name of an earl's daughter.

*The Honorable* often appears before the names of sons of earls, viscounts and barons who do not have titles. Their names should stand alone in news stories, however.

*The Honorable* also appears frequently before the names of unmarried daughters of viscounts and barons. In news stories, however, use a full name on first reference, a last name preceded by *Miss* on second.

Some examples:

*Queen Elizabeth gave her sister's husband, Antony Armstrong-Jones, the title Earl of Snowdon. Their son, David, is the Viscount Linley. They also have a daughter, Lady Sarah Armstrong-Jones. Lord Snowdon, a photographer, was known as Antony Armstrong-Jones before he received his title.*

BARONET, KNIGHT: Use *Sir* before a name if appropriate in the context; otherwise follow routine practice for names: *Sir Harold Wilson* on first reference, *Sir Harold* (not *Sir Wilson*) on second. Or: *Prime Minister Harold Wilson* on first reference, *Wilson* on second.

Do not use both an honorary title and a title of authority such as *prime minister* before a name.

Use *Lady* before the name of the wife of a baronet or knight.

For a woman who has received an honor in her own right, use *Dame* before her name if it is the way she is known or it is appropriate in the context: *Dame Margot Fonteyn* on first reference, *Dame Margot* on second.

## nobody

**noisome, noisy** *Noisome* means offensive, noxious.
*Noisy* means clamorous.

**nolo contendere** The literal meaning is, "I do not wish to contend." Terms such as *no contest* or *no-contest plea* are acceptable in all references.

When a defendant in a criminal case enters this plea, it means that he is not admitting guilt but is stating that he will offer no defense. The person is then subject to being judged guilty and punished as if he had pleaded guilty or had been convicted. The principal difference is that the defendant retains the option of denying the same charge in another legal proceeding.

### no man's land

**non-** Hyphenate all except the following words, which have specific meanings of their own:

nonchalance   nonentity
nonchalant    nonsense
nondescript   nonsensical

### non-aligned nations
A political rather than economic or geographic term. Although non-aligned nations do not belong to Western or Eastern military alliances or blocs, they profess not to be neutral, like Switzerland, but activist alternatives.

Do not confuse *non-aligned* with *Third World,* although many Third World nations belong to the non-aligned group. For example, Yugoslavia is a non-aligned nation because it does not belong to the Warsaw Pact, but it is not a Third World nation.

See the **Third World** entry.

**non-controversial** All issues are controversial. A *non-controversial issue* is impossible. A *controversial issue* is redundant.

**none** It usually means no single one. When used in this sense, it always takes singular verbs and pronouns: *None of the seats was in its right place.*

Use a plural verb only if the sense is no two or no amount: *None of the consultants agree on the same approach. None of the taxes have been paid.*

### non-restrictive clauses
See **non-essential clauses.**

**noon** Do not put a *12* in front of it.

### no one

**norm** A standard, model, or pattern for a group. See the **average, mean, median, norm** entry.

**north, northern, northeast, northwest** See the **directions and regions** entry.

**North America** See **Western Hemisphere.**

**North Atlantic Treaty Organization** *NATO* is acceptable in all references, but use it sparingly. A phrase such as *the alliance* is less burdensome to the reader.

**North Carolina** Abbrev.: *N.C.* See **state names.**

**North Central Airlines** See **Republic Airlines.**

**North Central region** As defined by the U.S. Census Bureau, the 12-state region is broken into eastern and western divisions.

The five *East North Central* states are Indiana, Illinois, Michigan, Ohio and Wisconsin.

The seven *West North Central* states are Iowa, Kansas, Minnesota, Missouri, Nebraska, North Dakota and South Dakota.

See **Northeast region; South;** and **West** for the bureau's other regional breakdowns.

**North Dakota** Abbrev.: *N.D.* See **state names.**

**Northeast region** As defined by the U.S. Census Bureau, the nine-state region is broken into two divisions—the *New England* states and the *Middle Atlantic* states.

Connecticut, Maine, Massachusetts, New Hampshire, Rhode Island and Vermont are the *New England* states.

New Jersey, New York and Pennsylvania are classified as the *Middle Atlantic* states.

See **North Central region; South;** and **West** for the bureau's other regional breakdowns.

**Northern Ireland** Use *Northern Ireland* after the names of all communities in datelines.

See **datelines** and **United Kingdom.**

**North Slope** The portion of Alaska north of Brooks Range, a string of mountains extending across the northern part of the state.

**Northwest Orient Airlines** *Northwest Airlines* is acceptable in all references.

Headquarters is in St. Paul, Minn.

**Northwest Territories** A territorial section of Canada. Do not abbreviate. Use in datelines after the names of all cities and towns in the territory.

If necessary, specify in the text whether the community

is in one of the three territorial subdivisions: *Franklin, Keewatin* and *Mackenzie.*
See **Canada.**

**nouns** The abbreviation *n.* is used in this book to identify the spelling of the noun forms of words frequently misspelled.

**Nova Scotia** One of the three Maritime Provinces of Canada. Do not abbreviate.
See **datelines.**

**November** See **months.**

**Novocain** A trademark for a drug used as a local anesthetic. It also may be called *procain.*

**nowadays** Not *nowdays.*

**Nuclear Regulatory Commission** This commission has taken over the regulatory functions previously performed by the Atomic Energy Commission.
*NRC* is acceptable on second reference, but *the agency* or *the commission* is preferred.

**nuclear terminology** In reporting on nuclear energy, include the definitions of appropriate terms, especially those related to radiation.

**core** The part of a nuclear reactor that contains its fissionable fuel. In a reactor core, atoms of fuel, such as uranium, are split. This releases energy in the form of heat which, in turn, is used to boil water for steam. The steam powers a turbine, and the turbine drives a generator to produce electricity.

**fission** The splitting of the nucleus of an atom, releasing energy.

**meltdown** The worst possible nuclear accident in which the reactor core overheats to such a degree that the fuel melts. If the fuel penetrates its protective housing, radioactive materials will be released into the environment.

**rad** The standard unit of measurement for absorbed radiation. A *millirad* is a thousandth of a rad. There is considerable debate among scientists as to whether there is any safe level of absorption.

**radiation** Invisible particles or waves given off by radioactive material, such as uranium. Radiation can damage or kill body cells, resulting in latent cancers, genetic damage or death.

**rem** The standard unit of measurement of absorbed radiation in living tissue, adjusted for different kinds of radiation so that one rem of any radiation will produce the same biological effect. A *millirem* is a thousandth of a rem.

A diagnostic chest X-ray involves between 20 millirems and 30 millirems of radiation. Each American, on average, receives 100 millirems to 200 millirems of radiation a year from natural "background" sources, such as cosmic rays, and man-made sources, such as diagnostic X-rays. There is considerable debate among scientists over the safety of repeated low doses of radiation.

**roentgen** The standard measure of X-ray exposure.

**uranium** A metallic, radioactive element used as fuel in nuclear reactors.

**numerals** A numeral is a figure, letter, word or group of words expressing a number.

Roman numerals use the letters *I, V, X, L, C, D* and *M*. Use Roman numerals for wars and to show personal sequence for animals and people: *World War II, Native Dancer II, King George VI, Pope John XXIII.* See **Roman numerals.**

Arabic numerals use the figures *1, 2, 3, 4, 5, 6, 7, 8, 9* and *0.* Use Arabic forms unless Roman numerals are specifically required. See **Arabic numerals.**

The figures *1, 2, 10, 101,* etc., and the corresponding words—*one, two, ten, one hundred one,* etc.—are called cardinal numbers. The term ordinal number applies to *1st, 2nd, 10th, 101st, first, second, tenth, one hundred first,* etc.

Follow these guidelines in using numerals:

LARGE NUMBERS: When large numbers must be spelled out, use a hyphen to connect a word ending in *y* to another word; do not use commas between other separate words that are part of one number: *twenty; thirty; twenty-one; thirty-one; one hundred forty-three; one thousand one hundred fifty-five; one million two hundred sev-*

enty-six thousand five hundred eighty-seven.

**SENTENCE START:** Spell out a numeral at the beginning of a sentence. If necessary, recast the sentence. There is one exception—a numeral that identifies a calendar year.

Wrong: *993 freshmen entered the college last year.*

Right: *Last year 933 freshmen entered the college.*

Right: *1976 was a very good year.*

**CASUAL USES:** Spell out casual expressions:
*A thousand times no! Thanks a million. He walked a quarter of a mile.*

**PROPER NAMES:** Use words or numerals according to an organization's practice: *20th Century Fox, Twentieth Century Fund, Big Ten.*

**FRACTIONS:** See the **fractions** entry.

**DECIMALS:** See the **decimal units** entry.

**FIGURES OR WORDS?**
For ordinals:
—Spell out *first* through *ninth* when they indicate sequence in time or location: *first base, the First Amendment, he was first in line.* Starting with *10th* use figures.

—Use *1st, 2nd, 3rd, 4th,* etc. when the sequence has been assigned in forming names. The principal examples are geographic, military and political designations such as *1st Ward, 7th Fleet* and *1st Sgt.* See examples in the separate entries listed below.

For cardinal numbers, consult the following separate entries:

| | |
|---|---|
| act numbers | latitude and |
| addresses | longitude |
| ages | mile |
| aircraft names | model num- |
| amendments to | bers |
| the Consti- | monetary units |
| tution | No. |
| betting odds | page numbers |
| century | parallels |
| channel | percentages |
| chapters | political |
| congressional | divisions |
| districts | proportions |
| course num- | ratios |
| bers | recipes |
| court decisions | room numbers |
| court names | route numbers |
| dates | scene numbers |
| decades | scores |
| decimal units | serial numbers |
| dimensions | sizes |

distances
district
earthquakes
election returns
fleet
formula
fractions
handicaps
heights
highway designations

spacecraft designations
speeds
telephone numbers
temperatures
years

SOME PUNCTUATION AND USAGE EXAMPLES:
—*Act 1, Scene 2*
—*a 5-year-old girl*
—*DC-10* but *747B*
—*a 5–4 court decision*
—*2nd District Court*
—*the 1980s, the 80s*
—*The House voted 230–205.* (Fewer than 1,000 votes.)
—*Jimmy Carter defeated Gerald Ford 40,827,292 to 39,146,157.* (More than 1,000 votes.)
—*Carter defeated Ford 10 votes to 2 votes in Little Junction.* (To avoid confusion with ratio.)
—*5 cents, $1.05, $650,000, $2.45 million*
—*No. 3 choice,* but *Public School 3*
—*0.6 percent, 1 percent, 6.5 percent*
—*a pay increase of 12 per-*

*cent to 15 percent.* Or: *a pay increase of between 12 percent and 15 percent.*
Also: *from $12 million to $14 million*
—*a ratio of 2-to-1, a 2-1 ratio*
—*a 4–3 score*
—*(212) 262-4000*
—*minus 10, zero, 60 degrees*

OTHER USES: For uses not covered by these listings: Spell out whole numbers below 10, use figures for 10 and above. Typical examples: *The woman has three sons and two daughters. He has a fleet of 10 station wagons and two buses.*

IN A SERIES: Apply the appropriate guidelines: *They had 10 dogs, six cats and 97 hamsters. They had four four-room houses, 10 three-room houses and 12 10-room houses.*

**nuns** See **sister.**

**Nuremberg** Use this spelling for the city in West Germany, instead of Nuernberg, in keeping with widespread practice.

**nylon** Not a trademark.

**oasis, oases**

**obscenities, profanities, vulgarities** Do not use them in stories unless they are part of direct quotations and there is a compelling reason for them.

When a profanity, obscenity or vulgarity is used, flag the story at the top:

**Editors: Language in 4th graf may be offensive to some readers.**

Then confine the offending language, in quotation marks, to a separate paragraph that can be deleted easily by editors who do not want it.

In reporting profanity that normally would use the words *damn* or *god,* lowercase *god* and use the following forms: *damn, damn it, goddamn it.* Do not, however, change the offending words to euphemisms. Do not, for example, change *damn it* to *darn it.*

If a full quote that contains profanity, obscenity or vulgarity cannot be dropped but there is no compelling reason for the offensive language, replace letters of an offensive word with a hyphen. The word *damn,* for example, would become *d—* or *———.*

When the subject matter of a story may be considered offensive, but the story does not contain quoted profanity, obscenities or vulgarities, flag the story at the top:

**Editors: The contents may be offensive to some readers.**

For guidelines on racial or ethnic slurs, see the **nationalities and races** entry.

**Occident, Occidental** Capitalize when referring to Europe, the Western Hemisphere or an inhabitant of these regions.

**Occidental Petroleum Corp.** Headquarters is in Los Angeles.

**Occupational Safety and Health Administra-**

**tion** *OSHA* is acceptable on second reference.

**occupational titles** They are always lowercase. See **titles.**

**occur, occurred, occurring** Also: *occurrence.*

**oceangoing**

**ocean** The five, from the largest to the smallest: Pacific Ocean, Atlantic Ocean, Indian Ocean, Antarctic Ocean, Arctic Ocean.

Lowercase *ocean* standing alone or in plural uses: *the ocean, the Atlantic and Pacific oceans.*

**October** See **months.**

**odd-** Follow with a hyphen:

odd-looking    odd-numbered

**odds** See **betting odds.**

**oddsmaker**

**off-, -off** Follow Webster's New World Dictionary. Hyphenate if not listed there.

Some commonly used combinations with a hyphen:

off-color    off-white
off-peak    send-off

off-season    stop-off

Some combinations without a hyphen:

cutoff    offside
liftoff    offstage
offhand    playoff
offset    standoff
offshore    takeoff

**off-Broadway, off-off-Broadway** See the **Broadway, off-Broadway, off-off-Broadway** entry.

**office** Capitalize *office* when it is part of an agency's formal name: *Office of Management and Budget.*

Lowercase all other uses, including phrases such as: the office of the attorney general, the U.S. attorney's office.

See **Oval Office.**

**officeholder**

**off of** The *of* is unnecessary: *He fell off the bed.* Not: *He fell off of the bed.*

**Ohio** Do not abbreviate. See **state names.**

**oil** In shipping, oil and oil products normally are measured by the ton. For news stories, convert these tonnage figures to gallons.

There are 42 gallons to

each barrel of oil. The number of barrels per ton varies, depending on the type of oil product.

To convert tonnage to gallons:

—Determine the type of oil.

—Consult the following table to find out how many barrels per ton for that type of oil.

—Multiply the number of tons by the number of barrels per ton. The result is the number of barrels in the shipment.

—Multiply the number of barrels by 42. The result is the number of gallons.

EXAMPLE: A tanker spills 20,000 metric tons of foreign crude petroleum. The table shows 6.998 barrels of foreign crude petroleum per metric ton. Multiply 6.998 × 20,000 = 139,960 barrels. Multiply 139,960 × 42 = 5,878,320 gallons.

TABLE: The table on the following page is based on figures supplied by the American Petroleum Institute:

**Oil, Chemical and Atomic Workers Interna-tional Union** The shortened forms *Oil Workers union, Chemical Workers union* and *Atomic Workers union* are acceptable in all references.

Headquarters is in Denver.

**OK, OK'd, OK'ing, OKs** Do not use *okay*.

**Oklahoma** Abbrev.: *Okla.* See **state names**.

**Oklahoma City** Stands alone in datelines.

**Old City of Jerusalem** The walled part of the city.

**Old South** The South before the Civil War. See **New South**.

**Old Testament** See **Bible**.

**old-time, old-timer, old times**

**Old West** The American West as it was being settled in the 19th century.

**Old World** The Eastern Hemisphere: Asia, Europe, Africa. The term also may be an allusion to European culture and customs.

**Olympic Airways** Headquarters is in Athens, Greece.

**olympics** Capitalize all references to the international athletic contests held every four years: *the Olympics, the Winter Olympics, the Olympic Games, the Games, an Olympic-sized pool.*

An Olympic-sized pool is 50 meters long by 25 meters wide.

Lowercase other uses: *a beer-drinking olympics.*

**on** Do not use *on* before a date or day of the week when its absence would not lead to confusion: *The meeting will be held Monday. He will be inaugurated Jan. 20.*

Use *on* to avoid an awkward juxtaposition of a date and a proper name: *John met Mary on Monday. He told Reagan on Thursday that the bill was doomed.*

Use *on* also to avoid any suggestion that a date is the object of a transitive verb: *The House killed on Tuesday a bid*

## OIL EQUIVALENCY TABLE

| Type of Product | Barrels Per Short Ton (2,000 lbs.) | Barrels Per Metric Ton (2,204.6 lbs.) | Barrels Per Long Ton (2,240 lbs.) |
|---|---|---|---|
| crude oil, foreign | 6.349 | 6.998 | 7.111 |
| crude oil, domestic | 6.770 | 7.463 | 7.582 |
| gasoline and naphtha | 7.721 | 8.511 | 8.648 |
| kerosene | 7.053 | 7.775 | 7.900 |
| distllate fuel oil | 6.580 | 7.253 | 7.369 |
| residual fuel oil | 6.041 | 6.660 | 6.766 |
| lubricating oil | 6.349 | 6.998 | 7.111 |
| lubricating grease | 6.665 | 7.346 | 7.464 |
| wax | 7.134 | 7.864 | 7.990 |
| asphalt | 5.540 | 6.106 | 6.205 |
| coke | 4.990 | 5.500 | 5.589 |
| road oil | 5.900 | 6.503 | 6.608 |
| jelly and petrolatum | 6.665 | 7.346 | 7.464 |
| liquefied pet. gas | 10.526 | 11.603 | 11.789 |
| Gilsonite | 5.515 | 6.080 | 6.177 |

to raise taxes. *The Senate post-poned on Wednesday its consideration of a bill to reduce import duties.*

**one-** Hyphenate when used in writing fractions:
one-half        one-third
Use phrases such as *a half* or *a third* if precision is not intended.
See **fractions.**

**one another** See the **each other, one another** entry.

**one man, one vote** The adjective form: *one-man, one-vote. He supports the principle of one man, one vote. The one-man, one-vote rule.*

**one-sided**

**one time, one-time** *He did it one time. He is a one-time winner. She is a one-time friend.*

**Ontario** This Canadian province is the nation's first in total population and second to Quebec in area. Do not abbreviate.
See **datelines.**

**operas** See **composition titles.**

**opinion polls** See the **polls and surveys** entry.

**opossum** The only North American marsupial. No apostrophe is needed to indicate missing letters in a phrase such as *playing possum.*

**oral, verbal, written** Use *oral* to refer to spoken words: *He gave an oral promise.*
Use *written* to refer to words committed to paper: *We had a written agreement.*
Use *verbal* to compare words with some other form of communication: *His tears revealed the sentiments that his poor verbal skills could not express.*

**ordinal numbers** See **numerals.**

**Oregon** Abbrev.: *Ore.* See **state names.**

**Oreo** A trademark for a brand of chocolate sandwich cookies held together by a white filling.
The use of the word by blacks indicates belief that another black is "black outside but white inside."

**Organization of American States** *OAS* is acceptable on second reference.

Headquarters is in Washington.

**Organization of Petroleum Exporting Countries** Use the full name for most first references. *OPEC* may be used on first reference in business oriented copy, but the body of the story should identify it as the shortened form of the name.

The 13 OPEC members: Algeria, Ecuador, Gabon, Indonesia, Iran, Iraq, Kuwait, Libya, Nigeria, Qatar, Saudi Arabia, United Arab Emirates, Venezuela.

Headquarters is in Vienna, Austria.

**organizations and institutions** Capitalize the full names of organizations and institutions: *the American Medical Association; First Presbyterian Church; General Motors Corp.; Harvard University, Harvard University Medical School; the Procrastinators Club; the Society of Professional Journalists, Sigma Delta Chi.*

Retain capitalization if *Co., Corp.* or a similar word is deleted from the full proper name: *General Motors.* See **company; corporation;** and **incorporated.**

SUBSIDIARIES: Capitalize the names of major subdivisions: *the Pontiac Motor Division of General Motors.*

INTERNAL ELEMENTS: Use lowercase for internal elements of an organization when they have names that are widely used generic terms: *the board of directors of General Motors, the board of trustees of Columbia University, the history department of Harvard University, the sports department of the Daily Citizen-Leader.*

Capitalize internal elements of an organization when they have names that are not widely used generic terms: *the General Assembly of the World Council of Churches, the House of Delegates of the American Medical Association, the House of Bishops and House of Deputies of the Episcopal Church.*

FLIP-FLOPPED NAMES: Retain capital letters when commonly accepted practice flops a name to delete the word *of: College of the Holy Cross, Holy Cross College;*

*Harvard School of Dental Medicine, Harvard Dental School.*

Do not, however, flop formal names that are known to the public with the word *of*: *Massachusetts Institute of Technology*, for example, not *Massachusetts Technology Institute.*

**ABBREVIATIONS AND ACRONYMS:** Some organizations and institutions are widely recognized by their abbreviations: *Alcoa, GOP, NAACP, NATO.* For guidelines on when such abbreviations may be used, see the individual listings and the entries under **abbreviations and acronyms** and **second reference.**

**Orient, Oriental** Capitalize when referring to the Far East nations of Asia and nearby islands or to an inhabitant of these regions.

Also: *Oriental rug, Oriental cuisine.*

**Orlon** A trademark for a form of acrylic fiber similar to nylon.

**orthodox** Capitalize when referring to membership in or the activities of an East-ern Orthodox church. See **Eastern Orthodox Churches.**

Capitalize also in phrases such as *Orthodox Judaism* or *Orthodox Jew.* See **Jewish congregations.**

Do not describe a member of an Eastern Orthodox church as a *Protestant.* Use a phrase such as *Orthodox Christian* instead.

Lowercase *orthodox* in nonreligious uses: *an orthodox procedure.*

**Orthodox Church in America** See **Eastern Orthodox churches.**

**Oscar, Oscars** See **Academy Awards.**

**oscillating theory** See **big-bang theory.**

**Ottawa** The capital of Canada stands alone in datelines.

**Ouija** A trademark for a board used in spiritual seances.

**ounce (dry)** Units of dry volume are not customarily carried to this level.

See **pint (dry).**

**ounce (liquid)** See **fluid ounce.**

**ounce (weight)** It is defined as 437.5 grains.

The metric equivalent is approximately 28 grams.

To convert to grams, multiply by 28 (5 ounces × 28 = 140 grams).

See **grain** and **gram.**

**out-** Follow Webster's New World. Hyphenate if not listed there.

Some frequently used words:

| | |
|---|---|
| outargue | outpost |
| outbox | output |
| outdated | outscore |
| outfield | outstrip |
| outfox | outtalk |
| outpatient (n., adj.) | |

**-out** Follow Webster's New World. Hyphenate nouns and adjectives not listed there.

Some frequently used words (all nouns):

| | |
|---|---|
| cop-out | hide-out |
| fade-out | pullout |
| fallout | walkout |
| flameout | washout |

Two words for verbs:

| | |
|---|---|
| fade out | walk out |
| hide out | wash out |
| pull out | |

**Outer Banks** The sandy islands along the North Carolina coast.

**out of bounds** But as a modifier: *out-of-bounds. The ball went out of bounds. He took an out-of-bounds pass.*

**out of court, out-of-court** *They settled out of court. He accepted an out-of-court settlement.*

**Oval Office** The White House office of the president.

**over** It generally refers to spatial relationships: *The plane flew over the city.*

*Over* can, at times, be used with numerals: *She is over 30. I paid over $200 for this suit.* But *more than* may be better: *Their salaries went up more than $20 a week.* Let your ear be your guide.

**over-** Follow Webster's New World. A hyphen seldom is used. Some frequently used words:

| | |
|---|---|
| overbuy | overrate |
| overexert | override |

See the **overall** entry.

**-over** Follow Webster's New World Dictionary. Hyphenate if not listed there.

Some frequently used words (all are nouns, some also are used as adjectives):

carry-over        stopover
holdover          walkover
takeover

Use two words when any of these occurs as a verb.

See **suffixes.**

**overall** A single word in adjectival and adverbial use: *Overall, the Democrats succeeded. Overall policy.*

The word for the garment is *overalls.*

**Overseas National Airways** Headquarters is in New York.

**owner** Not a formal title. Always lowercase: *Atlanta Braves owner Ted Turner.*

**Oyez** Not *oyes.* The cry of court and public officials to command silence.

**Ozark Air Lines** Headquarters is in St. Louis.

**Ozark Mountains** Or simply: *the Ozarks.*

# P

**Pablum** A trademark for a soft, bland food for infants.

In lowercase, *pabulum* means any over-simplified or bland writing or idea.

**pacemaker** Formerly a trademark, now a generic term for a device that electronically helps a person's heart maintain a steady beat.

**Pacific Ocean** See **oceans**.

**Pacific Standard Time (PST), Pacific Daylight Time (PDT)** See **time zones**.

**paddy wagon**

**page numbers** Use figures and capitalize *page* when used with a figure. When a letter is appended to the figure, capitalize it but do not use a hyphen: *Page 1, Page 10, Page 20A.*

One exception: *It's a Page One story.*

**paintings** See **composition titles**.

**palate, palette, pallet** *Palate* is the roof of the mouth.

A *palette* is an artist's paint board.

A *pallet* is a bed.

**Palestine Liberation Organization** Not Palestinian. *PLO* is acceptable on second reference.

**pan-** No hyphen when combined with a common noun:

panchromatic    pantheism

Most combinations with *pan-* are proper nouns, however, and both *pan-* and the proper name it is combined with are capitalized:

Pan-African    Pan-Asiatic
Pan-American

**Panama City** Use *PANAMA CITY, Fla.,* or *PANAMA CITY, Panama,* in datelines to avoid confusion between the two.

**Pan American World Airways** A *Pan Am airliner* is acceptable in any reference.

Headquarters is in New York.

**pantsuit** Not *pants suit*.

**pantyhose**

**papal nuncio** Do not confuse with an *apostolic delegate*. See the **apostolic delegate, papal nuncio** entry.

**Pap test (or smear)** After George Papanicolaou, the U.S. anatomist who developed this test for cervical and uterine cancer.

**parallel, paralleled, paralleling**

**parallels** Use figures and lowercase to identify the imaginary locater lines that ring the globe from east to west. They are measured in units of 0 to 90 degrees north or south of the equator.

Examples: *4th parallel north, 89th parallel south,* or, if location north or south of the equator is obvious: *19th parallel.*

See the **latitude and longitude** entry.

**pardon, parole, probation** The terms often are confused, but each has a specific meaning. Do not use them interchangeably.

A *pardon* forgives and releases a person from further punishment. It is granted by a chief of state or a governor. By itself, it does not expunge a record of conviction, if one exists, and it does not by itself restore civil rights.

A *general pardon,* usually for political offenses, is called *amnesty.*

*Parole* is the release of a prisoner before the sentence has expired, on condition of good behavior. It is granted by a parole board, part of the executive branch of government, and can be revoked only by the board.

*Probation* is the suspension of sentence for a person convicted, but not yet imprisoned, on condition of good behavior. It is imposed and revoked only by a judge.

**parentheses** See the entry in the **Punctuation** chapter.

**parent-teacher association** *PTA* is acceptable in all references. Capitalize when part of a proper name: *the Franklin School Parent-Teacher Association* or *the Parent-Teacher Association of the Franklin School.*

**pari-mutuel**

**Paris** The city in France stands alone in datelines.

**parish** Capitalize as part of the formal name for a church congregation or a governmental jurisdiction: *St. John's Parish, Jefferson Parish.*
Lowercase standing alone or in plural combinations: *the parish, St. John's and St. Mary's parishes, Jefferson and Plaquemines parishes.*
See **county** for additional guidelines on governmental jurisdictions.

**parishioner**

**Parkinson's disease** After James Parkinson, the English physician who described this degenerative disease of later life.

**Parkinson's law** After C. Northcote Parkinson, the British economist who came to the satirical conclusion that work expands to fill the time allotted to it.

**parliament** See **foreign legislative bodies.**

**parliamentary** Lowercase unless part of a proper name.

**parole** See the **pardon, parole, probation** entry.

**partial quotes** See **quotation marks** in the **Punctuation** chapter.

**particles** See **foreign particles.**

**part time, part-time** Hyphenate when used as a compound modifier: *She works part time. She has a part-time job.*

**party** See the **political parties and philosophies** entry.

**party affiliation** Let relevance be the guide in determining whether to include a political figure's party affiliation in a story.
Party affiliation is pointless in some stories, such as an ac-

count of a governor accepting a button from a poster child.

It will occur naturally in many political stories.

For stories between these extremes, include party affiliation if readers need it for understanding or are likely to be curious about what it is.

GENERAL FORMS: When party designation is given, use any of these approaches as logical in constructing a story:

—*Democratic Sen. Hubert Humphrey of Minnesota said* . . .

—*Sen. Hubert Humphrey, D-Minn., said* . . .

—*Sen. Hubert Humphrey also spoke. The Minnesota Democrat said* . . .

—*Rep. Morris Udall of Arizona is seeking the Democratic presidential nomination. Not: Rep. Morris Udall, D-Ariz., is seeking the Democratic* . . .

In stories about party meetings, such as a report on the Republican National Convention, no specific reference to party affiliation is necessary unless an individual is not a member of the party in question.

SHORT-FORM PUNCTUATION: Set short forms such as *D-Minn.* off from a name by commas, as illustrated above.

Use the abbreviations listed in the entries for each state. (No abbreviations for *Alaska, Hawaii, Idaho, Iowa, Maine, Ohio, Texas and Utah.*)

Use *R-* for Republicans, *D-* for Democrats, and three-letter combinations for other affiliations: *Sen. James Buckley, R-Con-N.Y., spoke with Sen. Harry Byrd, D-Ind-Va.*

FORM FOR U.S. HOUSE MEMBERS: The normal practice for U.S. House members is to identify them by party and state. In contexts where state affiliation is clear and home city is relevant, such as a state election roundup, identify representatives by party and city: *U.S. Reps. Thomas P. O'Neill Jr., D-Cambridge, and Margaret Heckler, R-Wellesley.* If this option is used, be consistent throughout the story.

FORM FOR STATE LEGISLATORS: Short-form listings showing party and home city are appropriate in state wire stories. For trunk wire stories, the normal practice is to say that the individual is a *Republican* or *Democrat.* Use a short-form listing only if the legislator's home city is relevant.

See **legislative titles**.

**pass** See the **adopt, approve, enact, pass** entry.

**passenger lists** When providing a list of victims in a disaster, arrange names alphabetically according to last name, include street addresses if available, and use a paragraph for each name:

*Jones, Joseph, 260 Town St., Sample, N.Y.*

*Williams, Susan, 780 Main St., Example, N.J.*

**passenger mile** One passenger carried one mile, or its equivalent, such as two passengers carried one-half mile.

**passer-by, passers-by**

**Passover** The week-long Jewish commemoration of the deliverance of the ancient Hebrews from slavery in Egypt. Occurs in March or April.

**pasteurize**

**pastor** See **religious titles** and the entry for the individual's denomination.

**patriarch** Lowercase when describing someone of great age and dignity.

Capitalize as a formal title before a name in some religious uses. See **Eastern Orthodox churches; religious titles;** and **Roman Catholic Church**.

**Patriot's Day** April 19, a legal holiday in Massachusetts.

**patrol, patrolled, patrolling**

**patrolman, patrolwoman** Capitalize before a name only if the word is a formal title. In some cities, the formal title is *police officer*.

See **titles**.

**payload**

**peacekeeping**

**peacemaker, peacemaking**

**peace offering**

**peacetime**

**peacock** It applies only to the male. The female is a *peahen*. Both are *peafowl*.

**peck** A unit of dry measure equal to eight dry quarts or one-fourth of a bushel.

The metric equivalent is approximately 8.8 liters.

To convert to liters, multiply by 8.8 (5 pecks × 8.8 = 44 liters).

See **liter**.

**pedal, peddle** When riding a bicycle or similar vehicle, you *pedal* it.

When selling something, you may *peddle* it.

**peddler**

**Peking** See the **Beijing** entry.

**pell-mell**

**penance** See **sacraments**.

**peninsula** Capitalize as part of a proper name: *the Florida Peninsula, the Upper Peninsula of Michigan.*

**penitentiary** See the **prison, jail** entry.

**Pennsylvania** Abbrev.: *Pa.* Legally a commonwealth, not a state.

See **state** and **state names**.

**Pennsylvania Dutch** The individuals are of German descent. The word *Dutch* is a corruption of *Deutsch,* the German word for "German."

**penny-wise** See **-wise**. Also: *pound-foolish.*

**Pentecost** The seventh Sunday after Easter.

**Pentecostalism** See **religious movements**.

**people, persons** Use *person* when speaking of an individual: *One person waited for the bus.*

The word *people* is preferred to *persons* in all plural uses. For example: *Thousands of people attended the fair. Some rich people pay few taxes. What will people say? There were 17 people in the room.*

*Persons* should be used only when it is in a direct quote or part of a title as in *Bureau of Missing Persons.*

*People* also is a collective noun that takes a plural verb when used to refer to a single race or nation: *The American people are united.* In this sense, the plural is *peoples: The peoples of Africa speak many languages.*

**people's** Use this possessive form when the word occurs in the formal name of a nation: *the People's Republic of Albania.*

Use this form also in such phrases as *the people's desire for freedom.*

**Pepsi, Pepsi Cola** Trademarks for a brand of cola soft drink.

**Pepsico Inc.** Formerly the Pepsi-Cola Co.

Headquarters is in Purchase, N.Y.

**percent** One word. It takes a singular verb when standing alone or when a singular word follows an *of* construction: *The teacher said 60 percent was a failing grade. He said 50 percent of the membership was there.*

It takes a plural verb when a plural word follows an *of* construction: *He said 50 percent of the members were there.*

It takes a plural verb when a plural word follows an *of* construction: *He said 50 percent of the members were there.*

**percentages** Use figures: *1 percent, 2.5 percent* (use decimals, not fractions), *10 percent.*

For amounts less than 1 percent, precede the decimal with a zero: *The cost of living rose 0.6 percent.*

Repeat *percent* with each individual figure: *He said 10 percent to 30 percent of the electorate may not vote.*

**periods** See the entry in the **Punctuation** chapter.

**perk** A shortened form of *perquisite,* often used by legislators to describe fringe benefits. In the state of New York, legislators also use the word *lulu* to describe the benefits they receive in lieu of pay.

When either word is used, define it.

**permissible**

**Persian Gulf** Use this long-established name for the body of water off the southern coast of Iran.

Some Arab nations call it the *Arabian Gulf.* Use *Arabian Gulf* only in direct quotations and explain in the text that the body of water is more commonly known as the *Persian Gulf.*

**personifications** Capitalize them: *Grim Reaper, John Barleycorn, Mother Nature, Old Man Winter, Sol,* etc.

**persons** See the **people, persons** entry.

**-person** Do not use coined words such as *chairperson* or *spokesperson* in regular text.

Instead, use *chairman* or *spokesman* if referring to a man or the office in general. Use *chairwoman* or *spokeswoman* if referring to a woman. Or, if applicable, use a neutral word such as *leader* or *representative.*

Use *chairperson* or similar coinage only in direct quotations or when it is the formal description for an office.

**persuade** See the **convince, persuade** entry.

**Peter Principle** It is: Each employee is promoted until he reaches his level of incompetence.

From the book by Laurence J. Peter.

**petty officer** See **military titles.**

**PG, PG-13** The *parental guidance* rating. See **movie ratings.**

**phase** See the **faze, phase** entry.

**Ph.D., Ph.D.s** The preferred form is to say a person *holds a doctorate* and name the individual's area of specialty.

See **academic degrees** and **doctor.**

**phenomenon, phenomena**

**Philadelphia** The city in Pennsylvania stands alone in datelines.

**Philippines** In datelines, give the name of a city or town followed by *Philippines:*
*MANILA, Philippines (AP)*

—

Specify the name of an individual island, if needed, in the text.

In stories: *the Philippines* or *the Philippine Islands* as the construction of a sentence dictates.

The people are *Filipinos.* The language is *Pilipino.*

**Photostat** A trademark for a type of photocopy.

## piano, pianos

**pica** A unit of measure in printing, equal to a fraction less than one-sixth of an inch. A pica contains 12 points.

**picket, pickets, picketed, picket line** *Picket* is both the verb and the noun. Do not use *picketer.*

## picnic, picnicked, picnicking, picnicker

**pico-** A prefix denoting one-trillionth of a unit. Move a decimal point 12 places to the left in converting to the basic unit: 2,999,888,777,666.5 picoseconds = 2.9998887776665 seconds.

**Piedmont Aviation** A *Piedmont airliner* is acceptable in any reference.

Headquarters is in Winston-Salem, N.C.

## pigeon

**pigeonhole** (n. and v.)

**Pikes Peak** No apostrophe. After Zebulon Montgomery Pike, a U.S. general and explorer. The 14,110-foot peak is in the Rockies of central Colorado.

**pile up** (v.) **pileup** (n., adj.)

**pill** Do not capitalize in references to oral contraceptives. Use *birth control pill* on first reference if necessary for clarity.

**pilot** Not a formal title. Do not capitalize before a name.

See **titles.**

**pingpong** A synonym for *table tennis.*

The trademark name is *Ping-Pong.*

**pint (dry)** Equal to 33.6 cubic inches, or one-half of a dry quart.

The metric equivalent is approximately .55 of a liter.

To convert to liters, multiply by .55 (5 dry pints × .55 = 2.75 liters).

See **liter** and **quart (dry).**

**pint (liquid)** Equal to 16 fluid ounces, or two cups.

The approximate metric equivalents are 470 milliliters or .47 of a liter.

To convert to liters, multi-

ply by .47 (4 pints × .47 =
1.88 liters).
See **liter.**

**Pinyin** The official Chinese
spelling system.
See **Chinese names.**

**pipeline**

**pistol** A pistol can be either an automatic or a revolver, but *automatic* and *revolver* are not synonymous. A
*revolver* has a revolving cylinder that holds the cartridges;
an *automatic* does not.
See **weapons.**

**Pittsburgh** The city in
Pennsylvania stands alone in
datelines.
The spelling is *Pittsburg* (no
*h*) for communities in Califor-
nia, Illinois, Kansas, New
Hampshire, Oklahoma and
Texas.

**plains** See **Great Plains.**

**planets** Capitalize the
proper names of planets: *Jupiter, Mars, Mercury, Neptune,
Pluto, Saturn, Uranus, Venus.*
Capitalize *earth* when used
as the proper name of our
planet: *The astronauts returned to Earth.*
Lowercase nouns and ad-

jectives derived from the
proper names of planets and
other heavenly bodies: *martian, jovian, lunar, solar, venusian.*
See **Earth** and **heavenly
bodies.**

**planning** Avoid the redundant *future planning.*

**plants** In general, lowercase the names of plants, but
capitalize proper nouns or adjectives that occur in a name.
Some examples: *tree, fir,
white fir, Douglas fir; Scotch
pine; clover, white clover, white
Dutch clover.*
If a botanical name is used,
capitalize the first word;
lowercase others: *pine tree
(Pinus), red cedar (Juniperus
virginiana), blue azalea (Calli-
carpa americana), Kentucky
coffee tree (Gymnocladus
dioica).*

**Plastic Wood** A trade-
mark for a brand of wood-fil-
ler compound.

**play titles** See **composition titles.**

**plead, pleaded, plead-
ing** Do not use the colloquial
past tense form, *pled.*

**Plexiglas** Note the single *s*. A trademark for plastic glass, generically called *plexiglass*.

**plow** Not *plough*.

**plurality** See the **majority, plurality** entry.

**plurals** Follow these guidelines in forming and using plural words:

MOST WORDS: Add *s*: *boys, girls, ships, villages*.

WORDS ENDING IN CH, S, SH, SS, X and Z: Add *es*: *churches, lenses, parishes, glasses, boxes, buzzes*. (*Monarchs* is an exception.)

WORDS ENDING IN IS: Change *is* to *es*: *oases, parentheses, theses*.

WORDS ENDING IN Y: If *y* is preceded by a consonant or *qu*, change *y* to *i* and add *es*: *armies, cities, navies, soliloquies*. (See PROPER NAMES below for an exception.)
Otherwise add *s*: *donkeys, monkeys*.

WORDS ENDING IN O: If *o* is preceded by a conso-nant, most plurals require *es*: *buffaloes, dominoes, echoes, heroes, potatoes*. But there are exceptions: *pianos*. See individual entries in this book for many of these exceptions.

WORDS ENDING IN F: Change *f* to *v* and add *es*: *leaves, selves*.

LATIN ENDINGS: Latin-root words ending in *us* change *us* to *i*: *alumnus, alumni*.
Most ending in *a* change to *ae*: *alumna, alumnae* (*formula, formulas* is an exception).
Those ending in *on* change to *a*: *phenomenon, phenomena*.
Most ending in *um* add *s*: *memorandums, referendums, stadiums*. Among those that still use the Latin ending: *addenda, curricula, media*.
Use the plural that Webster's New World lists as most common for a particular sense of a word.

FORM CHANGE: *man, men; child, children; foot, feet; mouse, mice;* etc.
Caution: When *s* is used with any of these words it indicates possession and must

be preceded by an apostrophe: *men's, children's,* etc.

WORDS THE SAME IN SINGULAR AND PLURAL: *corps, chassis, deer, moose, sheep,* etc.

The sense in a particular sentence is conveyed by the use of a singular or plural verb.

WORDS PLURAL IN FORM, SINGULAR IN MEANING: Some take singular verbs: *measles, mumps, news.*

Others take plural verbs: *grits, scissors.*

COMPOUND WORDS: Those written solid add *s* at the end: *cupfuls, handfuls, tablespoonfuls.*

For those that involve separate words or words linked by a hyphen, make the most significant word plural:

—Significant word first: *adjutants general, aides-de-camp, attorneys general, courts-martial, daughters-in-law, passers-by, postmasters general, presidents-elect, secretaries general, sergeants major.*

—Significant word in the middle: *assistant attorneys general, deputy chiefs of staff.*

—Significant word last: *assistant attorneys, assistant corporation counsels, deputy sheriffs, lieutenant colonels, major generals.*

WORDS AS WORDS: Do not use *'s: His speech had too many "ifs," "ands" and "buts."* (Exception to Webster's New World.)

See **words as words** entry.

PROPER NAMES: Most ending in *es* or *z* add *es: Charleses, Joneses, Gonzalezes.*

Most ending in *y* add *s* even if preceded by a consonant: *the Duffys, the Kennedys, the two Germanys, the two Kansas Citys.* Exceptions include *Alleghenies* and *Rockies.*

For others, add *s: the Carters, the McCoys, the Mondales.*

FIGURES: Add *s: The custom began in the 1920s. The airline has two 727s. Temperatures will be in the low 20s. There were five size 7s.*

(No apostrophes, an exception to Webster's New World guideline under "apostrophe.")

**SINGLE LETTERS:** Use *'s: Mind your p's and q's. He learned the three R's and brought home a report card with four A's and two B's. The Oakland A's won the pennant.*

**MULTIPLE LETTERS:** Add *s: She knows her ABCs. I gave him five IOUs. Four VIPs were there.*

**PROBLEMS, DOUBTS:** Separate entries in this book give plurals for troublesome words and guidance on whether certain words should be used with singular or plural verbs and pronouns. See also **collective nouns** and **possessives.**

For questions not covered by this book, use the plural that Webster's New World lists as most common for a particular sense of a word.

Note also the guidelines that the dictionary provides under its "plural" entry.

**p.m., a.m.** Lowercase, with periods. Avoid the redundant *10 p.m. tonight.*

**pocket veto** Occurs only when Congress has adjourned. If Congress is in session, a bill that remains on the president's desk for 10 days becomes law without his signature. If Congress adjourns, however, a bill that fails to get his signature within 10 days is vetoed.

Many states have similar procedures, but the precise requirements vary.

**podium** See the **lectern, podium, pulpit, rostrum** entry.

**poetic license** It is valid for poetry, not news or feature stories.

See **colloquialisms** and **special contexts.**

**poetry** See **composition titles** for guidelines on the names of poems.

Capitalize the first word in a line of poetry unless the author deliberately has used lowercase for a special effect. Do not, however, capitalize the first word on indented lines that must be created simply because the writer's line is too long for the available printing width.

**poinsettia** Note the *ia.*

**point** Do not abbreviate. Capitalize as part of a proper name: *Point Pleasant.*

**point (printing)** As a unit of measure in printing, a *point* equals a fraction less than a seventy-second of an inch. A pica contains 12 *points.* See **pica.**

**point-blank**

**Polaroid** A trademark for Polaroid Land instant-picture cameras and for transparent material containing embedded crystals capable of polarizing light.

**police department** In communities where this is the formal name, capitalize *police department* with or without the name of the community: *the Los Angeles Police Department, the Police Department.*

If a police agency has some other formal name such as *Division of Police,* use that name if it is the way the department is known to the public. If the story uses *police department* as a generic term for such an agency, put *police department* in lowercase.

If a police agency with an unusual formal name is known to the public as a *police department,* treat *police department* as the name, capitalizing it with or without the name of the community. Use

the formal name only if there is a special reason in the story.

If the proper name cannot be determined for some reason, such as the need to write about a police agency from a distance, treat *police department* as the proper name, capitalizing it with or without the name of the community.

Lowercase *police department* in plural uses: *the Los Angeles and San Francisco police departments.*

Lowercase *the department* whenever it stands alone.

**police titles** See **military titles** and **titles.**

**policy-maker** (n.) **policy-making** (n. and adj.)

**polio** The preferred term for *poliomyelitis* and *infantile paralysis.*

**Politburo** Acceptable in all references for the *Political Bureau of the Communist Party.* It is the chief policy-making body in the Soviet Union and other Communist nations.

**political divisions** Use Arabic figures and capitalize the accompanying word when used with a figure: *1st Ward, 10th Ward, 3rd Precinct, 22nd Precinct, the ward, the precinct.*

**political parties and philosophies** Capitalize both the name of the party and the word *party* if it is customarily used as part of the organization's proper name: *the Democratic Party, the Republican Party.*

Capitalize *Communist, Conservative, Democrat, Liberal, Republican, Socialist,* etc., when they refer to the activities of a specific party or to individuals who are members of it. Lowercase these words when they refer to political philosophy (see examples below).

Lowercase the name of a philosophy in noun and adjective forms unless it is the derivative of a proper name: *communism, communist; fascism, fascist.* But: *Marxism, Marxist; Nazism, Nazi.*

EXAMPLES: *John Adams was a Federalist, but a man who subscribed to his philosophy today would be described as a federalist. The liberal Republican senator and his Conservative Party colleague said they believe that democracy and communism are incompatible. The Communist said he is basically a socialist who has reservations about Marxism.*

*See* **convention** *and* **party affiliation.**

**politicking**

**politics** Usually it takes a plural verb: *My politics are my own business.*

As a study or science, it takes a singular verb: *Politics is a demanding profession.*

**polls and surveys** Stories based on public opinion polls should include the basic information for an intelligent evaluation of the results. In addition, such stories should be worded carefully to avoid exaggerating the results.

Information that should be in every story based on a poll should include the answers to the following questions.

1. How many people were interviewed? How were they selected? (Generally, only polls based on a random sample of the population are reliable.)

2. When was the poll taken? (Opinions can change quickly in response to events,

especially during election campaigns.)

3. Who paid for the poll? (Be wary of polls for candidates. The release of a candidate's poll is a campaign tactic.)

4. What is the sampling error for a poll and for subgroups mentioned in the story? (These figures should be provided by the polling organization. Such error margins are inversely related to sample size; the fewer people interviewed, the larger the sampling error. If opinions of a sub-group—like Roman Catholics, for example—are important, the sampling error for the sub-group should be included.)

5. How was the poll conducted—by telephone or in peoples' homes? (Polls conducted on street corners, in shopping malls or by mail generally should be avoided.)

6. What questions were asked and in what order? (Small differences in question wording can cause big differences in results. Exact question wording need not be included in a story unless it is a key to the results.)

Other areas for careful examination in poll stories are:

1. Exaggerating poll results. A poll based on 1,000 interviews saying one candidate has 46 percent support and another 44 percent backing does NOT say one candidate is "leading" the other. Only when the margin between the candidates is more than twice the sampling error can one candidate be said to be leading. If the gap is less than the error margin, the poll says the candidates are about even.

2. The results of earlier polls on the same topic can often be used to show trends in public opinion. However, take care if the polls are conducted by different polling organizations. Differing results might be caused by differing poll techniques.

3. In political polls, find out who makes up the base of the interviews for the results. Since everyone doesn't vote, pollsters base their results on registered voters alone, or, as election day draws near, "likely voters." If the results are based on "likely voters," ask the pollster how that group was identified.

4. No matter how good the poll, no matter how wide the margin, a poll does NOT say that one candidate will win an election. Polls can be wrong

and much can change the minds of the voters before they can cast their ballots.

**pom-pom,    pompon** *Pom-pom* is sometimes used to describe a rapid-firing automatic weapon. Define the word if it must be used.

A *pompon* is a large ball of crepe paper or fluffed cloth, often waved by cheerleaders or used atop a hat. It is also a flower that appears on some varieties of chrysanthemums.

**pontiff** Not a formal title. Always lowercase.

**pooh-pooh**

**pope** Capitalize when used as a formal title before a name; lowercase in all other uses: *Pope Paul spoke to the crowd. At the close of his address, the pope gave his blessing.*
See **Roman Catholic Church** and **titles.**

**Popsicle** A trademark for a brand of flavored ice on a stick.

**popular names** See **capitalization.**

**pore, pour** The verb *pore* means to gaze intently or steadily: *She pored over her books.*
The verb *pour* means to flow in a continuous stream: *It poured rain. He poured the coffee.*

**port, starboard** Nautical for left and right (when facing forward, toward the bow). Port is left. Starboard is right. Change to *left* or *right* unless in direct quotes.

**Portuguese names** See the **Spanish and Portuguese names** entry.

**possessives**    Follow these guidelines:

PLURAL NOUNS NOT ENDING IN S: Add *'s: the alumni's contributions, women's rights.*

PLURAL NOUNS ENDING IN S: Add only an apostrophe: *the churches' needs, the girls' toys, the horses' food, the ships' wake, states' rights, the VIPs' entrance.*

NOUNS PLURAL IN FORM, SINGULAR IN MEANING: Add only an apostrophe:    *mathematics' rules, measles' effects.* (But see INANIMATE OBJECTS below.)

Apply the same principle when a plural word occurs in the formal name of a singular entity: *General Motors' profits, the United States' wealth.*

**NOUNS THE SAME IN SINGULAR AND PLURAL:** Treat them the same as plurals, even if the meaning is singular: *one corps' location, the two deer's tracks, the lone moose's antlers.*

**SINGULAR NOUNS NOT ENDING IN S:** Add *'s:* *the church's needs, the girl's toys, the horse's food, the ship's route, the VIP's seat.*

Some style guides say that singular nouns ending in *s* sounds such as *ce, x,* and *z* may take either the apostrophe alone or *'s.* See SPECIAL EXPRESSIONS, but otherwise, for consistency and ease in remembering a rule, always use *'s* if the word does not end in the letter *s: Butz's policies, the fox's den, the justice's verdict, Marx's theories, the prince's life, Xerox's profits.*

**SINGULAR COMMON NOUNS ENDING IN S:** Add *'s* unless the next word

begins with *s: the hostess's invitation, the hostess' seat; the witness's answer, the witness' story.*

**SINGULAR PROPER NAMES ENDING IN S:** Use only an apostrophe: *Achilles' heel, Agnes' book, Ceres' rites, Descartes' theories, Dickens' novels, Euripides' dramas, Hercules' labors, Jesus' life, Jules' seat, Kansas' schools, Moses' law, Socrates' life, Tennessee Williams' plays, Xerxes' armies.*

**SPECIAL EXPRESSIONS:** The following exceptions to the general rule for words not ending in *s* apply to words that end in an *s* sound and are followed by a word that begins with *s: for appearance' sake, for conscience' sake, for goodness' sake.* Use *'s* otherwise: *the appearance's cost, my conscience's voice.*

**PRONOUNS:** Personal interrogative and relative pronouns have separate forms for the possessive. None involve an apostrophe: *mine, ours, your, yours, his, hers, its, theirs, whose.*

Caution: If you are using an apostrophe with a pronoun, always double-check to be sure that the meaning calls for a contraction: *you're, it's, there's, who's.*

Follow the rules listed above in forming the possessives of other pronouns: *another's idea, others' plans, someone's guess.*

**COMPOUND WORDS:** Applying the rules above, add an apostrophe or *'s* to the word closest to the object possessed: *the major general's decision, the major generals' decisions, the attorney general's request, the attorneys general's request.* See the **plurals** entry for guidelines on forming the plurals of these words.

Also: *anyone else's attitude, John Adams Jr.'s father, Benjamin Franklin of Pennsylvania's motion.* Whenever practical, however, recast the phrase to avoid ambiguity: *the motion by Benjamin Franklin of Pennsylvania.*

**JOINT POSSESSION, INDIVIDUAL POSSESSION:** Use a possessive form after only the last word if ownership is joint: *Fred and Sylvia's apartment, Fred and Sylvia's stocks.*

Use a possessive form after both words if the objects are individually owned: *Fred's and Sylvia's books.*

**DESCRIPTIVE PHRASES:** Do not add an apostrophe to a word ending in *s* when it is used primarily in a descriptive sense: *citizens band radio, a Cincinnati Reds infielder, a teachers college, a Teamsters request, a writers guide.*

Memory Aid: The apostrophe usually is not used if *for* or *by* rather than *of* would be appropriate in the longer form: *a radio band for citizens, a college for teachers, a guide for writers, a request by the Teamsters.*

An *'s* is required, however, when a term involves a plural word that does not end in *s: a children's hospital, a people's republic, the Young Men's Christian Association.*

**DESCRIPTIVE NAMES:** Some governmental, corporate and institutional organizations with a descriptive word in their names use an apostrophe; some do not. Follow the user's practice: *Actors Equity, Diners Club, the Ladies' Home Journal, the National Governors' Association, the Veterans Administration.* See separate entries for these and similar names frequently in the news.

QUASI POSSESSIVES: Follow the rules above in composing the possessive form of words that occur in such phrases as *a day's pay, two weeks' vacation, three days' work, your money's worth.*

Frequently, however, a hyphenated form is clearer: *a two-week vacation, a three-day job.*

DOUBLE POSSESSIVE: Two conditions must apply for a double possessive—a phrase such as *a friend of John's*—to occur: 1. The word after *of* must refer to an animate object, and 2. The word before *of* must involve only a portion of the animate object's possessions.

Otherwise, do not use the possessive form on the word after *of: The friends of John Adams mourned his death.* (All the friends were involved.) *He is a friend of the college.* (Not *college's,* because college is inanimate).

Memory Aid: This construction occurs most often, and quite naturally, with the possessive forms of personal pronouns: *He is a friend of mine.*

INANIMATE OBJECTS: There is no blanket rule against creating a possessive form for an inanimate object, particularly if the object is treated in a personified sense. See some of the earlier examples, and note these: *death's call, the wind's murmur.*

In general, however, avoid excessive personalization of inanimate objects, and give preference to an *of* construction when it fits the makeup of the sentence. For example, the earlier references to *mathematics' rules* and *measles' effects* would better be phrased: *the rules of mathematics, the effects of measles.*

**post-** Follow Webster's New World. Hyphenate if not listed there.

Some words without a hyphen:

| | |
|---|---|
| postdate | postnuptial |
| postdoctoral | postoperative |
| postelection | postscript |
| postgraduate | postwar |

Some words that use a hyphen:

post-bellum    post-mortem

**post office** It may be used but it is no longer capitalized because the agency is now the *U.S. Postal Service.*

Use lowercase in referring to an individual office: *I went to the post office.*

**potato, potatoes**

**pothole**

**pound (monetary)** The English pound sign is not used. Convert the figures to dollars in most cases. Use a figure and spell out *pounds* if the actual figure is relevant.

**pound (weight)** Equal to 16 ounces. The metric equivalent is approximately 454 grams, or .45 kilograms.

To convert to kilograms, multiply the number of pounds by .45 (20 pounds × .45 = 9 kilograms).

See **gram** and **kilogram.**

**pour** See the **pore, pour** entry.

**poverty level** An income level judged inadequate to provide a family or individual with the essentials of life. The figure for the United States is adjusted regularly to reflect changes in the Consumer Price Index.

**practitioner** See **Church of Christ, Scientist.**

**pre-** The rules in **prefixes** apply. The following examples of exceptions to first-listed spellings in Webster's New World are based on the general rule that a hyphen is used if a prefix ends in a vowel and the word that follows begins with the same vowel:

| | |
|---|---|
| pre-election | pre-establish |
| pre-eminent | pre-exist |
| pre-empt | |

Otherwise, follow Webster's New World, hyphenating if not listed there. Some examples:

| | |
|---|---|
| prearrange | prehistoric |
| precondition | preignition |
| precook | prejudge |
| predate | premarital |
| predecease | prenatal |
| predispose | pretax |
| preflight | pretest |
| preheat | prewar |

Some hyphenated coinage, not listed in the dictionary:

| | |
|---|---|
| pre-convention | pre-dawn |

**preacher** A job description, not a formal religious title. Do not capitalize.

See **titles** and **religious titles.**

**precincts** See **political divisions.**

**predominant, predominantly** Use these primary spellings listed in Webster's New World for the adjectival and adverbial forms. Do not use the alternatives it records, *predominate* and *predominately.*

The verb form, however, is *predominate.*

**prefixes** See separate listings for commonly used prefixes.

Generally, do not hyphenate when using a prefix with a word starting with a consonant.

Three rules are constant, although they yield some exceptions to first-listed spellings in Webster's New World Dictionary:

—Except for *cooperate* and *coordinate,* use a hyphen if the prefix ends in a vowel and the word that follows begins with the same vowel.

—Use a hyphen if the word that follows is capitalized.

—Use a hyphen to join doubled prefixes: *sub-subparagraph.*

**premier, prime minister** These two titles often are used interchangeably in translating to English the title of an individual who is the first minister in a national government that has a council of ministers.

*Prime minister* is the correct title throughout the Commonwealth, formerly the British Commonwealth. See **Commonwealth** for a list of members.

*Prime minister* is the best or traditional translation from most other languages. For consistency, use it throughout the rest of the world with these exceptions:

—Use *premier* for France and its former colonies.

—Use *premier* for the Communist nations of Eastern Europe and Asia.

—Use *chancellor* in Austria and West Germany.

—Follow the practice of a nation if there is a specific preference that varies from this general practice.

*Premier* is also the correct title for the individuals who lead the provincial governments in Canada and Australia.

See **titles.**

**premiere** A first performance.

## Presbyterian churches

There are four levels of authority in Presbyterian practice—individual congregations, presbyteries, synods and a general assembly.

Congregations are led by a pastor, who provides guidance in spiritual matters, and by a session, composed of ruling elders chosen by the congregation to represent the members in matters of government and discipline.

A presbytery is composed of all the ministers and an equal number of ruling elders, including at least one from each congregation, in a given district. Although the next two levels are technically higher, the presbytery has the authority to rule on many types of material and spiritual questions.

Presbyteries unite to form a synod, whose members are elected by the presbyteries. A synod generally meets once a year to decide matters such as the creation of new presbyteries and to pass judgment on appeals and complaints that do not affect the doctrine or constitution of the church.

A general assembly, composed of delegations of pastors and ruling elders from each presbytery, meets yearly to decide issues of doctrine and discipline within a Presbyterian body. It also may create new synods, divide old ones and correspond with general assemblies of other Presbyterian bodies.

The assembly also chooses the stated clerk and the moderator for a denomination. The stated clerk, the chief administrative officer, normally serves for an extended period. The moderator, the presiding officer, serves for a year.

The northern and southern branches of Presbyterianism merged in 1983 to become the Presbyterian Church (U.S.A.). Its membership totals 3 million. Formerly, Presbyterianism in the United States was concentrated in two bodies. The principal body in the north was the United Presbyterian Church in the United States of America. The Presbyterian Church in the United States was the principal southern body.

BELIEFS: The characteristic teachings rely heavily on the writings of John Calvin, a 16th-century French lawyer turned theologian who emphasized the "sovereignty of God." He taught that church government is a purely human organization, quasi-democratic in nature. Christ, rather than any human individual, is the only real head of the church.

Presbyterians believe in the Trinity and the humanity and divinity of Christ. Baptism, which may be administered to children, and the Lord's Supper are the only sacraments.

The basic doctrinal standard is the Westminster Confession of Faith, a document drawn up by an assembly of leaders who met from 1643 to 1648 in England.

CLERGY: All Presbyterian clergymen may be described as *ministers. Pastor* applies if a minister leads a congregation.

On first reference, use *the Rev.* before the name of a man or woman. On second reference, use only the last name of a man; use *Miss, Mrs., Ms.* or no title before the last name of a woman depending on her preference.

See **religious titles.**

OTHER OFFICIALS: The preferred form for elected officials such as *elders* and *dea-*

*cons* is to put the title after the name, with no religious title before the name. Capitalize *stated clerk, moderator, elder* and *deacon* when used before a name.

**presently** Use it to mean *in a little while* or *shortly,* but not to mean *now.*

**presidency**          Always lowercase.

**president** Capitalize president only as a formal title before one or more names: *President Reagan, Presidents Ford and Carter.*

Lowercase in all other uses: *The president said today. He is running for president. Lincoln was president during the Civil War.*

See **titles.**

FIRST NAMES: In most cases, the first name of a current or former U.S. president is not necessary on first reference. Use first names when necessary to avoid confusion: *President Andrew Johnson, President Lyndon Johnson.* First names also may be used for literary effect, or in feature or personality contexts.

For presidents of other nations and of organizations and

institutions, capitalize president as a formal title before a full name: *President Josip Broz Tito of Yugoslavia* (not *President Tito* on first reference), *President John Smith of Acme Corp.*

On second reference, use only the last name of a man. Use *Miss, Mrs. or Ms.* or no title before the last name of a woman, depending on her preference.

**presidential** Lowercase unless part of a proper name.

**Presidents Day** Not adopted by the federal government as the official name of the Washington's Birthday holiday. However, some federal agencies, states and local governments use the term.

See **Washington's Birthday.**

**Presidential Medal of Freedom** This is the nation's highest civilian honor. It is given by the president, on the recommendation of the Distinguished Civilian Service Board, for "exceptionally meritorious contribution to the security of the United States or other significant public or private endeavors."

Until 1963 it was known as the Medal of Freedom.

**presiding officer** Always lowercase.

**press conference** News conference is preferred.

**press secretary** Seldom a formal title. For consistency, always use lowercase, even when used before an individual's name.

(The formal title for the person who serves a U.S. president in this capacity is *assistant to the president for press relations.*)

See **titles.**

**pretense, pretext** A *pretext* is something that is put forward to conceal a truth: *He was discharged for tardiness, but the reason given was only a pretext for general incompetence.*

A *pretense* is a false show, a more overt act intended to conceal personal feelings: *My profuse compliments were all pretense.*

**priest** A vocational description, not a formal title. Do not capitalize.

See **religious titles** and the entries for the **Roman**

**Catholic Church** and **Episcopal Church.**

**prima-facie** (adj.)

**primary** Do not capitalize: *the New Hampshire primary, the Democratic primary, the primary.*

**primary day** Use lowercase for any of the days set aside for balloting in a primary.

**prime meridian** See **meridians.**

**prime minister** See the **premier, prime minister** entry.

**prime rate** The interest rate that commercial banks charge on loans to their borrowers with the best credit ratings.

Fluctuations in the prime rate seldom have an immediate impact on consumer loan rates. Over the long term, however, consistent increases (or decreases) in the prime rate can lead to increases (or decreases) in the interest rates for mortgages and all types of personal loans.

**prince, princess** Capitalize when used as a royal title before a name; lowercase when used alone: *Prince Charles, the prince.*
See **nobility.**

**Prince Edward Island** One of the three Maritime Provinces of Canada. Do not abbreviate.
See **datelines.**

**principal, principle** *Principal* is a noun and adjective meaning someone or something first in rank, authority, importance or degree: *She is the school principal. He was the principal player in the trade. Money is the principal problem.*
*Principle* is a noun that means a fundamental truth, law, doctrine or motivating force: *They fought for the principle of self-determination.*

**prior to** *Before* is less stilted for most uses. *Prior to* is appropriate, however, when a notion of requirement is involved: *The fee must be paid prior to the examination.*

**prison, jail** Do not use the two words interchangeably.

DEFINITIONS: *Prison* is a generic term that may be applied to the maximum security institutions often known as *penitentiaries* and to the medium security facilities often called *correctional institutions* or *reformatories*. All such facilities confine people serving sentences for felonies.

A *jail* is a facility normally used to confine people serving sentences for misdemeanors, people awaiting trial or sentencing on either felony or misdemeanor charges, and people confined for civil matters such as failure to pay alimony and other types of contempt of court.

See the **felony, misdemeanor** entry.

The guidelines for capitalization:

PRISONS: Many states have given elaborate formal names to their prisons. They should be capitalized when used, but commonly accepted substitutes should also be capitalized as if they were proper names. For example, use either *Massachusetts Correctional Institute-Walpole* or *Walpole State Prison* for the maximum security institution in Massachusetts.

Do not, however, construct a substitute when the formal name is commonly accepted: It is *the Colorado State Penitentiary*, for example, not *Colorado State Prison*.

On second reference, any of the following may be used, all in lowercase: *the state prison, the prison, the state penitentiary, the penitentiary*.

Use lowercase for all plural constructions: *the Colorado and Kansas state penitentiaries*.

JAILS: Capitalize *jail* when linked with the name of the jurisdiction: *Los Angeles County Jail*. Lowercase *county jail, city jail* and *jail* when they stand alone.

FEDERAL INSTITUTIONS: Maximum security institutions are known as *penitentiaries: the U.S. Penitentiary at Lewisburg* or *Lewisburg penitentiary* on first reference; *the federal penitentiary* or *the penitentiary* on second reference.

Medium security institutions include the word *federal* as part of their formal names: *the Federal Correctional Institution at Danbury, Conn.* On second reference: *the correctional institution, the federal prison, the prison*.

Most federal facilities used to house people awaiting trial or serving sentences of a year or less have the proper name *Federal Detention Center.* The term *Metropolitan Correctional Center* is being adopted for some new installations. On second reference: *the detention center, the correctional center.*

**prisoner of war** *POW* is acceptable on second reference.

Hyphenate when used as a compound modifier: *a prisoner-of-war trial.*

**private** See **military titles.**

**privilege, privileged**

**pro-** Use a hyphen when coining words that denote support for something. Some examples:

pro-abortion      pro-business
pro-labor         pro-life
pro-peace         pro-war

No hyphen when *pro* is used in other senses: *produce, profile, pronoun,* etc.

**probation** See the **pardon, parole, probation** entry.

**Procter & Gamble Co.** *P&G* is acceptable on second reference.

Headquarters is in Cincinnati.

**profanity** See the **obscenities, profanities, vulgarities** entry.

**professor** Never abbreviate. Capitalize when used as a formal title before a full name. Do not continue in second reference unless part of a quotation.

See **academic titles** and **titles.**

**profit-sharing** (n. and adj.) The hyphen for the noun is an exception to Webster's New World.

**Prohibition** Capitalize when referring to the period that began when the 18th Amendment to the Constitution prohibited the manufacture, sale or transportation of alcoholic liquors.

The amendment was declared ratified Jan. 29, 1919, and took effect Jan. 16, 1920. It was repealed by the 21st Amendment, which took effect Dec. 5, 1933, the day it was declared ratified.

**propeller**

**proper nouns** See **capitalization.**

**prophecy** (n.) **prophesy** (v.)

**proportions** Always use figures: *2 parts powder to 6 parts water.*

**proposition** Do not abbreviate. Capitalize when used with a figure in describing a ballot question: *He is uncommitted on Proposition 15.*

**prosecutor** Capitalize before a name when it is the formal title. In most cases, however, the formal title is a term such as *attorney general, state's attorney* or *U.S. attorney.* If so, use the formal title on first reference.

Lowercase *prosecutor* if used before a name on a subsequent reference, generally to help the reader distinguish between prosecutor and defense attorney without having to look back to the start of the story.

See **titles.**

**prostate gland** Not *prostrate.*

**Protestant, Protestantism** Capitalize these words when they refer either to denominations formed as a result of the break from the Roman Catholic Church in the 16th century or to the members of these denominations.

Church groups covered by the term include Anglican, Baptist, Congregational, Methodist, Lutheran, Presbyterian and Quaker denominations. See separate entries for each.

*Protestant* is not generally applied to Christian Scientists, Jehovah's Witnesses or Mormons.

Do not use *Protestant* to describe a member of an Eastern Orthodox church. Use a phrase such as *Orthodox Christian* instead.

See **religious movements.**

**Protestant Episcopal Church** See **Episcopal Church.**

**protester** Not *protestor.*

**prove, proved, proving** Use *proven* only as an adjective: *a proven remedy.*

**provinces** Names of provinces are set off from

community names by commas, just as the names of U.S. states are set off from city names: *They went to Halifax, Nova Scotia, on their vacation.*

Do not capitalize *province: They visited the province of Nova Scotia. The earthquake struck Shensi province.*

See **datelines.**

**proviso, provisos**

**provost marshal** The plural: *provost marshals.*

**PTA** See **parent-teacher association.**

**PT boat** It stands for *patrol torpedo boat.*

**Public Broadcasting Service** It is not a network, but an association of public television stations organized to buy and distribute programs selected by a vote of the members.

*PBS* is acceptable on first reference only within contexts such as a television column. Otherwise, do not use *PBS* until second reference.

**public schools** Use figures and capitalize *public school* when used with a fig-

ure: *Public School 3, Public School 10.*

If a school has a commemorative name: *Benjamin Franklin School.*

**publisher** Capitalize when used as a formal title before an individual's name: *Publisher Isaiah Thomas of the Massachusetts Spy.*

See **titles.**

**Puerto Rico** Do not abbreviate. See **datelines.**

**Pulitzer Prizes** These yearly awards for outstanding work in journalism and the arts were endowed by the late Joseph Pulitzer, publisher of the old New York World, and first given in 1917. They are awarded by the trustees of Columbia University on recommendation of an advisory board.

Capitalize *Pulitzer Prize,* but lowercase the categories: *Pulitzer Prize for public service, Pulitzer Prize for fiction,* etc.

Also: *She is a Pulitzer Prize winner. He is a Pulitzer Prize-winning author.*

**pull back** (v.) **pullback** (n.)

**pull out** (v.) **pullout** (n.)

**pulpit** See the **lectern, podium, pulpit, rostrum** entry.

**punctuation** Think of it as a courtesy to your readers, designed to help them understand a story.

Inevitably, a mandate of this scope involves gray areas. For this reason, the punctuation entries in this book refer to guidelines rather than rules. Guidelines should not be treated casually, however.

See the Punctuation chapter for separate entries under: **colon; comma; dash; ellipsis; exclamation mark; hyphen; parentheses; period; question mark; quotation marks;** and **semicolon.**

**pupil, student** Use *pupil* for children in kindergarten through eighth grade.

*Student* or *pupil* is acceptable for grades nine through 12.

Use *student* for college and beyond.

**Purim** The Jewish Feast of Lots, commemorating Esther's deliverance of the Jews in Persia from a massacre plotted by Haman. Occurs in February or March.

**push-button** (n., adj.)

**push up** (v.) **push-up** (n., adj.)

**put out** (v.) **putout** (n.)

**pygmy**

**Pyrex** A trademark for a brand of oven glassware.

**Q-and-A format** See **question mark** in **Punctuation** chapter.

**Qantas Airways** Headquarters is in Sydney, Australia.

**QE2** Acceptable on second reference for the ocean liner *Queen Elizabeth 2.*
(But use a Roman numeral for the monarch: *Queen Elizabeth II.*)

**Q-Tips** A trademark for a brand of cotton swabs.

**Quaalude** A trade name for a drug containing methaqualone. Not synonymous with illegal drugs containing methaqualone.

**Quakers** This informal name may be used in all references to members of the *Religious Society of Friends,* but always include the full name in a story dealing primarily with Quaker activities.

The denomination originated with George Fox, an Englishman who objected to Anglican emphasis on ceremony. In the 1640s, he said he heard a voice that opened the way for him to develop a personal relationship with Christ, described as the Inner Light, a term based on the Gospel description of Christ as the "true light."

Brought to court for opposing the established church, Fox tangled with a judge who derided him as a "Quaker" in reference to his agitation over religious matters.

The basic unit of Quaker organization is the weekly meeting, which corresponds to the congregation in other churches. A monthly meeting receives and records members, extends spiritual care and, if necessary, material aid for members of one or more weekly meetings.

A quarterly meeting consists of representatives from several monthly meetings.

Quarterly meetings unite into larger groups called yearly meetings, which are the rough equivalent of conventions, conferences, synods or dioceses in other faiths.

Capitalize references to a specific meeting, such as *the Yearly Meeting of the Philadelphia Society of Friends.* On second reference: *the yearly meeting* or *the meeting.*

Various yearly meetings form larger associations that assemble at intervals of a year or more. The largest is the Friends United Meeting. Its 15 yearly meeting members represent about half the Friends in the world.

Others include the Evangelical Friends Alliance and the Friends General Conference. Members of the conference include some yearly meetings that also are affiliated with the Friends United Meeting.

Overall, Friends count about 120,000 members in the United States and Canada and a total of 200,000 worldwide.

BELIEFS: Fox taught that the Inner Light emancipates a person from adherence to any creed, ecclesiastical authority or ritual forms. Many weekly meetings of worship involve silent meditation, in which any participant may speak when spiritually moved to do so. In others, there is a service of prayer and preaching.

CLERGY: There is no recognized ranking of clergy over lay people. However, meeting officers, called *elders* or *ministers,* are chosen by acclamation for their ability in leadership, but they do not go through an ordination ceremony. Many Quaker ministers, particularly in the Midwest and West, use *the Rev.* before their names and describe themselves as *pastors.*

Capitalize *elder, minister* or *pastor* when used as a formal title before a name. Use *the Rev.* before a name on first reference if it is a minister's practice. On second reference, use only the last name of a man; use *Miss, Mrs., Ms.* or no title before the last name of a woman depending on her preference.

See **religious titles.**

**quakes** See **earthquakes.**

**quart (dry)** Equal in volume to 67.2 cubic inches. The metric equivalent is approximately 1.1 liters.

To convert to liters, multiply by 1.1 (5 dry quarts × 1.1 = 5.5 liters).
See **liter.**

**quart (liquid)** Equal in volume to 57.75 cubic inches. Also equals 32 fluid ounces.

The approximate metric equivalents are 950 milliliters or .95 of a liter.

To convert to liters, multiply by .95 (4 quarts × .95 = 3.8 liters).
See **liter.**

**quasar** Acceptable in all references for a *quasi-stellar astronomical object,* often a radio source. Most astronomers consider quasars the most distant objects observable in the heavens.

**Quebec** The city in Canada stands alone in datelines.

Use *Quebec City* in the body of a story if the city must be distinguished from the province.

Do not abbreviate any reference to the province of Quebec, Canada's largest in area and second largest in population.
See **datelines.**

**queen** Capitalize only when used before the name of royalty: *Queen Elizabeth II.* Continue in second references that use the queen's given name: *Queen Elizabeth.*

Lowercase *queen* when it stands alone.

Capitalize in plural uses: *Queens Elizabeth and Victoria.*
See **nobility** and **titles.**

**queen mother** The mother of a reigning monarch. See **nobility.**

**questionnaire**

**quick-witted**

**quotation marks** See entry in **Punctuation** chapter.

**quotations in the news** Never alter quotations even to correct minor grammatical errors or word usage. Casual minor tongue slips may be removed by using ellipses but even that should be done with extreme caution. If there is a question about a quote, either don't use it or ask the speaker to clarify.

Do not routinely use abnormal spellings such as *gonna* in attempts to convey regional dialects or mispronunciations. Such spellings are appropriate, however, when relevant or help to convey a desired touch in a feature.

FULL vs. PARTIAL QUOTES: In general, avoid fragmentary quotes. If a speaker's words are clear and concise, favor the full quote. If cumbersome language can be paraphrased fairly, use an indirect construction, reserving quotation marks for sensitive or controversial passages that must be identified specifically as coming from the speaker.

CONTEXT: Remember that you can misquote some-

one by giving a startling remark without its modifying passage or qualifiers. The manner of delivery sometimes is part of the context. Reporting a smile or a deprecatory gesture may be as important as conveying the words themselves.

OFFENSIVE LANGUAGE: See the **obscenities, profanities, vulgarities** entry.

PUNCTUATION: See the **quotation marks** entry in the **Punctuation** chapter.

# R

**R** The *restricted* rating. See **movie ratings**.

**rabbi** See **Jewish congregations**.

**Rabbinical Assembly** See **Jewish congregations**.

**Rabbinical Council of America** See **Jewish congregations**.

**raccoon**

**race** Identification by race is pertinent:

—In biographical and announcement stories, particularly when they involve a feat or appointment that has not routinely been associated with members of a particular race.

—When it provides the reader with a substantial insight into conflicting emotions known or likely to be involved in a demonstration or similar event.

In some stories that involve a conflict, it is equally important to specify that an issue cuts across racial lines. If, for example, a demonstration by supporters of busing to achieve racial balance in schools includes a substantial number of whites, that fact should be noted.

Do not use racially derogatory terms unless they are part of a quotation that is essential to the story.

See the **obscenities, profanities, vulgarities** entry and the **nationalities and races** entry.

**rack, wrack** The noun *rack* applies to various types of framework; the verb *rack* means to arrange on a rack, to torture, trouble or torment: *He was placed on the rack. She racked her brain.*

The noun *wrack* means ruin or destruction, and generally is confined to the phrase *wrack and ruin*.

The verb *wrack* has substantially the same meaning

as the verb *rack,* the latter being preferred.

**racket** Not *racquet,* for the light bat used in tennis and badminton.

**radar** A lowercase acronym for *radio detection and ranging.*

**radical** In general, avoid this description in favor of a more precise definition of an individual's political views.

When used, it suggests that an individual believes change must be made by tearing up the roots or foundation of the present order.

Although *radical* often is applied to individuals who hold strong socialist or communist views, it also is applied at times to individuals who believe an existing form of government must be replaced by a more authoritarian or militaristic one.

See the **leftist, ultra-leftist** and **rightist, ultra-rightist** entries.

**radio** Capitalize and use before a name to indicate an official voice of the government: *Radio Moscow.*

Lowercase and place after the name when indicating only that the information was obtained from broadcasts in a city. *Havana radio,* for example, is the form used in referring to reports that are broadcast on various stations in the Cuban capital.

**radio station** The call letters alone are frequently adequate, but when this phrase is needed, use lowercase: *radio station WHEC.*

See **call letters.**

**railroads** Capitalize when part of a name: *the Illinois Central Gulf Railroad.*

Railroad companies vary the spellings of their names, using *Railroad, Rail Road, Railway,* etc. Consult the Official Railway Guide-Freight Service and the Official Railway Guide-Passenger Service for official spellings.

Use *the railroad* for all lines in second references.

Use *railroads* in lowercase for all plurals: *the Penn Central and Santa Fe railroads.*

See **Amtrak** and **Conrail.**

**rainstorm** See **weather terms.**

**raised, reared** Only humans may be *reared.*

Any living thing, including humans, may be *raised*.

**ranges** The form: *$12 million to $14 million*. Not: *$12 to $14 million*.

**rank and file** (n.) The adjective form: *rank-and-file*.

**rarely** It means seldom. *Rarely ever* is redundant, but *rarely if ever* often is the appropriate phrase.

**ratios** Use figures and hyphenate: *the ratio was 2-to-1, a ratio of 2-to-1, a 2-1 ratio*. As illustrated, the word *to* should be omitted when the numbers precede the word *ratio*.

Always use the word *ratio* or a phrase such as *a 2-1 majority* to avoid confusion with actual figures.

**ravage, ravish** To *ravage* is to wreak great destruction or devastation: *Union troops ravaged Atlanta*.

To *ravish* is to abduct, rape or carry away with emotion: *Soldiers ravished the women*.

Although both words connote an element of violence, they are not interchangeable. Buildings and towns cannot be *ravished*.

**rayon** Not a trademark.

**RCA Corp.** Formerly Radio Corporation of America. *RCA* is acceptable on second reference. RCA is now owned by General Electric Co.

Headquarters is in New York.

**re-** The rules in **prefixes** apply. The following examples of exceptions to first-listed spellings in Webster's New World are based on the general rule that a hyphen is used if a prefix ends in a vowel and the word that follows begins with the same vowel:

| | |
|---|---|
| re-elect | re-enlist |
| re-election | re-enter |
| re-emerge | re-entry |
| re-employ | re-equip |
| re-enact | re-establish |
| re-engage | re-examine |

For many other words, the sense is the governing factor:

| | |
|---|---|
| recover (regain) | re-cover (cover again) |
| reform (improve) | re-form (form again) |
| resign (quit) | re-sign (sign again) |

Otherwise, follow Webster's New World. Use a hyphen for words not listed there unless the hyphen would distort the sense.

**reader** See **Church of Christ, Scientist.**

**Realtor** The term *real estate agent* is preferred. Use *Realtor* only if there is a reason to indicate that the individual is a member of the National Association of Realtors.
See **service marks.**

**reared** See the **raised, reared** entry.

**rebut, refute** *Rebut* means to argue to the contrary: *He rebutted his opponent's statement.*
*Refute* connotes success in argument and almost always implies an editorial judgment. Instead, use *deny, dispute, rebut* or *respond to.*

**recipes** Always use figures. See **fractions.**
Do not use abbreviations. Spell out *teaspoon, tablespoon,* etc.
See the **food** entry for guidelines on when to capitalize the names of foods.

**recision** The preferred spelling is *rescission.*

**reconnaissance**

**Reconstruction** The process of re-organizing the Southern states after the Civil War.

**record** Avoid the redundant *new record.*

**rector** See **religious titles.**

**recur, recurred, recurring** Not *re-occur.*

**Red** Capitalize when used as a political, geographic or military term: *the Red army.*

**Red China** See **China.**

**red-haired, redhead, redheaded** All are acceptable for a person with red hair.
*Redhead* also is used colloquially to describe a type of North American diving duck.

**red-handed** (adj. and adv.)

**red-hot**

**redneck** From the characteristic sunburned neck acquired in the fields by farm laborers. It refers to poor, white rural residents of the South and often is a derogatory term.

**re-elect, re-election**

**refer** See the **allude, refer** entry.

**referable**

**reference works** Capitalize their proper names.

Do not use quotation marks around the names of books that are primarily catalogs of reference material. In addition to catalogs, this category includes almanacs, directories, dictionaries, encyclopedias, gazetteers, handbooks and similar publications.

EXAMPLES: *Congressional Directory, Webster's New World Dictionary, the AP Stylebook*. But: *"The Careful Writer"* and *"Modern American Usage."*

See the bibliography for the principal reference works used in preparing this book.

**referendum, referendums**

**reformatory** See the **prison, jail** entry.

**Reform Judaism** See **Jewish congregations.**

**refute** See the **rebut, refute** entry.

**regime** See the **government, junta, regime** entry.

**regions** See the **directions and regions** entry.

**reign, rein** The leather strap for controlling a horse is a *rein*, hence figuratively: *seize the reins, give free rein to, put a check rein on.*

*Reign* is the period a ruler is on the throne: *The king began his reign.*

**release times** Follow these guidelines:

TIME SET BY SOURCE: If a source provides material on condition that it not be published or broadcast until a specific time, the story should contain a boldface slug to that effect:

↑ **For Release 10 a.m. EST, Time set by source.** ←

MOVEMENT TIME SET BY SOURCE: If a source provides material on condition that it not be moved on any wire read by newspapers or broadcasters until a specific time, the request will be respected. Consult the General Desk if any problems arise.

RELEASE SPECIFIED BY SOURCE: If a source does not specify a particular hour but says material is for release in morning papers, the automatic release time for print and broadcast is 6:30 p.m. Eastern time.

If a source says only that material is for release in afternoon papers, the automatic release time for print and broadcast is 6:30 a.m. Eastern time.

In either case, the story should contain a boldface slug to that effect:

↑ **For Release 6:30 p.m. EST.** ←
↑ **For Release 6:30 a.m. EST.** ←

ENTERPRISE COPY: Stories sent in advance for a specified cycle and date are released for broadcast and morning papers at 6:30 p.m.; 6:30 a.m. if the advance was sent for afternoon papers.

**religious    affiliations** Capitalize the names and the related terms applied to members of the order: *He is a member of the Society of Jesus. He is a Jesuit.*

**religious    movements** The terms that follow have been grouped under a single entry because they are interrelated and frequently cross denominational lines.

**evangelical** Historically, *evangelical* was used as an adjective describing dedication to conveying the message of Christ. Today it also is used as a noun, referring to a category of doctrinally conservative Christians. They emphasize the need for a definite, adult commitment or conversion to faith in Christ and the duty of all believers to persuade others to accept Christ.

*Evangelicals* make up some conservative denominations and are numerous in broader denominations. Evangelicals stress both doctrinal absolutes and vigorous efforts to win others to belief.

The National Association of Evangelicals is an interdenominational, cooperative body of relatively small, conservative Protestant denominations. It has a total of about 2.5 million members and maintains headquarters in Wheaton, Ill.

**evangelism** The word refers to activity directed outside the church fold to influence others to commit themselves to faith in Christ, to his work of serving others and to infuse his principles into society's conduct.

Styles of evangelism vary from direct preaching appeals at large public meetings to practical deeds of caring in the name of Christ, indirectly conveying the same call to allegiance to him.

The word *evangelism* is derived from the Greek *evangelion,* which means the gospel or good news of Christ's saving action in behalf of humanity.

**fundamentalist** The word gained usage in an early 20th-century fundamentalist-modernist controversy within Protestantism. In recent years, however, *fundamentalist* has to a large extent taken on pejorative connotations except when applied to groups that stress strict, literal interpretations of Scripture and

separation from other Christians.

In general, do not use *fundamentalist* unless a group applies the word to itself.

**liberal** In general, avoid this word as a descriptive classification in religion. It has objectionable implications to many believers.

Acceptable alternative descriptions include *activist, more flexible* and *broadview.*

*Moderate* is appropriate when used by the contending parties, as is the case in the conflict between the moderate or more flexible wing of the Lutheran Church-Missouri Synod and conservatives, who argue for literal interpretations of biblical passages others consider symbolic.

Do not use the term *Bible-believing* to distinguish one faction from another, because all Christians believe the Bible. The differences are over interpretations.

**neo-Pentecostal, charismatic** These terms apply to a movement that has developed within mainline Protestant and Roman Catholic denominations since the mid-20th century. It is distinguished by its emotional expressiveness, spontaneity in worship, speaking or praying in "unknown tongues" and healing. Participants often characterize themselves as "spirit-filled" Christians.

Unlike the earlier Pentecostal movement, which led to separate denominations, this movement has swelled within major churches.

**Pentecostalism** A movement that arose in the early 20th century and separated from historic Protestant denominations. It is distinguished by the belief in tangible manifestations of the Holy Spirit, often in demonstrative, emotional ways such as speaking in "unknown tongues" and healing.

Pentecostal denominations include the Assemblies of God, the Pentecostal Holiness Church, the United Pentecostal Church Inc. and the International Church of the Foursquare Gospel founded by Aimee Semple McPherson.

**religious references** The basic guidelines:

DEITIES: Capitalize the proper names of monotheistic deities: *God, Allah, the Father, the Son, Jesus Christ, the Son of God, the Redeemer, the Holy Spirit,* etc.

Lowercase pronouns referring to the deity: *he, him, his, thee, thou, who, whose, thy,* etc.

Lowercase *gods* in referring to the deities of polytheistic religions.

Capitalize the proper names of pagan and mythological gods and goddesses: *Neptune, Thor, Venus,* etc.

Lowercase such words as *god-awful, goddamn, godlike, godliness, godsend.*

LIFE OF CHRIST: Capitalize the names of major events in the life of Jesus Christ in references that do not use his name: *The doctrines of the Last Supper, the Crucifixion, the Resurrection and the Ascension are central to Christian belief.*

But use lowercase when the words are used with his name: *The ascension of Jesus into Heaven took place 40 days after his resurrection from the dead.*

Apply the principle also to events in the life of his mother: *He cited the doctrines of the Immaculate Conception and the Assumption.* But: *She referred to the assumption of Mary into heaven.*

RITES: Capitalize proper names for rites that commemorate the Last Supper or signify a belief in Christ's presence: *the Lord's Supper, Holy Communion, Holy Eucharist.*

Lowercase the names of other sacraments. See the **sacraments** entry.

Capitalize *Benediction* and the *Mass.* But: *a high Mass, a low Mass, a requiem Mass.*

HOLY DAYS: Capitalize the names of holy days. See the **holidays and holy days** entry and separate entries for major Christian and Jewish feasts.

OTHER WORDS: Lowercase *heaven, hell, devil, angel, cherub, an apostle, a priest,* etc.

Capitalize *Hades* and *Satan.*

For additional details, see **Bible,** entries for frequently used religious terms, the entries for major denominations, **religious movements** and **religious titles.**

**Religious Society of Friends** See **Quakers.**

**religious titles** The first reference to a clergyman or clergywoman normally should include a capitalized title before the individual's name.

In many cases, *the Rev.* is the designation that applies before a name on first reference. Use *the Rev. Dr.* only if the individual has an earned doctoral degree (doctor of divinity degrees frequently are honorary) and reference to the degree is relevant.

On second reference to members of the clergy:

—To a man: Use only a last name if he uses a surname: *the Rev. Billy Graham* on first reference, *Graham* on second. If a man is known only by a religious name, repeat the title: *Pope Paul VI* or *Pope Paul* on first reference, *Pope Paul, the pope* (not Paul) or *the pontiff* on second; *Metropolitan Ireney* on first reference, *Metropolitan Ireney* or *the metropolitan* on second.

—To a woman: Use *Miss, Mrs., Ms.* or no title before her last name depending on her preference.

Detailed guidance on specific titles and descriptive words such as *priest* and *minister* is provided in the entries for major denominations. In general, however:

CARDINALS, ARCHBISHOPS, BISHOPS: The preferred form for first reference is to use *Cardinal, Archbishop* or *Bishop* before the individual's name: *Cardinal Timothy Manning, archbishop of Los Angeles.* On second reference: *Manning* or *the cardinal.*

Substitute *the Most Rev.* if applicable and appropriate in the context: *He spoke to the Most Rev. Joseph L. Bernardin, archbishop of Cincinnati.* On second reference: *Bernardin* or *the archbishop.*

Entries for individual denominations tell when *the Most Rev., the Very Rev.,* etc., are applicable.

MINISTERS AND PRIESTS: Use *the Rev.* before a name on first reference.

Substitute *Monsignor* before the name of a Roman Catholic priest who has received this honor.

Do not routinely use *curate, father, pastor* and similar words before an individual's name. If they appear before a name in a quotation, capitalize them.

RABBIS: Use *Rabbi* before a name on first reference. On second reference, use only the last name of a man; use *Miss, Mrs., Ms.* or no title before a woman's last name depending on her preference.

NUNS: Always use *Sister,* or *Mother* if applicable, before a name: *Sister Agnes Rita* in all references if the nun uses only a religious name; *Sister Clare Regina Torpy* on first reference if she uses a surname, *Sister Torpy* on second, or *Miss, Ms.* or no title as she prefers.

OFFICEHOLDERS: The preferred first-reference form for people who hold church office but are not ordained clergy in the usual sense is to use a construction that sets the title apart from the name by commas. Capitalize the formal title of an office, however, if it is used directly before an individual's name.

**reluctant, reticent** *Reluctant* means unwilling to act: *He is reluctant to enter the primary.*

*Reticent* means unwilling to speak: *The candidate's husband is reticent.*

**Reorganized Church of Jesus Christ of Latter Day Saints** Not properly described as a *Mormon church.* See the explanation under **Church of Jesus Christ of Latter-day Saints.**

**representative, Rep.** See **legislative titles** and **party affiliation.**

**republic** Capitalize *republic* when used as part of a nation's full, formal name: *the Republic of Argentina.*
See **datelines.**

**Republic Airlines** Formed by the merger of North Central Airlines and Southern Airways.
Headquarters is in Minneapolis.

**republican, Republican Party** *GOP* may be used on second reference.
See the **political parties and philosophies** entry.

**Republican Governors Association** No apostrophe.

**Republican National Committee** On second reference: *the national committee, the committee.*
Similarly: *Republican State Committee, Republican County Committee, Republi-*
can City Committee, the state committee, the county committee, the city committee, the committee.*

**reputation** See the **character, reputation** entry.

**rescission** Not *recision.*

**Reserve Officers' Training Corps** The *s'* is military practice. *ROTC* is acceptable in all references.
When the service is specified, use *Army ROTC, Navy ROTC* or *Air Force ROTC,* not *AROTC, NROTC* or *AFROTC.*

**resident** See the **citizen, resident, subject, national, native** entry.

**resistible**

**restaurateur** No *n.* Not *restauranteur.*

**restrictive clauses** See the **essential clauses, nonessential clauses** entry.

**restrictive phrases** See the **essential phrases, nonessential phrases** entry.

**Retail Clerks International Union** See **United**

**Food and Commercial Workers International Union.**

**Reuters** A private British news agency, named for Baron Paul Julius von Reuter, the founder.

The official name is *Reuters Ltd.* It is referred to as *Reuters.* When it is used as an adjective, the *s* is dropped: *a Reuter correspondent, a Reuter story.*

**Rev.** When this description is used before an individual's name, precede it with the word *the* because, unlike the case with *Mr.* and *Mrs.,* the abbreviation *Rev.* does not stand for a noun.

If an individual has a secular title such as *Rep.,* use whichever is appropriate to the context.

See **religious titles.**

**revolution** Capitalize when part of a name for a specific historical event: *the American Revolution, the Bolshevik Revolution, the French Revolution.*

*The Revolution,* capitalized, also may be used as a shorthand reference to the *American Revolution.* Also: *the Revolutionary War.*

Lowercase in other uses: *a revolution, the revolution, the American and French revolutions.*

**revolutions per minute** The abbreviation *rpm* is acceptable on first reference in specialized contexts such as an auto column. Otherwise do not use it until second reference.

**revolver** See **pistol** and **weapons.**

**Rh factor** Also: *Rh negative, Rh positive.*

**Rhode Island** Abbrev.: *R.I.* Smallest of the 50 states in total land area: 1,049 square miles.

See **state names.**

**Richter scale** See **earthquakes.**

**RICO** An acronym for *Racketeer Influenced, Corrupt Organizations Act.* Do not use.

**riffraff**

**rifle** See **weapons.**

**rifle, riffle** *To rifle* is to plunder or steal.

*To riffle* is to leaf rapidly through a book or pile of papers.

**right hand** (n.) **right-handed** (adj.) **right-hander** (n.)

**rightist, ultra-rightist** In general, avoid these terms in favor of more precise descriptions of an individual's political philosophy.

As popularly used today, particularly abroad, *rightist* often applies to someone who is conservative or opposed to socialism. It also often indicates an individual who supports an authoritarian government that is militantly anti-communist or anti-socialist.

*Ultra-rightist* suggests an individual who subscribes to rigid interpretations of a conservative doctrine or to forms of fascism that stress authoritarian, often militaristic, views.

See **radical** and the **leftist, ultra-leftist** entry.

**right of way, rights of way**

**right-to-work** (adj.) A *right-to-work* law prohibits a company and a union from signing a contract that would require the affected workers to be union members.

Federal labor laws generally permit such contracts. There is no federal right-to-work law, but Section 14B of the Taft-Hartley Act allows states to pass such laws if they wish. Many states have done so.

The repeal of Section 14B would have the effect of voiding all right-to-work laws. By itself, the repeal would not require workers to be union members, but in states that now have right-to-work laws, the repeal would open the way to contracts requiring union membership.

See **closed shop** for definitions of various agreements that require union membership.

**right wing** (n.) But: *right-wing* (adj.), *right-winger* (n.).

**Ringling Bros. and Barnum & Bailey Circus** Note the *and, &.*

Headquarters is in Washington.

**Rio Grande** Not *Rio Grande River. (Rio* means river.)

**rip off** (v.) **rip-off** (n., adj.)

**river** Capitalize as part of a proper name: *the Mississippi River*.

Lowercase in other uses: *the river, the Mississippi and Missouri rivers*.

**road** Do not abbreviate. See **addresses**.

**Roaring '20s** See **decades**.

**robbery** See the **burglary, larceny, robbery, theft** entry.

**rock 'n' roll**

**Rocky Mountains** Or simply: *the Rockies*.

**roll call** (n.) **roll-call** (adj.)

**Rolls-Royce** Note the hyphen in this trademark for a make of automobile.

**roly-poly**

**Roman Catholic Church** The church traces its origin to Christ's choice of the apostle Peter to lead his church on earth and his promise that "whatever you bind on earth shall be bound in heaven and whatever you loose on earth shall be loosed in heaven."

The church teaches that its bishops have been established as the legitimate successors of the apostles through generations of ceremonies in which authority was passed down by a laying-on of hands.

Responsibility for teaching the faithful and administering the church rests with the bishops. However, the church holds that the pope has final authority over their actions because he is the bishop of Rome, the office that it teaches was held by Peter at his death.

The shared teaching power —often called *collegiality*—of the bishops is particularly manifest when a pope summons an ecumenical council, a meeting of all bishops to regulate church worship and define new expressions of its teachings. Council actions must be approved by the pope, however, before they can take effect.

Although the pope is empowered to speak infallibly on faith and morals, he does so only in formal pronouncements that specifically state he is speaking from the chair (*ex cathedra)* of St. Peter. This rarely used prerogative was most recently invoked in 1950, when Pope Pius XII declared that Mary was assumed bodily into heaven.

The Curia serves as a form of governmental Cabinet. Its members, appointed by the pope, handle both administrative and judicial functions.

The pope also chooses members of the College of Cardinals, who serve as his principal counselors. When a new pope must be chosen, they meet in a conclave to select a new pope by majority vote. In practice, cardinals are bishops, but there is no requirement that a cardinal be a bishop.

In the Latin Rite used by Catholics in the Western world, there are no national "churches" in the sense that applies in other denominations. Bishops in various nations do, however, organize conferences that develop programs to further the needs of the church in their nations. The National Conference of Catholic Bishops is the national organization of Roman Catholic bishops in the United States. Its administrative arm is the United States Catholic Conference, with offices in Washington.

In the Eastern Rite, followed by many Roman Catholics who live in the Middle East or trace their origins to it, there are national churches. They and the archbishops (often called *patriarchs)* who head them have considerable autonomy in ritual and discipline, but they acknowledge the authority of the pope. See the **Eastern rite** entry.

In the United States, the church's principal organizational units are archdioceses and dioceses. They are headed, respectively, by archbishops and bishops, who have final responsibility for many activities within their jurisdictions and report directly to Rome. Although the seat of an archdiocese once served as a meeting place for the bishops of other dioceses within a region, there is little practical difference between the two in the Latin Rite. An archbishop, however, is required to report to Rome if he believes that abuses have occurred in a diocese within his region.

MEMBERSHIP: The church counts more than 600

million members worldwide. In the United States it has more than 48 million members, making it the largest single body of Christians in the nation.

BELIEFS: Roman Catholics believe in the Trinity—that there is one God who exists as three divine persons, the Father, the Son and the Holy Spirit. They believe that the Son became man as Jesus Christ.

Other beliefs include salvation through Christ, and everlasting heaven and hell.

The essential elements of belief are contained in the Bible and in "tradition," the body of teachings passed on both orally and in writing by the apostles and their successors.

The Mass is the central act of worship. Christ is believed to be present in the Holy Eucharist, which is consecrated during Mass.

In addition to the Holy Eucharist, there are six other sacraments—baptism, confirmation, penance (often called the sacrament of reconciliation), matrimony, holy orders, and the sacrament of the sick (formerly extreme unction).

CLERGY: Ranks below the pope are, in descending order, cardinal, archbishop, bishop, monsignor, priest and deacon. In religious orders, some men who are not priests have the title *brother*.

Capitalize *pope* when used as a title before a name: *Pope Paul VI, Pope Paul.* Lowercase in all other uses. See the **titles** entry.

The first-reference forms for other titles follow. Use only last names on second reference.

Cardinals: *Cardinal Timothy Manning.* The usage *Timothy Cardinal Manning,* a practice traceable to the nobility's custom of identifications such as *William, Duke of Norfolk,* is still used in formal documents but otherwise is considered archaic.

Archbishops: *Archbishop Joseph L. Bernardin,* or *the Most Rev. Joseph L. Bernardin, archbishop of Cincinnati.*

Bishops: *Bishop Bernard J. Flanagan,* or *the Most Rev. Bernard J. Flanagan, bishop of Worcester.*

Monsignors: *Monsignor Joseph E. Vogt.* Do not use the abbreviation *Msgr.* Do not use *the Rt. Rev.* or *the Very Rev.*—this distinction between types of monsignors no longer is made.

Priests: *the Rev. John J. Paret.* When necessary in quotations on second reference: *Father Paret.*

Deacons: *Deacon Mark Smith.*

Brothers: *Brother Thomas Garvey.*

Nuns: See the **sister** entry. See **religious titles.**

**Romania** Not *Rumania.*

**Romanian Orthodox Church** The Romanian Orthodox Church in America is an autonomous archdiocese of the Romanian Orthodox Church. The Romanian Orthodox Episcopate of America is an autonomous archdiocese within the Orthodox Church in America.

See **Eastern Orthodox churches.**

**Roman numerals** They use letters *(I, X,* etc.) to express numbers.

Use Roman numerals for wars and to establish personal sequence for people and animals: *World War I, Native Dancer II, King George V, Pope John XXIII, John Jones III.* See the **junior, senior** entry.

Use Arabic numerals in all other cases. See **Arabic numerals** and **numerals.**

In Roman numerals, the capital letter *I* equals 1, *V* equals 5, *X* equals 10, *L* equals 50, *C* equals 100, *D* equals 500 and *M* equals 1,000. Do not use *M* to mean million, as some newspapers occasionally do in headlines.

Other numbers are formed from these by adding or subtracting as follows:

—The value of a letter following another of the same or greater value is added: *III* equals 3.

—The value of a letter preceding one of greater value is subtracted: *IV* equals 4.

**Rome** The city in Italy stands alone in datelines.

**room numbers** Use figures and capitalize *room* when used with a figure: *Room 2, Room 211.*

**rooms** Capitalize the names of specially designated rooms: *Blue Room, Lincoln Room, Oval Office, Persian Room.*

**Roquefort cheese, Roquefort dressing** A certification mark for a type of blue cheese cured in Roquefort, France.

It is not a trademark.

**rosary** It is *recited* or *said,* never *read.* Always lowercase.

**Rosh Hashana** The Jewish new year. Occurs in September or October.

**rostrum** See the **lectern, podium, pulpit, rostrum** entry.

**ROTC** Acceptable in all references for *Reserve Officers' Training Corps.*

When the service is specified, use *Army ROTC, Navy ROTC,* or *Air Force ROTC,* not *AROTC, NROTC* or *AFROTC.*

**round up** (v.) **roundup** (n.)

**route numbers** Do not abbreviate *route.* See **highway designations.**

**Royal Dutch-Shell Group of Companies** This holding company, based in London and The Hague, owns substantial portions of the stock in numerous corporations that specialize in petroleum and related products.

Most have *Shell* in their names.

Among them is Shell Oil Co., a U.S. corporation, with headquarters in Houston.

**royal titles** See **nobility.**

**R.S.V.P.** The abbreviation for the French *répondez s'il vous plaît,* it means *please reply.*

**Rt. Rev.** See the entry for an individual denomination.

**rubber stamp** (n.) **rubber-stamp** (v. and adj.)

**rubella** Also known as *German measles.*

**runner-up, runners-up**

**running mate**

**rush hour** (n.) **rush-hour** (adj.)

**Russia, Soviet Union** *Soviet people* and *the Soviets* are acceptable umbrella terms in referring to all the people who live within the 15 republics that make up the *Union of Soviet Socialist Republics,* popularly known as *the Soviet Union.*

The Russian Soviet Federated Socialist Republic is the dominant state, and its leaders effectively control the other 14 republics. For this reason, *Russia, Russian* and *Russians* are acceptable synonyms for *Soviets* and *Soviet Union* when referring to the governmental apparatus. For example: *Russia is considering the U.S. proposal. The United States is negotiating with the Russians.*

Do not, however, use *Russia, Russian* or *Russians* in references to all the people of the Soviet Union. Make it *Soviet hockey team,* for example, not *Russian hockey team,* in a story about a group that includes Soviet citizens of many nationalities.

When relevant, identify the nationalities of the individuals involved. While a first reference might say *Soviet gymnast,* for example, indicate later in the story where the individual comes from in the Soviet Union.

In addition to the *Russians,* national groups within the Soviet Union include *Armenians, Georgians, Latvians, Lithuanians* and *Ukrainians.*

DATELINES: MOSCOW stands alone. Follow all other community names with *U.S.S.R.* In the body of a story use *Soviet Union* or the full name, not *U.S.S.R.*

Identify a republic in the text if relevant.

REPUBLICS: The Russian republic includes Moscow and pre-revolutionary Russia. It is the largest in area and population.

The other 14, from the most populous to the least populous, are: The Ukrainian, Byelorussian, Uzbeck, Kazakh, Georgian, Azerbaidzhan, Lithuanian, Moldavian, Latvian, Kirgiz, Tadzhik, Armenian, Estonian and Turkmen Soviet Socialist Republics.

The Ukrainian and Byelorussian republics have their own memberships in the United Nations.

**Russian names** When a first name in Russian has a close phonetic equivalent in English, use the equivalent in translating the name: *Alexander Solzhenitsyn* rather than *Aleksandr,* the spelling that would result from a transliteration of the Russian letter into the English alphabet.

When a first name has no close phonetic equivalent in English, express it with an

English spelling that approximates the sound in Russian: *Nikita,* for example.

For last names, use the English spelling that most closely approximates the pronunciation in Russian.

If an individual has a preference for an English spelling that is different from the one that would result by applying these guidelines, follow the individual's preference.

Women's last names have feminine endings. But use them only if the woman is not married or if she is known under that name *(the ballerina Maya Plissetskaya).* Otherwise, use the masculine form: *Victoria Brezhnev,* not *Brezhneva.*

Russian names never end in *off,* except for common mistransliterations such as *Rachmaninoff.* Instead, the transliterations should end in *ov: Romanov.*

**Russian Orthodox Church** See **Eastern Orthodox churches.**

**Russian Revolution** Also: *the Bolshevik Revolution.*

# S

**Sabbath** Capitalize in religious references; lowercase to mean a period of rest.

**Sabena Belgian World Airlines** A *Sabena airliner* is acceptable in any reference.

Headquarters is in Brussels, Belgium.

**saboteur**

**sacraments** Capitalize the proper names used for a sacramental rite that commemorates the life of Jesus Christ or signifies a belief in his presence: *the Lord's Supper, Holy Communion, Holy Eucharist.*

Lowercase the names of other sacraments: *baptism, confirmation, penance* (now often called *the sacrament of reconciliation), matrimony, holy orders,* and *the sacrament of anointing the sick* (formerly *extreme unction*).

See entries for the major religious denominations and **religious references.**

**sacrilegious**

**Safeway Stores Inc.** Headquarters is in Oakland, Calif.

**saint** Abbreviate as *St.* in the names of saints, cities and other places: *St. Jude; St. Paul, Minn.; St. John's, Newfoundland; St. Lawrence Seaway.*

But see the entries for **Saint John** and **Sault Ste. Marie.**

**Saint John** The spelling for the city in New Brunswick.

To distinguish it from *St. John's, Newfoundland.*

**salable**

**SALT** See **Strategic Arms Limitation Talks (Treaty).**

**Salt Lake City** Stands alone in datelines.

**salvo, salvos**

**SAM, SAMs** Acceptable on second reference for *surface-to-air-missile(s)*.

**San'a** It's NOT an apostrophe (') in the Yemen capital's name. It's a reverse apostrophe ('), or a single opening quotation mark.

**sandbag** (n.) The verbs: *sandbagged, sandbagging.* And: *sandbagger.*

**San Diego** The city in California stands alone in datelines.

**sandstorm** See **weather terms.**

**sandwich**

**Sanforized** A trademark denoting that a fabric has been pre-shrunk according to a particular standard.
A related trademark, *Sanforset,* describes a Sanforized fabric that has been treated to meet standards for smoothness.

**San Francisco** The city in California stands alone in datelines.

**sanitarium, sanitariums**

**San Marino** Use alone in datelines on stories from the Republic of San Marino.

**Santa Claus**

**Sardinia** Use instead of Italy in datelines on stories from communities on this island.

**Saskatchewan** A province of Canada north of Montana and North Dakota. Do not abbreviate.
See **datelines.**

**Satan** But lowercase *devil* and *satanic.*

**satellites** See **spacecraft designations.**

**satellite communications** The following are some generally used technical terms dealing with satellite communications.
—*uplink* The transmission from the ground to the satellite.
—*downlink* The transmission from the satellite to the ground.
—*foot print* The area on the ground in which a transmis-

sion from a particular satellite can be received.

—*earth station* Sending or receiving equipment on the ground for a satellite.

—*transponder* The equipment on a satellite which receives from the ground and sends to the ground. A satellite usually has a number of *transponders.*

—*geosynchronous* A satellite orbit in which the satellite appears to always be in the same place in reference to the earth. Most communications satellites are in geosynchronous orbits. Also *geostationary.*

**Saturday** See **days of the week**.

**Saturday Night Special** See **weapons**.

**Sault Ste. Marie, Mich., Sault St. Marie, Ontario** The abbreviation is *Ste.* instead of *St.* because the full name is *Sault Sainte Marie.*

**savings and loan associations** They are not banks. Use *the association* on second reference.

**savior** Use this spelling for all senses, rather than the alternative form, *saviour.*

**Scandinavian Airlines System** *SAS* is acceptable on second reference.

Headquarters is in Stockholm, Sweden.

**scene numbers** Capitalize *scene* when used with a figure: *Scene 2; Act 2, Scene 4.*

But: *the second scene, the third scene.*

**scheme** Do not use as a synonym for *a plan* or *a project.*

**school** Capitalize when part of a proper name: *Public School 3, Madison Elementary School, Doherty Junior High School, Crocker High School.*

**scissors** Takes plural verbs and pronouns: *The scissors are on the table. Leave them there.*

**Scot, Scots, Scottish** A native of Scotland is a *Scot.* The people are the *Scots,* not *the Scotch.*

Somebody or something is *Scottish.*

**scotch barley, scotch broth, scotch salmon, scotch sour**

**Scotch tape** A trademark for a brand of transparent tape.

**Scotch whisky** A type of whiskey distilled in Scotland from malted barley. The malt is dried over a peat fire.

Capitalize *Scotch* and use the spelling *whisky* only when the two words are used together.

Lowercase *scotch* standing alone: *Give me some scotch.*

Use the spelling *whiskey* for generic references to the beverage, which may be distilled from any of several grains.

The verb *to scotch* means to stamp out, put an end to.

**Scotland** Use *Scotland* after the names of Scottish communities in datelines.

See **datelines** and **United Kingdom**.

**Scripture, Scriptures** Capitalize when referring to the religious writings in the Bible.

See **Bible**.

**scuba** Lowercased acronym for *self-contained underwater breathing apparatus.*

**sculptor** Use for both men and women.

**scurrilous**

**Seaboard World Airlines** Headquarters is in New York.

**Sea Islands** A chain of islands off the coasts of South Carolina, Georgia and Florida.

Islands within the boundaries of South Carolina include Parris Island, Port Royal Island, and St. Helena Island.

Those within Georgia include Cumberland Island (largest in the chain), St. Simons Island and St. Catherines Island (no apostrophes), and Sea Island.

Amelia Island is within the boundaries of Florida.

Several communities have names taken from the island name—Port Royal is a town on Port Royal Island, Sea Island is a resort on Sea Island, and St. Simons Island is a village on St. Simons Island.

In datelines:

*PORT ROYAL, S.C. (AP)—*

*ST. SIMONS ISLAND, Ga. (AP)—*

**seaman** See **military titles**.

**Sears, Roebuck and Co.** Headquarters is in Chicago.

**seasons** Lowercase *spring, summer, fall, winter* and derivatives such as *springtime* unless part of a formal name: *Dartmouth Winter Carnival, Winter Olympics, Summer Olympics.*

**Seattle** The city in the state of Washington stands alone in datelines.

**second guess** (n.) The verb form: *second-guess.* Also: *second-guesser.*

**second hand** (n.)
**secondhand** (adj. and adv.) *Secondhand Rose had a watch with a second hand that she bought secondhand.*

**second-rate** (adj.) All uses: *A second-rate play. The play is second-rate.*

**second       reference** When used in this book, the term applies to all subsequent references to an organization or individual within a story.

Acceptable abbreviations and acronyms for organizations frequently in the news are listed under the organization's full name. A few prominent acronyms acceptable on first reference also are listed alphabetically according to the letters of the acronym.

The listing of an acceptable term for second reference does not mean that it always must be used after the first reference. Often a generic word such as *the agency, the commission* or *the company* is more appropriate and less jarring to the reader. At other times, the full name may need to be repeated for clarity.

For additional guidelines that apply to organizations, see the **abbreviations and acronyms** entry and **capitalization**.

For additional guidelines that apply to individuals, see **courtesy titles** and **titles**.

**secretary** Capitalize before a name only if it is an official corporate or organizational title. Do not abbreviate. See **titles**.

**secretary-general** With a hyphen. Capitalize as a formal title before a name: *Secretary-General Dag Hammarskjold.*

See **titles**.

**secretary of state** Capitalize as a formal title before a name. See **titles**.

**secretary-treasurer** With a hyphen. Capitalize as a formal title before a name. See **titles**.

**Secret Service** A federal agency administered by the Treasury Department.

The *Secret Service Uniformed Division,* which protects the president's residence and offices and the embassies in Washington, formerly was known as the Executive Protective Service.

**section** Capitalize when used with a figure to identify part of a law or bill: *Section 14B of the Taft-Hartley Act.*

**Securities and Exchange Commission** *SEC* is acceptable on second reference.

The related legislation is the *Securities Exchange Act* (no *and*).

**Security Council (U.N.)** *Security Council* may be used on first reference in stories under a United Nations datelines. Use *U.N. Security Council* in other first references.

Retain capitalization of *Security Council* in all references.

Lowercase *council* whenever it stands alone.

**Seeing Eye dog** A trademark for a guide dog.

**seesaw**

**self-** Always hyphenate:

self-assured    self-government
self-defense

**sell out** (v.) **sellout** (n.)

**semi-** The rules in **prefixes** apply, but in general, no hyphen.

Some examples:

semifinal    semiofficial
semi-invalid    semitropical

**semiannual** Twice a year, a synonym for *biannual.*

Do not confuse it with *biennial,* which means every two years.

**senate** Capitalize all specific references to governmental legislative bodies, regardless of whether the name of the nation or state is used: *the U.S. Senate, the Senate, the Virginia Senate, the state Senate, the Senate.*

Lowercase plural uses: *the Virginia and North Carolina senates.*

See **governmental bodies**.

The same principles apply to foreign bodies. See **foreign legislative bodies**.

Lowercase references to non-governmental bodies: *the student senate at Yale.*

**senator, Sen.** See **legislative titles** and **party affiliation**.

**senatorial** Always lowercase.

**send off** (v.) **send-off** (n.)

**senior** See the **junior, senior** entry.

**senior citizen** Use the term sparingly. See **elderly**.

**sentences** Capitalize the first word of every sentence, including quoted statements and direct questions:
*Patrick Henry said, "I know not what course others may take, but as for me, give me liberty or give me death."*

Capitalize the first word of a quoted statement if it constitutes a sentence, even if it was part of a larger sentence in the original: *Patrick Henry said, "Give me liberty or give me death."*

In direct questions, even without quotation marks: *The story answers the question, Where does true happiness really lie?*

See **ellipsis** in the **Punctuation** chapter and **poetry**.

**September** See **months**.

**sergeant** See **military titles**.

**serial numbers** Use figures and capital letters in solid form (no hyphens or spaces unless the source indicates they are an integral part of the code): *A1234567.*

**serviceable**

**service clubs** See the **fraternal organizations and service clubs** entry.

**service mark** A brand, symbol, word, etc. used by a supplier of services and protected by law to prevent a competitor from using it: *Realtor,* for a member of the National Association of Realtors, for example.

When a service mark is used, capitalize it.

The preferred form, however, is to use a generic term unless the service mark is essential to the story.

See **brand names** and **trademark**.

**sesquicentennial** Every 150 years.

**set up** (v.) **setup** (n. and adj.)

**Seven Seas** Arabian Sea, Atlantic Ocean, Bay of Bengal, Mediterranean Sea, Persian Gulf, Red Sea, South China Sea.

**Seven Sisters** The colleges are: Barnard, Bryn Mawr, Mount Holyoke, Radcliffe, Smith, Vassar and Wellesley.

Also a nickname for the world's largest privately operated oil companies: British Petroleum, Exxon, Gulf, Mobil, Royal Dutch-Shell, Standard Oil Co. of California and Texaco.

**Seventh-day Adventist Church** The denomination is traceable to the preaching of William Miller of New Hampton, N.Y., a Baptist layman who said his study of the Book of Daniel showed that the end of the world would come in the mid-1840s.

When the prediction did not come true, the Millerites split into smaller groups. One, influenced by visions described by Ellen Harmon, later Mrs. James White, is the precursor of Seventh-day Adventist practice today.

The General Conference, which meets every four years, has authority to make decisions that affect the denomination worldwide. In descending order of authority come divisions for various sections of the world, union conferences for major areas within a division, and, in the United States, state conferences. Members at each level participate in electing representatives to higher levels.

The office of the General Conference, located in Washington, lists U.S. membership at 500,000 and worldwide membership at 2.5 million.

BELIEFS: The description *adventist* is based on the belief

that a second coming of Christ is near. Believers hold that events leading to the coming began in the mid-1840s and will continue until the completion of a process that will identify those worthy of joining in the resurrection at the second coming of Christ.

*Seventh-day* derives from the contention that the Bible permits no deviation from observing the seventh day of the week as the Sabbath.

Baptism, by immersion, is reserved for those old enough to understand its meaning. Baptism and the Lord's Supper are the only sacraments.

CLERGY: The head of the General Conference holds the formal title of *president*. The formal titles for ministers are *pastor* or *elder*. Capitalize them when used immediately before a name on first reference. On second reference, use only the last name of a man; use *Miss, Mrs. or Ms.* or no title before the last name of a woman, depending on her preference.

The designation *the Rev.* is not used.

See **religious titles**.

**Seven-Up, 7Up** Trademarks for a brand of soft drink.

**Seven Wonders of the World** The Egyptian pyramids, the hanging gardens of Babylon, the mausoleum at Halicarnassus, the temple of Artemis at Ephesus, the Colossus of Rhodes, the statue of Zeus by Phidias at Olympia and the pharos or lighthouse at Alexandria.

**sewage, sewerage** *Sewage* is waste matter.

*Sewerage* is the drainage system.

**sex changes** Follow these guidelines in using proper names or personal pronouns when referring to an individual who has had a sex-change operation:

—If the reference is to an action before the operation, use the proper name and gender of the individual at that time.

—If the reference is to an action after the operation, use the new proper name and gender.

For example:

*Dr. Richard Raskind was a first-rate amateur tennis player. He won several tourna-*

*ments. Ten years later, when Dr. Renee Richards applied to play in tournaments, many women players objected on the ground that she was the former Richard Raskind, who had undergone a sex-change operation. Miss Richards said she was entitled to compete as a woman.*

**sexism** See the **man, mankind** and **women** entries.

**shah** Capitalize when used as a title before a name: *Shah Mohammed Reza Pahlavi of Iran.*

The Shah of Iran commonly is known only by this title, which is, in effect, an alternative name. Capitalize *Shah of Iran* in references to the holder of the title; lowercase subsequent references as *the shah.*

The practice is based on the guidelines in the **nobility** entry.

**shake up** (v.) **shake-up** (n. and adj.)

**shall, will** Use *shall* to express determination: *We shall overcome. You and he shall stay.*

Either *shall* or *will* may be used in first-person constructions that do not emphasize determination: *We shall hold a meeting. We will hold a meeting.*

For second- and third-person constructions, use *will* unless determination is stressed: *You will like it. She will not be pleased.*

See the **should, would** entry and **subjunctive mood**.

**shape up** (v.) **shape-up** (n. and adj.)

**Shariah** The legal code of Islam. It is roughly comparable to the Talmudic tradition in Judaism.

**Shavuot** The Jewish Feast of Weeks, commemorating the receiving of the Ten Commandments. Occurs in May or June.

**she** Do not use this pronoun in references to ships or nations.

Use *it* instead.

**Sheet Metal Workers International Association** The shortened form *Sheet Metal Workers union* is acceptable in all references.

Headquarters is in Washington.

**Sheetrock** A trademark for a brand of gypsum wallboard.

**shell** See **weapons**.

**Shell Oil Co.** This U.S. company, with headquarters in Houston, is part of the Royal Dutch-Shell Group of Companies. The group owns more than half of the stock in Shell Oil.

**sheriff** Capitalize when used as a formal title before a name. See **titles**.

**ships** See the **boats, ships** entry.

**shirt sleeve, shirt sleeves** (n.) **shirt-sleeve** (adj.)

**shoeshine, shoestring**

**shopworn**

**shortchange**

**short-lived** (adj.) *A short-lived plan. The plan was short-lived.*

**short ton** Equal to 2,000 pounds. See **ton**.

**shot** See **weapons**.

**shotgun** See **weapons**.

**should, would** Use *should* to express an obligation: *We should help the needy.*

Use *would* to express a customary action: *In the summer we would spend hours by the seashore.*

Use *would* also in constructing a conditional past tense, but be careful:

Wrong: *If Soderholm would not have had an injured foot, Thompson would not have been in the lineup.*

Right: *If Soderholm had not had an injured foot, Thompson would not have been in the lineup.*

See **subjunctive mood**.

**showcase, showroom**

**show off** (v.) **showoff** (n.)

**shrubs** See **plants**.

**shut down** (v.) **shutdown** (n.)

**shut-in**

**shut off** (v.) **shut-off** (n.)

**shut out** (v.) **shutout** (n.)

**(sic)** Do not use *(sic)* unless it is in the matter being quoted. To show that an error, peculiar usage or spelling is in the original, use a note to editors at the end of copy, after a dash:

———
↑ **Editors: The spelling cabob is in the original copy.** ←
Or:
↑ **Editors: The spelling jorga is correct.** ←

**Sicily** Use instead of Italy in datelines on stories from communities on this island.

**side by side, side-by-side** *They walked side by side. The stories received side-by-side display.*

**Sierra Nevada, the** Not *Sierra Nevada Mountains. (Sierra* means mountains.)

**sightseeing, sightseer**

**Simoniz** A trademark for a brand of auto wax.

**Sinai** Not *the Sinai.* But: *the Sinai Desert, the Sinai Peninsula.*

**Singapore** Stands alone in datelines.

**single-handed, single-handedly**

**sir** See **nobility**.

**sister** Capitalize in all references before the names of nuns.
If no surname is given, the name is the same in all references: *Sister Agnes Rita.*
If a surname is used in first reference, drop the given name on second reference: *Sister Clair Regina Torpy* in first reference, *Sister Torpy* on subsequent references, or use courtesy titles or no title as she prefers.
Use *Mother* the same way when referring to a woman who heads a group of nuns.
See **religious titles**.

**sister-in-law, sisters-in-law**

**sit down** (v.) **sit-down** (n. and adj.)

**sit in** (v.) **sit-in** (n. and adj.)

**sizable**

**sizes** Use figures: *a size 9 dress, size 40 long, 10 1/2B shoes, a 34 1/2 sleeve.*

**skeptic** See the **cynic, skeptic** entry.

**ski, skis, skier, skied, skiing** Also: *ski jump, ski jumping.*

**Skid Road, Skid Row** The term originated as *Skid Road* in the Seattle area, where dirt roads were used to skid logs to the mill. Over the years, *Skid Road* became a synonym for the area where loggers gathered, usually down among the rooming houses and saloons.

In time, the term spread to other cities as a description for sections, such as the Bowery in New York, that are havens for derelicts. In the process, *row* replaced *road* in many references.

Use *Skid Road* for this section in Seattle; either *Skid Road* or *Skid Row* for other areas.

**skillful**

**slang** In general, avoid slang, the highly informal language that is outside conventional or standard usage.
See **colloquialisms; dialect;** and **word selection**.

**slaying** See the **homicide, murder, manslaughter** entry.

**sledgehammer**

**sleet** See **weather terms**.

**sleight of hand**

**slowdown**

**slumlord**

**slush fund**

**small-arms fire**

**small-business man**

**smash up** (v.) **smashup** (n. and adj.)

**Smithfield Ham** A trademark for a ham dry-cured, smoked and aged in Smithfield, Va.

**Smithsonian Institution** Not *Smithsonian Institute.*

**smoke bomb, smoke screen**

**Smokey** Or *Smokey Bear.* Not *Smokey the Bear.*
But: *A smoky room.*

**smolder** Not *smoulder.*

**snowdrift, snowfall, snowflake, snowman, snowplow, snowshoe, snowstorm, snowsuit**

**so called** (adv.) **so-called** (adj.)

**socialist, socialism** See the **political parties and philosophies** entry.

**Social Security** Capitalize all references to the U.S. system.
The number groups are hyphenated: *123-45-6789.*
Lowercase generic uses such as: *Is there a social security program in Sweden?*

**social titles** See **courtesy titles.**

**Society for the Prevention of Cruelty to Ani-** mals *SPCA* is acceptable on second reference.
The *American Society for the Prevention of Cruelty to Animals* is limited to the five boroughs of New York City.
The autonomous chapters in other cities ordinarily precede the organization by the name of the city: On first reference, the *Philadelphia Society for the Prevention of Cruelty to Animals;* on second, the *Philadelphia SPCA* or *SPCA* as appropriate in the context.

**Society of Friends** See **Quakers.**

**Society of Professional Journalists, Sigma Delta Chi** In abbreviation called *SPJ,SDX.* Comma, no space.

**soft-spoken**

**solicitor** See **lawyer.**

**Solid South** Those Southern states traditionally regarded as supporters of the Democratic Party.

**soliloquy, soliloquies**

**song titles** See **composition titles.**

**son-in-law, sons-in-law**

**SOS** The distress signal.
*S.O.S* (no final period) is a
trademark for a brand of soap
pad.

**sound barrier** The speed
of sound, no longer a true barrier because aircraft have exceeded it. See **Mach number**.

**South** As defined by the
U.S. Census Bureau, the 16-
state region is broken into
three divisions.
 The four *East South Central* states are Alabama, Kentucky, Mississippi and Tennessee.
 The eight *South Atlantic*
states are Delaware, Florida,
Georgia, Maryland, North
Carolina, South Carolina,
Virginia and West Virginia.
 The four *West South Central* states are Arkansas, Louisiana, Oklahoma and Texas.
 See **North Central re-
gion**; **Northeast region**;
and **West** for the bureau's
other regional breakdowns.

**south, southern,
southeast, southwest** See
the **directions and regions**
entry.

**South America** See
**Western Hemisphere**.

**South Carolina** Abbrev.:
*S.C.* See **state names**.

**South Dakota** Abbrev.:
*S.D.* See **state names**.

**Southeast Asia** The nations of the Indochinese Peninsula and the islands southeast of it: Burma, Cambodia,
Indonesia, Laos, Malaysia,
New Guinea, the Philippines,
Singapore, Thailand and Vietnam.
 See **Asian subcontinent**
and **Far East**.

**Southeast Asia Treaty
Organization** *SEATO* is acceptable on second reference.

**Southern Airways** See
**Republic Airlines**.

**Soviet Union** Acceptable
in all references in the body of
a story for *Union of Soviet Socialist Republics*. But use
*U.S.S.R.* in datelines.
 See the **Russia, Soviet
Union** entry for guidance on
using *Soviet* and for a list of
the 15 republics that make up
the nation.

**Space Age** It began with the launching of Sputnik 1 on Oct. 4, 1957.

**space agency** See **National Aeronautics and Space Administration**.

**space centers** See **John F. Kennedy Space Center** and **Lyndon B. Johnson Space Center**.

**spacecraft designations** Use Arabic figures and capitalize the name: *Gemini 7, Apollo 11, Pioneer 10.*

**spaceship**

**space shuttle** Lowercase *space shuttle,* but capitalize a proper name.

The space shuttle is a reusable winged aircraft capable of carrying people and cargo into Earth orbit. It is designed to take off vertically with the aid of booster rockets. After an orbital mission, re-entry begins with the firing of engines that send the craft back into Earth's atmosphere. The final leg of the return trip is a powerless glide to a landing strip.

**Spanish-American War**

**Spanish and Portuguese names** The family names of both the father and mother usually are considered part of a person's full name. In everyday use, customs vary widely with individuals and countries.

The normal sequence is given name, father's family name, mother's family name: *Jose Lopez Portillo.*

On second reference, use only the father's family name *(Lopez),* unless the individual prefers or is widely known by a multiple last name *(Lopez Portillo).*

Some individuals use a *y* (for *and*) between the two surnames: *Jose Lopez y Portillo.* Include the *y* on second reference only if both names are used: *Lopez y Portillo.*

In the Portuguese practice common in Portugal and Brazil, some individuals use only the mother's family name on second reference. If the individual's preference is not known, use both family names on second reference: *Humberto Castello Branco* on first reference, *Castello Branco* on second.

A married woman frequently uses her father's family name followed by the particle *de* (for *of*) and her husband's name. A woman named *Irma Perez* who married a man named *Anibal Gutierrez* would be known as *Irma Perez de Gutierrez*. Use *Mrs. Gutierrez* on second reference.

**speaker** Capitalize as a formal title before a name. Generally, it is a formal title only for the speaker of a legislative body: *Speaker Thomas P. O'Neill.*
See **titles**.

**special contexts** When this term is used in this book, it means that the material described may be used in a regular column devoted to a specialized subject or when a particular literary effect is suitable.

Special literary effects generally are suitable only in feature copy, but even there they should be used with care. Most feature material should follow the same style norms that apply to regular news copy.

**species** Same in singular and plural. Use singular or plural verbs and pronouns depending on the sense: *The spe-*

*cies has been unable to maintain itself. Both species are extinct.*

**speeches** Capitalize and use quotation marks for their formal titles, as described in **composition titles**.

**speechmaker, speechmaking**

**speed of sound** See **Mach number**.

**speeds** Use figures. *The car slowed to 7 miles per hour, winds of 5 to 10 miles per hour, winds of 7 to 9 knots, 10-knot wind.*

Avoid extensively hyphenated constructions such as *5-mile-per-hour winds.*

**speed up** (v.) **speedup** (n. and adj.)

**spelling** The basic rule when in doubt is to consult this book followed by, if necessary, a dictionary under conditions described in the **dictionary** entry.

Memory Aid: Noah Webster developed the following rule of thumb for the frequently vexing question of whether to double a final consonant in forming the present participle and past tense of a verb:

—If the stress in pronunciation is on the first syllable, do not double the consonant: *combat, combating, combated; cancel, canceling, canceled.*

—If the stress in pronunciation is on the second syllable, double the consonant unless confusion would result: *jut, jutted, jutting.* An exception, to avoid confusion with *buss,* is *bus, bused, busing.*

**spill, spilled, spilling** Not *spilt* in the past tense.

**split infinitive** See **verbs**.

**spokesman, spokeswoman** But not *spokesperson.* Use *a representative* if you do not know the sex of the individual.

**spouse** Use when some of the people involved may be men. For example: *physicians and their spouses,* not *physicians and their wives.*

**spring** See **seasons**.

**springtime**

**sputnik** Usually lowercase, but capitalize when followed by a figure as part of a proper name: *Sputnik 1.*

**squall** See **weather terms**.

**square** Do not abbreviate. Capitalize when part of a proper name: *Washington Square.*

**squinting modifier** A misplaced adverb that can be interpreted as modifying either of two words: *Those who lie often are found out.*

Place the adverb where there can be no confusion, even if a compound verb must be split: *Those who often lie are found out.* Or if that was not the sense: *Those who lie are often found out.*

**Sri Lanka** Formerly Ceylon. Use *Sri Lanka* in datelines and other references to the nation.

The people may be called either *Sri Lankans* or *Ceylonese.*

Before the nation was called Ceylon, it was Serendip, whence comes the word *serendipity.*

**SRO** Acceptable on second reference for *standing room only.*

**S.S. Kresge Co.** Now known as *K mart.* Headquarters is in Troy, Mich.

**SST** Acceptable in all references for a *supersonic transport.*

**stadium, stadiums** Capitalize only when part of a proper name: *Yankee Stadium.*

**staffer(s)** Do not use for *staff member(s)* or *member(s) of the staff.*

**Stalin, Josef** Not *Joseph.*

**stanch, staunch** *Stanch* is a verb: *He stanched the flow of blood.*
*Staunch* is an adjective: *She is a staunch supporter of equality.*

**Standard & Poor's Register of Corporations** The source for determining the formal name of a business. See **company names**.
The register is published by Standard & Poor's Corp. of New York.

**standard-bearer**

**Standard Oil Co. (Indiana)** *Indiana Standard* or *Standard of Indiana* is acceptable on second reference.
*Amoco* is a company trademark.
Headquarters is in Chicago.

**Standard Oil Co. (New Jersey)** The former name of *Exxon Corp.*

**Standard Oil Co. of California** *Socal* is acceptable on second reference.
Headquarters is in San Francisco.

**Standard Oil (Ohio)** *Sohio* is acceptable on second reference.
Headquarters is in Cleveland.

**standard time** Capitalize *Eastern Standard Time, Pacific Standard Time,* etc., but lowercase *standard time* when standing alone.
See **time zones**.

**stand in** (v.) **stand-in** (n. and adj.)

**standing room only** *SRO* is acceptable on second reference.

**stand off** (v.) **standoff** (n. and adj.)

**stand out** (v.) **standout** (n. and adj.)

**starboard** Nautical for *right*. See **port, starboard** entry.

**"The Star-Spangled Banner"** But lowercase *the national anthem.*

**state** Lowercase in all *state of* constructions: *the state of Maine, the states of Maine and Vermont.*

Four states—Kentucky, Massachusetts, Pennsylvania and Virginia—are legally commonwealths rather than states. The distinction is necessary only in formal uses: *The commonwealth of Kentucky filed a suit.* For simple geographic reference: *Tobacco is grown in the state of Kentucky.*

Do not capitalize *state* when used simply as an adjective to specify a level of jurisdiction: *state Rep. William Smith, the state Transportation Department, state funds.*

Apply the same principle to phrases such as *the city of Chicago, the town of Auburn,* etc.

See also **state names**.

**statehouse** Capitalize all references to a specific statehouse, with or without the name of the state: *The Massachusetts Statehouse is in Boston. The governor will visit the Statehouse today.*

Lowercase plural uses: *the Massachusetts and Rhode Island statehouses.*

**state names** Follow these guidelines:

STANDING ALONE: Spell out the names of the 50 U.S. states when they stand alone in textual material. Any state name may be condensed, however, to fit typographical requirements for tabular material.

EIGHT NOT ABBREVIATED: The names of eight states are never abbreviated in datelines or text: *Alaska, Hawaii, Idaho, Iowa, Maine, Ohio, Texas* and *Utah.*

Memory Aid: Spell out the names of the two states that are not part of the continental United States and of the continental states that are five letters or fewer.

ABBREVIATIONS REQUIRED: Use the state abbreviations listed at the end of this section:

—In conjunction with the name of a city, town, village or military base in most datelines. See **datelines** for examples and exceptions for large cities.

—In conjunction with the name of a city, county, town, village or military base in text. See examples in **Punctuation** section. See **datelines** for guidelines on when a city name may stand alone in the body of a story.

—In short-form listings of party affiliation: *D-Ala., R-Mont.* See **party affiliation** entry for details.

The abbreviations, which also appear in the entries for each state, are:

| | | |
|---|---|---|
| Ala. | Md. | N.D. |
| Ariz. | Mass. | Okla. |
| Ark. | Mich. | Ore. |
| Calif. | Minn. | Pa. |
| Colo. | Miss. | R.I. |
| Conn. | Mo. | S.C. |
| Del. | Mont. | S.D. |
| Fla. | Neb. | Tenn. |
| Ga. | Nev. | Vt. |
| Ill. | N.H. | Va. |
| Ind. | N.J. | Wash. |
| Kan. | N.M. | W.Va. |
| Ky. | N.Y. | Wis. |
| La. | N.C. | Wyo. |

PUNCTUATION: Place one comma between the city and the state name, and another comma after the state name, unless ending a sentence or indicating a dateline: *He was travelling from Nashville, Tenn., to Austin, Texas, en route to his home in Albuquerque, N.M. She said Cook County, Ill., was Mayor Daley's stronghold.*

MISCELLANEOUS: Use *New York state* when necessary to distinguish the state from New York City.

Use *state of Washington* or *Washington state* when necessary to distinguish the state from the District of Columbia. (*Washington State* is the name of a university in the state of Washington.)

**State of the Union** Capitalize all references to the president's annual address.

Lowercase other uses: *"The state of the union is confused,"* the editor said.

**state police** Capitalize with a state name if part of the formal description for a police agency: *the New York State Police, the Virginia State Police.*

In most cases, *state police*

standing alone is a shorthand reference for *state policemen* rather than a reference to the agency. For consistency and to avoid hairline distinctions about whether the reference is to the agency or the officers, lowercase the words *state police* whenever they are not preceded by a state name.

See **highway patrol**.

**states' rights**

**statewide**

**stationary, stationery** To stand still is to be *stationary*.

Writing paper is *stationery*.

**station wagon**

**statute mile** It equals 5,280 feet, or approximately 1.6 kilometers.

To convert to approximate nautical miles, multiply the number of statute miles by .869.

See **kilometer; knot; mile;** and **nautical mile**.

**staunch** See the **stanch, staunch** entry.

**steady-state theory** See **big-bang theory**.

**stepbrother, stepfather** Also: *stepsister, stepmother.*

**steppingstone**

**stifling**

**St. John's** The city in the Canadian province of Newfoundland.

Not to be confused with *Saint John, New Brunswick.*

**St. Louis** The city in Missouri stands alone in datelines.

**stockmen's advisory** See **weather terms**.

**stool pigeon**

**stopgap**

**storm** See **weather terms**.

**storyteller**

**straight-laced, strait-laced** Use *straight-laced* for someone strict or severe in behavior or moral views.

Reserve *strait-laced* for the notion of confinement, as in a corset.

**strait** Capitalize as part of a proper name: *Bering Strait, Strait of Gibraltar.*

But: *the Bosporus* and *the Dardanelles.* Neither is followed by *Strait.*

**straitjacket** Not *straightjacket.*

**Strategic Arms Limitation Talks (Treaty)** *SALT* is acceptable on first reference to the talks or the treaty as long as it is made immediately clear which is being referred to.

Use *the arms talks, the talks, strategic arms treaty,* or *the treaties* in some references to avoid alphabet soup.

There are two treaties, one of which has not been ratified. *Talks* are the discussions with regard to the two treaties or to a new treaty.

*SALT 1* is the first treaty and *SALT 2* is the second.

**Strategic Defense Initiative** This is the official name of the research and development work on defense against a nuclear attack. *SDI* is the acronym and is acceptable on second reference. "Star Wars" has become synonymous with both and was derived from the movie series.

If used, it must always be within quotation marks.

**street** Abbreviate only with a numbered address. See **addresses.**

**strikebreaker**

**strong-arm** (v., adj.)

**strong-willed**

**student** See the **pupil, student** entry.

**Styrofoam** A trademark for a brand of plastic foam. Use the term plastic foam unless referring specifically to the trademark product.

**sub-** The rules in **prefixes** apply, but in general, no hyphen. Some examples:

| | |
|---|---|
| subbasement | submachine gun |
| subcommittee | suborbital |
| subculture | subtotal |
| subdivision | subzero |

**subcommittee** Lowercase when used with the name of a legislative body's full committee: a *Ways and Means subcommittee.*

Capitalize when a subcommittee has a proper name of its own: *the Senate Permanent*

*Subcommittee on Investigations.*

**subject** See the **citizen, resident, subject, national, native** entry.

**subjunctive mood** Use the subjunctive mood of a verb for contrary-to-fact conditions, and expressions of doubts, wishes or regrets:
*If I were a rich man, I wouldn't have to work hard.*
*I doubt that more money would be the answer.*
*I wish it were possible to take back my words.*
Sentences that express a contingency or hypothesis may use either the subjunctive or the indicative mood depending on the context. In general, use the subjunctive if there is little likelihood that a contingency might come true:
*If I were to marry a millionaire, I wouldn't have to worry about money.*
*If the bill passes as expected, it will provide an immediate tax cut.*
See the **should, would** entry.

**submachine gun** See weapons.

**subpoena, subpoenaed, subpoenaing**

**Sucaryl** A trademark for a brand of non-caloric sweetener.

**successor**

**suffixes** See separate listing for commonly used suffixes.
Follow Webster's New World Dictionary for words not in this book.
If a word combination is not listed in Webster's New World, use two words for the verb form; hyphenate any noun or adjective forms.

**suit, suite** You may have a *suit* of clothes, a *suit* of cards, or be faced with a *lawsuit.*
There are *suites* of music, rooms and furniture.

**Sukkot** The Jewish Feast of Tabernacles, celebrating the fall harvest and commemorating the desert wandering of the Jews during the Exodus. Occurs in September or October.

**summer** See **seasons.**

**summertime**

**sun** Lowercase. See **heavenly bodies.**

**sunbathe** The verb forms: *sunbathed, sunbathing.* Also: *sunbather.*

**Sun Belt** Generally those states in the South and West, ranging from Florida and Georgia through the Gulf states into California.

**Sunday** See **days of the week.**

**super** Avoid the slang tendency to use it in place of *excellent, wonderful,* etc.

**super-** The rules in **prefixes** apply, but in general, no hyphen. Some frequently used words:

superagency superhighway
supercarrier superpower
supercharge supertanker

As with all prefixes, however, use a hyphen if the word that follows is capitalized: *super-Republican.*

**Super Bowl**

**superintendent** Do not abbreviate. Capitalize when used as a formal title before a name.
See **titles.**

**superior court** See **court names.**

**supersede**

**supersonic** See **Mach number.**

**supersonic transport** *SST* is acceptable in all references.

**supra-** The rules in **prefixes** apply, but in general, no hyphen. Some examples:

supragovern- supranational
mental

**Supreme Court of the United States** Capitalize *U.S. Supreme Court* and also *the Supreme Court* when the context makes the *U.S.* designation unnecessary.

The chief justice is properly the *chief justice of the United States,* not *of the Supreme Court: Chief Justice William Rehnquist.*

The proper title for the

eight other members of the court is *associate justice*. When used as a formal title before a name, it should be shortened to *justice* unless there are special circumstances: *Justice Sandra Day O'Connor, Associate Justice Sandra Day O'Connor.*

See **judge.**

**supreme courts of the states** Capitalize with the state name *(the New Jersey Supreme Court)* and without the state name when the context makes it unnecessary: *the state Supreme Court, the Supreme Court.*

If a court with this name is not a state's highest tribunal, the fact should be noted. In New York, for example, the Supreme Court is a trial court. Appeals are directed to the Appellate Division of the Supreme Court. The state's highest court is the Court of Appeals.

**Supreme Soviet** The principal legislative body of the Soviet Union.

**surface-to-air missile(s)** *SAM(s)* may be used on second reference. Avoid the redundant *SAM missiles.*

**suspensive hyphenation** The form: *The 5- and 6-year-olds attend morning classes.*

**swastika**

**sweat pants, sweat shirt, sweat suit**

**Swissair** Headquarters is in Zurich, Switzerland.

**syllabus, syllabuses**

**synagogue** Capitalize only when part of a formal name.

**Synagogue Council of America** See **Jewish congregations.**

**synod** A council of churches or church officials. See the entry for the denomination in question.

# T

**Tabasco** A trademark for a brand of hot pepper sauce.

**tablecloth**

**tablespoon, tablespoonfuls** Equal to three teaspoons or one-half a fluid ounce.

The metric equivalent is approximately 15 milliliters.

See **liter** and **recipes.**

**table tennis** See **pingpong.**

**tabular matter** Exceptions may be made to the normal rules for abbreviations, as necessary to make material fit. But make any abbreviations as clear as possible.

**tailspin**

**tail wind**

**Taiwan** Use *Taiwan,* not *Formosa,* in references to the Nationalist government in Taiwan and to the island itself.

See **China.**

**take-home pay**

**take off** (v.) **takeoff** (n. and adj.)

**take out** (v.) **takeout** (n. and adj.)

**take over** (v.) **takeover** (n. and adj.)

**take up** (v.) **takeup** (n. and adj.)

**Talmud** The collection of writings that constitute the Jewish civil and religious law.

**Tammany, Tammany Hall, Tammany Society**

**tanks** Use Arabic figures, separated from letters by a hyphen: *M-60.* Plural: *M-60s.*

**tape recording** The noun. But hyphenate the verb form: *tape-record.*

**Tass** The Soviet government's news agency.

**tattletale**

**teachers college** No apostrophe.

**team** See collective nouns.

**teammate**

**teamster** Capitalize *teamster* only if the intended meaning is that the individual is a member of the International Brotherhood of Teamsters, Chauffeurs, Warehousemen and Helpers of America.

**Teamsters union** Acceptable in all references to the *International Brotherhood of Teamsters, Chauffeurs, Warehousemen and Helpers of America.*
See the entry under that name.

**tear gas** Two words. See also **Chemical Mace.**

**teaspoon** Equal to one-sixth of a fluid ounce, or one-third of a tablespoon.

The metric equivalent is approximately five milliliters.
See **liter.**

**teaspoonful, teaspoonfuls** Not *teaspoonsful.* See **recipes.**

**Technicolor** A trademark for a process of making color motion pictures.

**teen, teen-ager** (n.) **teen-age** (adj.) Do not use *teen-aged.*

**Teflon** A trademark for a type of non-stick coating.

**telecast** (n.) **televise** (v.)

**telephone numbers** Use figures. The forms: *(212) 621-1500, 621-1500, (212) MU 2-1500.* If extension numbers are given: *Ext. 2, Ext. 364, Ext. 4071.*
The use of parentheses around the area code is based on a format that telephone companies have agreed upon for domestic and international communications.

**TelePrompTer** A trademark for a type of cuing device.
It is no relation to Tele-

prompter Corp., a cable television company with headquarters in New York.

**Teletype** A trademark for a brand of teleprinters and teletypewriters.

**television program titles** Follow the guidelines in **composition titles.**

Put quotation marks around *show* only if it is part of the formal name. The word *show* may be dropped when it would be cumbersome, such as in a set of listings.

In text or listing, treat programs named after the star in any of the following ways: *"The Mary Tyler Moore Show," "Mary Tyler Moore"* or *the Mary Tyler Moore show.* But be consistent in a story or set of listings.

Use quotation marks also for the title of an episode: *"Chuckles Bites the Dust," an episode of "The Mary Tyler Moore Show."*

**television station** The call letters alone are frequently adequate, but when this phrase is needed, use lowercase: *television station WTEV.*

**telex, Telex** (n.) A communications system. Use lowercase when not referring to a specific company. Use uppercase only when referring to the company. Never used as a verb.

**telltale**

**temblor** See **earthquakes.**

**temperature-humidity index** See **weather terms.**

**temperatures** Use figures for all except *zero.* Use a word, not a minus sign, to indicate temperatures below zero.

Right: *The day's low was minus 10.*

Right: *The day's low was 10 below zero.*

Wrong: *The day's low was −10.*

Right: *The temperature rose to zero by noon.*

Right: *The day's high was expected to be 9 or 10.*

Also: *5-degree temperatures, temperatures fell 5 degrees, temperatures in the 30s* (no apostrophe).

Temperatures get *higher* or *lower,* but they don't get *warmer* or *cooler.*

Wrong: *Temperatures are*

*expected to warm up in the area Friday.*

Right: *Temperatures are expected to rise in the area Friday.*

See **Fahrenheit; Celsius;** and **weather terms.**

**Ten Commandments** Do not abbreviate or use figures.

**tenderhearted**

**tenfold**

**Tennessee** Abbrev.: *Tenn.* See **state names.**

**Tennessee Valley Authority** *TVA* is acceptable on second reference.

Headquarters is in Knoxville, Tenn.

**tera-** A prefix denoting 1 trillion units of a measure. Move a decimal point 12 places to the right, adding zeros if necessary, to convert to the basic unit: 5.5 teratons = 5,500,000,000,000 tons.

**terrace** Do not abbreviate. See **addresses.**

**Texaco Inc.** Headquarters is in Harrison, N.Y.

**Texas** Do not abbreviate. Second in total land area: 262,134 square miles.

See **state names.**

**texts, transcripts** Follow normal style guidelines for capitalization, spelling and abbreviations in handling a text or transcript.

Use quotation marks only for words that were quoted in the text by the person who spoke.

Identify a change in speakers by starting a paragraph with the new speaker's name and a colon. Use normal second-reference forms if the speaker has been identified earlier; provide a full name and identification if the individual is being mentioned for the first time.

Use *Q:* for *question* and *A:* for *answer* at the start of paragraphs when these notations are adequate to identify a change in speakers.

See **ellipsis** in the **Punctuation** chapter for guidelines on condensing texts and transcripts.

**Thai** A native or the language of Thailand.

*Siam* and *Siamese* are historical only.

Use *siamese* for the cat.

**Thanksgiving, Thanksgiving Day** The fourth Thursday in November.

**that (conjunction)** Use the conjunction *that* to introduce a dependent clause if the sentence sounds or looks awkward without it. There are no hard-and-fast rules, but in general:

—*That* usually may be omitted when a dependent clause immediately follows a form of the verb to say: *The president said he had signed the bill.*

—*That* should be used when a time element intervenes between the verb and the dependent clause: *The president said Monday that he had signed the bill.*

—*That* usually is necessary after some verbs. They include: *advocate, assert, contend, declare, estimate, make clear, point out, propose* and *state.*

—*That* is required before subordinate clauses beginning with conjunctions such as *after, although, because, before, in addition to, until* and *while: Haldeman said that after he learned of Nixon's intention to resign, he sought pardons for all connected with Watergate.*

When in doubt, include *that.* Omission can hurt. Inclusion never does.

**that, which, who, whom (pronouns)** Use *who* and *whom* in referring to people and to animals with a name: *John Jones is the man who helped me.* See the **who, whom** entry.

Use *that* and *which* in referring to inanimate objects and to animals without a name.

See the **essential clauses, non-essential clauses** entry for guidelines on using *that* and *which* to introduce phrases and clauses.

**theater** Use this spelling also in all names: *Shubert Theater.*

**theft** See the **burglary, larceny, robbery, theft** entry.

**their, there, they're** *Their* is a possessive pronoun: *They went to their house.*

*There* is an adverb indicating direction: *We went there for dinner.*

*There* also is used with the force of a pronoun for impersonal constructions in which the real subject follows the verb: *There is no food on the table.*

*They're* is a contraction for *they are.*

**theretofore** Use *until then.*

**Thermo-Fax** A trademark for a brand of photocopy machine.

**thermos** Formerly a trademark, now a generic term for any vacuum bottle, although one manufacturer still uses the word as a brand name.

Lowercase *thermos* when it is used to mean any vacuum bottle; use *Thermos* when referring to the specific brand.

**Third World** The economically developing nations of Africa, Asia and Latin America.

Do not confuse with nonaligned, which is a political term. See **non-aligned.**

**three-D** *3-D* is preferred.

**3M** The name of the company is Minnesota Mining & Manufacturing. Its products are known under the names *3M* and *Scotch.* The company is popularly known as *3M.* Headquarters is in St. Paul, Minn.

**three R's** They are: *reading, 'riting and 'rithmetic.*

**threesome**

**throwaway** (n. and adj.)

**thunderstorm** See **weather terms.**

**Thursday** See **days of the week.**

**tidbit**

**tie, tied, tying**

**tie in** (v.) **tie-in** (n. and adj.)

**tie up** (v.) **tie-up** (n. and adj.)

**time element** Use *today, this morning, this afternoon, tonight,* etc., as appropriate in stories for afternoon editions. Use the day of the week elsewhere. See the **today, tonight** and the **tomorrow, yesterday** entries.

Use *Monday, Tuesday,* etc., for days of the week within seven days before or after the current date.

Use the month and a figure for dates beyond this range. See **months** for forms and punctuation.

Avoid such redundancies as *last Tuesday* or *next Tuesday.* The past, present or future tense used for the verb usually provides adequate indication of which Tuesday is meant: *He said he finished the job Tuesday. She will return on Tuesday.*

Avoid awkward placements of the time element, particularly those that suggest the day of the week is the object of a transitive verb: *The police jailed Tuesday.* Potential remedies include the use of the word on (see the **on** entry), rephrasing the sentence, or placing the time element in a different sentence.

**time of day** The exact time of day that an event has happened or will happen is not necessary in most stories. Follow these guidelines to determine when it should be included and in what form:

SPECIFY THE TIME:
—Whenever it gives the reader a better picture of the scene: Did the earthquake occur when people were likely to be home asleep or at work? A clock reading for the time in the datelined community is acceptable, although *pre-dawn hours* or *rush hour* often is more graphic.

—Whenever the time is critical to the story: When will the rocket be launched? When will a major political address be broadcast? What is the deadline for meeting a demand?

DECIDING ON CLOCK TIME: When giving a clock reading, use the time in the datelined community.

If the story is undated, use the clock time in force where the event happened or will take place.

The only exception is a nationwide story or tabular listing that involves television or radio programs. Always use Eastern time, followed by *EDT* or *EST,* and specify whether the program will be broadcast simultaneously nationwide or whether times will vary because of separate transmissions for different time zones. If practical, specify those times in a separate paragraph.

ZONE ABBREVIATIONS: Use *EST, CDT, PST,* etc., after a clock time only if:
—The story involves travel or other activities, such as the closing hour for polling places

or the time of a televised speech, likely to affect persons or developments in more than one time zone.

—The item involves television or radio programs. (See above.)

—The item is undated.

—The item is an advisory to editors.

CONVERT TO EASTERN TIME? Do not convert clock times from other time zones in the continental United States to Eastern time. If there is high interest in the precise time, add *CDT, PST,* etc., to the local reading to help readers determine their equivalent local time.

If the time is critical in a story from outside the continental United States, provide a conversion to Eastern time using this form:

*The kidnappers set a 9 a.m. (3 a.m. EDT) deadline.*

See **time zones** for additional guidance on forms.

**times** Use figures except for *noon* and *midnight.* Use a colon to separate hours from minutes: *11 a.m., 1 p.m., 3:30 p.m.*

Avoid such redundancies as *10 a.m. this morning, 10 p.m. tonight* or *10 p.m. Monday night.* Use *10 a.m. today, 10 p.m. today* or *10 p.m. Monday,* etc., as required by the norms in **time element.**

The construction *4 o'clock* is acceptable, but time listings with *a.m.* or *p.m.* are preferred.

See **midnight** and **time zones.**

**time sequences** Use figures, colons and periods as follows: *2:30:21.65* (hours, minutes, seconds, tenths, hundredths).

**time zones** Capitalize the full name of the time in force within a particular zone: *Eastern Standard Time, Eastern Daylight Time, Central Standard Time,* etc.

Lowercase all but the region in short forms: *the Eastern time zone, Eastern time, Mountain time,* etc.

See **time of day** for guidelines on when to use clock time in a story.

Spell out *time zone* in references not accompanied by a clock reading: *Chicago is in the Central time zone.*

The abbreviations *EST, CDT,* etc., are acceptable on first reference for zones used within the continental United States, Canada and Mexico only if the abbreviation is linked with a clock reading: *noon EST, 9 a.m. PST.* (Do not set the abbreviations off with commas.)

Spell out all references to time zones not used within the continental United States: *When it is noon EDT, it is 1 p.m. Atlantic Standard Time and 7 a.m. Alaska Standard Time.*

One exception to the spelled-out form: *Greenwich Mean Time* may be abbreviated as *GMT* on second reference if used with a clock reading.

### tiptop

### titleholder

**titles** In general, confine capitalization to formal titles used directly before an individual's name.

The basic guidelines:

LOWERCASE: Lowercase and spell out titles when they are not used with an individual's name: *The president issued a statement. The pope gave his blessing.*

Lowercase and spell out titles in constructions that set them off from a name by commas: *The vice president, Nel-* *son Rockefeller, declined to run again. Paul VI, the current pope, does not plan to retire.*

COURTESY TITLES: See the **courtesy titles** entry for guidelines on when to use *Miss, Mr., Mrs., Ms.* or no titles.

The forms *Mr., Mrs., Miss* and *Ms.* apply both in regular text and in quotations.

FORMAL TITLES: Capitalize formal titles when they are used immediately before one or more names: *Pope Paul, President Washington, Vice Presidents John Jones and William Smith.*

A formal title generally is one that denotes a scope of authority, professional activity or academic accomplishment so specific that the designation becomes almost as much an integral part of an individual's identity as a proper name itself: *President Carter, Gov. Ella Grasso, Dr. Marcus Welby, Pvt. Gomer Pyle.*

Other titles serve primarily as occupational descriptions: *astronaut John Glenn, movie star John Wayne, peanut farmer Jimmy Carter.*

A final determination on

whether a title is formal or occupational depends on the practice of the governmental or private organization that confers it. If there is doubt about the status of a title and the practice of the organization cannot be determined, use a construction that sets the name or the title off with commas.

ABBREVIATED TITLES: The following formal titles are capitalized and abbreviated as shown when used before a name outside quotations: *Dr., Gov., Lt. Gov., Rep., Sen.* and certain military ranks listed in the **military titles** entry. Spell out all except *Dr.* when they are used in quotations.

All other formal titles are spelled out in all uses.

ROYAL TITLES: Capitalize *king, queen,* etc., when used directly before a name. See individual entries and **nobility.**

TITLES OF NOBILITY: Capitalize a full title when it serves as the alternative name for an individual. See **nobility.**

PAST AND FUTURE TITLES: A formal title that an individual formerly held, is about to hold or holds temporarily is capitalized if used before the person's name. But do not capitalize the qualifying word: *former President Ford, deposed King Constantine, Attorney General-designate Griffin B. Bell, acting Mayor Peter Barry.*

LONG TITLES: Separate a long title from a name by a construction that requires a comma: *Charles Robinson, undersecretary for economic affairs, spoke.* Or: The *undersecretary for economic affairs, Charles Robinson, spoke.*

UNIQUE TITLES: If a title applies only to one person in an organization, insert the word *the* in a construction that uses commas: *John Jones, the deputy vice president, spoke.*

ADDITIONAL GUIDANCE: Many commonly used titles and occupational descriptions are listed separately in this book, together with guidelines on whether and/or when they are capitalized. In these entries, the phrases *before a name* or *im-*

*mediately before a name* are used to specify that capitalization applies only when a title is not set off from a name by commas.

See **composition titles; legislative titles; military titles;** and **religious titles.**

**TNT** Acceptable in all references for *trinitrotoluene.*

**tobacco, tobaccos**

**Tobago** See the **Trinidad and Tobago** entry.

**today, tonight** Use in direct quotations, in stories intended for publication in afternoon newspapers on the day in question, and in phrases that do not refer to a specific day: *Customs today are different from those of a century ago.*

Use the day of the week in stories intended for publication in morning newspapers and in stories filed for use in either publishing cycle.

See **tonight.**

**Tokyo** Stands alone in datelines.

**tollhouse, tollhouse cookies**

**Tommy gun** Alternative trademark for Thompson submachine gun.

See **weapons.**

**tomorrow** Use only in direct quotations and in phrases that do not refer to a specific day: *The world of tomorrow will need additional energy resources.*

Use the day of the week in other cases.

**ton** There are three different types:

A *short ton* is equal to 2,000 pounds.

A *long ton,* also known as a *British ton,* is equal to 2,240 pounds.

A *metric ton* is equal to 1,000 kilograms, or approximately 2,204.62 pounds.

CONVERSION EQUATIONS:

Short to long: Multiply by .89 (5 short tons × .89 = 4.45 long tons).

Short to metric: Multiply by .9 (5 short tons × .9 = 4.5 metric tons).

Long to short: Multiply by 1.12 (5 long tons × 1.12 = 5.6 short tons).

Long to metric: Multiply

by 1.02 (5 long tons × 1.02 = 5.1 metric tons).

Metric to short: Multiply by 1.1 (5 metric tons × 1.1 = 5.5 short tons).

Metric to long: Multiply by .98 (5 metric tons × .98 = 4.9 long tons).

See **metric system.**

See **kiloton** for units used to measure the power of nuclear explosions.

See **oil** for formulas to convert the tonnage of oil shipments to gallons.

**tonight** All that's necessary is *8 tonight,* or *8 p.m. today.* Avoid the redundant *8 p.m. tonight.*

**tornado** See **weather terms.**

**Toronto** The city in Canada stands alone in datelines.

**Tory, Tories** An exception to the normal practice when forming the plural of a proper name ending in *y.*

The words are acceptable on second reference to the Conservative Party in Britain and its members.

**total, totaled, totaling** The phrase *a total of* often is redundant.

It may be used, however, to avoid a figure at the start of a sentence: *A total of 650 people were killed in holiday traffic accidents.*

**toward** Not *towards.*

**town** Apply the capitalization principles in **city.**

**town council** Apply the capitalization principles in **city council.**

**trade in** (v.) **trade-in** (n. and adj.)

**trademark** A trademark is a brand, symbol, word, etc., used by a manufacturer or dealer and protected by law to prevent a competitor from using it: *AstroTurf,* for a type of artificial grass, for example.

In general, use a generic equivalent unless the trademark name is essential to the story.

When a trademark is used, capitalize it.

Many trademarks are listed separately in this book, together with generic equivalents.

The U.S. Trademark Association, located in New York, is a helpful source of information about trademarks.

See **brand names** and **service marks.**

**trade off** (v.) **trade-off** (n. and adj.)

**traffic, trafficked, trafficking**

**trampoline** Formerly a trademark, now a generic term.

**trans-** The rules in **prefixes** apply, but in general, no hyphen. Some examples:

transcontinen-        transsexual
tal
transmigrate         transship
transoceanic         trans-Siberian

Also: *trans-Atlantic* and *trans-Pacific.* These are exceptions to Webster's New World in keeping with the general rule that a hyphen is needed when a prefix precedes a capitalized word.

**transcripts** See the **texts, transcripts** entry.

**transfer, transferred, transferring**

**Transjordan** Earlier name for Jordan.

**transsexuals** See **sex changes.**

**Trans World Airlines** A *TWA airliner* is acceptable in any reference.
Headquarters is in New York.

**travel, traveled, traveling, traveler**

**travelogue** Not *travelog.*

**treasurer** Capitalize when used as a formal title immediately before a name. See **titles.**
Caution: The secretary of the U.S. Department of the Treasury is not the same person as the U.S. treasurer.

**trees** See **plants.**

**tribes** See the **nationalities and races** entry.

**trigger-happy**

**TriMotor** The proper name of a three-engine airplane once made by Ford Motor Co.

**Trinidad and Tobago** In datelines on stories from this island nation, use a community name followed by either *Trinidad* or *Tobago*—but not both—depending on where the community is located.

**TriStar** The proper name that Lockheed Aircraft Corp. uses for its L-1011 jetliner.

**Trojan horse, Trojan War**

**troop, troops, troupe** A *troop* is a group of people or animals. *Troops* means several such groups, particularly groups of soldiers.

Use *troupe* only for ensembles of actors, dancers, singers, etc.

**tropical depression** See **weather terms.**

**Truman, Harry S.** With a period after the initial. Truman once said there was no need for the period because the *S* did not stand for a name. Asked in the early 1960s about his preference, he replied, "It makes no difference to me."

AP style has called for the period since that time.

**trustee** A person to whom another's property or the management of another's property is entrusted.

Do not capitalize if used before a name.

**trusty** A prison inmate granted special privileges as a trustworthy person.

Do not capitalize if used before a name.

**try out** (v.) **tryout** (n.)

**tsar** Use *czar.*

**T-shirt**

**tuberculosis** *TB* is acceptable on second reference.

**Tuesday** See **days of the week.**

**tune up** (v.) **tuneup** (n. and adj.)

**turboprop** See **aircraft terms.**

**turnpike** Capitalize as part of a proper name: *the Pennsylvania Turnpike.* Lowercase *turnpike* when it stands alone.

See **highway designations.**

**TV** Acceptable as an adjective or in such constructions as *cable TV*. But do not normally use as a noun unless part of a quotation.

**Twelve Apostles** The disciples of Jesus. An exception to the normal practice of using figures for 10 and above.

**20th Century Fox, Twentieth Century Fund, Twentieth Century Limited** Follow an organization's practice. See **company names**.

**typhoons** Capitalize typhoon when it is part of the name that weather forecasters assign to a storm: *Typhoon Tilda*.

But use *it* and *its*—not *she, her* or *hers*—in pronoun references.

And do not use the presence of a woman's name as an excuse to attribute sexist images of women's behavior to a typhoon.

See **weather terms**.

# U

**U** In Burmese names, *U* is an honorific prefix. It means something like "Mr.," and is used for adult males only. It should not be used. For example, *U Nu* is only *Nu* in all references. Women retain their given names after marriage. No courtesy titles apply.

**U-boat** A German submarine. Anything referring to a submarine should be *submarine* unless directly referring to a German vessel of World War I or II vintage.

**UFO, UFOs** Acceptable in all references for *unidentified flying object(s)*.

**UHF** Acceptable in all references for *ultrahigh frequency*.

**Ukrainian Catholic Church** See **Eastern Rite churches.**

**Ukrainian Soviet Socialist Republic** See the **Russia, Soviet Union** entry.

**ukulele**

**Ulster** A colloquial synonym for *Northern Ireland*. See **United Kingdom.**

**ultra-prefixes** The rules in **prefixes** apply, but in general, no hyphen. Some examples:

| | |
|---|---|
| ultramodern | ultrasonic |
| ultranational- ism | ultraviolet |

**ultrahigh frequency** *UHF* is acceptable in all references.

**un-** The rules in **prefixes** apply, but in general, no hyphen. Some examples:

| | |
|---|---|
| un-American | unnecessary |
| unarmed | unshaven |

**U.N.** Used as an adjective, but not as a noun, for United Nations.

See **United Nations.**

**Uncle Sam**

**Uncle Tom** A term of contempt applied to a black person, taken from the main character in Harriet Beecher Stowe's novel "Uncle Tom's Cabin." It describes the practice of kowtowing to whites to curry favor.

Do not apply it to an individual. It carries potentially libelous connotations of having sold one's convictions for money, prestige or political influence.

**under-** The rules in **prefixes** apply, but in general, no hyphen. Some examples:

   underdog      undersheriff
   underground   undersold

**undersecretary** One word. See **titles.**

**under way** Two words in virtually all uses: *The project is under way. The naval maneuvers are under way.*

One word only when used as an adjective before a noun in a nautical sense: *an underway flotilla.*

**unemployment rate** In the United States, this estimate of the number of unemployed residents seeking work is compiled monthly by the Bureau of Labor Statistics, an agency of the Labor Department.

Each month the bureau selects a nationwide cross section of the population and conducts interviews to determine the size of the U.S. work force. The work force is defined as the number of people with jobs and the number looking for jobs.

The unemployment rate is expressed as a percentage figure. The essential calculation involves dividing the total work force into the number of people looking for jobs, followed by adjustments to reflect variable factors such as seasonal trends.

**UNESCO** Acceptable on first reference for the *United Nations Educational, Scientific and Cultural Organization,* but a subsequent reference should give the full name.

**UNICEF** Acceptable in all references for the *United Nations Children's Fund.* The words *International* and

*Emergency,* originally part of the name, have been dropped.

**unidentified flying object(s)** *UFO* and *UFOs* are acceptable in all references.

**Uniform Code of Military Justice** The laws covering members of the U.S. armed forces.

**uninterested** See the **disinterested, uninterested** entry.

**union** Capitalize when used as a proper name for the Northern states during the Civil War: *The Union defeated the Confederacy.*

**union names** The formal names of unions may be condensed to conventionally accepted short forms that capitalize characteristic words from the full name followed by *union* in lowercase.

Follow union practice in the use of the word *worker* in shortened forms. Among major unions, all except the United Steelworkers use two words: *United Auto Workers, United Mine Workers,* etc.

When *worker* is used generically, make *autoworkers* one word in keeping with widespread practice; use two words for other job descriptions: bakery workers, mine workers, steel workers.

See the **local of a union** entry and the individual entries for these unions frequently in the news:

**Amalgamated Clothing and Textile Workers Union of America**

**Amalgamated Transit Union**

**American Federation of Government Employees**

**American Federation of Labor and Congress of Industrial Organizations**

**American Federation of Musicians**

**American Federation of State, County and Municipal Employees**

**American Federation of Teachers**

**American Federation of Television and Radio Artists**

**American Postal Workers Union**

**Bakery and Confectionery Workers' International Union of America**

**Bricklayers, Masons and Plasterers' Interna-**

tional Union of America

Brotherhood of Railway, Airline and Steamship Clerks, Freight Handlers, Express and Station Employees

Communications Workers of America

Hotel and Restaurant Employees and Bartenders International Union

International Association of Machinists and Aerospace Workers

International Brotherhood of Electrical Workers

International Brotherhood of Painters and Allied Trades of the United States and Canada

International Brotherhood of Teamsters, Chauffeurs, Warehousemen and Helpers of America

International Ladies' Garment Workers Union

International Longshoremen's and Warehousemen's Union

International Longshoremen's Association

Laborers' International Union of North America

National Association of Letter Carriers

Newspaper Guild, The

Oil, Chemical and Atomic Workers International Union

Sheet Metal Workers International Association

United Automobile, Aerospace and Agricultural Implement Workers of America

United Brotherhood of Carpenters and Joiners of America

United Electrical, Radio and Machine Workers of America

United Food and Commercial Workers International Union

United Mine Workers of America

United Rubber, Cork, Linoleum and Plastic Workers of America

United Steelworkers of America

**Union of Soviet Socialist Republics** Use *U.S.S.R.* in datelines from all cities except *Moscow*, which stands alone in datelines.

*Soviet Union* is acceptable

in all references in the body of a story.

See the **Russia, Soviet Union** entry for a list of the republics.

**union shop** See **closed shop.**

**unique** It means one of a kind. Do not describe something as *rather unique* or *most unique.*

**United Airlines** A subsidiary of Allegis Corp.

Headquarters is in Chicago.

**United Arab Emirates** Do not abbreviate, even in datelines.

Use *U.A.E.* (with periods) if quoted matter requires the abbreviation.

**United Automobile, Aerospace and Agricultural Implement Workers of America** The shortened forms *United Auto Workers* and *United Auto Workers union* are acceptable in all references.

*UAW* and *Auto Workers* are acceptable on second reference.

Use *autoworker* or *autoworkers* (one word, lowercase)

in generic references to workers in the auto industry.

Headquarters is in Detroit.

**United Brotherhood of Carpenters and Joiners of America** The shortened form *Carpenters union* is acceptable in all references.

Headquarters is in Washington.

**United Church of Christ** See Congregationalist churches.

**United Electrical, Radio and Machine Workers of America** The shortened form *Electrical Workers union* is acceptable in all references.

Headquarters is in New York.

**United Food and Commercial Workers International Union** Formed by the merger of the Retail Clerks International Union and the Amalgamated Meat Cutters and Butcher Workmen of North America.

The shortened form *Food and Commercial Workers union* is acceptable in all references.

Headquarters is in Washington.

**United Kingdom** It consists of Great Britain and Northern Ireland.

Great Britain (or Britain) consists of England, Scotland and Wales.

Ireland is independent of the United Kingdom.

See **datelines** and **Ireland.**

**United Methodist Church** See **Methodist churches.**

**United Mine Workers of America** The shortened forms *United Mine Workers* and *United Mine Workers union* are acceptable in all refernces.

*UMW* and *Mine Workers* are acceptable on second reference.

Use *mine workers* or *miners,* lowercase, in generic references to workers in the industry.

Headquarters is in Washington.

**United Nations** Spell out when used as a noun. Use *U.N.* (no space) only as an adjective.

The periods in *U.N.,* for consistency with U.S., are an exception to the first listing in Webster's New World Dictionary.

In datelines:
*UNITED NATIONS (AP)—*

Use *U.N. General Assembly, U.N. Secretariat* and *U.N. Security Council* in first references not under a United Nations dateline.

*General Assembly, the Secretariat* and *Security Council* are acceptable in all references under a United Nations dateline and on second reference under other datelines.

Lowercase *the assembly* and *the council* when they stand alone.

See **UNESCO** and **UNICEF.**

**United Presbyterian Church in the United States of America** It no longer exists. See **Presbyterian churches** entry.

**United Press International** A privately owned news agency formed in 1958 as a merger of United Press and International News Service.

Use the full name on first reference. *UPI* is acceptable on second reference.

The address is 1400 Eye St., Washington, D.C. 20005. The telephone number is (202) 898-8000.

**United Rubber, Cork, Linoleum and Plastic Workers of America** The shortened forms *United Rubber Workers* and *United Rubber Workers union* are acceptable in all references.

Capitalize *Rubber Workers* in references to the union or its members.

Use *rubber workers,* lowercase, in generic references to workers in the rubber industry.

Headquarters is in Akron, Ohio.

**United Service Organizations** *USO* is acceptable on second reference.

**United States** Spell out when used as a noun. Use *U.S.* (no space) only as an adjective.

---

For organizations with names beginning with the words United States, see entries alphabetized under U.S.

---

**United Steelworkers of America** The shortened forms *United Steelworkers* and *United Steelworkers*

*union* are acceptable in all references.

Capitalize *Steelworkers* in references to the union or its members.

Use *steel workers* (two words, lowercase) in generic references to workers in the steel industry. (Many Steelworkers are employed in other industries and thus are not steel workers.)

Headquarters is in Pittsburgh.

**United Synagogue of America** Not *synagogues.* See **Jewish congregations.**

**up-** The rules in **prefixes** apply, but in general, no hyphen. Some examples:

| | |
|---|---|
| upend | upstate |
| upgrade | uptown |

**-up** Follow Webster's New World Dictionary. Hyphenate if not listed there.

Some frequently used words (all are nouns, some also are used as adjectives):

| | |
|---|---|
| breakup | mix-up |
| call-up | mock-up |
| change-up | pileup |
| checkup | push-up |
| cleanup | roundup |
| close-up | runners-up |
| cover-up | setup |
| crackup | shake-up |

| | |
|---|---|
| follow-up | shape-up |
| frame-up | smashup |
| grown-up | speedup |
| holdup | tie-up |
| letup | walk-up |
| lineup | windup |
| makeup | |

Use two words when any of these occurs as a verb.

See **suffixes**.

**UPI** Acceptable on second reference for *United Press International*.

**uppercase** One word (n., v., adj.) when referring to the use of capital letters. An exception to Webster's New World in keeping with printers' practice.

**upside down** (adv.) **upside-down** (adj.) *The car turned upside down. She made an upside-down cake. The book is upside-down.*

**upstate** Always lowercase: *upstate New York.*

**upward** Not *upwards.*

**U.S.** Used as an adjective, but not as a noun, for *United States.*

**USAir** Formerly known as Allegheny Airlines. Allegheny Commuter airlines operate under contracts with USAir.

Headquarters is in Washington.

**U.S. Air Force** See **air force; military academies;** and **military titles.**

**U.S. Army** See **army; military academies;** and **military titles.**

**U.S. Coast Guard** See **coast guard; military academies;** and **military titles.**

**U.S. Conference of Mayors** The members are the mayors of cities with 30,000 or more residents. See *National League of Cities.*

Use *the conference* or *the mayors' conference* on second reference.

There is no organization with the name *National Mayors' Conference.*

**U.S. Court of Appeals** The court is divided into 12 circuits as follows:

District of Columbia Circuit.

1st Circuit: Maine, Massachusetts, New Hampshire, Rhode Island, Puerto Rico. Based in Boston.

364 U.S. Court of Appeals

2nd Circuit: Connecticut, New York, Vermont. Based in New York.

3rd Circuit: Delaware, New Jersey, Pennsylvania, Virgin Islands. Based in Philadelphia.

4th Circuit: Maryland, North Carolina, South Carolina, Virginia, West Virginia. Based in Richmond, Va.

5th Circuit: Louisiana, Mississippi, Texas. Based in New Orleans.

6th Circuit: Kentucky, Michigan, Ohio, Tennessee. Based in Cincinnati.

7th Circuit: Illinois, Indiana, Wisconsin. Based in Chicago.

8th Circuit: Arkansas, Iowa, Minnesota, Missouri, Nebraska, North Dakota, South Dakota. Based in St. Louis.

9th Circuit: Alaska, Arizona, California, Hawaii, Idaho, Montana, Nevada, Oregon, Washington, Guam. Based in San Francisco.

10th Circuit: Colorado, Kansas, New Mexico, Oklahoma, Utah, Wyoming. Based in Denver.

11th Circuit: Alabama, Florida and Georgia. Based in Atlanta.

The courts do not always sit in the cities where they are based. Sessions may be held in other major cities within each region.

REFERENCE FORMS: A phrase such as a *federal appeals court* is acceptable on first reference.

On first reference to the full name, use *U.S. Court of Appeals* or a full name, use *U.S. Court of Appeals* or a full name: *8th U.S. Circuit Court of Appeals* or *the U.S. Court of Appeals for the 8th Circuit.*

*U.S. Circuit Court of Appeals* without a circuit number is a misnomer and should not be used.

In shortened and subsequent references: *the Court of Appeals, the 2nd Circuit, the appeals court, the appellate court(s), the circuit court(s), the court.*

Do not create non-existent entities such as *the San Francisco Court of Appeals.* Make it *the U.S. Court of Appeals in San Francisco.*

JURISTS: The formal title for the jurists on the court is *judge: U.S. Circuit Judge Homer Thornberry* is preferred to *U.S. Appeals Judge Homer Thornberry,* but either is acceptable.

See **judge.**

**U.S. Court of Claims**
This court handles suits against the federal government. It is based in Washington.

**U.S. Court of Customs and Patent Appeals** This court handles appeals involving customs, patents and copyright. It is based in Washington.

**U.S. Court of Military Appeals** This court, not part of the judicial branch as such, is a civilian body established by Congress to hear appeals from actions of the Defense Department. It is based in Washington.

**U.S. Customs Court**
This court, based in New York City, handles disputes over customs duties that arise at any U.S. port of entry.

**U.S. District Courts**
There are 94. In shortened and subsequent references: *the District Court, the District Courts, the court.*

*Judge* is the formal title for District Court jurists: *U.S. District Judge Frank Johnson.* See **judge.**

**usher** Use for both men and women.

**U.S. Information Agency** Formerly the U.S. Communication Agency.

Use *U.S. Information Agency* on first reference. Lowercase *the communication agency* or the *agency* in second references.

**U.S. Military Academy** See **military academies.**

**U.S. Navy** See **navy; military academies;** and **military titles.**

**U.S. Postal Service** Use *U.S. Postal Service* or *the Postal Service* on first reference. Retain capitalization of *Postal Service* in subsequent references to the agency.

Lowercase *the service* when it stands alone. Lowercase *post office* in generic references to the agency and to an individual office: *I went to the post office.*

**U.S. Postal Service Directory of Post Offices** The reference for U.S. place names not covered in this book.

**USS** For *United States Ship*, *Steamer* or *Steamship*, preceding the name of a vessel: the *USS Iowa*.

In datelines:

*ABOARD USS IOWA (AP)—*

**U.S. Supreme Court** See **Supreme Court of the United States.**

**U.S. Tax Court** This is an administrative body within the U.S. Treasury Department rather than part of the judicial branch. It handles appeals in tax cases.

**USX Corp.** Formerly U.S. Steel.

**Utah** Do not abbreviate. See **state names.**

**U-turn** (n. and adj.)

# V

**v.** See **verbs.**

**vacuum**

**Valium** A trademark for a brand of tranquilizer and muscle relaxant. It also may be called *diazepam.*

**valley** Capitalize as part of a full name: *the Mississippi Valley.*

Lowercase in plural uses: *the Missouri and Mississippi valleys.*

**Vandyke beard, Vandyke collar**

**Varig Brazilian Airlines** Headquarters is in Rio de Janeiro.

**Vaseline** A trademark for a brand of petroleum jelly.

**Vatican City** Stands alone in datelines.

**V-E Day** May 8, 1945, the day the surrender of Germany was announced, officially ending the European phase of World War II.

**vegetables** See **food.**

**V-8** The engine.

**vendor**

**venereal disease** *VD* is acceptable on second reference.

**verbal** See the **oral, verbal, written** entry.

**verbs** The abbreviation *v.* is used in this book to identify the spelling of the verb forms of words frequently misspelled.

SPLIT FORMS: In general, avoid awkward constructions that split infinitive forms of a verb *(to leave, to help,* etc.) or compound forms *(had left, are found out,* etc.)

Awkward: *She was ordered*

to immediately leave on an assignment.

Preferred: *She was ordered to leave immediately on an assignment.*

Awkward: *There stood the wagon that we had early last autumn left by the barn.*

Preferred: *There stood the wagon that we had left by the barn early last autumn.*

Occasionally, however, a split is not awkward and is necessary to convey the meaning:

*He wanted to really help his mother.*

*Those who lie are often found out.*

*How has your health been?*

*The budget was tentatively approved.*

**Vermont** Abbrev. *Vt.* See **state names.**

**vernacular** The native language of a country or place. A vernacular term that has achieved widespread recognition may be used without explanation if appropriate in the context.

Terms not widely known should be explained when used. In general, they are appropriate only when illustrating vernacular speech.

See **colloquialisms** and **dialect.**

**verses** See **poetry** for guidelines on how to handle verses of poetry typographically.

**versus** Abbreviate as *vs.* in all uses.

**vertical takeoff aircraft** See the **V-STOL** and **VTOL** entries.

**very high frequency** *VHF* is acceptable in all references.

**Very Rev.** See **Episcopal Church; religious titles;** and **Roman Catholic Church.**

**Veterans Administration** No apostrophe. *VA* may be used on second reference.

When referring to VA hospitals, capitalize full names: *the Boston Veterans Administration Hospital* (or the *Boston VA Hospital* if second reference), but lowercase references such as *the VA hospital.*

**Veterans Day** Formerly Armistice Day, Nov. 11, the anniversary of the armistice that ended World War I in 1918.

The federal legal holiday, observed on the fourth Monday in October during the mid-1970s, reverted to Nov. 11 in 1978.

**Veterans of Foreign Wars** *VFW* is acceptable on second reference.

Headquarters is in Kansas City, Mo.

**veto, vetoes** (n.) The verb forms: *vetoed, vetoing.*

**VHF** Acceptable in all references for *very high frequency.*

**vice-** Use two words: *vice admiral, vice chairman, vice chancellor, vice consul, vice president, vice principal, vice regent, vice secretary.*

Several are exceptions to Webster's New World. The two-word rule has been adopted for consistency in handling the similar terms.

**vice president** Capitalize or lowercase following the same rules that apply to *president.* See **president** and **titles.**

Do not drop the first name on first reference.

**vice versa**

**Victrola** A trademark for a brand of record player.

**videotape** (n. and v.)

**videotex, teletext** Not *videotext. Videotex* is the generic term for two-way interactive data systems that transmit text and sometimes graphics via telephone lines or cable. A user can specify desired information and communicate with a host computer or other users through a terminal keyboard.

*Teletext* is a one-way system that transmits text material or graphics via a television or FM broadcast signal or cable TV system. The user can select material desired but cannot communicate with other users.

**vie, vied, vying**

**vienna bread, vienna coffee, vienna sausages** See **food.**

**Viet Cong**

**Vietnam** Not *Viet Nam.*

**Vietnam War**

**village** Apply the capitalization principles in **city**.

**VIP, VIPs** Acceptable in all references for *very important person(s)*.

**Virginia** Abbrev.: *Va.* Legally a commonwealth, not a state.
See **state** and **state names**.

**Virgin Islands** Use with a community name in datelines on stories from the U.S. Virgin Islands. Do not abbreviate.
Identify an individual island in the text if relevant.
See **datelines** and **British Virgin Islands**.

**viscount, viscountess** See **nobility**.

**vitamins** Lowercase *vitamin*, use a capital letter and/or a figure for the type: *vitamin A, vitamin B-12*.

**V-J Day** The day of victory for the Allied forces over Japan in World War II.
It is calculated both as Aug. 15, 1945, the day the fighting with Japan ended, and as Sept. 2, 1945, the day Japan officially surrendered.

**V-neck** (n. and adj.)

**Voice of America** *VOA* is acceptable on second reference.

**volatile** Something that evaporates rapidly. It may or may not be explosive.

**Volkswagen of America Inc.** The name of the U.S. subsidiary of the German company named *Volkswagen A.G.*
U.S. headquarters is in Englewood Cliffs, N.J.

**volley, volleys**

**Volunteers in Service to America** *VISTA* is acceptable in second reference.

**von** See **foreign particles**.

**voodoo**

**vote-getter**

**vote tabulations** Always use figures for the totals.
Spell out below 10 in other phrases related to voting: *by a five-vote majority, with three abstentions, four votes short of the necessary two-thirds majority.*

For results that involve fewer than 1,000 votes on each side, use these forms: *The House voted 230–205, a 230–205 vote.*

To make totals that involve more than 1,000 votes on a side easier to read, separate the figures with the word *to* to avoid hyphenated adjectival constructions. See **election returns** for examples.

**V-STOL** Acceptable on second reference for an aircraft capable of *vertical* or *short takeoff or landing.*

**VTOL** Acceptable on second reference for an aircraft capable of *vertical takeoff or landing.*

**vulgarities** See the **obscenities, profanities, vulgarities** entry.

**Wac, WAC** *Wac* is no longer used by the military but is an acceptable term in a reference to a woman who served in what used to be the *Women's Army Corps.*

*WAC* is acceptable on second reference to the corps.

**Waf, WAF** *Waf* no longer is used by the military but is acceptable in a reference to a woman who served in the Air Force.

*WAF* is acceptable on second reference to the *Women's Air Force,* an unofficial organizational distinction formerly made by the Air Force but never authorized by Congress.

**waiter** (male) **waitress** (female)

**Wales** Use *Wales* after the names of Welsh communities in datelines.

See **datelines** and **United Kingdom.**

**walk up** (v.) **walk-up** (n. and adj.)

**Wall Street** When the reference is to the entire complex of financial institutions in the area rather than the actual street itself, *the Street* is an acceptable short form.

See **capitalization.**

**war** Capitalize when used as part of the name for a specific conflict: *the Civil War, the Cold War, the Korean War, the Vietnam War, the War of 1812, World War II,* etc.

**warden** Capitalize as a formal title before a name. See **titles.**

**wards** Use figures. See **political divisions.**

**warhead**

**war horse, warhorse** Two words for a horse used in battle.

One word for a veteran of many battles: *He is a political warhorse.*

**warlike**

**warlord**

**Warner Communications Inc.** Headquarters is in New York.

The motion picture division is Warner Bros. Inc.

**warrant officer** See **military titles.**

**wartime**

**washed-up**

**Washington** Abbreviate the state as *Wash.*

Never abbreviate when referring to the U.S. capital.

Use *state of Washington* or *Washington state* and *Washington, D.C.,* or *District of Columbia* when the context requires distinction between the state and the federal district.

See **state** and **state names.**

**Washington's Birthday** Capitalize *birthday* in references to the holiday.

The date he was born is computed as Feb. 22. The federal legal holiday is the third Monday in February.

Some states and some organizations refer to it as *Presidents Day* but the formal name has not changed.

**wastebasket**

**waterspout** See weather terms.

**Wave, WAVES** *Wave* no longer is used by the military but is acceptable in a reference to a woman who served in the Navy.

*WAVES* is acceptable on second reference to the *Women Accepted for Volunteer Emergency Service,* an organizational distinction made for women during World War II but subsequently discontinued.

**weak-kneed**

**weapons** *Gun* is an acceptable term for any firearm. Note the following definitions and forms in dealing with weapons and ammunition:

**anti-aircraft** A heavy-caliber cannon that fires explosive shells. It is designed for defense against air attack. The form: *a 105mm anti-aircraft gun.*

**artillery** A carriage-mounted cannon.

**automatic** A kind of pistol designed for automatic or semiautomatic firing. Its cartridges are held in a magazine. The form: *a .22-caliber automatic.*

**buckshot** See **shot** below.

**bullet** The projectile fired by a rifle, pistol or machine gun. Together with metal casing, primer and propellant, it forms a *cartridge.*

**caliber** A measurement of the diameter of the inside of a gun barrel except for most shotguns. Measurement is in either millimeters or decimal fractions of an inch. The word *caliber* is not used when giving the metric measurement. The forms: *a 9mm pistol, a .22-caliber rifle.*

**cannon** A large-caliber weapon, usually supported on some type of carriage, that fires explosive projectiles. The form: *a 105mm cannon.*

**carbine** A short-barreled rifle. The form: *an M-3 carbine.*

**cartridge** See **bullet** above.

**Colt** Named for Samuel Colt, it designates a make of weapon or ammunition developed for Colt handguns. The forms: *a Colt .45-caliber revolver, .45 Long Colt ammunition.*

**gauge** This word describes the size of a shotgun. Gauge is expressed in terms of the number per pound of round lead balls with a diameter equal to the size of the barrel. The bigger the number, the smaller the shotgun. Some common shotgun gauges:

| Gauge | Interior Diameter |
|---|---|
| 10 | .775 inches |
| 12 | .729 inches |
| 16 | .662 inches |
| 20 | .615 inches |
| 28 | .550 inches |
| .410 | .410 inches |

The .410 actually is a caliber, but commonly is called a gauge.

The forms: *a 12-gauge shotgun, a .410-gauge shotgun.*

**howitzer** A cannon shorter than a gun of the same caliber employed to fire projectiles at relatively high angles at a target, such as opposing forces behind a ridge. The form: *a 105mm howitzer.*

**machine gun** An automatic gun, usually mounted on a support, that fires as long as the trigger is depressed. The forms: *a .50-caliber Browning machine gun.*

**Magnum** A trademark for a type of high-powered cartridge with a larger case and a larger powder charge than other cartridges of approximately the same caliber. The form: *a .357-caliber Magnum, a .44-caliber Magnum.*

**M-1, M-16** These and similar combinations of a letter and figure(s) designate rifles used by the military. The forms: *an M-1 rifle, an M-16 rifle.*

**musket** A heavy, smoothbore, large-caliber shoulder firearm fired by means of a matchlock, a wheel lock, a flintlock or a percussion lock. Its ammunition is a musket ball.

**pistol** A hand weapon. It may be a *revolver* or an *automatic.* Its measurement is in calibers. The form: *a .38-caliber pistol.*

**revolver:** A kind of pistol. Its cartridges are held in chambers in a cylinder that revolves. The form: *a .45-caliber revolver.*

**rifle:** A firearm with a rifled bore. It uses bullets or cartridges for ammunition. Its size is measured in calibers. The form: *a .22-caliber rifle.*

**Saturday Night Special** The popular name for the type of cheap pistol used for impulsive crimes, often committed on Saturday nights.

**shell** The word applies to military or naval ammunition and to shotgun ammunition.

**shot** Small lead or steel pellets fired by shotguns. A shotgun shell usually contains 1 to 2 ounces of shot. Do not use *shot* interchangeably with *buckshot,* which refers only to the largest shot sizes.

**shotgun** A small-arms gun with a smooth bore, sometimes double-barreled.

Its ammunition is shot. Its size is measured in gauges. The form: *a 12-gauge shotgun.*

**submachine gun** A lightweight automatic gun firing small-arms ammunition.

**weather-beaten**

**weather bureau** See **National Weather Service.**

**weatherman** The preferred term is *weather forecaster.*

**weather terms** The following are based on definitions used by the National Weather Service. All temperatures are Fahrenheit.

**blizzard** Wind speeds of 35 mph or more and considerable falling and/or blowing of snow with visibility near zero.

**coastal waters** The waters within about 20 miles of the coast, including bays, harbors and sounds.

**cyclone** A storm with strong winds rotating about a moving center of low atmospheric pressure.

The word sometimes is used in the United States to mean *tornado* and in the Indian Ocean area to mean *hurricane.*

**degree-day** A degree-day is a computation that gauges the amount of heating or cooling needed for a building. An uninsulated building will maintain an inside temperature of 70 degrees if the outside temperature is 65 degrees. A degree-day is a one-degree difference in this equilibrium for one day (a temperature of 64 degrees for 24 hours), or its equivalent such as a two-degree difference for half a day (a temperature of 63 for 12 hours).

A temperature of 10 below zero for 24 hours yields 75 degree-days. A temperature of 85 degrees for six hours yields five degree-days.

**dust storm** Visibility of one-half mile or less due to dust, wind speeds of 30 mph or more.

**flash flood** A sudden, violent flood. It typically occurs after a heavy rain or the melting of a heavy snow.

**flash flood warning** Warns that flash flooding is imminent or in progress. People in the affected area should take necessary precautions immediately.

**flash flood watch** Alerts the public that flash flooding is possible. Those in the affected area are urged to be ready to take additional precautions if a flash flood warning is issued or if flooding is observed.

**flood** Stories about floods usually tell how high the water is and where it is expected to crest. Such a story should also, for comparison, list flood stage and how high the water is above, or below, flood stage.
Wrong: *The river is expected to crest at 39 feet.*
Right: *The river is expected to crest at 39 feet, 12 feet above flood stage.*

**freeze** Describes conditions when the temperature at or near the surface is expected to be below 32 degrees during the growing season. Adjectives such as *severe* or *hard* are used if a cold spell exceeding two days is expected.
A freeze may or may not be accompanied by the formation of frost. However, use of the term *freeze* usually is re-stricted for occasions when wind or other conditions prevent frost.

**freezing drizzle, freezing rain** Synonyms for *ice storm.*

**frost** Describes the formation of thin ice crystals, which might develop under conditions similar to dew except for the minimum temperatures involved. Phrases such as *frost in low places* or *scattered light frost* are used when appropriate. The term *frost* seldom appears in state forecasts unless rather heavy frost is expected over an extensive area.

**funnel cloud** A violent, rotating column of air that does not touch the ground, usually a pendant from a cumulonimbus cloud.

**gale** Sustained winds within the range of 39 to 54 mph (34 to 47 knots).

**heavy snow** It generally means:
a. A fall accumulating to 4 inches or more in depth in 12 hours, or
b. A fall accumulating to 6 inches or more in depth in 24 hours.

**high wind** Normally indicates that sustained winds of 39 mph or greater are expected to persist for one hour or longer.

**hurricane or typhoon** A warm-core tropical cyclone in which the minimum sustained surface wind is 74 mph or more.

Hurricanes are spawned east of the international date line. Typhoons develop west of the line. They are known as cyclones in the Indian Ocean.

When a hurricane or typhoon loses strength (wind speed), usually after landfall, it is reduced to *tropical storm* status.

**hurricane categories** Hurricanes are ranked one to five according to what is known as the Saffir-Simpson scale of strength:

Category 1—Hurricane has central barometric pressure of 28.94 inches or more and winds of 74 to 95 mph, is accompanied by a 4-5 foot storm surge and causes minimal damage.

Category 2—Pressure 28.50 to 28.93 inches, winds from 96 to 110 mph, storm surge 6-8 feet, damage moderate.

Category 3—Pressure 27.91 to 28.49 inches, winds from 111 to 130 mph, storm surge 9-12 feet, damage extensive.

Category 4—Pressure 27.17 to 27.90 inches, winds from 131 to 155 mph, storm surge 13-18 feet, damage extreme.

Category 5—Pressure less than 27.17 inches, winds greater than 155 mph, storm surge higher than 18 feet, damage catastrophic.

Only two *Category 5* storms have hit the United States since record-keeping began: the 1935 Labor Day hurricane that hit the Florida Keys and killed 600 people and Hurricane Camille, which devastated the Mississippi coast in 1969, killing 256 and leaving $1.4 billion damage.

**hurricane eye** The relatively calm area in the center of the storm. In this area winds are light and the sky often is covered only partly by clouds.

**hurricane season** The portion of the year that has a relatively high incidence of hurricanes. In the Atlantic, Caribbean and Gulf of Mexico, this is from June through

November. In the eastern Pacific, it is June through Nov. 15. In the central Pacific, it is June through October.

**hurricane tide** Same as **storm tide.**

**hurricane warning** Warns that one or both of these dangerous effects of a hurricane are expected in specified coastal areas in 24 hours or less:

a. Sustained winds of 74 mph (64 knots) or higher, and/or

b. Dangerously high water or a combination of dangerously high water and exceptionally high waves, even though winds expected may be less than hurricane force.

**hurricane watch** An announcement for specific areas that a hurricane or incipient hurricane conditions may pose a threat to coastal and inland communities.

**ice storm, freezing drizzle, freezing rain** Describes the freezing of drizzle or rain on objects as it strikes them. *Freezing drizzle* and *freezing rain* are synonyms for *ice storm.*

**ice storm warning** Reserved for occasions when significant, and possibly damaging, accumulations of ice are expected.

**National Hurricane Center** The National Weather Service's National Hurricane Center in Coral Gables, Fla., has overall responsibility for tracking and providing information about tropical depressions, tropical storms and hurricanes in the Atlantic Ocean, Gulf of Mexico and Caribbean Sea.

The service's Eastern Pacific Hurricane Center in San Francisco is responsible for hurricane information in the Pacific Ocean area north of the equator and east of 140 degrees west longitude.

The service's Central Pacific Hurricane Center in Honolulu is responsible for hurricane information in the Pacific Ocean area north of the equator from 140 degrees west longitude to 180 degrees.

**nearshore waters** The waters extending to 5 miles from shore.

**offshore waters** The waters extending to about 250 miles from shore.

**sandstorm** Visibility of one-half mile or less due to sand blown by winds of 30 mph or more.

**severe blizzard** Wind speeds of 45 mph or more, great density of falling and/or blowing snow with visibility frequently near zero and a temperature of 10 degrees or lower.

**severe thunderstorm** Describes either of the following:
   a. Winds—Thunderstorm-related surface winds sustained or gusts 50 knots or greater.
   b. Hail—Surface hail three-quarters of an inch in diameter or larger. The word *hail* in a watch implies hail at the surface and aloft unless qualifying phrases such as *hail aloft* are used.

**sleet** (one form of ice pellet) Describes generally solid grains of ice formed by the freezing of raindrops or the refreezing of largely melted snowflakes. Sleet, like small hail, usually bounces when hitting a hard surface.

**sleet (heavy)** Heavy sleet is a fairly rare event in which the ground is covered to a depth of significance to motorists and others.

**snow avalanche bulletin** Snow avalanche bulletins are issued by the U.S. Forest Service for avalanche-prone areas in the western United States.

**squall** A sudden increase of wind speed by at least 16 knots and rising to 25 knots or more and lasting for at least one minute.

**stockmen's advisory** Alerts the public that livestock may require protection because of certain combinations of cold, wet and windy weather, specifically cold rain and/or snow with temperatures 45 degrees or lower and winds of 25 mph or higher. If the temperature is in the mid-30s or lower, the wind speed criterion is lowered to about 15 mph.

**storm tide** Directional wave(s) caused by a severe atmospheric disturbance.
   A *tidal wave* radiates from the center of an earthquake.

**temperature-humidity index** The temperature-humidity index indicates the combined effect of heat and air moisture on human comfort. A reading of 70 or below indicates no discomfort. A reading of 75 would indicate discomfort in half the population and all would feel uncomfortable with a reading of 79. The National Weather Service issues the *THI* between June 15th and September 15th.

**tornado** A violent rotating column of air forming a pendant, usually from a cumulonimbus cloud, and touching the ground. It usually starts as a funnel cloud and is accompanied by a loud roaring noise. On a local scale, it is the most destructive of all atmospheric phenomena.

**tornado warning** Warns the public of an existing tornado or one suspected to be in existence.

**tornado watch** Alerts the public to the possibility of a tornado.

**travelers'    advisory** Alerts the public that difficult traveling or hazardous road conditions are expected to be widespread.

**tropical depression** A tropical cyclone in which the maximum sustained surface wind is 38 mph (33 knots) or less.

**tropical storm** A warm-core tropical cyclone in which the maximum sustained surface winds ranges from 39 to 73 mph (34 to 63 knots) inclusive.

**typhoon** See **hurricane or typhoon** in this listing.

**waterspout** A tornado over water.

**wind chill index** Also known as the wind chill factor. No hyphen.
The *wind chill index* is a calculation that describes the combined effect of the wind and cold temperatures on exposed skin. The *wind chill index* would be minus 22, for example, if the temperature was 15 degrees and the wind was blowing at 25 mph—in other words, the combined effect would be the same as a temperature of 22 below zero with no wind.
The higher the wind at a given temperature, the lower the wind chill reading, although wind speeds above 45

## Heat Index Table
### Relative Humidity (Percentage)

Apparent Temperature

| Air Temp | 30 | 35 | 40 | 45 | 50 | 55 | 60 | 65 | 70 | 75 | 80 | 85 | 90 | 95 | 100 |
|---|---|---|---|---|---|---|---|---|---|---|---|---|---|---|---|
| 110 | 123 | 130 | 137 | 143 | 150 | | | | | | | | | | |
| 105 | 113 | 118 | 123 | 129 | 135 | 142 | 149 | | | | | | | | |
| 100 | 104 | 107 | 110 | 115 | 120 | 126 | 132 | 138 | 144 | | | | | | |
| 95 | 96 | 98 | 101 | 104 | 107 | 110 | 114 | 119 | 124 | 130 | 136 | | | | |
| 90 | 90 | 91 | 93 | 95 | 96 | 98 | 100 | 102 | 106 | 109 | 113 | 117 | 122 | | |
| 85 | 84 | 85 | 86 | 87 | 88 | 89 | 90 | 91 | 93 | 95 | 97 | 99 | 102 | 105 | 108 |
| 80 | 78 | 79 | 79 | 80 | 81 | 81 | 82 | 83 | 85 | 86 | 86 | 87 | 88 | 89 | 91 |
| 75 | 73 | 73 | 74 | 74 | 75 | 75 | 76 | 76 | 77 | 77 | 78 | 78 | 79 | 79 | 80 |
| 70 | 67 | 67 | 68 | 68 | 69 | 69 | 70 | 70 | 70 | 70 | 71 | 71 | 71 | 71 | 72 |

## Wind Chill Factor Table

| Wind MPH | \ | Air Temperature | | | | | | | | | | | | | |
|---|---|---|---|---|---|---|---|---|---|---|---|---|---|---|---|
| | | 35 | 30 | 25 | 20 | 15 | 10 | 5 | 0 | -5 | -10 | -15 | -20 | -25 | -30 | -35 |

Apparent Temperature

| Wind MPH | | 35 | 30 | 25 | 20 | 15 | 10 | 5 | 0 | -5 | -10 | -15 | -20 | -25 | -30 | -35 |
|---|---|---|---|---|---|---|---|---|---|---|---|---|---|---|---|---|
| 5 | – | 33 | 27 | 21 | 16 | 12 | 7 | 0 | -5 | -10 | -15 | -21 | -26 | -31 | -36 | -42 |
| 10 | – | 22 | 16 | 10 | 3 | -3 | -9 | -15 | -22 | -27 | -34 | -40 | -46 | -52 | -58 | -64 |
| 15 | – | 16 | 9 | 2 | -5 | -11 | -18 | -25 | -31 | -38 | -45 | -51 | -58 | -65 | -72 | -78 |
| 20 | – | 12 | 4 | -3 | -10 | -17 | -24 | -31 | -39 | -46 | -53 | -60 | -67 | -74 | -81 | -88 |
| 25 | – | 8 | 1 | -7 | -15 | -22 | -29 | -36 | -44 | -51 | -59 | -66 | -74 | -81 | -88 | -96 |
| 30 | – | 6 | -2 | -10 | -18 | -25 | -33 | -41 | -49 | -56 | -64 | -71 | -79 | -86 | -93 | -101 |
| 35 | – | 4 | -4 | -12 | -20 | -27 | -35 | -43 | -52 | -58 | -67 | -74 | -82 | -89 | -97 | -105 |
| 40 | – | 3 | -5 | -13 | -21 | -29 | -37 | -45 | -53 | -60 | -69 | -76 | -84 | -92 | -100 | -107 |
| 45 | – | 2 | -6 | -14 | -22 | -30 | -38 | -46 | -54 | -62 | -70 | -78 | 85 | -93 | -102 | -109 |

Winds of more than 45 mph add little to the chilling.

mph have little additional cooling effect.

**wind shear** It is caused when a mass of cooled air rushes downward out of a thunderstorm in what is called a *microburst,* hits the ground and rushes outward in all directions. Wind shear itself is described as a sudden shift in wind direction and speed. A plane flying through a microburst at low altitude, as on final approach or take-off, would at first experience a strong headwind and increased lift, followed by a strong tailwind and sharply decreased lift.

**winter storm warning** Notifies the public that severe winter weather conditions are almost certain to occur.

**winter storm watch** Alerts the public to the possibility of severe winter weather conditions.

**weather vane**

**Webster's New World Dictionary** See **dictionaries.**

**Webster's Third New International Dictionary** See **dictionaries.**

**Wednesday** See **days of the week.**

**weekend**

**weeklong**

**weights** Use figures: *The baby weighed 9 pounds, 7 ounces. She had a 9-pound, 7-ounce boy.*

**weirdo**

**well** Hyphenate as part of a compound modifier: *She is a well-dressed woman. She is well-dressed.*
See **hyphen** in the **Punctuation** chapter for guidelines on compound modifiers.

**well-being**

**well-to-do**

**well wishers**

**west, western** See the **directions and regions** entry.

**West** As defined by the U.S. Census Bureau, the 13-

state region is broken into two divisions.

The eight *Mountain division* states are Arizona, Colorado, Idaho, Montana, Nevada, New Mexico, Utah and Wyoming.

The five *Pacific division* states are Alaska, California, Hawaii, Oregon and Washington.

See **North Central region; Northeast region;** and **South** for the bureau's other three regional breakdowns.

**Western Hemisphere** The continents of North and South America, and the islands near them.

It frequently is subdivided as follows:

**Caribbean** The islands from the tip of Florida to the continent of South America, plus, particularly in a political sense, French Guiana, Guyana and Surinam on the northeastern coast of South America.

Major island elements are the Bahamas, Cuba, Hispaniola (the island shared by the Dominican Republic and Haiti), Jamaica, Puerto Rico, and the West Indies islands.

**Central America** The narrow strip of land between Mexico and Colombia. Located there are Belize, Costa Rica, El Salvador, Guatemala, Honduras, Nicaragua and Panama.

**Latin America** The area of the Americas south of the United States where Romance languages (those derived from Latin) are dominant. It applies to most of the region south of the United States except areas with a British heritage: the Bahamas, Barbados, Belize, Grenada, Guyana, Jamaica, Trinidad and Tobago, and various islands in the West Indies. Surinam, the former Dutch Guiana, is an additional exception.

**North America** Canada, Mexico, the United States and the Danish territory of Greenland. When the term is used in more than its continental sense, it also may include the islands of the Caribbean.

**South America** Argentina, Bolivia, Brazil, Chile, Colombia, Ecuador, Paraguay, Peru, Uruguay, Venezuela, and in a purely continental sense, French Guiana, Guyana and Suriname. Politically and psychologically, however, the latter three regard themselves as part of the Caribbean.

**West Indies** The term no longer is used extensively, but it applies to the Caribbean islands east of Puerto Rico southward to South America.

Major island elements are the nations of Barbados, Grenada, and Trinidad and Tobago, plus smaller islands dependent in various degrees on:

—Britain: British Virgin Islands, Anguilla, and the West Indies Associated States, including Antigua, Dominica, St. Lucia, St. Vincent and St. Christopher-Nevis.

—France: Guadeloupe (composed of islands known as Basse-Terre and Grande-Terre, plus five other islands) and Martinique.

—Netherlands: Netherlands Antilles, composed of Aruba, Bonaire, Curacao, Saba, St. Eustatius and the southern portion of St. Martin Island (the northern half is held by France and is part of Guadeloupe).

—United States: U.S. Virgin Islands, principally St. Croix, St. John and St. Thomas.

**West Germany** Use in datelines instead of the *Federal Republic of Germany.*

See **Berlin** and **East Germany.**

**West Indies** See **Western Hemisphere.**

**West Point** Acceptable on second reference to the *U.S. Military Academy.*

See **military academies.**

In datelines:

*WEST POINT, N.Y. (AP)—*

**West Virginia** Abbrev.: *W.Va.* (no space between *W.* and *Va.*). See **state names.**

**wheat** It is measured in bushels domestically, in metric tons for international trade.

There are 36.7 bushels of wheat in a metric ton.

**wheelchair**

**wheeler-dealer**

**whereabouts** Takes a singular verb:

*His whereabouts is a mystery.*

**wherever**

**which** See the **essential clauses, non-essential clauses** entry; the **that, which** entry; and the **who, whom** entry.

**whip** Capitalize when used as a formal title before a name. See **legislative titles** and **titles.**

**whiskey, whiskeys** Use the spelling *whisky* only in conjunction with *Scotch.*
See the **Scotch whisky** entry.

**white-collar** (adj.)

**White House** Do not personify it with phrases such as *the White House said.* Instead, use a phrase such as *a White House official said.*

**white paper** Two words, lowercase, when used to refer to a special report.

**whitewash** (n. and v. and adj.)

**who, whom** Use *who* and *whom* for references to human beings and to animals with a name. Use *that* and *which* for inanimate objects and animals without a name.
*Who* is the word when someone is the subject of a sentence, clause or phrase: *The woman who rented the room left the window open. Who is there?*
*Whom* is the word when someone is the object of a verb or preposition: *The woman to whom the room was rented left the window open. Whom do you wish to see?*
See the **essential clauses, non-essential clauses** entry for guidelines on how to punctuate clauses introduced by *who, whom, that* and *which.*

**wholehearted**

**wholesale price index** A measurement of the changes in the average prices that businesses pay for a selected group of industrial commodities, farm products, processed foods and feed for animals.
Capitalize when referring to the U.S. index, issued monthly by the Bureau of Labor Statistics, an agency of the Labor Department.

**whole-wheat**

**who's, whose** *Who's* is a contraction for *who is,* not a possessive: *Who's there?*
*Whose* is the possessive: *I do not know whose coat it is.*

**wide-** Usually hyphenated. Some examples:

| | |
|---|---|
| wide-angle | wide-eyed |
| wide-awake | wide-open |
| wide-brimmed | |

Exception: *widespread.*

**-wide** No hyphen. Some examples:

| | |
|---|---|
| citywide | nationwide |
| continentwide | statewide |
| countrywide | worldwide |
| industrywide | |

**widow, widower** In obituaries: A man is *survived by his wife,* or *leaves his wife.* A woman is *survived by her husband,* or *leaves her husband.*
Guard against the redundant *widow of the late.* Use *wife of the late* or *widow of.*

**widths** See **dimensions.**

**wigwag**

**wildlife**

**Wilkes-Barre, Pa.**

**will** See the **shall, will** entry and **subjunctive mood.**

**Wilson's disease** After Samuel A. Wilson, an English neurologist. A disease characterized by abnormal accumulation of copper in the brain, liver and other organs.

**Windbreaker** A trademark for a brand of wind-resistant sports jacket.

**wind chill index** See **weather terms.**

**window dressing** The noun. But as a verb: *window-dress.*

**wind-swept**

**wind up (v.) windup** (n. and adj.)

**wingspan**

**winter** See **seasons.**

**wintertime**

**wiretap, wiretapper**
The verb forms: *wiretap, wiretapped, wiretapping.*

**Wisconsin** Abbrev.: *Wis.* See **state names.**

**-wise** No hyphen when it means in the *direction* of or *with regard to.* Some examples:

| | |
|---|---|
| clockwise | otherwise |
| lengthwise | slantwise |

Avoid contrived combinations such as *moneywise, religionwise.*

The word *penny-wise* is spelled with a hyphen because it is a compound adjective in which *wise* means *smart,* not an application of the suffix *-wise.* The same for *street-wise* in *the street-wise youth.*

**Woman's Christian Temperance Union** Not *women's. WCTU* is acceptable on second reference.

**women** Women should receive the same treatment as men in all areas of coverage. Physical descriptions, sexist references, demeaning stereotypes and condescending phrases should not be used.

To cite some examples, this means that:

—Copy should not assume maleness when both sexes are involved, as in *Jackson told newsmen* or in *the taxpayer . . . he* when it easily can be said *Jackson told reporters* or *taxpayers . . . they.*

—Copy should not express surprise that an attractive woman can be professionally accomplished, as in: *Mary Smith doesn't look the part, but she's an authority on . . .*

—Copy should not gratuitously mention family relationships when there is no relevance to the subject, as in: *Golda Meir, a doughty grandmother, told the Egyptians today . . .*

—Use the same standards for men and women in deciding whether to include specific mention of personal appearance or marital and family situation.

In other words, treatment of the sexes should be evenhanded and free of assumptions and stereotypes. This does not mean that valid and acceptable words such as *mankind* or *humanity* cannot be used. They are proper.

See **courtesy titles; divorcee;** the **man, mankind** entry; and **-persons.**

**Women's Army Corps** See the **Wac, WAC** entry.

**Woolworth's** Acceptable in all references for F.W. Woolworth Co.

**word-of-mouth** (n. and adj.)

**words as words** The meaning of this phrase, which appears occasionally in this book and similar manuals that deal with words, is best illustrated by an example: In this sentence, *woman* appears solely as a word rather than as the means of representing the concept normally associated with the word.

When italics are available, a word used as a word should be italicized. Entries in this book use italics when a word or phrase is discussed in this sense. Note, for example, the italics used for *woman* in this sentence and in the example sentence.

Italics are not available to highlight this type of word use on the news wires. When a news story must use a word as a word, place quotation marks around it.

See **plurals.**

**word selection** In general, any word with a meaning that universally is understood is acceptable unless it is offensive or below the normal standards for literate writing.

This stylebook lists many words with cautionary notes about how they should be used. The entries in Webster's New World Dictionary provide cautionary notes, comparisons and usage guidelines to help a writer choose the correct word for a particular context.

Any word listed in Webster's New World may be used for the definitions given unless this stylebook restricts its use to only some definitions recorded by the dictionary or specifies that the word be confined to certain contexts.

If the dictionary cautions that a particular usage is objected to by some linguists or is not accepted widely, be wary of the usage unless there is a reason in the context.

The dictionary uses the description *substandard* to identify words below the norms for literate writing.

The dictionary provides

guidance on many idiomatic expressions under the principal word in the expression. The definition and spelling of *under way,* for example, are found in the "way" entry.

If it is necessary to use an archaic word or an archaic sense of a word, explain the meaning.

Additional guidance on the acceptability of words is provided in this book under:

| | |
|---|---|
| Americanisms | jargon |
| colloquialisms | special |
| dialect | contexts |
| foreign words | vernacular |

See also the **obscenities, profanities and vulgarities** entry.

**workday**

**working class** (n.)
**working-class** (adj.)

**workout**

**workweek**

**World Bank** Acceptable in all references for *International Bank for Reconstruction and Development.*

**World Council of Churches** This is the main international, interdenominational cooperative body of Anglican, Eastern Orthodox, Protestant and old or national Catholic churches.

The Roman Catholic Church is not a member but cooperates with the council in various programs.

Headquarters is in Geneva, Switzerland.

**World Court** This was an alternative name for the *Permanent Court of International Justice* set up by the League of Nations.

See the entry for the **International Court of Justice,** which has replaced it.

**World Health Organization** *WHO* is acceptable on second reference.

Headquarters is in Geneva, Switzerland.

**World Series** Or the *Series* on second reference. A rare exception to the general principles under **capitalization.**

**World War I, World War II**

**worldwide**

**worn-out**

**worship, worshiped, worshiping, worshiper**

**worthwhile**

**would** See the **should, would** entry.

**wrack** See the **rack, wrack** entry.

**write** (v.) **write-in** (n. and adj.)

**wrongdoing**

**Wyoming** Abbrev.: *Wyo.* See **state names.**

# XYZ

**X** The rating that denotes *individuals under 17 are not admitted.* See **movie ratings.**

**Xerox** A trademark for a brand of photocopy machine. Never a verb.

**X-ray** (n., v. and adj.) Use for both the photographic process and the radiation particles themselves.

**yam** Botanically, yams and sweet potatoes are not related, although several varieties of moist-fleshed sweet potatoes are popularly called *yams* in some parts of the United States.

**yard** Equal to three feet.
The metric equivalent is approximately 0.91 meter.
To convert to meters, multiply by .91 (5 yards × .91 = 4.55 meters).
See **foot; meter;** and **distances.**

**year-end** (adj.)

**yearlong**

**years** Use figures, without commas: *1986.* Use an *s* without an apostrophe to indicate spans of decades or centuries: *the 1890s, the 1800s.*
Years are the lone exception to the general rule in numerals that a figure is not used to start a sentence: *1976 was a very good year.*
See **A.D.; B.C.; centuries; historical periods and events;** and **months.**

**yellow journalism** The use of cheaply sensational methods to attract or influence readers. The term comes from the "Yellow Kid," a comic strip, in the New York World in 1895.

**yesterday** Use only in direct quotations and in phrases that do not refer to a specific day: *Yesterday we were young.*
Use the day of the week in other cases.

## yesteryear

**Yom Kippur** The Jewish Day of Atonement. Occurs in September or October.

**Young Men's Christian Association** *YMCA* is acceptable in all references.

Headquarters is in New York.

**Young Women's Christian Association** *YWCA* is acceptable in all references.

Headquarters is in New York.

**youth** Applicable to boys and girls from age 13 until 18th birthday. Use *man* or *woman* for individuals 18 and older.

**yo-yo** Formerly a trademark, now a generic term.

**Yukon** A territorial section of Canada. Do not abbreviate. Use in datelines after the names of communities in the territory.

See **Canada.**

## yule, yuletide

## zero, zeros

**zero-base budgeting** A process that requires an agency, department or division to justify budget requests as if its programs were starting from scratch, or from a base of zero. In theory this assures a review of all programs at budget time.

## zigzag

**Zionism** The effort of the Jews to regain and retain their biblical homeland. It is based on the promise of God in the Book of Genesis that Israel would forever belong to Abraham and his descendants as a nation.

The term is named for Mount Zion, the site of the ancient temple in Jerusalem. The Bible also frequently uses *Zion* in a general sense to denote the place where God is especially present with his people.

**ZIP codes** Use all-caps *ZIP* for *Zone Improvement Program,* but always lowercase the word *code*.

Run the five digits together without a comma, and do not put a comma between the state name and the ZIP code: *New York, N.Y. 10020.*

# SPORTS GUIDELINES AND STYLE

In 1983, all sports entries were moved into one section, making the use of the information more convenient.

Perhaps it is also an indication of how the coverage of sports continues to grow and how important it is to the overall news report.

Sports is entertainment. It is big business. It is news that extends beyond games, winners and losers.

It is also statistics—agate.

Writing about sports requires a broad understanding of law and economics and psychology and sociology and more.

As the appetite grows, so too does the need for writing with style and consistency.

The constant is the need to write with clarity and accuracy.

Good sports writing depends on the same writing and reporting tools as any other story.

A stylebook, a sports section of a stylebook, is an aid in reaching that goal.

# SPORTS GUIDELINES AND STYLE

## A

**All America, All-American** The Associated Press recognizes only one All-America football and basketball team each year. In football, only Walter Camp's selections through 1924, and the AP selections after that, are recognized. Do not call anyone an *All-America* selection unless he is listed on either the Camp or AP roster.

Similarly do not call anyone an *All-America basketball player* unless an AP selection. The first All-America basketball team was chosen in 1948.

Use *All-American* when referring specifically to an individual:

*All-American Pat Ewing,* or *He is an All-American.*

Use *All-America* when referring to the team:

*All-America team,* or *All-America selection.*

**Americas Cup** (golf)
**America's Cup** (yatching)

**archery** Scoring is usually in points. Use a basic summary. Example:

**(After 3 of 4 Distances)**
1. Darrell Pace, Cincinnati, 914 points.
2. Richard McKinney, Muncie, Ind. 880.
3. Etc.

**AstroTurf** A trademark for a type of artificial grass.

**athlete's foot, athlete's heart**

**athletic club** Abbreviate as *AC* with the name of a club, but only in sports summaries: *Illinois AC.* See the **volleyball** entry for an example of such a summary.

**athletic teams** Capitalize teams, associations and recognized nicknames: *Red Sox, the Big Ten, the A's, the Colts.*

**auto racing** Follow the form listed below for summaries.

Example:
Hampton, Ga. (AP)—The finish of

Sunday's $151,900 Atlanta 500 NAS-CAR Grand National stock car race with type of car, laps completed and winner's average speed:

1. David Pearson, Mercury, 328 laps, 126.094 mph.
2. Benny Parsons, Chevrolet, 328.
3. Etc.

In international events, insert the name of the driver's country after his name or, for a U.S. driver, his hometown, as in:

4. Mario Andretti, Nazareth, Pa., Ford, 328.

For point leaders:

**World Driver Leaders**
**(Points on 9-6-4-3-2-1 basis)**
1. Nicki Lauda, Austria, 47 points. 2. Emerson Fittipaldi, Brazil, 53. 3. Etc.

# B

**backboard, backcourt, backfield, backhand, backspin, backstop, backstretch, backstroke** Some are exceptions to Webster's New World, made for consistency in handling sports stories.

**badminton** Games are won by the first player to score 21 points, unless it is necessary to continue until one player has a two-point spread. Most matches go to the first winner of two games.

Use a match summary. See **racquetball** for an example.

**ball carrier**

**ballclub, ballpark, ball-player**

**baseball** The spellings for some frequently used words and phrases, some of which are exceptions to Webster's New World:

| | |
|---|---|
| backstop | passed ball |
| ballclub | put out (v.) |
| ballpark | putout (n.) |
| ballplayer | pinch hit (v.) |
| baseline | pinch-hit (n., adj.) |
| bullpen | |
| center field | pinch hitter (n.) |
| center fielder | |
| designated hitter | pitchout |
| | play off (v.) |
| doubleheader | playoff (n., adj.) |
| double play | |
| fair ball | RBI (s., pl.) |
| fastball | rundown (n.) |
| first baseman | sacrifice |
| foul ball | sacrifice fly |
| line | sacrifice hit |
| foul tip | shoestring catch |
| ground-rule double | shortstop |
| home plate | shut out (v.) |
| home run | shutout (n., adj.) |
| left-hander | |
| line drive | slugger |

| | |
|---|---|
| line up (v.) | squeeze play |
| lineup (n.) | strike |
| major league(s) | strike zone |
| (n.) | Texas leaguer |
| major-league | triple play |
| (adj.) | twi-night |
| major-leaguer | double- |
| (n.) | header |
| outfielder | wild pitch |

NUMBERS: Some sample uses of numbers: *first inning, seventh-inning stretch, 10th inning; first base, second base, third base; first home run, 10th home run; first place, last place; one RBI, 10 RBI. The pitcher's record is now 6-5. The final score was 1-0.*

LEAGUES: Use *American League, National League, American League West, National League East,* etc. On second reference: *the league, the pennant in the West, the league's West Division,* etc.

BOX SCORES: A sample follows.

The visiting team always is listed on the left, the home team on the right.

Only one position, the last he played in the game, is listed for any player.

Figures in parentheses are the player's total in that category for the season.

Use the *First Game* line shown here only if the game was the first in a doubleheader.

One line in this example— *None out when winning run scored*—could not have occurred in this game as played. It is included to show its placement when needed.

**First Game**
**PHILADELPHIA**

| | ab | r | h | bi |
|---|---|---|---|---|
| Stone lf | 4 | 0 | 0 | 0 |
| GGross lf | 0 | 0 | 0 | 0 |
| Schu 3 | 4 | 1 | 0 | 0 |
| Samuel 2b | 4 | 0 | 1 | 2 |
| Schmdt 1 | 4 | 0 | 0 | 0 |
| Virgil c | 4 | 2 | 2 | 1 |
| GWilson rf | 4 | 0 | 0 | 0 |
| Maddox c | 3 | 0 | 0 | 0 |
| Jeltz ss | 2 | 0 | 0 | 0 |
| KGross p | 3 | 0 | 1 | 0 |
| Tekulve p | 0 | 0 | 0 | 0 |
| **Totals** | **32** | **3** | **4** | **3** |

**SAN DIEGO**

| | ab | r | h | bi |
|---|---|---|---|---|
| Flannry 2 | 3 | 0 | 1 | 0 |
| Gwynn rf | 4 | 0 | 2 | 0 |
| Garvey 1 | 4 | 0 | 0 | 0 |
| Nettles 3b | 3 | 1 | 1 | 0 |
| Royster 3 | 0 | 0 | 0 | 0 |
| McRynl cf | 4 | 0 | 1 | 1 |
| Kennedy c | 4 | 0 | 1 | 0 |
| Martinez lf | 4 | 1 | 1 | 0 |
| Templtn ss | 4 | 0 | 2 | 1 |
| Dravcky p | 2 | 0 | 0 | 0 |
| Bmbry ph | 1 | 0 | 0 | 0 |
| Lefferts p | 0 | 0 | 0 | 0 |
| **Totals** | **33** | **2** | **9** | **2** |

| | |
|---|---|
| **Philadelphia** | 010 200 000 - 3 |
| **San Diego** | 000 200 000 - 2 |

None out when winning run scored.

Game Winning RBI - Virgil.
E. Templeton, GWilson. DP - Philadelphia 2. LOB - Philadelphia 3, San Diego 6. 2B - Templeton, Gwynn. HR - Virgil 2 (8).

| | IP | H | R | ER | BB | SO |
|---|---|---|---|---|---|---|
| **Philadelphia** | | | | | | |
| KGross W, 4-6 | 7 1-3 | 9 | 2 | 2 | 0 | 3 |
| Tekulve S, 3 | 1 2-3 | 0 | 0 | 0 | 1 | 0 |
| **San Diego** | | | | | | |
| Dravecky L, 4-3 | 7 | 4 | 3 | 1 | 1 | 2 |
| Lefferts | 2 | 0 | 0 | 0 | 0 | 1 |

HBP—Flannery by KGross. T—2:13. A-17,740.

LINESCORE: When a bare linescore summary is required, use this form:

| Philadelphia | 010 200 000—3 4 1 |
|---|---|
| San Diego | 000 200 000—2 9 1 |

K. Gross, Tekulve (8) and Virgil; Dravecky, Lefferts (3) and Kennedy. W - KGross, 4-6. LDravecky, 4-3. Sv - Tekulve (3). HRs - Philadelphia, Virgil 2 (8).

LEAGUE STANDINGS:
The form:

**All Times EDT**
**NATIONAL LEAGUE**

**EAST**

| | W | L | Pct. | GB |
|---|---|---|---|---|
| Pittsburgh | 92 | 69 | .571 | - |
| Philadelphia | 85 | 75 | .531 | 6½ |

**WEST**

| | W | L | Pct. | GB |
|---|---|---|---|---|
| Cincinnati | 108 | 54 | .667 | - |
| Los Angeles | 88 | 74 | .543 | 20 |

**(Night games not included)**
**Monday's Results**
Chicago 7, St. Louis 5
Atlanta at New York, rain.

**Tuesday's Games**
Cincinnati (Gullett 14-2 and Nolan 4-4) at New York (Seaver 12-3 and Matlack 6-1) 2, 6 p.m.
**Wednesday's Games**
Cincinnati at New York
Chicago at St Louis, night
Only games scheduled.

In subheads for results and future games, spell out day of the week as: *Tuesday's Games,* instead of *Today's Games.*

**basic summary** This format for summarizing sports events lists winners in the order of their finish. The figure showing the place finish is followed by an athlete's full name, his affiliation or hometown, and his time, distance, points, or whatever performance factor is applicable to the sport.

If a contest involves several types of events, the paragraph begins with the name of the event.

A typical example:

60-yard dash—1, Steve Williams, Florida TC, 6.0 2, Hasley Crawford, Philadelphia Pioneer, 6.1. 3, Mike McFarland, Chicago TC, 6.2. 4, Etc.
100—1, Steve Williams, Florida TC, 10.l. 2, Etc.

Additional examples are provided in the entries for many of the sports that are reported in this format.

Most basic summaries are a single paragraph per event, as shown. In some competitions with large fields, however, the basic summary is supplied under a dateline with each winner listed in a single paragraph. See the **auto racing and bowling** entries for examples.

For international events in which U.S. or Canadian competitors are not among the leaders, add them in a separate paragraph as follows:

Also: 14, Dick Green, New York, 6.8. 17, George Bensen, Canada, 6.9. 19, Etc.

In events where points, rather than time or distance, are recorded as performances, mention the word points on the first usage only:

1. Jim Benson, Springfield, N.J., 150 points. 2. Jerry Green, Canada, 149. 3. Etc.

**basketball** The spellings of some frequently used words and phrases:

| | |
|---|---|
| backboard | half-court |
| backcourt | press |
| backcourtman | halftime |
| baseline | hook shot |
| field goal | jump ball |
| foul line | jump shot |
| foul shot | layup |
| free throw | man-to-man |
| free-throw line | midcourt |
| frontcourt | pivotman |
| full-court press | play off (v.) |
| goaltending | playoff (n., |
| | adj.) |
| | zone |

NUMBERS: Some sample uses of numbers: *in the first quarter, a second-quarter lead, nine field goals, 10 field goals, the 6-foot-5 forward, the 6-10 center. He is 6 feet 10 inches tall.*

LEAGUE: *National Basketball Association* or *NBA.*

For subdivisions: *the Atlantic Division of the Eastern Conference, the Pacific Division of the Western Conference,* etc. On second reference: *the NBA East, the division, the conference,* etc.

BOX SCORE: A sample follows. The visiting team is always listed first.

In listing the players, begin with the five starters—two forwards, center, two guards—and follow with all substitutes who played.

Figures after each player's last name denote field goals, free throws, free throws attempted and total points.

Example:

**LOS ANGELES (114)**
Worthy 8-19 4-6 20, Rambis 4-6 0-0 8, Abdul-Jabbar 6-11 0-0 12, E. Johnson 8-14 3-4 19, Scott 5-14 0-0 10, Cooper 1-5 2-2 4, McAdoo 6-13 0-0 12, McGee 4-7 4-5 14, Spriggs 4-7 0-2 8, Kupchak 3-3 1-2 7. Totals 49-100 14-21 114.

**BOSTON (148)**
McHale 10-16 6-9 26, Bird 8-14 2-2 19, Parish 6-11 6-7 18, D. Johnson 6-14 1-1 13, Ainge 9-15 0-0 19, Buckner 3-5 0-0 6, Williams 3-5 0-0 6, Wedman 11-11 0-2 26, Maxwell 1-1 1-2 3, Kite 3-5 1-2 7, Carr 1-3 0-0 3, Clark 1-2 0-0 2. Totals 62-102 17-25 148.

Three-point goals - Wedman 4, McGee 2, Bird, Ainge, Carr. Fouled out - None. Rebounds - Los Angeles 43 (Rambis 9), Boston 63 (McHale 9).

Assists - Los Angeles 28 (E. Johnson 12), Boston 43 (D. Johnson 10).

Total fouls - Los Angeles 23, Boston 17. Technicals - Ainge. A-14,890.

## STANDINGS: The format for professional standings:

**Eastern Conference**
**Atlantic Division**

| | W | L | Pct. | GB |
|---|---|---|---|---|
| Boston | 43 | 22 | .662 | - |
| Philadelphia | 40 | 30 | .571 | 5½ |
| Etc. | | | | |

In college boxes, the score by periods is omitted because the games are divided only into halves.

**UCLA (69)**
Jackson 1-6 2-2 4, Maloncon 4-7 2-2 10, Wright 4-7 1-5 9, Gaines 4-6 1-2 9, Miguel 5-10 0-0 10, Butler 2-3 6-8 10, Hatcher 3-8 0-0 6, Immel 2-2 1-1 5, Haley 1-1 4-4 6, Miller 0-2 0-0 0, J. Jones 0-3 0-0 0, Dunlap 0-0 0-0 0. Totals 26-55 17-24 69.

**ST. JOHN'S (88)**
Berry 10-14 3-5 23, Glass 4-5 3-6 11, Wennington 5-9 4-4 14, Moses 5-6 0-0 10, Mullin 6-11 4-6 16, Jackson 1-3 5-5 7, Stewart 0-3 2-2 2, S. Jones 1-2 2-2 4, Bross 0-1 0-0 0, Rowan 0-2 0-0 0, Shurina 0-0 1-2 1, Coregy 0-0 0-0 0. Totals 32-56 24-32 88.

Halftime - St. John's 48, UCLA 35. Fouled out - None. Rebounds - UCLA 25 (Wright 9), St. John's 39 (Mullin 9). Assists - UCLA 18 (Gaines 5), St. John's 21 (Moses 8). Total fouls - UCLA 22, St. John's 20.
A-15,256

The format for college conference standings:

| | Conference | | | All Games | | |
|---|---|---|---|---|---|---|
| | W | L | Pct. | W | L | Pct. |
| **Missouri** | 12 | 2 | .857 | 24 | 4 | .857 |

**betting odds** Use figures and a hyphen: *The odds were 5-4; he won despite 3-2 odds against him.*

The word *to* seldom is necessary, but when it appears it should be hyphenated in all constructions: *3-to-2 odds, odds of 3-to-2, the odds were 3-to-2.*

**bettor** A person who bets.

**bicycle**

**billiards** Scoring is in points. Use a **match summary**. Example:

Minnesota Fats, St. Paul, Minn., def. Pool Hall Duke, 150-141.

**bobsledding, luge** Scoring is in minutes, seconds and tenths of a second. Extend to hundredths if available.

Identify events as *two-man, four-man, men's luge, women's luge.*

Use a basic summary. Example:

Two-man—1, Jim Smith and Dick Jones, Alaska Sledders, 4:20.77. 2, Tom Winner and Joe Finisher, Mountaineers, 4:31.14. 3, etc.

**bowl games** Capitalize them: *Cotton Bowl, Orange Bowl, Rose Bowl,* etc.

**bowling** Scoring systems use both total points and won-lost records.

Use the basic summary format in paragraph form. Note that a comma is used in giving pinfalls of more than 999.

Examples:

ST. LOUIS (AP)—Second-round leaders and their total pinfalls in the $100,000 Professional Bowlers Association tournament:
1. Bill Spigner, Hamden, Conn., 2,820.
2. Gary Dickinson, Fort Worth, Texas, 2,759.
3. Etc.
ALAMEDA, Calif. (AP)—The 24 match play finalists with their won-lost records and total pinfall Thursday night after tour rounds - 26 games - of the $65,000 Alameda Open bowling tournament:

1. Jay Robinson, Los Angeles, 5-3, 5,937.
2. Butch Soper, Huntington Beach, Calif., 3-5, 5,932.
3. Etc.

**boxing** The three major sanctioning bodies for professional boxing are the World Boxing Association, the World Boxing Council and the International Boxing Federation.

Weight classes and titles by organization:

108-111 pounds—Junior flyweight, WBA, IBF; light flyweight, WBC.

112-117 pounds—Flyweight, WBA, WBC, IBF.

118-121 pounds—Bantamweight, WBA, WBC, IBF.

122-125 pounds—Junior featherweight, WBA, IBF; super bantamweight, WBC.

126-129 pounds—Featherweight, WBA, WBC, IBF.

130-134 pounds—Junior lightweight, WBA, IBF; super featherweight, WBC.

135-139 pounds—Lightweight, WBA, WBC, IBF.

140-146 pounds—Junior welterweight, WBA, IBF; super lightweight, WBC.

147-153 pounds—Welterweight, WBA, WBC, IBF.

154-159 pounds—Junior

middleweight, WBA, IBF; super welterweight, WBC.

160-174 pounds—Middleweight, WBA, WBC.

160-164 pounds—Middleweight, IBF.

165-174 pounds—Super middleweight, IBF.

175-194 pounds—Light heavyweight, WBA, WBC, IBF.

195 pounds—Junior heavyweight, WBA; cruiserweight, WBC, IBF.

Over 195 pounds—Heavyweight, WBA, WBC, IBF.

Some other terms:

**kidney punch** A punch to an opponent's kidney when the puncher has only one hand free. An illegal punch. If the puncher has both hands free, a punch to the opponent's kidney is legal.

**knock out** (v.) **knockout** (n. and adj.) A fighter is knocked out if he takes a 10-count.

If a match ends early because one fighter is unable to continue, say that the winner stopped the loser. In most boxing jurisdictions there is no such thing as a technical knockout.

**outpointed** No *outdecisioned.*

**rabbit punch** A punch behind an opponent's ear. It is illegal.

SUMMARIES: Use a match summary.

Some examples, with the fighters' weights after their names and the number of rounds at the end:

Randy Jackson, 152, New York, outpointed Chuck James, 154, Philadelphia, 10.

Muhammad Ali, 220, Chicago, knocked out Pierre Coopman, 202, Belgium, 5.

George Foreman, 217, Hayward, Calif., stopped Joe Frazier, 214, Philadelphia, 2.

TALE OF THE TAPE:
An example:

SAN JUAN, Puerto Rico (AP)—The tale of the tape for the Jean Pierre Coopman-Muhammad Ali world heavyweight championship fight Friday night:

|  | Coopman | Ali |
|---|---|---|
| Age | 29 | 34 |
| Weight | 202 | 220 |
| Height | 6-0 | 6-3 |
| Reach | 75 | 80 |
| Chest Normal | 43 | 44 |
| Chest Expanded | 45 1/2 | 46 |
| Biceps | 15 | 15 |
| Forearm | 13 | 13 1/2 |
| Waist | 34 1/2 | 34 |
| Thigh | 25 1/2 | 26 |
| Calf | 15 | 17 |
| Neck | 17 | 17 1/2 |
| Wrist | 7 1/2 | 8 |

| | | |
|---|---|---|
| Fist | 12 1/2 | 13 |
| Ankle | 9 | 9 1/2 |

## SCORING BY ROUNDS:
An example:

NEW YORK (AP)—Scorecards for the Muhammad Ali-Joe Frazier heavyweight title fight Friday night:

Scoring by rounds:

**Referee Tom Smith**
AAA FFF AAA AFA FFF—A8-7

**Judge Bill Swift**
AAA FFF FFF AFA FFF—F10-5

**Judge Ralph Cohen**
AAA FFF FFF FFF AFF—F11-4

Scoring by points system:

**Referee Tom Smith**

| A | 10 | 10 | 10 | 10 | 10 | 10 | 10 |
|---|----|----|----|----|----|----|----|
| F | 10 | 9 | 9 | 9 | 9 | 9 | 9 |
| A | 10 | 10 | 10 | 9 | 9 | 9 | 10 |
| F | 10 | 10 | 9 | 10 | 10 | 10 | 10 |

Total—Ali 146, Frazier 143.

**Judge Ralph Cohen**

| A | 10 | 9 | 10 | 10 | 10 | 10 | 10 |
|---|----|---|----|----|----|----|----|
| F | 9 | 10 | 10 | 9 | 9 | 9 | 9 |
| A | 10 | 10 | 10 | 10 | 9 | 9 | 9 |
| F | 9 | 10 | 10 | 9 | 10 | 10 | 10 |

**box office** (n.) **box-office** (adj.)

**bullfight, bullfighter, bullfighting**

**bullpen** One word, for the place where baseball pitchers warm up, and for a pen that holds cattle.

## C

**Canada goose** Not Canadian goose.

**canoeing** Scoring is in minutes, seconds and tenths of a second. Extend to hundredths if available.

Use a basic summary. Example:

**Canoeing, Men**
**Kayak Singles, 500 meters**
Heat 1—Rudiger Helm, East Germany, 1:56.06. 2. Zoltan Sztanity, Hungary, 1:57.12. 3. Etc.

Also: 6. Henry Krawczyk, New York, 2:04.64.

First Repechage—1, Ladislay Soucek, Czechoslovakia, 1:53.30. 2. Hans Eich, West Germany, 1:54.23. 3. Etc.

**coach** Capitalize only when used without a qualifying term before the name of the person who directs an athletic team: *General Manager Red Auerback signed Coach Tom Heinsohn to a new contract.*

If *coach* is preceded by a qualifying word, lowercase it: *third base coach Frank Crosetti, defensive coach George Perles, swimming coach Mark Spitz.*

Lowercase *coach* when it

stands alone or is set off from a name by commas: *The coach, Tom Heinsohn, was charged with a technical.*

The capitalization of *coach* is based on the general rule that formal titles used directly before an individual's name are capitalized. See **titles** in main section.

**colt** A male horse 4 years and under.

**conferences** Here is a listing of major college conferences:

Atlantic Coast Conference: Clemson, Duke, Georgia Tech, Maryland, North Carolina, North Carolina State, Virginia, Wake Forest.

Big East: Boston College, Connecticut, Georgetown, Pittsburgh, Providence, St. John's, Seton Hall, Syracuse, Villanova.

Big Eight Conference: Colorado, Iowa State, Kansas, Kansas State, Missouri, Nebraska, Oklahoma, Oklahoma State.

Big Sky Conference: Boise State, Idaho, Idaho State, Montana, Montana State, Nevada-Reno, Northern Arizona, Weber State.

Big Ten Conference: Illinois, Indiana, Iowa, Michi-

gan, Michigan State, Minnesota, Northwestern, Ohio State, Purdue, Wisconsin.

Ivy League: Brown, Columbia, Cornell, Dartmouth, Harvard, Pennsylvania, Princeton, Yale.

Metro Collegiate Athletic Conference: Cincinnati, Florida State, Louisville, Memphis State, South Carolina, Southern Mississippi, Tulane, Virginia Tech.

Mid-American Conference: Ball State, Bowling Green, Central Michigan, Eastern Michigan, Kent State, Miami-Ohio, Northeastern Illinois, Ohio University, Toledo, Western Michigan.

Pacific Coast Athletic Conference: California-Irvine, California-Santa Barbara, Fresno State, Fullerton State, Long Beach State, Nevada-Las Vegas, New Mexico State, Pacific, San Jose State, Utah State.

Pacific 10 Conference: Arizona, Arizona State, California, Oregon, Oregon State, Southern California, Stanford, UCLA, Washington, Washington State.

Southeastern Conference: Alabama, Auburn, Florida, Georgia, Kentucky, Louisiana State, Mississippi, Mississippi State, Tennessee, Vanderbilt.

Southwest Conference: Arkansas, Baylor, Houston, Rice, Southern Methodist, Texas, Texas A&M, Texas Christian, Texas Tech.

Sun Belt Conference: Alabama-Birmingham, Jacksonville, North Carolina-Charlotte, Old Dominion, South Alabama, South Florida, Virginia Commonwealth, Western Kentucky.

Western Athletic Conference: Air Force, Brigham Young, Colorado State, Hawaii, New Mexico, San Diego State, Texas-El Paso, Utah, Wyoming.

**courtesy titles** On sports wires, do not use courtesy titles in any reference unless needed to distinguish among people of the same last name. See **courtesy titles** in main section.

**cross country** No hyphen, an exception to Webster's New World based on the practices of U.S. and international governing bodies for the sport.

Scoring for this track event is in minutes, seconds and tenths of a second. Extend to hundredths if available.

Use a basic summary. Example:

**National AAU Championship
Cross Country**
Frank Shorter, Miami, 5:25.67 2. Tom Coster, Los Angeles, 5:30.72 3. Etc.

Adapt the basic summary to paragraph form under a dateline for a field of more than 10 competitors. See the **auto racing** and **bowling** entries for examples.

See also the **track and field** entry.

**cycling** Use the basic summary format.

# D

**decathlon** Summaries include time or distance performance, points earned in that event and the cumulative total of points earned in previous events.

Contestants are listed in the order of their overall point totals. First name and hometown (or nation) are included only on the first and last events on the first day of competition; on the last day, first names are included only in the first event and in the summary denoting final placings.

Use the basic summary format. Include all entrants in summaries of each of the 10 events.

An example for individual events:

### Decathlon
### (Group A)

100-meter dash - 1. Fred Dixon, Los Angeles, 10.8 seconds, 854 points. 2. Bruce Jenner, San Jose State, 11:09, 783. 3. Etc.

Long jump - 1. Dixon 24-7 (7.34m), 889, 1,743. 2. Jenner, 23-6 (7.17m), 855, 1,638. 3. Etc.

Decathlon final - 1. Bruce Jenner, San Jose State, 8,524 points. 2. Fred Dixon, Los Angeles, 8,277. 3. Etc.

**discus** The disk thrown in track and field events.

**diving** Use a basic summary.

See **skating, figure** for the style on compulsory dives.

### E

**ERA** Acceptable in all references to baseball's *earned run average.*

### F

**fencing** Identify epee, foil and saber classes as: *men's individual foil, women's team foil,* etc.

Use a match summary for early rounds of major events, for lesser dual meets and for tournaments.

Use a basic summary for final results of major championships.

For major events, where competitors meet in a round-robin and are divided into pools, use this form:

Epee, first round (four qualify for semi-finals) Pool 1 - Joe Smith, Springfield, Mass., 4-1. Enrique Lopez, Chile, 3-2. Etc.

**figure skating** See **skating, figure** for guidelines on the summary form.

**filly** A female horse 4 years old and under.

**football** The spellings of some frequently used words and phrases:

| | |
|---|---|
| ball carrier | lineman |
| ballclub | line of scrim- |
| blitz (n., v.) | mage |
| end line | out of bounds |
| end zone | (adv.) |
| fair catch | out-of-bounds |
| field goal | (adj.) |
| fourth-and-one | pitchout (n.) |
| (adj.) | place kick |
| fullback | place-kicker |
| goal line | play off (v.) |
| goal-line stand | playoff (n., |
| halfback | adj.) |
| halftime | quarterback |

| | |
|---|---|
| handoff | runback (n.) |
| kick off (v.) | running back |
| kickoff (adj.) | split end |
| left guard | tailback |
| linebacker | tight end |
| | touchback |
| | touchdown |
| | wide receiver |

**NUMBERS:** Use figures for yardage: *The 5-yard line, the 10-yard line, a 5-yard pass play, he plunged in from the 2, he ran 6 yards, a 7-yard gain.* But: *a fourth-and-two play.*

Some other uses of numbers: *The final score was 21-14. The team won its fourth game in 10 starts. The team record is 4-5-1.*

**LEAGUE:** *National Football League,* or *NFL; United States Football League,* or *USFL.*

**STATISTICS:** All football games, whether using the one- or two-point conversion, use the same summary style.

The visiting team always is listed first.

Field goals are measured from the point where the ball was kicked—not the line of scrimmage. The goal posts are 10 yards behind the goal lines. Include that distance.

Abbreviate team names to four letters or less on the scoring and statistical lines as illustrated.

The passing line shows, in order: completions-attempts-had intercepted.

A sample agate package:

### Birmingham-Houston, Stats

| | | |
|---|---|---|
| Birmingham | 7 16 0 7— | 30 |
| Houston | 14 7 0 6— | 27 |

**First Quarter**

Hou—Harrell 23 pass from Dillon (Fritsch kick), 1:00

Bir—Jones 11 run with lateral after Mason 12 pass from Stoudt (Miller kick), 5:57

Hou—Harrell 6 run (Fritsch kick), 8:07

**Second Quarter**

Bir—FG Miller 47, 1:13

Bir—Caruth 6 run (Miller kick), 5:49

Hou—Johnson 36 pass from Dillon (Fritsch kick), 12:12

Bir—FG Miller 43, 14:33

**Fourth Quarter**

Bir—FG Miller 20, 3:42

Bir—Stoudt 1 run (kick failed), 9:09

Hou—Dillon 8 run (pass failed), 13:58

A - 13,202

| | Bir | Hou |
|---|---|---|
| First downs | 21 | 15 |
| Rushes-yards | 46-209 | 12-70 |
| Passing yards | 109 | 206 |
| Return yards | 75 | 112 |
| Comp-Att | 13-24-0 | 17-33-2 |
| Sacked-Yards Lost | 4-23 | 2-24 |
| Punts | 3-38 | 3-41 |
| Fumbles-lost | 1-1 | 2-0 |
| Penalties-yards | 3-25 | 12-69 |
| Time of Possession | 35:57 | 24:03 |

### INDIVIDUAL STATISTICS

RUSHING—Birmingham, Caruth 23-

84, Coles 14-59, Stoudt 8-50, Gant 1-5. Houston, Harrell 4-34, Fowler 5-26, Dillion 3-10.

PASSING—Birmingham, Stoudt 13-24-0 133. Houston, Dillion 17-33-2 283.

RECEIVING—Birmingham, Toler 4-53, Jones 3-15, McFaddon 2-38, Coles 2-12, Mason 1-12, Caruth 1-4. Houston, Johnson 5-108, McGee 3-59, McNeil 3-36, 2-27, Sanders 3-29, Verdin 1-24.

MISSED FIELD GOALS-Houston, Fritsch 32.

The rushing and receiving paragraphs for individual leaders show attempts and yardage gained. The passing paragraph shows completions, attempts, number of attempts intercepted, and total yards gained.

STANDINGS: The form for **professional standings:**

**American Conference**
**East**

| | W | L | T | Pct. | PF | PA |
|---|---|---|---|---|---|---|
| Baltimore | 10 | 4 | 0 | .714 | 395 | 269 |
| New England | 9 | 5 | 0 | .643 | 387 | 275 |
| Etc. | | | | | | |

The form for **college conference standings:**

**Conference**

| | W | L | T | Pts. | OP |
|---|---|---|---|---|---|
| UCLA | 6 | 1 | 0 | 215 | 123 |
| Etc. | | | | | |

**All games**

| | W | L | T | Pts. | OP |
|---|---|---|---|---|---|
| UCLA | 8 | 2 | 1 | 326 | 233 |
| Etc. | | | | | |

In college conference stand-

ings, limit team names to nine letters or fewer. Abbreviate as necessary.

**fractions** Put a full space between the whole number and the fraction. Do not separate with a *thin* symbol.

# G

**game plan**

**gelding** A castrated male horse.

**golf** Some frequently used terms and some definitions:

**Americas Cup** No possessive.

**birdie, birdies** One stroke under par.

**bogey, bogeys** One stroke over par. The past tense is *bogeyed*.

**eagle** Two strokes under par.

**fairway**

**Masters Tournament** No possessive. Use *the Masters* on second reference.

**tee, tee off**

**U.S. Open Championship** Use *the U.S. Open* or *the Open* on second reference.

NUMBERS: Some sample uses of numbers:

Use figures for handicaps: *He has a 3 handicap; a 3-handicap golfer; a handicap of 3 strokes; a 3-stroke handicap.*

Use figures for par listings: *He had a par 5 to finish 2-up for the round; a par-4 hole; a 7-under-par 64; the par-3 seventh hole.*

Use figures for club ratings: *a No. 5 iron, a 5-iron, a 7-iron shot, a 4-wood.*

Miscellaneous: *the first hole, the ninth hole, the 10th hole, the back nine, the final 18, the third round. He won 3 and 2.*

ASSOCIATIONS: *Professional Golfers' Association* (note the apostrophe) or *PGA*. *PGA Tour* is the official name. Use *tour* (lowercase) on second reference.

The same principle applies to the *Ladies Professional Golf Association* (no apostrophe, in keeping with *LPGA* practice).

SUMMARIES—Stroke (Medal) Play: List scores in ascending order. Use a dash before the final figure, hyphens between others.

On the first day, use the player's score for the first nine holes, a hyphen, the player's score for the second nine holes, a dash and the player's total for the day:

First round:

| | |
|---|---|
| Jack Nicklaus | 35-35—70 |
| Johnny Miller | 36-35—71 |

Etc.

On subsequent days, give the player's scores for each day, then the total for all rounds completed:

Second round:

| | |
|---|---|
| Jack Nicklaus | 70-70—140 |
| Johnny Miller | 71-70—141 |

Etc.

Final round, professional tournaments, including prize money:

| | | |
|---|---|---|
| Jack Nicklaus, | $30,000 | 70-70-68—278 |
| Johnny Miller, | $17,500 | 71-70-69—290 |

Use hometowns, if ordered, only on national championship amateur tournaments. Use home countries, if ordered, only on major international events such as the British Open. If used, the hometown or country is placed on a second line, indented one space:

| | |
|---|---|
| Arnold Palmer | 70-69-68-70—277 |
|   United States | |
| Tony Jacklin | 71-70-70-70—281 |
|   England | |

The form for cards:

| | |
|---|---|
| Par out | 444 343 544-35 |

| | |
|---|---|
| Watson out | 454 333 435-34 |
| Nicklaus out | 434 243 544-33 |
| Par in | 434 443 454-35—70 |
| Watson in | 434 342 443-31—65 |
| Nicklaus in | 433 443 453-33—66 |

SUMMARIES—Match Play: In the first example that follows, the *and 1* means that the 18th hole was skipped because Nicklaus had a 2-hole lead after 17. In the second, the match went 18 holes. In the third, a 19th hole was played because the golfers were tied after 18.

Jack Nicklaus def. Lee Trevino, 2 and 1.

Sam Snead def. Ben Hogan, 2-up.

Arnold Palmer def. Johnny Miller, 1-up (19).

**Grey Cup** The Canadian Football League's championship game.

**Gulfstream Park** The racetrack.

**gymnastics** Scoring is by points. Identify events by name: *sidehorse, horizontal bars,* etc.

Use a basic summary. Example:

Sidehorse—1. John Leaper, Penn State, 8.8 points. 2. Jo Tumper, Ohio State, 7.9. 3. Etc.

# H

**halfback**

**handball** Games are won by the first player to score 21 points or, in the case of a tie breaker, 11 points. Most matches go to the first winner of two games.

Use a match summary. Example:

Bob Richards, Yale, def. Paul Johnson, Dartmouth, 21-18, 21-19.

Tom Brenna, Massachusetts, def. Bill Stevens, Michigan, 21-19, 17-21, 21-20.

**handicaps** Use figures, hyphenating adjectival forms before a noun: *He has a 3 handicap, he is a 3-handicap golfer, a handicap of 3 strokes, a 3-stroke handicap.*

**hit and run** (v.) **hit-and-run** (n. and adj.) *The coach told him to hit and run. He scored on a hit-and-run. She was struck by a hit-and-run driver.*

**hockey** The spellings of some frequently used words:

| | |
|---|---|
| blue line | play off (v.) |
| crease | playoff (n., |
| face off (v.) | adj.) |

| faceoff (n., adj.) | power play power-play goal |
|---|---|
| goalie | |
| goal line | red line |
| goal post | short-handed |
| goaltender | slap shot |
| penalty box | two-on-one break |

The term *hat trick* applies when a player has scored three goals in a game. Use it sparingly, however.

LEAGUE: *National Hockey League* or *NHL.*

For NHL subdivisions: *the Patrick Division of the Campbell Conference, the division, the conference,* etc.

SUMMARIES: The visiting team always is listed first in the score by periods.

Note that each goal is numbered according to its sequence in the game.

The figure after the name of a scoring player shows his total goals for the season.

Names in parentheses are players credited with an assist on a goal.

The final figure in the listing of each goal is the number of minutes elapsed in the period when the goal was scored.

| Philadelphia | 3 0 0—3 |
|---|---|
| Edmonton | 2 2 1—5 |

First period—1, Philadelphia, Rick Sutter 1 (Ron Sutter, Smith, :46. 2, Edmonton, Coffey 10 (Huddy, Kurri), 4:22 (pp). 3, Philadelphia, Bergen 4 (Zezel, Crossman), 6:38 (pp). 4, Philadelphia, Craven 4 (Smith, Marsh), 11:32 (sh). 5, Edmonton, Huddy 3 (Coffey, Kurri), 18:23 (pp). Penalties—Poulin, Phi (high-sticking), 3:31; Hughes, Edm (high-sticking), 5:17; Messier, Edm (slashing), 5:59; Crossman, Phi, double minor (holding-unsportsmanlike conduct), 8:32; Hospodar, Phi (slashing), 16:38.

Second period—6, Edmonton, Anderson 10, :21. 7, Edmonton, Gretzky 15 (Coffey, Huddy), 12:53 (pp). Penalties—Tocchet, Phi (roughing), :48; Fogolin, Edm (roughing), :48; Paterson, Phi (hooking), 12:11; Allison, Phi (slashing), 17:39; Hunter, Edm (roughing), 17:39; Low, Edm (holding), 18:02; Crossman, Phi (holding), 19:07; Hunter, Edm (holding), 20:00.

Third Period—8 Edmonton, Gretzky 16 (Messier, Anderson), 3:422 (pp). Penalties—Hospodar, Phi (hooking), 2:46; Hunter, Edm (kneeing), 7:58.

Shots on goal—Philadelphia 10-6-7 23. Edmonton 101-32.

Penalty shots—Ron Sutter, Phi, 8:47 1st (missed).

Goalies—Philadelphia, Lindbergh at 8:56 2nd; reentered at start of 3rd, 10-9) Edmonton, Fuhr (23-20). A—17,498. Referee—Kerry Fraser.

STANDINGS: The form:

Campbell Conference
Patrick Division

| | W | L | T | Pts. | GF | GA |
|---|---|---|---|---|---|---|
| Philadelphia | 47 | 10 | 14 | 108 | 314 | 184 |
| NY Islanders | 45 | 17 | 9 | 99 | 310 | 192 |
| Etc. | | | | | | |

**horse races** Capitalize their formal names: *Kentucky*

*Derby, Preakness, Belmont Stakes,* etc.

**horse racing** Some frequently used terms and their definitions:

**colt** A male horse 4 years old and under

**horse** A male horse over 4 years old.

**gelding** A castrated male horse.

**filly** A female horse 2 to 5 years old.

**mare** A female horse 5 years and older.

**stallion** A male horse used for breeding.

**broodmare** A female horse used for breeding.

**furlong** One-eighth of a mile. Race distances are given in furlongs up through seven furlongs, after that in miles, as in *one-mile, 1 1-16 miles.*

**entry** Two or more horses owned by same owner running as a single betting interest. In some states two or more horses trained by same person but having different owners also are coupled in betting.

**mutuel field** Not *mutual field.* Two or more horses, long shots, that have different owners and trainers. They are coupled as a single betting interest to give the field not more than 12 wagering interests. There cannot be more than 12 betting interests in a race. The bettor wins if either horse finishes in the money.

**half-mile pole** The pole on a race track that marks one-half mile from the finish. All distances are measured from the finish line, meaning that when a horse reaches the quarter pole, he is one-quarter mile from the finish.

**bug boy** An apprentice jockey, so called because of the asterisk beside the individual's name in a program. It means that the jockey's mount gets a weight allowance.

**horses' names** Capitalize. See **animals** in main section.

# I

**IC4A** See **Intercollegiate Association of Amateur Athletes of America.**

**indoor** (adj.) **indoors** (adv.) *He plays indoor tennis. He went indoors.*

**injuries** They are *suffered* or *sustained,* not *received.*

**Intercollegiate Association of Amateur Athletes of America** In general, spell out on first reference.

A phrase such as *IC4A tournament* may be used on first reference, however, to avoid a cumbersome lead. If this is done, provide the full name later in the story.

# J

**judo** Use the basic summary format by weight divisions for major tournaments; the match summary for dual and lesser meets.

# K

**Kentucky Derby** *The Derby* on second reference. An exception to normal second-reference practice.

See **capitalization** in main section.

# L

**lacrosse** Scoring in goals, worth one point each.

The playing field is 110 yards long. The goals are 80 yards apart, with 15 yards of playing area behind each goal.

A match consists of four 15-minute periods. Overtimes of varying lengths may be played to break a tie.

Adapt the summary format in **hockey**.

**Ladies Professional Golf Association** No apostrophe after *Ladies.* In general, spell out on first reference.

A phrase such as *LPGA tournament* may be used on first reference to avoid a cumbersome lead. If this is done, provide the full name later in the story.

**left hand** (n.) **left-handed** (adj.) **left-hander** (n.)

**M**

**marathon** Use the formats illustrated in the **cross country** and **track and field** entries.

**mare** A female horse 5 years and older.

**match summary** This format for summarizing sports events applies to one vs. one contests such as tennis, match play golf, etc.

Give a competitor's name, followed either by a hometown or by a college or club affiliation. For competitors from outside the United States, a country name alone is sufficient in summaries sent for domestic use.

Example:

Jimmy Conners, Belleville, Ill., def. Manuel Orantes, Spain, 2-6, 6-3, 6-2, 6-1.

**metric system** See main section.

**motorboat racing** Scoring may be posted in miles per hour, points or laps, depending on the competition.

In general, use the basic summary format. For some major events, adapt the basic summary to paragraph form under a dateline. See the **auto racing** entry for an example.

**motorcycle racing** Follow the format shown under **auto racing.**

**N**

**National Association for Stock Car Auto Racing** Or *NASCAR*.

**National Collegiate Athletic Association** Or *NCAA*.

**numerals** See the main section on general use and entries on **betting odds, handicaps** and **scores.**

## O

**odds** See **betting odds.**

## P

**pingpong** A synonym for *table tennis.*

The trademark name is *Ping-Pong.*

**platform tennis** See **tennis.**

**play off** (v.) **playoff, playoffs** (n. and adj.) The noun and adjective forms are exceptions to Webster's New World Dictionary, in keeping with widespread practice in the sports world.

**postseason, preseason** No hyphen.

## R

**racket** Not *racquet,* for the light bat used in tennis and badminton.

**racquetball** Games are won by the first player to score 21 points, unless it is necessary to continue until one player has a two-point spread. Most matches go to the first winner of two games.

Use a match summary. Examples:

John Smith, Rutgers, def. Paul Giroux, Harvard, 21-8, 17-21, 22-20.
Frank Tivnan, Columbia, def. Tim Leland, Princeton, 21-17, 21-19.

**record** Avoid the redundant *new record.*

**right hand** (n.)
**right-handed** (adj.)
**right-hander** (n.)

**rodeo** Use the basic summary format by classes, listing points.

**rowing** Scoring is in minutes, seconds and tenths of a second. Extend to hundredths if available.

Use a basic summary. An example, for a major event where qualifying heats are required:

Single Sculls Heats (first two in each heat qualify for Monday's quarterfinals, losers go to repechage Friday): Heat 1 - 1, Peter Smith, Australia, 4:24.7. 2.

Etc. Heat 2 - 1, John Jones, Canada, 4:26.3. 7 2, Etc.

**runner-up, runners-up**

# s

**scores** Use figures exclusively, placing a hyphen between the totals of the winning and losing teams: *The Reds defeated the Red Sox 4-3, the Giants scored a 12-6 football victory over the Cardinals, the golfer had a 5 on the first hole but finished with a 2-under-par score.*

Use a comma in this format: *Boston 6, Baltimore 5.*

See individual listings for each sport for further details.

**skating, figure** Scoring includes both ordinals and points.

Use a basic summary. Examples:

**Men**
**(After 3 compulsory figures)**
Sergei Volkov, Soviet Union, 19-5 ordinals, 44.76 points. 2, John Curry, Britain, 21.5, 44.96. 3, Etc.
**Women's Final**
Dorothy Hamill, Riverside, Conn., 9.0 ordinals, 215 points. 2, Dianne de Leeuw, Netherlands, 20.0, 236. 3, Etc.

**skating, speed** Scoring is in minutes, seconds and

tenths of a second. Extend to hundredths if available.

Use a basic summary.

**ski, skis, skier, skied, skiing** Also: *ski jump, ski jumping.*

**skiing** Identify events as: *men's downhill, women's slalom,* etc. In ski jumping, note style where two jumps and points are posted.

Use a basic summary. Example:

90-meter special jumping—1, Karl Schnabel, Austria, 320 and 318 feet, 234.8 points. 2, Toni Innauer, Austria, 377-299, 232.9. 3, Etc. Also: 27, Bob Smith, Hanover, N.H., 312-280, 201.29, Etc.

**sports editor** Capitalize as a formal title before a name. See **titles** in main section.

**sports sponsorship** For general style see main section. For the titles or names of sports events use the commercial sponsor's name of the event on first reference. Example: *Buick Mr. Goodwrench Open.*

**stadium, stadiums** Capitalize only when part of a

proper name: *Yankee Stadium.*

**swimming** Scoring is in minutes, and if appropriate, seconds and tenths of a second. Extend to hundredths if available.

Most events are measured in metric units.

Identify events as *men's 440-meter relay, women's 100-meter backstroke,* etc. on first reference. Condense to *men's 440 relay, women's 100 backstroke* on second reference.

See the **track and field** entry for the style on relay teams and events where a record is broken.

Use a basic summary. Examples, where qualifying heats are required:

Men's 200-meter Backstroke Heats (fastest eight qualify for final Saturday night) heat 1 - 1, John Nabor, USC, 2:03.25. 2, Zoltan Verraszio, Hungary, 2:03.50. 3, Etc.

For diving events, adapt the format shown in the **skating, figure** entry.

**T**

**table tennis** See **ping-pong.**

**tennis** The scoring units are points, games, sets and matches.

A player wins a point if his opponent fails to return the ball, hits it into the net or hits it out of bounds. A player also wins a point if his opponent is serving and fails to put the ball into play after two attempts *(double faults,* in tennis terms).

A player must win four points to win a game. In tennis scoring, both players begin at *love,* or zero, and advance to 15, 30, 40 and game. (The numbers *15, 30* and *40* have no point value as such—they are simply tennis terminology for *1 point, 2 points* and *3 points.*) The server's score always is called out first. If a game is tied at 40-all, or *deuce,* play continues until one player has a two-point margin.

A set is won if a player wins six games before his opponent has won five. If a set becomes tied at five games apiece, it goes to the first player to win seven games. If two players who were tied at five games apiece also tie at six games apiece, they nomally play a tiebreaker—a game that goes to the first player to win seven points. In some cases, however, the rules call for a player to win by two games.

A match may be either a best-of-three contest that goes to the first player or team to win two sets, or a best-of-five contest that goes to the first player or team to win three sets.

Set scores would be reported this way: *Chris Evert Lloyd defeated Sue Barker 6-0, 3-6, 6-4.* Indicate tie-breakers in parenthesis after the set score: *7-6 (11-9).*

SUMMARIES: Winners always are listed first in agate summaries. An example:

**Men's Singles**
**First Round**

Jimmy Connor, Belleville, Ill., def. Manuel Orantes, Spain, 2-6, 6-3, 6-2, 6-1.

Bjorn Borg, Sweden, def. Jim Green, New York (default).

Arthur Ashe, New York, def. James, Peters, Chicao, 6-3, 4-3 (retired).

**track and field** Scoring is in distance or time, depending on the event.

Most events are measured in metric units. For those meets that include feet, make sure the measurement is clearly stated, as in *men's 100-meter dash, women's 880-yard run,* etc.

For time events, spell out *minutes* and *seconds* on first references, as in *3-minutes, 26.1 seconds.* Subsequent times in stories and all times in agate require a colon and decimal point: *3:34.4.* For a marathon, it would be *2 hours, 11 minutes, 5.01 seconds* on first reference, then the form *2:12:4.06* for later listings.

Do not use a colon before times given only in seconds and tenths of a second. Use progressions such as *6.0 seconds, 9.4, 10.1,* etc. Extend times to hundredths, if available: *9.45.*

In running events, the first event should be spelled out, as in *men's 100-meter dash.* Later references can be condensed to phrases such as *the 200, the 400,* etc.

For hurdle and relay events, the progression can be: *100-meter hurdles, 200 hurdles,* etc.

For field events—those that do not involve running—use these forms: *26 1/2* for *26 feet, one-half inch; 25-10 1/2* for *25 feet, 10 1/2 inches,* etc.

In general, use a basic summary. For the style when a record is broken, not the mile event in the example below. For the style in listing relay teams, note 1,000-meter relay.

60-yard dash—1, Steve Williams, Florida TC, 6.0 2, Hasley Crawford, Philadelphia Pioneer, 6.2 3, Mike McFarland, Chicago TC. 6.2 3. Etc.

100—1, Steve Williams, Florida TC 10.1. 2, Etc.

Mile—1, Filbert Bayi, Tanzania, 3:55.1, meet record; old record 3:59, Jim Beatty, Los Angeles TC. Feb. 27, 1963. 2. Paul Cummings, Beverly Hills TC. 3:56.1. 3, Etc.

Women's 880—1, Johanna Forman, Falmouth TC. 2:07.9. 2. Etc.

1,600-meter relay—1, St. John's, Jon Kennedy, Doug Johnson, Gary Gordon, Ordner Emanuel, 3:21.9. 2, Brown, 3:23.5. 3. Fordham, 3:24.1. 4, Etc.

Team scoring—Chicago TC 32. Philadelphia Pioneer 29, Etc.

Where qualifying heats are required:

Men's 100-meter heats (first two in each heat qualify for Friday's semifinals): Heat 1—1, Steve Williams, Florida TC. 10.1. 2, Etc.

# V

## volley, volleys

**volleyball** Games are won by the first team to score 15 points, unless it is necessary to continue until one team has a two-point spread.

Use a match summary. Example:

**National AAU Men's Volleyball**
**First Round**
New York AC def. Illinois AC 15-7, 12-15, 19-17.

Vesper Boat Club, Philadelphia, def. Harvard 15-7, 15-8.

# W

**water polo** Scoring is by goals. List team scores. Example:

World Water Polo Championship
First Round
United States 7, Canada 1
Britain 5, France 3
Etc.

**water skiing** Scoring is in points. Use a basic summary. Example:

World Water Skiing Championships
Men
Overall—1, George Jones, Canada, 1,987 points. 2, Phil Brown, Britain, 1,756. 3, Etc.
Slalom—1, George Jones, Canada, 73 buoys (two rounds). 2, Etc.

**weightlifting** Identify events by weight classes. Where both pounds and kilograms are available, use both figures with kilograms in parentheses, as shown in the examples.

Use a basic summary. Example:

Flyweight (114.5 lbs.)—1, Zygmont Smalcerz, Poland, 744 pounds (337.5 kg). 2, Lajos Szuecs, Hungary, 728 (330 kg). 3, Etc.

**World Series** Or *the Series* on second reference. A rare exception to the general principles under **capitalization**.

**wrestling** Identify events by weight division.

# Y

**yachting** Use a basic summary, identifying events by classes.

**yard** Equal to three feet.

The metric equivalent is approximately 0.91 meters.

To convert to meters, multiply by .91 (5 yards × .91 = 4.55 meters).

See **foot; meter;** and **distances.**

**yard lines** Use figures to indicate the dividing lines on a football field and distance traveled: *4-yard line, 40-yard line, he plunged in from the 2, he ran 6 yards, a 7-yard gain.*

**yearling** An animal 1 year old or in its second year. The birthdays of all thoroughbred horses arbitrarily are set at Jan. 1. On that date, any foal born in the preceding year is reckoned 1 year old.

# BUSINESS GUIDELINES AND STYLE

Covering business or economic news often intimidates reporters who seldom do it. It should not. Writing about business is not much different from covering a plane crash or a hockey game—you have to find out what happened, then explain it clearly.

This section of the Stylebook is intended to help you do that.

It includes an explanation of how to write one of the most common business stories, the quarterly earnings report issued by all publicly held corporations. And there are alphabetical definitions of business and economic terms and jargon.

A word of caution.

As with any specialty, technical terms and economic argot permeate the business world. Avoid jargon. Define technical terms. Do not assume your reader knows their meaning. Stories about corporations, business executives and economic trends increasingly are spreading beyond the business pages. We must cover these stories so they can be understood by the general public.

## COVERING CORPORATE EARNINGS REPORTS

Federal law requires all corporations whose stock is publicly traded to report revenues and profits or losses each three months. This is what business is all about—whether a corporation made money or lost it, and why.

Each of these stories should include certain basic information.

The lead should tell the reader what the company does if it is not a household word and should give the increase or decline of profits, either in percentage or absolute terms, along with the reason.

Comparisons of profits or losses and revenues should be made with the same period a year earlier. For example, the third quarter of this year compared to the third quarter of last year. This reduces seasonable variations that affect many businesses.

If the report is for the final quarter of the company's fiscal year, include the annual profit and revenue figures. Include the earnings-per-share figure, which simply is the profit divided by the number of shares of stock outstanding.

Include comments on the corporation's performance from the chief executive or outside analysts, and any background that puts the performance in perspective.

Here is an example of a concise and understandable story on Polaroid Corp.'s performance during the final quarter of 1981.

Note the third paragraph, which fits into a sentence the profits, earnings per share and revenues for the quarter, along with the numbers for the comparable quarter a year earlier.

Earnings stories are routine. But with thought, they can

pack a lot of information about a company into a small package.

---

## AM-Polaroid Earnings, 260
## Polaroid Earnings Plunge 95 Percent

CAMBRIDGE, Mass. (AP)—Polaroid Corp. said Thursday earnings plunged 95 percent in the final three months of 1981, in part because of the $30.4 million it set aside to cover the cost of reducing its work force by 11 percent.

Polaroid said other factors contributing to the decline were a slump in worldwide sales of photo products and the cost of introducing its new Polaroid Sun Cameras and phasing out older products.

For the fourth quarter, earnings were $1.7 million, or 6 cents a share, on revenue of $445.3 million, compared with earnings of $32.3 million, or 98 cents a share, on revenue of $460.6 million in the same 1980 period.

Profits for all of 1981 fell 64 percent to $31.12 million, or 95 cents a share, from $85.4 million, or $2.60 a share, in 1980. Sales of the instant camera giant were also down, slipping from $1.45 billion in 1980 to $1.42 billion in 1981.

Polaroid announced a plan several months ago to trim back its staff by offering early retirement incentives. The company says it has cut back worldwide employment by 2,000 workers or 11 percent of its work force.

Polaroid President William J. McCune Jr. said international sales declined 9 percent last year, partially due to worldwide economic decline and the weakening of foreign currencies against the dollar.

He said U.S. sales were up a modest 3 percent, including an increase in the company's share of the instant camera market.

Polaroid's technical and industrial photographic business continued to increase in dollar volume, he said.

# BUSINESS GUIDELINES AND STYLE

## A

**accounts payable** Current liabilities or debts of a business that must be paid in the near future (within one year).

**accounts receivable** Amounts due to a company for merchandise or services sold on credit. These are short-term assets.

**acquisitions** The process of buying or acquiring some asset. The term can refer to the purchase of a block of stock, or, more often, to the acquisition of an entire company.

**agricultural parity** The ratio between the price a farmer buys and sells, calculated from the same base period when farm incomes were considered equivalent to income standards of the economy. In the United States when parity falls below 100 for certain products, the farmer receives a percentage of the actual parity figure from the government.

**antitrust** Any law or policy designed to encourage competition by curtailing monopolistic power and unfair business practices.

**appreciation** Increase in value of property, as opposed to *depreciation.*

**arbitrage** Buying currency, commercial bills or securities in one market and selling them at the same time in another to make a profit on the price discrepancy.

**asset** Current cash and other items readily converted into cash, usually within one year.

**asset, fixed** Plant, land, equipment, long-term investments that cannot be readily liquefied without disturbing the operation of the business.

# B

**balance sheet** A listing of assets, liabilities and net worth showing the financial position of a company at a specific time. A bank's balance sheet is generally referred to as a statement of condition.

**balloon mortgage** A mortgage whose amortization schedule will not extinguish the debt by the end of the mortgage term, leaving a large payment (called balloon payment) of the remaining principal balance to be paid at that time.

**basis point** The movement of interest rates or yields expressed in hundredths of a percent.

**bear market** A period of generally declining stock prices.

**bearer bond** A bond for which the owner's name is not registered on the books of the issuing company. Interest and principal is thus payable to the bond holder.

**bearer stock** Stock certificates that are not registered in any name. They are negotiable without endorsement and transferable by delivery.

**Big Board** Acceptable on second reference for the *New York Stock Exchange.*

**blue chip stock** Stock in a company known for its long-established record of making money and paying dividends.

**bond ratings** The two most popular are prepared by Moody's Investors Service Inc. and Standard & Poor's Corp.
Moody's uses nine ratings. The range, from the designation for top-quality issues to the one for those judged the greatest risk, is: Aaa, Aa, A, Baa, Ba, B, Caa, Ca and C.
Standard & Poor's uses seven basic grades. The range, from top to bottom, is: AAA, AA, A, BBB, BB, B and D. Occasionally it adds a plus or minus sign on grades AA through BB.

**bonds** See **loan terminology.**

**book value** The difference between a company's assets and liabilities.

The *book value per share* of common stock is the *book value* divided by the number of common shares outstanding.

**brand names** When they are used, capitalize them.

Brand names normally should be used only if they are essential to a story.

Sometimes, however, the use of a brand name may not be essential but is acceptable because it lends an air of reality to a story: *He fished a Camel from his shirt pocket* may be preferable to the less specific cigarette.

Brand name is a non-legal term for *service mark* or *trademark*. See entries under those words in main section.

**bull market** A period of generally increasing market prices.

**bullion** Unminted precious metals of standards suitable for coining.

# C

**capital** When used in a financial sense, *capital* describes money, equipment or property used in a business by a person or corporation.

**capital gain, capital loss** The difference between what a *capital* asset cost and the price it brought when sold.

**cents** Spell out the word *cents* and lowercase, using numerals for amounts less than a dollar: *5 cents, 12 cents.* Use the $ sign and decimal system for larger amounts: *$1.01, $2.50.*

**central bank** A bank having responsibility for controlling a country's monetary policy.

**charge off** A loan that no longer is expected to be repaid and is written off as a bad debt.

**Chicago Board of Trade** The largest commodity trading market in the United States.

**Chicago Board Options Exchange (CBOE)** An exchange set up by the Chicago Board of Trade to trade stock options.

**closely held corporation** A corporation in which stock shares and voting control are concentrated in the hands of a small number of investors, but for which some shares are available and traded on the market.

**Co.** See **company.**

**collateral** Stock or other property that a borrower is obliged to turn over to a lender if unable to repay a loan.
See **loan terminology.**

**commercial paper** One of the various types of short-term negotiable instruments whereby industrial or finance companies obtain cash after agreeing to pay a specific amount of money on the date due.

**commodity** The products of mining or agriculture before they have undergone extensive processing.

**commodities futures contract** A contract to purchase or sell a specific amount of a given commodity at a specified future date.

**common stock, preferred stock** An ownership interest in a corporation.

If other classes of stock are outstanding, the holders of common stock are the last to receive dividends and the last to receive payments if a corporation is dissolved. The company may raise or lower common stock dividends as its earnings rise or fall.

When preferred stock is outstanding and company earnings are sufficient, a fixed dividend is paid. If a company is liquidated, holders of preferred stock receive payments up to a set amount before any money is distributed to holders of common stock.

**company, companies** Use *Co.* or *Cos.* when a business uses either word at the end of its proper name: *Ford Motor Co., American Broadcasting Cos.* But: *Aluminum Company of America.*

If *company* or *companies* appears alone in second reference, spell the word out.

The forms for possessives:

*Ford Motor Co.'s profits, American Broadcasting Cos.' profits.*

See main section for specific company names.

**company names** Consult the company or Standard & Poor's Register of Corporations if in doubt about a formal name. Do not, however, use a comma before *Inc.* or *Ltd.*

See the **organizations and institutions** entry in main section. Also note names of specific companies in main section.

**conglomerate** A corporation that has diversified its operations, usually by acquiring enterprises in widely varied industries.

**consumer credit** Loans extended to individuals or small businesses usually on an unsecured basis, and providing for monthly repayment. Also referred to as installment credit or personal loans.

**convertible bond** See **loan terminology.**

**Corp.** See **corporation.**

**corporate names** See **company names.**

**corporation** An entity that is treated as a person in the eyes of the law. It is able to own property, incur debts, sue and be sued.

Abbreviate *corporation* as *Corp.* when a company or government agency uses the word at the end of its name: *Gulf Oil Corp., the Federal Deposit Insurance Corp.*

Spell out *corporation* when it occurs elsewhere in a name: *the Corporation for Public Broadcasting.*

Spell out and lowercase *corporation* whenever it stands alone.

The form for possessives: *Gulf Oil Corp.'s profits.*

**cost-plus**

**coupon** See **loan terminology** for its meaning in a financial sense.

**cross rate** The rate of exchange between two currencies calculated by referring to the rates between each and a third currency.

# D

**debt service** The outlay necessary to meet all interest and principal payments during a given period.

**default** The failure to meet a financial obligation, the failure to make payment either of principal or interest when due or a breach or nonperformance of the terms of a note or mortgage.

**deflation** A decrease in the general price level, which results from a decrease in total spending relative to the supply of available goods on the market. Deflation's immediate effect is to increase purchasing power.

**depreciation** The reduction in the value of capital goods due to wear and tear or obsolescence.

*Estimated depreciation* may be deducted from income each year as one of the costs of doing business.

**discount** Interest withheld when a note, draft or bill is purchased.

**discount rate** The rate of interest charged by the Federal Reserve on loans it makes to member banks. This rate has an influence on the rates banks then charge their customers.

**dividend** In a financial sense, the word describes the payment per share that a corporation distributes to its stockholders as their return on the money they have invested in its stock.

See **profit terminology.**

**dollars** Always lowercase. Use figures and the *$* sign in all except casual references or amounts without a figure: *The book cost $4. Dad, please give me a dollar. Dollars are flowing overseas.*

For specified amounts, the word takes a singular verb: *He said $500,000 is what they want.*

For amounts of more than $1 million, use the *$* and numerals up to two decimal places. Do not link the numerals and the word by a hyphen: *He is worth $4.35 million. He is worth exactly $4,351,242. He proposed a $300 billion budget.*

The form for amounts less

than $1 million: *$4, $25, $500, $1,000, $650,000.*

See **cents.**

**Dow Jones & Co.** The company publishes The Wall Street Journal and Barron's National Business and Financial Weekly. It also operates the Dow Jones News Service.

For stock market watchers, it provides the Dow Jones industrial average, the Dow Jones transportation average, the Dow Jones utility average, and the Dow Jones composite average.

Headquarters is in New York.

**downside risk** The probability that the price of an investment will fall.

**dumping** The selling of a product in a foreign market at a price lower than the domestic price. It is usually done by a monopoly when it has such a large output that selling entirely in the domestic market would substantially reduce the price.

**durable goods** Long-lasting goods such as appliances that are bought by consumers.

**E**

**employee** Not *employe.*

**equity** When used in a financial sense, *equity* means the value of property beyond the amount that is owed on it.

A *stockholder's equity* in a corporation is the value of the shares he holds.

A *homeowner's equity* is the difference between the value of the house and the amount of the unpaid mortgage.

**Eurodollar** A U.S. dollar on deposit in a European bank, including foreign branches of U.S. banks.

**extraordinary loss, extraordinary income** See **profit terminology.**

**F**

**factor** A financial organization whose primary business is purchasing the accounts receivable of other firms, at a discount, and taking the risk and responsibilities of making collection.

**federal funds, federal funds rate** Money in excess of what the Federal Reserve says a bank must have on hand to back up deposits. The excess can be lent overnight to banks that need more cash on hand to meet their reserve requirements. The interest rate of these loans is the federal funds rate.

**firm** A business partnership is correctly referred to as a *firm: He joined a law firm.*
Do not use *firm* in references to an incorporated business entity. Use *the company* or *the corporation* instead.

**fiscal, monetary** *Fiscal* applies to budgetary matters. *Monetary* applies to money supply.

**fiscal year** The 12-month period that a corporation or governmental body uses for bookkeeping purposes.
The federal government's fiscal year starts three months ahead of the calendar year— fiscal 1984, for example, ran from Oct. 1, 1983, to Sept. 30, 1984.

**float** Money that has been committed but not yet credited to an account, like a check that has been written but has not yet cleared.

**f.o.b.** Acceptable on first reference for **free on board.**

**force majeure** A condition permitting a company to depart from the strict terms of a contract because of an event or effect that can't be reasonably controlled.

**freely floating** Describes an exchange rate that is allowed to fluctuate in response to supply and demand in the foreign markets.

**full faith and credit bond** See **loan terminology.**

**G**

**general obligation bond** See **loan terminology.**

**H**

**hedging** A method of selling for future delivery whereby a dealer protects himself from falling prices between the time he buys a product and the time he re-sells or processes it. A miller, for example, who buys wheat to convert to flour will sell a similar quantity of wheat he doesn't own at near the price at which he bought his own. He will agree to deliver it at the same time his flour is ready for market. If at that time the price of wheat and therefore flour has fallen, he will lose on the flour but can buy the wheat at a low price and deliver it at a profit. If prices have risen, he will make an extra profit on his flour which he will have to sacrifice to buy the wheat for delivery. But either way he has protected his profit.

**holding company** A company whose principal assets are the securities it owns in companies that actually provide goods or services.

The usual reason for forming a holding company is to enable one corporation and its directors to control several companies by holding a majority of their stock.

**I**

**Inc.** See **incorporated.**

**income** See **profit terminology.**

**incorporated** Abbreviate and capitalize as *Inc.* when used as a part of a corporate name. It usually is not needed, but when it is used, do not set off with commas: *J.C. Penney Co. Inc. announced* . . .

See **company names.**

**Index of Leading Economic Indicators** A composite of 12 economic measurements that was developed to help forecast likely shifts in the U.S. economy as a whole.

It is compiled by the Commerce Department.

**inflation** A sustained increase in prices. The result is a decrease in the purchasing power of money.

There are two basic types of inflation:

—*Cost-push inflation* occurs when rising costs are the chief reason for the increased prices.

—*Demand-pull inflation* occurs when the amount of money available exceeds the amount of goods and services available for sale.

**infrastructure** An economy's capital in the form of roads, railways, water supplies, educational facilities, health services, etc., without which investment in factories can't be fully productive.

**International Monetary Fund** *IMF* is acceptable on second reference. Headquarters is in Washington.

A supply of money supported by subscriptions of member nations, for the purpose of stabilizing international exchange and promoting orderly and balanced trade. Member nations may obtain foreign currency needed, making it possible to correct temporary maladjustments in their balance of payments without currency depreciation.

**L**

**leverage** The use of borrowed assets by a business to enhance the return of the owner's equity. The expectation is that the interest rate charged will be lower than the earnings made on the money.

**liabilities** When used in a financial sense, the word means all the claims against a corporation.

They include accounts payable, wages and salaries due but not paid, dividends declared payable, taxes payable, and fixed or long-term obligations such as bonds, debentures and bank loans.

See **assets.**

**liquidation** When used in a financial sense, the word means the process of converting stock or other assets into cash.

When a company is liquidated, the cash obtained is first used to pay debts and obligations to holders of bonds and preferred stock. Whatever cash remains is distributed on a per-share basis to the holders of common stock.

**liquidity** The ease with which assets can be converted to cash without loss in value.

**loan terminology** Note the meanings of these terms in

describing loans by governments and corporations:

**bond** A certificate issued by a corporation or government stating the amount of a loan, the interest to be paid, the time for repayment and the collateral pledged if payment cannot be made. Repayment generally is not due for a long period, usually seven years or more.

**collateral** Stock or other property that a borrower is obligated to turn over to a lender if unable to repay a loan.

**commercial paper** A document describing the details of a short-term loan between corporations.

**convertible bond** A bond carrying the stipulation that it may be exchanged for a specific amount of stock in the company that issued it.

**coupon** A slip of paper attached to a bond that the bondholder clips at specified times and returns to the issuer for payment of the interest due.

**default** A person, corporation or government is in default if it fails to meet the terms for repayment.

**debenture** A certificate stating the amount of a loan, the interest to be paid and the time for repayment, but not providing collateral. It is backed only by the corporation's reputation and promise to pay.

**full faith and credit bond** An alternative term for general obligation bond, often used to contrast such a bond with a moral obligation bond.

**general obligation bond** A bond that has had the formal approval of either the voters or their legislature. The government's promise to repay the principal and pay the interest is constitutionally guaranteed on the strength of its ability to tax the population.

**maturity** The date on which a bond, debenture or note must be repaid.

**moral obligation bond** A government bond that has not had the formal approval of either the voters or their legislature. It is backed only by the government's "moral obligation" to repay the principal and interest on time.

**municipal bond** A general obligation bond issued by a state, county, city, town, village, possession or territory, or a bond issued by an agency or authority set up by one of these governmental units. In general, interest paid on municipal bonds is exempt from federal income taxes. It also usually is exempt from state and local taxes if held by someone living within the state of issue.

**note** A certificate issued by a corporation or government stating the amount of a loan, the interest to be paid and the collateral pledged in the event payment cannot be made. The date for repayment is generally more than a year after issue but not more than seven or eight years later. The shorter interval for repayment is the principal difference between a note and a bond.

**revenue bond** A bond backed only by the revenue of the airport, turnpike or other facility that was built with the money it raised.

**Treasury borrowing** A *Treasury bill* is a certificate representing a loan to the federal government that matures in three, six or 12 months. A *Treasury note* may mature in one to 10 years or more. A *Treasury bond* matures in seven years or more.

# M

**margin** The practice of purchasing securities in part with borrowed money, using the purchased securities as collateral in anticipation of an advance in the market price. If the advance occurs, the purchaser may be able to repay the loan and make a profit. If the price declines, the stock may have to be sold to settle the loan. The margin is the difference between the amount of the loan and the value of the securities used as collateral.

**monetary** See the **fiscal, monetary** entry.

**money market** The market for various money market instruments.

**moral obligation bond**
See **loan terminology.**

**municipal bond** See
**loan terminology.**

**N**

**National Labor Rela-
tions Board** *NLRB* is acceptable on second reference.

**net income, net profit**
See **profit terminology.**

**New York Stock Ex-
change** *NYSE* is acceptable
on second reference as an adjective. Use *the stock exchange* or *the exchange* for
other references.

**note** For use in a financial
sense, see **loan terminology.**

**O**

**option** The word means
an agreement to buy or sell
something, such as shares of
stock, within a stipulated time
and for a certain price.

A *put option* gives the
holder the right to sell blocks
of 100 shares of stock within a
specified time at an agreed-
upon price.

A *call option* gives the
holder the right to buy blocks
of 100 shares of stock within a
specified time at an agreed-
upon price.

**over the counter** A
term for the method of trading when securities are not
listed on a recognized securities exchange.

**P**

**preferred stock** See the
**common stock, preferred
stock** entry.

**price-earnings ratio**
The price of a share of stock
divided by earnings per share
for a 12-month period. Ratios
in AP stock tables reflect
earnings for the most recent
12 months.

For example, a stock selling
for $60 per share and earning
$6 per share would be selling
at a price-earnings ratio of 10-
to-1.

See **profit terminology.**

**prime rate** The interest
rate that commercial banks
charge on loans to their bor-

rowers with the best credit ratings.

Fluctuations in the prime rate seldom have an immediate impact on consumer loan rates. Over the long term, however, consistent increases (or decreases) in the prime rate can lead to increases (or decreases) in the interest rates for mortgages and all types of personal loans.

**profit-taking** (n. and adj.) Avoid this term. It means selling a security after a recent rapid rise in price. It is inaccurate if the seller bought the security at a higher price, watched it fall, then sold it after a recent rise but for less than he bought it. In that case, he would be cutting his losses, not taking his profit.

**profit terminology** Note the meanings of the following terms in reporting a company's financial status. Always be careful to specify whether the figures given apply to quarterly or annual results.

The terms, listed in the order in which they might occur in analyzing a company's financial condition:

**revenue** The amount of money a company took in, including interest earned and receipts from sales, services provided, rents and royalties.

The figure also may include excise taxes and sales taxes collected for the government. If it does, the fact should be noted in any report on revenue.

**sales** The money a company received for the goods and services it sold.

In some cases the figure includes receipts from rents and royalties. In others, particularly when rentals and royalties make up a large portion of a company's income, figures for these activities are listed separately.

**gross profit** The difference between the sales price of an item or service and the expenses directly attributed to it, such as the cost of raw materials, labor and overhead linked to the production effort.

**income before taxes** Gross profits minus company-wide expenses not directly attributed to specific products or services. These expenses typically include interest costs, advertising and sales costs, and general administrative overhead.

**net income, profit, earnings** The amount left after taxes have been paid.

A portion may be committed to pay preferred dividends. Some of what remains may be paid in dividends to holders of common stocks. The rest may be invested to obtain interest revenue or spent to acquire new buildings or equipment to increase the company's ability to make further profits.

To avoid confusion, do not use the word *income* alone—always specify whether the figure is *income before taxes* or *net income*.

The terms *profit* and *earnings* commonly are interpreted as meaning the amount left after taxes. The terms *net profit* and *net earnings* are acceptable synonyms.

**earnings per share** The figure obtained by dividing the number of outstanding shares of common stock into the amount left after dividends have been paid on any preferred stock.

**dividend** The amount paid per share per year to holders of common stock. Payments generally are made in quarterly installments.

The dividend usually is a portion of the earnings per share. However, if a company shows no profit during a given period, it may be able to use earnings retained from profitable periods to pay its dividend on schedule.

**return on investment** A percentage figure obtained by dividing the company's assets into its net income.

**extraordinary loss, extraordinary income** An expense or source of income that does not occur on a regular basis, such as a loss due to a major fire or the revenue from the sale of a subsidiary. Extraordinary items should be identified in any report on the company's financial status to avoid creating the false impression that its overall profit trend has suddenly plunged or soared.

**protective tariff** A duty high enough to assure domestic producers against any effective competition from foreign producers.

## R

**receivership** A legal action in which a court appoints a *receiver* to manage a business while the court tries to resolve problems that could ruin the business, such as insolvency. *Receivership* is often used in federal bankruptcy court proceedings. But it also can be used for non-financial troubles like an ownership dispute.

In bankruptcy proceedings, the court appoints a trustee called a *receiver* who attempts to settle the financial difficulties of the company while under protection from creditors.

**recession** A falling-off of economic activity that may be a temporary phenomenon or could continue into a depression.

**retail sales** The sales of retail stores, including merchandise sold and receipts for repairs and similar services.

A business is considered a *retail store* if it is engaged primarily in selling merchandise for personal, household or farm consumption.

**revenue** See **profit terminology.**

**revenue bond** See **loan terminology.**

**revolving credit** Describes an account on which the payment is any amount less than the total balance, and the remaining balance carried forward is subject to finance charges.

**rollover** The selling of new securities to pay off old ones coming due or the refinancing of an existing loan.

## S

**savings and loan associations** They are not banks. Use *the association* on second reference.

**service mark** A brand, symbol, word, etc. used by a supplier of services and protected by law to prevent a competitor from using it: *Realtor,* for a member of the National Association of Realtors, for example.

When a service mark is used, capitalize it.

The preferred form, however, is to use a generic term unless the service mark is essential to the story.

See **brand names** and **trademark.**

**short** An investment term used to describe the position held by individuals who sells stock that they do not yet own by borrowing from their broker in order to deliver to the purchaser.

A person selling short is betting that the price of the stock will fall.

**short covering** The purchase of a security to repay shares borrowed from a broker.

**short sale** A sale of securities which are not owned by the sellers at the time of sale but which they intend to purchase or borrow in time to make delivery.

**small-business man**

**spin off** A distribution that occurs when the company forms a separate company out of a division, a subsidiary or other holdings. The

shares of the new company are distributed proportionately to the parent company holders.

**spot market** A market for buying or selling commodities or foreign exchange for immediate delivery and for cash payment.

**spot price** The price of a commodity available for immediate sale and delivery. The term is also used to refer to foreign exchange transactions.

**Standard & Poor's Register of Corporations** The source for determining the formal name of a business. See **company names.**

The register is published by Standard & Poor's Corp. of New York.

**stockbroker**

**stock market prices** Use fractions rather than decimals, spelling out the fraction if it is not linked with a figure: *The stock went up three-quarters of a point. The stock went up 1 1/2 points.*

# T

**trademark** A trademark is a brand, symbol, word, etc., used by a manufacturer or dealer and protected by law to prevent a competitor from using it: *AstroTurf,* for a type of artificial grass, for example.

In general, use a generic equivalent unless the trademark name is essential to the story.

When a trademark is used, capitalize it.

Many trademarks are listed separately in this book, together with generic equivalents.

The U.S. Trademark Association, located in New York, is a helpful source of information about trademarks.

See **brand names** and **service marks.**

**Treasury bills, Treasury bonds, Treasury notes** See **loan terminology.**

# U

**union names** The formal names of unions may be condensed to conventionally accepted short forms that capitalize characteristic words from the full name followed by *union* in lowercase.

Follow union practice in the use of the word *worker* in shortened forms. Among major unions, all except the *United Steelworkers* use two words: *United Auto Workers, United Mine Workers,* etc.

See entry in main section for more detail and references.

# W

**Wall Street** When the reference is to the entire complex of financial institutions in the area rather than the actual street itself, *the Street* is an acceptable short form.

See **capitalization.**

**wholesale price index** A measurement of the changes in the average price that businesses pay for a selected group of industrial commodities, farm products, processed foods and feed for animals.

Capitalize when referring to the U.S. index, issued monthly by the Bureau of Labor Statistics, an agency of the Labor Department.

# Y

**yield** In a financial sense, the annual rate of return on an investment, as paid in dividends or interest. It is expressed as a percentage obtained by dividing the market price for a stock or bond into the dividend or interest paid in the preceding 12 months. See **profit terminology.**

# A GUIDE TO PUNCTUATION

There is no alternative to correct punctuation. Incorrect punctuation can change the meaning of a sentence, the results of which could be far-reaching.

Even if the meaning is not changed, bad punctuation, however inconsequential, can cause the reader to lose track of what is being said and give up reading a sentence.

The basic guideline is to use common sense.

—Punctuation is to make clear the thought being expressed.

—If punctuation does not help make clear what is being said, it should not be there.

"The Elements of Style" by E.B. White and William Strunk Jr. is a bible of writers. It states:

"Clarity, clarity, clarity. When you become hopelessly mired in a sentence, it is best to start fresh; do not try to fight your way through against terrible odds of syntax. Usually what is wrong is that the construction has become too involved at some point; the sentence needs to be broken apart and replaced by two or more shorter sentences."

This applies to punctuation. If a sentence becomes cluttered with commas, semicolons, and dashes, start over.

These two paragraphs are full of commas and clauses; all of it equals too much for the reader to grasp:

*The Commonwealth Games Federation, in an apparent effort to persuade other nations to ignore the spiraling boycott, ruled Sunday that Budd, a runner who has had a storied past on and off the track, and Cowley, a swimmer who competes for the University of Texas, were ineligible under the Commonwealth Constitution to compete for England in the 10-day event to be held in Edinburgh, Scotland, beginning July 24.*

*The decision on Budd, who has been the object of a number of demonstrations in the past, and Cowley followed an earlier announcement Sunday by Tanzania that it was joining Nigeria, Kenya, Ghana and Uganda in boycotting the games because of Britain's refusal to support economic sanctions against South Africa's white-led government.*

# PUNCTUATION MARKS AND HOW TO USE THEM

**ampersand (&)** Use the *ampersand* when it is part of a company's formal name: *Baltimore & Ohio Railroad, Newport News Shipbuilding & Dry Dock Co.*

The *ampersand* should not otherwise be used in place of *and.*

**apostrophe (')** Follow these guidelines:

POSSESSIVES: See the **possessives** entry in main section.

PLURAL NOUNS NOT ENDING IN *S:* Add *'s: the alumni's contributions, women's rights.*

PLURAL NOUNS ENDING IN *S:* Add only an apostrophe: *the churches' needs, the girls' toys, the horses' food, the ships' wake, states' rights, the VIPs' entrance.*

NOUNS PLURAL IN FORM, SINGULAR IN MEANING: Add only an apostrophe: *mathematics' rules, measles' effects.* (But see INANIMATE OBJECTS below.)

Apply the same principle when a plural word occurs in the formal name of a singular entity: *General Motors' profits, the United States' wealth.*

NOUNS THE SAME IN SINGULAR AND PLURAL: Treat them the same as plurals, even if the meaning is singular: *one corps' location, the two deer's tracks, the lone moose's antlers.*

SINGULAR NOUNS NOT ENDING IN S: Add *'s: the church's needs, the girl's toys, the horse's food, the ship's route, the VIP's seat.*

Some style guides say that singular nouns ending in *s* sounds such as *ce, x,* and *z* may take either the apostrophe alone or *'s.* See SPECIAL EXPRESSIONS, but otherwise, for consistency and ease in remembering a rule, always use 's if the word does not end in the letter s: *Butz's policies, the fox's den, the justice's verdict, Marx's theories, the prince's life, Xerox's profits.*

SINGULAR COMMON NOUNS ENDING IN S: Add 's unless the next word begins with s: *the hostess's invitation, the hostess' seat; the witness's answer, the witness' story.*

SINGULAR PROPER NAMES ENDING IN S: Use only an apostrophe: *Achilles' heel, Agnes' book, Ceres' rites, Descartes' theories, Dickens' novels, Euripides' dramas, Hercules' labors, Jesus' life, Jules' seat, Kansas' schools, Moses' law, Socrates' life, Tennessee Williams' plays, Xerxes' armies.*

SPECIAL EXPRESSIONS: The following exceptions to the general rule for words not ending in s apply to words that end in an s sound and are followed by a word that begins with s: *for appearance' sake, for conscience' sake, for goodness' sake.* Use 's otherwise: *the appearance's cost, my conscience's voice.*

PRONOUNS: Personal interrogative and relative pronouns have separate forms for the possessive. None involves an apostrophe: *mine, ours, your, yours, his, hers, its, theirs, whose.*

Caution: If you are using an apostrophe with a pronoun, always double-check to be sure that the meaning calls for a contraction: *you're, it's, there's, who's.*

Follow the rules listed above in forming the possessives of other pronouns: *another's idea, others' plans, someone's guess.*

COMPOUND WORDS: Applying the rules above, add an apostrophe or 's to the word closest to the object possessed: *the major general's decision, the major generals' decisions, the attorney general's request, the attorneys general's request.* See the **plurals** entry for guidelines on forming the plurals of these words.

Also: *anyone else's attitude, John Adams Jr.'s father, Benjamin Franklin of Pennsylvania's motion.* Whenever practical, however, recast the phrase to avoid ambiguity: *the motion by Benjamin Franklin of Pennsylvania.*

JOINT POSSESSION, INDIVIDUAL POSSESSION: Use a possessive form after only the last word if ownership is joint: *Fred and Sylvia's apartment, Fred and Sylvia's stocks.*

Use a possessive form after both words if the objects are individually owned: *Fred's and Sylvia's books.*

DESCRIPTIVE PHRASES: Do not add an apostrophe to a word ending in *s* when it is used primarily in a descriptive sense: *citizens band radio, a Cincinnati Reds infielder, a teachers college, a Teamsters request, a writers guide.*

Memory Aid: The apostrophe usually is not used if *for* or *by* rather than *of* would be appropriate in the longer form: *a radio band for citizens, a college for teachers, a guide for writers, a request by the Teamsters.*

An *'s* is required, however, when a term involves a plural word that does not end in *s: a children's hospital, a people's republic, the Young Men's Christian Association.*

DESCRIPTIVE NAMES: Some governmental, corporate and institutional organizations with a descriptive word in their names use an apostrophe; some do not. Follow the user's practice: *Actors Equity, Diners Club, the Ladies' Home Journal, the National Governors' Association,* the Veterans Administration. See separate entries for these and similar names frequently in the news.

QUASI POSSESSIVES: Follow the rules above in composing the possessive form of words that occur in such phrases as *a day's pay, two weeks' vacation, three days' work, your money's worth.*

Frequently, however, a hyphenated form is clearer: *a two-week vacation, a three-day job.*

DOUBLE POSSESSIVE: Two conditions must apply for a double possessive—a phrase such as *a friend of John's*—to occur: 1. The word after *of* must refer to an animate object, and 2. The word before *of* must involve only a portion of the animate object's possessions.

Otherwise, do not use the possessive form on the word after *of: The friends of John Adams mourned his death.* (All the friends were involved.) *He is a friend of the college.* (Not *college's,* because *college* is inanimate.)

Memory Aid: This construction occurs most often, and quite naturally, with the possessive forms of personal pronouns: *He is a friend of mine.*

INANIMATE OBJECTS: There is no blanket rule against creating a possessive form for an inanimate object, particularly if the object is treated in a personified sense. See some of the earlier examples, and note these: *death's call, the wind's murmur.*

In general, however, avoid excessive personalization of inanimate objects, and give preference to an *of* construction when it fits the makeup of the sentence. For example, the earlier references to *mathematics' rules* and *measles' effects* would better be phrased: *the rules of mathematics, the effects of measles.*

OMITTED LETTERS: *I've, it's, don't, rock 'n' roll, 'Tis the season to be jolly. He is a ne'er-do-well.* See **contractions** in main section.

OMITTED FIGURES: *The class of '62. The Spirit of '76. The '20s.*

PLURALS OF A SINGLE LETTER: *Mind your p's and q's. He learned the three R's and brought home a report card with four A's and two B's. The Oakland A's won the pennant.*

DO NOT USE: For plurals of numerals or multiple-letter combinations. See **plurals.**

**brackets** They cannot be transmitted over news wires. Use parentheses or recast the material.

See **parentheses.**

**colon (:)** The most frequent use of a colon is at the end of a sentence to introduce lists, tabulations, texts, etc.

Capitalize the first word after a colon only if it is a proper noun or the start of a complete sentence: *He promised this: The company will make good all the losses.* But: *There were three considerations: expense, time and feasibility.*

EMPHASIS: The colon often can be effective in giving emphasis: *He had only one hobby: eating.*

LISTINGS: Use the colon in such listings as time elapsed *(1:31:07.2),* time of day *(8:31 p.m.),* biblical and legal citations *(2 Kings 2:14; Missouri Code 3:245–260).*

DIALOGUE: Use a colon for dialogue. In coverage of a trial, for example:

*Bailey: What were you doing the night of the 19th?*

*Mason: I refuse to answer that.*

Q AND A: The colon is used for question-and-answer interviews:

*Q: Did you strike him?*
*A: Indeed I did.*

INTRODUCING QUOTATIONS: Use a comma to introduce a direct quotation of one sentence that remains within a paragraph. Use a colon to introduce longer quotations within a paragraph and to end all paragraphs that introduce a paragraph of quoted material.

PLACEMENT WITH QUOTATION MARKS: Colons go outside quotation marks unless they are part of the quotation itself.

MISCELLANEOUS: Do not combine a dash and a colon.

**comma (,)** The following guidelines treat some of the most frequent questions about the use of commas. Additional guidelines on specialized uses are provided in separate entries such as **dates** and **scores.**

For detailed guidance, consult "The Comma" and "Misused and Unnecessary Commas" in the Guide to Punctuation section in the back of Webster's New World Dictionary.

IN A SERIES: Use commas to separate elements in a series, but do not put a comma before the conjunction in a simple series: *The flag is red, white and blue. He would nominate Tom, Dick or Harry.*

Put a comma before the concluding conjunction in a series, however, if an integral element of the series requires a conjunction: *I had orange juice, toast, and ham and eggs for breakfast.*

Use a comma also before the concluding conjunction in a complex series of phrases: *The main points to consider are whether the athletes are skillful enough to compete, whether they have the stamina to endure the training, and whether they have the proper mental attitude.*

See the **dash** and **semicolon** entries for cases when elements of a series contain internal commas.

WITH EQUAL ADJECTIVES: Use commas to separate a series of adjectives equal in rank. If the commas could be replaced by the word *and* without changing the sense, the adjectives are equal: *a thoughtful, precise manner; a dark, dangerous street.*

Use no comma when the

last adjective before a noun outranks its predecessors because it is an integral element of a noun phrase, which is the equivalent of a single noun: *a cheap fur coat* (the noun phrase is *fur coat); the old oaken bucket; a new, blue spring bonnet.*

**WITH NON-ESSENTIAL CLAUSES:** A non-essential clause must be set off by commas. An essential clause must not be set off from the rest of a sentence by commas.

See the **essential clauses, non-essential clauses** entry in the main section.

**WITH NON-ESSENTIAL PHRASES:** A non-essential phrase must be set off by commas. An essential phrase must not be set off from the rest of a sentence by commas.

See the **essential phrases, non-essential phrases** entry in the main section.

**WITH INTRODUCTORY CLAUSES AND PHRASES:** A comma is used to separate an introductory clause or phrase from the main clause: *When he had tired of the mad pace of New York, he moved to Dubuque.*

The comma may be omitted after short introductory phrases if no ambiguity would result: *During the night he heard many noises.*

But use the comma if its omission would slow comprehension: *On the street below, the curious gathered.*

**WITH CONJUNCTIONS:** When a conjunction such as *and, but* or *for* links two clauses that could stand alone as separate sentences, use a comma before the conjunction in most cases: *She was glad she had looked, for a man was approaching the house.*

As a rule of thumb, use a comma if the subject of each clause is expressly stated: *We are visiting Washington, and we also plan a side trip to Williamsburg. We visited Washington, and our senator greeted us personally.* But no comma when the subject of the two clauses is the same and is not repeated in the second: *We are visiting Washington and plan to see the White House.*

The comma may be dropped if two clauses with expressly stated subjects are short. In general, however, favor use of a comma unless a particular literary effect is desired or if it would distort the sense of a sentence.

**INTRODUCING DI-**

RECT QUOTES: Use a comma to introduce a complete one-sentence quotation within a paragraph: *Wallace said, "She spent six months in Argentina and came back speaking English with a Spanish accent."* But use a colon to introduce quotations of more than one sentence. See **colon.**

Do not use a comma at the start of an indirect or partial quotation: *He said his victory put him "firmly on the road to a first-ballot nomination."*

BEFORE ATTRIBUTION: Use a comma instead of a period at the end of a quote that is followed by attribution: *"Rub my shoulders," Miss Cawley suggested.*

Do not use a comma, however, if the quoted statement ends with a question mark or exclamation point: *"Why should I?" he asked.*

WITH HOMETOWNS AND AGES: Use a comma to set off an individual's hometown when it is placed in apposition to a name: *Mary Richards, Minneapolis, and Maude Findlay, Tuckahoe, N.Y., were there.* However, the use of the word *of* without a comma between the individual's name and the city name generally is preferable: *Mary Richards of Minneapolis and Maude Findlay of Tuckahoe, N.Y., were there.*

If an individual's age is used, set if off by commas: *Maude Findlay, 48, Tuckahoe, N.Y., was present.* The use of the word *of* eliminates the need for a comma after the hometown if a state name is not needed: *Mary Richards, 36, of Minneapolis and Maude Findlay, 48, of Tuckahoe, N.Y., attended the party.*

WITH PARTY AFFILIATION, ACADEMIC DEGREES, RELIGIOUS AFFILIATIONS: See separate entries under each of these terms.

NAMES OF STATES AND NATIONS USED WITH CITY NAMES: *His journey will take him from Dublin, Ireland, to Fargo, N.D., and back. The Selma, Ala., group saw the governor.*

Use parentheses, however, if a state name is inserted within a proper name: *The Huntsville (Ala.) Times.*

WITH YES AND NO: *Yes, I will be there.*

IN DIRECT ADDRESS: *Mother, I will be home late. No, sir, I did not take it.*

SEPARATING SIMILAR WORDS: Use a comma to separate duplicated words that otherwise would be confusing: *What the problem is, is not clear.*

IN LARGE FIGURES: Use a comma for most figures higher than 999. The major exceptions are: street addresses *(1234 Main St.),* broadcast frequencies *(1460 kilohertz),* room numbers, serial numbers, telephone numbers, and years *(1876).* See separate entries under these headings.

PLACEMENT WITH QUOTES: Commas always go inside quotation marks.

See **semicolon.**

## compound adjectives
See the **hyphen** entry.

**dash (—)** Follow these guidelines:

ABRUPT CHANGE: Use dashes to denote an abrupt change in thought in a sentence or an emphatic pause: *We will fly to Paris in June—if I get a raise. Smith offered a plan—it was unprecedented—to raise revenues.*

SERIES WITHIN A PHRASE: When a phrase that otherwise would be set off by commas contains a series of words that must be separated by commas, use dashes to set off the full phrase: *He listed the qualities*

*—intelligence, humor, conservatism, independence—that he liked in an executive.*

ATTRIBUTION: Use a dash before an author's or composer's name at the end of a quotation: *"Who steals my purse steals trash."—Shakespeare.*

IN DATELINES: *NEW YORK (AP)—The city is broke.*

IN LISTS: Dashes should be used to introduce individual sections of a list. Capitalize the first word following the dash. Use periods, not semicolons, at the end of each section. Example: *Jones gave the following reasons:—He never ordered the package. — If he did, it didn't come. —If it did, he sent it back.*

WITH SPACES: Put a space on both sides of a dash in all uses except the start of a paragraph and sports agate summaries.

LOCATION ON KEYBOARDS: On most manual typewriters, the dash must be indicated by striking the hyphen key twice. On most video display terminals, however, there is a separate key that should be used to provide the unique dash symbol with one keystroke.

**ellipsis ( . . . )** In general, treat an ellipsis as a three-letter word, constructed with three periods and two spaces, as shown here.

Use an ellipsis to indicate the deletion of one or more words in condensing quotes, texts, and documents. Be especially careful to avoid deletions that would distort the meaning.

Brief examples of how to use ellipses are provided after guidelines are given. More extensive examples, drawn from the speech in which President Nixon announced his resignation, are in the sections below marked CONDENSATION EXAMPLE and QUOTATIONS.

SPACING REQUIREMENTS: In some computer editing systems the thin space must be used between the periods of the ellipsis to prevent them from being placed on two different lines when they are sent through a computer that handles hyphenation and justification.

Leave one regular space—never a thin—on both sides of an ellipsis: *I . . . tried to do what was best.*

PUNCTUATION GUIDELINES: If the words that precede an ellipsis constitute a grammatically complete sentence, either in the original or in the condensation, place a period at the end of the last word before the ellipsis. Follow it with a regular space and an ellipsis: *I no longer have a strong enough political base. . . .*

When the grammatical sense calls for a question mark, exclamation point, comma or colon, the sequence is word, punctuation mark, regular space, ellipsis: *Will you come? . . .*

When material is deleted at the end of one paragraph and at the beginning of the one that follows, place an ellipsis in both locations.

CONDENSATION EXAMPLE: Here is an example of how the spacing and punctuation guidelines would be applied in condensing President Nixon's resignation announcement:

*Good evening. . . .*

*In all the decisions I have made in my public life, I have always tried to do what was best for the nation. . . .*

*. . . However, it has become evident to me that I no longer have a strong enough political base in Congress.*

*. . . As long as there was a base, I felt strongly that it was*

necessary to see the constitutional process through to its conclusion, that to do otherwise would be . . . a dangerously destabilizing precedent for the future.

QUOTATIONS: In writing a story, do not use ellipses at the beginning and end of direct quotes:

"It has become evident to me that I no longer have a strong enough political base," Nixon said.

Not ". . . it has become evident to me that I no longer have a strong enough political base . . . ," Nixon said.

HESITATION: An ellipsis also may be used to indicate a pause or hesitation in speech, or a thought that the speaker or writer does not complete. Substitute a dash for this purpose, however, if the context uses ellipses to indicate that words actually spoken or written have been deleted.

SPECIAL EFFECTS: Ellipses also may be used to separate individual items within a paragraph of show business gossip or similar material. Use periods after items that are complete sentences.

## exclamation point (!)

Follow these guidelines:

EMPHATIC EXPRESSIONS: Use the mark to express a high degree of surprise, incredulity or other strong emotion.

AVOID OVERUSE: Use a comma after mild interjections. End mildly exclamatory sentences with a period.

PLACEMENT WITH QUOTES: Place the mark inside quotation marks when it is part of the quoted material: "How wonderful!" he exclaimed. "Never!" she shouted.

Place the mark outside quotation marks when it is not part of the quoted material: I hated reading Spenser's "Faerie Queene"!

MISCELLANEOUS: Do not use a comma or a period after the exclamation mark:

Wrong: "Halt!", the corporal cried.

Right: "Halt!" the corporal cried.

## hyphen (-)

Hyphens are joiners. Use them to avoid ambiguity or to form a single idea from two or more words.

Some guidelines:

AVOID AMBIGUITY: Use a hyphen whenever ambiguity would result if it were omitted: The president will speak to small-business men. (Businessmen normally is one word. But *the president will speak to small businessmen* is unclear.)

Others: *He recovered his health. He re-covered the leaky roof.*

COMPOUND MODIFIERS: When a compound modifier—two or more words that express a single concept—precedes a noun, use hyphens to link all the words in the compound except the adverb *very* and all adverbs that end in *ly: a first-quarter touchdown, a bluish-green dress, a full-time job, a well-known man, a better-qualified woman, a know-it-all attitude, a very good time, an easily remembered rule.*

Many combinations that are hyphenated before a noun are not hyphenated when they occur after a noun: *The team scored in the first quarter. The dress, a bluish green, was attractive on her. She works full time. His attitude suggested that he knew it all.*

But when a modifier that would be hyphenated before a noun occurs instead after a form of the verb *to be,* the hyphen usually must be retained to avoid confusion: *The man is well-known. The woman is quick-witted. The children are soft-spoken. The play is second-rate.*

The principle of using a hyphen to avoid confusion explains why no hyphen is required with *very* and *-ly* words. Readers can expect them to modify the word that follows. But if a combination such as *little-known man* were not hyphenated, the reader could logically be expecting *little* to be followed by a noun, as in *little man.* Instead, the reader encountering *little known* would have to back up mentally and make the compound connection on his own.

TWO-THOUGHT COMPOUNDS: *serio-comic, socio-economic.*

COMPOUND PROPER NOUNS AND ADJECTIVES: Use a hyphen to designate dual heritage: *Italian-American, Mexican-American.*

No hyphen, however, for *French Canadian* or *Latin American.*

PREFIXES AND SUFFIXES: See the **prefixes** and **suffixes** entries, and separate entries for the most frequently used prefixes and suffixes.

AVOID DUPLICATED VOWELS, TRIPLED CONSONANTS: Examples: *anti-*

*intellectual, pre-empt, shell-like.*

WITH NUMERALS: Use a hyphen to separate figures in **odds, ratios, scores,** some **fractions** and some **vote tabulations.** See examples in entries under these headings.

When large numbers must be spelled out, use a hyphen to connect a word ending in *y* to another word: *twenty-one, fifty-five,* etc.

SUSPENSIVE HYPHENATION: The form: *He received a 10- to 20-year sentence in prison.*

**parentheses ( )** In general, use parentheses around logos, as shown in the **datelines** entry, but otherwise be sparing with them.

Parentheses are jarring to the reader. Because they do not appear on some news service printers, there is also the danger that material inside them may be misinterpreted.

The temptation to use parentheses is a clue that a sentence is becoming contorted. Try to write it another way. If a sentence must contain incidental material, then commas or two dashes are frequently more effective. Use these alternatives whenever possible.

There are occasions, however, when parentheses are the only effective means of inserting necessary background or reference information. When they are necessary, follow these guidelines:

WITHIN QUOTATIONS: If parenthetical information inserted in a direct quotation is at all sensitive, place an editor's note under a dash at the bottom of a story alerting copy desks to what was inserted.

PUNCTUATION: Place a period outside a closing parenthesis if the material inside is not a sentence *(such as this fragment).*

*(An independent parenthetical sentence such as this one takes a period before the closing parenthesis.)*

When a phrase placed in parentheses *(this one is an example)* might normally qualify as a complete sentence but is dependent on the surrounding material, do not capitalize the first word or end with a period.

MATERIAL FROM OTHER AREAS: If a story contains information from outside the datelined city, put the material in parentheses only if the correspondent in the datelined community was cut off from incoming communications. See **dateline selection.**

INSERTIONS IN A PROPER NAME: Use parentheses if a state name or similar information is inserted within a proper name: *The Huntsville (Ala.) Times.* But use commas if no proper name is involved: *The Selma, Ala., group saw the governor.*

NEVER USED: Do not use parentheses to denote a political figure's party affiliation and jurisdiction. Instead, set them off with commas, as shown under **party affiliation.**

Do not use *(cq)* or similar notation to indicate that an unusual spelling or term is correct. Include the confirmation in an editor's note at the top of a story.

**periods (.)** Follow these guidelines:

END OF DECLARATIVE SENTENCE: *The stylebook is finished.*

END OF A MILDLY IMPERATIVE SENTENCE: *Shut the door.*

Use an exclamation point if greater emphasis is desired: *Be careful!*

END OF SOME RHETORICAL QUESTIONS: A period is preferable if a statement is more a suggestion than a question: *Why don't we go.*

END OF AN INDIRECT QUESTION: *He asked what the score was.*

MANY ABBREVIATIONS: For guidelines, see the **abbreviations and acronyms** entry. For the form of a frequently used abbreviation, see the entry under the full name, abbreviation, acronym or term.

INITIALS: *John F. Kennedy, T.S. Eliot* (No space between *T.* and *S.,* to prevent them from being placed on two lines in typesetting.)

Abbreviations using only the initials of a name do not take periods: *JFK, LBJ.*

ELLIPSIS: See **ellipsis.**

ENUMERATIONS: After numbers or letters in enumerating elements of a summary: *1. Wash the car. 2. Clean the basement.* Or: *A. Punctuate properly. B. Write simply.*

PLACEMENT WITH QUOTATION MARKS: Periods always go inside quotation marks. See **quotation marks.**

**question mark (?)** Follow these guidelines:

END OF A DIRECT

QUESTION: *Who started the riot?*

*Did he ask who started the riot?* (The sentence as a whole is a direct question despite the indirect question at the end.)

*You started the riot?* (A question in the form of a declarative statement.)

INTERPOLATED QUESTION: *You told me—Did I hear you correctly?—that you started the riot.*

MULTIPLE QUESTION: Use a single question mark at the end of the full sentence:

*Did you hear him say, "What right have you to ask about the riot?"*

*Did he plan the riot, employ assistants, and give the signal to begin?*

Or, to cause full stops and throw emphasis on each element, break into separate sentences: *Did he plan the riot? Employ assistants? Give the signal to begin?*

CAUTION: Do not use question marks to indicate the end of indirect questions:

*He asked who started the riot. To ask why the riot started is unnecessary. I want to know what the cause of the riot was. How foolish it is to ask what caused the riot.*

QUESTION AND ANSWER FORMAT: Do not

use quotation marks. Paragraph each speaker's words:

*Q: Where did you keep it?*
*A: In a little tin box.*

PLACEMENT WITH QUOTATION MARKS: Inside or outside, depending on the meaning:

*Who wrote "Gone With the Wind"?*

*He asked, "How long will it take?"*

MISCELLANEOUS: The question mark supersedes the comma that normally is used when supplying attribution for a quotation: *"Who is there?" she asked.*

**quotation marks (" ")**
The basic guidelines for open-quote marks (") and close-quote marks ("):

FOR DIRECT QUOTATIONS: To surround the exact words of a speaker or writer when reported in a story:

*"I have no intention of staying," he replied.*

*"I do not object," he said, "to the tenor of the report."*

*Franklin said, "A penny saved is a penny earned."*

*A speculator said the practice is "too conservative for inflationary times."*

RUNNING QUOTATIONS: If a full paragraph of

quoted material is followed by a paragraph that continues the quotation, do not put close-quote marks at the end of the first paragraph. Do, however, put open-quote marks at the start of the second paragraph. Continue in this fashion for any succeeding paragraphs, using close-quote marks only at the end of the quoted material.

If a paragraph does not start with quotation marks but ends with a quotation that is continued in the next paragraph, do not use close-quote marks at the end of the introductory paragraph if the quoted material constitutes a full sentence. Use close-quote marks, however, if the quoted material does not constitute a full sentence. For example:

*He said, "I am shocked and horrified by the incident.*

*"I am so horrified, in fact, that I will ask for the death penalty."*

But: *He said he was "shocked and horrified by the incident."*

*"I am so horrified, in fact, that I will ask for the death penalty," he said.*

DIALOGUE OR CONVERSATION: Each person's words, no matter how brief, are placed in a separate paragraph, with quotation marks at the beginning and the end of each person's speech:

*"Will you go?"*
*"Yes."*
*"When?"*
*"Thursday."*

NOT IN Q-and-A: Quotation marks are not required in formats that identify questions and answers by *Q:* and *A:*. See the **question mark** entry for example.

NOT IN TEXTS: Quotation marks are not required in full texts, condensed texts or textual excerpts. See **ellipsis.**

COMPOSITION TITLES: See the **composition titles** entry for guidelines on the use of quotation marks in book titles, movie titles, etc.

NICKNAMES: See the **nicknames** entry.

IRONY: Put quotation marks around a word or words used in an ironical sense: *The "debate" turned into a free-for-all.*

UNFAMILIAR TERMS: A word or words being introduced to readers may be placed in quotation marks on first reference:

*Broadcast frequencies are measured in "kilohertz."*

Do not put subsequent references to *kilohertz* in quotation marks.

See the **foreign words** entry.

AVOID UNNECESSARY FRAGMENTS: Do not use quotation marks to report a few ordinary words that a speaker or writer has used:

Wrong: *The senator said he would "go home to Michigan" if he lost the election.*

Right: *The senator said he would go home to Michigan if he lost the election.*

PARTIAL QUOTES: When a partial quote is used, do not put quotation marks around words that the speaker could not have used.

Suppose the individual said, *"I am horrified at your slovenly manners."*

Wrong: *She said she "was horrified at their slovenly manners."*

Right: *She said she was horrified at their "slovenly manners."*

Better when practical: Use the full quote.

QUOTES WITHIN QUOTES: Alternate between double quotation marks ("or") and single marks ('or'):

*She said, "I quote from his letter, 'I agree with Kipling that "the female of the species is more deadly than the male," but the phenomenon is not an unchangeable law of nature,' a remark he did not explain."*

Use three marks together if two quoted elements end at the same time: *She said, "He told me, 'I love you.'"*

PLACEMENT WITH OTHER PUNCTUATION: Follow these long-established printers' rules:

—The period and the comma always go within the quotation marks.

—The dash, the semicolon, the question mark and the exclamation point go within the quotation marks when they apply to the quoted matter only. They go outside when they apply to the whole sentence.

See **comma.**

**semicolon (;)** In general, use the semicolon to indicate a greater separation of thought and information than a comma can convey but less than the separation that a period implies.

The basic guidelines:

TO CLARIFY A SERIES: Use semicolons to separate elements of a series when individual segments contain material that also must be set off by commas:

*He leaves a son, John Smith of Chicago; three daughters,*

*Jane Smith of Wichita, Kan., Mary Smith of Denver, and Susan, wife of William Kingsbury of Boston; and a sister, Martha, wife of Robert Warren of Omaha, Neb.*

Note that the semicolon is used before the final *and* in such a series.

Another application of this principle may be seen in the cross-references at the end of entries in this book. Because some entries themselves have a comma, a semicolon is used to separate references to multiple entries, as in: *See the* **felon, misdemeanor** *entry;* **pardon, parole, probation;** *and* **prison, jail.**

See the **dash** entry for a different type of connection that uses dashes to avoid multiple commas.

TO LINK INDEPENDENT CLAUSES: Use a semicolon when a coordinating conjunction such as *and, but* or *for* is not present: *The package was due last week; it arrived today.*

If a coordinating conjunction is present, use a semicolon before it only if extensive punctuation also is required in one or more of the individual clauses: *They pulled their boats from the water, sandbagged the retaining walls, and boarded up the windows; but even with these precautions, the island was hard-hit by the hurricane.*

Unless a particular literary effect is desired, however, the better approach in these circumstances is to break the independent clauses into separate sentences.

PLACEMENT WITH QUOTES: Place semicolons outside quotation marks.

# A GUIDE TO COMPUTER TERMS

Computers have rapidly reached a point where they affect every aspect of living. The following defines and gives correct spellings for common computer terms. Also listed are jargon words and terms to be avoided.

# Computer Terms

**AC** An abbreviation for *alternating current.* Spell out.

**ADP** An abbreviation for *automatic data processing.* Spell out.

**AI** An abbreviation for *artificial intelligence.* Spell out.

**alphanumeric** (adj) A term for information composed of letters, symbols and numerals.

**ASCII** An acronym for *American Standard for Computer Information Interchange.* It is used for communications among most computers and is usually sent in a seven-bit word length.

**asynchronous, asynchronous communication** Computer activity that has no time or schedule control but in which the comple-

tion of one task is followed by the start of another. See **synchronous, synchronous communication.**

**analog** Not *analogue. Analog* computers work like an electrical slide rule. They are very fast but do not have the capability of storing large amounts of data or the logical facilities of a digital computer. *Analog* computers were the starting point of the modern computer.

**ANSI** Abbreviation for *American National Standards Institute.* Spell out on first reference. Use of the term *ANSI COBOL* or *ANS COBOL* is incorrect. Spell out the name *American National Standards COBOL.* See **COBOL.**

**answerback** (n.) The response of one computer to another saying it has received data from the other.

**artificial intelligence** A computer that thinks like a human. Currently, computers cannot apply experience, logic, and prediction to problem solving. They act only on instructions either from the program or from the user.

**assembler** A type of program. Do not use *assembler program,* which is redundant.

**assembler instruction, assembler language** Do not use *assembly.* A system of putting together a program.

**assembler language** Lowercase when this term is used as the shortened, informal name of a particular *assembler language* or when referring to the language in general. Use initial capitals when this term is part of the complete formal name of a language.

**async** Jargon for *asynchronous.* Avoid.

**auto-answer** Avoid. Use *automatic calling* for the noun, *calls automatically* for the verb.

**auxiliary storage** Means data storage other than main memory, such as that on a disk storage unit.

**BASIC** A programming language. Acronym for *Beginners' All-Purpose Symbolic Instruction Code.* Use of acronym on first reference is acceptable if it is identified as a programming language. For example: *That model of a personal computer uses the programming language, BASIC.*

**batch processing** (n.) **batch-processing** (adj.) A method of processing data in chunks. Information and instructions are put into the computer for handling as a single unit.

**baud** A unit used to measure speed of transmission based on the number of bits sent per second.

**big iron** Jargon for large, mainframe computers. Avoid.

**binary digit** Can be abbreviated as *bit* on first reference.

**bit** Acceptable on all references as an acronym for *binary digit.* Actual data transmitted takes the form of electrical impulses. These can be thought of as either *on* or *off* or *1 and 0.* The pulses are bits.

**boot, reboot** Start or restart a computer program with a set series of instructions telling the machine to, in turn, call up other instructions and follow them. It comes from the phrase *picking himself up by his own bootstraps.*

**BPI** Abbreviation for *bytes per inch.* Spell out on first reference.

**bpi** Abbreviation for *bits per inch.* Spell out on first reference.

**BPS** Abbreviation for *bytes per second.* Spell out on first reference.

**bps** Abbreviation for *bits per second.* Spell out on first reference.

**breadboard** An experimental model of any electronic device. The term is derived from the time when circuit prototypes were laid out on a breadboard-sized piece of wood.

**bubble memory** A storage device that does not lose data when power is turned off.

**buffer** Generally a device used to temporarily store information being transferred from one unit to another. The purpose of a *buffer* is to compensate between different speeds of the exchanging units. *Buffers* may be between memory and an output inside a computer, between two computers or between a computer and a printer.

**bug** (n.) Jargon for an error in the system. Avoid.

**bulletin board** In videotex, a bulletin board consists of public messages contributed by individual computer users. The messages can be read by anyone connected to the system.

**button** Use *key.*

**byte** A unit of storage usually the size of one character of information.

**cabletext** Distribution of data and graphics via a cable TV system.

**central processing unit** The nerve center of a computer. The part of the computer that actually processes data being put in or taken out.

**chip** A semiconductor containing interconnected electronic circuits and devices that all together perform specific tasks for a computer.

**clock** A computer clock provides pulses at fixed intervals controlling the activities of the computer.

**COBOL** A programming language. Acronym for *Common Business-Oriented Language*. Use of *COBOL* on first reference is acceptable if identified as a programming language.

**CD-ROM** An acronym for a *compact disk* acting as a *read-only-memory* device.

**computer-aided** (adj.)

**CAD** An acronym for *computer-aided design*. Spell out on the first reference.

**CADAM** An acronym for *Computer-Graphics Augmented Design and Manufac-turing*, a trademark of the Lockheed Corp. Do not confuse with the generic term *CAD/CAM*. Spell out on first reference.

**CAD/CAM** An acronym for *computer aided design/ computer aided manufacture*. Spell out on first reference.

**core, core storage** The main memory of the computer. The term is based on the use of ferrite cores capable of holding a magnetic charge. These are no longer used.

**CP/M** Abbreviation for *Control Program for Microcomputer*. A general purpose operating system for 8- and 16-bit microcomputers. It was the first disk-based-system software product designed for microcomputers and is a trademark of the Digital Research Corp.

**console** Do not use interchangeably with *station* or *terminal*. A *console* is usually a controlling unit of the computer used by programmers and technicians to maintain or make changes in the programming and operation.

**cps** Abbreviation for *characters per second*. Spell out on first reference.

**CPU** Abbreviation for *central processing unit*. Do not use. See **central processing unit**. For full-size computers, *central processing unit* is often synonymous with *mainframe*.

**CRT** Abbreviation for *cathode ray tube*. Do not use. *CRT* is not synonymous with *terminal, workstation* or *display*. It is only the tube on which there is a display.

**cursor** (n.) A flashing square, underline or similar display on the screen indicating the point at which the next character typed will appear.

**daisy printwheel** (n.) **daisywheel** (adj.) **daisywheel printer** (n.) A wheel on which characters are arranged in a circular pattern. Used in high-speed printers.

**DASD** Acronym for *direct access storage device*. Spell out. For second reference, *storage unit* or *disk storage unit* is acceptable.

**data bank** (n. and adj.) A storage system for large amounts of information.

**data communication** Not *data communications*.

**data processing** (n. and adj.) Do not hyphenate the adjective.

**DC** Abbreviation for *direct current* or *data communication*. Spell out.

**debug** (v.) Jargon for removing problems from the system. Avoid.

**diagnostic** Do not use this word alone to mean *diagnostic message, diagnostic program* or *diagnostic test*. Running a *diagnostic program* finds out if the computer is performing properly and if not, why.

**digital** A computer that uses numbers to perform logical and numerical calculations, usually in a binary form.

**direct access** (n.) **direct-access** (adj.) The operator has the ability to issue instructions and retrieve infor-

**mation** without having to go through any other system.

**disk** Not *disc*. Means *hard disk, fixed disk* or *magnetic disk storage device*. Not an abbreviation for *diskette*.

**diskette** A generic term that means *floppy diskette*. Not synonymous with *disk*.

**DOS** An acronym for *disk operating system*. Spell out. It is composed of one or more diskettes on which data can be stored and one or more disk drives to read the information stored on the disks.

**dot matrix printer** Synonym for *matrix printer*. Uses pins thrust against the ribbon to make a series of dots in the form of a character.

**duplex** A system that allows simultaneous two-way transmissions.

**end user** (n.) **end-user** (adj.) The individual or organization that actually makes use of the computer to perform specific tasks.

**ergonomics** (n.) A system of adapting work and working conditions to the needs and comfort of the worker.

**error checking** (n.) A part of a computer program that constantly reviews the operation and reports on errors in processing.

**file name** The computer identification of a specific block of information.

**file protection** (n.) A system for preventing access to or change or destruction of a block or blocks of information stored in a computer.

**first generation, second generation, third generation** The first generation computers used electron tubes like the old radio tubes, the second moved to transistors and the third went to semiconductor chips.

**floppy disk** Use *diskette*.

**flowchart** A diagram showing the sequence of operations performed in a computer. It also can be applied to general business and manufacturing operations.

**FORTRAN** A programming language. Acronym for

*Formula Translation.* Use of acronym on first reference is acceptable if it is identified as a programming language.

**front-end processor** See **front-end system.**

**front-end system** Copy preparation terminals, including writing, editing and ad preparation.

**gigabyte** 1,073,741,824 bytes of storage.

**gigo** Acronym for *garbage in, garbage out.* Jargon. Do not use. It means that if flawed data is put into a computer, flawed data will be produced by the computer.

**global search** (n. and adj.) A search that covers all data stored in a computer.

**half-duplex** Capable of sending and receiving transmissions but not simultaneously.

**halt** A computer program comes to a stop while trying to perform a task. Usually the program can be resumed after being *booted.*

**hard copy** Use *copy.*

**hard disk** Use *disk.*

**hardware** The physical equipment of a computer. The actual wires, disks, chips, circuit boards and other devices.

**holograph** A three-dimensional image generated by a computer.

**information industry** Preferred term for the data processing industry.

**information processing** Should be used when referring to both data and word processing.

**input** (n.) Do not use as a verb.

**integrated circuit** A circuit containing interconnected electronic circuits and devices formed on a single body of a semiconductor. See **chip** and **semiconductor.**

**intelligent terminal** A programmable terminal.

**interface** (n. and adj.) Acceptable only when a more specific word is not available. Do not use as a verb.

**I/O** Abbreviation for *input/output*. Spell out.

**IPL** Abbreviation for *initial program load*. Do not use as a verb. Use: *The systems engineer loaded the initial program.*

**JCL** Abbreviation for *job control language*. Spell out.

**K** Abbreviation for *kilobyte*. It means 1,024 bytes. Similarly, *64k* means 64 times 1,024 bytes or 65,536 bytes, not 64,000. Leave no space between *K* and the preceding number, as in *128K of storage*. The abbreviation *K* should not be used to mean 1,000 as in *$25k*.

**KB** Another abbreviation for kilobyte. *K* is preferred.

**keyboard**

**keypad**

**keypunch** Do not use *keypunch* in the name of a device designated as *card punch*.

**kilobyte** It is 1,024 bytes. Abbreviations are *K* or *KB*. Leave no space between *K* or *KB* and the preceding number, as in *128K of storage*.

**LAN** Acronym for *local area network*. Spell out. An interconnected group of personal computers and a main computer.

**laser** Acronym for *light amplification by stimulated emission or radiation*. Acceptable in all references.

**log off** (v.) **log-off** (n. and adj.) **log on** (v.) **log-on** (n. and adj.) A process by which a person identifies himself to the computer to gain admission to it. An individual who wants to use the computer must type a code on a terminal keyboard. To log off, another code is typed.

**MIS** An acronym for *management information system(s)*. Spell out. A system designed specifically to help in management decision making. It may also perform routine processing.

**mainframe** A full-size central computer. Also the central processing unit of a computer system.

**main memory** The internal memory of a computer. The direct access storage of the computer as opposed to peripheral storage units such as disks. *Main memory* is often synonymous with *random access memory.*

**MB** Abbreviation for *megabyte,* which is 1,048,576 bytes. Similarly, *5MB* means five times 1,048,576, not 5,000,000. Leave no space between *MB* and the preceding number, as in *5MB of storage.*

**megabyte** It is 1,048,576 bytes. Abbreviation is *MB.* Leave no space between *MB* and the preceding number, as in *5MB of storage.*

**menu** A display of a list of options on a terminal screen of tasks that can be performed by the terminal or the computer.

**microcomputer** A very small computer that has a processor, a small number of terminals and a storage system. Primarily used as a personal computer or for a small office system. Storage generally is less than that of a minicomputer.

**microfiche** A small sheet of microfilm on which can be stored a number of pages of documents.

**microfilm** A film on which documents are photographed in reduced size.

**microprocessor** The processor of a microcomputer.

**microsecond** One-millionth of a second.

**millisecond** One-thousandth of a second.

**minicomputer** A compact computer with greater storage and processing capacity and capable of handling more terminals than a *microcomputer.*

**mips** Acronym for *million instructions per second.* Spell out on first reference.

**modem** Literally: *modulate, demodulate.* A device that allows computers to communicate with a central data base via a phone line.

**MOS** Abbreviation for *metal-oxide semiconductor.*

**multiplexer** A system for transmitting or receiving simultaneously two or more signals over a single circuit.

**MDS** An acronym for *multipoint distribution system*. Transmission by microwave, usually for pay television. Range is about 25 miles.

**multiprocessor** Two or more processors linked to a central unit that assigns work.

**nanosecond** One-billionth of a second.

**network architecture** The basic layout of a computer and its attached systems such as terminals and the paths among them.

**non-volatile** In computer terminology, this means it will not be destroyed if the machine loses power. *A bubble memory is non-volatile.*

**OCR** Abbreviation for *optical character reader* or *optical character recognition*. Spell out. An optical character reader is a system for putting information into a computer from a printed page.

**offline, online** Usually a storage or processing system not directly accessible in an *offline* system. An *online* system has information storage

and processing immediately accessible by the user.

**output** (n.) Do not use as a verb.

**parity** A check of computer word length in transmissions between two computers. *Parity* is either odd or even. For proper transmission and receipt, the computers must have the same *parity*.

**PBX** Abbreviation for *private branch exchange*. Spell out. A *private branch exchange* is a telephone system within an organization and owned by the organization. It usually is operated by a computer and connects to regular telephone company lines for outside calls.

**peripheral** (n.) (adj.) Equipment and machines that can be connected to a computer. Examples include disk systems, buffers, special input and output devices, and terminals.

**personal computer** A version of a microcomputer designed for individual use. They vary greatly in size and capacity. Do not use the abbreviation *PC.*

**picosecond**    One-trillionth of a second.

**prioritize** Never. Use *set priorities* instead.

**PROM** An acronym for *programmable read-only memory*. Spell out. See **ROM**.

**RAM** An acronym for *random access memory*. Spell out. An area of computer memory that can be manipulated by the user.

**real time** (n.) **real-time** (adj.) Instantaneous. Used to describe computers that have no delay in receiving an instruction and processing it. Analog computers are *real-time* computers.

**ROM** An acronym for *read only memory*. Spell out. An area of computer memory where operating instructions and other programs reside permanently. Programs in this area of the computer can be activated, but not altered by the user.

**semiconductor** A substance such as silicon that has poor conductivity at low temperatures but which has conductivity improved by minute additions of voltage. Semiconductors form the basis of transistors and computer chips.

**sign off, sign on** (v.), **sign-off, sign-on** (n. and adj.) See **log off.**

**stand-alone** (adj.) Not dependent on a main computer for processing. Many personal computers are used in a stand-alone situation.

**synchronous, synchronous communication** Computer activity that is controlled by time and schedule. The task cannot be performed except on a strict schedule.

**telecommunication** (n. and adj.) The transmission of information over radio waves, microwaves, optical fibers or wires.

**teletext** A one-way system that transmits text material or graphics via a TV or FM broadcast signal or cable TV system. User can select material desired but cannot communicate with other users.

**throughput** The productivity of a computer. The

number of functions it can handle in a specified time.

**tie line** A direct telephone line not dependent on dialing a telephone company assigned number. It also may be a line that is activated by just picking up the receiver.

**time sharing** A system in which a computer is required to work on a variety of operations concurrently. The computer goes from one instruction to another, performing each task in sequence. Some systems also are given priorities to certain tasks and do them on demand without regard to sequence. Time sharing is common when a number of companies or divisions of a company use the same computer.

**Touch-Tone** A trademark of AT&T.

**user friendly** Avoid. For example: *The system is easy to use,* not *the system is user friendly.*

**utilize** Avoid. *Use* is almost always the better word.

**V** Abbreviation for *volt.* Spell out.

**VDT** Abbreviation for *visual display terminal,* commonly used term in the U.S. Spell out.

**VDU** Abbreviation for *visual display unit,* commonly used term in Australia, Canada and Europe. Spell out.

**videotex** Not *videotext.* The generic term for two-way interactive data systems that transmit text and sometimes graphics via telephone lines or cable. User can specify desired information and communicate with host computer or other users through terminal keyboard.

**word** When used in referring to computers, a *word* is a basic unit of data in computer memory. A *word* consists of a predetermined number of characters or bits. *Word* length is seven bits, a 24-bit *word.*

**word processing** (adj.) Do not hyphenate the adjective.

# BIBLIOGRAPHY

Following are reference books used in the preparation of The Associated Press Stylebook. They are the accepted reference sources for material not covered by the Stylebook.

**First reference for spelling, style, usage and foreign geographic names:**

*Webster's New World Dictionary of the American Language,* Second College Edition; Prentice Hall Press, Division of Simon & Schuster, Inc., New York.

**Second reference for spelling, style and usage:**

*Webster's Third New International Dictionary of the English Language,* Unabridged; G. & C. Merriam Co., Springfield, Mass.

**Second reference for foreign geographic names:**

*National Geographic Atlas of the World,* National Geographic Society, Washington, D.C.

**First reference for place names in the 50 states:**

*U.S. Postal Service Directory of Post Offices;* U.S. Postal Service, Washington, D.C.

**For aircraft names:**

*Jane's All the World's Aircraft;* Jane's Yearbooks, London, and Franklin Watts Inc., New York.

**For military ships:**

*Jane's Fighting Ships;* Jane's Yearbooks, London, and Franklin Watts Inc., New York.

**For non-military ships:**

*Lloyd's Register of Shipping;* Lloyd's Register of Shipping Trust Corp. Ltd., London.

**For railroads:**
*Official Railway Guide—Freight Service,* and *Official Railway Guide—Passenger Service, Travel Edition;* Official Railway Guide, New York.

**For federal government questions:**
*Official Congressional Directory;* U.S. Government Printing Office, Washington, D.C.

**For foreign government questions:**
*Political Handbook of the World;* McGraw-Hill Book Co., New York.

**For the formal name of a business:**
*Standard & Poor's Register of Corporations, Directors and Executives;* Standard & Poor's Corp., New York.

**For religion questions:**
*Handbook of Denominations in the United States;* Abingdon Press, Nashville, Tenn., and New York.
*Yearbook of American and Canadian Churches;* Abingdon Press, Nashville, Tenn., and New York, for the National Council of Churches of Christ in the U.S.A., New York.

Other references consulted in the preparation of the AP Stylebook:

Bernstein, Theodore M. *The Careful Writer: A Modern Guide to English Usage.* Atheneum, 1965.

Bernstein, Theodore M. *More Language That Needs Watching.* Channel Press, 1962.

Bernstein, Theodore M. *Watch Your Language.* Atheneum, 1958.

*The Chicago Manual of Style,* 13th Edition. University of Chicago Press, 1982.

Follett, Wilson (edited and completed by Jacques Barzun). *Modern American Usage.* Hill & Wang, 1966.

Fowler, H. W. *A Dictionary of Modern English Usage.* Oxford University Press, 1965.

Morris, William and Morris, Mary. Harper *Dictionary of Contemporary Usage.* Harper & Row, 1975.

Shaw, Harry. *Dictionary of Problem Words & Expressions.* McGraw-Hill Book Co., 1975.

Skillin, Marjorie E. and Gay, Robert M. *Words Into Type*. Prentice-Hall Inc., 1974.

Strunk, William Jr. and White, E. B. *The Elements of Style*, Second Edition. The Macmillan Co., 1972.

Also consulted were the stylebooks of the Boston Globe, Indianapolis News, Kansas City Star, Los Angeles Times, Miami Herald, Milwaukee Journal, Milwaukee Sentinel, Newsday, New York Times, Wilmington (Del.) News-Journal, and the U.S. Government Printing Office.

# LIBEL MANUAL

# FOREWORD

What follows is not a textbook on libel. It is a guide for The Associated Press staff. It explains fundamental principles in libel for working writers and editors.

This manual will make no reader an expert on libel. It will, we hope, make everyone aware of what libel is and how to avoid it.

Underlying all the guidance in this book is one basic rule for the AP staff: If a legal problem develops with a story, or if guidance is needed in the handling of a story, consult the General Desk. Nothing in the manual alters this rule.

As is the case in other fields of the law, the law of libel is not static. We have seen dramatic changes in the past 20 years—not all in the same direction. And the new interpretations go on even as this is written.

What does not change is our promise to ourselves to be accurate and to be fair.

For his help with this manual we are indebted to retired General News Editor Samuel G. Blackman.

LOUIS D. BOCCARDI
President and
General Manager

## Chapter 1

# INTRODUCTION

Associate Justice John Marshall Harlan remarked that "the law of libel has changed substantially since the early days of the Republic."

And it has changed substantially since he made that observation more than a decade ago. Recent years have seen the Supreme Court of the United States decide several cases that made headlines and truly can be called landmarks.

But the working journalist remembers: The news stories which generate the most claims of injury to reputation—the basis of libel—are run-of-the-mill. Perhaps 95 of 100 libel suits are in that category and result from publication of charges of crime, immorality, incompetence or inefficiency.

A Harvard Nieman report makes the point: "The gee-whiz, slam-bang stories usually aren't the ones that generate libel, but the innocent-appearing, potentially treacherous minor yarns from police courts and traffic cases, from routine meetings and from business reports."

Most of these suits based on relatively minor stories result from factual error or inexact language—for example, getting the plea wrong or making it appear that all defendants in a case face identical charges.

Libel even lurks in such innocent-appearing stories as birth notices and engagements. The fact that some New York newspapers had to defend suits recently for such announcements illustrates the care and concern required in every editorial department.

Turner Catledge, retired managing editor of The New York Times, says in his book, "My Life and the Times," that he learned over the years that newspapers must be extremely careful in checking engagement announcements. He noted that "sometimes people will call in the engagement of two people who hate each other, as a practical joke."

In short, there is no substitute for accuracy. But, of course, this does not mean that accurately reporting libelous assertions automatically absolves the journalist of culpability.

Accurate reporting will not prevent libel if there is no privilege, either the constitutional privilege or the fair report privilege.

A fair and impartial report of judicial, legislative and other public and official proceedings is privileged—that is, not actionable for libel. But it is important to know, for instance, what constitutes judicial action. In many states there is no privilege to report the filing of the summons and complaint in a civil suit until there has been some judicial action.

Many libel suits occur in the handling of court and police news, especially criminal courts. Problems can arise in stories about crime and in identifying a suspect where there has been no arrest or where no charge has been made.

Don't be deluded into thinking a safe approach is to eliminate the subject's name. If the description—physical or otherwise—readily identifies him to those in his immediate area, the story has, in effect, named him.

When accusations are made against a person, it is always well to try for balancing comment. The reply must have some relation to the original charges. Irrelevant countercharges can lead to problems with the person who made the first accusation.

The chief causes of libel suits are carelessness, misunderstanding of the law of libel, limitations of the defense of privilege (including the First Amendment privilege) and the extent to which developments may be reported in arrests. These are discussed in detail in this manual, which is "must" reading for every Associated Press staff member. It should be reviewed periodically.

## Chapter 2

## LIBEL, DEFENSES and PRIVILEGE

Libel is injury to reputation.

Words, pictures or cartoons that expose a person to public hatred, shame, disgrace or ridicule, or induce an ill opinion of a person are libelous.

Actions for civil libel result mainly from news stories that allege crime, fraud, dishonesty, immoral or dishonorable conduct, or stories that defame the subject professionally, causing financial loss either personally or to a business.

There is only one complete and unconditional defense to a civil action for libel: that the facts stated are PROVABLY TRUE. (Note well that word, PROVABLY.) Quoting someone correctly is not enough. The important thing is to be able to satisfy a jury that the libelous statement is substantially correct.

A second important defense is PRIVILEGE. Privilege is one of two kinds—absolute and qualified.

Absolute privilege means that certain people in some circumstances can state, without fear of being sued for libel, material which may be false, malicious and damaging. These circumstances include judicial, legislative, public and official proceedings and the contents of most public records.

The doctrine of absolute privilege is founded on the fact that on certain occasions the public interest requires that some individuals be exempted from legal liability for what they say.

Remarks by a member of a legislative body in the discharge of official duties are not actionable. Similarly, libelous statements made in the course of legal proceedings by participants are also absolutely privileged, if they are relevant to the issue. Statements containing defamatory matter may be absolutely privileged if publication is required by law.

The interests of society require that judicial, legislative and similar official proceedings be subject to public discussion. To that extent, the rights of the individual about whom damaging statements may be made are subordinated to what are deemed to be the interests of the community.

We have been talking about absolute privilege as it applies to participants in the types of proceedings described here.

As applied to the press, the courts generally have held that privilege is not absolute, but rather is qualified. That means that it can be lost or diluted by how the journalist handles the material.

Privilege can be lost if there are errors in the report of the hearing, or if the plaintiff can show malice on the part of the publication or broadcast outlet.

An exception: Broadcasters have absolute privilege to carry the broadcast statements of political candidates who are given air time under the "equal opportunity" rules.

The two key points are:

1—Does the material at issue come from a privileged circumstance or proceeding?

2—Is the report a fair and accurate summation?

Again, the absolute privilege legislators enjoy—they cannot be sued, for example, for anything said on the floor of the legislature—affords total protection.

The journalist's protection is not as tight. But it is important and substantial and enables the press to report freely on many items of public interest which otherwise would have to go unreported.

The press has a qualified privilege to report that John Doe has been arrested for bank robbery. If the report is fair and accurate, there is no problem.

Statements made outside the court by police or a prosecutor or an attorney may not be privileged unless the circumstances indicate it is an official proceeding. However, some states do extend privilege to these statements if made by specified top officials.

Newspapers and broadcasters often carry accounts going beyond the narrow confines of what is stated in the official charges, taking the risk without malice because they feel the importance of the case and the public interest warrant doing so.

The source of such statements should be specified.

Sometimes there are traps.

In New York and some other states, court rules provide that the papers filed in matrimonial actions are sealed and thus not open to inspection by the general public.

But sometimes litigants or their lawyers may slip a copy of the papers to reporters. Publication of the material is dangerous because often the litigants come to terms outside of court and the case never goes to trial. So privilege may never attach to the accusations made in the court papers.

In one such case, the vice president of a company filed suit alleging that he was fired because the newspaper published his wife's charges of infidelity. The newspaper responded that its report was a true and fair account of court proceedings. The New York Court of Appeals rejected that argument on grounds that the law makes details of marital cases secret because spatting spouses frequently make unfounded charges. The newspaper appealed to the Supreme Court of the United States. But it lost.

Unless some other privilege applies, there is danger in carrying a report of court papers that are not available for public inspection by reason of a law, court rule or court order directing that such papers be sealed.

As stated earlier, a fair and accurate report of public and official proceedings is privileged.

There has never been an exact legal definition of what

constitutes an official proceeding. Some cases are obvious—trials, legislative sessions and hearings, etc.

Strictly speaking, conventions of private organizations are not "public and official proceedings" even though they may be forums for discussions of public questions. Hence, statements made on the floor of convention sessions or from speakers' platforms may not be privileged.

Statements made by the president of the United States or a governor in the course of executive proceedings have absolute privilege for the speaker, even if false or defamatory. However, this absolute privilege may not apply to statements having no relation to executive proceedings.

President Kennedy once was asked at a news conference what he was going to do about "two well-known security risks" in the State Department. The reporter gave names when the president asked for them. This was not privileged and many newspapers and radio stations did not carry them. The Associated Press did because it seemed in the public interest to report the incident fully. No suits resulted.

After a civil rights march, George Wallace, then governor of Alabama, appeared on a television show and said some of the marchers were members of Communist and Communist-front organizations. He gave some names, which newspapers carried. Some libel suits resulted.

The courts have ruled that publishing that a person is a Communist is libelous on its face if he is not a Communist.

"The claimed charge that the plaintiff is a Nazi and a Communist is in the same category . . . The current effect of these statements is the decisive test. Whatever doubt there may have been in the past as to the opprobrious effect on the ordinary mind of such a change . . . recent events and legislation make it manifest that to label an attorney a Communist or a Nazi is to taint him with disrepute." (*Levy vs. Gelber, 175 Misc. 746*)

The fact that news comes from official sources does not

eliminate the concern. To say that *a high police official said* means that you are making the accusation. A statement that a crime has been committed and that the police are holding someone for questioning is reasonably safe, because it is provably true. However, there are times when the nature of the crime or the prominence of those involved requires broader treatment. Under those circumstances, the safest guide is whatever past experience has shown as to the responsibility of the source. The source must be trustworthy and certain to stand behind the information given.

## REPETITION OF LIBEL

In reporting the filing of a libel suit, can we report the content of the charge? By so doing, do we compound the libel, even though we quote from the legal complaint?

Ordinarily, a fair and impartial report of the contents of legal papers in a libel action filed in the office of the clerk of the court is privileged. However, many states do not extend privilege to the filing of court actions; in such a case there is no privilege until the case comes to trial or until some other judicial action takes place.

But we have found that it is safe, generally speaking, to repeat the libel in a story based on the filing of a suit.

## FAIR COMMENT AND CRITICISM

The publication of defamatory matter that consists of comment and opinion, as distinguished from fact, with reference to matters of public interest or importance, is covered by the defense of fair comment.

Of course, whatever facts are stated must be true.

The right of fair comment has been summarized as follows:

"Everyone has a right to comment on matters of public interest and concern, provided they do so fairly and with an honest purpose. Such comments or criticism are not libelous, however severe in their terms, unless they are written maliciously. Thus it has been held that books, prints, pictures and statuary publicly exhibited, and the architecture of public buildings, and actors and exhibitors are all the legitimate subjects of newspapers' criticism, and such criticism fairly and honestly made is not libelous, however strong the terms of censure may be." *(Hoeppner vs. Dunkirk Pr. Co., 254 N.Y. 95)*

# CRIMINAL LIBEL

The publication of a libel may result in what is considered a breach of the peace. For that reason, it may constitute a criminal offense. It is unnecessary to review that phase of the law here because the fundamental elements of the crime do not differ substantially from those that give rise to a civil action for damages.

## Chapter 3

# PUBLIC OFFICIALS, PUBLIC FIGURES, PUBLIC ISSUES

In a series of decisions commencing in 1964, the Supreme Court established important First Amendment protections for the press in the libel area.

But in more recent decisions, the tide in libel has been running against the press, particularly in the unrelenting narrowing of the definition of a public figure. This was the single most active area of libel law in the decade of the '70s.

While the full impact of the later decisions is not yet clear, a review of the rulings since the mid-1960s shows the trend.

Three basic cases established important precedents. They did so in a logical progression. The cases were:

—New York Times vs. Sullivan (1964).
—Associated Press vs. Walker (1967).
—Gertz vs. Robert Welch (1974).

In the New York Times case, the Supreme Court ruled in March 1964 that public officials cannot recover damages for a report related to official duties unless they prove actual malice.

To establish actual malice, the official was required to prove that at the time of publication, those responsible for the story knew it was false or published it with reckless disregard of whether it was true or false.

The decision reversed a $500,000 libel verdict returned in Alabama against The New York Times and four black ministers. The court said:

"The constitutional guarantees (the First and 14th Amendments) require, we think, a federal rule that prohibits a public official from recovering damages for a defamatory falsehood relating to his official conduct unless he proves that the statement was made with 'actual malice'—that is, with knowledge that it was false or with reckless disregard of whether it was false or not."

This does not give newspapers absolute immunity against libel suits by officials who are criticized. But it does mean that when a newspaper publishes information about a public official and publishes it without actual malice, it should be spared a damage suit even though some of the information may be wrong.

The court said it considered the case "against the background of a profound national commitment to the principle that debate on public issues should be uninhibited, robust and wide open, and that it may well include vehement, caustic and sometimes unpleasantly sharp attacks on government and public officials."

The ruling in The New York Times case with respect to public officials was extended by the Supreme Court in June 1967 to apply also to public figures.

In so holding, the court reversed a $500,000 libel judgment won by former Maj. Gen. Edwin A. Walker in a Texas state court against The Associated Press.

The AP reported that Walker had "assumed command" of rioters at the University of Mississippi and "led a charge of students against federal marshals" when James H. Meredith was admitted to the university in September 1962. Walker alleged those statements to be false.

The court said: "Under any reasoning, Gen. Walker was a public man in whose public conduct society and the press had a legitimate and substantial interest."

The rulings in The New York Times and The Associated Press cases were constitutional landmark decisions for freedom of the press and speech. They offered safeguards not previously defined. But they did not confer license for defamatory statements or for reckless disregard of the truth.

The AP decision made an additional important distinction.

In the same opinion, the court upheld an award granted Wallace Butts, former athletic director of the University of Georgia, against Curtis Publishing Co. The suit was based on an article in the Saturday Evening Post accusing Butts of giving his football team's strategy secrets to an opposing coach prior to a game between the two schools.

The court found that Butts was a public figure, but said there was a substantial difference between the two cases. Justice Harlan said: "The evidence showed that the Butts story was in no sense 'hot news' and the editors of the magazine recognized the need for a thorough investigation of the serious charges. Elementary precautions were, nevertheless, ignored."

Chief Justice Warren, in a concurring opinion, referred to "slipshod and sketchy investigatory techniques employed to check the veracity of the source." He said the evidence disclosed "reckless disregard for the truth."

The differing rulings in The Associated Press and the Saturday Evening Post cases should be noted carefully. The AP-Walker case was "hot news"; the Post-Butts story was investigative reporting of which journalists are doing more and more.

Extension of the Times rule in one case was based on a column by Drew Pearson which characterized a candidate for the United States Senate as "a former small-time bootlegger." The jury held that the accusation related to the private sector of the candidate's life. Reversing this judgment, the Supreme Court said:

"We therefore hold as a matter of constitutional law that a charge of criminal conduct, no matter how remote in time or place, can never be irrelevant to an official's or a candidate's fitness for office for purposes of application of the 'knowing falsehood or reckless disregard' rule of New York Times vs. Sullivan."

Another case was brought by a Chicago captain of detectives against Time magazine, which had quoted from a report of the U.S. Civil Rights Commission without making clear that the charges of police brutality were those of the complainant whose home was raided and not the independent findings of the commission. The court described the commission's documents as "bristling with ambiguities" and said Time did not engage in a "falsification" sufficient to sustain a finding of actual malice.

The progression of the New York Times, AP and Metromedia cases was interrupted in June 1974 with the Supreme Court's decision in the case of Gertz vs. Robert Welch Inc.

Gertz, a lawyer of prominence in Chicago, had been attacked in a John Birch Society publication as a Communist. There were additional accusations as well.

Gertz sued and the Supreme Court upheld him, ruling that he was neither a public official nor a public figure.

The decision opened the door to giving courts somewhat wider leeway in determining whether someone was a public person.

This case also opened the way to giving state courts the right to assess what standard of liability should be used in testing whether a publication about a private individual is actionable. It insisted, however, that some degree of fault, at least negligence, be shown.

For instance, some state courts have established a negligence standard (whether a reasonable person would have done the same thing as the publisher under the circumstances). The New York courts follow a gross negligence test. Others still observe the actual malice test in suits by private individuals against the press.

Bear in mind that the significance of the Gertz decision

still is being developed, as new cases arise and are adjudicated. But at a minimum it opened the way to judgments the three earlier cases would seem to have barred.

More recently, in the case of Time vs. Firestone, the Supreme Court again appears to have restricted the public figure and public issue standards.

The case stemmed from Time magazine's account of the divorce of Russell and Mary Alice Firestone. The magazine said she had been divorced on grounds of "extreme cruelty and adultery." The court made no finding of adultery. She sued.

She was a prominent social figure in Palm Beach, Fla., and held press conferences in the course of the divorce proceedings. Yet the Supreme Court said she was not a public figure because "she did not assume any role of special prominence in the affairs of society, other than perhaps Palm Beach society, and she did not thrust herself to the forefront of any particular public controversy in order to influence resolution of the issues involved in it."

As in the Gertz case, the decision opened the way to findings within the states involving negligence, a standard less severe than the actual malice standard that was at the base of three earlier landmark cases.

Supreme Court decisions, starting with Gertz and extending through Firestone and more recent cases, have consistently narrowed the class of persons to be treated as public figures under the Times-Sullivan and AP-Walker standards.

Two 1979 rulings by the Supreme Court illustrate the narrowing of the protections that seemed so wide only a few years earlier:

Sen. William Proxmire of Wisconsin was sued for $8 million by Ronald Hutchinson, a research scientist who had received several public grants, including one for $50,000. Proxmire gave Hutchinson a "Golden Fleece" award, saying Hutchinson "has made a fortune from his monkeys and in the process made a monkey of the American taxpayer." Hutchinson sued. The Supreme Court found that, despite the receipt of substantial public funds, Hutchinson was not a public figure. The court also ruled that Proxmire's news release was not protected by congressional immunity.

Ilya Wolston pleaded guilty in 1957 to criminal contempt for failing to appear before a grand jury investigating espionage. A book published in 1974 referred to these events. Wolston alleged that he had been libeled. In ruling on Wolston vs. Reader's Digest, the Supreme Court said that he was not a public figure. The court said people convicted of crimes do not automatically become public figures. Wolston, the court said, was thrust into the public spotlight unwillingly.

In effect, the court extended the Firestone concept of unwilling notoriety to criminal as well as civil cases.

Thus the pattern through Gertz, Firestone, Proxmire and Reader's Digest is clear. The Times rule has been left standing but it is tougher and tougher to get in under it.

The court is rejecting the notion that a person can be a public figure simply because of the events that led to the story at issue. The courts are saying that public figure means people who seek the limelight, who inject themselves into public debate, etc. The courts are saying that involvement in a crime, even a newsworthy one, does not make one a public figure.

This means that the broad "public official" and "public figure" protections that came out of the Times and AP cases remain, but for shrinking numbers of people who are written about.

At the same time, the "reckless disregard of the truth" and "knowing falsity" standards of the Times decision also slip away, becoming applicable to fewer people as the public figure definition narrows.

And those standards are being replaced in state after state with simple negligence standards. In other words, the plaintiff, now adjudged to be a private citizen because of the recent rulings, must now prove only that the press was negligent, not reckless.

The difference is more than semantic. This development suggests that press lawyers will be relying more on some of the old standbys as defenses—plaintiff's inability to prove falsity, privilege, fair comment—and this puts the ball right back with editors and reporters.

The Supreme Court in 1986 held, however, in Philadelphia Newspapers vs. Hepps, that, at least where a newspaper has published statements on a matter of public concern, a private figure plaintiff cannot prevail without showing the statements at issue are false. This case provides that the common law rule requiring a defendant to prove truth is supplanted by a constitutional requirement that the plaintiff demonstrate falsity when the statements involved are of public concern.

Another recent Supreme Court decision that provoked wide press controversy came in the case of Herbert vs. Lando.

The court ruled in 1979 that retired Army Lt. Col. Anthony Herbert, a Vietnam veteran, had the right to inquire into the editing process of a CBS "60 Minutes" segment, produced by Barry Lando, which provoked his suit. Herbert had claimed the right to do this so that he could establish actual malice.

The decision formalizes and calls attention to something that was at least implicit in the Times case, namely, that a plaintiff had the right to try to prove the press was reckless or even knew that what it was printing was a lie. How else could this be done except through inquiry about a reporter's or editor's state of mind?

So the ruling reminds plaintiffs' lawyers that they can do

this and will, no doubt, be responsible for far more of this kind of inquiry than the press has had to face before.

A crucial test will be how far judges will let plaintiffs' lawyers range in their discovery efforts. Will they let the plaintiff widen the embrace of inquiry into stories other than the one at issue? Will they let the plaintiff rummage about the news room, probing unrelated news judgments, examining the handling of other unrelated stories, demanding to know why this investigative piece survived while that one died quietly on the kill hook?

That the questions are being prompted by the Herbert-Lando ruling is the best response to those who say that the decision didn't really mean much.

The preliminary answer to these questions appears to be that there has been some widening of this sort of inquiry by plaintiffs newly alerted to this area by the Lando ruling.

The press should be certain that files include contemporaneous memorandums that will testify later to the care taken with the story and the conviction that it was true and fair.

There was a footnote in the Proxmire case which has had a marked effect on the way libel cases are litigated. Footnote 9 questioned the practice of dismissing libel actions early in the course of litigation. The lower courts have paid serious attention to this footnote, with the result that more and more libel actions are being tried before a jury.

In a 1986 decision, Anderson vs. Liberty Lobby, however, the Supreme Court held that summary judgment should be granted in libel actions against public officials and public figures unless the plaintiff can prove actual malice with "convincing clarity" or by "clear and convincing evidence." This rule should facilitate the early dismissal of unmeritorious claims without the expense and burden of proceeding to trial.

The huge jury verdicts that often result have caused much concern among legal commentators and the press. A number of remedies have been proposed, but it remains unclear at this point whether the Supreme Court will take any action to stem the tide of runaway million-dollar jury verdicts of recent years.

An indication that the Supreme Court is facing this problem appeared in its 1984 opinion in Bose vs. Consumers Union. Bose Corp. sued Consumer Reports over its publication of disparaging comments concerning Bose's loudspeaker systems and obtained a damage judgment of about $211,000. The Court of Appeals, after a careful review of the record, reversed. The Supreme Court endorsed this process, underscoring the need for appellate courts in libel cases to make an independent review of the record—a standard of scrutiny that does not apply in most other appeals. For the foreseeable future, the press will continue to rely on the willingness of the appeals courts to overturn excessive jury verdicts.

## SUMMARY OF FIRST AMENDMENT RULES

The gist of the principles established in the cases discussed above may be summarized as follows:

A. The Public Official Rule: the press enjoys a great protection when it covers the affairs of public officials. In order to successfully sue for libel, a public official must prove actual malice. This means the public official must prove that the editor or reporter had knowledge that the facts were false or acted with reckless disregard of the truth.

B. The Public Figure Rule: the rule is the same for public figures and public officials. That is, a public figure must prove actual malice. The problem is that it is very difficult in many cases to predict who will be classified as a public figure. In general, there are two types of public figures:

1. General Purpose Public Figures: this is an individual

who has assumed the role of special prominence in the affairs of society and occupies a position of persuasive power and influence. An example is the entertainer Johnny Carson.

2. Limited Purpose Public Figures: this is a person who has thrust himself or herself into the vortex of a public controversy in an attempt to influence the resolution of the controversy. An example would be a vocal scientist who has lectured and published articles in an attempt to influence a state legislature to ban fluoridation of water.

C. The Private Figure Rule: a private figure is defined in the negative. It is someone who is not a public figure. The rule of law for libel suits brought by private figures varies from state to state. The variations fall into three general categories:

1. A number of states follow the same rule for private figures and public figures. They require private figures to prove actual malice. These states include Alaska, Colorado, Indiana and Michigan.

2. One state, New York, requires private figures to prove that the publisher acted in a "grossly irresponsible manner." To date, no other state has adopted this rule.

3. Most states require private figures to prove only negligence. Negligence is a term of art that is difficult to define. As a rule of thumb, a careless error on the part of the journalist will often be found to constitute negligence.

These distinctions become important after the story has moved on our wires when there is a challenge and we are preparing our legal defenses. These distinctions do not apply in our preparations of stories. We do not have a standard that lets us go easier with ourselves if the story concerns a public official/figure and be tougher on ourselves if it concerns a private figure.

## Chapter 4

# THE RIGHT OF PRIVACY

The right of privacy is a doctrine that has been developing in the past century. It is recognized by statute in only a few states, including New York, but courts increasingly are taking cognizance of it. It is clearly an area to be watched.

The doctrine is based on the idea that a person has the right to be let alone, to live a private life free from publicity.

In 1890, two Boston lawyers wrote in the Harvard Law Review:

"The press is overstepping in every direction the obvious bounds of propriety and decency."

It is of interest that one of those lawyers, who later became Justice Brandeis, said years later in one of his dissents:

"The makers of our Constitution undertook to secure conditions favorable to the pursuit of happiness. They recognized the significance of man's spiritual nature, of his feelings and of his intellect. They knew that only a part of the pain, pleasure and satisfactions of life are to be found in material things. They sought to protect Americans in their beliefs, their thoughts, their emotions and their sensations. They conferred, as against the government, the right to be let alone—the most comprehensive of rights and the right most valued by civilized men." *(Olmstead vs. United States, 277 U.S. 438, 478)*

When a person becomes involved in a news event, voluntarily or involuntarily, he forfeits the right to privacy. Similarly, a person somehow involved in a matter of legitimate public interest, even if not a bona fide spot news event, normally can be written about with safety.

However, this is different from publication of a story or

picture that dredges up the sordid details of a person's past and has no current newsworthiness.

Paul P. Ashley, then president of the Washington State Bar Association, said in a talk on this subject at a meeting of The Associated Press Managing Editors Association:

"The essence of the wrong will be found in crudity, in ruthless exploitation of the woes or other personal affairs of private individuals who have done nothing noteworthy and have not by design or misadventure been involved in an event which tosses them into an arena subject to public gaze."

Here are details of a few cases brought in the name of right of privacy:

—A leading case centering on publication of details of a person's past concerned a man who as a child prodigy in 1910 had attracted national attention. In 1937, The New Yorker magazine published a biographical sketch of the plaintiff. He alleged invasion of privacy.

The court said "he had cloaked himself in obscurity but his subsequent history, containing as it did the answer to the question of whether or not he had fulfilled his early promise, was still a matter of public concern. The article . . . sketched the life of an unusual personality, and it possessed considerable popular news interest."

The court said further:

"We express no comment on whether or not the newsworthiness of the matter printed will always constitute a complete defense. Revelations may be so intimate and so unwarranted in view of the victim's position as to outrage the community's notions of decency. But when focused upon public characters, truthful comments upon dress, speech, habits, and the ordinary aspects of personality will usually not transgress this line. Regrettably or not, the misfortunes and frailties of neighbors and 'public figures' are subjects of considerable interest and discussion to the rest of the population. And when such are the mores of the community, it would be unwise for a court to bar their expression in the newspapers, books, and magazines of the day."

—The unsavory incidents of the past of a former prostitute, who had been tried for murder, acquitted, married and lived a respectable life, were featured in a motion picture. The court ruled that the use of her name in the picture and the statement in advertisements that the story was taken from true incidents in her life violated her right to pursue and obtain happiness.

Some courts have ruled that a person who is recognizable in a picture of a crowd in a public place is not entitled to the right of privacy. But if a camera singled him out for no news-connected reason, then his privacy is invaded, some courts have ruled.

Another example of spot news interest: A child was injured in an auto accident in Alabama. A newspaper took a picture of the scene before the child was removed and ran it. That was spot news. Twenty months later a magazine used the picture to illustrate an article. The magazine was sued and lost the case, the court ruling that 20 months after the accident the child was no longer "in the news."

In another case, a newspaper photographer in search of a picture to illustrate a hot-weather story took a picture of a woman sitting on her front porch. She wore a housedress, her hair in curlers, her feet in thong sandals. The picture was taken from a car parked across the street from the woman's home. She sued, charging invasion of privacy. A court, denying the newspaper's motion for dismissal of the suit, said the scene photographed "was not a particularly newsworthy incident," and the limits of decency were exceeded by "surreptitious" taking and publishing of pictures "in an embarrassing pose."

A woman took her two children to the county fair and went with them into the funhouse. A newspaper photographer took her picture just as a jet of air blew up her dress. She sued, and the Supreme Court of Alabama upheld the damages.

The rules in New York state on the right of privacy that are applicable to unauthorized publication of photographs in a single issue of a newspaper may be summarized generally as follows:

1. The plaintiff may recover damages if the photograph is published in or as part of an advertisement, or for advertising purposes.

2. There is liability if the photograph is used in connection with an article of fiction in any part of a newspaper.

3. There may be no recovery under the statute for publication of a photograph in connection with an article of current news or immediate public interest.

4. Newspapers publish articles that are neither strictly news items nor strictly fictional in character. They are not the responses to an event of peculiarly immediate interest, but though based on fact, are used to satisfy an ever-present educational need. Such articles include, among others, travel stories, stories of distant places, tales of history personages and events, the reproduction of items of past news and surveys of social conditions. These are articles educational and informative in character. As a general rule, such cases are not within the purview of the statute. *(Lahiri vs. Daily Mirror Inc., Misc. Reports, N.Y. 162, p780)*.

The Supreme Court of the United States ruled in January 1967 that the constitutional guarantees of freedom of the press are applicable to invasion-of-privacy cases involving reports of newsworthy matters.

The ruling arose out of a reversal by the Supreme Court of a decision of a New York court that an article with photos in Life magazine reviewing a play, "The Desperate Hours," violated the privacy of a couple who had been held hostage in a real-life incident. In illustrating the article, Life posed the actors in the house where the real family had been held captive.

The family alleged violation of privacy, saying the article gave readers the impression that the play was a true account of their experiences. Life said the article was "basically truthful."

The court said:

"The line between the informing and the entertaining is too elusive for the protection of (freedom of the press). Erroneous statement is no less inevitable in such case than in the case of comment upon public affairs, and in both, if innocent or merely negligent, it must be protected if the freedoms of expression are to have the 'breathing space' that they 'need to survive.'

"We create grave risk of serious impairment of the indispensable service of a free press in a free society if we saddle the press with the impossible burden of verifying to a certainty the facts associated in a news article with a person's name, picture or portrait, particularly as related to non-defamatory matter."

The court added, however, that these constitutional guarantees do not extend to "knowing or reckless falsehood." A newspaper still may be liable for invasion of privacy if the facts of a story are changed deliberately or recklessly, or "fictionalized." As with The New York Times and The Associated Press decisions in the field of libel, the "Desperate Hours" case does not confer a license for defamatory statements or for reckless disregard of the truth.

# Chapter 5

# APPLYING THE RULES

We already have defined libel and explained the defenses available to the press. Let's now look at some applications.

In a society in which standards of right living are recognized by most people, any accusation that a member of society has violated such standards must be injurious. Members of a community establish in the minds of others an estimate of what they are believed to be. Injury to that reputation may mean business, professional or social ruin.

One court decision put the matter this way:

"The law of defamation is concerned only with injuries to one's reputation . . .

"Embarrassment and discomfort no doubt came to her from the publication, as they would to any decent woman under like circumstances. Her own reaction, however, has no bearing upon her reputation. That rests entirely upon the reactions of others. We are unable to find anything in this article which could appreciably injure plaintiff's reputation." *(Kimmerle vs. New York Evening Journal Inc., 262 N.Y. 99)*

The traditional rule was that defamation was concerned only with injuries to one's reputation. That rule was altered in 1974 by the Gertz case, which held that emotional distress is also an element of damages in libel.

In order to be libelous, it is not necessary that a publication impute criminal activity. The following was held to be libelous:

### "Pauper's Grave For Poor Child"

"Unless financial aid is forthcoming immediately, the body of a 4-year-old boy who was run over Tuesday will be interred in Potter's Field, burying ground of the homeless, friendless and penniless, who die or are killed in New York City. The parents of this youngster are in dire financial straits, and at this writing have no alternative but to let their son go to his final rest in a pauper's grave."

The court said:

"It is reasonably clear, therefore, that in some cases it may be a libel if the plaintiff has been written up as an object of pity . . . The reason is that in libel the matter is defamatory not only if it brings a party into hatred, ridicule or contempt by asserting some moral discredit upon his part, but also if it tends to make him be shunned or avoided, although it imputes no moral turpitude to him." *(Katapodis vs. Brooklyn Spectator Inc., 287 N.Y. 17)*

A publication that does not discredit a person as an individual may nonetheless damage a person's professional status.

A story stated that after a man's body had been taken from the water in which he had been swimming, he was pronounced dead by a doctor. Later, the youth was revived. The doctor sued because of the implication that he had been unable to determine whether a person was living or dead.

Similarly, a publication may affect a business.

Companies are naturally sensitive to news stories that reflect on their business prospects and practices. There have been many such news stories in the field of environmental and consumer protection. The issues are complicated, and the legal aspects not always clear. Formal charges and allegations should be reported precisely and fairly.

Likewise, there is no alternative to precision in reporting any criminal charge.

Not only what is written, but the instruments used in transmitting it, must be considered in handling news. It is safer to say *acquitted* or *innocent,* rather than *not guilty,* because of the danger that the negative may be dropped in transmission.

An essential element of an action for libel is that the complainant be identifiable to a third party. Nevertheless, the omission of names will not, in itself, provide a shield against a claim for libel. As was pointed out earlier, there may be enough details for the person to be recognizable.

A story may, by the use of a general description or name, make a libelous charge against an organized group. It is possible that any member of the group could bring an action on the story.

If the material is libelous and not privileged, then the question turns to proof.

Can the substance be established by documents, by testimony from trustworthy persons or by material from privileged sources? Hearsay evidence is not enough. It is not enough to show that somebody gave you the unprivileged information. The issue turns on proof.

Another libel pitfall is the mistaken identity case. There is no complete defense when a newspaper confuses a famous individual with a person bearing a similar name who gets into a scrape. Petty thieves running afoul of the law may give the names of famous people—often old-time athletes—in the hope of getting leniency from a judge.

A few years ago a man charged with a minor crime appeared in Magistrate's Court in New York and gave as his name that of a once-great baseball pitcher. The magistrate gave the prisoner a suspended sentence. The real baseball player was a prosperous auto salesman, who threatened multiple suits when he read the story in the newspapers.

# CLOSED COURTROOMS

In 1980, in Richmond Newspapers vs. Virginia, the Supreme Court ruled that under the First Amendment, criminal trials are presumptively open to the public and the media and may be closed only when it is necessary to protect some interest that outweighs the interest in access. A trial judge must articulate findings, on the record, to support any closure. This decision marked the first time in the nation's history that the right to find out what a branch of government is doing had been afforded direct and specific constitutional protection.

In 1982, in Globe Newspapers vs. Superior Court, the Supreme Court recognized that the constitutional right of access to criminal trials applies even with respect to a sex-offense trial involving a minor victim. The court struck down a statute mandating closure in such cases. While it said that the states have a significant interest in protecting minor victims of sexual assault from the trauma of testifying in open court, the Supreme Court held that trial judges must determine on a case-by-case basis whether this interest outweighs the presumption of openness and stated that any closure order must be "narrowly tailored to protect that interest" without unduly infringing on First Amendment rights.

The Supreme Court further held in 1984 in Press-Enterprise vs. Superior Court that the constitutional right of access to criminal trials encompasses the right to attend jury selection.

In 1986, in a second case called Press-Enterprise vs. Superior Court, the Supreme Court ruled that the First Amendment right to access attaches to preliminary hearings in a criminal case unless specific findings are made on the record to demonstrate that closure is essential to preserve higher values and is narrowly tailored to serve that interest. If the interest asserted is the defendant's right to a fair trial, the preliminary hearing may not be closed unless there is a "substantial probability" that the right to a fair trial will be prejudiced by publicity that closure would prevent and that reasonable alternatives to closure cannot adequately protect the right to a fair trial.

The Associated Press has distributed the following statement to be read in court by its reporters when confronted with an attempt to close a criminal proceeding.

The statement allows the reporter, when permitted to address the court, to state the basic press position and to seek time for counsel to appear to make the legal argument.

The following statement can be read verbatim, although if any parts are not applicable to a specific case they can be changed or omitted.

May it please the Court, I am (name) of The Associated Press (or newspaper). I respectfully request the opportunity to register on the record an objection to the motion to close this proceeding to the public and to representatives of the news media. The Associated Press (or newspaper) requests a hearing at which its counsel may present to the court legal authority and arguments that closure in this case is improper.

The United States Supreme Court has now firmly held that the press and the public have a constitutional right to attend criminal trials and pretrial proceedings and may not be excluded unless the court makes findings on the record that closure is required to preserve higher values and is narrowly tailored to serve that interest. There is, therefore, a presumption of openness which is firmly rooted in the Constitution and essential to proper functioning of the criminal justice system.

The Associated Press (or newspaper) takes the position that the defendant should be required to make the following showing in order to prevail on a motion to close this proceeding:

—First, the defendant must demonstrate that by conducting this proceeding in public the defendant's right to a fair trial will be prejudiced by publicity which closure would prevent. The defendant must demonstrate therefore that disclosures made in this hearing will prejudice the case and that these disclosures would not otherwise be brought to the attention of potential jurors.

—Second, the defendant must demonstrate that none of the alternatives to an order closing this proceeding would effectively protect the right to a fair trial. Among the alternatives available to protect the defendant's rights are: a careful and searching voir dire, continuance, severance, change of venue, peremptory challenges, sequestration and admonition of the jury.

—Third, the defendant must demonstrate that closure will be effective in protecting the right to a fair trial. In the present case there has already been substantial publicity concerning the facts. The defendant must demonstrate that any prejudice to the right of a fair trial would result from publicity given to disclosures made in this proceeding, and not to previously published facts or allegations.

—Finally, the defendant must establish that reasonable alternatives to closure cannot adequately protect the defendant's free trial rights.

The Associated Press (or newspaper) believes that there has been substantial public interest generated by this case. The public has a right to be informed of future developments, and the court should avoid any impression that justice is being carried on in secrecy.

The public has a right to know how the court system is handling criminal matters, what kind of deals may be struck by prosecutors and defense lawyers, what kind of evidence may be kept from the jury, and what sort of police or prosecutorial acts or omissions have occurred. For these reasons, The Associated Press (or newspaper) objects to the motion for closure and respectfully requests a hearing in which it can present full legal arguments and authority.

The Supreme Court has never addressed the question of whether there is a First Amendment right of access to civil trials and pretrial proceedings. Several federal appeals courts, employing the reasoning of the Supreme Court's criminal trial access decisions, have ruled that both civil trials and pretrial proceedings are presumptively open to the press and public.

# PHOTO CAPTIONS

The art of writing captions for LaserPhotos can be elusive to many journalists simply because, for the most part, so little time is spent at it.

But it is no mystery. Adherence to a few basic rules, the mastery of simple mechanical preparations, and a touch of writing flair will result in readable, widely published captions.

## CAPTION CONTENT

The caption's job is to describe and explain the picture to the reader.

The challenge is to do it interestingly, accurately, always in good taste.

A further challenge is to write the caption, whenever appropriate, in a sprightly, lively vein.

An APME Continuing Study Committee put together Ten Tests of a Caption. They are:

1. Is it complete?
2. Does it identify, fully and clearly?
3. Does it tell when?
4. Does it tell where?
5. Does it tell what's in the picture?
6. Does it have the names spelled correctly, with the proper name on the right person?
7. Is it specific?
8. Is it easy to read?

9. Have as many adjectives as possible been removed?
10. Does it suggest another picture?

And rule No. 11, the Cardinal Rule, never, never to be violated:

> *NEVER WRITE A CAPTION*
> *WITHOUT SEEING THE PICTURE.*

## STYLE REQUIREMENTS

Caption style rules that deal with spelling, capitalization, abbreviations, grammar, titles, etc., are precisely the same as for the news wires.

There are some mechanical style requirements for captions alone, however.

Most LaserPhotos will carry a caption setup like this.

**(NY 14) NEW YORK, Feb. 18—WANNA BUY A PUSSYCAT?—Subway riders cuddle kittens found abandoned in a cardboard box on a subway platform in New York Friday. A sign attached to the box read "Kittens For Sale, $2 Each," but the seller was nowhere to be found. The box and its batch of six pussycats were taken to the American Society for the Prevention of Cruelty to Animals shelter in Manhattan. (AP LaserPhoto) (jtm-61405mbr/dns) 1986**

**Figure 1**

The various parts of the caption are as follows:

**(NY 14)** The call letters of the network station where the transmitter is located, and picture number in the station's sequence of offerings on a given day.

**NEW YORK** The name of the city where the picture was

made. Identify the state, too, if there could be doubt about the city's location.

**Feb. 18** The date the picture is transmitted. The time element of when the picture was made should be included in the body of the caption.

**WANNA BUY A PUSSYCAT?** The overline. Just a few bright words to put across the point of the picture, attract the reader's attention, or evoke a smile. Use verbs in overlines, avoid labels and lifeless phrases.

**(AP LaserPhoto)** The credit immediately follows the body of the caption.

**jtm** The initials of the caption writer.

**61405** The day of the week the picture was transmitted —in this case 6 for Friday—and the time the caption was written on a 24-hour clock.

**mbr/dns** The source of the picture—in this case a *member (mbr), The Daily News (dns)*. If the picture is from an AP staff photographer, the photographer's initials should be used. Other possible designations include *handout (ho), stringer (str)*.

**1986** The year of transmission, for library reference.

There are times when the credit *(AP LaserPhoto)* will be carried in a different way. For example: *(Tass photo via AP LaserPhoto), (Hsinhua photo via AP LaserPhoto), (Department of Defense photo via AP LaserPhoto), (NBC-TV photo via AP LaserPhoto),* etc.

These special credit lines are carried at the insistence of the source or because we want to make clear just what the source of the photo was, because of possible influence on its content.

## THE UNDATED CAPTION

When a picture is taken from files, regardless of where that file is—member, stringer or the AP file—use an undated caption.

> **(NY 3-Jan. 6) INDUSTRIALIST DIES—Tom Smith, president of Industrial Industries, died Tuesday in Kansas City where he was attending a convention. He was 68 years old. (AP LaserPhoto) (jcy31040fls) 1985 (EDS: This is a 1983 file picture)**

Note that the caption used on this file photo does not carry a dateline, carries a reference to *files (fls)* as a source, and provides an editor's note telling when the photo was made.

The undated style is used so that there is no confusion about the picture being made on the day of the news event.

## CAPTIONS FOR ADVANCES

Many pictures we transmit on the LaserPhoto network are moved in advance. As with stories, these pictures must carry word to editors regarding publication date.

Captions for AP advances should carry the date and cycle in which the picture will be printed, along with information that will connect the picture to a story in situations in which a story also is provided.

Here is a sample advance caption:

> **(ADVANCE FOR FRIDAY PMS, FEB. 18, WITH STORY SLUGGED BETS BY BURT BERLINER)**
>
> ---
>
> **(NY20-Feb. 12) A BET A DAY KEEPS THE BLAHS AWAY —Suzy Q. Smith cheers her favorite horse and jockey**

on to what she hopes will be a first-place win Saturday at New York's Aqueduct Racetrack. Ms. Smith says betting on the horses brought new excitement into her life. She is one of an increasing number of people who are betting more money despite America's skyrocketing cost of living. (AP LaserPhoto) (rjk71600stf/bb) 1986.

## TRANSMISSION PREPARATION

There are basically two sizes of captions—a long version, which runs along the 10-inch dimension of the print, and a short version, runs along the 8-inch dimension. See **Figures 2** and **3** for examples.

There will be cases in which the print you transmit will be smaller than 8 × 10 inches, generally for mugshots. In such cases, the caption should be measured and written to fit neatly on the picture, as in **Figure 4. Figure 5** shows improper mounting.

On occasion you will want to "combo" pictures, which means setting up two or more small prints in one transmission. Pictures must be the same size if comboed. See **Figure 6** for correct procedure. **Figure 7** shows incorrect mounting.

**Figure 2**

**LONG AND SHORT CAPTIONS**

**Figure 3**

**Figure 4**

Wrong

**Figure 5**

**MUGSHOT CAPTIONS**

**Figure 6**

Wrong

**Figure 7**

**COMBOED CAPTIONS**

When transmitting pictures, always place the photo in the laser transmitter as follows: The 10-inch dimension of the picture should enter the transmitter. Do not insert the 8-inch dimension. The photo image always should face away from you as you insert the print. See **Figure 8**.

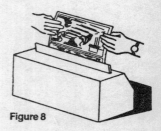

**Figure 8**

# FILING
# THE WIRE

These guidelines seek to help editors at newspapers and AP offices handle copy easily and efficiently.

The three principal objectives of the coding are:

—Assurance that stories will be routed promptly to the proper editor.

—Assurance that directories showing only the first slug line on a story will be as informative as possible.

—The ability to have a computer system automatically link leads, adds, inserts, subs, etc. to previous copy.

## CODING REQUIREMENTS

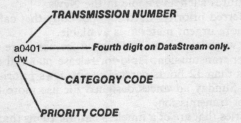

TRANSMISSION NUMBER

a0401 ——————— Fourth digit on DataStream only.
dw

CATEGORY CODE

PRIORITY CODE

Every **transmission number** begins with a letter of the alphabet. The principal letters reserved for nationwide transmissions are:

**a** and **b**—Spot news and/or advances.

**f**—News designed primarily for financial pages.

**s**—Sports copy.

The letter in the transmission number is identified in some technical contexts as a Service Level Designator.

Transmission numbers are placed on stories by computers. The remaining codes described in these pages must be placed on stories by staff members.

**Priority codes** are used by AP bureaus to assure that stories move on the wires in the order of their urgency. At newspapers, the codes can be used by computer systems to determine the order in which stories come to an editor's attention.

The principal priority codes, in order of urgency, and their use:

**f**—Flash, highest priority, seldom used.

**b**—Bulletins, first adds to bulletins, kill notes.

**u**—Urgent, high-priority copy, including all corrections. It must be used on all items that carry an URGENT slug. It also may be used on items that lack this slug but must move on an urgent basis.

**r**—Regular priority: digests, advisories, indexes, digest stories, other major stories that break too late for the digest, special fixtures such as People in the News.

**d**—Deferred priority. Used for spot copy that can be delayed if more urgent material is available.

**a**—For weekday advances designed for use more than 12 hours after transmission. Hold-for-release material sent for use in less than 12 hours carries a spot news priority.

**s**—For Sunday advances designed for use more than 12 hours after transmission.

**w**—Stories that are of a timeless nature. Items that review the history of an event. For example, a list of the number of casualties suffered in World War II by each participating country.

**x,y,z**—For internal routing among AP bureaus.

**Category codes** are designed to help newspapers with computer systems sort copy into the electronic equivalents of putting paper copy on domestic stories in one pile, Washington stories in a second, international stories in a third, etc.

A space appears between the priority code and the category code when a story is transmitted. A space also appears between the two when a story is being edited on the screen of many AP computer terminals. However, some terminals require that there be no space between the two, although the space is inserted at the time of transmission.

The principal category codes and their use:

**a**—Domestic, non-Washington general news items.

**b**—Special events.

**e**—Selected entertainment copy.

**f**—News copy, regardless of dateline, designed primarily for use on financial pages. When a major story of financial interest also moves as part of the general news service, editors should be advised that the same story has been routed to both financial desks and news desks.

**i**—International items, including stories from the United Nations, U.S. possessions, and undated roundups keyed to foreign events.

**l**—Selected "lifestyle" copy.

**n**—Stories of state or regional interest under domestic datelines. If a regional item has a Washington dateline, use the *w* category. If a regional item is designed primarily for financial pages, use the *f* category regardless of the dateline.

**p**—National political copy. (Used in election years only.)

**q**—Use only for the result or period score of a single sports event. The code is designed to help newspaper computer systems build a list of scores or ignore individual scores and wait for transmissions that group them.

**s**—Sports stories, standings, results of more than one event.

**v**—Advisories about stories that may carry any of the category letters. This code is used primarily for news digests, news advisories, lists of transmitted advances and indexes.

**w**—Washington-datelined stories. Change to the *a* or *b* category code if a subsequent lead shifts the dateline to a different city.

## KEYWORD SLUG LINE

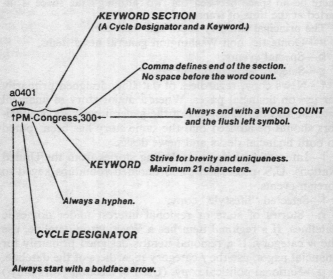

**KEYWORD SECTION**
(A Cycle Designator and a Keyword.)

Comma defines end of the section.
No space before the word count.

Always end with a WORD COUNT
and the flush left symbol.

**KEYWORD**
Strive for brevity and uniqueness.
Maximum 21 characters.

Always a hyphen.

**CYCLE DESIGNATOR**

Always start with a boldface arrow.

Every item transmitted on AP news and sports wires must begin with a **keyword slug line.** There are no exceptions.

Every keyword slug line must have at least a keyword section. Up to three other sections, as shown in examples that follow, are used when necessary.

The commas that appear in the example are critical for operations of many AP computers. On high-speed AP circuits, the commas are replaced by spaces, and all other spaces in the line are eliminated, to conform with industry-wide specifications for automatic routing of copy in newspaper computer systems.

Always end the keyword slug with the flush left symbol. (← or <).

The **keyword section** of the line consists of a cycle designator and a keyword or keywords. A boldface symbol or upperrail ( ↑ or /\ ) precedes the cycle designator. This is followed by the cycle designator, a hyphen and the keyword. A comma marks the end of the section.

Because the keyword section provides the basic identification of a story for automatic linkup routines, it must be repeated in exactly the same form on all subsequent leads, adds, inserts, subs, etc. filed for a story.

There are three **cycle designators:**

↑ **AM**—Indicates that morning newspapers have first use of the story.

↑ **PM**—Indicates that afternoon newspapers have first use of the story.

↑ **BC**—Indicates that the item is for use by either AMs or PMs—immediately if it is a spot item, or on the publication date if it is an advance.

The *BC*-designation is used on all Sunday advances.

The **keyword** should provide an indication of the story's content.

The following standards apply:

—Overall, the keyword should not exceed a total of 21 letters and/or figures. (Rule of thumb: *If you have to count the letters, the keyword is too long.)*

—Commonly accepted abbreviations and acronyms such as *Scotus* for Supreme Court of the United States and *Xgr* for legislature are encouraged where applicable.

Provide a **word count** estimate at the end of the keyword slug line.

When using a CRT to edit or write a story, use the word count key or obtain the estimate by counting the number of lines and multiplying by 10. Include lines that have only one or two words—this helps compensate for lines with more than 10 words.

When a story will run more than one take, the first take should give the word count for that take followed by a hyphen and the total wordage estimate for the story (do not use a comma if the total is more than 999 words, for example 1020).

No take of a story should exceed an estimated 750 words on most slow-speed wires, 1,500 words on high-speed wires.

Do not put a space before the word count or a comma after it. End with the flush left symbol and strike the return key.

## VERSION SECTION

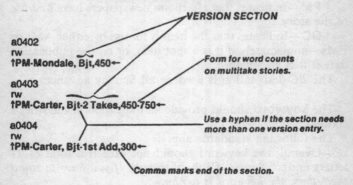

a0402
rw
↑PM-Mondale, Bjt,450←

*VERSION SECTION*

*Form for word counts on multitake stories.*

a0403
rw
↑PM-Carter, Bjt-2 Takes,450-750←

*Use a hyphen if the section needs more than one version entry.*

a0404
rw
↑PM-Carter, Bjt-1st Add,300←

*Comma marks end of the section.*

The **version section** of the keyword slug line is designed to give editors and computer systems a quick indication of whether to place an item at the top, bottom or middle of previous takes sent under the same keyword.

The terms that follow are the only ones that should appear in the version section of a keyword slug line. When more than one term is necessary, separate them with a hyphen. Use figures as indicated.

The version vocabulary is broken into two lists. Do not use more than one of the items from this first list in a keyword slug line. If a term from the second list is needed, it must follow any term from this list:

**Bjt**
**1st Ld, 2nd Ld,**
**10th Ld,** etc.
**Adv 01, Adv 31,** etc.
**Advisory**
**KILL**
**WITHHOLD**
**ELIMINATION**

**CORRECTIVE**
**CLARIFICATION**

A term from the second list may stand alone in the version section if no term from the first list is needed. Some stories require two items from the second list. If that is the case, the order in which the terms appear is not critical, but they must be separated by a hyphen. The second list:

**2 Takes, 3 Takes,** etc.
**1st Add, 2nd Add,** etc.
**Insert**
**Sub**
**Correction**
**Writethru**
**Box** (Sports only.)

## REFERENCE NUMBER SECTION

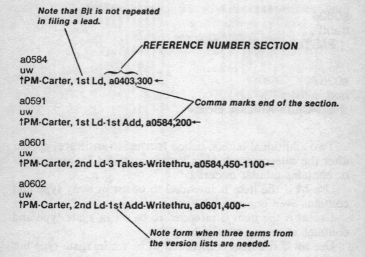

Note that Bjt is not repeated
in filing a lead.

*REFERENCE NUMBER SECTION*

a0584
uw
↑PM-Carter, 1st Ld, a0403,300 ←

a0591
uw
↑PM-Carter, 1st Ld-1st Add, a0584,200 ←

*Comma marks end of the section.*

a0601
uw
↑PM-Carter, 2nd Ld-3 Takes-Writethru, a0584,450-1100 ←

a0602
uw
↑PM-Carter, 2nd Ld-1st Add-Writethru, a0601,400 ←

*Note form when three terms from
the version lists are needed.*

The **reference number** is the transmission number used on a previous take of a story. List only one in a keyword line.

Follow these norms:

—Cite the number of the most recent lead if you are sending a new lead, sub, insert, correction, advisory, etc.

—If you are filing an add, cite only the transmission number on the immediately preceding take of the story.

—If a story has moved in many pieces and you think editors should have more reference numbers than the one in the keyword line, list them on a line below the keyword slug line.

# FORMAT IDENTIFIERS

a0624
dabt
↑ **PM-Temperatures,300**←


s0357
rsat
↑ **BC-Celts-Knicks, Box,**←


Two additional letters, called **format identifiers,** appear after the category code if an item is intended for agate and/or contains tabular material.

Use **bt** if the item is intended to be set in body type and contains even one tabular line.

Use **at** if the item is intended to be set in agate type and contains even one tabular line.

Use **ax** if the item is intended to be set in agate type but contains no tabular lines.

Some CRT screens automatically show **bx** if the item has not been coded for agate or tabular composition.


# SPECIAL NOTE TO MEMBERS

### KEYWORD FORMAT—Slow-speed

Newspapers that receive the A Wire and other circuits operating at 66 words per minute will notice that slugs appear with the commas intact.

### KEYWORD FORMAT—DataStream

As indicated in the introduction on the keyword, the commas in the keyword slug line are replaced by spaces when stories are sent on DataStream at 1,200 words per minute.

Any spaces in the line as originally typed are removed automatically to meet the industry standards for the keyword line in high-speed transmissions.

In addition to the information placed in the keyword slug by editors, the computers that transmit DataStream add a four-digit filing date with a hyphen in the middle and a four-digit word count. The computer makes the word estimate by counting the number of characters in the story and dividing by six.

Here is how one of the slugs shown earlier would look on DataStream:

u w PM-Reagan 2ndLd-Writethru a5840 02-06 0455

## FORMAT IDENTIFIERS on DataStream

The letters **at, bt,** etc., shown in the examples of **format identifiers** do not appear on DataStream. However, they help generate non-printing characters that are sent in this location to convey the same information about whether the item is meant to be set in agate or body type and whether it contains tabular material.

# PROOFREADERS' MARKS

| | |
|---|---|
| ¶ ATLANTA (AP)—The organization | indent for paragraph |
| said Thursday. It was the first | paragraph |
| the last attempts. | |
| With this the president tried | no paragraph |
| the Jones Smith company is not | transpose |
| over a period of sixty or more years | use figures |
| there were 9 in the group. | spell it out |
| Ada, Oklahoma, is the hometown | abbreviate |
| The Ga. man was the guest of | don't abbreviate |
| prince edward said it was his | uppercase |
| as a result This will be | lowercase |
| the ac cuser pointed to them | remove space |
| In these times it is necessary | insert space |
| the order for the later devices | retain |
| The ruling a fine example | insert word |
| according to the this source | delete |
| according to the this source | delete |

| | |
|---|---|
| **BF** ⊐ By DONALD AMES ⊏ | bold face, center |
| J.R. Thomas ⌉ | flush right |
| ⌊ J.R. Thomas | flush left |
| ⋀ | insert comma |
| ⋁ | insert apostrophe |
| ⋁ ⋁ | insert quotation marks |
| ⊗ or ⊙ | insert period |
| = | hyphen |
| ⊢⊣ | dash |

## About the AP

The Associated Press is a non-profit, cooperative news service founded in 1848. In the mid-1980s, the AP was serving nearly 1,400 newspaper and 3,900 broadcast members in the United States. AP services were printed and broadcast abroad by more than 8,500 subscribers in 116 countries.

The news service, with headquarters in New York City, has 132 bureaus and correspondent posts in the United States and 82 abroad. It employs more than 1,500 full-time reporters, editors and photographers worldwide. Its budget exceeds $200 million a year.

**HEADQUARTERS**
**The Associated Press**
**50 Rockefeller Plaza**
**New York, N.Y. 10020**
**(212) 621-1500**

Following are telephone numbers for frequently called departments and desks at the AP's headquarters in New York City. The area code is 212.

AP Newsfeatures
621-1820
Digital Stocks
621-1540
Financial Desk
621-1680
Foreign Desk
621-1663

General Desk
621-1600
New York City Bureau
621-1670
Photo Desk
621-1900
Racing Desk
621-1638
Service Desk
621-1595
Sports Desk
621-1630
World Desk
621-1650

## U.S. Bureaus

Following are telephone numbers for AP bureaus in the United States.

750 West 2nd Ave., Suite 102
P.O. Box 2175, Federal Station
Anchorage, **Alaska** 99501
  **(907) 278-4383**
  **(907) 278-7549**

505 N. Second St. Suite 120
Phoenix, **Arizona** 85004
  **(602) 258-8934**
  **(602) 271-8188**

1101 West Second Street
Little Rock, **Arkansas** 72201-2003
  **(501) 374-5536**

1111 South Hill St., Room 263
Los Angeles, **California** 90015-2296
  **(213) 746-1200**

318 Fox Plaza,
1390 Market St.,
San Francisco, **California**
94102-5474
**(415) 621-7432**

1444 Wazee St., Suite 130
Denver, **Colorado** 80202-1395
**(303) 825-0123**

241 Asylum St.
Hartford, **Connecticut** 06103-0437
**(203) 246-6876**

2021 K St. N.W., Suite 606
Washington, **D.C.** 20006-1082
**(202) 833-5300**

9100 N.W. 36th Street
Miami, **Florida** 33137-5079
**(305) 594-5826**

One CNN Center, South Tower
Atlanta, **Georgia** 30303-2705
**(404) 522-8971**
**(404) 522-8972**

P.O. Box 2956, Main St. Station
Hawaii News Agency Building
Suite 500
Honolulu, **Hawaii** 96802-2956
**(808) 536-5510**

230 North Michigan Ave.
Chicago, **Illinois** 60601-5968
**(312) 781-0500**

Star News Building
307 N. Pennsylvania St.
P.O. Box 1950
Indianapolis, **Indiana** 46206-1950
**(317) 639-5501**

1001 First Interstate Bank Building
Sixth and Locust
P.O. Box 1741
Des Moines, **Iowa** 50306-1741
**(515) 243-3281**

Courier-Journal Building
525 West Broadway
Room 407-A
Louisville, **Kentucky** 40202
**(502) 583-7718**

1001 Howard Ave., Suite 200A
New Orleans, **Louisiana** 70113-2077
**(504) 523-3931**

222 St. Paul Place, Suite 400
Baltimore, **Maryland** 21202
**(301) 539-3524**

184 High Street
Boston, **Massachusetts** 02110
   **(617) 357-8100**

660 Plaza Drive, Suite 2400
Detroit, **Michigan** 48207
   **(313) 259-0650**

Business and Tech Center,
511 11th Ave. South
Minneapolis, **Minnesota** 55415
   **(612) 332-2727**

215 West Pershing Road
Suite 221
Kansas City, **Missouri** 64108-
1850
   **(816) 421-4844**

Room C West Building
1300 Cedar Street,
P.O. Box 5810
Helena, **Montana** 59604-5810
   **(406) 442-7440**

The Monitor Building
3 N. State St., P.O. Box 1296
Concord, **New Hampshire**
03301
   **(603) 224-3327**

Airport International Plaza
Route 1 & 9 South
Newark, **New Jersey** 07114
   **(201) 642-0151**

P.O. Box 1845
Albuquerque, **New Mexico**
87103-1845
   **(505) 822-9022**

645 Albany-Shaker Road
P.O. Box 11010
Albany, **New York** 12211-0010
   **(518) 458-7821**

50 Rockefeller Plaza
New York, **New York** 10020
   **(212) 621-1670**

4020 Chase Blvd., Suite 300
219 McDowell Street
Raleigh, **North Carolina** 27607-
3933
   **(919) 833-8687**

Dispatch Building, 4th Floor
34 South Third Street
P.O. Box 1812
Columbus, **Ohio** 43216
   **(614) 228-4306**

Old Daily Oklahoman Building
500 North Broadway
Oklahoma City, **Oklahoma**
73102-6288
   **(405) 236-0663**

1320 S.W. Broadway
Portland, **Oregon** 97201-3487
   **(503) 228-2169**

Suite 250
One Franklin Plaza
Philadelphia, **Pennsylvania**
19102
  **(215) 561-1133**

1091 Assembly Street
P.O. Box 1435
Columbia, **South Carolina**
29202-1435
  **(803) 799-6418**
  **(803) 799-5510**

Banner-Tennessean Building
1100 Broadway
P.O. Box 22990
Nashville, Tennessee 37202-
2990
  **(615) 244-2205**

Southland Center
Suite 2100
Dallas, **Texas** 75201
  **(214) 220-2022**

116 Regents Street
P.O. Box 11129
Salt Lake City, **Utah** 84147
  **(801) 322-3405**

Suite 1380
700 East Main Street
Richmond, **Virginia** 23219-2684
  **(804) 643-6646**

210 Boren North
P.O. Box 2144
Seattle, **Washington** 98111-
2144
  **(206) 682-1812**

Room 206
Charleston Newspapers Building
1001 Virginia Street East
P.O. Box 1713
Charleston, **West Virginia**
25326-1713
  **(304) 346-0897**

Journal Square
918 Ninth Fourth Street
Milwaukee, **Wisconsin** 53203-
1596
  **(414) 225-3580**

## *Zip*

## KNOCKS OUT THE PRESS!

"A box of toys, epigrams, firecrackers, political pot shots, Talmudic maunderings, whistles and screams."
—**John Leonard,** *New York Times*

"Apple here has perfected an interesting fictional technique by incorporating real figures into his story. . . . But Apple brings his well-known figures into a totally new and purely imaginative context . . . *Zip* is no less than the life-force itself, a force strongly felt in this extraordinarily funny and serious little book that stretches the limits of the novel just a bit more." —*Chicago Sun-Times*

"If you skip this book because you don't like boxing (or communists) I can only say that it would be like skipping Mark Twain because you don't like boys."
—*Boston Sunday Globe*

"There's magic here. From the Goldstein's cellar in Detroit to the fight of the century in Havana—with J. Edgar Hoover as stakes—is a zany distance to travel, and Apple's a good-humored guide." —*New Republic*

"The lunacy that sparked and fizzed in Apple's first book, *The Oranging of America,* returns to light up this absurd, delightful tale." —*Cosmopolitan*

"Apple's irreverent imagination has never been friskier . . . a masterful manipulator of proper names and improper language is throwing a helluva party." —*Kirkus Reviews*

*more . . .*

"His prose has the humor and poise of Bellow's or Roth's." —*Washington Post*

"Remember Budd Schulberg's unscrupulous Sammy Glick on the make in Hollywood? Max Apple's first novel has this same breakneck narrative drive, with the added embellishments of quick wit and a runaway imagination . . . it is refreshing to frolic with so brisk a writer."

—*Saturday Review*

# A Novel
## of the Left
### and the Right

# MAX·APPLE

**WARNER BOOKS**

A Warner Communications Company

I would like to express my gratitude to the National Endowment for the Arts for the grant which made it possible for me to finish this work.

*Zip* is a work of fiction and its content derives entirely from my imagination. Where I have used real names or what seem to be physical descriptions of real people, it is done purely in the interest of fiction. In any serious sense the similarities between the characters in this novel and the real lives of any persons living or dead are unintended and coincidental.

—Max Apple

WARNER BOOKS EDITION

This Warner Books Edition is published by arrangement with the author.

Warner Books, Inc.
666 Fifth Avenue
New York, N.Y. 10103

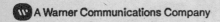 A Warner Communications Company

Printed in the United States of America

First Warner Books Printing: February, 1986

10  9  8  7  6  5  4  3  2  1

*For Bashy and for Rachmiel*

# ZIP

# 1

Let me steal nothing more from you, Jesús, my middle-weight. The story is all yours, conqueror of the roped-off ring, hero of the dusty Third World streets. In history you will stand as an image of the possible, a breaker of boundaries. But when I first saw you, all I could offer was $1.65 per hour as a breaker of batteries.

Even in your desperation you shined. Nearly asleep on the porch of our tiny office, jacketless in the ice cold Michigan November, you arose to let me enter. In the midst of your shivering, even there, I could see your dignity.

"Señor," you said, "I am an innocent man waylaid by circumstance."

Circumstance Ira Goldstein understands, innocence too. I give you my extra jacket, a dollar advance for breakfast, and then your own fifteen-pound sledge-hammer to beat the lead free of battery casing, the precious lead that keeps Momma and me in business. Momma thinks I'm crazy to hire someone whom I find sleeping outside the office door.

"This is no romantic story about orphans," she says. "This is the real world. In the real world you're the orphan and I'm the widow. And this is a junkyard, not a charity for drunken Mexicans."

Jesús listens to it all. His body is tense. His young cheeks have no hint of beard. You can see at once that

1

he has learned to roll with insults. He hands me my jacket. "Jesús will go. Thanks, buddy," he says.

"Wait," I say, "my mother talks like this all the time. She has become hardened by the business world because of tough breaks. Give her a few weeks and she'll be bringing you homemade sponge cake."

Frieda laughs. "All right," she says, "lead is forty-six cents a pound with this Mexican and forty-six cents without him. Maybe with a little help you'll get out more too."

Momma's desire for me to get out, her never-ending passion to do right for her only child, enters into each of her decisions. You, Jesús, a waif on the doorstep, you have no obligations. Earn a living, stay out of jail, register to vote—for you this is plenty. But for me the business of daily life has to lead to a direct dividend. Two hundred dollars a week, a reasonably good house, a color TV, a one-year-old pickup, a good credit rating, all this is not enough. Grandma needs offspring. The pressure is on my loins to produce. But before those loins even have a chance, the mouth has to make small talk, the eyes have to look straight at the girls who terrify me, the hands have to make promising gestures. In one of the books that she carried with her from Lithuania Grandma shows me significant passages that guarantee eternal life to those who live long enough to witness a great-grandchild. It is 1966, and Grandma is no superstitious fool. She knows the odds are long, but she trusts the wisdom of the past. Also, to encourage me can do no harm. "Get some zip," she says. "Go out, get married."

She and Frieda don't want me to be trapped by the burden of themselves. They would gladly live alone in poverty if necessary just so their twenty-four-year-old Ira could find a nice girl and live as bland a life as any salesman in Detroit.

Five days a week I man the scale, and roam the yard full of battery carcasses and rusted radiators. But to Momma and Grandma I am a prince among these ruins. They don't understand why the girls of Detroit are not marching in groups around our house to demand that I go out more. Grandma thinks I should begin to telephone fathers to ask their permission; Momma wants me to attend more mixers at the community center.

While they plan my future, you, Jesús, a stranger, you save my life. When I am in the greatest peril, I see for the first time your speed and power. From the perch of my own fear I learn to trust you. It's three below zero in the office. Moses Robinson has me backed against the wall. "Who says a ton is two thousand pounds? If it was two thousand pounds they'd call it two tons." He wants to be paid on the basis of a 1000-pound ton. He is wild, irrational, mean. He weighs at least 240. Frieda screams, "Give him whatever he wants, he'll kill you!" And it looks as if he might.

"Pay, Jewman," he says, "or you'll be brushin' your teeth through your ass." I see the gold rims of his teeth, the pores of his black skin. I am too paralyzed to move, but my mother is beside me handing him money.

"I want the Jewman to give it to me. I want a receipt." He is smiling an ugly, triumphant smile. Then Jesús steps into the tiny office.

"Señor," he says to Moses Robinson, "leave this man alone. He is telling you the truth. A ton is two thousand pounds."

"Mind your own fucking business," Robinson says, "or I'll wipe the shit off the walls with you too."

Jesús smiles. He is ready. "Try it," he says. Robinson turns toward Jesús.

Frieda pulls me to the door. She wants me to run to the truck and go for help. "Wait," I say. "I don't want to leave Jesús here alone. Robinson was a fighter. He went

3

ten rounds with Ezzard Charles." My father took me to see that fight. When I first met Moses Robinson I idolized him. Now he is a hulk, aging but powerful, moving in on young Jesús.

Of course Robinson throws the first punch, and of course Jesús destroys him with clean and effortless punches like a television policeman. Jesús spreads Robinson across the floor. The black man is more embarrassed than hurt. I write his receipt for a thousand pounds and hand him his cash. He departs in silence.

"Thank you," Frieda says. "You have saved Ira from a beating, maybe death. We can never thank you enough."

And what way, Jesús, did I find to thank you—the way of exploitation and greed. The way of setting every man against every other man. I know what you have written about those years. I agree. My penitence is complete and yet do you remember how innocent we both were? You were eighteen years old, Jesús, fresh from street crime, and what did I know? I read *Sport* magazine and *Ring*, and still daydreamed about playing for the Detroit Tigers. That night I imagined us in center ring, me holding your glove aloft as the TV cameras ground out our image and the roar of the crowd declared us winners forever. It was almost the first good dream I had been able to sustain in years. My father was there too: Abe, risen from the grave to be in your corner. He wore a shirt that said *Jesús*. His face was indistinct, but I recognized him from the stoop of his shoulders. He didn't say much. His resurrection was not important when we were going for the championship. This my father understood. In returning, as in life, he shunned the spotlight. It was so real that I could taste your sweat when we hugged.

"What are you going to do, Ira," Howard Cosell

asked, "now that your fighter has won the champion-ship? How are you going to top a success like that?"

"Howard," I tell him and the millions watching, "we're going to Florida. I'm getting for my mother and grandmother a small condominium in a Jewish neigh-borhood. It's good-bye forever to the scrap business. And the cold Michigan winters. They will clip coupons and eat fresh ocean fish."

"But what about you, the architect of this splendid triumph?"

"I, Howard, am going to marry Karen Cole, who sat across from me in tenth grade study hall. She used to go steady with football players, but now she has matured and recognizes my worth. Her tits point skyward. Girls envy her lift and posture. If she is watching I want to say 'Hi, Karen, I have not forgotten you.' I will watch over Jesús and develop other promising talent. Florida is a good home base for working with Latins. Of course I'll give lots of money to the United Jewish Appeal and may even let Jesús fight an exhibition in Israel. I'll do what I can for world peace as well."

"Good luck," Howard Cosell wishes me as I spread the ropes for Jesús and follow him out of the ring through the cheering mass into the wintergreen-smelling locker room.

"Where did you get the idea of starting this young Puerto Rican on the road to the championship?" Cosell asks. He has followed me to the locker room. I tell him about the Moses Robinson incident. "Naturally," he says. "You saw a super talent and you were determined to develop it to its full potential. This is one of the problems with the contemporary world. Nobody works to his potential. The black men in your scrap yard, for example, could break dozens more batteries each, and you yourself could take three night classes per semester rather than two. And the brain as we all know scarcely gets any use at all. Instead of daydreaming about naked girls you could learn a little about the stock market and tax laws. Would this kill you? And while you're at it, how about studying a little Hebrew, to give *nachas* to your grandmother. How many years does she have left? Show a little respect. Don't run out of the room when she asks you to point out the department store sales in the newspaper. Not everyone is as interested as you are in the Vietnam war. Grandma wants Hudson's and Wurzburg's to stay in business too, just like you want Hanoi. You weren't born yet in the Depression when Hudson's gave your mother a job and kept the family going on her eight dollars a week. For that you'll owe them always. On white sale days, on end-of-month clearances, Grandma wants to repay her debt to Hudson's and get a few bargains too."

"I agree," I tell him, "but it was in order to develop all the fine qualities of life that I pursued my career as a manager and gave Jesús the inspiration and financial backing that he needed."

"But your grandmother," he chides me, "she never wanted her only grandson to end up like this, in the boxing ring with half-naked brutes and gamblers and loose women of all kinds."

"Sacrifices have to be made. In this century there is little purity. My grandma lives in another world. To her a supermarket is as revolutionary as space travel. I have given up trying to modernize her."

"Does this mean," Cosell asks, "that you no longer will come home from school and translate for her some of the English classics into Yiddish? Does it mean that you will not watch TV with her as you watched *I Love Lucy* and the *$64,000 Question* in your childhood?

"And how about her bad leg. Now that you are a famous manager and an international celebrity, are you

6

going to neglect wrapping her arthritic knee in the red flannel that she says helps her? Are you going to insist that she remove the copper bracelet that keeps her wrist from aching? Is she going to be too much of an embarrassment—this remnant of Lithuania who can't even write English?"

Jesús interrupts. "Listen, boys, Ira is tired. So am I. The fighter and manager need some rest. And we've got strategy to work on, especially while his father, Abe, is around to help us out. Did you boys know that Abe was a fight fan? Yes, much more than his son Ira. Had Abe been alive I would have been an even surer thing."

The locker room is awash in cold beer and champagne. Frieda brings in trays of cold cuts and homemade strudel. How the fight fans and reporters dig into the strudel. This everyone loves. This was the strudel that Dr. Shimmer used to snack on—Dr. Shimmer who signed Abe's death certificate, who called one night to say that Abe Goldstein had rolled a seven but life must go on. How he loved that strudel that Frieda used to give him when he visited Abe's hospital room. He held it away from his white gown so the crumbs wouldn't disturb other patients. He chewed in small, slow bites. All the time that he snacked he left the cold hard stethoscope on Abe's heart. Frieda and little Ira huddled at the side of the bed, waiting for the report on the heart. Today the heart is good, bad, so-so? Always noncommittal, Dr. Shimmer merely said, "OK." He wrote notes. Not for you to peek at, little Ira. He wrote these notes for the nurses, whose high starched rumps you longed for even in those days, barely past your Bar Mitzvah. Your poor father's veins so choked by cholesterol that barely enough blood slipped through to keep his legs cold and clammy. And you, being an open pig about circulation, getting hard-ons for the nurses. If you're not careful you'll end up no better than Abe. Remember what Miss

7

Davis said, "You must be kind to your heart." Miss Davis says, "It never gets a total rest, it works all day and all night. How would you like to work as hard as your heart works?" It is a question, Miss Davis, that has stayed with me. Thanks to you, I rest my hardy little worker lest I exploit him and the heart goes on to strike me dead. "An ingrate," says the heart, "he lies, he abused me, he didn't keep his head down the way you said to, Miss Davis. He played with himself too much, making me pump all that extra blood to his groin. He ran nonstop home from school. He lived in fear of bad grades. From him I never got a moment's rest. Since third grade he has never during the day taken those twenty-five deep, slow breaths that you told him about. He has not imagined himself on a nice calm beach with the sun just so, a light breeze across his flesh and the ocean making a soothing noise in the background. He is pigging me up. He might just as well stick two hands all the way down his throat and squeeze the last ventricular throb out of me."

From my father's death I learned adversity, and adversity, like experience and Miss Davis, is a good teacher. From experience you learn that every cloud has a silver lining. Arteries, however, should be lined only with their quick, moist, supple selves. No extraneous matter for an artery, or it will tell that sturdy heart of yours. And hearts need arteries more than they need rest. This, Miss Davis, you failed to tell me, this I gleaned along the way. The Fleischmann's pamphlet has a colorful drawing of an artery filled with cholesterol. The artery is a nice glossy pink, the cholesterol is dark as motor oil, thick as birthday cake. It lies there, making it tough on your blood. Now, this blood is bothering nobody, minding its own business, carrying some good nutrients here, a few waste products there. Blood is congenial. It is the symbol of Brotherhood Week. The body's own little whore, it goes to any man. The Red Cross takes blood from you and gives it to someone who needs it more. The Red Cross is like Robin Hood; and blood, Dr. Shimmer, we know it as a self-evident truth, blood is better than money. In the pamphlet given free by Fleischmann's margarine, a cutaway drawing shows the cholesterol in peaks and valleys, like flames nipping at the blood as it goes through a narrow place. The definition of a hero: Someone who defends a narrow place against great odds. This I learned from Dr. Arthur, English 201. Not as valuable as Miss Davis's dictum on rest, but still, what is more heroic than the heart defending a narrow place, the quickly clogging artery? The odds against the heart are literally infinite. Still it works; it puffs itself up, it goes overtime, it seeks alternate routes—the smaller country arteries where the traffic is lighter, but in a pinch. . . . And if the heart, defending the closing artery against the odds is heroic, then get this Dr. Shimmer, Dr. Arthur, Miss Davis, Frieda still in grief. Get this everyone who can use it: Of those who die each year, more than half are the result of heart ailments. And each one of these millions died a hero's death as surely as any Norseman of old who wanted Valhalla enough to stick a dull knife into his chest at the first sign of sickness.

"Why look for other heroes," Howard Cosell says, "when right in front of us we have this eighteen-year-old kid with the knife scars of the barrio barely healed upon him, this eighteen-year-old who tonight showed us what manhood was all about. Did he back away from spades with knives? Not this kid. Hard as nails. He listened to his manager. He watched out for low blows, and punched from the shoulder. I'll tell you something, folks," Howard says, "this is off the record but you know I'd like to see the day that Johnson and Mc-Namara and Rusk and all the rest of them get into trunks and come out in the open to spar a few with Ho Chi Minh, Brezhnev, and Mao. Ira is nobody's fool. You might laugh at him for tying up with Latinos and Italians and black men in this brutal sport, but who's to say that it's not the wave of the future."

Ah, the future, Howard, if only you're right about that. That is what Grandma wants from me. The grandchild in my loins and the girl somewhere in the crowd, if only the future would bring those elements together and make of them a little boy in a skullcap carrying a *siddur* and moving in silent prayer beside Grandma. If the future holds such a phantom, Howard, then it's better than championships, better than big cash purses.

"Get some zip," Grandma says, "before cancer and arthritis put me underground. Find a girl. How hard can that be?"

Harder, Grandma, than training a graceful middleweight; although in this case, thanks to Jesús, these things coincide. What I have not yet seen in a girl I dare approach, I see at once in Jesús: the elegant virtues of nature. He has everything. But middleweight contenders are not an item born, otherwise every strong misfit in Detroit might step through the ropes of the Motor City Arena to capitalize on his brute force. No, in the ring it takes more than strength, more than meanness. Jesús is not even especially powerful, not at all like the tattooed men who move refrigerators for a living or the muscle boys who glory in their triceps. No self-consciousness for Jesús. He takes his body for granted. A swift combination is as instinctive to him as reaching for a handkerchief during the pollen season is to a hay fever sufferer. The eye spots an opening, the fists are there before any other part knows what's happened.

But even when you start with everything, as Jesús did,

there are still months of learning before the swift puncher can cross the ring to meet his equal. Jesús has the rhythms of a winner, but only in short spurts. He throws three swift punches, then drops his arms. He has a tendency to look around the room, so that a fast punching bag gives him one for one. His brilliant speedy jab Jesús throws with his wrist alone, neglecting to add the sweet kiss of power from his left shoulder.

Sometimes after a long day among the batteries, radiators, and burned-out car bodies, Jesús and I barely have the energy for two hours at the gym. On those days when we're both tired, or at the times when Jesús is too lazy to skip rope or hit the bag, or too sure of himself to put on the protective cup or the headgear—at times like this I wonder why we keep at it. I consider the odds against glory, the uninsured risk of cuts and broken bones. Then I think of the reality of me at the scale weighing lead, Jesús in the yard smashing batteries. When we are down, Jesús and I read each other's moods.

"Madison Square in the spring, boss," Jesús says, and I arise from my stool. He can relieve my melancholy by shadow boxing, by dancing in the ring without lifting a glove against his sparring partner. Yes, to encourage Ira takes little, Jesús, only a few flashes of your brilliance, but how can I translate that enthusiasm to Frieda, who trusts me with our savings although the lead market is way off?

"Ira," she says, "for you I'd do anything. Maybe this is my failure as a mother. But who can say no to a son orphaned at fourteen, and from a father like Abe? I say to myself, 'would Abe say no to him'? About a boxer he would never say no. Who would believe that grown Jewish men could be like this. Like father like son. Still I thank God that you take after him. He left us better than money. Character is what he left."

When we begin, Jesús, you are still a part of the long

11

daydream from which I cannot seem to awaken. It is this that has taken my "zip." I can't explain it to Grandma, not even to Dr. Shimmer. It's as if between me and the world there is a sheet of Saran Wrap. Through it I see everything, the way other people do, but somehow I'm kept at a distance by that almost invisible layer. Then, after watching your moves for a while, my hopes for your career seem to raise the plastic sheet like a stage curtain. With you I am ready to be unwrapped.

Still, to make you more than a sloppy gym-sparring partner takes money. An engraved robe can run $200, regulation boxing gloves are $85, mouthpieces $12.50 each. There are doctor bills and $75 a month just to hit the bag in the gym and get two clean towels a day.

You would think that nothing could be simpler than two men in the ring stalking each other. The physics is clear. Two striving to become one. Yes, the second law of thermodynamics rules the cosmos, but money rules the ring. For Frieda I try to make it look like a sure thing. "He is so good, Momma, that I don't see how we can lose. Even if he doesn't get to be champion or even one of the best in his weight class, he'll still earn his keep."

"But owning another man."

"Not owning him, just managing him, just his career. You manage him—like the bank manages your money. You don't give it to them."

But we know now, Jesús, how right my mother's instinct was. I recall your remarks printed in *Pravda* as they were translated by *The New York Times*, "The beginning of the alienation of labor is the management by one individual of the affairs of another individual." Your statement stung me to the heart. Although I never intended it to become an exploitative relationship, I see

12

now that always secretly, unconsciously, I was using you for my own ends.

And Grandma, she whom you liked best of all in our family, she calls you a shvartzer, fails to distinguish you from the noisy blacks moving into our neighborhood who threaten her as she takes her daily two-block walk with the aid of a cane which she would gladly use against the colored children who spit in her path. To Grandma you never stop being a threat. When I move you to our basement, to a cozy little room adjacent to the ninety-pound hanging bag, Grandma calls a locksmith. She bolts herself into her room. She refuses to pronounce your name.

"It's *Hayzus*, Grandma. In Puerto Rico it's as common as Jack or Bob."

"I won't stay alone in the house with a schvartzer devil." I call in the rabbi to explain to her that you are legitimate. A professional fighter. A Puerto Rican, not a shvartzer. You are living in the basement so that we can save money while you build a reputation and a career for both of us. You are as safe as a devout Jew loaded with *mezuzahs* and prayers against circumstantiality.

The rabbi, too, is suspicious. "What man keeps someone in his basement and teaches him to hit other men?"

"A manager," I say. "An entrepreneur. A potential big giver to Jewish charities."

"Notwithstanding," he says, "it smacks of the gentiles."

We descend to the fighter in his lair. Eighteen-year-old Jesús in the small, wood-paneled basement room watching the afternoon movie on a fuzzy twelve-inch Motorola. The rabbi is seventy-five. He was a friend of my grandfather, whom I never knew. He officiated at Abe's funeral. He threw the first scoop of dirt; he ac-

13

companied me in the Kaddish, saying it slowly, clearly, so that I did not miss any of those tricky Aramaic syllables.

He examines the ninety-pound bag, itself a hundred-dollar investment. He smells it but does not touch. The bag moves lightly in the air. The chain creaks. To him you are a caged animal, smooth, brown, awesome. He thinks of me as the man with the chair in the den of lions and tigers.

"From this people earn a living?" he asks.

"Millions," I say. "It is safe and clean. Policed by the state board, and supervised by doctors. There have been great Jewish fighters, too."

"Ira," he says, "your grandfather of blessed memory was a sage. He was more devout than most rabbis. Wisdom dripped from his fingertips. He died young. Your father, too, slipped into eternity in the midst of his prime. Only you has the angel of death spared. Only you to watch over the declining years of your grandmother and your mother."

Is this the only reason I have been spared, I think, only to watch over these women, not to live as Ira Goldstein, who once played in the Little Leagues and who may yet gather diplomas, women, and fortune in the wide world of the gentiles?

"Rabbi," I say, "you know that she will listen to you. Don't approve of my venture. This I'm not asking. Tell her only not to be afraid that Jesús will slit her throat. He is honest and sincere and hardworking. As soon as he earns a little money, he will move into a delux apartment. I couldn't let him stay in a single room on Woodward Avenue without even a hot plate and so much noise that he is up half the night. A boxer must guard his body. Food and rest and training—these are his Torah."

"And your mother? Frieda approves of this?"

"She lets me do as I please. Rabbi, I'm twenty-four, I'm not a boy. At my age other men are in the world in the midst of success. They have wives and families."

"So why not you too?"

"I will, Rabbi, God willing, in time I will too. But now there is this to do. When my destined bride appears, I will recognize her." I only say this to impress him, to put into my small talk the hum of predestination, the glitter of divine planning. And yet when Debby does appear to me, it is as Destiny. How you saw her, Jesús, I know not, nor does she. She remembers the rally in front of Cobo Hall, her Ho Chi Minh sign, the hot breeze of the evening—and suddenly you, helping her hold the sign aloft in the wind. And I, somewhere deep in the crowd, waited months longer for Destiny, for her whom you culled out of the protest march.

"Ira," you said, "can I use the pickup on Saturday night?" You who gave me yourself, could I deny you a truck? For you it was monasticism—the training, the running, the sleeping long. On Saturday night you had to break the bonds. I understood. I envied. I gave you the truck.

"For shame," Frieda says, "a Jewish girl. Someone should tell her father."

"Keep out of it," I say, "it's none of our business. We don't own the man. His private life is his own business. As long as it doesn't hurt his training." You are always home by midnight, up by seven, working out on the ninety-pounder. Your taped fists awaken me. I drink coffee as I watch the light sweat break onto your shoulders. You jump rope. From eight to nine you run over the freezing Detroit streets all the way to the corner of Greenfield and Six Mile Road and back. I make us a breakfast of eggs, rolls—and because of you—even meat in the morning: little kosher sausages tasting like the pork that inspired their creation.

15

I train you by the book, by the several books I have borrowed from the Detroit Public Library. *My Life* by Willy Pep, *The Career of a Boxer* by William and Alan Boyd, and *So You Want to Fight* by the editors of *Ring*. But there is no absolute routine. No book can read the individual body—the hungers, the instincts, the capacity for pain. To this day I wonder how I—a fan but with no experience in the ring—how I noticed in that single explosive moment with Moses Robinson all the nonphysical elements that make a winner. How did I spot your native intelligence, your ambition, your confidence—the smoldering hate which for so long lay within you?

"I do not like it," the rabbi says. "A young man like you should not dwell so close to paganism. The Romans did this kind of sport. On the grounds of our Temple they despoiled us with arenas of torture. Of this business I will not approve. But I will tell your grandmother that the fighter is no threat to her life. It is your life that he threatens."

"Even the shvartzer finds a Jewish girl. But not our Ira," Grandma says when she hears of your Saturday-night adventures. We watch *The Lawrence Welk Show*. Frieda takes a bath. I read Grandma the evening paper and call her attention to the clearance at Sears. I wonder what you do and who the girl is. You return silently. In the morning you offer no stories, no explanations, but your fists seem extra fresh. I imagine you embracing a lewd Jewess—as coy as the punching bag, as soft as the fifteen-ounce training gloves.

Grandma notices the happy couples dancing on the TV screen, and Lawrence Welk surrounded by singing sisters. "On New Year's Eve," Grandma says, "and all the other *goyische yom tovs*, Lawrence Welk brings his own family to sing and dance. You should see how beautiful they look. They hug him every minute. The grandchildren pour out of his lap. Not everyone can be so lucky."

16

No longer do you go to Goldstein's We Buy Junk and Batteries. Not there, where rust and infection thicken the air, not there do I store my investment. Grandma gradually unbolts herself and learns the difference between a Puerto Rican and a black, a nicety that I have forced upon her. "You'll see," she tells me, "one day you'll come home and find my blood on the Armstrong linoleum. In advance I forgive you for what this wild man will do to me. Can he help it? You bring a wild goy into your house, you have to expect terror."

The way you are with her, Jesús, shows me something that I admire more than your power and courage in the ring. With her you are gentle and patient. When Frieda joins me at the shop early, you carry upstairs to Grandma her boiled egg, her hot Sanka and toast. You leave the tray outside her door. You are not offended that she won't unlock the door until she hears your footsteps at the bottom of the stairs. Once she is dressed and moving around the house, she trusts you more. Sometimes together you scan the newspaper looking for sales. You, too, she has forgiven in advance.

Everything she can forgive, but not Solomon. From Grandma you learn the name of the villain, the details of his crimes. "Next to Hitler is Solomon." This I remember from my childhood. Abe used to laugh it off. He did not hate Solomon. "Competition is the name of the game. Business is business," Abe Goldstein said. Solomon's big trucks roared into gas stations, paid top price for the batteries, and left Abe only the loyal few who liked him more than a few dollars extra.

"He had it on his mind to kill your father—and he did," Grandma says. "With such aggravation who could live?"

"Don't listen to her," Frieda says, "Solomon is not such a monster. She doesn't know the whole story. The man suffers plenty."

From you he suffers, Momma, from being deprived of what Grandma and I and the battery business have every day. Was my need for money so great, Momma, that I sent you there to the pits of capitalism to barter yourself so that I could hire Miguel León to train Jesús for one month? Where I have never been, there I let you wander: to Solomon, the king of midwestern scrap. Solomon, the father of the fragmentizer. Solomon, whose machines chew up a car every fourteen seconds, whose semis and railroad cars feed the oxygen furnaces of Gary and Pittsburgh. Magnets litter his desk. Momma, in shame, averts her eyes from the girlie calendars that advertise heavy machinery. Solomon's four telephones ring blood. His pinky ring glows in the dark. An extra set of false teeth floats in a gold-rimmed Solomon Iron and Steel glass.

"Copper is dying," he shouts down the long corridor of typists and metal buyers. "The Africans are trying to put us out of business. Screw their black asses. Buy zinc from Arizona and chrome from Rhodesia. I don't want to look at copper until the price goes to eighty cents. Hide all my pennies."

"Frieda," he says, acknowledging her presence on the leather chair, "what is a diamond like you doing in such a business? Look at the mud on your shoes. You should be in the beauty shop at Saks or in your own Miami condominium. Look at you waiting for me to calm down. Look at you, a high-class widow, an educated woman, still young enough to marry, sitting in a junk-yard office."

"I want to borrow money."

"For investing?"

Frieda shakes her head.

"For taxes?"

"No."

"For retirement of debt?"

18

"For a middleweight," Frieda says, "with a brutal left hook."

Solomon breaks into smiles.

"You mean that slippery Mexican who pals around with Ira?"

Frieda nods.

"For this you come to the King of Detroit to borrow money?"

"For this."

"To keep me company at a UJA dinner you're too busy. A movie, a play, a ride in my Cadillac—all this is too much to ask from Frieda Goldstein. But if, God forbid, her son needs money to throw around on his Mexican boyfriend to buy dope and weapons, then she comes to ask. For me nothing, for him everything."

"He is flesh and blood. You're a stranger. Why do you do this, Solomon? Why do you torture me every time I see you? Can't you say, 'Frieda, I'm sorry?' Can't you answer straight like a bank or a rich *goy*?"

"How much does Ira need?"

"Four thousand now, maybe two more in six months. By then Jesús should be earning his expenses. We'll sign notes and pay back with prime rate interest."

"It breaks my heart, Frieda." Solomon lowers his voice, closes the door. "It breaks my heart to see you like this because your son isn't man enough to run his own life. A solid, hardheaded businesswoman like you coming to borrow money for a prizefighter. Who would believe it?"

Solomon eyes his extra set of teeth. "It's a strange world Frieda, *landsleit* like us, our parents from the same small town in Lithuania. If we'd stayed there and Hitler had left us alone, what would we own now between us, a featherbed and six copper pans? Here we've got everything."

"You mean you've got everything, Solomon. To us a

19

hundred dollars a day is still a big deal. If I had everything, I wouldn't be coming to you now for a middleweight loan."

"Frieda," Solomon says, rising from his chair, "Frieda, for you I wouldn't refuse anything. Ask for my balers, my semis, my load luggers, even my fragmentizer. Only ask and see what happens. But for your son and his Mexican, am I a crazy man, Frieda? Did I build Solomon Iron and Metal from a pushcart to an empire by handing out thousands to prizefighters? I didn't give a nickel to Joe Louis, a national treasure, when he had his tax troubles. Why should I support a Mexican who if he could get past my fence and my dogs would steal my wallet and cut my throat out. It's like giving money to the Arabs."

"All right, Solomon. Enough. I understand. I know it sounds risky. The difference is, I trust my son's judgment and you don't. Still, a secured loan is a secured loan whether it's to a Mexican or to the Chase Manhattan Bank."

"What's the security?"

Frieda pulls her diamond ring with difficulty over a swollen knuckle. "A gift from Abe in '42, when business was good for the first time in years. Three-and-a-half carats." From her purse she removes a jeweler's letter. "Appraised value, sixty-five hundred dollars, slight imperfection not visible to naked eye, blue-white pear cut, platinum setting."

Solomon holds the ring in his large red hand. "Had you married me I could have given you one of these every year, every month if you'd wanted. From a working lifetime this is all he gave you, this trinket?"

"Solomon, it was enough. Do I get the loan or not?"

"Laverne," Solomon yells down the corridor to a secretary, "come in for dictation. Eight and a quarter interest. This ring stays in my vault for security. The lawyer will send a copy."

So Abe's diamond, the only love gift you have, this you mortgaged for your son's whim. Oh, Momma, I wish I had been like other well-meaning sons who lead their parents to lose everything in the stock market or on can't-miss franchises. I wish that instead of Jesús I had met one of the imitators of Colonel Sanders, and with him led you astray more conventionally. I wish that I had found my zip and a head for business early in life. I wish that I had showered you with grandchildren and dividend checks. But Momma, I now believe that Solomon was yours as Jesús became mine.

He takes the ring from your outstretched finger. He throws it in an empty ink well. He pulls you toward him. For my middleweight, Momma, you are the collateral.

# 2

The path from the locker room to the canvas ring is laced with craters. A worn-out blue rug runs the length of the walk. Popcorn crunches beneath the eighty-dollar boxing shoes. Castro calls this your immersion in the cauldron of capitalism. All revolutionaries, Fidel says, make the long march. Mao's went through the mountains and along the Yellow River. Fidel himself traversed the wilds of Camagüey and Oriente Province. Jesús Martinez Goldstein, your long march is through catcalls of bored men. Some reach out to slap at your back where the tight bronze muscles twinkle beneath the robe. All around us flies the flag. Old Glory emblazoned even on the ceiling of this converted armory. The national anthem is the prayer of Jesús, the moment of silence before the pure theater of the fight takes over. Because, Jesús, once that bell rings all of our analytic planning vanishes. It is, as Fidel says, "total physics." When I read your statement that "The laws of physics rule the ring as surely as the proletariat will rule the world," I thought to myself, Is this the man who stepped through the ropes that March 15, 1965, to face Otis Leonard of the scuffed shoes and drippy nose? The crowd is with you automatically. The crowd such as it is, three hundred or so strong, is a collection of derelicts, fans and wild-eyed heroin people full of smiles. But that night I don't even notice them. It is only you I am focusing upon, you and the beginning of my own long march to glory.

The curly hair of Jesús, the wily black eyes, the teeth whiter than the canvas floor, the powerful arms—all of this is visible to the naked eye. The fight fan sees more. He notices the natural footwork, the economy of movement, the power that operates all through the body and is unleashed like inevitability when it finally pushes out from the pillowy glove.

As casually as your jabs rip the flesh of Otis Leonard on that night, with that same lightness of manner you approached Debby, held her banner, whispered into her pampered ear some revolutionary slogans of your own. She recalls your speed. "One kiss and he is all over me," she says, "his hands go toward my underwear. Fighter," she says to you, "I'm not your below-the-belt punching bag."

For me you have discovered her. Just as I did the groundwork for Fidel and Brezhnev and the unnamed millions whom you will liberate, you, Jesús, find the answer to Grandma's prayers. Debby is twenty when you find her in the crowded rally. Your eye is good. She stands out. Her sharp gentile-like nose, her pale skin and the flame of her anger appeal to you. She is the kind of girl who ruined my adolescence.

"What did Plato say about screwing women?" you ask me, and then I know that your Jewish girl is only a refugee from the land of cashmere sweaters and Ford Thunderbirds, not yet ready to embrace the future in the lunges of a Puerto Rican fighter. Secretly I am glad.

"Plato believed in friendship," I tell you, "in non-romantic love."

"Bullshit," you say. For weeks the pickup stays home on Saturday night, but you roam the streets disdaining Jewesses for the light-hipped girls who do not mention Plato. You are home by midnight. As the record grows,

23

so does the discipline. Six four-round victories. One each Wednesday night. All knockouts.

Sal Contrato, the promoter, on a whim names you Goldstein. "It might get some Jews back into the armory," he says. "They spend a lot on refreshments. When they left boxing, they took the class with them. They moved into hockey and basketball. Jews are gregarious people. They like team sports."

Some are not so gregarious. Like me, I love the loneliness of the ring, even along the apron where I await my man for the minute between rounds. But, Jesús, you are the crowd's man. You laugh at the name Goldstein, but you take it on; you let Contrato emblazon it across your robe. While Ali is beginning to inspire a whole generation of black men to adopt Muslim names, you, the middleweight hero of the people, go for the archness of a Hebrew name. All of you is contradictions. "The most versatile Communist ideologue since Trotsky," Fidel calls you, but to Grandma you remain the dangerous basement dweller, the shadow between herself and her family, the evil eye on her grandson's future.

Let me tell you about the evil eye. Yes, I know that the postrevolutionary world will have no place for such nonsense. Even in our time it has been a fading superstition, but don't forget that I was raised by your friend, Grandma. As a child I worried about the evil eye. More than polio I feared it. Because the evil eye is something that a friend, too, can throw at you in a sort of accidental way. It can be a Freudian slip with cosmic power. Suppose you happen to look particularly good some day, an acquaintance notices it. Now, he means no harm but that little voice of envy within him shoots out a millisecond of "may pimples scar him for life," and the damage is done, virtually without the realization of the perpetrator. We live in a world where unformed thoughts are as powerful as deeds. "Watch out,"

Grandma warns me, "for ladies with goiters, men who limp, children with running noses." And I am equally wary of the hunchback, the flea-bitten, the partially paralyzed, and the sane, whole healthy ones who say "come here little boy," and try to pinch your cheek. I am the only child of an only child. On both sides of the family. To me "uncle" and "aunt" are abstractions; my cousins collect pensions.

If you think that I hovered over you trying to protect you—my investment—from accidental mishap, imagine how Grandma guarded me from the evil eye. Until I was school age she washed my face daily in her urine, and made me swear never to tell Momma. Of course she rinsed me off with clean water, but it was there as an invisible protection against the evil eye. As I grew older I made up my own little superstitions. Various objects had powers to protect me, but I stepped on cracks in the sidewalk and walked beneath ladders. I could have broken mirrors too, if I had had the chance. With you, Jesús, I tried to keep my body from touching the ropes as I moved between the second and third strands, and I never let you touch the water bucket.

At home I insist that you eat your meals on our excellent Wedgwood bone china. Frieda rebels at first but then gives in. "Who are we saving it for?" I ask, a reference she knows to the years of frugality that earned her this china. She was so secretive—sneaking it into the house in unmarked bags, one big plate at a time—but too proud to keep from sticking the hard-won plate in that black mahogany chest with the glass doors. They called it the china closet, but to me it was the safety deposit box, the secret place in the house. When Abe carried a lot of cash, he would make a round wad of bills, turn the little key in the middle of the glass doors and drop the bills smack into the china teapot, carefully replacing its top. Every other valuable document went into those

25

Wedgwood dishes. My parents' Hebrew marriage certificate lay in the covered vegetable dish next to my grandfather's citizenship papers and passport, the truck title, the house deed; and, when it came in the mail, it was with pure instinct that I laid Abe's death certificate neatly beside them. The china was Frieda's only extravagance. She took pleasure in announcing the difficulty she endured to be able to buy it. She defended each piece, "I saved money all year by not letting the butcher salt the meat for ten cents a pound extra. It adds up to a few nice dishes." Each piece of Wedgwood sat on its own plastic stand. They were like green-and-white troops behind the glass doors. Before we had you, Jesús, the china closet was the last defense of the Goldstein family. When the day of judgment came, Frieda and I would open the dark doors, and with the teapot and vegetable dish leading the way, that china would march out to defend us—shielding the documents, the cash, the petty martyrdom of her sacrifices, shielding all with its power as an "investment." "Investment" still was a magical word. You, too, were an investment, Jesús, that's why I wanted you to eat your meals on those dishes. I want my investments to know each other. The fighter and the china—now that is a portfolio for all the world to envy.

And against that envy, that universal evil eye, I don't even have the strength of Grandma's piss. So I worry always, Jesús, that you will be injured in sparring at the gym, that somebody's flower pot will fall on your head and kill you along Seven Mile Road. Traffic, bathtub slips, choking, freak diseases—all these things can trip up a budding career. And we have no insurance. Frieda says, "How can you worry so about him and then every Wednesday night send him out with someone who wants to hit him as hard as he can? It doesn't make sense."

She disappears sometimes in the evening. She never

used to. Is it Solomon? Has my fighter's career sent my mother forever into his grasp? Jesús, do you know the family comedy? Do you know that Frieda in her late forties is still sought by our enemy Solomon? Grandma told me stories. I grew up thinking him a young rapist. When I finally saw him, he was short, bald, and toothless. Frieda could knock him out in one round.

As a modern man, Jesús, I did the best I could for you against the evil eye, but even if I were as careful as Grandma I could not have conjured a defense against ideology. I saw the stacks of *Ramparts* and *The Daily Worker* beside your basement cot. I knew that you craved the front lines of the anti-war movement, but how could I believe that your career did not come before all these matters?

Otis Leonard, J. R. Thomson, Brutus Phillips, Jordan Simms, Al Truax, Jimmy Malone—all these black and white middleweights went down like bowling pins before your onslaught. Their wives and girl friends wept bitter tears at ringside. You whipped these men so quickly that your robe barely seemed to leave your shoulders. On some Wednesdays there was no sweat on your limbs. You dressed without a shower and went home to read. I smelled Madison Square Garden or the Coliseum in Los Angeles.

Days in the battery business lost all meaning. I stopped being careful; the acid shredded my work pants and left burns upon my thighs. Grandma put aside her fears. Her arthritis stiffened her wrists. She needed you to help her around the house. She pretended you were an ordinary domestic, a *shabbas goy*, whose duty was to make her comfortable. She sent you to the drugstore for Mercurochrome and let you dab it on her nails as a remedy against the swelling. In your own memoirs you wrote, "The old lady, the grandmother, was the only one in that group of capitalistic lackeys who understood the

27

value of labor. She had no contempt for the ordinary man. Her understanding was marred by religion just as Marx points out—the Jew sees only other Jews, not mankind. Within the severe limits of her historical perspective she treated me well. The rest of them exploited my strength, she used me only to aid herself in time of legitimate need and to turn on her electric appliances on Friday night and Saturday."

All the time, Jesús, I was fooled. I thought you put up with her Old World insults and understood the trouble I had gone to before she reconciled herself to your presence in the house. The whole thing you present in a very strange way in that little book that has caused me such embarrassment. You make it seem as if I even stood in the way of your political education. You say that I censored your reading material, and yet all I did was look for big print to protect you from eyestrain. "He never inquired of my plans for the future," you wrote. "He treated me as if I was a piece of machinery which, with good care, might return an astronomical percentage on his investment. A speculative but fairly substantial piece of capital goods." And what you say about gangsters, this makes no distinctions between the Mafia and Solomon and me. While it was going on, you were deadly quiet. Only the murmurings about Plato as you whacked at the big bag outside your bedroom door gave me an inclination that Debby was disturbing you. Everything else you kept to yourself until the Kid Sangrilla fight, and by then you were big news and beyond my power to direct.

It is true I went to Debby as a pimp. I was fearful. For all I knew she would resent me at once. Even her address would have been enough to scare me away in most circumstances. In six years of night school I had never visited a student apartment. From the classroom to the pickup to home was my route. Those happy people going out for pizzas and throwing Frisbees to each other were no friends of mine. They even carried their books differently. Until I became your manager I held no hopes to compare with theirs. You were my equalizer. For your sake I went intending to plead with the girl to loosen up, to forget Plato and think about the middle-weight championship.

You were already picked as a comer by *Ring*, had eleven impressive wins, and were almost ready for a solid diet of ten-rounders. But I noticed that your defensive moves were slow against Truax; and Malone, your eleventh opponent, landed a right cross on your chin that put you on the canvas. You went down like butter melting. I had to fight all my instincts to keep from jumping into the ring to pick you up. Of course your showmanship and power saved the moment, even turned it to your advantage. You shook the bewilderment out of your curly hair, beckoned him with an open glove and then pointed to the spot near the far post where, with one vicious uppercut that reminded everyone of Kid Gavilan's bolo punch, you put Malone away. The *Free Press* printed that picture of you pointing to the spot. "Just like Babe Ruth," the caption said. But while the sports page touted the uncanny accuracy of your prediction, I went a few blows back to remember you stunned, on your back, looking for help in the empty air. Yes, I worried about my investment. A loss could set us back months, maybe forever. The crowd likes consecutive strings; it is the no-hitter psychology, the vision of perfection. For this I risk a meeting with the girl who I think has perhaps slowed you down. With difficulty I pry her address from you.

For my own sake and for Grandma's entrance to eternity I do not seek out the lairs of Jewish girls. But for you, my investment, my Puerto Rican middleweight, my silent star to be, for you I overcome shyness, put beneath my arm a folded copy of the *Ring* issue that lists you, and climb her stairs.

Devastation hangs from the walls of Debby Silvers' living room. Ho Chi Minh and the red banner fly amid black-and-white snapshots of napalmed children and griefstricken mothers. Legless refugees sell souvenirs. She sits on a water bed eating M&Ms. She reads a book called *The Structure of Music*. At once I recognize that she is the end of my quest. She beckons me to her water bed, the only furniture. I tremble with lust. For a moment, Jesús, I forget you. Her brown nipples cast shadows through the soft Indian shirt. Her thighs flower in blue jeans.

"I am the manager of Jesús Goldstein." She laughs at my formality.

"Ira, I know all about you." She smiles but her look is fierce, as if the atrocities upon the wall had been performed upon her parents, yesterday. She moves barefoot through the clutter of her room to make instant coffee.

"I, too, am against the war," I tell her. Her entire body grows rigid.

"I can't talk about that. I have to read my Aesthetics assignment. If I start talking about it, I can't make myself study. I just want to go and sit in front of the White House and fast until they stop it all."

I thumb through *The Structure of Music*. I tell her that the only music I really listen to is the sound of the bell at the end of a round.

"Don't make light of yourself," she says. "Jesús tells me you have been like a brother to him, and saved him from the viciousness of life on the New York streets."

Why didn't you include that in your memoirs instead of that portrait of your manager as a vicious capitalist? And if you didn't believe it, why did you tell Debby and predispose her to liking me? Had you told her I was a reactionary, there is no doubt you would have ruined my future.

Perhaps the angels intervened on my side. Those same angels who helped Dr. Shimmer deliver Frieda from danger, those angels who were at the side of his forceps during that long, hard labor that extracted me and that makes me feel guilty. "Twenty-two hours," Grandma says. "Abe went to shul to say psalms." They added another Hebrew name so that the angel of death might be fooled. And out I popped, worth every second of that agony, and the angels go to work immediately seeking out a bride for me. They have a tough time too, these angels. Grandma knows. In this respect her stories are not different from the fairy tales of the gentile world. There I learn about fairy godmothers who concern themselves with the individual welfare of a wretch like Cinderella. From Grandma's stories I know that the weaker angels, the ones not busy guiding the events of the wise men, these concern themselves with finding proper matches for young Jewish men and women. These intervening angels, and not lust or money or congenial personality, determine our brides. They check history for mates. They work under severe limitations. Life is short, the fertile season shorter still. They are limited by geography and most of all by the small number of Jews. "What if the angels accidentally find me a *shiksa*?" I used to ask.

"Spinoza," she said. "This one will grow up to shame us all. In the other world I'll be forced to avoid the glory of the Lord because this apostate is growing into a wild Yankee. *Shiksa feh*." She spits. I grow into the age of wet dreams, never daring to ask again about the possible mistake of an angel. The evil eye I know I'll recognize should it come at me through the layers of urine, but a young gentile woman? How, after all, will I be able to resist that? I know, Grandma, that the Holocaust should weigh heavily on me. I know what losses we suffered. But really, what bothers me the most are all the Jewish brides that perished before the angels even had a chance to evaluate them. I was born on Pearl Harbor Day. While other Americans sat silently beside radios, shocked and afraid, Frieda screamed for twenty-two hours in Butterworth Hospital, screamed at the indifferent nurses already busy with Jap hating, screamed at Abe, at Grandma, at Dr. Shimmer himself, who later enlisted in the reserves and pranced around the clinic in khaki on Thursday afternoons.

Grandma's theory is that I was deposited extra deep in Frieda because of the danger of elevators. Now, the Jap and the Nazi—these dangers she did not comprehend. But a crowded elevator at Hudson's and her Frieda big with child and carrying the pressure cooker that they bought on sale to steam my baby vegetables, this is a danger that even the angels can't protect from. The elevators can make you vomit with their speed, but worst of all they expose the big belly to elbows, shoves and "Excuse me, I want out here" on every floor. Handbags smash at Frieda, briefcases, umbrellas. Grandma is all hands trying to protect me from these elevator strangers. And until I see Debby on that water bed, I have done nothing to repay that prenatal care.

So thank you Jesús, and thank you, angels, for not leading me to shiksas; and though Debby claims to be a nonbeliever, for Grandma's purposes she counts. Still, here I am confronting my destined love, and what do I do? I try to convince her to be "good" to my fighter, to stop bothering him with Plato and start doing what radical girls are known for.

She laughs at me. "I've seen *The Great White Hope*. I know that women can ruin the careers of big black brutes. You want me to screw him, Ira, is that what you have come here for?"

"No," I say, "of course not." I hope that the angels are not listening. With such a frank tongue how will she stand beneath the *chuppah* surrounded by flowers and beaming relatives? Still, I get a hard-on. The embarrassment alone is enough to make me flee.

"Ira," she says, "don't run away." She holds my hand, keeps me on the water bed. "Jesús told me you are shy, lonely. I know the risks you take on his behalf. I know that you borrowed money from Solomon. I know who he is. In high school I went out a few times with Darrell, one of his sons. He had a mania for bowling. On our second date he bought me a big black ball with my initials on it. I refused to take it, and I thought he would cry. Everyone knows what a bastard Solomon is. His own sons hate him. To be in debt to him is like mortgaging yourself to Satan. Jesús appreciates what you are doing. So do I.

"You know, Ira," she tells me, "I am not a pacifist, only a protester against this war. I believe aggression should be released in a healthy way. For Jesús, the ring is healthy. As far as the sex goes, he can take care of himself, you don't have to help him out. He talks about Plato because I am trying to educate him away from hard-line Marxism toward a more general utopian theory."

This is the first time that I hear about the Marxism. To me you never say a word. Of course I guessed—and so did Frieda—that you probably had a reason for leaving New York, a police record, an involvement in dope or numbers. But who in 1965 thinks of Marxism? You are an anachronism, you belong in the fifties, though then as a middleweight you would have had to take on Tony Zale and La Motta and Sugar Ray himself.

33

"What do you mean by his Marxism?" I ask in honest innocence. "He wants to make a million in the ring."

"Don't be so sure, Ira. There are things he would not compromise." From her I learn some of your story. Your birth on the Island in poverty. Your mother's escape from a cruel husband aboard an Eastern Airline's flight full of carefree tourists. Her marriage in New York to Diego Martinez, who began by organizing popsicle cart pushers, and rose to power in the International Socialist movement. "His stepfather spent most of the fifties in jail. Jesús grew up around freethinkers. He met Norman Thomas. But due to circumstance they neglected his education. What he knows are propaganda tracts. He honestly believes Gus Hall will someday be elected president."

"He never talks politics to me," I say, "only boxing."

"I draw it out. I am interested. He thought because I am in the movement I am one of them. I was sure he had told you."

So, I thought to myself, my middleweight is a Communist, so what? Also, I thought, it comes full circle. Grandma too palled around with the Communists, the more serious kind in Odessa in 1917. Before she married Zayde she knew the boys who wanted to change the world. "Communists, Zionists, freethinkers of all kinds," she said, "wanted to marry me and take me away from the righteous path. My father chose for me. He picked your grandfather Meyer, a Talmud *chochem*. You could burn the whole city of Odessa around him and if he was reading about a section of Torah, he wouldn't notice anything else."

So, Grandma, two generations, a war and a continent later, one of these Communists catches up with us. In fact, on Wednesday nights we own him for up to thirty fighting minutes. This is what America means. Everything can happen here.

"I didn't mean to betray a confidence," Debby is saying. As she moves closer to me I think not of Marxists but of those nipples only inches from my arm. This, or perhaps the word Communist itself, brings back to me the memory of the one sexual pleasure of my life: Sharon Shapiro on that night in October when President Kennedy said he was going to stop the Russians from putting missiles into Cuba. If only every day brought threats like that one. Sharon Shapiro stood up and screamed in the Italian restaurant. The owner said, "The President is going to speak," and he put on the TV. I could still eat, but not Sharon Shapiro, my blind date, the niece of Sylvia Karp. Sharon Shapiro of Briarwood, Illinois, I hope you are not reading this. It was my good fortune to be with her for the apocalypse. She worked on JFK's campaign. She had a framed letter of thanks. She was virtually going steady with an anthropologist from Harvard.

"It's war," she sobbed aloud, even though the President asked us to remain calm. She ran to the pay phone to see if they wanted her back in Briarwood, Illinois, for these dreadful hours or minutes that might be everyone's last. Her father, a lawyer—a calm man whom she trusted—told her to stay put at Aunt Sylvia's, he would call her in the morning. "If there is a morning," Sharon Shapiro said. She had no time for lack of intensity. "When the end of the world may be this close," Sharon said, "we cannot guard our emotions. Think of how terrible it must be for him."

With JFK, Sharon Shapiro suffered. She could not look at her spaghetti. Decisions had to be made. Khrushchev counts his missiles, looks over his grandchildren, contemplates the gleaming walls of the Kremlin, and decides that Kennedy, after all, might be the greatest fool in history. The Russian destroyers glide serenely toward the Caribbean, their sailors vaguely aware of the American F-4s flying rhythmically through the clouds as if to lead the way toward the island of happy brown comrades.

President Jack and brother Bob come in from playing touch football in three-hundred-dollar suits. They huddle in the White House. Jackie, still pale from her miscarriage, cancels engagements: "The President and Mrs. Kennedy regret to inform you that because we may be momentarily involved in World War, we will be unable to attend the opening at the Museum of Modern Art." From the Kennedys she learns that catastrophe is no excuse for rudeness. Sharon thanks the waiter, checks her makeup in a pocket mirror. Jack and Bob, Dean Rusk, McNamara and the joint chiefs stay put in the White House beside ticker tapes and twenty-foot maps of the earth laid out flat and calm as if by a pre-Columbus cartographer.

While John F. Kennedy and Nikita Khrushchev face each other across a dark, lonely ocean, like lovers competing for the fertile little slit of Cuba lying beneath her bearded master, that night Sharon Shapiro—who hardly knows me—takes between her drawn lips my moist phallus. "Before we are cast into the oblivion of geologic time," she says, "I want to try this. About this I have always been curious. Let me."

Oh, Sharon Shapiro, I let you and I thank you, and I excuse you now and in the thousand times that I have relived that moment.

"I should have been with David tonight. What happened should have happened with David."

Yes, I believe you but maybe David doesn't deserve everything. He must have you now. You returned to Illinois the next day and never even sent me a note. Sylvia Karp told me one day in the supermarket that you were married. Since on that night you could not blow your David or John F. Kennedy, so you did me, there on the edge of the universe in your Aunt Sylvia Karp's recreation room. If I would dare to tell Grandma about this, I would ask her if the angels were finally getting around to doing their job for me and were testing a few models before making their decision. I don't honestly know if I am a virgin as I sit beside Debby on the water bed. I have never asked about the technicalities. Sharon Shapiro seems like a war experience. That night she had me too believing that the mushroom-shaped cloud coming up from Miami would be our last vision. "Detroit is a primary target," she reminded me, "an industrial center. We may be the first to go. But what difference do a few minutes make."

So, I think it is as an almost complete male virgin that you find me, Debby, panting upon your water bed. The procurer become the seducer.

From Sharon Shapiro I have learned that at the world's end people dabble still in idle curiosity. Socrates, at the end, said he owed someone a chicken; and my own father, more humble than Socrates, said, "I'm hungry." Oh, my father, I know what you meant but the nurse didn't. While you grabbed your heart, she left you to fetch skim milk from the pantry. "He said he was hungry," she told Dr. Shimmer, who excused her literalism.

"It's all right, Nurse Phillips," Dr. Shimmer told her, "he didn't know what he was saying, a dying gasp." Dr. Shimmer fills out the morgue forms. I am fourteen, looking down at my silver ID bracelet, at the big solid square letters that say IRA. Twenty feet down the hall Abe is laid out. Nurse Phillips gives me his teeth and glasses in a clean white envelope. I take them home. I never tell Frieda or Grandma, who have forgotten these trinkets of daily life, but I still have my father's upper bridge and his bifocals in my desk drawer right beside Webster's Dictionary.

"It's late," Debby says. "Have you accomplished your mission? Do you still want me to go to bed with your fighter? Or," she asks, reading my look, my hunger, as Nurse Phillips failed to read Abe's, "would you rather keep me for yourself?"

You, Debby, are no Sharon Shapiro. Not for you are coyness and curiosity. You are as straightforward as a Cliff's Outline.

Across the water bed you come toward me. You kick off your sandals so they won't weigh you down. I feel as if I'm twenty feet deep in that bed. I sit expectantly, the way kids do at the bottom of swimming pools waiting for the buoyant water to lift them to fresh breath. When you kiss me do you know what I am thinking, I am thinking "enough, this is enough." There is a Hebrew song, "Dayanu," recounting in a folksy way all sorts of miracles and the chorus sings out after each one, "Dayanu" ("It would have been enough"). The lyrics mention the crossing of the Red Sea, the gift of the Sabbath, the splendor of the Ten Commandments—each one would have been enough. The chorus would settle for a gesture, a promise; the chorus could have withstood, if necessary, another thousand years of slavery in Egypt. And for me, too, Debby, it would have been enough if you had only kissed me the way you did while I sat there still holding *Ring* magazine in my sweaty left hand. You could have licked your lips with your small tongue and waited for me to try something else. Or you could have said "it's wrong," or "I hardly know you," and still I would have walked away from your apartment grateful and fulfilled.

It would have been enough, Debby, if having kissed me and then having moved back to look me over and assess the effect of yourself upon me, it would have been enough if I had seen only that saucy teasing look come over you, that smile that said "Lucky Ira, I'm going to get you. You're as trapped here as the sufferers on the walls. Lie back and enjoy it." That look alone I enjoyed more than anything I had ever seen. I would not have traded that look and the sense of anticipation that it carried with it for the combined favors of all the Playboy bunnies of all time.

When you reached down to pull *The Ring* from my grasp and tossed it carelessly on the floor, then I knew for sure that it was not just kissing but everything. And once my hands were free of the boxing magazine it was as if every thought of Jesús went with the magazine into the rubble beside the bed.

My hands, Debby, my hands knew what to do. With Sharon Shapiro I remember that they didn't know. If I had put them on top of her head it might have embarrassed her or caused her discomfort. And using them to grab some part of her seemed wrong. In fact, only her back was available to me while she bent into my lap. I remember putting my hands on her Aunt Sylvia's tweed couch, which was rough and uncomfortable.

But for you, my destined one, the hands knew more than I did. Before the rest of me, the hands got zip. Maybe these hands know the difference between passion and curiosity. For me the second kiss, the feel of all of you pressed against me, the motion of both of us upon the waters—this too would have been enough. But the hands are going everywhere, to the breasts, they go. . . . Enough. I am thinking this is enough. Then the belly. Okay, enough, and those fingers, like tourists, shop along the wide boulevard of the thighs. My mind is singing "dy—dy—anu, dy—dy—anu," the Hebrew ditty of modesty; my eager hands are dancing to a wilder rhythm. Finally, the Dayanu voice blends with our movements. The mind keeps on with this song, but it is no longer the one I chanted at the Seder between the second and third cups of wine. In the midst of Dayanu, a small miracle happens: Zip passes through me, and it is not merely the charge of sexuality. In fact, if I were not so busy I would stop to wonder at the appearance of such a thing. That my body could go through the proper motions, I had always known, but whether my mind would let it, of this I wasn't so sure.

It might have happened in other ways. I could have experienced such euphoria in the middle of a mathematics problem or while reading a poem or even while watching a boxing match. But as a special sign, as if I needed it, through you, I discover zip. The mind and the body together, this secret pleasure I learn from you on our first night. Grandma, I thank you for praying that I might acquire zip, and Debby, to you I am forever grateful for this moment. But zip, I learn, is not a steady thing, not like money in the bank. "It's called postcoital depression," you say as I lie there contemplating what must be a turning point in my life.

"Whatever you call it," I mumble into your shoulder, "Dayanu. It's enough."

# 3

My draft notice sends Grandma packing. You, Jesús, carry the old trunks down from the attic. "My great-grandparents were Russian citizens," she says, "they'll take us back in a minute. We've still got friends in Odessa. But you, you'll have to stay here. Only relatives can go back with me. In Russia their fighters would kill you. They have big Kalmuks from Siberia. They fight with whips, not like here."

If Grandma only knew whom she was snubbing in her desire to save me by getting back to Russia. "Anti-Semitism everywhere," she says. "Who ever heard of Vietnams, and still they're after Jews."

Frieda is more practical. While Grandma packs for emigration, she goes to Dr. Shimmer for certification of my marginal high blood pressure, my flat feet, and my hay fever—wild around pollen counts and sure to blow the whole army out of Vietnam when I start sneezing in the jungles.

But with Debby Silvers at my side I go the hero's route. Hundreds cheer. I like it, I know how Jesús must feel. I hold my draft card aloft, Debby raises the Zippo lighter. "Hell no, we won't go!" young men behind me are chanting. Memorial candles are the only light as we stand ceremonially in front of the library beneath a soaring American flag. It feels like Yom Kippur.

For the sins of Johnson, forgive us, O Lord; for the

sins of B52s, and marines—yes, even for the sins of good intentions and for the sins we have not committed but only thought and for the ones we have not even thought. For everything let this Zippo lighter atone.

And also for sins I am committing upon the girl with the lighter—if in this age these are still sins—forgive these too, Heavenly Father.

I hold the card until my fingertips crackle. Those Buddhist monks who burn themselves alive are for a second my fellowship of pain. Debby sucks my fingers. You, Jesús, ignorant of what I am doing, are asleep in your cozy quarters. To you I am now a deceitful master. Because of her I hide my private life. I leave you alone except for our daily training sessions. "Tell him," Debby says. But I cannot risk her, not yet. If I have to choose, it is her, not my middleweight. Fame and fortune can go out the window.

But you hardly notice my new life. Since the Babe Ruth–like incident you have become the dandy of sportswriters. They call almost every day. They stop in at the gym. Bill Green of the *Free Press* calls you "The Crab" because of the way you tend to jab with an almost open fist, as if you would rather claw and snatch. The name sticks. Like Goldstein you laugh it off. All things come easily to you. "Bring on the champion," laughs Crab Goldstein. "I'm ready for everybody."

Then the arena closes. While I am up in the air with the draft, fearing Canada may be my only alternative, Sal Contrato decides Motor City Auditorium is his living grave. He wants the stock car racing business with his brother-in-law. "Shit, this is Motor City ain't it? We'll give 'em motors. Boxing is as dead in this town as a good whorehouse, when all these broads are giving it away. In the forties your boy would have drawn a paying crowd to training sessions. Now they want football. Let fucking Henry Ford give 'em football."

"Sal," I plead, "what about Jesús coming into his own? Where will I book his fights?"

"Take him to Vegas. There's still a little action there, and if things don't work out, a fast Mexican can earn plenty as a pit man." For the first time since I imagined you in the ring, my hope honestly falters. When we needed money for a real trainer, I didn't hesitate. I asked Frieda to go to Solomon. For a month of Miguel León, the prince of trainers, she risked her diamond. For my whims as a manager she risked the scorn of her lady friends. Bad enough that the mother runs a battery junk yard, the son takes up a new business—a boxing manager. Some family. Would you believe they're only two generations from rabbis in Vilna. Only three generations from considerable money in the timberlands of Russia. Whose daughter would you wish upon such people? When finally there is a daughter ready to risk it and opponents primed for ten-round main events, Sal closes the Detroit market. This is monopoly power out to get my Marxist. In a free economy we could fight on street corners and charge onlookers the way kids sell lemonade.

Jesús, my creation, what could I do? If I had not felt guilty for taking somehow from you, although accidentally, your Platonic woman, I might have let it all go at that moment. But I thought I still owed you, and I did—even now I'll admit that. I owed you the chance you had earned with your fast hands.

For you, I stayed with boxing. For me, my mother went finally to Solomon forever.

# 4

"Peace, peace," Solomon said, "there is no peace." All six of his phones rang, their lights flashed in the air. To his right a ticker tape whirred out metal futures. When Solomon was down, not even the thought of 1929 could make him answer the phone. Secretaries, buyers, transportation officials all sat in the waiting room. Busy men across the country were put on hold. "To have all this," he said aloud, "and yet die unfulfilled."

"Please, Mr. Solomon." Through the oak door came the voice of Maureen, his executive secretary. "Please just see Mr. Sanderson. He came from Toronto. He has to catch a noon flight back. You made the appointment months ago."

"Throw the son of a bitch out," Solomon roared through the door, "Throw them all out. I'm closed for the day. Can't I take a rest? Even the goddamn computers break down." Maureen cleared the waiting room and the phone lines. She opened the Muzak speaker to his office. Solomon took the pillow from his closet and lay down on his Brazilian leather couch.

It was 1936. Frieda had graduated from high school, wore her hair in a tight bun. She lived above the bakery and carried its aromas with her. *Challa* in her smile, sugar donut lips, Solomon hungered for everything. He bought fresh bread before each meal in the hope of ei-

44

ther seeing her come down the outside wooden staircase, her legs in colored hose, a book in her hand, or seeing her during her working hours, surrounded by the rolls and cookies, measuring out with those small and beautiful hands the pounds and dozens. Through the glass case Solomon watched her crisp movement. On Saturday night he waited for her until eighteen minutes after the sun set, and they let her out. She had to be home by midnight. In the summer the sun didn't set until nine-thirty. All week he daydreamed about their two hours together while he ran the scale for greedy Epstein, who cheated every peddler.

They were landsleit, he and Frieda. Both born in Detroit within a year of the time their parents emigrated from Russia to Michigan. His family were freethinkers, as happy to escape Jewish ritual as Russian persecution. The Weiners never strayed from orthodoxy. Detroit was Gehenna to them. They even applied for return visas to Europe but cousins dissuaded them, brought them dishes, pots, chipped in to help open the tiny bakery so old Weiner would have his own shop and not have to work on the Sabbath. Their only child, Frieda, they raised like a memorial candle to the old ways. Her innocence glowed. On Saturday she wore long white dresses. Even as a child he loved to see her walking down the street beside her stiff black-gowned father.

When they passed Solomon, old man Weiner spat. He hated the Solomons from the old country, where they were pariahs and he a prince of the synagogue. Their equality in America he did not recognize. Little Frieda looked on in shame at her father's rudeness. Solomon fell so deeply in love that he longed to have a Bar Mitzvah, to win her by skillful Biblical paraphrasing or whatever it was these people valued. His own father raised him to be a socialist and a universalist. Solomon often told people that if his old man were alive he would

45

be mortified by his son's success. "A pinko to the heart," Solomon said. "We sat home every night waiting for Revolution just like the religious Jews awaited the Messiah. By the time I was a teen-ager I knew that money was all that mattered. His universal socialism never got him more than nine dollars a week. But I think even my father, who lived for his ideals, could have been bought off for a fifty-dollar bill. I don't believe anyone ever gave him the chance."

In school when he read *Romeo and Juliet*, Solomon knew that Shakespeare spoke only to him. He wrote her long love letters in badly spelled Yiddish and English. He longed for friends like Mercutio, for meddling clergy, for anything that might bring him close to her. When she was sixteen, old Weiner died, stiffened in his regular chair at the synagogue. They knew he was dead only because he failed to stand at the appropriate moment.

Solomon waited out the mourning time and thought he had a chance. For a week Frieda cried. For the next month she would not smile. For a year she heard no music or idle talk. When she was seventeen he proposed wildly as she tried to run away from him down a Woodward Avenue alley. He caught her behind the Florsheim Shoe store. Their feet were in a small mud puddle. With two hands she still held her long skirt aloft for the run. Against the dark, wet bricks he pressed her, laid his lips to her chin, to her neck. She stood motionless, terrified, expecting Satan to leap from the eaves trough. Solomon cried, mortified himself, lay down in the mud, promised suicide if she spurned him. He was wet and muddy. Frieda laughed, ran from him to the sunlight of the street. "Don't chase me into alleys," she called back to him, "Come to the house like other boys. Momma will let you."

For another year he courted her on Saturday nights. Other men wanted her. Every week brought new matches offered to her mother. Money was theirs for the choosing. A big clothing store owner wanted her for his son. A pharmacist with four stores, doctors, lawyers—everyone who saw Frieda wanted her for his own or for his son. Without old Weiner to guide them Frieda's mother wavered among the suitors. "Meyer didn't care about wealth," she said. "He wanted a good family. Even as far back as the great-grandparents. If possible, he wanted rabbis on both sides of the family. I'm just an ignorant woman, how can I choose the right man for a girl like Frieda?"

While Bertha wavered among the choices for her daughter, in her heart Frieda chose strange, wild Solomon, a confessed eater of pork, an offspring of wild atheists, hardly more civilized than a gentile. He followed her through the city. She felt his dark eyes always looking at her. At home, sometimes, through slits in the window shades, she suspected him. He alone of all the suitors dared to kiss her, touch her. He had nothing to offer. Only his passion, his youth, his possibility. His own family laughed at him for courting the one they called the "Queen of the Jews." His father, the socialist, taunted him. "They'll have you grow earlocks yet and run to the synagogue three times a day. You'll forget the working classes. The world is full of women. Pick someone who will be a help in the class struggle. What can this silly girl do, pray?"

Solomon was prepared, if asked, to adopt her gods, her ways. For her he would change his dress, his manner —anything. One Saturday afternoon as he stood outside the bakery awaiting the setting sun, hoping for an afternoon glimpse of her, he saw her mother go out with a group of women. He heard them talk of an afternoon with sick Mrs. Rosen. They wouldn't return until evening. He tortured himself by waiting an hour, then rushed up the wooden staircase. She awakened from a nap to open the door, asked him to leave; her mother would find out, neighbors would see. She blocked the door with her body. He brushed against her as he moved through. From downstairs, from the cold ovens came the aromas of yesterday's dough. Frieda herself still pink and warm from sleep let him enter the room, forgetting for a moment the monumental risk. In her presence Solomon was all instinct. His hands moved toward her. Talk was superfluous.

"No, Solomon," she said. Her father's spirit hovered. She pummelled the back of his head with her soft slippers, scratched at him—but not with all her strength. Her father's treasure, the Queen of the Jews, was just an eighteen-year-old high school graduate who secretly practiced the Charleston, who wore lipstick and the kind of underwear her mother didn't know about. If she lacked Solomon's intensity of passion, her own was still sufficient to the task. They fell to the ground, her flannel nightgown, his gabardine suit, wrinkled in embrace. His cufflinks tickled her ears. Her father's soul howled from the grave. All these months she had avoided with her mouth those lips that she knew to be unclean. She suffered his kisses upon her cheeks, but now her lips, too, he touched and the soft flesh of her neck and breasts.

"Meyer called me from the grave," her mother said later. "There I was sitting at Mrs. Rosen's bedside when I heard Meyer say as clear as I ever heard anything, 'leave this old lady and go home to your daughter.' "

With the outer door not even closed she found them locked in embrace. Bertha poured the hot water from the tea kettle on him, burning too the exposed breast of her daughter, making him scream more for having to part from his beloved than from pain. With the tea kettle still aloft, she chased him down the stairs. The neighbors saw.

"Nothing happened, Momma," Frieda sobbed.

"Harlot," Bertha called her, not even offering butter for the burned bosom of her only child.

In fasting and in penitence and in pain Frieda stayed in her room until Monday. The rabbi knocked at her door. Abe awaited her in the living room. They tied knots in a handkerchief. No gifts were exchanged. Abe had rabbis on both sides of his family, although he himself had no particular gift for scholarship. Solomon knew him as one of the peddlers whom he regularly cheated at the Epstein Brothers scale.

"In such a way your father made a choice for you," Bertha said. "He warned me that if I did not do the duty of a parent you would end up like the beasts."

In a small and quiet wedding ceremony, Frieda circled her new husband seven times. He was a big, slow-moving man. Rabbinic blood had not made him argumentative. He too had been born in the New World, in Detroit. For their honeymoon he took her to Navin Field to watch the Tigers and the Yankees. Although she always remembered her guilt about that Saturday afternoon, Frieda did not regret her marriage. She loved Abe Goldstein and the sweet slow-moving son who so much resembled him.

Solomon left Detroit the day of her wedding. He hid outside the synagogue thinking that even at the last minute he might murder the would-be groom and take his place. No one noticed the spurned man. He took the first bus to the east. He stopped at Pittsburgh because he was carsick. For a year his own parents did not know his whereabouts. When he returned to Detroit a decade later, rich and arrogant, his heart was full of vengeance.

He married Irene Kay—her real name and her stage name. She sang at the piano bar that was Solomon's first nighttime stop in Detroit. He ate a heavy beefsteak, drank wine, watched men and women on the dance floor. Irene Kay's silky voice moved them. He liked her leaning over the piano with a microphone in her hand. He had checked the credit rating of Goldstein's Batteries & Scrap. They were not even listed.

"A fucking peddler has my treasure, and all my money can't do anything." He sent Frieda a letter telling her he was back, offering to give Abe $25,000 to let her go.

"My dear friend," Frieda wrote to him. "It is my pleasure to see you have so much money. In these days who has money like that—only you and Rockefeller. The knowledge of your success makes me happy. I knew you would be a successful person. Although Abe is not successful, we have, thank God, enough for our needs. Please don't think about me and what might have been. This is a closed book. Each person goes the way of destiny. Mine is Abe, yours is riches. Marry someone soon. This will calm you and keep you from loneliness in your old age."

He sent a waiter with a note and a hundred dollars to Irene Kay. The next week they were married. She bore him three healthy boys. He built a house in Sherwood Estates with a nursery for the children. Irene Kay lived in splendid isolation. When she died, the boys went to boarding schools. Summers they travelled or lived at camps or dude ranches. Solomon paid all the bills and required no post cards. They led their own lives and rarely saw their father. Two of the boys were married and ran one of Solomon's companies. He never visited his grandchildren.

Frieda pushed past the secretaries.

"Mr. Solomon won't see anyone, I'm sorry."

"Solomon!" Frieda called out as she knocked. "It's Frieda Goldstein." He opened the door and spit hot phlegm at his secretary.

I can hardly stand telling it. Thirty years late, Solomon gets what he wants: my mother. She comes in to plead my case. They can't advance their fighter's career without a local arena. How can they go somewhere else? The thought of Ira and the fighter alone in Las Vegas makes her shiver. They also have no money for this. He breaks down. Frieda holds him in her arms. His silent ticker tape, his unlit phone lines, and his warm tears move her. They bump against the desk, scattering ashtrays and magnets.

"My life is cursed without you," Solomon says. "It is one long day, these thirty years. I earn these millions to keep myself from falling apart." She notices his big soft earlobes, the age spots on his hands. Her own breasts sag in his arms. She has trouble catching her breath from his kiss.

"Life catches all of us," she says. "Abe never got the chance to watch me grow old."

"To me," Solomon says, "you're still the Frieda upstairs above the bakery, the bride I never got."

"I've got varicose veins, now, Solomon, and spots of battery dirt here on my index finger that nothing seems to wash out. And Momma is old and hates you as much as ever."

He hugs her as if she is a cashier's check.

"Once you got away, and look what happened to me."

"What happened to you should happen to everyone."

"Not the money, everyone thinks only of Solomon's money. What do I care for the money, strange *goyim* will spend it when I'm dead. Yes, that's what my sons are. Bill and Bob and Darrell—even the names are strange to me. They're big and blond. They drink beer and go to church on Sunday. What can I say, they're good citizens, but from me—from my heart and my blood—they took nothing."

"Solomon," she says, "how can you say that about your own sons?" She is thinking of me, Ira, the little jewel of her body, the reason she and Grandma keep going on cold dark days. Me, her sweet Ira who is about to be drafted into the army. To Frieda you can't say anything bad about sons; she holds up her Ira as if he were St. Francis. Just to be a boy is nothing. A son, that's something. Ira became a real son young, while others were still boys being boys. He wore Dad's watch, his Masonic ring, his gold tie bar. He tried to lower his voice and steer the car underhanded like Abe did. A boy imitating a dead father—there's a touching thought. And this boy, this *mensch* who honors his mom and grandma —him they're going to send to Vietnam.

"Not if I can help it they won't," Solomon says. He takes Frieda's two hands and leads her to the plate glass window at the rear of the office. The King of Detroit Scrap, emerging from his own dark melancholy, is strangely gentle. In silence they watch the slow grinding force of the fragmentizers. Cranes hang at odd angles over hundred-foot piles of refuse. Half-loaded railroad cars litter the landscape.

Oh Momma, I understand what must be happening to you. Suddenly in his office, looking out at the empire of rust, you have a vision of what life might have been. A life of your own balers and semis, of secretaries engraving checks, of cheerful good mornings from employees, and conversation with customers who are not drunk or exhausted.

I had the same hopes for you, Momma, only they were to come true from my efforts not from Solomon's. I would rise from tending the scrap yard to a position of power and brilliance in the world. It's not such a wild fantasy. Every day on the Johnny Carson show aren't there actors and writers and other stars telling us how they rose from humble origins to become what they are now. I have been working, Momma, these six years in night school to make something better of myself. I know

52

you don't want me to work like my father did. "Ira has Abe's personality," you say, "but God willing he'll have better luck in the world."

Grandma says your luck is determined at birth, and my birth emerged out of torturous labor, shrouded from the world by Pearl Harbor Day. Could there be anything lucky about such a birth?

"You can never know," Grandma says, "you just have to wait." So I wait through six years of night school, dreaming that I will be the first medical doctor or supreme court justice or international businessman who has ever gathered all his knowledge and diplomas exclusively in night classes. "Yes," I will tell Johnny Carson, "I missed some of the fun, some of the social life that day students probably experience, but none of that really bothered me. In my youth I was not frivolous. I wanted to become something so that my mother would be able to retire from the scrap business and my grandmother could have some pleasure in seeing our family tradition of excellence emerge again after a lot of setbacks on this continent."

"He's not just anybody," Grandma says at my graduation. "After all, look who his grandfather was." She is the main speaker at this event. All of the important people at the university have given her this exceptional honor. It is their way of being proud of me. I stand among my fellow graduates, all of us as tired as if we were in class, most of us a decade or two older than regular graduates. Our ceremony, too, takes place at night.

Grandma wears academic robes which are only slightly fuller than her black dresses. A few thin hairs appear beneath the mortarboard. I am number one in the class. Xerox and IBM send telegrams competing for my services. Their personnel managers offer me blank checks. "Fill in any amount," they tell me, "any amount.

Don't be shy. We can't do this for everyone, but in a special case there are no rules." Even the Detroit Tigers try to lure me back to sports with a bonus of $50,000 and a guarantee of no minor-league play, but I'm already in my mid-twenties, too old for games. "You should have offered when I was eighteen," I tell the GM, "then I would have signed for peanuts. Years of night school take a lot out of a young prospect. I don't have my old speed or reflexes. Now instead of playing for the Tigers, I'll just invest wisely for a few years and then I'll buy the team."

Grandma is impatient with all the sports talk. "Bring in the businessmen," she says. "Not in public, not at graduation," I say, "wait at least until the ceremony is over."

The president of the university gives Momma and Grandma honorary diplomas to thank them for all they've done for me. Together the three of us march down the aisle. "I should only live to see the wedding," Grandma says.

Yes, it is my wedding she is awaiting, Momma, not yours. My rich spouse, my worldly success, my offspring —you, Momma, are the lost generation. Having delivered me and then suffered your own bad luck, you have been moved out of the path of our family's destiny.

But luck still plays her own tricks. Grandma is right, everyone has to wait. There in the enclosure of his fortune Solomon stands ready to tear asunder once and for all the three of us as we await my future.

The tears stream down his tanned cheeks. Your brown work oxfords, Momma, have left grease stains on his carpet, your boy's windbreaker makes noises against his custom-made suit. Yours is the success story, Momma, yours the rise from humble origins. There on his Brazilian leather sofa high above thirty-three acres of recycling equipment, Solomon fulfills his dream of you.

The crane operators lean out of their cabs to observe their boss in ecstasy. Millionaires from all over the country continue to wait for Solomon to reengage his telephone. This time Grandma has no premonition. This time, Momma, you are old enough.

# 5

Caluccio Salutatti, in Detroit on Party business, read the-
obituaries at the end of the sports section. Across from
the deaths, Caluccio looked at the picture of the smiling
Crab Goldstein raising an Everlast glove. The Party had
never gone in much for sports. Entertainers were better
educated. But since the end of the blacklist days entertainers had found new causes. You could comb Hollywood and not find a Communist. And the new-style
radicals—most of them thought Stalin was a German.
Everyone was looking to the East these days. Vietnam,
Thailand, Burma, China—these were your hot spots.
Caluccio missed the good old days when people worried
about losing Europe. He had spent some months in jail
and a lot of years on the road. In Belgrade, in Prague, in
Sofia, in Warsaw, he could be greeted by important people on the street. In Detroit he was just an old man in a
shiny suit.

"Sonofabitch," Caluccio murmured in his native Italian, "if that ain't the Martinez kid." Professional
Communists never forget a face. That is one of the
things that goes on in cell meetings. J. Edgar Hoover
knew this. They spend twenty minutes of every meeting
on memory practice. They try to meet in rooms with lots
of angles, with pictures on the walls or exotic surroundings of some kind. They prefer old buildings. They train
the mind to associate, to put today's secret orders men-

56

tally on, say, the dirty wastebasket in the corner. If they are ever captured and grilled, they are taught to remember single items rather than the entire wastebasket. It is an old trick. The Dale Carnegie people teach it to executives. Salutatti was a master of memory. He saw the picture of Jesús Goldstein, recognized it and brought to mind the entire Martinez file. He allowed himself to say aloud, "I wondered what happened to that kid." Caluccio stayed in a cheap hotel downtown. The FBI watched every step. He went to a pay phone to call the *Free Press* for Goldstein's home phone number. Caluccio wondered what the kid was like, wondered what part of the old days had rubbed off and whether the kid, in spite of everything, had kept some ideology. "He's still got that baby face, like his mother. I'd know him anywhere."

"Jesús Martinez," Caluccio said, when the fighter came upstairs to answer his phone call. Grandma watched with obvious suspicion. "You remember Caluccio Salutatti, Caluccio with the safe house in the Bronx?" The fighter broke into warm smiles of recognition. "I haven't seen you since you were maybe ten years old. Has it been tough on you, kid? I'll bet so. You know none of us ever forgot Martinez. There's a fund and a scholarship in his name. The rest of the barrio ain't fit to shine his shoes. They deserve what they're getting. I'm glad you think so too."

In the course of the conversation, Caluccio dropped some signs and coded messages. The fighter responded to several in kind. "He remembers something," Caluccio thought, "maybe Martinez did not die in vain." They arranged to meet at the zoo in front of the elephants. Jesús could be doing roadwork. It would not look suspicious.

With pain, Caluccio allowed himself a rare moment for a working Communist organizer. He allowed himself to remember the inglorious end of fellow worker, Sylvester Martinez. For a while Salutatti and Martinez were partners the way Jack Webb and Ben Alexander were in *Dragnet*. In light moments Martinez actually called Salutatti Sergeant Friday. Sometimes, they cruised the east coast in a '56 Ford. Salutatti specialized in small Italian businessmen and organized labor. Martinez had the more difficult work of organizing the immigrant masses pouring up from the Island. They had a tiny budget. The FBI men who followed them could afford the Holiday Inn across the highway from the nameless roadside cabins they were forced to choose. And Martinez's own apartment—what a living chaos. His wife's two children from a first marriage, six of his own from several women, and assorted comrades or just down-and-out Puerto Ricans who came to Martinez for help. Fast Spanish talking filled the apartment day and night. The kids ate and slept on the run. In the squalor important decisions had to be made.

Martinez, his belly too round for a belt, snapped his suspenders against his chest as he considered options. "Salutatti," he used to say, "you, with a big quiet house in the Bronx, you can afford to be philosophical. Here, I got to make judgments every five minutes. Not everything can be pure. Here, Lenin couldn't think so good either."

Martinez, in delusions of grandeur, thought of himself and Salutatti as America's Lenin and Trotsky. He thought that when the time came, the government would send him in a sealed train from Harlem to Washington, D.C. He would go on all the networks and declare martial law. People would stay home while all nondomestic property was seized. In a few weeks they would organize parades in every major city. Reformed capitalists would march arm in arm with workers they had previously exploited. Martinez and Salutatti would organize a new and enlightened government. There would be no secret

58

police, only an army well trained against counterrevolution.

"Martinez, you dreamer. Not in our lifetime."

"It's what keeps me going," the heavyset Puerto Rican told his partner. "If I didn't have the living example of Comrade Lenin I too would go to the church along with my poor brothers who do not trust me when I tell them the world is theirs."

In the house of Martinez, in the hope of revolution, in the midst of Harlem, Jesús "Crab" Goldstein reached boyhood, learned his politics and his fast, shifty footwork. He was the eldest stepson, the offspring of Maria and Rodrigo Sanchez. Maria left Sanchez in a drunken stupor on the Island, fled with her two small sons to New York. She met Martinez. He took her in. There was no official marriage, but everyone knew her as his wife. The FBI was upset that her welfare check went to a Communist organizer, but they were powerless. Every month they watched the signature, hoping to put Martinez away for forgery. Maria knew no politics and little English. She mothered her own boys and the Martinez group of six neglected ones. She tried to clean up the apartment. Salutatti remembers the softness of her skin, a tiny, frail woman who smiled much in spite of the hard times. Salutatti used to bring them leftovers on Monday from big Italian meals.

On the weekend Martinez had chances to make real money on numbers. People would have bought anything from him. He was a neighborhood leader, but the fat Communist would not let organized crime near his doorstep. When nine-year-old Jesús once hit a number, Martinez locked him in the closet for a whole day. He wanted his children to grow up untainted. He wanted them to be able to hold up their heads with pride in Moscow. Every Friday they took baths and put on clean clothes. He made them shine their shoes. They stood against the wall at attention. Then they practiced walking up Ninety-sixth Street pretending it was Lenin Square and they were on their way to the Kremlin. They marched to the storefront which Martinez called his lecture hall. On Friday afternoons he spoke to a few dozen —the faithful. The FBI men waited outside. They admired the nice, clean habit of a family walk.

Jesús never learned to read too well, but he knew the catch phrases of the revolution. He knew what "symps" were, and he awaited the dictatorship of the proletariat. He daydreamed of being a socialist realist. He spat at churches and felt a personal obligation to steal hubcaps and, when possible, radios from all Cadillacs, Buicks, and Chryslers. Jesús thought Moscow must be as easy to get to as Connecticut. Since coming to New York he had not travelled farther than Salutatti's house in the Bronx. There, they gathered once in 1952 to meet Jean-Paul Sartre and Pierre Legois, who were in New York to address committees of the United Nations. The war in Korea was booming. Five-year-old Jesús heard that Eisenhower had of late become a fascist. Martinez did not like the French comrades: "They talk too much," he said. Young Jesús noticed their lightweight suits and the way they made big motions with their hands. These two Frenchmen were the first slender comrades the boy had seen. Everyone who came to Martinez's apartment seemed to be trying to match Martinez's weight as well as his ideals. Salutatti had a backyard with fruit trees. The boys picked some apples for the skinny Frenchmen. Jesús kept a few for his mother. When Martinez saw him holding back on his gift, he quickly accused the boy of accumulating capital. "To each according to his needs," he lectured to his stepson, "you know that."

"Mama needs too. She is as skinny as they are."

Martinez slapped the boy. "Your mama is skinny by choice. Big meals sit all around her. These men lose their appetites with hard work for the Revolution—they read books all day and night. Their eyes are weak. Their stomachs too. Give them the apples." He turned Jesús' pockets inside out. Two small apples fell to the ground. Sartre picked them up and carried them to the thin Spanish lady on the sofa. He kissed her on each cheek.

"If he weren't a comrade, I would have thrown him out the window," Martinez said on the subway ride home. "He wanted to make me look like a tyrant. They are trying to do the same to Stalin. In France, nothing is honorable."

Salutatti, who loved his partner's dedication, knew there would be trouble with the family. A man who gives his life to the Party can't have a wife and six children. Salutatti had aunts, nieces, nephews. This was plenty. Martinez did not agree. "The family is the microcosm of the State. Before there can be a just State there must be a just family. Before there can be a just family there must be women and small ones."

Martinez wanted them to learn Russian, but he did not know it himself. Maria tried to practice good English. She studied grammar books at home with the children. They did not go to school. Martinez and the Board of Education were in the midst of a legal suit. He did not want his children to pledge allegiance to a government he did not support. Salutatti thought it a silly issue. The Party would have preferred Martinez not to press it. He persisted with a legal-aid lawyer who hoped for a career with the ACLU.

On the streets where Jesús Martinez spent his days and some of his nights nobody cared about his stepfather's politics. Jesús had two gifts: speed and peripheral vision. He could see so far around himself that nobody dared come at him from behind. His fast hands pummelled boys much bigger than he was. Jesús never lost a street fight. He could feel safe without a knife.

Mama was proud that he went weaponless, that he joined no gangs, that with her he tried to practice good English. She wanted Martinez to send all the children to school, but she had no strength to argue with him. His whole business was arguing. People came from the Bronx and Brooklyn, from other states, from Cuba too, just to argue. Maria kept out of his way. He grew heavier and argued more but made fewer demands on her at night. She prayed that none of the children would become drug addicts or Communists. Martinez did not allow her to go to church, but to herself and for her children she prayed every day. She loved them all, his and hers alike, but Jesús was her pride. He never complained. Too little food, too little sleep, not enough attention from her—nothing seemed to bother the boy. He was quiet but jovial. He learned early to stay out of Martinez's way.

After school he worked in the supermarket. The manager said a boy like that would be a store manager himself someday.

Concerning the end of the Martinez family, Caluccio had heard several reports. He was out of the country so he could not be sure about the accuracy. There was a speedy trial that involved no politics. Maria's first husband, Rodrigo Sanchez, had also come to New York. He lived as a petty thief for several years before he spotted them one Friday afternoon headed down Ninety-sixth Street for Martinez's lecture. He remembered the slim thighs of his wife, the warm sun of Puerto Rico and their innocent days as fourteen-year-old lovers. He immediately hated the fat one who marched ahead of her. He eyed the line of children not knowing which were his. Maria walked with her head down and did not see her former husband. Sanchez watched as they sat in the last of the four rows and listened to the fat one talk to them and a few others. He followed them to the Amsterdam

Avenue apartment. The family took off their Friday afternoon clothes and hung them in their one closet. Martinez too removed his lecture suit to replace it with his size fifty-six bib overalls and flannel shirt.

Sanchez wanted his wife and sons. True, years had passed, but blood is thick. He came in to demand. Maria and Jesús were in the bedroom going over the helping verb "have." Martinez was snapping the bib of his overalls. The other children had scattered.

"My wife and my sons, fat one!" Sanchez screamed, bursting into the room. "My wife is mine and my boys for my old age. Turn them over." Martinez did not know the man. He had forgotten Maria's other husband. All children were the same to the Marxist, his own or someone else's.

Sanchez, full of drink and possibly heroin, waved a pistol. Martinez thought he was one of Franco's fascists out for revenge. In unison Jesús and his mother were saying, "I have learned and shall have learned." When Sanchez burst into the bedroom, Maria too failed to recognize her young husband in this dissolute gunman. He threw himself at her as if in love. Martinez rushed in. The gun went off several times. Blood lined the floors, stained the shoes of Jesús as he ran next door for help.

The Party did not replace Martinez among the Puerto Ricans. They wrote off the whole minority as a bad investment. Maria died clutching her grammar book. Sanchez was sentenced to two life terms. At twelve, Jesús was without a mother and two fathers. The State offered to put him in a year-round fresh-air camp and teach him a trade. He disappeared, returning eight years later as Crab Goldstein.

# 6

My mother, you who for twenty-two hours screamed at my birth, who for nineteen months nursed me close to your heart, you who shared with me alone in all the world the blood and body of Abe Goldstein—you now go over to the enemy, and in the wake of your defection there my fighter and I linger. You say you did not convince him to buy Motor City Auditorium, he wanted it as a tax shelter. You say the exclusive right to promote Jesús that was part of the package did not interest him. You think it is just a coincidence that suddenly Solomon has become my Master. He who might have been my father. You are now putting him in that position. Yes, Grandma told me everything about you two long ago, before my Bar Mitzvah.

Grandma tells me fewer stories now. She is concerned mainly with her hair. For years it has been thinning though it is barely gray. She wraps it in a bun that keeps disappearing. Gradually you see more and more of the bone comb, less and less of the hair around it. Pink patches of scalp peek out everywhere. She cries about her hair, shows me pictures of herself with thick black curls.

After Grandma's bath, Momma tells her about Solomon. Grandma splashes around like a seal for about twenty minutes, then Frieda or I help her out. Her arthritic leg is not strong enough to trust. When I help, I avert my eyes. She covers herself with a towel too. Of forbidden spots I see only her smooth elbows and upper arms. Grandma's dresses are wrist length and high-collared. In Europe she would have worn a wig. Her single concession to the twentieth century is to abandon the wig. But as her hair dwindles I think she may yet go back to one.

Grandma has rules for everything. For bathing the water has to be almost to the top of the tub, and there must be a towel to sit on, so you don't slip. And there has to be a very fine Ace comb to lace her scalp after washing the hair. This is to get the lice out. On a freight train during World War I Grandma got lice. For the next half century she scrapes her scalp in memory.

She comes out of the tub all pink and perspiring. She sits in her bed propped up by the huge feather pillows she carried across Russia and then shipped, along with herself, directly to Detroit. Neither Frieda nor I are allowed to do any of the maintenance work on these pillows. Grandma makes the cases and the inner linings herself. She pounds them fluffy every day, and once every few months on dry sunny days—with great effort —she puts them in the yard for fresh air.

"With the right pillow you'll always sleep well," she says. She laughs at Americans who lay their heads on foam rubber or cotton or dacron.

After the bath, when she is warm and comfortable, is the best time for stories. I bring her hot tea with lemon and preserves, and she is ready to tell me all. Most of the Solomon stories I heard after baths or on nights when the thunder woke me and Frieda let me go to sleep with Grandma. For the rest of the night I was comforted by stories of the thundery nights in Lithuania when the straw roof leaked and sometimes the animals had to get right in the house with you.

Freshly bathed, her sore knee wrapped in flannel, her

fingernails painted in dull Mercurochrome, propped up by the pillows that she knows are the secret of rest—at times like this Grandma is a powerful being. Her frail, old body is covered and comfortable. Her voice coming out of the bed is strong and young. Her stories are full of hate.

The night Frieda tells us about Solomon, Grandma and I are looking through the *Detroit News* spread on the blanket before her. It is nine p.m. Jesús is already asleep in his basement room after an eight-mile run in cold weather and a high-protein supper. Grandma is thinking of rubbing a little bit of petroleum jelly onto her hair to see if it will help.

When I see Frieda's face, I guess what she is going to tell us. The hints have been obvious to me but not to Grandma. Frieda's eyes are red, her fists are clenched. I wish that I could make it easier for her, but, though I will be silent, she knows I am on Grandma's side. The tears come before the announcement.

"I'm almost fifty years old, Momma, already ten years a widow. The man loves me. He has loved me for years. He's not what you think."

Grandma collapses into her pillows. Her pinkness vanishes. The *Detroit News* falls to the floor. She does not say anything.

"Nothing has to change for you," Frieda says through tears.

Grandma pushes her blankets down and with both hands tears a large rip in her nightgown as a sign of mourning.

"I'm doing it, Momma," Frieda says, "no matter what." She runs from the room.

"Thirty years later," Grandma says, "the old shamelessness returns. Meyer, don't blame me. See," she says to me, "he's pulling my hair out every night. Next it will be my skin."

66

Her hair in the next two weeks falls away in clumps. She is completely bald and will have no wig. She covers her naked scalp with a red bandana.

Solomon, coy and rich, comes to court Grandma. He brings her a three-year subscription to the *Forward* and an illustrated prayer book from Jerusalem. "I'm an old man too," he says, "let me have a few years of peace on earth."

Grandma takes off her red bandana, shows him her cracking, bald scalp. "Lice and vermin," she says, "the two of you have destroyed my thick curls. I go to the grave like a man."

"Listen, Bobbe," he says, "I'll get you wigs from Paris, France, and Chasidic dresses to cover your neck and elbows. In my house you'll eat the finest kosher off Limoges china. For Saturday shvartzeh maids will pre-tear your toilet tissues, lights and televisions will be off throughout the house. I'll have rabbis come every day just to keep you company, and if you want Israel, you can go any day of the week. If I ask, the prime minister himself will meet you at the airport."

"Vermin," she says, "away from me." She covers her eyes with her sleeve.

"Bobbe," says the steel man, "Solomon is not used to begging favors. In the world I give orders. Strong men run at the sound of my voice. But you don't know, Bobbe, what it's like to want. For thirty years I fall asleep every night saying to myself, 'Frieda.' When the boy was little, I used to have my driver take me around and around the park just so I could see her face while she played with him in the sand. My anger I took out on Abe. Who could blame me? He had her, what good was my money? I gave up; I married a shiksa. In her arms I thought of only Frieda."

"Stop," Grandma yells, "infidel. Companion of Satan."

"Hear me out," he says. "You, whose righteousness has driven me to be a tyrannical millionaire—against you I hold no anger. I was young, I should have waited a few more months, then I would have had her. So for those few minutes of folly, I waited thirty years. Only Moses had such patience."

"You are to Moses," Grandma says, "like a flea to the Statue of Liberty."

"Now, when I am old and have long ago given up, she says, it is time. She tells me this. Ask her, Bobbe, Frieda herself. Ten years a widow. She could have had me any time and now, suddenly she is ready."

I listen from Jesús' basement room where the two of us are packing his bag. Solomon is sending him to train at a run-down resort in Mt. Clemens. There are hot springs where a few old people still come for the baths. Solomon owns the resort, a dining room ringed by cabins. There are less than sixty guests. He will build a ring in the casino and convert one of the cabins to a steam room. Jesús can run his ten miles in peace along quiet country roads. As they discuss water temperature and swollen joints, the few arthritic Jews who can't afford Miami or Hot Springs will suffer one more indignity—a boxer in their midst.

To me, Solomon has tried to be reasonable. "I'm going to help you with the fighter," he says, "and after that you'll have a job for life. Don't worry, it will have nothing to do with my sons and you don't have to like me either. Just don't torture your Momma, it's enough that your Bobbe is doing it."

I can't look him in the eye. I just hear Grandma saying for all those years, "Next to Hitler is Solomon."

What if Hitler, back from Argentina and newly rich from land and cattle, wanted to promote Jesús. Would I let Hitler, too, say to me, "Sonny, I never meant your father any harm. He was not an aggressive businessman.

Even if I had left his customers alone it wouldn't have made any difference. Some people are just not cut out for the business world. Now, Abe, he would have been fine working for someone else. It's like your Grandma says about you, 'no zip.' "

And all you men of affairs—I think of all of you Hitlers and Solomons and Johnsons—what have you gotten us with all of your fabled zip? You've bled Europe and Asia.

"Not I," Solomon says, "I've made honest millions in the scrap of the Midwest. And all I ever wanted was your mother."

"Jesús," I say, "what do you think of our promoter and the luxurious training camp that we'll now have?"

"Fucking warmonger," Jesús says, punching the big bag and bringing a new wail from Grandma upstairs.

"Old lady," Solomon says, "cursed be your curses if you don't let your daughter marry me and live our last years in peace and plenty. Because of you acid has eaten away the gloss of her fingernails and hard grease is embedded in those dear hands. Because of your stubbornness the boy has become a laggard, a manager of fighters, a ne'er-do-well, an ambitionless softy like his father."

"You shouldn't dare to mention his father's name," Grandma says. She winds herself in her gray shawl crocheted by Aunt Sarah with the heart ailment. She hides her face behind it, as if to shield herself from the words of Frieda's suitor.

"Thirty years ago I should have come to you and said, 'I'm taking her, that's all there is to it.' But I was afraid—who knows of what. I was just afraid. And you stole her away, leaving me bereft in my young manhood."

"Out of my house, parasite and blasphemer." Grandma looks for her walking stick. I hear her scuffling on the floor above me. I want to help her. I want to go up there and hit him in the soft belly. "This one in memory of my father," I'll say, "and this one for Grandma." When he's down, I'll kick him in the false teeth. Grandma will go for the butcher knife and cut him ear to ear. But I haven't got the zip. I stay downstairs. As I listen I instinctively clutch the hand of Jesús. Now that Solomon has taken my mother, this fast-punching middleweight is my comforter.

"Bobbe," he says, "while you have been hating me for a few seconds of lust, I have bought banks and insurance companies. And without my donations that little hovel of a synagogue you go to would have closed years ago when the city first declared it a fire hazard. Wise up, old woman. Your daughter wants me now. She wants to step out of this dingy house, out of the griminess of her tiny battery shop, out of her nickel-and-dime existence into everything I can give to my new wife whom I have loved and desired forever."

"Better to be dead," Grandma says, "and have for company the bare earth than to live in Miami Beach with you, a blasphemer and the offspring of generations of atheists."

"So for the sins of my fathers, for this too I am responsible. Not just for what I had to do to make a living in this jungle but for what some peasant ancestor pulled off in southern Russia in Abraham Lincoln's time, for this too you blame me."

"For everything," Grandma says. "You and Hitler."

"Then sit in your own stink, old woman. Frieda is coming with me. Already she is at my house in the master suite, surrounded by maids, furs, and French perfumes. She sits in all this splendor crying for you, so I came here hoping you could be reasonable. But now, rot here if you like. The boy is going to be busy with his fighter. The battery shop she's already closed. Sit here

70

all alone and mourn your hair, foolish woman. I'll give you one last chance. Do you want to be in the Jewish home? With one phone call I get you a private room and guarantee a kosher salt-free diet."

"A pox on both of you," Grandma says. "May you have as many boils as I once had curls." She raises her stick in the air and brings it down at him. Solomon catches it and twists it loose from her arm. "So violence also the righteous perform." Across his knee he cracks the stick, her protector against the neighborhood of boys and dogs. "Rot here alone, as broken as your stick."

"Have pity, monster," Grandma wails, "have pity on this bald head. Give me back my only child." She strips the bandana from her and lays her bald head on the table. Her jaw droops, her eyes close. "Give her back or do me the favor please to chop off my head before you leave."

"Never," Solomon says. "Live long and alone and suffer for your mistakes."

When he slams the door, Jesús and I rush upstairs. I hold Grandma in my arms. Her eyes are closed. She murmurs in Hebrew to the pious grandfather whom they tell me was fierce and wise in his day.

On the couch she dabs at her eyes with the bandana, then replaces it quickly, ashamed of her naked scalp in the presence of Jesús.

"I have no daughter," Grandma says.

"You've got me," I say. She hugs me and cries against my breast. Jesús takes to our training camp resort his punching bags, three sets of gloves, two pairs of boxing shoes, and his hopes for the championship. I take Grandma into the wilderness of Mt. Clemens.

# 7

Of course, I have not entirely lost my mother. Even Grandma does not force me into the mourning she is now pursuing. She goes to the synagogue at seven, says Kaddish, comes home to a nice bowl of Cream of Wheat, which Jesús or I have made for her. She kibbitzes with the old folks at the resort. I never tell her that Solomon owns the place. In Mt. Clemens she thrives in the midst of mourning. It is as if she never had a daughter and was raised to spend her declining days in a fighters' training camp.

Every day Momma calls me. There are tears in her voice. Neither Grandma nor I attended her wedding.

"His sons didn't come either," Momma says. "We were like middle-aged orphans. It was a sad wedding. Ira," Momma says, "do I have to explain to you?"

"No, Momma," I say.

"Loneliness happens to everyone. One afternoon in his office when I went to talk about Jesús, it just struck me that I loved him still. It sounds crazy."

"Momma, I understand and I don't make judgments." I lie for the sake of the hours of labor, the months of breastfeeding, the years of tender care.

"You're taking care of her?" Frieda asks.

"You know I am."

"Your reward will be in this world as well as the next.

72

For what you're doing for us Solomon is revising his will."

"It's not necessary, Momma."

"But if I knew she was alone I would lose my mind."

"She's OK, Momma. She likes Mt. Clemens. She has her own cabin. In the dining room they cook for her with salt substitute. I give her all three pills every morning."

"God will bless you for this, Ira."

I hardly see Momma now. She lets the chauffeur drive her around town. She lords it over the Hadassah women who scorned her when she drove a pickup truck and earned her living in an honorable way. I think she is secretly happy to be rid of us too. After all, only Grandma and I are mementos of the past. Without us to clutter the landscape, she can imagine that she did run off with Solomon in 1936 and has been living in quiet luxury ever since. Still, I don't for a second doubt her love. She calls every day; she sends checks that I don't cash because Solomon pays all our expenses here. She probably thinks that this marriage will eventually do me some real good. Already my standing in the Jewish community must have zoomed along with hers.

But Grandma, Jesús, and I are thirty miles from Detroit. Here on the shores of Silver Lake we busy ourselves with training. Jesús and Grandma awaken at six. She goes to the synagogue, he does the roadwork. At eight we breakfast, then I plan strategy with George Danton, the Italian whom Solomon has hired as Jesús' full-time trainer. In 1940, Danton spent a year as a pharmacy student. He carries a prescription pad, though he can only write memos for liniments. He has charted and timed all of Jesús' muscle reflexes and says that he will be able to detect any slowdown in reflex action. "This way," George says, "we'll be able to save him from becoming a punching bag. As soon as I see a twentieth of a second's slowdown, I'll say, 'hustle his ass out of the ring.' I'll know two years before the results start showing up in action. This is preventive medicine."

In his spare time George offers to help out with Grandma's arthritis and circulation. She has taken a few baths here since all services are free to us, but she says the water is dirty. She won't show George her head, but he says that he can, under some circumstances, coax new hair out.

"*Goyishe kop*," Grandma calls him, but sometimes they play gin rummy together while Jesús takes his afternoon naps. The three of them keep busy. It is I who have almost nothing to do. Momma insisted that we close the battery shop as soon as she went to Solomon. I think she promised him that. He wanted no reminders, especially not of her in an old pickup truck. I didn't argue. My disgust with the battery business was an old story. I gave Eli Brown, who had worked for us all these years, the keys to the office and told him he could use the land if he wanted to.

"Ira," Eli Brown says, "I'm glad you and Frieda's gettin' out of this business. It's made for a shvartzer. You just watch my black ass hustle some good money outta this."

Eli cut down at its base the old "Goldstein We Buy Junk and Batteries" sign. I remember that Abe had paid one hundred dollars for that sign. Grandma and I had walked over one afternoon, just to see that brand new emblem as tall as an office building. We both thought Abe was a successful businessman. "If not for Solomon," Grandma tells me, "we would be millionaires." Until I am eight or nine and her arthritis hits the knee, Grandma and I walk for miles through all kinds of neighborhoods. Sometimes Frieda and Abe don't even know that I skip school to take the bus with Grandma to

74

Hudson's, where she can spend hours in housewares looking at the cooking utensils. She picks up every pan in the display, holds it about waist high, pretending she's in front of a hot oven. She plays with them the way I pound my fist into the centers of baseball mitts in the sporting goods department where she lets me spend a few minutes on the way out.

"Cheap *dreck*," she says. "Tin." She hates aluminum, and they never have any inexpensive copper. But Grandma knows that she has the king of pots, a twelve-quart copper one "that you couldn't buy in America no matter how much money you've got." She wraps it in wax paper and only uses it for gefilte fish on Passover. Like the china, it is another of our hopeless guarantees. Grandma knows she has the best pot, but she'll only use it a few days a year. The rest of the time she has to spend denigrating Hudson's housewares. Salesladies are afraid of us. When they come to offer help, Grandma is not embarrassed to be a critic. "You should be ashamed," she says, "to offer such merchandise. In two days this will turn black. And on these, when the enamel cracks, you can poison a whole house."

We never buy anything. All her American pots we purchase for green stamps—which is my department. Grandma gets the stamps from Frieda and stores them in a big shopping bag in her chiffonier. Every three or four months, usually on a Sunday afternoon, she pulls the stamps out and I wet a sponge to paste them in the books. Since Abe gets stamps when he buys gas for the truck, we build up a big supply—about fifteen books a year if Frieda is careful to shop only on double stamp day.

And the green stamp catalogue is Grandma's favorite reading material. Unlike the newspaper, where she has to guess amid a lot of words and smiling human models at what the actual item is, in the catalogue the bright pictures are self-explanatory. For green stamps we buy luxuries. In the S&H Redemption Center she does not practice thrift; there she criticizes none of the merchandise. There, everything is a bargain. We have a Seth Thomas kitchen clock in decorator colors, two webbed lawn chairs, a hammock, a set of Rogers silverplate in a wooden case—even West German steak knives. By the time we read the small print on the blades that says "Germany," we have already used the knives and can't return them. As far as I know they are our only German item. Grandma won't speak to a Jew in a Volkswagen. When she recognizes a German car on the street, she spits.

Until I learn about the Holocaust in school I don't really know why we hate Germany, but I know that my hate is real. Hitler and the Germans killed Grandma's brother, Esserkey. Anglicized, that's me, Ira. All I know is that the Germans killed him and his wife and his five children. I don't know why or how, but two years after he is killed, when I am born, his name is there waiting for me. I didn't know that the Germans killed other people too. I thought it was only her Esserkey whose picture I have seen in a big Russian fur coat. Grandma does not forgive the Germans nor does she stop mourning her baby brother. When I learn that millions of other Jews died like her Esserkey, I don't feel any worse.

In Mt. Clemens, Jesús and George Danton are the only gentiles among the guests. For some reason these health baths became the only Jewish resort in the Detroit area. At one time they were very plush, you can see this from the ornate plumbing fixtures and the chandeliers. But the resort is now very shabby. The bedspreads are worn thin, and there is rust in the sinks. For us, Solomon makes sure the rooms have new beds and chairs.

The details of Jesús' training are still up to me, but Solomon wants him to be maintained like an expensive fighter. For this he hires George Danton, who imposes the rules of "Rest, Exercise, and No Distractions." Danton has trained many a winner and knows ring strategy, he says, from A to Z. "You got to keep a fighter away from pussy. This is one of the main things. When I trained Lazerevitch for his big fights with Sugar Ray, I used to bring him pictures of naked women. 'Mr. L.,' I would say, 'exactly one hour after you lace that coon you are going to be humping this bitch. It is all arranged, believe me. Before the iodine is dry on your cuts, you're going to be making her scream for more. I've got the bridal suite in the Book Cadillac Hotel reserved and waiting. She knows who you are; she's seen your picture in the sports page. She's as excited as you are. Believe me, big fella, what you're gonna get is worth waiting for.'

"After every big fight I always had that room at the Book Cadillac and a big, strong whore waiting for him. Of course he was too tired to do anything—except in the second Robinson fight, when Sugar Ray knocked him out in two. Even though that just about ruined his career, I sent him over to the whore anyway. He claimed it was the best piece of ass he ever had.

"You got to keep a fighter hungry. This is the whole principle. When he steps through the ropes, you want him to think that the other man is responsible for keeping him from everything in the world. You want him to think, 'if only I can deck this son of a bitch, then I can get it all—money, snatch, the easy life.' This is the psychology of the ring."

"I don't think this is the best way to handle Jesús," I

tell him. "Jesús is a smart fellow. He reads, he knows politics and women. If he wants something he'll know how to get it. He won't wait for you to promise him some after-the-fight pleasures."

"Don't tell George Danton how to handle a Latin middleweight. Who trained Issac Logart and Kid Gaston and Emmanuel Torrero?"

So I sit around the tourist cabins of Mt. Clemens and let George Danton handle the training schedule. Maybe he is right. Jesús has not complained. Here at the resort he is a lot less restless than he was in Detroit. There are only the old men and women, a few bath attendants, and the resort servants. It is a quiet life. In two months, when the redecorating of Motor City Auditorium is completed, Jesús is going to take on his first ten-rounder. Solomon has hired publicity agents who come to Mt. Clemens about once a week for photographs. He is going to sponsor the first fight on local television preceded by a fifteen-minute special on the elegance of the new auditorium. The publicity man wants to tape me telling them how I discovered Jesús, but I refuse. It must be the evil eye that I fear. I almost hope that Solomon will change his mind about television, but I know that there can be no big time without the TV. He knows what he's doing.

The publicity people say he is making the old armory into the most modern boxing arena in the world. It will be designed in a circle with the ring in the middle. The balcony will be a cocktail lounge where people can sit at small tables and look down at the fight. There are microphones in each corner so the crowd can hear the between-the-rounds talk, and the referee will be wired so the sound of all the blows will reach everyone, not just the lucky few at ringside. Girls in bikinis will disrobe each fighter and carry the round number cards. They are working on special designs for the trunks. Everything

78

will be up to date, and they want to build up the local hope, Jesús Crab Goldstein, so that in a few months the Motor City Auditorium can be host to a World Championship.

In all the activity on the days that the publicity people and the TV crews are in camp to film, I hardly notice the old man in the shiny suit waiting for Jesús near the road where he does his running. I notice that he is dressed more formally than the resort guests, but I only catch a glimpse. At night, I drift to sleep trying to dream of Debby Silvers calling for me on her water bed; the man in the iridescent suit gets in the way somehow and scares me.

For the wrong reason, Jesús, I tremble in the cot of my tourist cabin. Get this. I think it's the Mafia. I think that young Jesús, for a grand or two in advance, has decided to take a dive. I've seen it in the movies. You'll be sorry, you'll end up as a wrestler. I'm afraid that the gangsters will come after me if I say anything. Who knows about this world of Mafia gangsters? Now if these were Jewish gangsters, like the old Purple Gang that Frieda and Abe used to talk about, then who would be afraid? Before I was born Frieda lived in their neighborhood. "They were perfect gentlemen. They didn't carry guns; they made less noise than regular neighbors." Whenever there was talk about crime, Frieda always mentioned them. It was the Golden Age of Crime. The way Momma carried on about them it's surprising that I didn't become an outlaw. If any course in school had been called "Preparing for the Purple Gang," I, Ira Goldstein, would have been the first to sign up. What they did she never talked about. But drive up on a dark night and they are there to open the car door for you. Need a blood transfusion in an emergency, the Purple Gang is there to help faster than the Red Cross. A small loan, a little food—this is the Depression, don't forget—

always the Gang is there to count on. And on the Sabbath and the Holy Days: "You should have seen them. It was like a parade. They took off their wide-brimmed felt hats and put on black skullcaps. They wore flowers in their lapels; their faces shined. You saw them walking down Livernois Avenue early in the morning and you knew there was a God in heaven. And if ever in a real pinch you needed a tenth man to make up that quorum for prayer, that *minyan*, then the Purple Gang would never let you down."

I used to think that the reason they were such successful criminals, Momma, was because God watched over them because of their piety and politeness. And, anyway, what sorts of crimes did Jewish criminals commit? They didn't murder or rob. Probably they just roughed up anti-Semites who without the Purple Gang would have roamed Detroit in those days being junior Nazis. Yes, at an early age I knew all about Father Coughlin, about the German Bundt groups and Henry Ford. Because of him our pickups were always Chevys. "Not a dollar to such an anti-Semitic *momzer*," Momma said. "Never a Ford, not even a used one." I used to daydream that the Purple Gang would one day get their hands on Hitler, Solomon, and Henry Ford, and rush them off to the synagogue all dressed up to listen to a two-hour sermon. Then, if they didn't change their ways, the Gang would do what the Gang had to do. They would do it the way Rev. Lieberman used to handle the chickens. First you say a blessing. Then you twist Henry Ford's neck back and slit his jugular until all the blood shoots out. Every chicken that I watched him slaughter for us had the name of one of our enemies. I understood history. I never used this for personal vengeance. Only enemies of America, Democracy, and the Jewish people got this treatment. I could take care of my own battles; the Purple Gang stood way back in the mountains of the thirties, like Robin Hood in the forest. When we needed them, they would strike for us. "When will there be another Purple Gang, Momma?" I used to ask her, "and where are they now?"

"Some are in jail. Some moved away from Detroit and went into other business. Who knows? I never knew any of them personally by name." But if not for the Purple Gang, Momma, what other Jewish heroes would I have had?

The Gang moved quickly against the enemies of Zion. They came out of retirement, closed their other businesses, escaped from prisons where they were unjustly held. They met in the middle of the night, not far from our house, near the bakery on Six Mile Road, the very bakery where Zeide of blessed memory once worked and where you, Momma, were attacked on that warm afternoon by the lust-crazed Solomon. The Gang meant business. "There are too many Hitlers," the Gang said. "Everywhere you look there are little Hitlers. They are ruining Abe's business, they are causing prices to rise, and coercing people—even Jews—to drive Ford automobiles. And the Jewish Hitlers—like Solomon—these are even more troublesome. Against them it's a regular civil war."

The Gang invaded Europe. They erased the numbers from the arms of the Camp victims. They resettled people by the millions in northwest Detroit and in Chicago too, on the west side in the big apartments near Cousin Sophia, where there were always vacancies because the shvartze lived so close. The original Hitler they tortured for two weeks, and, when he was dead, his eternal job was to shine the shoes of the scribes in Heaven. And Solomon, for him the Gang decreed poverty. A life of a scrap peddler and battery picker-upper. Like Abe, only worse. A life marked by many flat tires, faulty alternators, a life of much grease and little company on long boring rides. A life of no hitchhikers and all meals taken at roadside EAT signs from homely waitresses. Yes, this was the decree of the Gang. Throughout the land they dispersed. They appeared at Bnai Brith meetings and gave autographs. These were not one-sided men. They could talk about more than crime and Hitler. At the B.B. meetings they were full of warm anecdotes about the Tigers and the great Jewish slugger, Hank Greenberg.

Now, once the Gang had disposed of the Hitlers, they set themselves the task of promoting new Jewish sports talent, talent like say, Jesús Goldstein, who at least sounded Jewish and would do until a more legitimate member of the chosen folk emerged as a ranking contender in any weight division. The Gang declared that no Italian gangsters had better monkey around with this Jesús Goldstein, or else.

Ay, Jesús, it would have been so easy had only your man in the iridescent suit been an average Mafioso. But what can the Gang do with Communists? Against Stalin, against Trotsky (an enemy like Solomon), against the whole Red Army, what can even the Gang do? Had you settled for crime, Jesús, I could have helped you. I could have said, "My friend and protege, what is there to gain by throwing a fight? Solomon can pay you more than they can. If they threatened you, we could have hired Pinkerton's to guard all of Mt. Clemens. But you went beyond all of my guesses, all of my worries. For you there was only one Gang I could call on, though it broke my heart to do it. I did it Jesús because I am a good citizen. Do you know that no matter how much I oppose the war, I have nightmares about the Chinese coming in to kill us all at night. Not reasonable I know, but I was raised to "Know The Nearest Shelter." My blood was typed free of charge by the health department. I wore all through junior high a little plastic tag saying A+ that might, if the Russians bombed us, save me from every-thing but the fallout. I believe, Jesús, that we are living in the land of opportunity. Doesn't your career prove it? Never mind that Abe didn't get too many choices, I consider that he did all right. Wasn't he present in 1945 at all four home games in the Tigers-Cubs Series? Didn't he have ringside seats at the first La Motta-Robinson fight? Wasn't he a regular at all Union High home football and basketball games? Yes, Jesús, somehow it sank in—what I said in high school in the I Speak for Democracy contest where I took an honorable mention. It stayed in my heart. I might burn my draft card but not my birthright. Here, when there are Hitlers we know what to do. Here, you are free to be a Nazi, a Communist, a hippie, anything—only somebody's got to watch out for the public welfare. I believe it, Jesús, and no matter how many times you call me a fascist, I'm not sorry. When I found out who Caluccio Salutatti was, I called the FBI.

# 8

Jesús. Friend, brother, comrade—you who bore my name before the masses. You who helped me attend to Grandma; you—wide-mouthed, sturdy, quick-jabbing, hopeful prospect. You, whose fists brought me out of the doldrums of the battery business; you, old pal, I turned in without a qualm. Maybe it was the way that greasy Italian looked that finally convinced me. He lurked. He waited for you at the path to the woods, near the lake, inside his car—never where people might get a good look at him. I didn't know where you went with him or what you talked about. At the same time, I was worried about my relations to my country. Call it guilt if you want to, but burning the draft card made me feel responsible. "Vietnam," I said, "is one thing, everything else is another matter."

So who am I going to go to when you tell me proudly that Salutatti is a big shot in the American Communist Party. Should I tell Solomon—your promoter, my stepfather? How do you like that, Jesús, the first time I use that word. But that's what he is, a stepdad, a stand-in for Abe, a pinch-hitter in the seventh inning. So if I tell Stepdad he'll probably stop your career on the spot and pick up another fighter to fill his auditorium, unless Momma can stop him. And her I don't want to ask. Already I have driven her to Solomon. No more. Let her be Mrs. Solomon and live happily ever after.

Still, when I contacted the local office I never expected it to go so far. I thought that maybe an FBI man would come out to Mt. Clemens and give you a little lecture and maybe show an instructional film like Miguel León did about footwork or something else to wise you up. I didn't think they would take it so seriously. After all, what secrets does a boxer have? I just didn't want the responsibility of a well-known Communist hanging around the training camp. I wanted the FBI to get rid of him, not you.

Believe it or not, Grandma understands. "They ruined everything in Odessa," she says. "You couldn't walk through the streets without a hundred leaflets. They were worse than the Czar's men, and so many were young Jewish boys who should have been in yeshivas instead of littering the streets." She says that any Communists here must be trying to devalue our money. She tells me to call the police, but she doesn't know it is you whom the Communist is seeking. In your book you say, "The fascist police did not surprise me. I was expecting all along that they would attempt to ruin my career and to cause suspicion to fall upon my accomplishments. Nothing comes from the techniques of terror. They succeeded only in frightening my manager; the people did not succumb to the lies. Crab Goldstein and the truth proved more powerful than J. Edgar Hoover."

Comrade, I don't know about that. Hoover treats you like Iwo Jima. He comes to Detroit on an air force plane, and helicopters to Mt. Clemens. Even though I have read some ugly things about the man, I am nervous and even impressed as I wait for him in the one hotel in town. Imagine, Hoover, who knew Al Capone and John Dillinger and probably even the Purple Gang, coming to Mt. Clemens to see me just because I told the Detroit office of the FBI about the Italian. I am in the lobby a good half hour early. At this time I still don't think I am doing anything to damage you. Read this, my middle-weight, don't skip here, see how it really was. Yes, I am impressed that Hoover cares about us, but I think he must have had business in Detroit anyway and is just making a little side trip to Mt. Clemens. Of course, I can't help being overcome by the attention. It's like writing a letter to General Motors complaining about your car and having the president of the company fly down to take it on a test drive. And Hoover, no matter what we think of him these days, is the epitome of virtue. Though he may be mistaken now, I remember how right he was in all the TV dramas of my youth. I am not anti-FBI on that day in Mt. Clemens, and I'm not now as I write. Events have a way of taking over. I don't blame J. Edgar.

He comes off the helicopter, rounder and balder than I thought he would be. A short old man carrying a brief-case, probably not packing a rod. He swats at a fly, shakes hands. There is no secrecy. Here we are out in the open of the Hotel Sherwood, nine empty stories in the center of Mt. Clemens, and the leader of the Free World's anti-crime forces is addressing me, a nobody.

"Goddamn," he says, "it's hot here. Haven't they got any air conditioning? The fucking helicopter is cooler than this." His three aides go to the manager to request a fan. He doesn't make any small talk. He just sits at our table looking uncomfortable. In a few minutes the three of them come back with the manager and two fans, the manager asks for and gets an autograph for his son. Hoover opens the briefcase. He extracts files. "Born 1941," he says, "Turner Street School, Union High, member of Latin Club," he reads the tiny litany of my accomplishments. Then he pulls out a huge file on Salu-tatti and shows me a photograph that I easily identify.

"What the hell are you mixed up with them for?" he asks. The papers flap in the wind of the fans. I don't know why he is being so gruff to me. I tell him I'm not mixed up at all. That's why I reported it. He has not read in the record of my life that I burned my draft card, but this is what I'm worrying about. This is a federal offence; if he wants to, he can take me in right now. Imagine how it would look on the front page of the *Detroit Jewish News*, Momma, your son handcuffed by J. Edgar Hoover himself, being taken by helicopter to the federal penitentiary. There has not been an arrest by Hoover himself in three decades. To strike fear into the hearts of draft-card burners and others in the anti-war movement, Hoover himself comes out of the limbo of the bureaucracy to make this arrest. Capone, Dillinger, Bugsy Siegel and Ira Goldstein: notches on the handcuffs of J. Edgar.

In court they will bring up my infatuation with the Purple Gang; my desire for Debby Silvers, a known radical; and, of course, the coup de grace, my Communist associations.

"I'm not mixed up in anything," I say. "I reported it."

"Watch yourself, boy," Hoover says, "there are temptations along every road." Out of his briefcase he pulls that issue of *Ring* that lists Jesús as a contender, and describes him in one paragraph.

"Is he really as fast as they say?" Hoover asks.

"Every bit. He'll be a serious contender as soon as he gets a few ten-rounders under his belt."

"Goddamn," Hoover says.

I am trembling, afraid that he will take me in an instant, as soon as I blink or cough.

"Salutatti," he says, "is a smart cookie. We think he was after Joe Louis and probably would have had Cassius Clay if the Black Muslims hadn't beaten him to the punch."

"You mean the Communists are after boxers?"

Hoover smiles at his aides. "My young friend," he says, "when they say they're going to win, they mean business. Do you think they're going to win by recruiting John Does in the streets of Detroit? The top is riddled," he says, "always has been. Look at Hollywood, New York, D.C. They like to keep it quiet. Our job is to stay in touch with it. We watch their moves. We use counter-intelligence."

I feel like I am in an old movie somewhere in the tropics. The sound of the fans suggests banana trees outside. The three men in suits watching us, the brief-case, the quietness of the lobby, the serious look on everybody's face mean that the stakes are high. Hoover and his men just stare at me as if they expect me to crack in the silence and confess. "Never," I say to my-self. I sip the coke I ordered before Hoover arrived and wait for the next move.

"You like boys?" he asks.

"I like girls more," I say.

"What about the middleweight, boys or girls?"

"A girlchaser," I say, "a regular ass man, if you'll forgive the expression."

"Ever make any bets on his fights?"

"Never. I never even thought of it. I haven't in my entire life ever made a bet except with a friend, which is perfectly legal."

"You know the names of any of his other associates?"

Here, Debby, I take a risk. For you, I lie, even to J. Edgar Hoover. When they strap me to the lie detector, I will fail and probably go down in history as a subversive because I don't want them to go to your apartment and see the Vietnamese suffering on the walls. I don't want the three aides to push you around on the water bed, and slap your breasts to make you talk. It's bad enough that I'm involved, you I will protect.

"No," I say, "his private life, if he has one, he keeps to himself."

Hoover gets up and walks around the room. "I like these corner mirrors," he says. "In the big cities they've remodeled the hotels. You don't find places like this. If they'd air-condition the goddamn thing, a person could actually stay here."

Now it's easy to look back at Hoover and say, "What a buffoon, what a silly egomaniac." But on that afternoon in 1966, as I watch him looking at his series of reflections in the corner mirrors, I think to myself, Here I am for the first time in the actual presence of a great man. Some people are not as easily impressed by greatness as I am, but to me a public name, someone who has been on television, has a terrible power over me.

If you can be honest with yourself, Jesús, for just a second, try this. Imagine that it is not Hoover and Ira Goldstein in the lounge of the Sherwood Hotel. Imagine instead that it is Lenin and Jesús Crab Goldstein. Lenin has just flown in from Switzerland to watch you work out, and he wants some information about your manager. Aren't you a little awed by this Titan? Don't you think that Lenin in the mirror looks superhuman? Here you are a little-known middleweight sitting next to one of the great men of the twentieth century. Hundreds of millions of people listen to everything he says. Wars, kingdoms, empires fall from his pockets. He dumps cigar ash and the boundaries of Europe crumble. He writes a pamphlet and thousand-year-old churches are abandoned like fat women. Well, maybe you could resist the glance of a man like that. Maybe you, Jesús, could look the twentieth century in the face and give it a light, playful jab, maybe you could spit in its eye. I'm made of other stuff. I look at Hoover's unbelievable thickness. He looks like a small safe. His suit is that same dark green, within him are the jewels of law and order; everything that makes it possible for you and me, Jesús, to be making our way against all odds into the big time. Nobody else, not the Chief Justice, certainly not President Johnson with his big bulging ears and sloppy grin could fill me with such awe. Hoover is timeless, solid. He is not only the green of floor safes, but also of mail boxes and telephone company service vans. He exists to make sure that everything actually works. The man is hot, cranky, perhaps even unworthy of his power, but the image in those mirrors is the eagle flying right off a half-dollar. Don't forget that President Kennedy has only been dead for three years and there are less than 10,000 casualties in Vietnam and the Black Panthers are still only Oakland bandidos.

J. Edgar Hoover turns to look me square in the eye. "Son," he says. In an affectionate gesture he reaches up to put a hand on my shoulder. I can't take any more. I confess.

"In March I burned my draft card, sir." I hold out my hands ready for the cuffs. His three aides look up from their martinis, their open jackets exposing the shadow of revolvers. Hoover removes his hand from my shoulder. He goes back to the table to check my file. He glares at his aides.

"Nobody's perfect," he says. "We're lucky if we note ten percent of the burners." With his gold Cross ballpoint he writes into my file, "draft card burned." I read it upside down. It looks Russian. "Do you remember the exact date."

"March 11," I say.

How can I forget that after the burning I went with Debby Silvers back to the water bed? How can I forget the Vaseline that she smoothed on my burned fingertips kept moist in her mouth on the long walk back to her apartment. The pain was good. Burning the card was too easy. I wanted to suffer a little and to be comforted by her—the red fingertips, the white blisters, the Vaseline, the aloe vera plant she rubbed on me, the butter and then after all the ointments the smooth liquidity of herself, not like Sharon Shapiro blowing me out of apocalyptic curiosity. No, this time, on March 11, 1966, Debra Silvers desired nobody else, only me, a silly sympathetic liberal who couldn't even burn a draft card without hurting himself.

She arose from love and checked her clock. "I have an exam in the morning. Art History. I hate to do this to you, but really I've still got to study."

And while she studied Picasso and Max Ernst, I walked through the surreal ghetto of Detroit not afraid of the shadowy black men who seemed to leer at impossible angles along the cold street. This time there was no doubt. I had really done it. And, Grandma, if fornication counts a little toward the great-grandchild that you need to reach heaven, then tonight has been a momentous occasion for you as well. The angels who arrange my destiny waited four years after throwing Sharon Shapiro my way; they waited these four years because they didn't want to involve me in idle business. They wanted me to be free so that I could do a bang-up job in the battery business and bring lots of recycled lead to market.

"Take it easy, Big Shot," the angels warn. "Don't let a piece of ass go to your head. After all, you're twenty-four, everyone else starts at sixteen with shvartze whores from right in this neighborhood where you have no business walking around at one a.m. To these shvartze, all you are is a walking wristwatch. One good lay and you think you're Superman. They'll cut it off yet if you're not careful. You think because you're not going to Vietnam that they can't get you on the streets of Detroit?

"Listen," say the angels, "because you've got on your mind a naked girl with an art book between her legs six blocks from here, you're walking around where only a few months ago the U.S. Army had to go in tanks and shoot these shvartze just like they were Viet Cong. You want to live to have another erection, then run away from here quick."

But already it may be too late. Behind me are footsteps, the kind that have taps and high heels. I hear the sound of a leather coat against thighs. I am afraid to turn. I stop in the middle of the broken sidewalk. They take me under each arm as if they are a mother and father leading me down the aisle.

"Relax, brother," the man says. "We ain't going to do any damage to your sweet white ass." The woman who holds my other arm is tall and light-skinned. She pats my hand and smiles. They both have leather coats and are perfumed and hip. "We ain't going to hurt nobody, brother, we just saw you walking along and we thought this white boy better get some help or he might not make it home by hisself. Don't you know that this ain't open territory?"

"I was taking a walk. I burned my draft card." Yes, I blurt it out to them just as I would to J. Edgar Hoover, as if this single small act of defiance will keep them from murdering me.

"Honey, that's nothin', we burned the whole fucking town." They laugh and I join them.

"Look at you," say the angels, "arm in arm with shvartze. If this is what you wanted, why didn't you go when you were sixteen with all the other boys to the whorehouses. In those days you could find women like this one for ten dollars, and not be afraid for your life. For all these years we watch him. For the sake of his grandfather's soul we do an extra good job screening for him through a thousand applicants among women from all over the Midwest. And now when we find him one right here in Detroit, now he goes out to pal around with the pimps and their women, laughing about burning down a city where the army had to kill forty-five people before they quieted down. It was a regular pogrom and he laughs."

"Sweetheart," the girl says, "where are you heading? We are going to escort you. You're getting a safe passage courtesy of two happy niggers." They laugh but this time I don't. I tell her where my car is parked. They hold me bridegroom-style all the way. We pass other blacks. Everyone smiles at us. Remnants of the recent riot are everywhere. All the store windows are boarded. Entire buildings lie blackened along the block like rotten teeth in a mouth. My escorts rub alongside me.

"This young man been out looking for pussy. Yes, I believe this white fella is out lookin' for it." The man says this and they giggle again.

"No," I say, almost wanting to boast, "no, I was just walking, not looking for anything."

"Well, you found some pussy, didn't you, man. Well, there she is. Look on your other side, that's pussy, man, ain't that what you call it?"

She smiles and purses her lips as if to kiss me.

"What's the matter, white boy, you afraid to say pussy."

"Pussy," I say looking at her. She really is beautiful. I think of Debby Silvers—small, compact, energetic, the opposite of this tall, slow-moving negress.

"Twenty-four years he waits," the angels say, "and now he's going to do it twice in one night." And you know, I would have. If I was not afraid that they were planning to kill me, I would have invited them both to Debby's apartment and asked them to be quiet while she studied. And I would have done it again, right there on the water bed with the black girl while her friend watched and gave me advice on how experienced men who have been doing it since they were eleven operate in such circumstances. But the angels overestimate me.

"Please don't kill me," I ask her, she whom I have just called "pussy" and who clings to me in the dark street.

"Honey," she says, "I ain't even goin' to fuck you. We're just takin' a walk too. Don't be scared of us. We're the two happiest niggers in Detroit right now. Can't you see that?"

I don't tell J. Edgar Hoover anything else about March 11. But later on that night, when I was home and the fear had left me, I realized that they must have been very high, probably on heroin. They did just want to walk with me. And they kissed me on each cheek as I got into the pickup. "Lock your door, honey," she called out to me, "there's bad niggers too."

So when I tell J. Edgar Hoover that on March 11 I burned my draft card, I am only telling him a small part of the story of that day.

"You burned your draft card," Mr. Hoover is saying, "and you are the manager of a member of the Communist Party. You're twenty-four years old, are unmarried and have no previous record. You are a high school graduate and still a student."

"Part time," I tell him.

"Well, I guess the record is straight now and complete, isn't it?"

"As far as I know."

Mr. Hoover loosens his tie. He seems to feel better now that the fan has cooled the room. He sips for the first time from his own martini, which looks regal alongside my watery Coke.

"Young man," he says, "you've got yourself into the middle of something, you know that, don't you."

"I don't know what's going on, that's why I called your office."

"You did the right thing. You see, we knew anyway. We've been watching Salutatti for years. I can tell you at what hour of the day he moves his bowels. We knew he was meeting the fighter, but, you see, we didn't know how far the conspiracy stretched. We didn't know if you were part of it."

"I'm not sure there is any conspiracy. Jesús is still training normally. I don't think he's any threat to anyone. I just wish you could do something to keep that guy away from our training camp."

J. Edgar Hoover looks up at heaven blocked from his view by the off-white ceiling of the Sherwood Hotel. "If only I could round up every Communist and ship him off to Russia; ah, if I could do that, young man, then I could spend my days on the beaches and golf courses. I could retire and enjoy the fruits of my long labor in behalf of this nation. We have in this democracy a mixed blessing. The ones that want to kill you, throw your body to the dogs and take everything you have—they've got the same rights you do. They can go around and do anything they want to. Until there's evidence all we can do is watch. And now we're watching your fighter. And you."

"But what can Jesús do? He's harmless even if he is a Communist."

"Do you have any idea what a world champion is worth to the International Communist movement? Probably as much as the atom bomb. Do you know what people in Africa and Asia think of when they think about us? They think about our cars and hot dogs and our movie stars and our champions. Do you know that Cassius Clay three years ago turned the Black Muslims from a bunch of freaky Chicago Negroes into a world-wide movement? He did it with one sentence in the middle of the ring after he knocked out Liston. Now you hardly ever meet an Otis or a Washington. They're all Muhameds. Du Bois couldn't do it, and Malcolm X couldn't do it, and Martin Luther King can't do it either. But that cocky rascal Cassius Clay, he did it.

"Now suppose that in the middle of World War II, Joe Louis had declared himself a Nazi. What would have happened to our morale then? Thank God we had a patriotic champion when we really needed him. And Ali, for all the harm he's doing, he might as well be a Communist. How would it look all over the world if our heavyweight champion is a Black Muslim and our middleweight champ a card-carrying Communist? How does this make our generals and our congressmen look in the eyes of the world?"

The Director of the FBI looks straight at me. "I'm not blaming you for anything, young man. As far as I'm concerned the draft-card business can be forgotten. A few crazy kids are nothing compared to a Marxist champion.

"You know," he says, "the FBI is powerless to stop anyone from winning a fight. The gangsters can fix a fight whenever they want to. We've got evidence to prove it. But if your Jesús is as fast as he seems to be and if he can take a punch, there's not a thing the federal government can do to stop him. And if he pays his taxes, we can't get him later either."

I am awaiting Mr. Hoover's offer to become a spy. I remember *I Led Three Lives* when we first got our television set. It came on between Arthur Godfrey and wrestling. Herbert Philbrick fought the Communist conspiracy every week. Men like Salutatti plagued him from phone booths all over New York. To his own wife and children he never explained a thing. Years later his friends by watching TV realized why Philbrick spent so much time in pay phones.

Yes, Jesús, I am prepared to spy on you. I am prepared to seek out safe phones. I am prepared to casually eavesdrop whenever possible. I am prepared to look over your mail, although I don't think you have ever received a single letter. I am prepared to tell Hoover at what hour you have bowel movements, what you eat, and what you talk about. And I can do all this without feeling guilty, Jesús, because I don't think I am betraying you, because I think you are innocent, because I don't believe a few odd facts in the possession of the FBI can possibly do you any harm. In fact, Jesús, if I can do these few things I will feel relieved. If you can consort with important Communists and not worry about what this will do to me, why can't I tell Mr. Hoover a few things about you? You know that I would never compromise your career, your health, or your safety. Maybe it's idle for me to try to convince you that I meant no harm. The FBI was watching anyway; they knew before I told them. Salutatti knew they followed him; you knew you were being watched. Until that afternoon I was the only innocent one.

J. Edgar Hoover puts the files back in his briefcase. The three aides finish their drinks and button their jackets. They unplug the fans.

"Here is a phone number," Hoover says, handing me a business card. "Call us collect if you have any information."

"Do you want me to call at certain times?" I ask.

"No," he says, "it's a twenty-four-hour switchboard."

"But what should I look out for, sir?" I ask him. I still don't know what any of this is about. "What shall I try to do?"

"Try to be a good citizen," Mr. Hoover says, "as you were when you phoned us. Try to stand up for freedom and democracy whenever you can." He shakes my hand. "Some day," he says, "I'll see you at ringside. Apart from all the business aspects of this investigation, I'm a real fan."

# 9

With less trouble than Jesús had with Otis Leonard, this easily does Debby excel in art history. "I wrote a descriptive essay on the architecture of arenas," she says, "without ever having seen one. I wrote it based entirely on what you and Jesús told me and on some sketches of the Roman Forum that we studied in class. You know that nothing much has changed. The Romans did the best they could for comfortable seating. The passageways and aisles are about the same width and the Romans never had any pillars to block their vision."

What can I tell you, Debby, you who suffer for the Vietnamese and put off your own pleasures for the sake of homework and exams. What can you tell someone who studies economics and art history while the angels who have been planning my destiny for twenty-four years, these angels and I, sit around and wait to hear your test scores? Yet the angels don't really care about your grades. They want a good mother for Grandma's great-grandchild. After all, her guarantee of eternal bliss ought at least to be sure of a good Jewish upbringing. I want to ask you, Debby, while you tell me about Roman architecture and Keynesian economics, I want to ask you if maybe sometime in the future on Friday nights you'll light candles and cover your eyes and make those half-circle motions. with your hands that Grandma makes as if she is trying to pull the flames toward her. I want to ask you if twenty years from now when the war is over and you're forty-one and looking at the slope of old age, I want to ask you what you'll be like then. Will you collect money for the March of Dimes and the UJA, and make sure that our children take their medicine on time and wear warm clothes in winter? When I'm not a manager and you're not a student and an activist, what will we be?

"You'll be like all people," the angels say, "you'll live in a nice house. You'll go to work in the morning and to bed at night. If you're lucky you'll earn enough money to have a big plaque with your name on it on the wall of a synagogue. After you're dead, they'll light up that name every year on the anniversary of your death."

"But in between that plaque and now, the in-between —my life—that's what I'm curious about."

"About that," say the angels, "there's nothing to be curious. Only silly people worry about that—people like Mrs. Epstein who go to psychiatrists because they've got money to burn. If you've got time to worry about your life, then you're not working hard enough."

The angels are right. When I went every morning at seven to Goldstein's We Buy Junk and Batteries, I didn't worry about my life. I worried about the price of lead and copper and about the transmission on the pickup. Now, in the luxury of a training camp, I sit here while Jesús works and I wonder about my life.

"Why didn't you wonder when your father died," the angels say, "and you were fourteen and had to decide whether to help your mother after school or try out for the high school baseball team?

"Big shot second baseman every afternoon from three to six throws a ball around while Frieda stays alone at the dirty yard, a small dog for protection and company. Why didn't you wonder then if getting three hits the

100

entire season was reason enough to leave your own mother, a lonely widow, alone all spring?"

"He's like his father," Frieda says, never blaming me. "For sports he'll do anything. A boy has got to play. He's got sorrow enough; leave him alone now. Baseball is good for him."

Every time at bat I pressed to get a hit in memory of my father, who taught me years ago the level swing. On the Turner School field he hit fungos to me until I could go back on a fly ball at the crack of the bat and run right up to the edge of the brick building before I turned to spot the ball.

"For defense, you've got instincts," the coach says, "but at the plate there's trouble." The trouble is I want to please the memory of my Daddy. I want him who died before I ever played in an organization beyond Little League, I want him to know that I'm taking a level cut and watching the ball all the way. But I want that hit so much that I lunge at the ball, I strike out, I dribble ground balls to the left of the mound. No amount of hustle gets me on base. I do not hit my weight. "Three hits," I tell Momma, "in two and a half months."

"So what," she says, "you had fun." I let her think so to make her happy, but it was no fun, Momma, going up to the plate and seeing the disappointment of my own teammates. It was no fun batting ninth and hoping to be hit by a pitch—but not too hard—so I could get on base and use my speed. I wanted to hold back, to stay calm, to watch the ball the way Daddy taught me to, but when I was finally there, in the silence between the pitcher and the batter, there I lost all my concentration. The bat became just a heavy stick with tape on it. I could hear the umpire chewing gum. I swung before the ball left the pitcher's hand, stopped myself, swung again off balance and half mad in my anxiety to get on base. Jesús, if you were like that you would never last one round. No, we

101

are opposites. You, middleweight, you shine under pressure. The ring enlarges you the way I used to disappear in the batter's box.

And, Debby, I want you the way I have desired nothing since those base hits. I worry, too, about losing you by my lunging anxiety, my awkwardness. You walk to school among crowds the way Betty and Veronica did in the Archie comic books. You and your friends talk a lot about the terrible war, but I can see by the way you tease one another that your own lives are not as grim as you pretend. You try, Debby, to integrate me into the company of the undergraduates, but I am as ill at ease among them as if I were a Viet Cong. I can talk sports or a little politics too, if I have to, but really what I want when you have me there among your friends—I really want them all to go off to a rally and leave us alone together. When they leave, you stop smoking, you smile less, you notice how much I want you. Then, laughing, you tell me, "Ira, all you like to do is fuck and go to the movies." You try to tease me as if I'm one of the friends from your classes, but I don't know how to respond. I offer to learn other pleasures, dining out, the theater, opera, ballet, museums of all kinds.

"No," Debby says, "I know that you'd do a lot of things just to please me, but it's got to be spontaneous or it's no good. I don't want to train you to like going to the museum. If you don't respond to art, you just don't. I'm surprised you don't just because you're a sensitive person, but I'm not going to teach you. Someday, when you want to, when you're ready, you'll look at a painting or a piece of sculpture and see the world whole, right there before your eyes."

Not me, Debby. All I'll ever see is what Grandma calls a *getch*, an idol. To me, a museum is a Philistine temple right in downtown Detroit. When I first read about Samson, the Detroit Art Museum was the very building I imagined him pulling down. Delilah stood there on Woodward Avenue watching the gray limestone crumble around her, regretting deceit, honoring, but too late, the long-haired Hebrew who liked only screwing and going to the movies.

The museums, the Masonic Temples, even some of the parks with their big, gray horsemen all remind me of Baal and Astarte. Just to be a Cub Scout I have to get Grandma's interpretation of whether I can go into the basement of the Catholic church where the meetings are held.

"Don't take off your hat," Grandma warns me. "Not if there are idols there. If you take off your hat, it's the same as bowing down to them."

"Don't be silly," Frieda and Abe tell me, "go to the meetings and do what everyone else does. There are other Jewish boys in the group. The den mother herself is a Hadassah lady." But when it comes down to it, Grandma, I keep my little blue cub scout beanie on. During "The Star Spangled Banner," during the silent prayer, during the pledge to the flag and the scout's salute my cap stays on. The Virgin Mary near the coat rack, the saints in the crevices are waiting for my hair to peek out.

"Good for you," Grandma says when I tell her, but after a few meetings I quit cub scouts. Week after week I cannot face the pressure of so many idols.

"This is the twentieth century," Debby reminds me, "when are you going to stop believing what your grandmother told you when you were six years old?"

At any time I'm ready, Debby. I'm ready to believe that I can take my hat off in church, ready to believe that Solomon is not a Hitler, ready to give up the evil eye, the angels, the Messiah carrying his shofar in a silver case. I'm not only ready, maybe I already have given up. Am I not here at Solomon's resort, sculpting in the flesh of Jesús a career as pagan as any in old Rome?

"It's true," Debby says, "that you're involved in a business that is almost universally looked down upon. But I don't hold that against you because all of your intentions are good. I believe in intentions. That's why I don't trust political leaders. They all want power. What do you want?"

I want you, Debby, and a championship for Jesús. I want Momma and Grandma back in one house and Solomon far away counting his money. I want our child wearing his hat if he has to among the Freemasons and the Scouts. I want boxing to return to Detroit the way it was in the heyday of Joe Louis. I want a pennant for the Tigers. I want to hit .360 and watch myself swing the bat slow motion in an instructional film. I want my father back in the pickup giving me yellow leather mittens so that I can help him load batteries without getting acid on my hands. I want to know what our life will be like in twenty years and in forty and in sixty. And after that too.

"For the first time," the angels say, "he's talking a little like a Talmud *chochem*. He wants to live long and know things. Who doesn't? But it's not so easy. You've made your list, now go out and do 699 good deeds every day. Follow the ten commandments and all the customs down to their slightest nuance."

"No," I say, "I can't." It took all I had to keep my hat on. But I'll have good intentions. Debby believes this is enough.

The angels moan like the crowd when a hero strikes out. They span the dark green earth spying out Jewesses in the pampas of the Argentine, in the wild loneliness of Australia. In Kansas City at the Jewish Community

Center, beside the pools of exotic hotels in Miami Beach, at delicatessens in Mexico City, in every corner of the Holy Land itself—they seek out an alternate bride.

"No luck," say the angels.

"Destiny," says the would-be groom.

"I've got to study," says Debby, "maybe next week."

# 10

In your published memoirs, Jesús, I do not recognize you. Of course, I am hurt when you refer to your manager as "the tool of the FBI and the CIA, and the Judas Iscariot of the Antiwar Movement," but I think that all of the venom that is in that book has been put there by someone other than you. The ghost writer provided by your Soviet publisher managed to get in all the name calling. The real Jesús is hidden in that propaganda pamphlet. Only in one small section—when you relate your first conversation with Tom Hayden—only there do I hear Jesús uncensored by the Soviets. Let me quote briefly the one honest fragment of that document.

From the *Memoirs* of Jesús the Crab (pp. 48–51):

Tom Hayden, he says, "Crab, why are you letting them exploit you?"

I say, "Tom, what the hell. I spent a lot of hours whittling my fingernails in reform school. What the hell. Fight for money or fight for your life."

He says, "Man, join us. We're fighting to change the world."

I say, "Martinez he always said he is changing the world. Fucker got his dick shot off. This changed the world?" Hayden does not know that Marx shoots out my ass. He thinks I am one dumb Islander and he has got to tell me what is happening in D.C., in Nam, in what he calls Latin America. I say, "I want some good fights in Detroit. I want knockdowns and big crowds and solid guarantees."

He says, "What about all that is going down in Nam. You want to associate yourself with all that?"

I say I am gunning to be champ, not president.

He says, "Same thing."

I say, "'You bring that crowd of marchers down to Motor City and you swell my gate, then I march with you."

He says, "If we swell your gate, that warmonger Solomon will get richer. Man, we are not paying taxes, we are not paying the phone company, we boycott the table grape. You expect us to pay admissions to a man who sells metals to General Dynamics and fabricated steel to Lockheed? You don't know the new radicals, my man, if you think we'd go to support a warmonger just to get a little publicity and a good man on our side. If you didn't want to be one with us," he says, "why did you come out here to the rallies, to the teach-ins? Why didn't you just stay in the gym and pack your nuts in hot towels?"

I say, "Hayden, I pack my nuts with your kind of Revolution. Where I come from we used to say, 'Stalin says, we do.'"

"Holy shit," Hayden says. "Where do you come from?"

"From the barrio," I say, "but I'm the stepson of Martinez, Stalin's honcho on Manhattan."

"You got credentials," Hayden says, "like nobody else in the Movement. But this makes you a liability. We are not Moscow-oriented. To us Moscow is as responsible as Washington. With us you would be more respectable as a Maoist."

I say, "Hayden, I left all that behind me. I come to the rallies to keep my finger in the pie. I look for new friends and girls."

"You're no idealist, Señor."

"I'm a middleweight."

"Well," he says, "see if we're there when on Wednesday night you step through the ropes with Kid Sangrilla. And I'll tell you this, Comrade, deck Kid Sangrilla and we'll have every welfare mother in Wayne County picketing your gym and Solomon's junkyard. Kid Sangrilla's mother is one of us. She marches. She organizes welfare protests. She says her son is mentally off and should not be in the ring."

"The Boxing Commission says he is A-OK," I tell him.

"The Boxing Commission is in Solomon's pocket," he says. "The whole city of Detroit is his handkerchief. They'd like you to kill Sangrilla. Why not give his mother a little more grief."

I say, "Sangrilla fought a draw with Chico Vejar, beat Kenny Lane, Luther Rawlings, Carelia Valdez. He has plenty of class and nobody can say there is a glass jaw on that face."

"The man's talent is not in question," Hayden says. "He has an IQ of seventy-six. He should be in a hospital not a boxing ring. He is also thirty-three years old and wears corrective shoes. His mother has been trying for years to keep him from fighting. He is outlawed in seventeen states. All I can tell you," Hayden says, "is that if you fight him you are on the other side. We've been with Mrs. Sangrilla on lots of welfare issues, we're not about to desert her when her only son's welfare is at stake. This is like a little Vietnam and you are the gunship, Comrade. Think about it. Are you going to be as hard-hearted as Stalin? Look what it got him. His own daughter hates the bastard."

"Hayden," I say, "I've got no love for capitalism and its attendant vices, but a contract is a contract. Come Wednesday night I'll be in the ring."

"Comrade," he says, "we are taking on Lyndon Johnson and the whole fucking army. We are not going to shy away from a punk middleweight."

Hayden and I we start as adversaries, end as friends.

# 11

At the Salt Springs Resort, Jesús, you respond to the routine of the training camp. Your whole heart goes into your fists and your legs. Maybe it's the discipline George imposes or perhaps it is the secluded calm of Mt. Clemens that has turned you into such a dedicated pro. You who used to skip your run whenever possible and never do any timing, work on the light bag; you who ate Hershey bars and pizzas when I turned my back, you now train as if you have recognized your true vocation.

I see your dedication, Jesús, even though I am looking for something else. Openly and without apologizing I have searched your cabin for propaganda pamphlets, and in a moment of real paranoia I even checked the ring posts for hidden microphones. But Jesús the Communist, Jesús the watched is serene, dedicated, innocent of conspiracy, and a stranger to laziness. In his Mt. Clemens training camp, amid the uniformly aged resort guests the body of Jesús the Crab blossoms.

It is Grandma who gives me trouble. Of course, I have not anticipated that this would be easy. I've left every evening open so that while George and Jesús go over the details of footwork and practice incidental calisthenics, I am trying to introduce Grandma among the fifty-two current guests of the resort. The lounge is filled with the noise of complaint as the guests discuss each day the effects of the mineral water. Mrs. Rappaport's ulcer is better because they've upped the temperature two degrees. Mr. Berman's gout shows no improvement; he raises his swollen toe from a sheepskin slipper. Folded sections of the Detroit newspapers lie scattered on the floor. There are bridge games in progress and a color TV that nobody watches.

On our first evening Grandma walks in, eyes the room, and announces, "My daughter has become a harlot. Look at me," she says, "and see what can happen to anyone." She points to the rip in her dress signifying mourning. She has no tears, only anger. The guests, accustomed to chronic senility, go back to their conversations. I sit on a vinyl sofa, I hold Grandma's hands and convince her to leave the guests alone. "They are sick people, full of their own tsuris," I tell her. Grandma agrees to write out her case against Frieda so that it can be published and available forever throughout the Yiddish-speaking world. But to anyone who inquires about her complaints, Grandma will still tell the whole story. One of the guests asks me in the dining room if the fighter killed my mother.

"My fighter," I tell him truly, "is as gentle as the mineral baths. He punishes himself more than anyone else."

This, Jesús, I know is a fact. George Danton gives you little leisure. He wears a jump rope for a belt so that you'll never be without an extra three minutes of rope skipping. Before lunch and dinner he slaps at your bobbing, feinting head until you both break into a new sweat. Ten hours every night you sleep and two hours each afternoon. The rest is punishment. In this training camp I understand that the grace of your movements has not come from an easy life. Only someone accustomed to pain can embrace and endure what George puts you through.

When I trained you, I counted your pulse beat after

every run; I put ice packs on your face in case there were invisible bruises. I carried a jacket for you the way batboys trail a pitcher who gets on base. Just as Frieda made me take cod liver oil, so I spooned it down you every morning in case the eggs, juice, toast, and sausages were not quite enough for the kind of ferocity that had to grow within you.

But George Danton, your professional trainer, handles you as if you're a racing car out on a testing track. "Ten miles every morning," he decrees, "even before orange juice." Heavy with sleep, and sockless on these cold mornings, Jesús, you wind your way through the woods surrounding the coronary victims and other invalids of the Salt Springs Resort.

I eat breakfast and wait for you. I watch the guests enter the dining hall on stiff limbs and with hands pressing against aches at the small of the back. I listen to the complaints of the sleepless and the chronically ill. And while they take their bran flakes and prune juice, their hot oatmeal or their corn flakes, you race along their perimeter as if to mock the pain of their every step.

Still, they don't resent you, these old Jews of Mt. Clemens. They respond to you the way Grandma did— as if you are from a race superior in strength to the human but barbarous in your heart. They don't envy power that is directed solely at hitting another man. If you got up so early and ran so fast to distribute newspapers or to deliver milk and then came home to count your profits in front of a grateful wife, this they would understand. The profit from a sale not from a punch, this is the profit that makes men men.

Did you think of me as one of them, Jesús, when you wrote that I was a "capitalist lackey, a petit bourgeoisie, with the soul of a dry goods merchant"? Maybe I am that, Jesús, maybe in spite of all my efforts to think of your work as a job like any other, maybe I never quite

111

succeeded in making that grand leap that separates your body from your self. For George it is no problem. The fighter he trains is a machine that has to perform to a certain set of efficiency standards. When the training hours are over, he treats you as if you're not the person into whose hardened gut he has, scarcely an hour before, slammed an eight-pound leather ball. I never hit you with the medicine ball, never slapped at your face in the reflex exercise. It was hard enough to rub iodine into cuts.

And yet, I know that George is right. "When I smack the ball into his belly," George says, "I'm keeping him from puking his guts out when Kid Sangrilla unloads a right hook below his heart." Yes, George, you're right and so are the Marines and the Boy Scouts and everyone else who specializes in making men tough enough to brave the punches. But I still can't do it. "That's why Solomon hired a pro to do the training," George says. "Did you ever watch a horse trainer beat the shit out of one of those thoroughbreds? You haven't seen anything until you've seen that. Those horses run their hearts out in the Kentucky Derby because they know they'll get their leather hides whipped for ten hours if they don't. What I'm doing with Jesús is nothing. The real problem is one of those two-hundred-and-sixty-pound heavy-weights that you have to sweat down to two-twenty in a month without making him too weak to stand up. When they said, 'do you want this job?' all I asked was the man's weight. When they said 'middleweight,' I said, 'you've got yourself the best trainer in the land.'"

Yes, George, you know your business. Under your tutelage I can see Jesús flourish. For you he skips rope to a metronome, he sprints the final mile of his run, he tapes his ankles as tightly as his hands. You have made him see his body as an instrument. The mind of Jesús is elsewhere—on girls perhaps, or on some dark covenant of the Communist Party—but his fists and his footwork are all here, all in the ring, all dynamite and lightning. The sparring partners complain. Young blacks from Detroit, we pay them twenty dollars a day plus room and board to move around in the ring with a man who could cut their life short with one swing. "He hits too hard," all three say. George buys them padded vests, the kind that deflect bullets, and tells Jesús to punch as hard as he can to the ribs. "If he gets used to marshmallow punching now, he'll do it in a real fight too. Boxing is instinct, habit. You got to do it right all the time. I feel sorry for the sparring partners. I raise their salaries to thirty dollars a day, and let them use the leased Oldsmobile that Solomon has given us. They button their vests and stay.

About your own pain, Jesús, you are silent.

When you come in so thirsty from the roadwork, your leg muscles swollen with blue veins, your face a dull red from heat and exhaustion, when I see you this way I think, This is enough. This is all that the track stars go through. In a few minutes, the breath comes back and they're almost normal. For you, when the pain of the long run is over, when the muscles are relaxed, then you begin the real punishment. You drink a quart of the water and dextrose that George Danton makes up for you, you unlace the sneakers and lace up the black mid-calf fighting shoes.

It is only eight a.m. Your day is just beginning. For you there are still medicine balls to stomach, the fast bag for forty-five minutes, two three-round sparring matches. Your hands will be taped so tightly that I worry about your circulation. Your fine thin eyebrows George will coat with petroleum jelly for protection against cuts. You refuse the headgear while sparring and your curls

113

droop in sweat. You who do not cut easily are daily stained by blood, usually from the nose or lip of a sparring partner.

Grandma rarely watches you train. A few of the resort guests drift into the ring room, particularly when you spar, but largely, you are ignored at the Salt Springs Resort. In the casino amid the round tables and cane chairs, there George has constructed your training ring. The room has a capacity of two hundred. Since there are only fifty-two paying guests there is plenty of space for a ring. George has used the little stage to install a set of wall pulleys, the light and heavy bags. In fact, the new ring with its white canvas floor hardly upsets the decor of the room. At eight p.m., while Jesús readies himself for bed, the bingo caller enters the ring. From this majestic perch the voice of the caller reaches even the hard of hearing.

George Danton, who supervised the remodeling of the Casino, did his best to maintain the relaxed atmosphere of the room.

"What the hell," he says, "the old folks have paid to come here and soak their asses and get some good meals. I don't think we should get in their way any more than we have to."

After the first few days the guests pay no more attention to the sparring in the ring or the punching at the bag than they do the waiters clearing tables in the adjacent dining room. While gambling or *schmoozing* they drink the bottled seltzer water that until a few years ago you could buy in some Detroit supermarkets. Jesús likes the mineral water squirted into his face between rounds. "A hit, George," he says, as the trainer squirts from two feet away toward Jesús' open mouth.

I am happy, Jesús, that you and George are friendly and playful with each other. Now that we are so isolated I shouldn't be your only contact with the outside world.

114

A fighter needs company. He is all loneliness and concentration in the ring. When he crosses the ropes, he needs to know that there are people who like him even if his jab was a little slow. George and you are like puppies cuffing one another, gesturing with your hands as you discuss defensive maneuvers. You two are the professionals. I sit back at one of the dining tables and drink the seltzer water that reminds me of Passover, when Daddy used to buy Grandma the Mt. Clemens water to help her digestion during a week of heavy meals and lots of matzo.

"He likes it out here," George Danton reassures me. "Every fighter likes training camp no matter what they say. Everything else just gets in the way when there's training on your mind. Here, it's all there is."

In the early afternoon, after a light but high-protein lunch, Jesús tapers off. A little rope skipping and some eye exercises that George says will help his reflexes, then an hour or two at the almost deserted beach. On most afternoons all four of us go. For Grandma I carry from the resort a big umbrella that I stick into the sand to shade her. There are hundreds of them in a shed, a reminder of better days at Salt Springs. Jesús spreads himself out on a big white towel emblazoned with a red crab, and lets George give him a rubdown right there in the sand.

"I break my fucking back doing it," George says, "but what the hell, he don't like the trainer's table. I won't force him because—who knows?—maybe there's some good comes from lying in the warm sand." Jesús dozes while George labors above him. Grandma sits in the old-fashioned cotton beach chair that lowers into four different positions. I like that chair and the umbrella too, so much heavier than the modern aluminum and plastic ones but more comfortable. I lower my own chair to three-quarters reclining Grandma won't move from the first notch. She sits as straight as if she's expecting someone to honk the horn for her at any minute. Even at the beach she wears a dress long enough to cover her knees and elbows. Her concession to the heat is to open the top button and tie a handkerchief around her neck, not a big cowboy bandana like she wears on her head, but a tiny, flowered kerchief that covers the bones at the base of her neck but still lets some of the warm breeze down into her dark long dress.

Grandma takes a book with her but the glare bothers her. When she asks me to, I read aloud to her—slowly because my Yiddish reading is faulty, picked up from the *Forward* rather than from formal instruction. "Turkey talk," George Danton calls it when I start reading to her. Jesús dozes right through it, but George moves away to a spot near the trash barrel so he can concentrate on boxing and not get caught up in our "mumbo jumbo."

"Antesmeet," Grandma calls George because he complains when the waiter refuses to bring him milk with his hamburger at the Salt Springs dining room. The three waiters, Negroes well past retirement age, are so accustomed to the kosher rules that they scold him more than Grandma does.

"There is no way," George says, "that a Jew who eats like this can get the right amounts of protein. I don't believe that Barney Ross did it."

Jesús has never compained about the kosher diet that of necessity has become his. He eats all those east European delicacies, the matzo balls, the kugels, the chopped liver. Against George's wishes, he now and then has some pickled herring after his run. "That kind of eating will turn him into a rabbi and a tub of lard," George says. He weighs Jesús every morning and every night, but Jesús, no matter what he does or how he eats, stays at 159.

"I've seen this kind," George says, "steady all the way, then two days before the weigh-in they balloon out like women with false pregnancies. I'd rather have him at 156 ½—that would give us some leeway."

The books Grandma brings are yellow and so brittle that some of the pages break in my hands. They belonged to her husband Meyer, and they were all printed in Vilna or Prague or Grodna early in the century. The one I have been reading to her is an argument against anarchism written by a religious socialist long before the Russian Revolution. "What good will it do," he wonders in passionate Yiddish, "to explode the Czars only to release the mob and the Cossacks onto the Jews? Beware, little brother," he warns, "beware of your friends who tell you that they will be with you in the good days to come. For us there will never be good in this cursed land."

Grandma is not moved by any of the early socialist and Zionist rhetoric. She looks at the water, the sand, at Jesús peaceful on his towel and she says, "Nu, Meyer, I've lived to see this."

"Grandma," I tell her, "there's lots of people that pay a fortune to spend days like this. When the weather is this good, you couldn't do better even at Miami Beach."

"Miami Beach is for her," Grandma says. She never mentions Frieda's name, it is always "her." "Miami Beach is for the harlots and the gamblers."

I don't argue. The sun puts me into a stupor too. I think of Debby, studying for exams now, still not convinced that I should be living in seclusion with Grandma and Jesús.

Only once in the past month have I seen her. And even then we had to make love quickly because she had an SDS meeting and two quizzes the next day. Debby is an honor student; would the angels pick less for me, grandson of genuine Talmud *chochem*? She understands too, what I am like, why I can't be as casual with her as the fraternity boys and the other campus people she knows.

"You don't have to be so nervous or so quick," she says, but I see her books piled on the desk, I hear her Baby Ben alarm ticking beside the water bed.

"I don't want to be in your way," I tell her.

"Lovers are never in each other's way."

She kisses me and goes to make instant coffee. Only when she says it do I fully realize that we are, in fact, lovers. The word has not come into my mind before. Probably I've repressed it for fear of the evil eye.

I lie on her water bed thinking about it. Debby studies. She runs the eraser tip of a pencil through her hair. She rocks a little, as if she is praying. She underlines with a yellow Hi-Liter. I watch the movements from behind. The underlining is a furious gesture of the elbow as if she is rowing a boat. She takes a study break every half hour. We roll around on the water bed.

I've tried to tell Grandma about Debby. I want to give her something to look forward to. I want to break the bond that vengeance has put on her mind. But she doesn't really listen to me very much. At the beach she stares at the water; in the dining room she will watch Jesús work out, and swat at flies with her cane. It is as if there is only so much zip between us, and now that I have a little it seems to be draining hers.

"That's crazy," Debby says, "why should you feel guilty because you're asserting yourself a little? She's old, Ira, her tiredness has nothing to do with you."

You're right, Debby, but even you, my love, as wonderful as you are, even with you it isn't the way I dreamed it would be, the way Grandma told me it would be.

"To get married," she said, "you have to say a good *Haftorah*. You have to be able to go into a shul, and when her father says to you, 'You can say a Haftorah?' you'll answer, 'of course,' and you'll do it so well that he'll be proud to have you for a son-in-law."

So I labored, Grandma, learning that segment from Isaiah for my Bar Mitzvah, but not the way other boys did for the presents only. No, Grandma, I studied and I sang, getting the notes just right, because even then at thirteen I was getting ready for proving myself. I was getting ready for the day when I would walk into a synagogue that glows like the ring at a main event. The other people would be introduced—minor dignitaries— while I bided my time at the rabbi's right, looking straight ahead, not even checking the words in the book, full of confidence. When I stepped forward and the cantor called my name out in Hebrew, "Ira, Son of Abraham," the fathers of eligible daughters all looked carefully at their books. They were going to check for errors. Fathers, after all, value their daughters. "This Ira, Son of Abraham, will have to be something very special," they are thinking. And the angels are warning me. "Don't blow it, Mr. Cocksure. You knew your Bar Mitzvah reading by heart for more than a year and still Mr. Turetsky said you made three mistakes. Mr. Cocksure will come in and smile at the crowd, look at the stained glass windows, and then forget how to sing the simplest note. It's happened lots of times."

"Not today," I sing out. And as I perform, my voice makes the old ladies put their handkerchiefs to their eyes. The chapter of Isaiah the Prophet that I sing to the ancient cadence causes the fathers in the audience to renew their belief. When I am finished they rouse themselves from wonder to shake my hand. Long life and strength they wish me, and then they lead their daughters down the aisle, one by one. Each girl dressed in bridal costume has been waiting who knows how long for someone to sing such a Haftorah. They all march to

119

"Here Comes the Bride." The fathers are proud, and promise rich dowries. The girls hidden behind veils promise even greater riches. One by one the blue-suited dads, the white-gowned girls, they line up like Miss America candidates.

And there I am, Ira on the stage amid rabbis, cantors, Torahs—the panoply of several thousand years all coinciding in this moment. The dads lead the girls down the aisle. Each father carries a wine glass for me to step on. We assemble beneath a quickly constructed *chuppa*. There are so many brides that you can hardly see me. Instead my voice, only thirteen and not breaking yet, my clear, high boyish voice resounds in my Haftorah over and over. "Enough," say the fathers, "say 'I do,' and break the wine glass." The girls hold their breaths and the white veils hang in all their stiffness.

"Grandma," I say, "pick me one. Let's start early on the great-grandchild. What's the damage? I won't quit school. I'll study twice as hard. Holy men in Europe were married at thirteen."

Yes, Debby, by heroics in the synagogue I once thought I would find love—by my ancient song and not by my young middleweight.

"You worry too much about all the details of everything," Debby says. "Save up your worries for the big things. With me it's the war and school. You're scattering your worries too much. Consolidate them. It gives you perspective."

It's true that while I lie here on your water bed I have no perspective. I wait only for the closing of your book. But back in Mt. Clemens I wonder what we'll do when the summer is over. Grandma asks me nothing. She has put herself completely in my hands. I wonder what we'll do when Salt Springs closes for the season. Will Solomon send us to train in the tropics, or will Jesús, Grandma, George, and I move back to our old house so

Frieda can try every day to win back her mother's love?

And what if Jesús loses even to Kid Sangrilla? I don't think it can happen, Jesús is too fast and powerful. But someday his legs will be heavy, his guard will drop, his mouthpiece will go flying across the canvas. Someday I'll be kneeling in the ring with smelling salts beneath his nose. What then for Jesús? If he has money it's one thing, but can I count on Solomon to make sure that a battered and senseless Jesús will never have to work the small town circuit?

"Ira," Debby says, "why can't you just relax? Enjoy the moment. I love you. Jesús loves you. Everything is going along smoothly enough." She says this one day when a UPI reporter in the *Detroit News* predicts that the war in iVetnam will be over in a few months. Johnson is just waiting for the elections, the reporter believes. Debby is ecstatic.

Instead, Johnson escalates and so do I. "If not now, when?" the rabbis ask. I ask Debby if when school is over she will join us. The fighter, the trainer, the grandmother, the manager, and now the bride—sharing a life and a career. I know that Jesús might resent this, but I am willing to risk it. I am counting on the fact that he will find plenty of girls for himself once he stops training. And if he marries too, there will be a happy six of us, always at ringside.

"I don't know about that," Debby says. "There's graduate school, and right now with the way things are in the world I don't know if I can just live my personal life as if it was all that mattered."

This is the age of communes. Debby's friends are banding together in groups much larger than our tiny tribe would be. They are living in old farmhouses or in villages. In eastern Michigan, near Mt. Clemens, there is a group of former students who come sometimes to use the mineral baths and pay the five-dollar one-day rate.

The Salt Springs guests who see nothing offensive about a gym in their casino can't stand the long-haired men coming to use the baths.

"*Schmutz*," say the waiters.

"Feh," say the guests.

They make their own sign and post it near the bathhouse. "Weekly and Season Guests Only."

I know that this commune style is the kind of life Debby thinks would be romantic and politically important. But with Grandma and Jesús I bring along baggage too much for those new people who desire only small children and home-grown vegetables.

"Let's leave it the way it is for now, Ira," she says, "let's not press things."

# 12

Because of the new arena and Kid Sangrilla's mother, the press covers Jesús' fight with Sangrilla the way only heavyweight championships are covered. The scheduled ten-round main event is nobody's concern but ours. There is only one TV camera inside the auditorium; there are four outside where the mob roams. Mrs. Estelle Sangrilla has organized the welfare mothers of Detroit. They are there with her, maybe five hundred angry young women. The black churches are represented, and about two hundred SDS white students have come by chartered bus from Ann Arbor. The welfare women carry signs that say "Boxing Is Out to Murder a Defective Child." The churchmen say boxing is part of the violence that makes Vietnam possible. The SDS people have signs enumerating Solomon's ties with the Defense Department. "The arena is a front for General Dynamics," Tom Hayden is yelling through a bullhorn. All this attention has drawn the biggest Detroit boxing crowd in decades. Solomon has sold all 12,000 scats. Only Billy Graham has previously sold out the arena. There are hundreds of police and special deputies encircling the crowd. Eldridge Cleaver is outside exhorting young black men to fight the oppressive white society instead of each other.

In the basement locker room, Jesús, George Danton

and I hear the noises from outside. Jesús is on the trainer's table where George is giving him a final quick rubdown. His taped hands lie at his sides. He is silent as a mummy, so relaxed that he seems asleep. Yesterday he weighed in at 158¼, but he has eaten three big meals and is already several pounds heavier. How I envy his ability to relax, to almost fall asleep in the midst of all this turmoil only a few minutes before his first televised main event.

For me it is not easy. Debby is out there—one of the picketers against me. I find myself the ally of Solomon, Hoover, big business, and imperialism. Just a few months ago I was part of the Movement, now my own colleagues are picketing outside my dressing room window.

"Can I help it," I tell Debby, "that Solomon owns the arena and the exclusive right to promote Jesús? Can I help it that Kid Sangrilla signed to fight us? The boxing commission and the health department say he's sane enough and strong enough to fight. This is Jesús' first big chance. It has nothing to do with politics." (I haven't told her about Hoover.)

"If you had any principles," she says, "you wouldn't let Jesús do this."

"Jesús wants to fight Sangrilla. I couldn't stop him if I wanted to. You should see the show he is putting on for the TV people. He loves to be interviewed."

She snaps her mouth shut and runs away from me. I want her more than the middleweight championship, more than an end to the war, but I stand there outside the main dining room of the resort and watch her run to her Volkswagen and drive away from me. This is the first time I have seen her in three weeks. Jesús, Hoover, and Grandma have kept me occupied in Mt. Clemens. Debby knows that I am heartbroken at my mother's marriage, she knows that this is Jesús' big chance, and still she wants me to stop it because her SDS friends don't like Solomon.

"I hate him more than they do," I tell her. "I grew up hating him. Grandma is in mourning because of him. If Kid Sangrilla's mother thinks he's making a fool of her son, how do you think I feel when he's taken my mother?"

"Oh, you poor Hamlet," she says, "get off your ass and do something. Disown your mother. Picket him."

"And what about Jesús?"

"Let him go with Solomon if he wants to; he's just an unreconstructed Stalinist."

I hear Tom Hayden in her voice. Her small dark features are pointed in anger. To kiss her would be acupuncture.

Grandma comes out to join us. She still carries her walking stick, but in Mt. Clemens there are only squirrels to swat. Her bald head is sweating beneath the red bandana. Her cuticles are painted in Mercurochrome which has dripped down her fingers like blood. In her old age, in her stooped arthritic slowness, Grandma still towers over Debby Silvers.

*"Sholom Aleichem,"* Grandma says.

"I admire you, Mrs. Weiner," Debby says. "You have the courage of your convictions. Your grandson is too weak-willed to do what he knows is right."

"Who's this cockroach?" Grandma asks me, *"Vas veel zee?"*

I tell her Debby's name. I want to tell her everything. I want her to know that in the loins of this cockroach lie her own hope for eternal life. I want Grandma to know that this is the one the angels have selected for me. But I can't say it in front of Debby, who hates me at this time and would hardly understand Grandma's superstition in her most generous moments. But Grandma has anticipated me.

125

"A board with a hole in it," she says. "Too skinny. And mean. Look at those eyes. I wouldn't give you a nickel for one like this."

"You won't have to," Debby says. She goes toward the path leading to the parking lot. I pursue her. Grandma spits and goes back to the dining room.

"She doesn't mean to be rude. It's just the way Grandma talks."

Jesús, loose and sweating in the midst of his ten-mile run, jogs past us. "He knows," Debby says, "I told him. I don't hide things." Jesús waves, throws a kiss toward Debby and disappears behind the elms. George Danton is following him on an English bicycle, and keeping track of his time and distance. The sun shines, birds sing, the air is clean.

"You're worse than a Hamlet," Debby says, "you're a Svengali. You start the whole terrible thing and then you just stand back and watch it happen."

"I don't even know what a Svengali is." She drives away without explaining.

I have tried all week to call Debby. She hangs up. Frieda called twice to warn me there would be trouble outside the arena, but not to worry, Solomon had plenty of armed guards whose job was to protect Jesús and me. Solomon wanted her to go to the fight. She refused. They were going to the Bahamas instead for the weekend. "Can you believe it," my mother says, "me going on a three-hour plane ride to only stay for two days?" Solomon has already taken her for a long weekend to Paris. In the summer they're going to Greece and Israel for two weeks. How can I disown her? Didn't she work hard all those years in the battery yard? Didn't she resist the temptations of such wealth for a decade? Debby, from her safe middle-class life cushioned by charge accounts and braces, doesn't know what it was like for Frieda to ride around in an old pickup while the Hadassah ladies tooted the horns of their Thunderbirds at her. She doesn't know what it was like to spend day after day arguing with peddlers over a nickel or a dime more for each battery and then hoping that nobody would steal the new purchases before they could be broken and the lead sold. She doesn't know the smell of the hot plastic cases in the air, or the sting of the acid on your skin. For me, Solomon is spoiled forever. Grandma has done her job too well. But how can I blame my mother for giving in, for wanting at forty-eight to spend a weekend in Paris or the Bahamas instead of at "Goldstein's We Buy Junk and Batteries"? I only wonder how she had the stamina to wait all those years. If she had done it right away, right after Abe died, maybe I could have been overcome then by a few simple bribes—a baseball glove, a new bicycle, a skiing trip. With such a stepfather I might have gone to Harvard or Yale and known at twenty-four who Svengali was without having to look him up in the World Book that Abe bought for my eighth birthday. Yes, he bought it from a door-to-door salesman. Yes, he believed the sales pitch, and yes, he paid two dollars a week for three years. But I don't think he got a bad deal. He used to tell me, "We've got it all here, everything from A to Z." He ran his thumbnail along the hard spines. The noise of his finger across all those volumes is to me, even now, the sound of knowledge. I recall it when I am studying for an exam. I can see his hand stop at the M–N volume, open the red cover and look through those shiny pages for Napoleon, right across the column from Naples. The shining waters and the splendid Emperor.

We really used to study those books. He'd say, "Just close your eyes and pick a book." He'd spin me around so I didn't know where I was from A to Z, and then the first one I'd touch he would take out. While still blindfolded I'd open to a page and there we'd start. Goldfish, Geneva, pen, penis, Wolsey, working classes . . . I had an alphabetical education. I remember more of the things we read that way than anything I ever learned in school. And Abe, though he'd never finished high school, was a wonderful quizzer. He loved facts. "Who was the first soldier killed in the American Revolution? Who was the first Jewish Supreme Court Justice? Who holds the National League home-run record?" When I learned the answers to all of his stumpers, we went through the encyclopedia looking for new "hard-but-not-impossible questions." "Impossible is not fair," Abe taught me.

Impossible it must have been for those ten years for Frieda to even let herself imagine what it would be like to go to the Bahamas for a weekend or drive a Cadillac or have a charge account at Saks. And now that it had happened how she must regret those wasted years.

And Grandma, for whose ancient grudge she denied herself and me everything, now takes no pleasure in life except the compilation of the case against her daughter. She is writing it out. Every evening after she completes her prayers she sits down with her green-and-black fountain pen and begins in Yiddish to strengthen her case. Her writing is bad since she can barely close her hand enough to hold the pen. She writes on unlined stationery with the name SALT SPRINGS RESORT at the top of each page.

"To the whole world," she writes. "Everyone should know what can happen in any family. Death you expect. Also pogroms, small meannesses from your friends, to be ignored by your grandchildren, arthritis—all this is normal. But live with a daughter forty-eight years. To think in her body runs the blood of one of the Almighty's true saints, dead before his time, too good for this world. To think that at the age when people are getting ready for social security she runs away to sleep with Satan himself. To me she's dead, but other parents can learn from this . . ."

Grandma, Grandma, what can we learn. When you told me the Solomon stories, I thought of him as a big dark bearlike man who hid in alleys waiting for young girls. Why didn't you tell me, Grandma, how he wanted her for all those years? I was ten and asking all the usual questions before Abe told me he never saw Frieda until the day they were engaged. To Frieda, Grandma, to the daughter you now curse, the span that made me must seem like a long, unjust interruption in her life. Abe and I are accidents created by you. Solomon, who is next to Hitler, Grandma, maybe he deserved her all along.

I can imagine myself his real son. I am a little shorter, a little thinner. I wear a pinky ring and keep lots of bills in a silver money clip. I drive around in a convertible. Girls like Debby Silvers call me every day. So do stockbrokers. He and Momma are gone most of the time, on cruises. They bring me expensive presents from all over the world. Instead of Abe's World Book, Solomon has bought for his only son a complete library as big as the Junior Adult Room at the Bridge Street Branch where Frieda used to take me twice a week. And it's not just the money, Grandma, it feels good to have a real live Dad, even if he's gone a lot of the time.

Solomon, can you teach me to shoot pool the way Abe did? "Always think two shots in advance," Abe says, "and never let your cue ball rest in a corner." Behind the back or one-handed without a bridge, Abe can sink any shot on the table. People in the midst of games they are paying for stop to watch him. I am proud of my dad. I put the blue chalk on the tip of his cue stick; I make sure there is talcum powder for his hand.

With me he is patient, but I can't line my shots up like he does. After about two feet my vision falters. I can't see straight lines to the pocket like he does.

"Daddy," I ask him, "why can't we have our own pool table? I would practice all the time."

"Then you'd be so good that I wouldn't have a chance against you." Why didn't it ever bother you, Daddy, that you couldn't afford a table and had to take me to the YMCA in a bad neighborhood where it was hard to find a parking place?

Had Grandma let her marry Solomon I would be managing an empire now instead of a middleweight. I would own horses if I wanted sport, and I would have a billiard table in the den. "Think two shots in advance," you teach me, dead father, but how far in advance are you thinking when Grandma with her eyes swollen from two days of crying comes to your house with the rabbi? Are you thinking of me at that time, of your battery business, of your heart attack nineteen years into the future? No, you're thinking only of the dark-eyed, beautiful Frieda in the last row of the women's section of the synagogue looking so childlike beside her tall strong mother. You're not thinking beyond kissing her, beyond sleeping with her every night for nineteen years. You're not even thinking of me, who will grow up only half-fathered, half-educated, not even able to decide what he should do at the moment he and his fighter have been awaiting.

Outside the armory, another romance is beginning. Tom Hayden and Jane Fonda are meeting. She is in Detroit shooting a new movie and has come over to lend her sympathy to the protestors. She is still wearing heavy makeup and the 1920's costume of the film. Her cheeks are heavy with rouge, her voice is cracking from a day of takes in a crowd scene. In fact, what she has just left is only slightly more chaotic than the scene outside the armory. Hayden recognizes her, calls her to the make-shift speaker's platform right above our locker room window.

"Hey, you can see right up her dress from here," George Danton says. Jesús comes off the trainer's table to join George at the window. Jesús raises his taped hands to his eyes so he can see better.

"I wish I could promise you her after you deck Sangrilla," George says. Jesús smiles. We can barely pick out her voice, but she is talking to the crowd. Hayden raises her fist into the air as if he is the referee and she the new champion. The sequins of her flapper dress sparkle at us. Jesús, still smiling, taps on the window. Nobody can hear him. He climbs on a chair to unlock the window, opens it, and calls out to Hayden who is silent now awaiting the next angry speaker.

Hayden comes to the window. He has to get down on all fours to see into the locker room. "Stalin's boy," he says, "so you're going through with it after all. I thought you would. You belong with the Solomons of this world. You've always been their ally. We may not stop this one, but after tonight's publicity Kid Sangrilla will never get another fight."

"You think I keel him," Jesús says in a broader accent than I have ever heard him use.

"You might," Hayden says, "it wouldn't be out of character, would it?"

"C'mon down," Jesús says. "We negotiate. Bring the girl."

"Hold on," I say, "the semi-final has already started. In twenty minutes we've got to go upstairs."

"Save the girl for later," George Danton says. He is worried too. "Later. You can even do it here in the locker room, but you can't risk anything before a fight. Kid Sangrilla may be a dummy but that don't affect his right hook."

Hayden is already halfway through the window. The only way to enter is head first. Jesús catches him under the arms and pulls the tall, thin radical into the dressing room. Hayden looks around. He doesn't recognize me but he stood only a few feet away the night I burned my draft card. Jesús is still on the chair awaiting Jane Fonda. Her upper body slides through the small opening. She is a heavier bundle than Hayden. Jesús holds her in those taped hands then lowers her easily to the ground. He closes the window.

"Goddamn," George Danton says, "we got no business having these rabble-rousers in here. Why don't the two of you and all your buddies go raise hell with some politicians? Boxing's got enough trouble without this."

Jane Fonda shakes her long red-gold hair and pulls at it as if she caught some spider webs on her journey through the window.

"Jesus Christ it smells down here," she says. "I thought this was supposed to be such a fancy building."

"They didn't remodel the locker rooms," I say. "Down here it's the same gladiator pit it's always been."

"You know that and you still go along with this kind of exploitation," Hayden says to me. "You know how much money Solomon will make tonight?"

"I don't care," I say, "as long as Jesús gets his paycheck. It will be the first time he ever earned more than five hundred dollars."

Jane Fonda sits down on George's stool. She crosses her long legs and lights a cigaret.

"Not in here," George says, "too much carbon monoxide will get in Jesús' lungs. If it goes more than six rounds he could feel it."

"Fuck off," she says.

George looks around for support. "If you don't give a shit," he says to me, "then I don't either. For all I care he can come out for the opening bell with a hard-on.

What do you want to have, a whorehouse and a political meeting or a dressing room? A fighter should be concentrating in these last twenty minutes. He ought to be thinking nothing but Kid Sangrilla. He ought to close his eyes and see in his head Sangrilla moving sideways and snapping that jab. He ought to be thinking defense and footwork. Any man who goes into the ring with snatch on his mind is a full step-and-a-half slower. All the wrong involuntary nerves respond. You got to keep all those synapses and nerve endings taut, ready to go. He should be a rubber band from the waist up, putty from below. I've never even seen a woman allowed into a dressing room."

"Who's this nut?" Jane asks.

"Jesús' trainer, George Danton."

"Well listen, Mr. George Danton, do you know who I am?"

"I don't care if you're the Queen of Sheba and wipe your ass with pomegranates, you don't belong here now. Afterwards it's OK."

Jane Fonda drops cigaret ash on the linoleum. "Listen, buster," she says, "I don't know where you get your ideas, but I didn't come here to screw any middleweights. I've just spent eleven hours pretending I was a whore with gangrene during World War I. I'm tired. I need a cigaret. If you're so worried about your young man's lungs, get him a gas mask. We've got hundreds on the set, I'll send you one." She blows smoke rings at George. He kicks over the water bucket.

"Why did you want to talk to us?" Hayden says. "Do you want to change your mind and join the protest?"

"George is not wrong," Jesús says slowly. "I like the girl."

"Everybody likes her," Hayden says. "She's a movie star. She earns a lot of money because a million guys want to get in her pants."

Jane laughs. "Ten million," she says.

"If she comes across right now," Jesús says, "I call off the fight."

I don't even know what to say. I just sit there and let Hayden and Jesús carry on. I haven't hesitated to alienate the one genuine girl friend I've ever had, the hope for Grandma's eternity and my own happiness, her I've spurned so that Jesús can have his chance—and here he is ready to barter his future for a fast encounter with a movie star.

Hayden is not so stunned. "We don't operate that way," he says. "Maybe Stalin and Beria carried on little experiments like this, trading sexual favors for inconsequential political victories, but we don't exploit our women any more than we send mental defectives out to line the pockets of General Dynamics. If you've got to prove your manhood this way, Crab, then you're fascist to the core."

While Hayden talks, Jesús is looking straight at Jane Fonda. She has put out her cigaret. She stretches her arms and yawns. "Don't be so solemn about everything, Tom," she says.

"With her," Jesús says, "I would make the revolution." He walks to the stool and embraces her. Her dress makes a lot of noise. Jesús' hands are taped tightly. Only his fingertips can move. They stand in the middle of the dressing room oblivious to us.

"I knew it," George Danton says, "you can kiss the crown good-bye. I hope they both get the triple clap."

"Jane," Hayden says, "I appreciate the gesture but this won't do any good. We'll actually make our point better if the fight does go ahead. I don't think there's really any chance that he'll hurt Kid Sangrilla. I mean you can go ahead with him if you want to, it's none of my business, but it's not for the cause."

Jane raises her knee hard into Jesús' crotch. It cracks

loudly against his protective cup. Still, he bends in pain. Jane bends too, to rub her kneecap. Hayden takes her arm and leads her through the doorway. When he opens the door, I see Caluccio Salutatti on a folding chair at the end of the hallway, his sharkskin almost glowing in the dark.

"Jesús," I say, "I don't know what you want in this world, but I'm beginning to think it's not the championship."

He smiles at me. He rubs his crotch to make sure the pain is gone. "Keep your eyes on the right," he says. "I'll make them forget Kid Gavilan and Sugar Ray."

A messenger comes running down the corridor to tell us Jesús is about to be introduced. George puts the silk robe over his smooth shoulders and laces up the gloves. Jesús "Crab" Goldstein pounds his fists together. "Don't worry, boys," he says. He walks up the corridor into the gleaming arena where the thousands wait. Four spotlights pick us up. The ring is blindingly white. Bells are ringing. "Ass is not ideology," Jesús whispers in my ear, "I take him in three."

# 13

Later, when I find the notebook and some of the letters from Salutatti, a little of what happened makes sense, although I can hardly believe the Communist Party and the FBI put so much emphasis on one fighter. I suppose I'm still too naïve for politics. If six years later Agnew could sell out for a few thousand and Nixon for a few hundred thousand, then maybe everyone was right to make such a fuss about Jesús Goldstein's brief career in the summer of 1966.

Salutatti's aims are very straightforward. He wants you so that they can stage championship fights throughout eastern Europe. Belgrade, Warsaw, Prague, Sofia, even Moscow and Leningrad, he writes, would welcome an American champion. "It would be six times better than the Olympics," he says in one of his letters. "You could do more for the cause in a single year than your father Martinez did in his lifetime. The Puerto Rican children need someone to admire, not just a fighter but a political leader. You can become their Fidel. Train hard, and when the time comes we will be ready. Everyone is with you. The cold war is happening on the athletic fields, in the parliaments and in the universities. You, Jesús, are the soldier of the hour."

I don't remember seeing Salutatti again on the night of the Kid Sangrilla fight. In fact, though lots of people, including three FBI agents, have interviewed me about that night, I almost feel as if I wasn't there.

The Jane Fonda episode only takes a few minutes but it puts me on another track. You, Jesús, you can do it. You can try to seduce a girl—even if you are only kidding—a few minutes before a televised prizefight. I believe that for you it is possible. You are so relaxed that you could sleep until you hear the ring announcer call your name. But I am disoriented. If J. Edgar Hoover brings out all my patriotism, then Jane Fonda brings out all my hero worship. Right here in our locker room, Jesús, we had a movie queen. Almost an equal of Marilyn Monroe. To you this doesn't mean anything. You try to screw her like you try Debby and maybe every other girl you meet. But, Jesús, to me a movie star is almost as holy as Hoover or the Pope. I am looking at Kid Sangrilla but I am thinking of Jane Fonda. Maybe it's because once I actually see the Kid, I understand why his mother and the welfare people are protesting. I want to stop it too, when I look across the ring at his unblinking blue-green eyes. He is a short, grotesquely well-built man. It looks like someone has sewn muscles along his arms and back almost haphazardly. From across the ring I can hear him snorting through his maimed nose. He is openly strong but anyone can see his unhealthiness. His eyebrows have grown together, his ears look as if they've been beaten against his skull. The ugly little man is smiling at us, and Jesús, dancing in our corner, throws him a kiss with both open gloves.

George Danton is still raving against women. He rubs Jesús' back under the robe. "Whole fucking place smells like perfume. They jazz up the armory and make it a French whorehouse. Joe Louis never even let a woman touch his glass of milk or press his clothes on the day of a fight."

We have to wait a long time in the ring because there

are so many celebrities to introduce. I am not listening to the names but how can I miss the tremendous cheer for J. Edgar Hoover, who moves easily through the ropes, shakes hands with Sangrilla and then very sincerely comes over to say, "Good luck, son" to Jesús. Not a wink to me, not a sign of suspicion toward Jesús.

"A real pro," I think. Jesús is laughing so hard that his mouthpiece falls out. "Everything is cute tonight, huh middleweight," George says. "Nookie is cute and the FBI is a riot and boy oh boy is it going to be hilarious when that ugly dummy slams you on your bony ass."

For me the rest is blurry. I remember only the atmosphere. The noise, the smell, the solemn look on Hoover's face as he climbed through the ropes, the way Diana Ross pulled at the top of her dress before she sang "The Star Spangled Banner." I remember the smooth feel of Jesús' skin, the weight of the water bucket, my own sweaty palms and nervous heart. I remember the precise timbre of the bell and the gray hairs sprouting from the nose of George Danton. After the first long look, I have no further impression of Kid Sangrilla. He is King Kong across the ring. I hear the uneven snort of his breath, heavy even before the fight has begun. I remember the lisping voice of the referee as he tells us briefly the rules of the Michigan Boxing Commission.

I think that for me the fight itself has forever melted into everything else that happened on that night. And yet, I stood at the northeast corner of the ring and watched Jesús trade blows with the Neanderthal man. I know that I was worried about Jesús, was proud of his speed and counter-punching—although none of the actual exchanges are now visible in my mind's eye as so much of the atmosphere still is.

And yet the voice of the arena manager in my ear in

the midst of round three, that I remember like my first glimpse of Debby.

"Maybe I shouldn't tell you this now," he is yelling directly into my head, "but they said to. Your grandma just had a stroke in Mt. Clemens. I've got a number you're supposed to call; it's in the office. You can get it after the fight."

I know that he walked down the steps and along the aisle and that I stood there, at least until the end of the round, but I was no longer seeing Jesús and Kid San-grilla. I saw Grandma alone in that Mt. Clemens cabin, her Mercurochromed fingers gone stiff, her bald head pale and showing its large pores. In the last minute and a half that I spent at the apron of the ring I heard—in the midst of Solomon's new arena and the voices of twelve thousand fans, in all that uproar—I heard the sound of my Grandma's stiff body hitting the desk as she wrote. I heard the sages of Israel gathering above the ring to greet her soul, which was coming here for a quick good-bye to me, her "boychick," her ticket to eternity who had not had the zip to guarantee her an easy pas-sage. The sages of Israel glowed in the spotlights, their beards fanned the prizefighters. At the bell I raced down the aisle toward the arena manager's office.

So, FBI, of course I am telling you the truth. When the tumult broke loose, I was in the office trying to reach Mrs. Wiseman—the lady with the stooped back and three sons who were specialists and had sent her to Mt. Clemens to relax. I was trying to reach Mrs. Wiseman to find out what hospital Grandma had been taken to, what doctor attended her, if she was conscious.

I didn't even smell the stink bombs until half the audience had left. Mrs. Wiseman beat the tear gas to my eyes by several minutes.

"She was just at her desk like always," Mrs. Wiseman

tells me, "writing I don't have to tell you what, when I hear this sound. You know through the Salt Springs resort walls you can hear a quiet burp, but this was a real rattling noise like throwing a chain against the wall. 'Bertha,' I yelled to her. I said it in Yiddish, 'Whatcha doin', what's all the noise about? You OK?' See, I was worried right away that the noise came from a person. It was that kind of noise, loud like a machine but still a person noise. So, when she didn't answer me and she didn't come to the door when I knocked, I got Billy with the passkey and we went in to find her spread out there on the desk. Her head was turned so sideways that I thought at first somebody had come in from behind and choked her to death.

" 'Artificial respiration,' I yelled to Billy, and laid her down and squeezed her sides and pulled her arms up while he called for the ambulance. I would have gone with her but my sons warned me, no excitement. I told the ambulance Mt. Sinai because they've got kosher meals there, but who knows where those two hoodlums took her. They picked her up like she was potatoes."

"Was she alive?" I am screaming into the phone. The noise is all around me, the crowd is running blindly for the exits. There are screams everywhere. Spilled Coke and beer flood the new carpets. I've looked dozens of times at the chaos on the videotape. The cameraman fled but the TV camera automatically recorded the effect of the stink bombs and the tear gas. The fighters continue long after the audience has turned its back. The crowd seems full of outlaws, for people tie handkerchiefs sloppily over their mouths. The security guards are also coughing helplessly. Even when the referee climbs through the ropes to run away, Jesús and Kid Sangrilla keep it up. Tears are streaming from Jesús' eyes as his body appears like an angel from behind the facade of smoke in the middle of the ring. As the smoke spreads, you see only a stray arm, the arch of a shoe, the top of a head. You can't tell whether it is Jesús or Kid Sangrilla. Finally, the videotape becomes all smoke. There is no sign of either fighter leaving the ring. Twenty minutes later when the firemen enter in their gas masks, the automatic camera shows the air clearing in the empty auditorium. It shows the handbags and jackets lying forgotten in the seats. It shows the nation's most elegant new arena as forlorn as a fresh widow. It does not show Jesús or Kid Sangrilla, and most important of all, it does not show J. Edgar Hoover.

It was hours before anyone even knew Hoover was gone. The morning papers treated the story lightly.

In 1966 a few stink bombs, some tear gas, and the disruption of a public event were nothing special. The early papers treated the disrupted fight as a funny story, one of the few instances of SDS levity. The national news even ran a segment of the videotape that showed the ring encased in smoke with a fragment of arm sticking out—Jesús' debut on network television.

Yes, for hours I guess it looked like a very funny story to the people who were following it. I wasn't. My eyes were still stinging from the tear gas when I reached Mt. Sinai hospital. I had put all thoughts of the fight out of my mind. I was sure that Hayden and Sangrilla's mother had carefully arranged to ruin Jesús' important match. I told myself all the way to the hospital that I would try to pick up the pieces when Grandma was better. But I suspected without being able to really think it, that Grandma was already dead.

It takes at least half an hour in the hospital to find out whether or not she is actually there. Then a cheerful nurse leads me to a hallway on the third floor, where they have put Grandma "temporarily, until we have a vacant room." Nobody can tell me how she is. When I see her, they don't have to. My powerful, opinionated

Grandma is lying there, open-eyed, clearly uncomfortable, and totally oblivious. Her face has an expression similar to Kid Sangrilla's. She cannot recognize me or even hear me. I want to tell her that she'll be okay, she'll be home in a few days and live yet to see that long-awaited great-grandchild, but I can't force myself to say anything. I move a chair against the stretcher, and hold her damp hand.

With only a couple of breaks for coffee I sit there with her all night. At two a.m. an intern tells me she might go at any second. At six-thirty they move her to a private room.

At seven o'clock, two FBI agents introduce themselves, close the door of the hospital room and tell me that Mr. Hoover is missing. I am too tired to care. I am thinking of calling Frieda in Nassau even though I know that Grandma wouldn't want me to. "You're a suspect," one of the FBI men says to me. "Where's your fighter?"

"I've been in this hospital all night. The last I saw he was in the ring waiting for round four. I don't know what went on in the armory. I was in the office trying to find out about Grandma when all the smoke hit. Jesús must be asleep. We have two rooms in the Book Cadillac Hotel in his name. If he's not there he and George might have gone back to Mt. Clemens. They must be wondering where I am."

"We've checked the Book Cadillac and we've checked Mt. Clemens," the FBI man says. "We've checked everywhere. You weren't too easy to locate either."

"That's not my fault."

"The fighter's missing and Mr. Hoover is missing. You can't say that's just a coincidence."

"I don't know anything. Look at my grandma. That's all that I'm worried about. Go ask Tom Hayden and the welfare mothers and the anti-Solomon protestors where Hoover is. I didn't throw the smoke bombs."

"They didn't either," he says. "C'mon with us."

"I'm not leaving my Grandma. She may die at any second."

They take me between them and hold my elbows. "Don't give us any trouble, buddy. There's not much to do for the old lady. We checked that too. Nobody can save her. But if we don't save Mr. Hoover I am personally going to castrate every pinko longhair in Wayne County."

"But I met Hoover. I gave him information."

"Maybe," they say as they pull me from room 340. "Maybe you helped to set him up for the kidnap."

"Who can kidnap the head of the FBI?"

"Communists," the agent says, "the international Communist conspiracy that all of you think is such a laugh. Hoover is missing, the middleweight is missing, and Caluccio Salutatti is missing. There's a lot of questions here and not much time. Your balls don't have a much better chance than your grandma's heart."

# 14

J. Edgar Hoover was not a big eater. Cold cereal in the morning, salad at noon, early dinner with wine. Nothing fancy, but always on schedule. His desk was clean as a mirror. He saved cigar bands in the upper right-hand corner of the top drawer of his desk. Fan mail was filed alphabetically and always answered. He hoped to eradicate crime but he was pledged to create order. Nothing could be mislaid in the world of Mr. Hoover. "Everything in its place and a place for everything," he used to tell new members of the staff.

Contrary to his popular image, Mr. Hoover was not tough, mean, or ruthless. He was easy to work for. He liked a clean, error-free typed page no matter what it said. He signed his name in small meticulous letters. He never used initials and he hated interoffice memos. The Depression and Prohibition converged to force his solid-looking jaw into the public eye. Given any choice Mr. Hoover would have preferred to manage a local insurance company office.

Jesús "Crab" Goldstein took a cigar from the inner pocket of Mr. Hoover's blue suit. He bit the top and gently spat the tobacco toward the G-man's foot. Mr. Hoover looked away, noticing that the middleweight discarded the band and the cellophane without first seeking a waste basket. Mr. Hoover felt nauseous. There was still tear gas in his lungs and in his eyes. Also, they were flying at a low altitude into a head wind.

"What are you going to do with me?" Mr. Hoover asked of the cocky cigar smoker.

Goldstein inhaled, coughed, shrugged his shoulders. He smiled. "Jesús the Crab, he only hurt people in the ring. You got no worries, bossman."

"I haven't worried since the depths of the Great Depression," Mr. Hoover answered. "I stopped worrying when the Dust Bowl grew fertile once more. I found my vocation and after that I let the criminal types do the worrying."

"Jesús the Crab is no criminal, bossman. This here's just good fun. You see pretty soon. In politics there is lots of joking around."

"Kidnapping is no joke, son, not in any country. And doing what you did to that arena, that too was a criminal offense—not to speak of the moral outrage. You made a fool out of one of God's unfortunates tonight. Kid Sangrilla needed to be treated like an equal. You robbed him of what may well be his last fight."

"This business is more important than boxing. You wait. Caluccio, he'll explain it to you."

"Son," Mr. Hoover said, "I've heard the Communist line in many a tongue. We monitor east European radio. I've got your slogans coming out of my ears. I came to see a good fight tonight, there was nothing political. Hell, G-men have to relax too. And you know I can't really relax while you're blowing cigar smoke and pointing a gun at me."

Jesús put away his pistol and crushed the cigar beneath his sleeve. "Sorry, bossman. The gun is not loaded. Caluccio just told me to keep an eye on you. I guess a ranking middleweight don't need a gun to watch an old man."

"After tonight, son, you'll never be ranked again.

You'll be scratched from the pages of the *Ring*, obliterated from any WBA-sanctioned events; you'll have to get your bouts behind the Iron Curtain." Mr. Hoover looked wistfully into the clear brown eyes of the Puerto Rican middleweight. "You know, son, it didn't have to turn out this way. You had a great chance to outrun your past. I read criminals like they're comic books. They can't look me in the eye. I walk past a line-up and point out the man every time. We've tried it in D.C., just to test me out. The local police can't believe it. It is uncanny. But what about those forked sticks that point toward the ground when there's water? They're uncanny too. I believe in the unknown. And I am not afraid. Criminals are afraid. They can't look into the eyes of J. Edgar Hoover. You're not a criminal, son. I'm sorry they led you astray. Someday you'll appreciate this country and the opportunity you threw away."

Jesús laughs, "Bossman, Jesús the Crab did not throw away nothin'. We just picked up guaranteed money in the bank and the big thing, the champeenship."

The small plane dips in the wind. The middleweight stumbles against the legs of J. Edgar Hoover. The FBI director helps the young fighter to regain his balance. The sun is rising. Beneath them the red clay of Georgia is moving toward the Florida swamps.

"There is nothing like being in a plane at dawn," Hoover says. "Even under these conditions I can't look at it without being touched by the splendor of nature."

"Yeh, it's something all right," Jesús says. "You know, Hoover, you ain't much like what I thought you would be."

"My fate," answers the director. "Nobody expects anything but a square jaw and a forty-five cradled near my ribs. I haven't even carried a gun in twenty years. You saw that when you frisked me. Criminals expect me to be like them, you expected me to be worse than you are."

"That's right."

"My boys will turn the world sideways until they find me. You may kill me, but you won't be able to hide me away. You know that, don't you?"

"Bossman, Jesús the Crab ain't gonna hurt you. You take it easy, in a few hours we'll be in Caracas."

"So that's where you're taking me."

"Maybe there, maybe Montevideo. Caluccio's not sure himself."

"Why are you spiriting me so far south?"

"Caluccio's got friends there. It's too hard to hide you in Detroit or Chicago."

J. Edgar Hoover leans back against the hard cushions of the Piper airplane. He has not addressed any questions to Caluccio Salutatti whom he knows to be a Communist, a criminal, and the organizer of his kidnapping. Nor has he taken any notice of the pilot. The fighter is still wearing his trunks, though the gloves and the tape have been removed from his hands. Mr. Hoover is not sure who pulled him out of the smoky arena. He thought it was his own men. Coughing and choking, he followed someone blindly to a car and ended up at a small airport. The fighter and Salutatti awaited him there carrying guns. Now he was on his way to Venezuela.

I've had too long and glorious a career, Hoover thinks, to end it kidnapped by a punk fighter and an over-the-hill Communist. Still, the world doesn't give too many choices. Kennedy didn't know what was awaiting him in Dallas. Lincoln went to see a play.

Just in case he is about to die, Hoover lets his mind toss images of his entire life before him. He sees the lady in the red dress telling a group of them in the Chicago office that John Dillinger is in the Biograph Theatre watching a double feature. Two of the boys goose her. The dress is very, very red. "Listen, hombres," she says, "after being John Dillinger's girl, I could take on a herd of elephants. Many a night he has threatened to shoot off my nipples. Life has not been a cakewalk. Still, no matter what you are thinking, it is no easy decision to rat on him. Even a bastard like that expects loyalty." The boys fondle her some more then get into the Chevy and head for the Biograph Theatre. They do not believe her. Too many times they have staked out the supposed lair of a famous criminal only to find themselves playing peeping tom to innocent folk.

Joe Allen drives. Bernie and Slim are in the front too. Hoover sits alone with the lady in red. The back seat of the Chevy is itchy, hard, very similar to the feel and texture of the seat he is now occupying. The lady sobs quietly into a white handkerchief. She is a small, well-muscled woman of Hungarian lineage, twenty-four years old. She has broad lips. She is no criminal. She leans against Mr. Hoover as if to ask comfort for her tears. "Grab her ass, J.," Joe Allen says. He can see them through the rear-view mirror.

"Keep your eyes on the road, Joe, in a few minutes you may have to face down a killer."

"Looks like you'll be facing down a beaver." The boys all laugh. Prohibition, with its long workdays, still brought a lot of laughs. Agents worked closely with each other. It was romantic to capture criminals. People really went to the post office to look at the "wanted" posters. Kids knew the vital statistics of famous criminals the way they now know football players.

Leaning against his blue suit, depositing flecks of tear and dandruff, she didn't seem to Mr. Hoover to be the girl friend of Public Enemy Number One. He saw someone led astray by the glamor of the illicit. He saw innocence shrouded by villainy. He saw a person falsely clad in a garish red dress.

"I'm from Indiana too," Hoover says, remembering her background file card. "It's for people like you that I want the world to be clean." She leans closer, dabs at a few more tears.

"Dillinger deserves to be put away forever," she says. "I hope it's you guys who do it. You're nice." The boys in the front seat are snickering.

A few minutes later they are at the Biograph Theatre and Joe Allen is dead. So is Dillinger. It happens before Hoover and the lady in red even make it out of the back seat. She is putting on lipstick; Hoover waits to hold the door open for her. They are planning to let her wait in the drugstore across the street. Hoover feels for his steel gun. She pulls at her silk hose. Dillinger, bored by the second feature, is on his way out. There are popcorn hulls on his trousers. The boys recognize him. He sees the sun reflect off their guns. He opens up. So do they. Hoover pushes the lady onto the seat, protecting her with his body. Her lips move against his neck. In ten minutes the photographers are everywhere. A routine afternoon becomes the beginning of a legend.

A few days after the coroner's hearing, the lady in red calls him. She is lonesome. Her friends, though knowing what a bad man she had, think her untrustworthy. She wants to talk to Mr. Hoover about a possible career in public service.

In the same black Chevy, he takes her for a ride. They go along Lakeshore Boulevard. She reminisces about her days in crime. "Once you like a fellow enough, you just start to think of it as his job. I even told some of my friends that my guy was a travelling salesman and we were gonna get married when he had a steady territory. Imagine that."

Mr. Hoover is persistently drawn to innocence. Had they met under more conventional circumstances he could go for this blonde, now clothed in drab blue as if to compensate for the dress that brought her notoriety. In the pantheon of women he has known she stays near the top—perhaps because the Dillinger case put the FBI in the limelight, perhaps for a more personal reason. Perhaps he is mistaken that night to look away when she says, "I want someone steady, like other girls have. I could make him happy." Hoover looks at her and sees a generation of girls gone wrong—hair bobbing, sequined dresses, white slavery, convertible cars. He looks at her and sees real beauty hung openly like a side of beef in a cooler. He looks at her and thinks of what it might be like to have a little bungalow in Oak Park, a couple of kids, a nine-to-five job with no travel.

"There will always be wrongdoing," she says. "I think that if we just keep our distance from it—as I swear I will from now on—then maybe that's enough. I mean, you could have a different career, couldn't you?"

He knows the moment she asks that his answer will be a turning point. Like Achilles, J. Edgar Hoover sees his options as the choice between a happy life or one given to the pursuit of perfection. When she walks up the steps of her apartment building and he stands at the outside door listening to the click of her high heels, he understands that his is a destiny plucked from the company of women.

"I chose," he announces over the hum of the engines. "I chose to fight and combat all attacks on innocence. Whether by individuals or by governments."

He opens his eyes.

"You're still dreaming, *Federale*," Caluccio Salutatti says. "Your eyes are open but you're dreaming about combating somebody. Your combating days are over. We've got a nice little rest home in Caracas for you. It's got lots of room and green grass and fresh air. The perfect spot for an FBI gringo."

"You're not scaring me, Salutatti. I know you like a brother. We've tailed you since 1947. I know who we're going to Caracas to meet. I know the street address, even the time of meeting. I know the code words you'll use and what your brother-in-law in Pittsburgh will say when he hears about this."

Salutatti lights a cigaret. "Mr. FBI, you think you know it all, don't you? You think everyone's going to roll over and give up because J. Edgar Hoover has memorized a few facts. Well, buddy, your goose is cooked. I hope you're a smart enough cop to know that.

"I've waited a lot of years for this, Hoover. You can't know what it's like to be followed for twenty years. Just to torture you I'm going to have you tailed for a few weeks so you'll know what it's like to have no privacy. You'll just go ahead and be a tourist, and we'll see you every time you take a leak."

Hoover looks the Communist in the eye. "Do what you want, Salutatti, I figured to retire anyway in a year or two. History has already had its say about J. Edgar Hoover. You got a lot less than you think by nabbing me. And you cost your boy here the chance to get a shot at the championship. That could have been a bigger propaganda boost than kidnapping an old crime fighter."

"Mr. J. Edgar Hoover, you didn't tail me close enough, I guess. We just insured Jesús the biggest fight of all time. We can fuck *Ring* magazine and the Madison Square Garden and all that capitalist junk. We're going to have a fight free and open to all the people of the world. There will be no hundred-dollar ringside seats, no fancy ladies in fur coats, no five-million-dollar gate. This fight will belong to the people; and you, Señor, you will be the fattest purse of the twentieth century."

"You see, Hoover," the Crab says, "Caluccio planned

all this with my career in mind. The fight of the century; we're gonna have it in Caracas."

"Hush, Kid," Salutatti says. "We don't need to give anything away. Who knows how they've got him wired."

By early afternoon, after a long refueling stop in Orlando, they are flying over Cuba. Just in case there is trouble in Florida, they hide Hoover under an Indian blanket while fueling. They give him a salami sandwich and a beer. Nobody questions them in Orlando. As they fly over Cuba, Salutatti and Jesús sing the hymn to the liberation of the land. Hoover joins them. "I know that too," he says, "and every other Communist national anthem. I know that totalitarian governments always have songs and flags galore but rarely a national flower or a symbol like our eagle or Uncle Sam. We have a course at the FBI Academy on the psychology of the liberation movements. We spend three months on Cuba."

Salutatti laughs, "You could spend your life on Cuba without understanding what is going on." He pulls the shade. "Let's take a nap. We got two hours until we stop again in Honduras. From there I'll call Fidel. If we went right to Cuba, it would make him look bad. You, Mr. Hoover," he says, "you can relax too. We're out of the U.S.A. You can be a regular tourist now." He reaches for Hoover's wallet, takes out the badge, holds it up to the light as if it's a jewel. "I'll keep it for you, Chief," he says, "until we get you home safe and sound."

# 15

I am jailed with the permission of President Johnson. No lawyer sees me, no charges are filed. "War powers act," an FBI agent tells me. "You can shove your constitutional rights until we find the boss."

I don't protest. Events and the exhaustion of the night in the hospital have been too much. I lie in my prison cot not asleep but too dazed to respond to the cacophony around me. They have me in a small cell adjacent to a business office in the Wayne County Sheriff's office. The FBI has virtually taken over the place. Local deputies lean on filing cabinets and drink Cokes. They are as puzzled as I am. I ask only that they keep me informed about Grandma. At eleven a.m. someone tells me that the hospital reports that she is stable. At noon they bring me a prison lunch. Nobody grills me. They just seem to want me to be close to them. Telephone tips from around the country come in every few minutes. FBI men dot a big map with the locations of the tips. Local police are dispatched to investigate each possibility.

Two voices are dominant. Ray Willis, the FBI's number two man, and Jerome Price, a Negro agent, head of the Detroit office. Willis's voice is gruff and heavy; the Negro sounds as musical as Harry Belafonte. On and off I sleep through the afternoon. Just before dinner I awaken. The map which I can see in the next room is full of dots on the west coast.

"How's my grandma?" I yell.

"Stable at four p.m.," comes the musical voice. "We didn't want to wake you. Are you feeling better now? Supper will be up in a few minutes." Price sounds so calm that I think maybe they have already found Hoover and are relaxing.

"No," he says when I ask, "it's just that we're settling in for a long grind. There's no point in panicking. That won't bring the chief back any sooner. We also feel a lot better about you. You look cleaner by the hour. Tonight you can have some company."

I wash, eat, and am wearing a clean prison shirt. How am I different from Trotsky, from the Purple Gang, from Eldridge Cleaver, whom I have recently read for the first time? My dreams of my heroic self would be coming true if only I were sitting in this prison as Samson sat among Philistines, repenting errors, waiting for one big chance to save his people. "Yes," I say when I ask myself if I would stay here forever to save the state of Israel. Yes, too, for the beleaguered Vietnamese, even the blacks of the South, but that's it. For the sake of Mr. Hoover I resent even one day taken from a not so busy life.

Grandma, alone, taking your last breaths. I hope if you awaken you'll know at least that you are in Mt. Sinai and not in one of those Catholic hospitals where the last thing a pious Jew might see is some pagan image. From that at least you are safe. My cell, too, is at least secular; if I should be persecuted, imprisoned, tortured, ruined in body and in mind, at least it will be as a good old American. This is not the kind of ghetto suffering your brother Esserkey knew. Where else but in America could a nice Jewish boy from a religious home even be suspected of masterminding the kidnapping of J. Edgar Hoover? Yes: I am here counting my blessings as Kate Smith used to tell us to. I am looking on the sunny side of things, absolutely certain that very decent black agent, Price, will make sure that I get a square deal. He will call Debby. She will come to me dressed in white. In a gesture of class Price will lock us together into the cell and then close that office door behind him.

"I've come to join you," she says, "for the sake of the times we're in, for the sake of your grandma who desires your offspring, for the sake of all the oppressed, all the forlorn." She pulls off her turtleneck shirt, her white linen skirt, her white anklets and tennis shoes. She stands before me with her blue-black eyes and square bangs looking like Veronica in the old Archie comic books. And I, I am as sexless as Jughead. I can't do it here on the narrow cot. I'm tired, also afraid that as a political prisoner I may meet my end among these FBI loyalists.

On one bare breast she wears a clenched-fist black power button, from her other bosom a golden silhouette of Chairman Mao dangles. "I am the Revolution," she says—not very dramatically because when I start to cry she quickly pulls off the emblems. "I was only trying to make you feel important. Ira, please, I know you're not a Communist; I know that you're innocent. I thought you might get a kick out of it. After all, you're famous now. You made the NBC news tonight and your picture is in all the papers."

"I don't want to be a Lee Harvey Oswald," I tell her. Already, I can imagine Frieda giving book-length interviews the way Oswald's mother has. She will tell everyone her Ira was innocent but nobody will believe her any more than I believe Oswald's mother. "I want an inquiry too," I tell her still sobbing. "I want a Warren Commission and a senate investigation. Even if they kill me I want everyone to know I was innocent."

"Ira," she says, hugging me in her naked arms. "Ira, nobody's going to kill you. See this belly now flat and

155

hard against you, you've got to pump it up, make me big with seed, let the good times roll. Don't let being in jail get you down. Nowadays it's a mark of honor to be arrested. Only the uncommitted people, the businesss types stay safely at home. People like us are arrested all the time. My last year's roommate, Rhonna, was arrested four times for SDS stuff. Her father is a rich doctor. He bailed her out and all her friends too."

When I touch her pale arms, my thumbprints stain her with blue ink. "Did they hold a number underneath you," she asks, "and take your picture too?"

"Yes," I tell her, "I am among the legions of crime." The thumbprints cling like tattoos.

"Oh Ira, c'mon," she says. "I don't care if the FBI catches us." She lounges on the cot where I know that on days past murderers must have coughed and masturbated. I notice the thin lines around her elbow, the softness rising from her thighs. "Not in jail," I say. "Not now."

"It's romantic. We may never have another chance in prison." Fully clothed I sit beside her. "You know," Debby says, "we underestimated Jesús. I thought of him as rough and untutored, but with good instincts."

"To me, he was the first chance I ever had to really do something in the world," I say. "Even though it's all turning on me now, I'm still glad. Without this I would never have met you." We embrace again. It is a tender scene. The manager and the girl friend hugging on the prison cot; the fighter and J. Edgar Hoover in a lethal embrace somewhere else in the wide world.

"You'll get out of this somehow," Debby says. "I used to think innocent people were always redeemed, but that was before Vietnam. Still, I know they can't keep you for long without charges. I just hope Jesús hasn't killed Hoover. Do you really think he could kill someone?"

156

This has never occurred to me. In all the months, Jesús, I never found the killer instinct in your gloves. You were more like an artist. After you finished your work, you just wanted to clean up the mess. And your work was, after all, those fast gloves, those dancing feet. The punches are almost beside the point when the rest of you is so dazzling. I used to wonder if the opponents were as amazed by your style as I was, if half your successful punches might land only because the other man is hypnotized by the stealthy rhythm of your jab.

George Danton, who rarely praised you, told me once in private that he had never seen anyone, not even a bantamweight, with faster hands. "If he's not a champ," George said, "it'll be our fault. He's got everything."

But whose fault is it, George, that Jesús has now vanished after disrupting his first main event and is charged with kidnapping J. Edgar Hoover? Whose fault is it that the fast hands long for the Iron Curtain? In the long history of Communist sympathizers this is an entirely new chapter. Bomb secrets have been stolen, codes deciphered, penultimate secrets exchanged, but all subversively, all in those phone booths of *I Led Three Lives*. You, Jesús, brought Communism out in the open. A full half decade before the women and the gays you and your tiny minority stole the headlines. Unlike the Arab terrorists killing at random, you practice selection as carefully as the anarchists used to. Hoover, of course, is your best target. I wonder now if you were cunning enough to use me. Did you knowingly seduce me into phoning the FBI, and were you and the Italian actually spying on Hoover when he came to Mt. Clemens?

"What can they want Hoover for," Debby says. "If it was something to do with stopping the war, I would be proud to go to jail with you. But Jesús never seemed to care about the war. And that terrible Salutatti, the FBI says, is a Stalinist. I think this is just a criminal act, independent of politics. Maybe they just have an old score to settle with Hoover. He has been bothering Communists for a long time."

The outer door opens. Price, Willis, and four more men enter. Debby covers herself with her arms, but everything is still visible.

"It's okay, sweetie," Price says, "we ain't recording anything. We just came to watch. It gets pretty dull out there taking anonymous tips for eighteen hours straight. Just go ahead and do whatever you had in mind. Agents are supposed to watch." The men chuckle. Debby lowers her arms. "If the manager won't do it, any of us can replace him," Price says. "It's perfectly legal."

Some of this I am not dreaming. Agent Price is really here in my cell. His tie is loose. His smile is full of relief.

"Good news, Ira," he says, "the chief is safe and sound. We just heard from the embassy in Caracas. Venezuela doesn't want to get involved, but Castro came to the rescue. Your stepdad is going to be in charge of the negotiations. They'll all be in Cuba by tonight."

"When will I get out of here?"

"Not until I get the OK from D.C. But don't worry, if you're still here when the fight comes on, Jerome Price guarantees you a nineteen-inch color TV right in this cell. After all, Goldstein is your fighter and no matter what happens it is sure gonna be the greatest fight of the century."

# 16

In Nassau, Solomon is sunbathing at the private beach of the William and Mary Hotel. He sits in a striped canvas chair. Frieda alongside him, in a one-piece swimsuit complete with short skirt, is reading a novel by Isaac Bashevis Singer. "My mother came from this world," she says, "to her it's not funny. How does Singer make funny stories out of suffering?"

"He does it to make a buck," Solomon says. "They all do." With Frieda beside him, Solomon forgets business. He smells the sun, the wind, the air. He stops chewing cigars and grinding his teeth. He is so relaxed that his tongue swims at the bottom of his mouth. This is the life I always wanted, he thinks. Nothing else matters. On the island there is no industry, no machinery and no noise of heavy equipment. He makes no deals, takes no calls, talks only to Frieda.

"Next year," he says, "I'm going to retire. Who needs more than we already have? We'll travel half the year and do *mitzvahs* the rest of the time. No kidding, Frieda, I'm ready to start being a good man. I'm almost sixty. It's time."

"You've always been good," she says, not looking up from her book.

"No," he says, "I've lied and cheated on weights. I have committed adultery too."

"Because you married a woman you didn't love. A lot of your errors, Solomon, blame on me. Our years apart, they were my error—at least since Abe died. I should have come to you after the first year."

Solomon remembers: In his mind the decades spew forth profits. World War II made everything possible. His small bales mushroomed. For the war effort he bought waste paper, inner tubes, burlap. There was no waste. Everything turned to profits. His three trucks moved through Pennsylvania. People trusted Solomon's broad, honest face. He knew how to talk to rural folks, old mechanics who had saved up a few hundred radiators as a cushion against hard times, farmers with rusting useless threshers they were too lazy to cart away. Solomon convinced them all to sell their refuse. He sent portable torches along to cut the steel in the open fields, and forklifts to load it onto his trucks. He mechanized before he knew what the word meant. He paid high wages so the unions couldn't touch him. After the war, Solomon bought an arsenal at auction. He purchased tanks, jeeps, parts of mortars, machine guns, millions of rounds of ammunition. Anything that was steel, and broken, Solomon bid on. He flew to Guam to examine stockpiles, to San Francisco and New York for financing. For a few weeks in 1946 Solomon owned more military equipment than many nations in the world.

Most he sold without even touching, but a few hundred salvagable tanks and jeeps he moved to Pittsburgh. He rented acreage. He paid mechanics and body men to work on them in their spare time. On Sundays, when Solomon had nothing to do, he would drive to his acres of gory surplus vehicles and imagine that he was a general passing before troops. The air filled with cheers and the sound of saluting arms. At the reviewing stand, Frieda waited in a wide-brimmed hat with a veil. President Roosevelt and Arthur Vandenberg, the senator from Michigan, had also flown in to congratulate him. The Hun was beneath their feet; the Jap, too, lay prostrate begging mercy.

"Solomon," FDR says, "they also serve who buy and reprocess scrap." Frieda is proud—and so much more beautiful than Eleanor Roosevelt.

"I did my duty, sir, as I saw it in these hard war years. Now I want to sell everything and go back to Detroit, which I've missed throughout the war. After all, I've still got family there."

The president understands. Senator Vandenberg is happy to have him back in the area of the Great Lakes.

On the sale of the war vehicles to foreign governments and dealers, Solomon earns, in 1946, more than a million dollars. He comes back to Detroit hoping to find Frieda.

A black bellhop runs down the beach toward the couple. "Mr. Solomon," he yells, "there's a very important message for you. An emergency. It's from the secretary of state of your great republic."

Thus Solomon, a longtime broker of steel becomes a go-between of the flesh. He tells the secretary of state that Ira must surely be innocent, afraid of what Frieda will do when she hears her boychick is in jail. Solomon is not stunned by anything. He never liked J. Edgar Hoover and had not personally met Jesús. The fighter was one of his wedding gifts to Frieda. He would have bought her son much more to make him stay away, he would yet.

"The whole thing is crazy," he tells Secretary Rusk, "these are not Communists, they're madmen."

"I agree," Rusk says, "but for the time being we have to deal with them. They asked for you to negotiate. They want a legal contract. We've got to go along. Most of Washington would just as soon let them have Hoover and be done with it, but we've got to get him back. If people think we can't protect Hoover from the Communists, they'll be afraid to walk the streets. It's a matter of national pride.

"They want the fight in the Sports Palace in Havana. Castro is apparently in on it too. They want world-wide TV with the networks paying the going rate; no blackmail, they say, just entertainment. They won't charge admission. Anyway, as crazy as it is, we've got to give them what they want. It's all peanuts as long as we get Hoover back. Agree to anything they want. The National Security Council says they are no threat. Moscow is as astonished by the kidnapping as we are. Their man says it's okay with the Kremlin if we go in and shoot them all. But we want this to be as peaceful and as quick as possible. You know we've already had a lot of trouble with the Dominican Republic. The president doesn't want any new problems with Cuba. Really, it's a good thing that they asked for you as a negotiator. The president wanted to send Averill Harriman too, but it's just as well to leave as much as we can in private hands."

Solomon calls his office. His secretary tells him that Frieda's mother is in critical condition. Solomon is afraid to send her back, afraid that a deathbed request from the old lady will tear his Frieda from him once again.

"Make sure she's got the best doctors," he says, "and don't ever tell anyone that I knew about this. I'm not telling Frieda. She has to go to Cuba with me."

So, Momma, while I lie in the Wayne County Jail looking at the ceiling and worrying about Grandma, you and Solomon ply the diplomatic route. "How exciting," the Hadassah ladies will say. "Imagine meeting Castro and negotiating for the government." They will wonder what you are wearing as you step down from the special air force jet that the president has sent for your use.

Cuban soldiers line the runways. Red flags float in the breeze. You are proud of yourself, Momma, and not very worried about Mr. Hoover. Why should you be? What's the FBI chief to Frieda Goldstein? He's out risking his neck every day against killers. Sometimes you just have to ransom him. It's like in business. Sometimes you just have to bribe the Castros of this world if you want things to go smoothly. Frieda understands. What she wonders about is Jesús in the middle of the kidnapping.

From the beginning Frieda kept her distance from Jesús. Grandma prepared more meals for him than Frieda did, even carried them downstairs, since she didn't like him eating with us. Frieda in the four months that she had Jesús as our boarder hardly spoke to him. At night she showered, watched TV, talked to Grandma about business, and caught up on gossip with a few friends on the telephone. She had no interest in middleweights.

"Will they blame Ira for any of this?" she wants to know. "Will people blame him because Jesús became a criminal?"

"No," Solomon tells her. The gentle stepfather spares Momma knowledge of my imprisonment and Grandma's stroke. The gentle stepfather is accustomed to multimillion-dollar negotiations. Solomon feels honored to be representing America. On the plane he and Frieda drink wine sent to them as a gift by the president. "May you have mazel on your venture," signed, "Lyndon Johnson," is attached to the bottle of wine. Imagine, Momma, Lyndon Johnson wishing you luck, all the reporters waiting for news, and you worrying how you are going to talk to people in Cuba if they don't know English.

In the hands of Solomon lies the fate of J. Edgar

Hoover, and more. My future, too, lies in his thick grip, as does the future of progressive socialists throughout the world who hide for a few days fearful of reprisals for this daring act. The World Communist Press condemns Salutatti. "Piracy," *Pravda* says. "A stupid crime," from the French Party Press. The Chinese News Agency doesn't even mention the event.

"You're wrong," Salutatti cables Moscow. "Think what you will of me, but this act finally brings us back into the news. We have become as tame as salesmen," Salutatti cables. "Let us give the revolution one big boost. Jesús the Crab, Salutatti, and Hoover do not matter. Let the world wake up to the issues. I am proud. Lenin would be proud. Castro understands. Let the best man win. But for fifteen rounds or less, let the world know that there are still men fighting peacefully for our ideals, fighting the battle in the shops, in the parks, on the wide capitalist streets where it must be fought. Win or lose, Caluccio Salutatti gives his all for the Party."

"Too many years in America," Fidel tells him after reading the text, "too much emotionalism." He slaps the thick back of his comrade. "Still, Salutatti, you understand the dramatic moment. Moscow is too dull. If not for us Cubans, the Yankees would have already forgotten Communism. This will be a good fight?"

Fidel greets Solomon and Frieda at the Havana airport. The soldiers do not look very military. They squat or sit on the black asphalt. Fidel is wearing a white linen suit and a Panama hat.

"This is purely a business deal," the premier says. "I took off my uniform to make you understand this. Today, I am F. Castro, a promoter. I am not endorsing anything about this fight."

"I understand," Solomon says. They work out the contract.

Momma is awed by Solomon's businesslike attitude. He is not nervous. He speaks up to Castro, arguing for every advantage. He could have been president, she thinks, maybe he will be yet. He's only fifty-nine.

For Jesús and Salutatti, Fidel gets guaranteed immunity from prosecution world-wide. For Cuba he gets all the TV proceeds plus ownership of the videotape. For Hoover, Solomon negotiates unconditional release the moment the fight is concluded. In case of a draw, Hoover is still to be freed. But Fidel keeps an option for a second fight also to be held in Havana in case the fight is a draw.

Representing both the United States government and Ralph "Tiger" Williams, the middleweight champion, Solomon agrees to terms. My stepfather personally offers to pay Tiger Williams $150,000 for agreeing to participate and to risk his championship in such a spectacular fashion.

"Naw," says the Tiger. "I'll do it for my country. Give the money to the boys' clubs where I got my start."

Tiger Williams figures he will knock Jesús out in less than five. "That boy has never gone ten; he's two years away from an honest title fight. Tiger will show the Communists."

Salutatti is not worried. "Even if we lose, it's a victory. We'll have a hundred million Americans watching. *The Daily Worker* never sells more than a thousand copies. The Third World will understand."

Hoover has a comfortable room in what was once the Havana Hilton. Frieda and Solomon are just down the hall. Jesús and Salutatti are at the National Boxing Farm, training for their fight, which has been arranged for two weeks. Castro allows Hoover to take a call from the president. "Just pretend it's a two-week vacation," Johnson suggests. "Sit in the sun, enjoy the girls. If anybody in Washington needs a vacation, it's you. Cuba used to be a helluva spot," Johnson says, "girls, gambling, hotsy totsy music. You could get anything in Cuba. That sonofabitch Castro (yeah, get that, I know your men are listening), that sonofabitch has made Cuba as dull as Poland."

The president also calls Solomon. "I'm having a good time, Mr. President. My wife is with me. It's kind of a honeymoon."

Johnson asks Solomon's age.

"A second marriage."

"Well, when all this crapola is over and we get Hoover back where he belongs, you and the little lady can just hightail it down to the ranch to spend some time with Lady Bird and me. You hear that . . . you bring us Hoover back in one piece and you'll have a barbecue biggern what we clamp on the astronauts."

Frieda worries about the pressure on Solomon. In Havana he chews cigars that Americans would pay two dollars apiece for. He spits brown leaf around government offices. The Cubans are not looking for trouble, Solomon gets what he wants: the fight in two weeks rather than three, an American referee, the pre-fight physical just like in the States, eight-ounce gloves, the three-knockdown rule. Solomon argues everything. Overnight he becomes knowledgeable about the sport.

In the heat of the afternoon, while Cuban fight negotiators take the siesta, Solomon and Hoover stroll along the beach. Frieda stays in, afraid of too much afternoon sun.

"Being a hostage," Hoover says, "is not so bad." He laughs. The sand squirts beneath his bare feet. "This wouldn't be a bad life, would it? Good meals, walks in the afternoon, early to bed, nice climate year round, and no paperwork to clog your mind. I wonder how these Cubans keep track of anything. While I've been here I

166

haven't cared a bit about any state secrets, I haven't once asked Castro what his ultimate plans are for Guantanamo, or snooped around the sugar crop. The truth is we know everything important. What I've been trying to find out is how these Cubans go about daily life, especially in government—you know, statistics, reports, memos, the whole thing."

"Nobody writes anything down," Solomon says. "I haven't seen a pen on the island. They all carry little pocket diaries when they talk to me. They open them to check the calendar on the inside cover. I've negotiated for three days and nobody has taken a note. I ask them how they can guarantee anything. They say that only capitalists worry about legalisms. Maybe they're right."

"Castro sure can talk," Hoover says. "We've got hundreds of hours on tape, but in person he's really something. If he ran for office in the States, he could out-argue anybody in Congress."

They roll their trousers to the knee and let the warm Caribbean surf foam around them.

"I had a pen pal in Cuba when I was a kid," Hoover says. "Antonio Duran. We corresponded until I went to college. We traded photographs. I always thought I would meet him someday, but we lost touch. You know how those things are. I tried to find him the first time I came here, in the thirties. I located his mother in a slum. She said he was a fisherman somewhere. She hadn't seen him in years. She said he couldn't write English. I wonder who wrote me those long letters."

"Life is strange," Solomon says, "full of surprises. I've made many a fortune and had bitter days in spite of it. Now I represent my country and walk on the beach with Mr. FBI. If you lived in Detroit, we could be friends."

"When I retire," Hoover says, "I'll sure as hell move out of Washington, D.C., fast. But Detroit is not my idea of the best place. Somewhere around here, down in the Keys maybe."

While you talk, men, while I lie bored in my cell, Grandma floats on the edges of her arteries. She, too, is in the warmer climes. Her brothers and sisters surround her. The challah is covered, her father's little silver wine goblets are on the table. Everything is ready. Her husband Meyer comes, wearing his black robes. Learning drips from his long fingers. Her father hugs the bridegroom, each man's long curly sideburns caressing the other's. She hides among her sisters, but, when Meyer moves toward the table to say the blessing for the challah, it is her eye that he seeks among the chattering women.

"Oh Tata," she thinks, "I'm too young for him. And how can I talk to a man with such knowledge? What will we say to each other when we're alone?"

"Women always know what to say," Tata tells her, but she never learns. With Meyer through the years, much is silence. In Odessa, in Detroit, on the boat, everywhere Meyer thinks and Bertha walks beside him sharing the silence. The sound of the little girl finally brings her the company she wants. Such a child restores the world. Even Meyer looks up from the Talmud for her, holds her on his lap while he sips tea, and lets her try to pull the sugar cube from between his teeth.

Yes, once little Frieda is born, Grandma's world turns back to happiness and talk, and they make a decent living in the bakery. Detroit is not Odessa, but she learns to forget her brothers and sisters and sit by the cash register making change in those tiny American coins.

The girl is like a leaf. She and Meyer so big, and Frieda pale, thin, beautiful, holding the hand of her mother and father on those wonderful Saturday afternoon walks when people sat on their porches nodding good shabbas; and Bertha felt like a princess beside this silent man whom all Detroit respected and who, her father told her in Odessa, would one day wrestle in the next world with the souls of Maimonides and the Rambam.

Oh, Grandma, in the deep shade of your veins, in the shrinking hypothalamus, in the hardened synapses of your nerves, in all the fancy physiology that I learned in school—where now can I find you? Agent Price stands beside me. Every day he brings me to you like a present, so that for a half hour I can watch your facial muscles contort, your closed eyelids flutter, your hard breaths push the white sheets up. You exhale in a rhythmical whisper—like Snow White's dwarfs going off to work. Death is on the empty trays, in the intravenous bottle, on the dark face of the TV where I see myself reflected, another shadow passing. Oh, Grandma, in all this craziness I just want to lie down beside you now and snuggle up like I did on the nights when the thunder woke me, and listen to you tell me stories about hunchbacks in Odessa and people who slept on the stoves and your little brother Esserkey before Hitler killed him. For so many years we waited together for something to happen. We waited for the angels to pluck out my bride and bring her home for your approval and Momma's delight. We waited for the Messiah together, Moses incarnate, who would blow a jazzy shofar and bring us back all the dead—including first of all your Meyer and my own daddy and make us one big happy family forever after. Instead, Grandma, while the Messiah lingered I brought you a Puerto Rican middleweight and the FBI. And as for Frieda, would you let Moses blow the shofar for her even while she lives? Frieda, your little girl, is not even here, Grandma, to wait with us for the angel you didn't

169

tell me about. For you, Grandma, I want the world to come to be full of pious Jews, and Christians who respect us for it, big meals, holidays, dresses with long sleeves, soft cooked, low-salt foods.

Price leaves us for a while when the nurse tells him to, and with me alone, Grandma, you are lucky enough to spend your final minutes. I shiver for both of us. I feel your soul move through the air as graceful as one of Jesús' jabs. The intravenous fluid drips into your bruised arm. The noise in the hallway is loud. Trays clatter, a nurse's aide compliments someone on a hairdo. You, who for days have been only a whistle, are now not even that. My hands are heavy on my knees. I do not go near you. I hold no mirror under your nose, offer no last kisses, no wails, no tears. When Agent Price returns, Debby is with him, clad in a charcoal gray dress like a Catholic schoolgirl.

"Oh, Ira," she says, holding me as tightly as people do in such scenes in the movies. "Oh, Ira. I love you. I'll help to make it easier for you, honest I will." Price has his head bowed. A nurse or two come in and feel around under the sheet. There is no panic. A cleaning lady enters prematurely to mop the floor.

"You were like her son," Debby says. "You can be proud of what you did for her at the end. We'll name our daughter after her, when all this is over." Debby kisses me and finally the tears come for Grandma, for the great confusion of Jesús and Frieda, and J. Edgar Hoover, and the Communists who popped up like flares in Grandma's long and lonely life.

It feels as if she is my child, this old lady who for days has been a shadow on the bed. One of her hands brushes the button that raises and lowers the bed, the other lies against the remote control TV selector. Her hands are still soft and fine. The interior veins that dried

170

out did not affect those hands that guarded me from everything.

"Ira," Debby says, "for you the world is just beginning. For both of us."

"Call Frieda," I say, as nurses sweet and efficient move my Grandma to a less crowded place.

# 17

Jesús of the fast ankles, the bolo punch, the head feint; Jesús of the clawing jab, the blinding hook; Jesús Crab Goldstein, as you prepare for your moment in history, do you train as George Danton would want you to? Is there steady roadwork, medicine balls to the stomach, two three-round warm-ups before lunch and dinner, shadow boxing at bedtime? I would have made sure, Jesús, no matter what the circumstances, that you were ready. I would have sharpened reflexes, prepared a high-protein diet, kept the press at a distance. If ever you needed us, Jesús, if ever George Danton and Ira Goldstein, your trainer and your manager, should have been with you, it was in those two weeks of pre-fight training at the National Boxing Camp in Cuba. But who aside from a few diehard boxing fans really cared about the fight itself when there was J. Edgar Hoover, suspended above the ring in a hanging basket like a topless dancer. Even during the live action of the match the TV cameras zoom in on Hoover, who watches from what is actually a very good seat. He is keeping score and, as his score-card later demonstrates, he is a very honest and de-tached judge.

The crowd is yours, Jesús, the way no crowd has ever belonged to a performer. For them you are Judy Garland, Frank Sinatra, and Hitler, all rolled into one shining middleweight. There are banners, there are people outside who just want to be near you, and there is a love that transcends sport and politics within that arena. Jesús the Crab is their national anthem. You wear the single color of the revolution, while Hoover's basket is decorated in red, white, and blue—not in the simple regimental style of the flag but in blotchy colors painted in spurts and various geometric shapes. Although Jesús is dark brown and Tiger Williams sleek and black as a streamlined panther, red is the dominant color. Red banners, red flags, the blood-red ropes of the ring.

Your final gift, Jesús, is to have me flown here to be at ringside, your guest for the evening. Debby, too, you have invited. I am anxious but with her there are problems. Her father doesn't want her to go. He is astonished to learn how involved his little girl is with this conspiracy. "I thought she was just going to anti-war rallies," he says. It takes phone calls from Solomon in Cuba and from the assistant secretary of state for Latin American Affairs to convince Debby's father. President Johnson personally guarantees her safety, so does Castro. To their minds this is just a quirky request from Jesús. They don't want to antagonize him needlessly. The government can afford to send a plane for us.

Right from jail the agents take me to the airport. I have only been out of mourning for Grandma for a few days. I didn't have to go through the seven-day mourning period, only sons and daughters are held to that by Jewish law, but at the end I was all she had. And what difference did it make to me in prison? There I sat anyway on a low cot next to an uncovered toilet, bereft of entertainment, Momma my only company.

Yes, Momma came back for the funeral and spends her days in the cell with me, her nights in the cheap hotel across the street. This week she has been the old Frieda, untainted by Solomon's gaudy millions. Grief has reduced her. She wears no jewelry or makeup.

"Ira," she says, "what will I do? I can't walk into his house without seeing her everywhere. I didn't feel guilty while she was alive. I knew how crazy her hate was. But now from the grave she is getting me. The only place I am comfortable is here in jail with you. The hotel has too many mirrors." Frieda, having just returned from Cuba, doesn't want me to go either. At the airport she and Debby's father comfort one another.

Debby and I are alone in an Air Force DC-8. A young lieutenant is our steward. He serves drinks, offers us sandwiches and magazines. "We're the friendly skies too," he says. "I envy the two of you getting to see the fight. Any of us would give a month's salary for a ticket."

But according to the terms of the contract all tickets are free. Jesús wants to be the people's champion. The seats are distributed from the arena box office on a first-come basis. The ringsiders have waited seven days for their tickets. People guard their places in line with drawn knives. There have been six murders this week in separate incidents relating to the ticket line. The American press covers the brutality of the wait as if it is a battle zone. The ace reporters from Vietnam are here, making analogies for all they're worth.

They keep us two hours at that airport, and then we are taken directly to the arena—V.I.P.s from Detroit, Debby and I to the ringside. I am remembering, Jesús, the flow of your body beneath my fingers, your solid confidence buoying my shaky hands as I knead the flesh of your shoulders. You look as fearless here in Cuba with the whole world watching, as you were in the Motor City Auditorium when Otis Leonard stepped through the ropes and asked for his second to hold a Kleenex to his nose. Those red satin trunks emblazoned with the hammer and sickle become you, so does that goatee that I never let you grow for fear of skin infection. Salutatti does not worry about infection He

174

doesn't care about your future in the ring. It is all and everything, all tonight. The goatee has not made you resemble Lenin, but it does bring out the romance of your background, the myth of sun and carefree natives. The beads I would not have allowed either. You do not need such accompaniment to remind everyone that you represent the unrepresented.

Solomon fumes at ringside. "None of this was in the contract," he tells Howard Cosell who is covering the fight for American television, "none of this at all. Hoover is supposed to be at the airport, not here in a hanging basket. If they pull too many more shenanigans, we'll just ask Tiger Williams to get out of the ring and let the Marines rescue Mr. Hoover."

"That's what a lot of Americans would like to see happen," Howard Cosell says, "but here we are at the meeting ground of sport and politics, ladies and gentlemen, where in a few brief moments the game that is no longer a game will begin."

For me, Howard, it never was a game, nor a business either. For me it was a coming-out party, a manager's sweet-sixteen. I wonder if Grandma would have watched. Probably not, Jesús; probably she would have stayed in her cabin in Mt. Clemens, continuing the list of her complaints against Momma. As soon as I get back I will destroy Grandma's notebook. This fresh torture Frieda does not need.

Jesús is throwing kisses, leaning his torso far over the ropes. Those wild Cubans are grasping the air as if foul balls or hockey pucks are actually coming at them. They hug one another as the glance and the outstretched arm of Jesús move in their direction. Strong men, workers accustomed to whole days in the sun, swoon when Jesús raises his arms and the red robe falls like crushed velvet at his feet. This is the international moment and all 45,000 in the Sports Palace know it. Lenin was a light-

175

weight, Stalin a dark counterpuncher. The rest were a bunch of nameless contenders awaiting the time when a Jesús Goldstein would come forth from the cradle of the enemy in his crimson trunks, shed his robe, and let his brown body gleam before the eyes of the world. Jesús, I can see from ringside that this is not boxing. There is no concentration in your glance; your shoelaces are not even pulled tight. I hope that George Danton is not watching. But how can he not watch? Who in America is not tuned in? The networks are not selling any advertising: You are the news, Jesús—for the first time a prime-time live boxing match presented by the network news.

Jesús is dancing in the ring, throwing kisses to all sides. So loud is the roar of the fans that Howard Cosell's voice is inaudible. There is Jesús in the middle of the ring, in the middle of the world, being loved in high decibels. He laughs a long laugh and seems to scream his own affection back to the crowd. Only superhuman restraint keeps them from tearing down the ropes just to touch their hero. My middleweight, you have it all—at this moment the world is between your hands. Tiger Williams, the champ shadow boxing in the opposite corner, might as well be in Miami Beach sipping a cocktail. Nobody sees him, nobody cares that he is 84–2 with 66 knockouts. Nobody cares about his eleven brothers and sisters in Oakland, California; his deaf aunt; his background as a star of boys' clubs and later, golden gloves events. At this moment, Jesús, while the fans scream as you are presented to them—at this moment I forgive you. Not that you have harmed me very much, but I forgive you, Jesús, for not going the usual route with me at your side. I forgive you for not waiting two more years and two dozen ten-rounders for a chance at a man like Tiger Williams. I forgive you because, right now I see that you are more important than the championship. When the cameras zero in on J.

Edgar Hoover, I see no malice in his look either. He waves to the American people; he throws two kisses of his own. Even in his ridiculous basket Mr. Hoover hangs in the Cuban sky as a distinguished man. His blue suit is well pressed, his shoes shined. This is a great sportsman at an international event.

Jesús has refused all interviews. Tiger Williams, once he has thanked his family and the boys' clubs, has nothing more to say. "I'm a good boxer," he says, "check the record. The record is where it's at."

But you're wrong, Tiger. Momma's wedding and Grandma's death and my own love affair with Debby—from here, Tiger, I can tell you that the record does not speak for itself. You are just lucky, Tiger, to be uncomplicated by even a draw. For the rest of us the record is not even kept. Jesús has just jumped outside the record book. He is now like one of those great race horses parading past the grandstand on Derby day while princes and millionaires gaze at the beauty of his strength in the sunlight and know that all their accomplishments are small stuff compared to such an animal.

I forgive you, Jesús, because you are right. Mr. Hoover, sportsman that he is, forgives you because you are beautiful. All across America and throughout the free world, fans and people who have never seen a match are watching tonight to see you demolished by the quiet champion. America needs a big win tonight. If the fix was on, it would be worth millions. It would be a fix bigger than the Mafia could conceive. A fix to revive a whole country sick of Vietnam and roving teen-age radicals and dope and irreverence from all sides.

Momma beside her TV probably doesn't see your glory, Jesús. She is too worried about my future. "Who ever thought he could do such a thing?" she says to herself. Her only worry is Ira. But, Momma, everyone else who is watching knows that Ira doesn't matter right

177

now. That brown, half-naked Puerto Rican has touched us with glory. The rest of our lives will be notable only because we knew him. His presence swells the arena. It can't go on much longer. The announcer has been trying for five minutes to quiet the crowd, but the Cubans will not stop cheering. Jesús, enjoy your moment. I, who love and forgive, I see what is coming.

Half mad from this single month in prison, I feel prophetic. I see the fight before it happens. I feel the fists of Tiger Williams here in the crowd more than you seem to in the glowing ring.

For the first two rounds you toy with Tiger Williams. In the clinches you blow in his ear; you caress his back like a lover. When you duck his powerful punches—any one of which could ruin you—you make no attempt to counterattack him. It is as if you are Fred Astaire, there only coincidentally in the ring with a fighter. It's as if some business apart from boxing has brought you there, so you dance through the motions almost embarrassed by this lunging black man flogging the air so near to your person.

A light sweat breaks over your body. On the color TV you gleam. The audience is quiet now. They realize more than you do, Jesús, what one of those punches could do to the side of your head or the space between your lungs. Tiger Williams is relentless. He is a patriot fighting for his country as well as a professional champion who knows his trade. There is fire and ice in him. For a decade he has been fighting obscure Latin Americans, a few Europeans, and an occasional American midwesterner. But until this night his reputation has been known only to a few serious fight fans. He has bled in the dark, a middleweight champion in an age dominated by team sports. Nothing can stop the mechanical onslaught of Tiger Williams. The crowd understands his power. Some of those punches will have to land on the smiling face as they already have begun to pound out a rhythm on the ribs.

J. Edgar Hoover in the hanging basket is never forgotten. One camera is always focused on him, as if for protection. His image is shown in the upper right-hand corner of the screen. It reminds us constantly that this is no ordinary athletic event. Hoover roots for Tiger Williams. In a quiet and dignified way he lifts his arms in pleasure when the Tiger attacks, lets his program drop to his knee when Jesús outmaneuvers the champ. But he does nothing histrionic. Hoover does not act as if his own life might be at stake. An experienced soldier of fortune, he gazes down at the battle beneath him, sips from his glass of white wine, and seems content to let Fortune have her way with him.

Hoover on this night, Jesús, Hoover is smarter than all of us. He hangs there calmly watching a fight. He is J. Edgar Hoover and what else is there to prove? The rest of us come out fighting at every bell. Faith in capitalism, genetics, zip—whatever it is that I lacked to become a moneyearning man of the world—that Hoover has in excess. He is tranquil above the swelling mass, quiet in the roar. He is the prize, the occasion of all this spectacle, and he stays calm as a Lake Michigan fisherman on a warm summer afternoon.

"It gives me the creeps," Debby says, "to see him so relaxed up there. I wish he would bang his fist and say he has to go to the bathroom or something."

Between the rounds Jesús does not sit in his corner. During the minute of rest, he courts his fans; he stands at mid-ring, tired and exposed, soaking in their approval. He walks to the ropes, gestures with both hands at his chest, and pulls out, in mime, his heart, which he throws toward the dim masses.

Tiger Williams spits into the bucket.

Debby squeezes my sweating hand. "When it's all

over, Ira, everything, let's move to a little cottage in Vermont or Maine and be farmers." Flashbulbs blind us from all sides. "He said without you, Ira, he would never have had a career. In spite of everything you should be proud."

And you know something, Debby, Jesús—everyone who remembers that night—I am proud. Nobody in that screaming audience, none of the would-be catchers of his heart, is more proud of Jesús than I am. The world has only been with him for a few minutes, but I can feel in my palms the impact of his fists as I caught his jabs over the months of practice. I can see in the international hero the breaker of batteries, holding a sledgehammer over his shoulder in the Detroit winter. Yes, Jesús, history has carried you past Detroit, past me, and into the beatitude of this moment. But I know as I look at you that you are what I dreamed you would be. True I dreamed it otherwise—less spectacularly—but still I dreamed it while you were in the gym or the junkyard or in the basement watching TV. I always had in my mind the idea of what you might become: Jesús the strong, Jesús the conqueror, Jesús the best of men. What else does champion mean?

The blue-black arms of Tiger Williams cut the air. His power makes a noise, and the sweat flies from his body with each punch.

Suddenly Jesús is disembodied. His feet dance away from some of the blows, but he is clearly somewhere else. His eye is glazed, but in wonder, not in pain. Tiger Williams is a machine, a harvester; Jesús is the gift of nature growing carelessly in the wind and fine weather. The blue-black arms find landing places, but Jesús could care less.

I am up in my seat. "Stop it," I am screaming to his corner, "throw in the towel. Williams will kill him." Salutatti does not look my way. Jesús has not been down

180

yet, but all of the punches are landing now. Williams sets his feet and puts his full weight into each blow. His arms are tired from the constant swinging. "Stop the fight," I am yelling to Salutatti, to Debby, to the back-pedaling referee, his white shirt now spotted with the blood of Jesús.

Debby clutches my arm. "He'll be our friend, Ira, when all of it is over. He'll visit us every summer. He'll play with our children. Oh God, don't let them kill him." She sobs against my shoulder. The entire world is up begging Jesús to fall, to stop the onslaught, to go down like a boxer, not stand there like a bloodied martyr.

Williams himself steps back for a moment to gaze at the standing form of his adversary and to catch his breath for another savage flurry. Jesús is like a cloud. He is not stumbling, not faltering, but rolling smoothly across the surface of the ring. His motion is continual. For over sixty seconds he has not even raised his arms in defense. They lie as if paralyzed at his sides, although the legs work as efficiently as ever. The legs are doing a kind of boxer's waltz, circling away from the opposite corner smoothly, automatically, just as he learned to do in Miguel León's instructional film. He is all instinct now. For many seconds he has been out on his feet and I see, suddenly, that he will never fall.

Jesús has trained outside of his body. He is standing now in the realms of pure spirit. He is a block of marble and Tiger Williams some petty Michelangelo chipping away at him. Jesús will fall, but only in geologic time, when the arena withers to sandstone and the great grandchildren of Tiger Williams huddle in the cities of the twenty-second century. I look up at Hoover. He, too, is shaking his head in disbelief. Nobody wants it to go on. The referee looks at Salutatti as if to ask his permission to end it. The Italian sneers and punches the air, his signal for the fight to continue. The contract has called for an end to the technical-knockout rule. The referee can stop the fight only with permission from the manager of the stricken fighter. He, too, is a helpless witness to what now seems Salutatti's plan to execute Jesús on worldwide television.

"It's not Hoover that he's kidnapped, Jesús," I am yelling, "it's you. Go down. Go down and you'll live to fight again and screw girls like Jane Fonda. Oh, Jesús, please." I am sobbing, too, now. Tiger Williams is covered with the blood of Jesús. He has slowed his punches and aims each one as if he is a butcher cutting out a sirloin tip for a demanding customer.

Grandma, what is he proving now? Your shvartzer-Puerto Rican-orphan-communist-assman—what is he proving to anyone, and why is he holding his young life in the air as exposed as your poor bald head against the hospital pillow? The mouthpiece is gone and his teeth are all over the ring. His eyes are closed. His nose is not identifiable in the bloodied recess of his face. I don't know, Bobbe, where it comes from, but for the first time in my life comes the zip of Ira Goldstein. I push Debby aside as if she's a pickpocket. I part the ropes so quickly that they snap like rubber bands. When the referee approaches, my glare alone sends him to a neutral corner. I do not hear the audience. If they're still screaming, their roar is only white noise. I see slowness and silence. Tiger Williams, tired and in tears, points to his piece of work. He spits out his mouthpiece. "The motherfucker won't go down. He wants to git kilt. If I have to, I'll do it." I motion him aside with a nod of my head.

The wet and battered body of Jesús Goldstein I approach. As I come to him I close my own eyes to avoid seeing what two minutes of such ferocity has done to his smiling Latin features. I hug Jesús. The referee tries to part us, but I hug tight and lock my arms around him. "No more, Jesús, no more." My voice is calm. "Dr.

Shimmer will clean you up, my man, and in a few days you'll be good as new."

With his eyes still closed and through his bloody, toothless mouth Jesús' voice comes to me. "Fuck off, Ira," he says. "In the next round I level that coon."

The bell saves me. Cuban police haul me to the back of the arena. From my roost far from ringside, among the noisy rabble, Jesús, I watch as Salutatti orders J. Edgar Hoover's basket lowered into the ring. Yes, the fight is over. Salutatti has admitted the end. The basket comes slowly down, and Hoover in his blue suit and kidskin shoes steps into the blood-stained ring. He shakes the glove of Tiger Williams. The American TV cameras are on these two, but the crowd does not even see them. For in the middle of the ring, Jesús has entered the basket of Hoover's captivity and now, blinded and beaten as he is, Jesús is being raised aloft. Slowly, like the flag, he ascends. He raises his arms now to throw bloodied kisses. Debby has pushed her way to my side at the rear of the arena. The policemen forget me in the spectacle. She takes my hand and leads me out of the auditorium.

"I wanted to save him."

"I know," she says, "you did your best." She pulls me toward Vermont. When I look back for one last glimpse of Jesús, he is nearing the rafters, ascending still.